T0305136

Handbook of Corporate Equity Derivatives and Equity Capital Markets

For other titles in the Wiley Finance series
please see www.wiley.com/finance

Handbook of Corporate Equity Derivatives and Equity Capital Markets

Juan Ramirez

A John Wiley and Sons, Ltd., Publication

This edition first published 2011
© 2011 John Wiley & Sons, Ltd

Registered Office

John Wiley & Sons Ltd, The Atrium, Southern Gate, Chichester, West Sussex, PO19 8SQ, United Kingdom

For details of our global editorial offices, for customer services and for information about how to apply for permission to reuse the copyright material in this book please see our website at www.wiley.com.

Library of Congress Cataloging-in-Publication Data

Ramirez, Juan, 1961–
    Handbook of corporate equity derivatives and equity capital markets / Juan Ramirez.
        p. cm. — (The Wiley finance series)
    Includes bibliographical references and index.
    ISBN 978-1-119-97590-8
    1. Derivative securities—United States. 2. Options (Finance)—United States. I. Title.
    HG6024.U6R36 2011
    332.63′2—dc22

                                                                2011016272

A catalogue record for this book is available from the British Library.

ISBN 978-1-119-97590-8 (hardback) ISBN 978-1-119-97855-8 (ebk)
ISBN 978-1-119-95077-6 (ebk) ISBN 978-1-119-95078-3 (ebk)

Set in 10/12pt Times by Aptara Inc., New Delhi, India
Printed in Great Britain by Antony Rowe Ltd, Chippenham, Wiltshire

To my wife Marta and our children, Borja, Martuca and David

Contents

Preface   xvii

About the Author   xix

1   Main Strategic Equity Derivative Instruments   1
  1.1   Equity Forwards   1
     1.1.1   Equity Forwards   1
     1.1.2   Example of a Cash-settled Equity Forward on a Stock   2
     1.1.3   Example of a Physically Settled Equity Forward on a Stock   3
     1.1.4   Calculating the Forward Price of a Stock   4
  1.2   Equity Swaps   6
     1.2.1   Total Return Equity Swaps   6
     1.2.2   Price Return Equity Swaps   7
     1.2.3   Case Study: Physically Settled Total Return Equity Swap on
              Deutsche Telekom   7
     1.2.4   Case Study: Cash-settled Total Return Equity Swap on
              Deutsche Telekom   12
     1.2.5   Determination of the Initial Price   15
     1.2.6   Determination of the Settlement Price   16
     1.2.7   Equity Notional Resets   17
     1.2.8   Case Study: Total Return Equity Swap on EuroStoxx 50   17
     1.2.9   Compo Equity Swaps   21
     1.2.10 Quanto Equity Swaps   23
     1.2.11 Uses of Equity Swaps   25
  1.3   Stock Lending and Borrowing   26
     1.3.1   Stock Lending and Borrowing   26
     1.3.2   Stock Lending/Borrowing Transaction Flows   27
     1.3.3   Counterparty Credit Risk   28
     1.3.4   Advantages of Stock Lending and Borrowing   29
     1.3.5   Drawbacks of Stock Lending and Borrowing   29
  1.4   Call and Put Options   30
     1.4.1   Call Options   30
     1.4.2   Put Options   33

	1.4.3	European vs. American Style	36
	1.4.4	Time Value vs. Intrinsic Value	36
	1.4.5	In, At or Out-of-the-money	37
	1.4.6	Variables that Influence an Option Price	38
	1.4.7	Historical Volatility vs. Implied Volatility	40
	1.4.8	Put–Call Parity	41
	1.4.9	Options' Sensitivities, the "Greeks"	42
	1.4.10	Delta Hedging	44
	1.4.11	Offsetting Dividend Risk	45
	1.4.12	Adjustments to Option Terms Due to Other Corporate Actions	46
	1.4.13	Volatility Smile	47
	1.4.14	Implied Volatility Term Structure	48
	1.4.15	Composite and Quanto Options	49
1.5	Dividend Swaps		50
	1.5.1	Dividend Swaps	50
	1.5.2	Applications of Dividend Swaps	50
	1.5.3	Risks	52
	1.5.4	Main Dates in a Dividend Distribution	52
	1.5.5	Case Study: Single-stock Dividend Swap	52
	1.5.6	Case Study: Index Dividend Swap	56
	1.5.7	Pricing Implied Dividends	58
1.6	Variance Swaps and Volatility Swaps		58
	1.6.1	Variance Swaps Product Description	59
	1.6.2	Calculation of the Realized Volatility and the Realized Variance	61
	1.6.3	Volatility Swaps Product Description	62
	1.6.4	Volatility Swaps vs. Variance Swaps	63
	1.6.5	Applications of Variance and Volatility Swaps	63
2	**Equity Capital Markets Products**		**65**
2.1	Main Equity Capital Markets Products		65
	2.1.1	Capital Increase Products	65
	2.1.2	Secondary Placement Products	66
	2.1.3	Equity-linked Products	66
2.2	Initial Public Offerings		66
	2.2.1	Product Description	66
	2.2.2	Benefits of Going Public	67
	2.2.3	Drawbacks of Going Public	67
	2.2.4	The IPO Process	68
	2.2.5	Phase 1: Preparation of the Company	68
	2.2.6	Phase 2: Preparation of the Offering	69
	2.2.7	Phase 3: Marketing of the Offering	75
	2.2.8	Phase 4: Placement of the Offering	77
	2.2.9	Key Success Factors Affecting an IPO	80
	2.2.10	Key Risk Factors Affecting an IPO	81
	2.2.11	Case Study: Visa's IPO	82
2.3	Case Study: Google's Dutch Auction IPO		85

2.4   Rights Issues (or Rights Offerings)   87
    2.4.1   Product Description   87
    2.4.2   Main Definitions of a Rights Issue   88
    2.4.3   Advantages and Weaknesses of a Rights Issue   89
    2.4.4   Rights Offerings Success Factors   90
    2.4.5   Calculation of the TERP   90
    2.4.6   Case Study: ING's EUR 7.5 billion Rights Issue   91
2.5   Rights Issues of Convertible Bonds   95
    2.5.1   Case Study: Banco Popolare Rights Issue of a Convertible Bond   95
2.6   Accelerated Book-Buildings   98
    2.6.1   Product Description   98
    2.6.2   Advantages and Weaknesses of an ABB   99
    2.6.3   Estimating the Discount   99
    2.6.4   Case Study: IPIC's Disposal of 11.8% of Barclays   100
2.7   At the Market Offerings   100
    2.7.1   Product Description   100
    2.7.2   Case Study: US Treasury Placement of Citigroup Shares   101

3   Convertible Bonds and Mandatory Convertible Bonds   103
3.1   Introduction to Convertible Bonds   103
    3.1.1   What are Convertible Bonds?   103
    3.1.2   Convertible vs. Exchangeable Bonds – Exchange Property   104
3.2   Who Buys Convertible Bonds?   105
3.3   Convertible Bonds: The Issuer Perspective   106
3.4   Case Study: Infineon's Convertible Bond   107
    3.4.1   Main Terms of Infineon's Convertible Bond   107
    3.4.2   Conversion Price, Ratio, Premium and Lockout Period   108
    3.4.3   Hard No Call Period, Hard Call and Soft Call Options   109
    3.4.4   Put Rights   110
    3.4.5   Additional Clauses: Cash Option, Cash Top-up, Lock-up
           Period, Tax Call   111
    3.4.6   Value of a Convertible Bond at Maturity   112
    3.4.7   Value of a Convertible Bond during its Life   112
3.5   Delta Share Repurchase Strategy   114
3.6   Mandatory Convertible Bonds   115
3.7   Rationale for Issuing Mandatory Convertibles   115
3.8   Rationale for Investing in Mandatory Convertibles   116
3.9   Fixed Parity Mandatory Convertibles   116
    3.9.1   Case Study: Banco Santander's Fixed Parity
           Mandatory Convertible   116
3.10   Variable Parity Mandatory Convertibles   118
3.11   Dividend Enhanced Convertible Securities   118
    3.11.1   Conversion Mechanics of a DECS   118
    3.11.2   Anatomy of a DECS   120
    3.11.3   Embedded Derivatives in a DECS   121
    3.11.4   Pricing a DECS   122
3.12   Case Study: UBS's DECS   122

3.13   Special Clauses in Convertibles   124
      3.13.1   Dividend Protection Clauses   124
      3.13.2   Coupon Deferral Clauses   125
      3.13.3   Call Option Make-whole Clauses   126
      3.13.4   Change-of-control Make-whole Clauses   126
      3.13.5   Clean-up Call Clauses   127
      3.13.6   Net Share Settlement Clauses   127
3.14   Contingent Convertibles: FRESHES, CASHES and ECNS   127
      3.14.1   Case Study: Fortis's FRESH Instrument   128
      3.14.2   Case Study: Unicredit's CASHES Instrument   131
      3.14.3   Case Study: Lloyds ECN   136
      3.14.4   Case Study: Rabobank's SCN   139

4 Strategic Equity Transactions around Convertible/Exchangeable Bonds   141
4.1   Issuing an Exchangeable with a Third-party Guarantee   141
      4.1.1   Case Study: Controlinveste's Exchangeable Bonds on
              Portugal Telecom   141
      4.1.2   Transaction Overview   142
      4.1.3   Dividend Swap and Transaction Flows during the First Four Years   143
      4.1.4   Transaction Flows in Case of Exchanges or at Maturity   145
      4.1.5   Exchange Property Pledge and other Security Mechanisms   146
      4.1.6   Attractiveness of the Transaction to the Issuer and to BCP   147
4.2   Issuing a Convertible Through a Third Party   147
      4.2.1   Case Study: Novartis LEPOs and Put Options with Deutsche Bank   147
      4.2.2   Transaction Overview   147
      4.2.3   Deutsche Bank's Exposure to Novartis's Stock Price   149
      4.2.4   Effect of Deutsche Bank's Zero-coupon Convertibles on the
              Exchange Price   151
      4.2.5   Attractiveness of Deutsche Bank's Zero-coupon Exchangeables to
              Investors   152
      4.2.6   Advantages to Novartis and Relevance of a Call Right   152
4.3   Crystallizing a Gain in a Convertible Investment Through Warrants   153
      4.3.1   Case Study: Richemont Warrants Issue on Back of Convertible
              Preference Shares   153
      4.3.2   Warrants' Terms   154
      4.3.3   Analysis of R&R's Position   154
      4.3.4   Main Benefits to Richemont of the Warrants Issue   155
      4.3.5   Effect on BAT's Stock Price of the Warrants Issue   156
4.4   Monetizing a Stake with an Exchangeable Plus a Put   156
      4.4.1   Case Study: Deutsche Bank's Exchangeable into Brisa   156
      4.4.2   Transaction Overview   157
      4.4.3   Analysis of Deutsche Bank's Overall Position   158
4.5   Increasing Likelihood of Conversion with a Call Spread   161
      4.5.1   Case Study: Chartered Semiconductor's Call Spread with
              Goldman Sachs   161
      4.5.2   Goldman Sachs's Overall Position   162
      4.5.3   CSM's Overall Position   163

		4.5.4	Attractiveness of the Transaction to CSM	166
		4.5.5	Additional Remarks	167
	4.6	Decreasing Likelihood of Conversion with a Call Spread		169
		4.6.1	Case Study: Microsoft's Convertible Plus Call Spread	169
	4.7	Double Issuance of Exchangeable Bonds		169
		4.7.1	Case Study: ABC's Double Exchangeable	169
	4.8	Buying Back Conversion Rights		172
		4.8.1	Case Study: Cap Gemini's Repurchase of Conversion Right from Société Générale	172
	4.9	Buying Back Convertible/Exchangeable Bonds		175
		4.9.1	Case Study: TUI's Convertible Bond	175
	4.10	Pre-IPO Convertible Bonds		178

5 Hedging and Yield Enhancing Strategic Stakes — **181**

	5.1	Hedging a Strategic Stake		181
		5.1.1	Hedging with a Put Option	181
		5.1.2	Hedging with a Put Spread	184
		5.1.3	Hedging with a Collar	186
		5.1.4	Hedging with a Put Spread Collar	188
		5.1.5	Hedging with a Fly Put Spread	189
		5.1.6	Hedging with a Knock-out Put	191
		5.1.7	Summary of Main Hedging Strategies	193
		5.1.8	Hedging with Ladder Puts	193
		5.1.9	Hedging with Variable Premium and Variable Expiry Timer Puts	195
		5.1.10	Hedging with Pay-later Puts	197
	5.2	Yield Enhancement of a Strategic Stake		199
		5.2.1	Lending the Stock	199
		5.2.2	Selling Part of the Upside with a Call	200
		5.2.3	Monetization of Dividend Optionality	202
		5.2.4	Reduction of Dividend Withholding Taxes with a Stock Lending Strategy	204
		5.2.5	Reduction of Dividend Withholding Taxes with a Converse Strategy	205

6 Disposal of Strategic Stakes — **207**

	6.1	Most Common Disposal Strategies		207
		6.1.1	Case Study Assumptions	207
		6.1.2	Market Dribbling Out or Gradual Sale	208
	6.2	Deterministic Disposal Strategies		209
		6.2.1	ABB – Block Trade	209
		6.2.2	Mandatory Exchangeable Bond	211
		6.2.3	Indirect Issue of an Exchangeable Bond	211
	6.3	Enhanced Disposal Strategies		212
		6.3.1	Direct Issue of an Exchangeable Bond	213
		6.3.2	Sale of a Call Option	214
		6.3.3	One-speed Range Accrual	216

	6.3.4	Double-speed Range Accrual	220
	6.3.5	Double-speed Range Accrual with Final Call	221
	6.3.6	Double-speed Range Accrual with Deduction	222
	6.3.7	Double-speed Range Accrual with Knock-out	222
6.4	Derecognition Strategies		224
	6.4.1	Sale + Cash-settled Equity Swap	224
	6.4.2	Physically Settled Equity Swap + Call Option	227
6.5	Combination of ABB and a Call Option/Exchangeable		229
	6.5.1	Case Study: Germany's Disposal of Fraport with JP Morgan's Collaboration	229

7 Strategic Equity Derivatives in Mergers and Acquisitions — **235**

7.1	Keeping Voting Rights in Proxy Contests		237
	7.1.1	Case Study: Montalban Partners' Disposal of Gold International	237
7.2	Submitting Resolutions to an AGM		239
	7.2.1	Case Study: Laxey's Stock Lending Transaction	240
7.3	Increasing Likelihood of Success of a Merger Arbitrage Position		242
	7.3.1	Case Study: Perry's Equity Swaps with Bear Stearns and Goldman Sachs	242
7.4	Avoiding Mandatory Offer Rules		247
	7.4.1	Case Study: Agnelli Family Equity Swap with Merrill Lynch	247
7.5	Increasing Likelihood of Success of a Takeover		251
	7.5.1	Case Study: Unipol's Takeover of BNL and Call/Put Combination with Deutsche Bank	251

8 Stock Options Plans Hedging — **257**

8.1	Main Equity-based Compensation Plans		257
	8.1.1	Main Equity-based Compensation Plans	257
	8.1.2	Terminology of Stock Option Plans and SARs	258
8.2	IFRS Accounting for Equity-based Compensation Plans		259
	8.2.1	Accounting for Stock Options Plans	261
	8.2.2	Accounting for Stock Appreciation Rights	263
8.3	Case Study: ABC's ESOP and SAR		265
	8.3.1	Main Terms of ABC's ESOP and SAR	265
	8.3.2	Accounting for ABC's ESOP	266
	8.3.3	Accounting for ABC's SAR	270
8.4	Main ESOP/SAR Hedging Strategies		273
	8.4.1	Underlying Risks in ESOPs and SARs	273
	8.4.2	Hedging with Treasury Shares	274
	8.4.3	Hedging with Equity Swaps	275
	8.4.4	Hedging a SAR with an Enhanced Equity Swap	279
	8.4.5	Hedging with Standard Call Options	280
	8.4.6	Hedging with Auto Call Options	282
	8.4.7	Hedging with Timer Call Options	282
8.5	HSBC's Performance Share Plan		283
	8.5.1	Terms of HSBC's Performance Share Plan	283

	8.5.2	Accounting for the Plan	284
	8.5.3	Hedging the Plan	285

9 Equity Financings — **287**
	9.1	Case Study: Equity Collateralized Bond	287
		9.1.1 Bond Terms	287
		9.1.2 Main Documents of the Financing	288
		9.1.3 Parties to an Equity Financing	289
		9.1.4 Accounts in an Equity Financing	290
		9.1.5 Credit Enhancement Tools	291
		9.1.6 Early Termination Events	292
		9.1.7 Events of Default	295
		9.1.8 Syndicating the Equity Financing with a Credit Default Swap	297
		9.1.9 Recourse vs. Non-recourse Equity Financings	299
	9.2	Sale + Equity Swap	300
		9.2.1 Transaction Description	300
		9.2.2 Equity Swap Terms	300
		9.2.3 Equity Swap Flows	305
		9.2.4 Advantages and Weaknesses	307
	9.3	Prepaid Forward + Equity Swap + Pledge	308
		9.3.1 Product Description	308
		9.3.2 Equity Derivatives Terms	308
		9.3.3 Transaction Flows	314
		9.3.4 Advantages and Weaknesses	316
	9.4	Repo Financing	316
		9.4.1 Product Description	316
	9.5	Stock Loan Financing	317
		9.5.1 Product Description	317
	9.6	Put Financing	318
		9.6.1 Product Description	318
		9.6.2 Advantages and Weaknesses	319
	9.7	Collared Financing	320
		9.7.1 Product Description	320
		9.7.2 Advantages and Weaknesses	321
	9.8	Revolving Margin Loan Facilities	322
		9.8.1 Case Study: Oil SPE's Revolving Margin Loan Facility	322

10 Share Buybacks and Other Transactions on Treasury Shares — **327**
	10.1	Open Market Repurchase Programs	327
	10.2	Accelerated Repurchase Programs	329
		10.2.1 Case Study: Hewlett Packard's ASR with Merrill Lynch	329
	10.3	VWAP-Linked Repurchase Programs	332
		10.3.1 Execution on a Best Effort Basis	332
		10.3.2 Execution on a Guaranteed Basis	333
		10.3.3 Advantages and Weaknesses of a VWAP-linked Strategy	333

		10.3.4	Execution at a Discounted VWAP	334
		10.3.5	Execution at a Capped VWAP	337
	10.4	Prepaid Collared Repurchase Programs		338
		10.4.1	Case Study: Hewlett Packard's PCRP with BNP Paribas	339
	10.5	Deep-in-the-money Call Purchase		340
		10.5.1	Case Study: ABC's Acquisition of a Deep-in-the-money Call Option	341
	10.6	Asian Call Purchase		343
	10.7	Publicly Offered Repurchase Programs		345
		10.7.1	Case Study: Corporacion Dermoestetica's Public Offer to Acquire Own Shares	345
	10.8	Public Offer of Put Options		346
		10.8.1	Case Study: Swisscom's Public Offer of Put Options	346
	10.9	Private Sale of a Put Option		347
	10.10	Acquisition of Shares with a Range Accrual		348
		10.10.1	One-speed Range Accrual	348
		10.10.2	Double-speed Range Accrual	352
		10.10.3	Double-speed Range Accrual with Final Put	354
	10.11	Other Transactions on Treasury Shares		355
		10.11.1	Case Study: ABC's Restructuring of Call on Own Shares	355
		10.11.2	Case Study: Gilead's Share Repurchase Program Financed with Convertible Bonds	361
11	**Bank Regulatory Capital**			**365**
	11.1	An Overview of Basel III		365
		11.1.1	Precedent Bank Regulatory Capital Accords	365
		11.1.2	The Capital Ratio	366
		11.1.3	Bank Regulatory Capital	367
		11.1.4	Risk-weighted Assets	367
	11.2	Tier 1 Capital		369
		11.2.1	Common Equity Tier 1 Capital	369
		11.2.2	Additional Tier 1 Capital	373
	11.3	Tier 2 Capital		376
		11.3.1	Criteria for Inclusion in Tier 2 Capital	376
		11.3.2	Trigger Conditions for Hybrid Instruments	379
	11.4	Deductions from Common Equity Tier 1 Capital		380
		11.4.1	Goodwill and Other Intangible Assets (Except Mortgage Servicing Rights)	380
		11.4.2	Deferred Tax Assets	380
		11.4.3	Cash Flow Hedge Reserve	382
		11.4.4	Shortfall of the Stock of Provisions to Expected Losses	383
		11.4.5	Gain-on-sale Related to Securitization Transactions	383
		11.4.6	Gains and Losses on Fair Valued Own Liabilities due to Changes in Own Credit Risk	383
		11.4.7	Defined Benefit Pension Fund Assets and Liabilities	383
		11.4.8	Treasury Stock	385
		11.4.9	Reciprocal Stakes in Unconsolidated Financial Companies	385

	11.4.10	Less than 10% Stakes in Unconsolidated Financial Companies	385
	11.4.11	Significant Stakes in Unconsolidated Financial Companies	387
	11.4.12	Combined Deduction of Significant Investments in Unconsolidated Financial Entities, MSRs and DTAs	388
	11.4.13	Basel II 50/50 Deductions	389
11.5	Other Capital Buffers		389
	11.5.1	Capital Conservation Buffer	389
	11.5.2	Countercyclical Buffer	391
11.6	Transitional Arrangements		392
	11.6.1	Transitional Period	392
	11.6.2	Capital Instruments Failing Criteria for Eligibility in Capital	393
11.7	Leverage Ratio		393
11.8	Liquidity Coverage Ratio		394
11.9	Net Stable Funding Ratio		396
11.10	Case Study: Calculation of Minority Interests		397
11.11	Case Study: Creating Minority Interests		399
11.12	Case Study: Reducing Risk Weighting		401
11.13	Case Study: Releasing Common Equity		401
11.14	Case Study: Reducing an Unconsolidated Financial Stake		403
11.15	Case Study: Commerzbank's Capital Structure Enhancement with Credit Suisse		404

Bibliography   407

Index   409

Preface

This book tries to fill a gap in the financial literature. I was always frustrated by the lack of public information available on strategic equity. However, it is not surprising. Strategic equity transactions take place behind Chinese walls because often these transactions are highly confidential and market sensitive. Sometimes, investment banks and their clients try to avoid publicly disclosing a strategic equity transaction when it is part of an M&A transaction or aimed at circumventing specific accounting, tax and/or regulatory treatments.

The objective of this book is not to provide an exhaustive guide on strategic equity solutions. There are infinite possibilities in structuring strategic equity deals with different features in order to achieve a strategic objective. Instead, this book tries to be a useful reference and source of ideas. Although no two strategic equity transactions are the same, there are common threads that run through most strategic equity transactions (see Figure 0.1). This book is a summary of my work helping senior corporate and financial institutions executives to make sound strategic equity decisions in the following situations:

- Equity capital markets situations, especially regarding convertible bonds and mandatory convertible bonds.
- Hedge, yield enhancement and disposal of strategic stakes.
- Mergers and acquisitions.
- Stock options plan hedging.
- Equity financings.
- Share buybacks and other transactions on treasury shares.

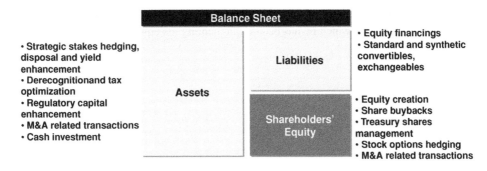

Figure 0.1 Main strategic equity transactions covered.

- Bank regulatory capital arbitrage.
- Tax-driven situations.

I strongly recommend this book to:

- **CFOs and treasurers of corporations** who are about to make a strategic equity decision. This book will help to devise a value-maximizing strategy and to assess if the entity is able to bear the risks associated with its implementation. This book is also useful in making an independent evaluation of the merits and risks of proposed structures to the company by its investment banks.
- **Equity derivatives, equity capital markets and corporate finance professionals at investment banks** looking to identify new strategic equity opportunities to sell to clients, to propose to clients innovative solutions and/or to quickly gain a specialized expertise in the strategic equity field.
- **Equity and credit research analysts** looking to better understand the rationale behind a particular strategic equity transaction entered into by an entity. This book can be useful to identify potential risks stemming from the transaction.
- **Private equity firms and hedge funds** looking to profit from a specific strategic situation of a company. This book can provide ideas about how to maximize profit while reducing the associated risk.
- **Accounting professionals** who are looking to understand a financial transaction before deciding its accounting treatment. This book can be useful to suggest a change in the product profile so a more favorable accounting treatment can be applied.
- **Legal/tax professionals** who are involved in strategic equity transactions and who are looking to gain a deeper knowledge of these transactions. This book can also help to devise a certain solution with a more favorable legal/tax treatment.
- **MBA students** who are looking to broaden their financial knowledge. This book complements some of the financial courses taught in an MBA, such as corporate finance, financial derivatives and strategic management. This book can also be useful to MBA students seeking an equity derivatives or equity capital markets position at an investment bank, or a position in the treasury or strategic development team of a corporation.

Besides its financial orientation, the book has two important objectives: to be practical and easy to read. In order to achieve the first objective, the book uses an extensive number of cases, many of them real situations. In order to achieve the second objective, I have also included around 200 figures (yes, I am a bit of a masochist). I hope that the reader finds this book a useful reference.

The opinions expressed in this book are those of the author alone and do not reflect the positions of the banks in which he has been implementing his equity derivatives practice.

About the Author

Juan Ramirez currently works in an international bank and is responsible for the marketing of strategic derivatives to the Iberian corporate and institutional clients. After earning a bachelor degree in electrical engineering at the ICAI University in Madrid, he joined the consumer products group at Arthur Andersen where he spent five years gaining a substantial exposure to the accounting world. After earning an MBA degree from the University of Chicago, Mr Ramirez moved to London to work at Chase Manhattan (currently JP Morgan). He has also worked at Lehman Brothers, Barclays Capital and Banco Santander.

Mr Ramirez has devoted more than 15 years to marketing structured derivatives solutions. During the last seven years he has been working in strategic equity transactions with a strong accounting, capital markets, tax and regulatory angle. Mr Ramirez is married and has three children.

1

Main Strategic Equity
Derivative Instruments

This chapter provides a good understanding of the equity derivative instruments most widely used by equity derivatives professionals. This is the most complex and technical chapter of this book. It aims to solidify the reader's technical knowledge of these instruments. I have also tried to emphasize the practical aspects of these instruments when applied to strategic equity transactions. I start with a discussion of less complex instruments such as equity forwards and equity swaps. I continue covering stock lending transactions – although not derivative instruments, they nonetheless are a key component of strategic equity transactions. Options are addressed next, starting with the basics and progressing to an explanation of option sensitivities and delta-hedging. Finally, I include more specialized equity derivative products such as dividend swaps, variance swaps and volatility swaps.

1.1 EQUITY FORWARDS

1.1.1 Equity Forwards

Equity forwards allow an investor to take bullish or bearish views on an underlying stock, a basket of stocks or a stock index.

- A **physically settled equity forward** is an agreement between two counterparties whereby one counterparty – the buyer – agrees to buy from the other counterparty – the seller – a specified number of shares of a specified stock or basket of stocks, at a specified time in the future – the settlement date – at a pre-agreed price – the forward price. This instrument is called a physically settled forward, because the underlying shares are delivered by the seller to the buyer. The buyer and the seller pay no upfront premium to enter into the equity forward.
- A **cash-settled equity forward** is an agreement between two counterparties whereby one counterparty – the buyer – receives at a specified time in the future – the settlement date – from the other counterparty – the seller – the appreciation of the underlying stock, basket of stocks or stock index, above a pre-agreed price – the forward price. Conversely, the seller receives from the buyer the depreciation of the underlying below the forward price. This forward is called a cash-settled forward, because no underlying shares are delivered to the buyer at maturity. Only cash is paid by one party to the other. The buyer and the seller pay no upfront premium to enter into the equity forward.
- Often a forward can be both cash-settled and physically settled, giving one of the two counterparties the right to choose the type of settlement just prior to maturity.

An equity forward agreement is formalized through a confirmation. The confirmation is generally legally subject to the terms and clauses of the International Swaps and Derivatives

Association (ISDA) Master Agreement signed between the two counterparties. As its name suggests, once signed, the Master Agreement governs all past and future individual derivative transactions entered into between the two counterparties.

1.1.2   Example of a Cash-settled Equity Forward on a Stock

Let's assume that our entity ABC Corp. has a positive view on Deutsche Telekom (DTE) stock for the next three months. As a result, ABC is considering entering into an equity forward. As seen earlier, a forward can be either physically settled or cash-settled. In a physically settled equity forward the buyer will pay to the seller an amount equal to the forward price multiplied by the number of shares, and the seller will deliver to the buyer the number of shares. In a cash-settled forward the appreciation or depreciation of the shares relative to the forward price is exchanged between the two counterparties. Because ABC is not interested in receiving DTE shares at maturity, ABC enters into a 3-month cash-settled equity forward on 10 million shares of DTE, with the following terms:

Equity Forward Main Terms	
Buyer	ABC Corp.
Seller	Gigabank
Trade date	20-September-20X1
Shares	Deutsche Telekom
Number of shares	10 million
Forward price	EUR 15.00
Settlement price	The closing price of the shares on the valuation date
Valuation date	20-December-20X1
Exchange	Eurex
Settlement method	Cash settlement
Cash settlement amount	The absolute value of:
	Number of shares $\times$ (Settlement price $-$ Forward price)
	With the convention that:
	If Settlement price $>$ Forward price, the amount shall be paid by the seller
	If Settlement price $<$ Forward price, the amount shall be paid by the buyer
Settlement date	23-December-20X1 (three exchange business days after the valuation date)

During the life of the equity forward, the flows between the two counterparties are the following.

At inception, the forward agreement is signed by the counterparties. No flows take place, as the buyer and the seller pay no upfront premium to enter into the equity forward.

Until maturity of the forward, no flows take place.

At maturity, the "settlement price" will be calculated on the "valuation date". In this example, the settlement price is the closing price of DTE stock on 20 December 20X1 (i.e., the valuation date). Immediately after, the "cash settlement amount" will be calculated as the absolute value

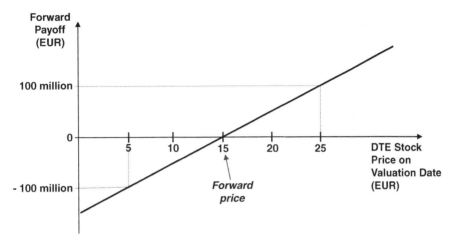

Figure 1.1   Equity forward payoff at maturity.

of the product of (i) the "number of shares" and (ii) the difference between the settlement price and the forward price. Three potential scenarios may take place:

- If DTE stock has appreciated relative to the forward price (i.e., the settlement price is greater than the forward price), ABC would receive from Gigabank the stock appreciation times the number of shares (i.e., the cash settlement amount) on the settlement date.
- Conversely, if DTE stock has depreciated relative to the forward price (i.e., the settlement price is lower than the forward price), ABC would pay to Gigabank the stock depreciation times the number of shares (i.e., the cash settlement amount) on the settlement date.
- If DTE stock has ended up at the same level as the forward price (i.e., the settlement price is equal to the forward price), no cash flows take place.

Let us assume that on the valuation date (20 December 20X1), DTE stock closes at EUR 18.00. The settlement price would then be EUR 18.00. ABC would receive from Gigabank EUR 30 million [= 10 million shares × (18.00 – 15.00)] on the settlement date (23 December 20X1).

Let us assume instead that on the valuation date (20 December 20X1), DTE stock closes at EUR 13.00. The settlement price would then be EUR 13.00. ABC would pay to Gigabank EUR 20 million [= 10 million shares × (15.00 – 13.00)] on the settlement date (23 December 20X1).

Figure 1.1 shows the profit or loss to ABC as a function of DTE's stock price at maturity. Therefore, DTE's maximum profit is unlimited while its maximum loss is limited to EUR 150 million (= 10 million shares × 15.00) reached if DTE's stock price is zero at maturity.

1.1.3   Example of a Physically Settled Equity Forward on a Stock

Let us assume that our entity, ABC Corp., plans to acquire 10 million shares of Deutsche Telekom (DTE) in three months' time. ABC is worried that DTE's stock price might increase

Figure 1.2 Physically settled equity forward, settlement at maturity.

during the next three months. As a result, ABC enters into a physically settled forward on 10 million shares of DTE, with the following terms:

Equity Forward Main Terms	
Buyer	ABC Corp.
Seller	Gigabank
Trade date	20-September-20X1
Shares	Deutsche Telekom
Number of shares	10 million
Forward price	EUR 15.00
Exchange	Eurex
Settlement method	Physical settlement
Settlement date	23-December-20X1

During the life of the equity forward, the flows between the two counterparties are the following.

At inception, the forward agreement is signed by the counterparties. No flows take place, as the buyer and the seller pay no upfront premium to enter into the equity forward.

Until maturity of the forward, no flows take place.

At maturity, "on the settlement date", the buyer – ABC – will pay to the seller – Gigabank – an amount equal to the forward price multiplied by the number of shares, and the seller – Gigabank – will deliver to the buyer – ABC – the number of shares of DTE, as shown in Figure 1.2. In other words, ABC will pay EUR 150 million (= 10 million × 15.00) in exchange for 10 million shares of DTE.

1.1.4 Calculating the Forward Price of a Stock

The easiest way to calculate a forward price of a stock is to come up with a riskless strategy, like the following:

- At inception, we buy one share of the stock paying the then prevailing stock price (i.e., the spot price). This purchase is financed at an interest rate. The overall cash flow at inception is zero, as the financing amount is invested in the stock.
- Also at inception, we will enter into a forward to sell the shares on a specific date (the maturity date).
- During the life of the forward, we will be lending the shares and receiving a fee, called the borrowing fee. We will invest any borrowing fee received until maturity at the then prevailing interest rate.
- During the life of the forward, we will be receiving the dividends distributed to the share. In our case the dividend would be paid to us by the stock borrower. We will invest the dividends until maturity.

- At maturity, we will sell the shares through the forward receiving the forward price, repay the financing, receive the amount resulting from the investment of the received dividends and receive the amount resulting from the investment of the received borrowing fee.

The cash flows at maturity are as follows:

$$\text{Forward price} - \text{Financing repayment amount} + \text{Reinvested dividends} + \text{Reinvested borrowing fee}$$

This cash flow has to be zero if no arbitrage opportunities are present (i.e., if the forward was priced accordingly). Therefore:

$$\text{Forward price} - \text{Financing repayment amount} + \text{Reinvested dividends} + \text{Reinvested borrowing fee} = 0$$

The amounts due to the reinvestment of the dividends and the fee are equivalent to their future value to maturity (FV). Rearranging the terms:

$$\text{Forward price} = \text{Financing repayment amount} - \text{FV(dividends)} - \text{FV(borrowing fee)}$$

Therefore, dividends paid out by the underlying stock, which lower the stock price on the ex-dividend date, have a negative effect on the value of the forward. The borrowing fee received for lending the stock also has a negative effect on the value of the forward.

The financing repayment amount can be expressed as the sum of (i) the spot price and (ii) the interest rate carry. As a result:

$$\textbf{Forward} = \textbf{Spot} + \textbf{Interest rate carry} - \textbf{FV(dividends)} - \textbf{FV(borrowing fee)}$$

If the forward matures in less than a year, the interest carry is calculated as:

$$\textbf{Interest carry} = \textbf{Spot} \times \textbf{Interest rate} \times \textbf{Day count fraction}$$

The following table summarizes the impact on the forward price of an increase in the specified variable, assuming everything else is equal:

	Forward price
Spot price	↑
Interest rate	↑
Dividends	↓
Borrowing fee	↓

As an example, let us assume that a stock is trading at EUR 100. The 3-month interest rate is 5% Actual/360. The company pays a EUR 2 dividend in one month (i.e., in 31 days). The borrowing fee is 0.20% annual Actual/365. The forward interest rate starting in one month and with a 2-month maturity is 4% annual Actual/360. The theoretical 3-month forward, assuming 92 calendar days in the period, is calculated as follows:

$$\text{Forward} = 100 + [100 \times 5\% \times 92/360] - [2 \times (1 + 4\% \times 62/360)] \\ - [100 \times 0.20\% \times 92/365]$$

Thus, the forward price is 99.21.

1.2 EQUITY SWAPS

Equity swaps are a convenient way to gain either long or short exposure to an equity underlying. The underlying can be a stock, a basket of stocks or a stock index. Based on the type of settlement, an equity swap can be either:

- A **cash-settled equity swap** – an agreement between two counterparties where one party receives the appreciation (and pays the depreciation) of a stock, a basket of stocks or a stock index in exchange for the payment of a stream of interest flows and sometimes the receipt of dividend payments. The other party has the opposite position.
- A **physically settled equity swap** – an agreement between two counterparties whereby one counterparty agrees to buy from the other counterparty the underlying shares and pays a pre-agreed amount in exchange for the payment of a stream of interest flows and sometimes the receipt of dividend payments.

An equity swap is an over-the-counter transaction between two counterparties. It is formalized through a confirmation. The confirmation is generally legally subject to the terms and clauses of the ISDA agreement signed between the two counterparties that sets out their obligations. Hereafter, I will be using the terms as set out by ISDA to cover the mechanics of an equity swap.

1.2.1 Total Return Equity Swaps

A **total return equity swap** is a transaction in which one party –the equity swap receiver – has a position equivalent to a long position in a stock, a basket of stocks or an equity index, while the other party – the equity swap payer – has the opposite position in the same underlying. In a total return equity swap, the equity amount payer and the equity amount receiver exchange during the life of the equity swap three strings of cash flows (see Figure 1.3):

- The **equity amount** reflects the price performance of a long position in the underlying stock relative to its initial price – the **reference price**. The **equity amount receiver** is the counterparty that benefits if the stock performance is positive. Conversely, the **equity amount payer** is the counterparty that benefits if the stock performance is negative.
- The **floating amount** reflects the cost of carrying the underlying stock. It is paid by the equity amount receiver to the equity amount payer. The floating amount is quoted as a floating interest rate plus a fixed spread. The floating rate is typically Libor, Euribor or a similar benchmark rate. The fixed spread is set at swap inception. Typically, the floating amount payments are made every three months, based on the equity swap notional.
- The **dividend amount** reflects the benefits of carrying the underlying stock. It is paid by the equity amount payer to the equity amount receiver.

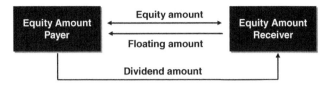

Figure 1.3 Total return equity swap cash flows.

The equity swap is called a total return equity swap because the equity amount receiver receives not only the appreciation of the stock price relative to the reference price but also the dividends distributed to the underlying stock. The equity amount receiver also pays the floating amount, which in a way resembles the interest payments of financing an investment with a notional equal to the equity amount. Therefore, the equity swap mimics a fully financed long position in the stock.

1.2.2 Price Return Equity Swaps

A **price return equity swap** is a transaction in which one party – the equity swap receiver – has a position equivalent to a long position in only the **price** of a stock, a basket of stocks or an equity index, while the other party – the equity swap payer – has the opposite position in the same underlying. In a price return equity swap, the equity amount payer and the equity amount receiver exchange during the life of the equity swap two strings of cash flows (see Figure 1.4):

- The **equity amount** reflects the price performance of a long position in the underlying stock relative to its initial price – the **reference price**. The appreciation of the stock price is received by the **equity amount receiver** from the **equity amount payer**. If, on the other hand, the stock depreciates, then the absolute value of the depreciation is paid to the equity amount payer from the equity amount receiver.
- The **floating amount** reflects the cost of carrying the underlying stock. It is paid by the equity amount receiver to the equity amount payer.

The equity swap is called a price return equity swap because the equity amount receiver receives only the appreciation of the stock relative to the reference price. The equity amount receiver does not receive the dividends distributed to the underlying stock. Therefore, the equity swap does not mimic a long position in the stock. On a stock that pays no dividends, a total return equity swap and a price return equity swap are the same instrument.

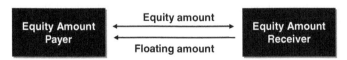

Figure 1.4 Price return equity swap cash flows.

1.2.3 Case Study: Physically Settled Total Return Equity Swap on Deutsche Telekom

In this subsection, I will cover in detail the mechanics of a physically settled total return equity swap on a stock with an example. Let us assume that ABC Corp. has 10 million shares of Deutsche Telekom (DTE), worth EUR 140 million. ABC wants to raise financing while maintaining economic exposure to the DTE stock. To raise the financing, ABC agrees with Gigabank to execute a sale of the DTE stake and to simultaneously enter into a physically settled total return equity swap.

Flows of the Transaction

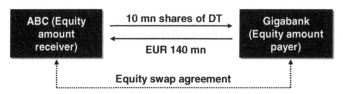

Figure 1.5 Flows on trade date.

The flows of the transaction on the trade date are as follows (see Figure 1.5):

- ABC sells its stake in DTE to Gigabank at the then prevailing stock price of EUR 14 per share. Thus, ABC raises EUR 140 million. Normally, the sale is executed through the stock exchange (i.e., ABC does not face Gigabank directly in the sale).
- ABC and Gigabank enter into a physically settled total return equity swap. The equity swap obliges ABC to buy back its DTE stake in one year's time at the same EUR 14 price per share.

The transaction flows during the life of the equity swap are as follows (see Figure 1.6):

- ABC pays an interest, the floating amount, to Gigabank based on the EUR 140 million equity swap notional.
- Gigabank pays to ABC an amount, the dividend amount, equivalent to the dividends distributed to the underlying DTE shares. This amount is paid on the same date the dividends are paid by DTE to its shareholders.

Figure 1.6 Flows during the life of the equity swap.

The transaction flows at maturity (i.e., on the settlement date of the equity swap) are as follows (see Figure 1.7):

- Through the physical settlement of the equity swap, ABC buys back its stake in DTE from Gigabank at a price of EUR 14 per share. ABC then pays EUR 140 million to Gigabank in exchange for 10 million shares of DTE.

It can be seen that all these flows are equivalent to Gigabank providing a EUR 140 million loan to ABC collateralized by 10 million shares of DTE. In theory, Gigabank should be offering better financing terms to ABC than in a standard loan because in case of ABC becoming insolvent, Gigabank can sell the DTE stock in the market and partially or totally repay the loan.

Figure 1.7   Flows on the settlement date of the equity swap.

Main Terms of the Equity Swap

The main terms of the equity swap are shown in the following table:

Physically Settled Total Return Equity Swap Terms	
Party A	ABC Corp.
Party B	Gigabank
Trade date	12-December-20X1
Effective date	15-December-20X1
Termination date	15-December-20X2
Underlying currency	EUR
Equity amount part	
Equity amount payer	Party B (Gigabank)
Equity amount receiver	Party A (ABC Corp.)
Shares	Deutsche Telekom common shares
Calculation agent	Party B (Gigabank)
Physical settlement	Applicable
Number of shares	10 million
Initial price	EUR 14.00
Equity notional amount	EUR 140 million
	Number of shares × Initial price
Settlement date	15-December-20X2
Floating amount part	
Floating amount payer	Party A (ABC Corp.)
Notional amount	The equity notional amount
Payment dates	At the end of each quarter (15-Mar-20X2, 15-Jun-20X2, 15-Sep-20X2 and 15-Dec-20X2)
Floating rate option	EUR-Euribor fixed on the second local business day preceding the last floating amount payment date. The floating rate for the initial period would be determined two local business days prior to the effective date
Designated maturity	3 months
Spread	Plus 120 bps (1.2%)
Floating rate day count fraction	Actual/360
Dividend amount part	
Dividend amount	100% of the paid amount
Dividend payer	Party B (Gigabank)
Dividend receiver	Party A (ABC)
Dividend period	The period commencing on, and including, the third scheduled trading day preceding the effective date and ending on, and including, the termination date
Dividend payment date	The date of the payment of the dividend by the issuer of the shares
Reinvestment of dividends	Not applicable

The **trade date** is the date on which the two counterparties to the equity swap agree on the terms of the equity swap. In our case, ABC and Gigabank agreed on the equity swap terms on 12 December 20X1.

The **effective date** is the date on which the equity swap starts. In our case, the equity swap started on 15 December 20X1. On this date, Gigabank had already put in place its initial hedge. Also, the interest period usually starts on the effective date.

The **termination date** is the date on which the equity swap ceases to exist. In our case, the termination date was 15 December 20X2. In other words, the equity swap term was one year.

The equity amount part

The **equity amount part** represents the information regarding the equity underlying and the way the equity swap will be settled. In our example, the equity swap will be **physically settled**, meaning that on the **settlement date** the equity amount receiver would be receiving the **number of shares** of DTE in exchange for the **equity notional amount**. The equity notional amount was determined as follows:

$$\text{Equity notional amount} = \text{Number of shares} \times \text{Initial price}$$
$$\text{Equity notional amount} = 10 \text{ million shares} \times 14$$
$$= \text{EUR } 140 \text{ million}$$

The floating amount part

The **notional amount** as defined in the floating amount part of the equity swap confirmation is the underlying quantity upon which floating amount payment obligations are computed. Normally this notional amount equates to the equity notional amount. Thus, in our case the notional amount was EUR 140 million.

In our example, ABC will pay Euribor 3-month plus 120 basis points at the end of each quarter. The Euribor 3-month rate is set two business days prior to the beginning of the interest period. The interest (i.e., the **floating amount**) to be paid at the end of each quarterly period is calculated as:

$$\text{Floating amount} = \text{Notional amount} \times (\text{Euribor 3-month} + 1.20\%) \times \text{Actual days}/360$$

The "360" that appears in the formula is the denominator of the **floating rate day count**. **Actual days** are the number of calendar days in the interest period.

Let us assume that the Euribor 3-month two business days prior to 15 December 20X1 was fixed at 3.30%. Let us assume further that there were 91 calendar days in the period from 15 December 20X1 to 15 March 20X2. At the end of the interest period (i.e., on 15 March 20X2) ABC paid the following floating amount (see Figure 1.8):

$$\text{Floating amount} = 140 \text{ million} \times (3.30\% + 1.20\%) \times 91/360 = \text{EUR } 1,592,500$$

The dividend amount part

The **dividend amount** reflects the benefits of carrying the underlying stock, mainly cash dividends distributed to the underlying shares. If an ex-dividend date falls in the dividend

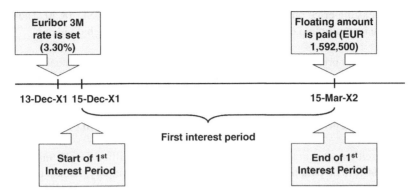

Figure 1.8 First floating amount period.

period (i.e., in our case the period between the effective date and the termination date), an amount equal to a percentage of the paid amount by the issuer of the stock is paid by the dividend payer – Gigabank – to the dividend receiver – ABC. In our example, Gigabank has to pay 100% of the ordinary and extraordinary cash or stock dividends declared in the currency of the company announcement. Stock/scrip dividends are included at the equivalent cash amount. The dividend amount is paid on the same date on which the issuer of the shares pays the dividend to the shareholders. Note that in this example, dividends are not reinvested.

In our case, the "dividend amount" was defined as "100% of the paid amount". When an issuer declares a dividend, the amount declared is called the "**gross dividend**" (i.e., the paid amount). The issuer of the shares – DTE – may levy a withholding tax when distributing dividends to Gigabank. As an example, let us assume that Gigabank receives what is called a "**net dividend**", for example 85% of the gross dividend. As a result, Gigabank would incur an additional cost if it pays 100% of the gross dividends to ABC. In order to not incur this additional cost, the dividend payer – Gigabank – pays to the dividend receiver – ABC – a dividend amount net of any withholding taxes or other taxes or duties in connection with the receipt of such dividend, equating to the dividend it receives from DTE. In this example, the "dividend amount" would be defined as "85% of the paid amount".

Reinvestment of Dividends

Sometimes, in a total return equity swap dividends are reinvested until maturity or until the next equity notional is reset. The reinvestment does not assume that the dividend proceeds are invested in money market instruments. Instead, the dividend proceeds are assumed to be reinvested in the same stock, at the closing of the ex-dividend date. Let us assume that the initial price of an equity swap on 10 million shares of a specific stock was USD 17.90. The equity swap effective date was 15 December 20X1 and its termination date was 15 December 20X2. During the life of the equity swap, the underlying stock paid two cash dividends:

- A gross dividend of USD 0.5 per share. Its ex-dividend date was 10 March 20X2. The closing price of the stock on 10 March 20X2 was USD 18.10.
- A gross dividend of USD 0.6 per share. Its ex-dividend date was 10 September 20X2. The closing price of the stock on 10 September 20X2 was USD 18.30.

The stock closing price on the equity swap valuation date was USD 18.50. The settlement price needs to be multiplied by the adjustment factors related to each dividend:

Settlement price = USD $18.50 \times$ Adjustment factor$_1 \times$ Adjustment factor$_2$
Adjustment factor = $1 +$ [Dividend/(Share price on ex-dividend date)]
Adjustment factor$_1 = 1 + (0.50/18.10) = 1.02762$
Adjustment factor$_2 = 1 + (0.60/18.30) = 1.03279$
Settlement price = USD $18.50 \times 1.02762 \times 1.03279 =$ USD 19.63

The cash settlement amount would then be USD 17.3 million [= 10 million shares $\times$ $(19.63 - 17.90)$] to be paid by the equity amount payer to the equity amount receiver.

1.2.4 Case Study: Cash-settled Total Return Equity Swap on Deutsche Telekom

In this subsection, I will cover in detail the mechanics of a cash-settled total return equity swap on a stock using a similar example. In this case, ABC believes that the stock of Deutsche Telekom (DTE) will increase in value over the next 12 months. ABC does not own DTE stock at inception and it is not interested in acquiring any DTE shares at maturity. ABC acquires the economic equivalent of a long position in the stock with a cash-settled total return equity swap.

Main Terms of the Equity Swap

The main terms of the equity swap are shown in the following table:

Cash-settled Total Return Equity Swap Terms	
Party A	ABC Corp.
Party B	Gigabank
Trade date	12-December-20X1
Effective date	15-December-20X1
Termination date	15-December-20X2
Underlying currency	EUR
Equity amount part	
Equity amount payer	Party B (Gigabank)
Equity amount receiver	Party A (ABC Corp.)
Shares	Deutsche Telekom common shares
Exchange	Euronext
Calculation agent	Party B (Gigabank)
Cash settlement	Applicable
Number of shares	10 million
Initial price	EUR 14.00
Equity notional amount	EUR 140 million
	Number of shares $\times$ Initial price
Settlement price	The price per share at the valuation time on the valuation date
Valuation time	At the close of trading on the exchange
Valuation date	12-December-20X2 (the third exchange business day preceding the settlement date)
Settlement date	15-December-20X2 (the termination date)

Cash-settled Total Return Equity Swap Terms

Floating amount part

Floating amount payer	Party A (ABC Corp.)
Notional amount	The equity notional amount
Payment dates	At the end of each quarter (15-Mar-20X2, 15-Jun-20X2, 15-Sep-20X2 and 15-Dec-20X2)
Floating rate option	EUR-Euribor fixed on the second local business day preceding the last floating amount payment date. The floating rate for the initial period would be determined two local business days prior to the effective date
Designated maturity	3 months
Spread	Plus 120 bps (1.2%)
Floating rate day count fraction	Actual/360

Dividend amount

Dividend amount	100% of the paid amount
Dividend payer	Gigabank
Dividend receiver	ABC Corp.
Dividend period	The period commencing on, and including, the third scheduled trading day preceding the effective date and ending on, and including, the valuation date
Dividend payment date	The date of the payment of the dividend by the issuer of the shares
Reinvestment of dividends	Not applicable

Flows of the Transaction

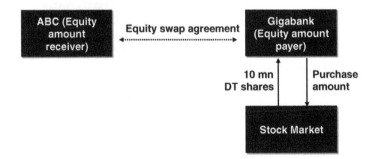

Figure 1.9   Flows on trade date.

The flows of the transaction on the trade date are as follows (see Figure 1.9):

- ABC and Gigabank enter into the cash-settled total return equity swap on 10 million shares of DTE. The initial price is set at EUR 14.00.
- Gigabank initially hedges its position by buying 10 million DTE shares in the stock market.

The flows of the transaction during the life of the equity swap are as follows (see Figure 1.10):

- ABC pays an interest, the floating amount, to Gigabank based on the EUR 140 million equity swap notional. The floating amount is identical to the physically settled equity swap covered in our previous case.

Figure 1.10 Flows during the life of the equity swap.

- Gigabank pays to ABC an amount, the dividend amount, equivalent to the dividends distributed to the underlying DTE shares. This amount is paid on the same date the dividends are distributed by DTE to its shareholders. The dividend amount is identical to the physically settled equity swap covered in our previous case.

The flows of the transaction at maturity (i.e., on settlement date of the equity swap) are as follows (see Figure 1.11):

- Gigabank unwinds its hedge, selling 10 million shares of DTE in the market.
- ABC and Gigabank settle the equity swap after calculating the settlement amount.

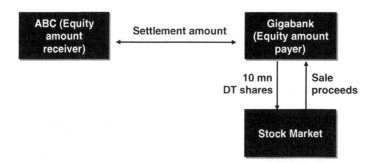

Figure 1.11 Flows on the settlement date of the equity swap.

On the valuation date, 12 December 20X2, the settlement amount would be calculated as:

Settlement amount = Number of shares × (Settlement price − Initial price)
Settlement amount = EUR 10 million × (Settlement price − 14.00)

The settlement price would be the closing price of DTE stock on the valuation date − 13 December 20X2.

- If the settlement amount is positive, the equity amount payer – Gigabank – would pay to the equity amount receiver – ABC – the settlement amount. For example, if the settlement price is EUR 17.00, ABC would receive from Gigabank EUR 30 million [= 10 million × (17.00 − 14.00)].
- If the settlement amount is negative, the equity amount receiver – ABC – would pay to the equity amount payer – Gigabank – the absolute value of the settlement amount. For example, if the settlement price is EUR 12.00, Gigabank would receive from ABC EUR 20 million [= Absolute value of 10 million × (12.00 − 14.00)].

1.2.5 Determination of the Initial Price

Commonly the bank facilitating the equity swap, Gigabank in our case, would initially be hedging its market exposure under the equity swap. The start of the execution of the hedge would start on trade date. Due to the fact that the delta of an equity swap is either 100% or minus 100%, the bank needs initially either to buy or to sell the **number of shares**. In our case, because Gigabank was exposed to a rising stock price and the number of shares was 10 million, Gigabank needed to buy 10 million DTE shares at the beginning of the transaction.

The **initial price** is commonly set according to one of the following three ways:

1. The acquisition/sale price of the shares executed in one block.

    In our previous case, the physically settled total return equity swap on Deutsche Telekom, Gigabank acquired the shares to initially hedge its position directly from ABC in one single transaction. In that case, the shares were acquired by Gigabank at EUR 14 per share. Therefore, the initial price was set at EUR 14 because it was the price at which Gigabank put in place its initial hedge. In this situation, the initial price is known on the trade date. No initial hedging period is needed.

2. The volume-weighted average price per share at which the bank puts in place its initial hedge.

    In most transactions, the initial hedge is put in place in the market during a period called the initial hedging period. When the size of the transaction is large relative to the average daily volume of the underlying, the initial hedge is executed during several days (see Figure 1.12). Let us assume that Gigabank had to buy the shares in the market. In order to not affect the stock price, and to comply with stock exchange regulations, Gigabank would try to not exceed 20% of the daily volume for DTE stock. If the daily volume average of DTE stock is 20 million shares, Gigabank would need 2.5 days to buy the 10 million DTE shares [= 10 million/(20 million × 20%)]. More formally, the initial price would be defined as: "the weighted average execution price at which Gigabank buys the shares between the trade date and the last day during which Gigabank puts in place its hedge position, on a best effort basis as determined and notified by the calculation agent. This last day will be the effective date. Gigabank shall notify ABC of the weighted average execution price at which Gigabank buys the shares on a daily basis whilst it is putting in place its hedge position."

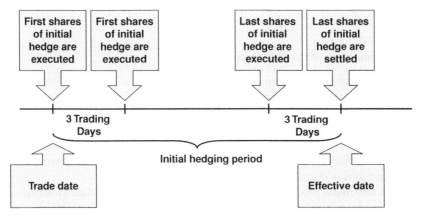

Figure 1.12 Initial hedging period.

The problem with this method of setting the initial price is that ABC is exposed to a poor execution by Gigabank. If Gigabank is not careful, the execution price might underperform the volume-weighted average price of the DTE stock during the period.

The effective date becomes the date on which the last shares of the initial hedge are settled. Because Gigabank has acquired shares during the initial hedging period, it has to finance the acquisition of these shares. As a result, ABC has to compensate Gigabank for the expense incurred by paying to Gigabank an initial floating amount on the effective date. This initial floating amount is calculated as the sum, for each day of the initial hedging period, of the acquisition expense:

$$\text{Acquisition expense} = (\text{Shares acquired}) \times (\text{Initial floating rate} + \text{Spread}) \times \text{Days}/360$$

where:

Shares acquired = Number of shares settled on such day
Initial floating rate = Euribor rate fixed two days prior to the first day of the initial
                         hedging period
Days = Number of calendar days from such day until the effective date

3. The average of the VWAP over a number of days.

Less frequent is to set the reference price as the average of an official price of the stock during a predetermined number of days. The most widely used official price is the volume-weighted average price (VWAP) of the day. For example, in our case the initial price could have been defined as "the arithmetic average of the daily volume-weighted average price over three exchange business days after the trade date". The advantage for ABC is that the calculation of the initial price is transparent, not depending on how Gigabank executes the hedge.

In our case, Gigabank puts in place its initial hedge by buying 10 million DTE shares in the market. Let us call the average price at which Gigabank buys these 10 million shares the "hedging price". Therefore, Gigabank is running the risk of any deviations of the hedging price relative to the average VWAP during the pre-agreed three days. It obliges Gigabank to acquire the shares in each of the three days, trying to mimic the VWAP for that day. If this risk is substantial, Gigabank would take it into account by requesting a higher spread from ABC.

1.2.6 Determination of the Settlement Price

One moment before the valuation time on the valuation date, the bank counterparty to the equity swap is either long or short the underlying number of shares. In our case, Gigabank was long 10 million shares of DTE. Therefore, at the valuation time on the valuation date Gigabank would need to sell 10 million shares immediately.

When the settlement mode is physical settlement, on the settlement date Gigabank will sell the 10 million shares to ABC at the initial price. In this case, the hedge unwind by Gigabank is not an issue, as it is executed in one block.

When the settlement mode is cash settlement, on the settlement date Gigabank and ABC will settle a cash amount (the settlement amount) but no shares will be exchanged between the two counterparties. At the same time, Gigabank will be unwinding its hedge by selling

10 million shares in the market. As a result, Gigabank would be exposed to any deviation of the price at which it sells the stock relative to the settlement price. Commonly, in a cash-settlement equity swap the settlement price is defined in one of the following ways:

- The closing price of the shares on a specific day. The valuation time is defined as "the close of the regular trading session on the valuation date". In order to mitigate its risk, Gigabank would need to sell the 10 million DTE shares at the closing, which can have a substantial impact on the stock closing price. Therefore, this definition of the settlement price makes sense when the number of shares of the underlying is small relative to its average daily volume.
- The arithmetic average of the daily VWAP over a pre-established number of days. In our case, it is expected that the hedge unwind would take three trading days. The settlement price would then be defined as "the arithmetic average of the daily volume-weighted average price over three exchange business days prior to and including the valuation date". As discussed in the previous subsection on determination of the initial price, in order to mitigate its risk, Gigabank would need to sell the shares during each of the pre-established days, trying to replicate the VWAP of such day. As each day Gigabank is running the risk of not achieving the VWAP, Gigabank would take it into account by requesting a higher spread from ABC.
- The volume-weighted average price per share at which the bank unwinds its hedge. More formally, "the weighted average execution price at which Gigabank sells the shares of its hedge position during the three exchange business days prior to, and including, the valuation date, on a best effort basis as determined and notified by the calculation agent. Gigabank shall notify ABC of the weighted average execution price at which Gigabank sells the shares on a daily basis whilst it is unwinding its hedge position." With this definition of the settlement price, Gigabank is not exposed to any market risks related to the unwinding of its hedge. However, ABC is exposed to a lower than expected sale price due to a bad execution by Gigabank. A lower than expected sale price will imply a lower than expected settlement price, diminishing ABC's profit (or enlarging its loss).

1.2.7 Equity Notional Resets

In our previous case, the equity notional was settled at the end of the equity swap life. It is not unusual that the equity notional is reset periodically, commonly coinciding with the payment of the floating amount. Long-term equity swaps generally reset quarterly, with the two counterparties exchanging payments based on the previous three months' returns. This makes the long-term equity swap equivalent to a series of three-month equity swaps. Of course, the inclusion of equity notional resets makes sense only for cash-settlement equity swaps. Equity swaps with equity notional resets help to reduce the counterparty credit risk associated with long-term transactions.

1.2.8 Case Study: Total Return Equity Swap on EuroStoxx 50

Although quite similar to a cash-settled equity swap on a stock, an equity swap on a stock index has some specific features. In this case I will try to address these peculiarities. Let us assume that ABC Corp. has the view that the main European stock index, the EuroStoxx 50 is going to have a strong performance during the next 12 months. In the following case, ABC obtains through a cash-settled total return equity swap an economic exposure to the EuroStoxx 50 index without physically owning the stocks members of the index. The main terms of the equity swap are shown in the following table:

Terms of a Total Return Equity Swap on a Stock Index	
Party A	ABC Corp.
Party B	Gigabank
Trade date	12-December-20X1
Effective date	15-December-20X1
Termination date	15-December-20X2
Underlying currency	EUR
Equity amount part	
Underlying index	EuroStoxx 50 index
Type of return	Total return
Calculation agent	Party B (Gigabank)
Number of baskets	100,000 (for avoidance of doubt, the number of baskets is in EUR being 10,000 contracts $\times$ 10 EUR tick value)
Initial index level (Index$_0$)	3,500
Equity notional amount	EUR 350 million (Number of baskets $\times$ Index$_0$)
Equity amount	Equity notional amount $\times$ [(Index$_T$ − Index$_0$)/Index$_0$]
Equity amount payer	Party B (Gigabank)
Equity amount receiver	Party A (ABC Corp.)
Index$_T$	Level of the index at the closing of the valuation date
Cash settlement	Applicable
Settlement currency	EUR
Valuation date	12-December-20X2
Settlement date	15-December-20X2
Floating amount part	
Floating amounts payer	Party A (ABC Corp.)
Floating amount	The equity notional amount
Payment dates	At the end of each quarter (15-Mar-20X2, 15-Jun-20X2, 15-Sep-20X2 and 15-Dec-20X2)
Floating rate option	EUR-Euribor fixed on the second local business day preceding the last floating amount payment date. The floating rate for the initial period would be determined two local business days prior to the effective date
Designated maturity	3 months
Spread	Plus 100 bps (1.0%)
Floating rate day count fraction	Actual/360
Dividend amount part	
Dividend amount payer	Party B (Gigabank)
Dividend amount receiver	Party A (ABC Corp.)
Dividend amounts	Number of baskets $\times$ Dividend per basket
Dividend period	Each quarterly period, coinciding with each interest period

Flows of the Transaction

The flows of the transaction on the trade date are as follows (see Figure 1.13):

- ABC and Gigabank enter into the cash-settled total return equity swap on 100,000 baskets of the EuroStoxx 50 index. The initial index level is set at EUR 3,500.

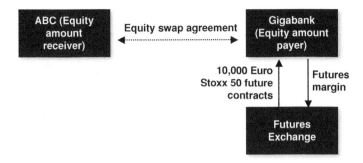

Figure 1.13 Flows on trade date.

• Gigabank initially hedges its position by buying 10,000 contracts of EuroStoxx 50 index futures. Gigabank posts initial margin at the futures exchange. This flow is not part of the equity swap.

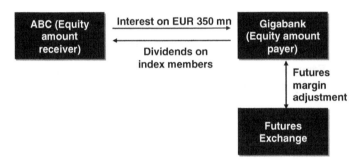

Figure 1.14 Flows during the life of the equity swap.

The flows of the transaction during the life of the equity swap are as follows (see Figure 1.14):

• ABC pays an interest, the floating amount, to Gigabank. ABC pays Euribor 3-month + 100 bps on the EUR 350 million equity notional amount.
• Gigabank pays to ABC an amount, the dividend amount, equivalent to the dividends distributed to the underlying stocks of the EuroStoxx 50 index during the dividend period. This amount is paid on the same date the floating amount is paid. The dividend amount is calculated by multiplying the "number of baskets" by the "dividend per basket" (to be defined later).
• Gigabank, on a daily basis, posts additional margin (or recovers some of the margin posted) to the futures exchange. This flow is not part of the equity swap.

The flows of the transaction at maturity (i.e., on the settlement date of the equity swap) are as follows (see Figure 1.15):

• Gigabank unwinds its hedge, selling 10,000 contracts of EuroStoxx 50 index futures. Gigabank receives the margin posted at the futures exchange.
• ABC and Gigabank settle the equity swap after calculating the equity amount. If the equity amount is positive, the index has appreciated and Gigabank pays to ABC the equity amount.

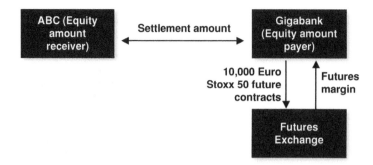

Figure 1.15   Flows on the settlement date of the equity swap.

If, on the other hand, the equity amount is negative, the index has depreciated and ABC pays to Gigabank the absolute value of the equity amount.

On valuation date, 12 December 20X2, the equity amount would be calculated as:

$$\text{Equity amount} = \text{Equity notional amount} \times [(\text{Index}_T - \text{Index}_0)/\text{Index}_0]$$

or also:

$$\text{Equity amount} = \text{Number of baskets} \times (\text{Index}_T - \text{Index}_0)$$
$$\text{Equity amount} = \text{EUR } 100{,}000 \times (\text{Index}_T - 3{,}500)$$

Index_T is the closing price of the EuroStoxx 50 index on the valuation date – 13 December 20X2.

- If the equity amount was positive, the equity amount payer – Gigabank – would pay to the equity amount receiver – ABC – the equity amount on the settlement date. For example, if Index_T was 4,000, ABC would receive from Gigabank EUR 50 million [= 100,000 × (4,000 – 3,500)].
- If the equity amount was negative, the equity amount receiver – ABC – would pay to the equity amount payer – Gigabank – the absolute value of the equity amount on the settlement date. For example, if Index_T is 3,000, Gigabank would receive from ABC EUR 50 million [= Absolute value of 100,000 × (3,000 – 3,500)].

Calculation of the Dividend per Basket

As seen earlier, Gigabank pays to ABC an amount, the dividend amount, equivalent to the dividends distributed to the underlying stocks of the EuroStoxx 50 index during the dividend period. In our case, the dividend period was each quarterly period during the life of the equity swap. Thus, the dividend amount is paid on the same date the floating amount is paid (i.e., at the end of each quarterly period). The dividend amount is calculated as:

$$\text{Dividend amount} = \text{Number of baskets} \times \text{Dividend per basket}$$

The "Dividend per basket" is calculated as:

$$\sum_s \sum_i \frac{n_{is} \times d_{is}}{D_i}$$

where:

    i means each weekday (each a "Relevant day$_i$") in the relevant dividend period.

    s means, in respect of each Relevant day$_i$, each share (each a "Share") that is comprised in the index on such a relevant day.

    d_{is} means, in respect of each Share$_i$ and a Relevant day$_t$:

        (a) if an ex-dividend date in respect of such Share$_i$ falls on such Relevant day$_t$, an amount equal to the relevant dividend in respect of such Share$_i$ and such Relevant day$_t$; or

        (b) otherwise, zero (0).

    n_{is} means, in respect of each Share$_i$ and a Relevant day$_t$, the number of such free-floating Share$_i$ comprised in the index, as calculated and published by the index sponsor on such Relevant day$_t$.

    D_i means, in respect of each Relevant day$_t$, the official index divisor, as calculated and published by the index sponsor on such Relevant day$_t$.

    "Relevant dividends" means "All dividends" for every period, for member stocks of the index that trade ex-dividend in that period, and for which the index sponsor does not adjust the index. If the index sponsor adjusts the index for part of a dividend, the remaining part is considered the relevant dividend.

    "All dividends" means:

- "Declared cash dividend" – an amount per Share$_i$ as declared by the issuer of such Share$_i$ where the ex-dividend date falls on such Relevant day$_t$, before the withholding or deduction of taxes at the source by or on behalf of any applicable authority having power to tax in respect of such a dividend, and shall exclude any imputation or other credits, refunds or deductions granted by any applicable authority having power to tax in respect of such dividend and any taxes, credits, refunds or benefits imposed, withheld, assessed or levied thereon and/or

- "Declared cash equivalent dividend" – the cash value of any stock dividend declared by the issuer of such Share$_i$ where the ex-dividend date falls on such Relevant day$_t$ (or, if no cash value is declared by the relevant issuer, the cash value of such stock dividend as determined by the calculation agent), calculated by reference to the opening price of such ordinary shares on the ex-dividend date applicable to that stock dividend.

1.2.9 Compo Equity Swaps

Through a compo equity swap, an investor can express a view that foreign stocks will rise or decline, taking also a position in the related foreign currency. A compo swap equity swap is equivalent to a direct foreign stock investment executed in an equity swap form. Therefore, a compo equity swap is an equity swap in which the underlying is denominated in a currency (the foreign currency) other than the currency in which the equity swap is denominated (the domestic currency). The initial and final values of the underlying are denominated in the foreign currency and are converted into the domestic currency using the exchange rate prevailing at the time the initial and final values are calculated. Although the equity swap is denominated in the investor's base currency, the investor is exposed to currency risk.

    Let us assume that ABC, a EUR-based entity, thinks that the S&P 500 index will rise strongly during the next 12 months. The S&P 500 index is denominated in USD. ABC also thinks that the USD will appreciate relative to the EUR. ABC enters into a compo price return equity swap with Gigabank with the following terms:

Terms of a Compo Price Return Equity Swap on a Stock Index

Party A	ABC Corp.
Party B	Gigabank
Trade date	12-December-20X1
Effective date	15-December-20X1
Termination date	15-December-20X2
Underlying currency	USD
Initial exchange rate (FX_0)	1.2500
Final exchange rate (FX_T)	The USD/EUR exchange rate as published on Bloomberg WMCO page on the valuation date at 04:00 p.m. London time
Equity amount part	
Underlying index	S&P 500 index
Type of return	Price return
Calculation agent	Party B (Gigabank)
Number of baskets	100,000
Initial index level ($Index_0$)	USD 1,200
Equity notional amount	EUR 96 million (Number of baskets $\times$ $Index_0/FX_0$)
Equity amount	Number of baskets $\times$ ($Index_T/FX_T - Index_0/FX_0$)
Equity amount payer	Party B (Gigabank)
Equity amount receiver	Party A (ABC Corp.)
$Index_T$	Level of the index at the closing of the valuation date
Cash settlement	Applicable
Settlement currency	EUR
Valuation date	12-December-20X2
Settlement date	15-December-20X2
Floating amount part	
Floating amounts payer	Party A (ABC Corp.)
Floating amount	The equity notional amount
Payment dates	At the end of each quarter (15-Mar-20X2, 15-Jun-20X2, 15-Sep-20X2 and 15-Dec-20X2)
Floating rate option	EUR-Euribor fixed on the second local business day preceding the last floating amount payment date. The floating rate for the initial period would be determined two local business days prior to the effective date
Designated maturity	3 months
Spread	Plus 20 bps (0.20%)
Floating rate day count fraction	Actual/360
Dividend amount part	**Not applicable**

The mechanics of the compo equity swap are quite similar to the cash-settled equity swap case covered previously.

The flows of the transaction on the trade date are as follows:

- ABC and Gigabank enter into the cash-settled compo price return equity swap on 100,000 baskets of the S&P 500 index. The initial index level ($Index_0$) is set at USD 1,200. The initial USD/EUR exchange rate (FX_0) is set at 1.2500.
- Gigabank initially hedges its position by buying 400 contracts of S&P 500 index futures. Gigabank posts initial margin at the futures exchange.

The flows of the transaction during the life of the equity swap are as follows:

- ABC pays an interest, the floating amount, to Gigabank. ABC pays Euribor 3-month + 20 bps on the EUR 96 million equity notional amount. Note that although the underlying stock index is denominated in USD, the floating amount is denominated in EUR.
- In this example there is no dividend amount, as it is a price return swap. Therefore, Gigabank keeps the dividends distributed to the underlying stocks of the S&P 500 index during the life of the equity swap. As a result, Gigabank compensates ABC by charging a lower spread (20 basis points in our case).

The flows of the transaction at maturity (i.e., on the settlement date of the equity swap) are as follows:

- Gigabank unwinds its hedge, selling 400 contracts of the S&P 500 index futures. Gigabank receives back the margin posted at the futures exchange.
- ABC and Gigabank settle the equity swap after calculating the equity amount. If the equity amount is positive, Gigabank pays to ABC the equity amount. If, on the other hand, the equity amount is negative, ABC pays to Gigabank the absolute value of the equity amount.

On the valuation date, 12 December 20X2, the equity amount would be calculated as:

$$\text{Equity amount} = \text{Number of baskets} \times (\text{Index}_T/\text{FX}_T - \text{Index}_0/\text{FX}_0)$$

Index_T is the closing price of the S&P 500 index on the valuation date – 12 December 20X2. FX_T is the USD/EUR exchange rate on the valuation date.

If the equity amount was positive, the equity amount payer – Gigabank – would pay to the equity amount receiver – ABC – the equity amount on the settlement date. For example, if Index_T is 1,600 and FX_T is 1.10, ABC would receive from Gigabank EUR 49,454,545.46 [= $100,000 \times (1,600/1.10 - 1,200/1.25)$].

If the equity amount was negative, the equity amount receiver – ABC – would pay to the equity amount payer – Gigabank – the absolute value of the equity amount on the settlement date. For example, if Index_T is 1,000 and FX_T is 1.30, Gigabank would receive from ABC EUR 19,076,923.08 (= Absolute value of [$100,000 \times (1,000/1.30 - 1,200/1.25)$]).

It is important to note that ABC is exposed to both the S&P 500 index and the USD/EUR exchange rate performances. ABC benefits from a rising S&P 500 index and/or from a declining USD/EUR FX rate. Conversely, ABC loses from a declining S&P 500 index and/or from a rising USD/EUR FX rate.

1.2.10 Quanto Equity Swaps

Through a quanto equity swap, an investor can express a view that foreign stocks will rise or decline, without taking a position in the foreign currency. Contrast this with a compo equity swap, in which the investor takes long or short exposure to the foreign stocks and the foreign currency. Therefore, a quanto equity swap is an equity swap in which the underlying is denominated in a currency (the foreign currency) other than that in which the equity swap is denominated (the domestic currency). The final value of the underlying is denominated in the foreign currency and is converted into the domestic currency using the exchange rate prevailing at inception. As a result, the investor is not exposed to currency risk.

Let us assume that ABC, a EUR-based entity, thinks that the S&P 500 index will rise strongly during the next 12 months. ABC is unsure of the USD behavior relative to the EUR, preferring to take currency exposure out of its position. ABC enters into a quanto price return equity swap with Gigabank with the following terms:

Terms of a Quanto Price Return Equity Swap on a Stock Index

Party A	ABC Corp.
Party B	Gigabank
Trade date	12-December-20X1
Effective date	15-December-20X1
Termination date	15-December-20X2
Underlying currency	USD
Initial exchange rate (FX_0)	1.2500

Equity amount part

Underlying index	S&P 500 index
Type of return	Price return
Calculation agent	Party B (Gigabank)
Number of baskets	100,000
Initial index level ($Index_0$)	USD 1,200
Equity notional amount	EUR 96 million (Number of baskets $\times$ $Index_0/FX_0$)
Equity amount	Number of baskets $\times$ ($Index_T/FX_0 - Index_0/FX_0$)
Equity amount payer	Party B (Gigabank)
Equity amount receiver	Party A (ABC Corp.)
$Index_T$	Level of the index at the closing of the valuation date
Cash settlement	Applicable
Settlement currency	EUR
Valuation date	12-December-20X2
Settlement date	15-December-20X2

Floating amount part

Floating amounts payer	Party A (ABC Corp.)
Floating amount	The equity notional amount
Payment dates	At the end of each quarter (15-Mar-20X2, 15-Jun-20X2, 15-Sep-20X2 and 15-Dec-20X2)
Floating rate option	EUR-Euribor fixed on the second local business day preceding the last floating amount payment date. The floating rate for the initial period would be determined two local business days prior to the effective date
Designated maturity	3 months
Spread	Plus 20 bps (0.20%)
Floating rate day count fraction	Actual/360

Dividend amount part	**Not applicable**

The flows of the transaction on the trade date are as follows:

- ABC and Gigabank enter into the cash-settled quanto price return equity swap on 100,000 baskets of the S&P 500 index. The initial index level ($Index_0$) is set at USD 1,200. The initial USD/EUR exchange rate (FX_0) is set at 1.2500.
- Gigabank initially hedges its position by buying 400 contracts of S&P 500 index futures. Gigabank posts initial margin at the futures exchange.

The flows of the transaction during the life of the equity swap are as follows:

- ABC pays an interest, the floating amount, to Gigabank. ABC pays Euribor 3-month + 20 bps on the EUR 96 million equity notional amount. Note that although the underlying stock index is denominated in USD, the floating amount is denominated in EUR.
- In this example there is no dividend amount, as it is a price return swap. Therefore, Gigabank keeps the dividends distributed to the underlying stocks of the S&P 500 index during the life of the equity swap. As a result, Gigabank compensates ABC by charging a lower spread (20 basis points in our case).

The flows of the transaction at maturity (i.e., on the settlement date of the equity swap) are as follows:

- Gigabank unwinds its hedge, selling 400 contracts of the S&P 500 index futures. Gigabank receives back the margin posted at the futures exchange.
- ABC and Gigabank settle the equity swap after calculating the equity amount. If the equity amount is positive, the index has appreciated and Gigabank pays to ABC the equity amount. If, on the other hand, the equity amount is negative, the index has depreciated and ABC pays to Gigabank the absolute value of the equity amount.

On the valuation date, the equity amount would be calculated as:

$$\text{Equity amount} = \text{Number of baskets} \times (\text{Index}_T/\text{FX}_0 - \text{Index}_0/\text{FX}_0)$$

Index_T is the closing price of the S&P 500 index on the valuation date – 12 December 20X2. FX_0 was the USD/EUR exchange rate – 1.2500 – on the effective date – 15 December 20X1.

- If the equity amount was positive, the equity amount payer – Gigabank – would pay to the equity amount receiver – ABC – the equity amount on the settlement date. For example, if Index_T is 1,600, ABC would receive from Gigabank EUR 32 million [= 100,000 × (1,600/1.25 – 1,200/1.25)].
- If the equity amount was negative, the equity amount receiver – ABC – would pay to the equity amount payer – Gigabank – the absolute value of the equity amount on the settlement date. For example, if Index_T is 1,000, Gigabank would receive from ABC EUR 16 million (= Absolute value of [100,000 × (1,000/1.25 – 1,200/1.25)]).

It is important to note that ABC is exposed only to the S&P 500 index and not to the USD/EUR exchange rate. ABC benefits from a rising S&P 500 index, independently of the behavior of the USD/EUR FX rate. Conversely, ABC loses from a declining S&P 500 index, independently of the behavior of the USD/EUR FX rate. Thus, a quanto equity swap is a valuable tool for equity investors to manage their exposure when investing in foreign equity markets without being saddled with foreign currency exposure.

1.2.11 Uses of Equity Swaps

Equity swaps can be particularly useful in a number of situations, for example:

- **To diversify a portfolio**. Equity swaps give economic exposure to a stock, basket of stocks or an equity index without legal ownership of the underlying. For example, an asset manager is bullish on a specific sector and wants to get a long exposure to the sector without buying the underlying stocks. The asset manager can buy an equity swap on the index that best tracks that sector. Note, however, that certain benefits of physical ownership are not obtained, such as the voting rights. Unlike a futures position, an equity swap does not require rolling positions.

- **To protect a portfolio**. Equity swaps reduce economic exposure to a stock, basket of stocks or an equity index while maintaining legal ownership of the underlying. For example, an asset manager wants to underweight a specific sector but does not want to sell the underlying stocks. The asset manager can go short an equity swap on the index that best tracks that sector.
- **To finance a portfolio**. An investor may seek to raise financing without using the traditional debt capital markets. The investor sells its portfolio and maintains an economic exposure to the portfolio by going long an equity swap on it. By selling the portfolio, the investor raises cash.
- **To obtain synthetic borrow and lending**. Where investors are unable to borrow or lend stocks, they can use equity swaps to borrow or lend stock synthetically. For example, say a certain stock is difficult to borrow, and an investor is seeking to benefit from lending the stock out. If an investor is unable to lend stocks, he/she can sell the stock and enter into a long total return swap. The swap counterparty can lend the stock out, being able to pass on the benefit by charging a lower financing rate to the investor.

1.3   STOCK LENDING AND BORROWING

Sometimes the benefit from lending stock out can be significant. For example, a stock may be expensive to borrow because it is involved in a merger or acquisition. If an investor in the stock does not lend the stock out, he/she will forgo the opportunity to outperform without taking any major additional risk.

1.3.1   Stock Lending and Borrowing

A stock lending and borrowing, or securities lending and borrowing, agreement is a contract between two counterparties whereby one counterparty – the stock borrower – borrows a stock from the other counterparty – the stock lender – with a commitment by the borrower to return equivalent stock at a future date. In return for borrowing the stock, the borrower pays a fee – the lending fee – and posts collateral.

A securities lending and borrowing agreement is formalized through a confirmation. The confirmation is generally legally subject to the terms and clauses of the Global Master Securities Lending Agreement (GMSLA) signed between the two counterparties that sets out their obligations.

In securities lending, the lender effectively retains all the benefits of ownership, other than the voting rights. The borrower can use the securities as required – perhaps by selling them or by lending them on to another party – but is liable to the lender for all the benefits distributed to the underlying shares, such as dividends or stock bonuses. The voting rights are transferred to the borrower in a stock lending transaction. If the lender wants to exercise its right to vote, it should recall the stock in good time so that a proxy voting form can be completed and returned to the registrar by the required deadline.

Open Borrow vs. Guaranteed Borrow

In general, a stock lending and borrowing transaction has no fixed maturity – an **open maturity**, and either party can terminate the transaction early on demand. This transaction is called an **"open borrow"**.

Sometimes, a stock lending and borrowing transaction has a **fixed maturity** and neither party can terminate the transaction early, unless agreement by both parties. In other words, the stock lender guarantees the availability of the stock to the stock borrower during the term of the transaction. This transaction is called a **"guaranteed borrow"**.

1.3.2 Stock Lending/Borrowing Transaction Flows

Flows at Inception

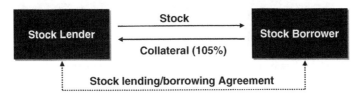

Figure 1.16   Stock lending/borrowing flows at inception.

At inception, three processes take place (as shown in Figure 1.16):

- The securities lending and borrowing agreement is agreed and signed by the two counterparties.
- The stock is transferred from the lender custody account to the borrower custody account. Legal title passes to the borrower, so he/she can sell or on-lend the stock.
- Collateral is posted by the borrower. Loaned stock is generally collateralized, reducing the lender's credit exposure to the borrower. Commonly, the borrower can post cash or other liquid securities. The market value of the collateral posted is typically 105% of the market value of the stock borrowed.

Flows during the Life of the Stock Lending and Borrowing Agreement

During the life of the stock lending and borrowing agreement, the following processes take place (as shown in Figure 1.17):

- The borrower pays a lending fee – the borrowing fee – to the lender.
- The lender pays interest to the borrower on the cash collateral. The interest is commonly calculated on a daily basis.

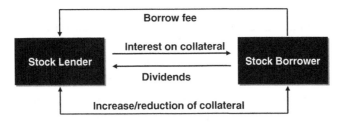

Figure 1.17   Stock lending/borrowing flows during the life of the agreement.

- The borrower pays the lender an amount equivalent to the dividends distributed to the borrowed shares. This amount is called the "**manufactured dividend**".
- Collateral is readjusted on a daily basis, so the market value of the collateral posted is 105% of the market value of the stock borrowed.

Flows at Maturity or Upon Early Termination

At maturity of the agreement, or upon early termination, the following processes take place (as shown in Figure 1.18):

- The stock is returned from the borrower custody account to the lender custody account.
- Collateral is returned by the lender to the borrower.

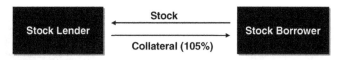

Figure 1.18   Stock lending/borrowing flows at maturity (or early termination).

1.3.3   Counterparty Credit Risk

Following an event of default, the stock lending and borrowing agreement provide for the non-defaulting counterparty to calculate its exposure to the defaulting counterparty. From a stock lender point of view, the net exposure is calculated as the cost of repurchasing the lent securities less the funds raised from the sale of the collateral. A deficit represents a claim on the defaulting counterparty in administration.

The stock lender is credit exposed to the stock borrower. Following an event of default, the non-defaulting stock lender has no claim on the defaulting stock borrower to return the lent securities as securities lending/borrowing is legally a transfer of ownership. However, in the event that the borrower defaults, the stock lender would set off the market value of the collateral against the market value of the lent stock. The lender owns the collateral and can either sell it, in the case of collateral other than cash, or use it, in the case of cash collateral, in order to repurchase the lent stock. This way, the stock lender is restored to its original position of owning the lent stock. There are several events that trigger the credit risk exposure to the borrower:

- During the life of the agreement, if the stock significantly increases in value, the stock borrower is required to post additional collateral and the borrower may fail to meet this obligation.
- During the life of the agreement, the stock borrower may fail to pay the manufactured dividend.
- During the life of the agreement, the stock borrower may fail to pay the borrow fee.
- At maturity, or upon early termination, the borrower may fail to return the stock. It would oblige the stock lender to buy back the lent stock in the market using the posted collateral. This collateral may not be sufficient to pay for the stock.

To reduce the credit risk exposure to the stock borrower, "**haircuts**" are employed. In other words, the stock borrower is required to provide collateral with a market value greater than the market value of the stock borrowed. Typically the haircut is 5% of the market value of the borrowed/lent stock (i.e., the collateral posted is 105% of the stock market value). Additionally, most stock-lending transactions are agreed on an open borrow basis, meaning that either counterparty can cancel the transaction with a short notice period. In a deteriorating credit environment, the stock lender can reduce his/her exposure in very short order.

The stock borrower is also credit exposed to the stock lender. There are several events that trigger the credit risk exposure to the lender:

• During the life of the agreement the stock lender may become insolvent, failing to pay the interest on the cash collateral.
• During the life of the agreement the stock lender may fail to return collateral in the case of a fall in value of the borrowed stock.
• At maturity, the stock lender may fail to return collateral. If the lender's insolvency takes place immediately after a sharp decline of the stock, the collateral posted may well exceed the market value of the stock, generating a loss for the stock borrower.

The credit risk to the stock lender may be very relevant if the lender is a major owner of the stock. The stock lender's insolvency may trigger a widespread sale of the stock, increasing the probability of a large loss for the stock borrower. However, most stock lending transactions are agreed on an open borrow basis, meaning that either counterparty can cancel the transaction with a short notice period. In a deteriorating credit environment, the stock borrower can reduce his/her exposure in very short order.

1.3.4 Advantages of Stock Lending and Borrowing

There are many positive aspects of stock lending and borrowing, for example:

• It allows stock investors to earn additional income by lending their stock on to third parties, enhancing the return of their stock portfolios.
• It allows stock investors to raise financing when the stock is lent against cash collateral.
• It supports many trading and risk management strategies that otherwise would be extremely difficult to execute.
• It increases the liquidity of the securities market by allowing securities to be borrowed temporarily; thus reducing the potential for failed settlements and their associated penalties.
• It is easy to implement and at a low cost. There are no depository or transaction costs on the lent stocks during the life of the transaction.
• It allows for early termination. There is the possibility for both counterparties to end the transaction at any time if the maturity is on an open basis.

1.3.5 Drawbacks of Stock Lending and Borrowing

There are some negative aspects of stock lending and borrowing, for example:

• The stock lender losses the voting rights associated with the lent shares.
• The stock lender is credit exposed to the stock borrower.
• The stock borrower is credit exposed to the stock lender.
• It may add selling pressure to the market on illiquid stocks by assisting stock short sellers.
• It may increase tax authorities' scrutiny of the investor as stock lending and borrowing transactions have sometimes been used to implement tax arbitrage schemes.

1.4 CALL AND PUT OPTIONS

In this section I will cover plain vanilla options. A vanilla option, also called a standard option, is a call or put in its most basic form. Options are a means for their buyers to gain either long or short exposure to an equity underlying with a limited downside.

1.4.1 Call Options

Call options allow an investor to take bullish views on an underlying stock, a basket of stocks or a stock index.

- A physically settled European call option provides the buyer – the holder – the right, but not the obligation, to buy a specified number of shares of an equity underlying at a predetermined price – the strike price – at a future date – the expiration date. In return for this right, the buyer pays an upfront premium for the call.
- A cash-settled European call option provides the buyer the appreciation of a specified number of shares of an equity underlying above a predetermined price – the strike price – at a future date – the expiration date. The buyer pays an upfront premium for the call.

At expiry, the holder of the call will exercise the option if the share price of the underlying stock is higher than the strike price. Thus, if the share price ends up lower than the strike price, the holder will not exercise the call. The holder has unlimited upside potential, while his/her loss is limited to the option premium paid.

As an example, let us assume that on 3 June 20X1, ABC is looking to buy IBM stock in six months' time. ABC believes that the stock of IBM will significantly increase in value over the next six months and acquires from Gigabank a European call option on one million IBM shares. On 3 June 20X1, IBM stock is trading at USD 150. The physically settled call option has the following terms:

Physically Settled Call Option – Main Terms	
Buyer	ABC Corp
Seller	Gigabank
Option type	Call
Trade date	3-June-20X1
Expiration date	3-December-20X1
Option style	European
Shares	IBM
Number of options	1 million
Option entitlement	One share per option
Strike price	USD 180.00 (120% of the spot price)
Spot price	USD 150.00
Premium	2.66% of the notional amount
	USD 4 million (i.e., USD 4 per share)
Premium payment date	Two currency business days after the trade date (5-June-20X1)
Notional amount	Number of options × Spot price
	USD 150 million
Settlement method	Physical settlement
Settlement date	6-December-20X1 (three exchange business days after the expiration date)

By buying the call option ABC has the right, but not the obligation, to buy on the "settlement date" one million shares of IBM at a strike price of USD 180 per share. Because upon exercise ABC would be buying the underlying stock, the call is a physically settled call. ABC pays to Gigabank a premium of USD 4 million on 5 June 20X1. Because it is European-style, the option can only be exercised at expiry. On the expiration date, 3 December 20X1, ABC would be assessing whether to exercise the option, as follows:

- If IBM's stock price is greater than the USD 180 strike price, ABC would exercise the call. On the "settlement date" ABC would receive from Gigabank one million shares of IBM in exchange for USD 180 million. For example, if at expiry IBM stock is trading at USD 210, ABC would exercise the call option paying USD 180 per share for a stock worth USD 210 per share.
- If IBM's stock price is lower than or equal to the USD 180 strike price, ABC would not exercise the option.

In a similar example, let us assume that ABC is not interested in having the right to buy one million shares of IBM but instead in receiving the appreciation of one million shares of IBM above USD 180. ABC then buys a cash-settled European call option on IBM stock with the following terms:

Cash-settled Call Option – Main Terms	
Buyer	ABC Corp
Seller	Gigabank
Option type	Call
Trade date	3-June-20X1
Expiration date	3-December-20X1
Option style	European
Shares	IBM
Number of options	1 million
Option entitlement	One share per option
Strike price	USD 180.00 (120% of the spot price)
Spot price	USD 150.00
Premium	2.66% of the notional amount
	USD 4 million (i.e., USD 4 per share)
Premium payment date	5-June-20X1 (two currency business days after the trade date)
Notional amount	Number of options × Spot price
	USD 150 million
Automatic exercise	Applicable
Settlement price	The closing price of the shares on the valuation date
Settlement method	Cash settlement
Cash settlement amount	The maximum of:
	(i) Number of options × (Settlement price – Strike price), and
	(ii) Zero
Cash settlement payment date	6-December-20X1 (three exchange business days after the expiration date)

ABC pays, on 5 June 20X1, a USD 4 million premium. On expiration date, ABC will exercise the call if IBM's stock price – the settlement price – is above the USD 180 strike price. What if ABC forgets to exercise the call? The contract includes a term, "automatic exercise", which prevents the buyer from forgetting to exercise an in-the-money option. In our option, the "automatic exercise" term is defined as "applicable", meaning that if the option is in-the-money on expiration date, it would automatically be exercised. More precisely, on 6 December 20X1 ABC would be receiving the "cash settlement amount". This amount is calculated as follows:

- If the "settlement price" is greater than the USD 180 strike price, the option would be exercised and ABC would receive an amount equivalent to Number of options × (Settlement price − Strike price) = 1 million × (Settlement price − 180). In other words, ABC receives from Gigabank the appreciation of the shares above USD 180. For example, if at expiry IBM stock price has risen to USD 210, the call would be exercised and ABC would receive from Gigabank USD 30 million [= 1 million shares × (210 − 180)]. Taking into account the USD 4 million initial premium paid, the overall payoff for ABC would be a profit of USD 26 million (= 30 million − 4 million).
- If the settlement price is lower than or equal to the USD 180 strike price, the cash settlement amount would be zero. The option would not be exercised and, thus, ABC would receive nothing. Taking into account the USD 4 million initial premium paid, the overall payoff for ABC would be a loss of USD 4 million.

Options strategies are often described using "payoff" graphs which show the value of an option (i.e., the cash settlement amount) on the expiration date after subtracting the upfront premium. Figure 1.19 shows the payoff for ABC under the IBM call. Note that in the graph the USD 4 million option premium has been taken into account ignoring timing differences. In reality, the premium is paid upfront while the payout of the option is received shortly after the option expiration date.

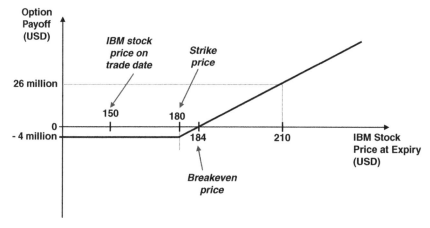

Figure 1.19   Payoff to the buyer of the call option.

The graph shows that there is a positive payoff for ABC, the option buyer, if the stock price at expiration is greater than the USD 184 breakeven price. The breakeven price is calculated as the sum of the USD 4 per share call premium and the USD 180.00 strike. By the same reasoning, there is a negative payoff if the stock price at expiration is lower than the breakeven price. The graph also shows that for a buyer of a call the upside is unlimited while the downside is limited to the initial premium paid.

Conversely, the seller of the IBM call, Gigabank, has a positive payoff if the stock price at expiration is lower than the breakeven price (see Figure 1.20). Applying the same reasoning,

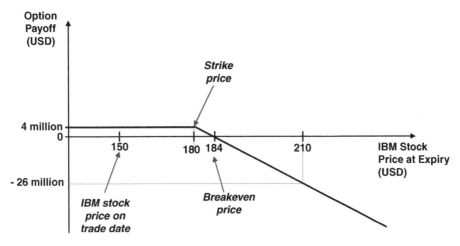

Figure 1.20   Payoff to the seller of the call option.

there is a negative payoff for the seller of the option if the stock price at expiry is greater than the breakeven price. The graph also shows that for a seller of a call the upside is limited to the initial premium received, while there is an unlimited downside.

1.4.2   Put Options

Put options allow an investor to take bearish views on an underlying stock.

- A physically settled European put option provides the buyer – the holder – the right, but not the obligation, to sell a specified number of shares at a predetermined price – the strike price – at a future date – the expiration date. In return for this right, the buyer pays an upfront premium for the put.
- A cash-settled European put option provides the buyer the depreciation of a specified number of shares below a predetermined price – the strike price – at a future date – the expiration date. The buyer pays an upfront premium for the put.

As an example, let us assume that on 3 June 20X1 ABC has a bearish view on IBM stock. ABC believes that IBM stock price will significantly fall over the next six months and acquires from Gigabank a European put option on one million IBM shares. On 3 June 20X1, IBM stock is trading at USD 150. Let us assume further that ABC is not interested in having the right to sell one million shares of IBM but instead in having the right to receive the depreciation of IBM's stock below USD 120. The cash-settled put option has the following terms:

Cash-settled Put Option – Main Terms	
Buyer	ABC Corp
Seller	Gigabank
Option type	Put
Trade date	3-June-20X1
Expiration date	3-December-20X1
Option style	European

Cash-settled Put Option – Main Terms	
Shares	IBM
Number of options	1 million
Option entitlement	One share per option
Strike price	USD 120.00 (80% of the spot price)
Spot price	USD 150.00
Premium	1.33% of the notional amount
	USD 2 million (i.e., USD 2 per share)
Premium payment date	5-June-20X1 (two currency business days after the trade date)
Notional amount	Number of options × Spot price
	USD 150 million
Settlement price	The closing price of the shares on the valuation date
Settlement method	Cash settlement
Cash settlement amount	The maximum of:
	(i) Number of options × (Strike price – Settlement price), and
	(ii) Zero
Cash settlement payment date	6-December-20X1 (three exchange business days after the expiration date)

ABC pays, on 5 June 20X1, a USD 2 million premium. At expiry, the holder of the put – ABC – will exercise the option if IBM's stock price is lower than the USD 120 strike price. Putting it in a more formal way, on the "cash settlement payment date" (6 December 20X1) ABC would be receiving the "cash settlement amount". This amount is calculated as follows:

- If the settlement price is lower than the USD 120 strike price, the option would be exercised and ABC would receive an amount equivalent to Number of options × (Strike price – Settlement price) = 1 million × (120 – Settlement price). In other words, ABC would receive from Gigabank the depreciation of the shares below USD 120. For example, if at expiry IBM stock price has fallen to USD 110, ABC would exercise the put, receiving from Gigabank USD 10 million [= 1 million shares × (120 – 110)]. Taking into account the USD 2 million initial premium paid, the overall payoff for ABC would be a profit of USD 8 million (= 10 million – 2 million).
- If the "settlement price" is greater than or equal to the USD 120 strike price, the option would not be exercised and ABC would receive nothing as the cash settlement amount would be zero. Taking into account the USD 2 million initial premium paid, the overall payoff for ABC would be a loss of USD 2 million.

Figure 1.21 shows the payoff for ABC under the IBM put. The graph illustrates the value of the option (i.e., the cash settlement amount) on the expiration date after subtracting the USD 2 million upfront premium. Note that in the graph the option premium has been taken into account ignoring timing differences. In reality, the premium is paid upfront and the payout of the option is received shortly after the option's expiration date.

The graph shows that there is a positive payoff for the option buyer if the stock price at expiry is lower than the USD 118 breakeven price. The breakeven price is calculated as the USD 120 strike minus the USD 2 per share premium. Applying the same reasoning, there is a negative payoff if the stock price at expiry is greater than the USD 118 breakeven price. The graph also shows that the upside is limited while the downside is limited to the initial premium

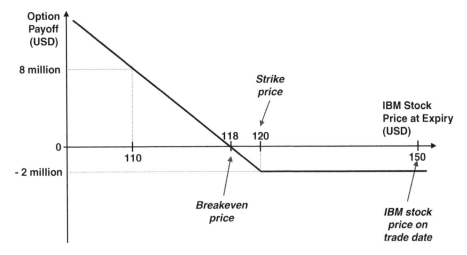

Figure 1.21 Payoff to the buyer of the put option.

paid. In our example, the maximum upside for ABC is USD 118 million (= 120 million – 2 million), reached when IBM stock price trades at zero on the expiration date.

The seller of the IBM put, Gigabank, has a positive payoff if the stock price at expiry is greater than the USD 118 breakeven price (see Figure 1.22). Applying the same reasoning, there is a negative payoff for the seller of the option if the stock price at expiry is lower than the USD 118 breakeven price. The graph also shows that the upside is limited to the initial premium received, while there is a limited downside. The maximum downside for Gigabank is USD 118 million (= 120 million – 2 million), reached if IBM stock price trades at zero on the expiration date.

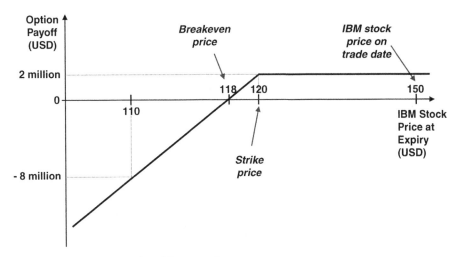

Figure 1.22 Payoff to the seller of the put option.

1.4.3   European vs. American Style

If an option can only be exercised on the expiry date it is called a **European-style** option. If an option can be exercised at any time up to the expiry date it is called an **American-style** option. Options can have more elaborate exercise schedules.

1.4.4   Time Value vs. Intrinsic Value

The value of an option before expiry is comprised of the sum of two components: its intrinsic value and its time value.

$$\text{Total value} = \text{Intrinsic value} + \text{Time value}$$

The intrinsic value of an option is the value it would have if it were exercised immediately. The intrinsic value of a call option is calculated as follows:

- When the stock price is above the strike price, the call option is said to have intrinsic value. This is because, were the call to expire at that moment there would be a positive cash payout.
- When the stock price is below or at the strike price, the call option is said to have no intrinsic value. This is because, were the call to expire at that moment there would be no cash payout.

$$\text{Call intrinsic value} = \text{Number of options} \times \text{Max}[(\text{Stock price} - \text{Strike price}), 0]$$

The intrinsic value of a put option is calculated as follows:

- When the stock price is below the strike price, the put is said to have intrinsic value. This is because, were the put to expire at that moment there would be a positive cash payout.
- When the stock price is above or at the strike price, the put is said to have no intrinsic value. This is because, were the put to expire at that moment there would be no cash payout.

$$\text{Put intrinsic value} = \text{Number of options} \times \text{Max}[(\text{Strike price} - \text{Stock price}), 0]$$

The time value of an option is the portion of the value of an option that is due to the fact that it has some time to expiration. The time value of an option represents the possibility that the option may finish in-the-money or further in-the-money. The time value will progressively erode as the option approaches its expiration date. At expiry there will be no time value. The time value component is calculated as the difference between the total value of an option and its intrinsic value:

$$\text{Time value} = \text{Total value} - \text{Intrinsic value}$$

Figure 1.23 illustrates the intrinsic value and time value components of a call option on 1 million IBM shares, a USD 180 strike and 6 months to expiration, assuming a 4% interest rate, a 2% dividend yield and a 30% implied volatility (note that the y-axis has not been graphed using a linear scale to better highlight the concepts). The total value of the option has been calculated using an option pricing model. For example, assuming IBM's spot price at USD 210, the total value of the call option would be USD 37 million. The intrinsic value

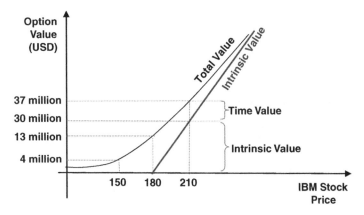

Figure 1.23   Intrinsic value vs. time value of a call option.

would be USD 30 million [= 1 million × (210 − 180)]. Therefore, the option time value would be USD 7 million (= 37 million − 30 million). The following table summarizes the intrinsic value and time value components for three stock price scenarios:

Spot price	USD 150	USD 180	USD 210
Intrinsic value	0	0	USD 30 million
Time value	USD 4 million	USD 13 million	USD 7 million
Total value	USD 4 million	USD 13 million	USD 37 million

1.4.5 In, At or Out-of-the-money

Options which have intrinsic value are described as being "**in-the-money**". By the same reasoning, options which have no intrinsic value (e.g., in a call option, if the share price is below the strike price) are called "**out-of-the-money**". If the option expires out-of-the-money, the holder will not exercise the option. An option is called "**at-the-money**" if the stock price is at the strike price.

Description	Call	Put	Intrinsic value
In-the-money	Stock price > Strike	Stock price < Strike	Yes
At-the-money	Stock price = Strike	Stock price = Strike	No
Out-of-the-money	Stock price < Strike	Stock price > Strike	No

Based on our previous call option on IBM with a strike price of USD 150:

Spot price	USD 150	USD 180	USD 210
Strike	USD 180	USD 180	USD 180
Moneyness	Out-of-the-money	At-the-money	In-the-money

At expiry, there will be no time value and there will be two different scenarios:

- The option expires in-the-money and there is a positive cash payout; or
- The option expires out-of-the-money and is worthless.

1.4.6 Variables that Influence an Option Price

Option prices are calculated using mathematical models. Most banks use in-house variations of the Black–Scholes model. In this section, I will not cover option pricing models as there are plenty of excellent books on the subject. However, I think it is important to understand how options are affected by the variables that drive option prices. Let us assume that we are already long a call or a put option. Ongoing valuation of the option depends on the following seven variables (see Figure 1.24):

Figure 1.24   Variables that affect an option valuation.

1. The **spot price**. It is the current price of the underlying stock. In the case of a call, as the stock price rises the value of the call increases. In the case of a put, as the stock price falls the value of the put increases, assuming everything else is equal.

	Call	Put
Spot price increases	↑	↓
Spot price decreases	↓	↑

2. The **strike price**. It is the exercise price of the option. It can be expressed as either an absolute level or a percentage of the spot price. Market participants commonly use the latter. A higher strike price means a lower call value, and a lower strike price means a higher call value. A higher strike price means a higher put value, and a lower strike price means a lower put value.

3. The **time to expiration**. It is the time period remaining to expiration. It is calculated as the difference, commonly in days, between the expiration date and the current date. Generally, the longer the time until expiration, the greater the value of an option. In other words, the longer the time until expiration, the higher the probability that the option will expire with a larger positive value. Note that sometimes changes in time to expiration have an ambiguous effect on European options due to the potential adverse effect of dividend payments during the life of the option.

	Call	Put
Time to expiration increases	↑	↑
Time to expiration decreases	↓	↓

4. The **implied volatility**. It is the expected volatility of the underlying during the life of the option. It is an estimation of the amplitude in the movement of the underlying stock price. Because the option payoff is asymmetric (i.e., the maximum payoff is larger than the premium paid), the higher the volatility, the more likely that a large movement of the stock price will translate into a larger payoff. Therefore, the higher the implied volatility, the more expensive is the option. The implied volatility is an annualized statistic expressed in percentage terms.

	Call	Put
Implied volatility increases	↑	↑
Implied volatility decreases	↓	↓

5. The **expected dividends** to be distributed to the underlying shares. If the company of the underlying stock decides to increase the dividends to be paid during the life of the option, this will cause a larger than expected drop in the stock price once it goes ex-dividend. Higher dividends lower the forward price, thus reducing the price of the call and increasing the price of the put.

	Call	Put
Expected dividends increase	↓	↑
Expected dividends decrease	↑	↓

6. The **interest rate**. Purchasing a call is comparable to buying a portion of the underlying stock. In a perfect market and in absence of dividends, the stock is expected to appreciate identically to an investment in a riskless interest rate instrument. As a result, an increase in interest rates implies that the underlying stock will rise higher. A call price will increase as the interest rate increases. Similarly, a put price will decrease as the interest rate increases.

	Call	Put
Interest rate increases	↑	↓
Interest rate decreases	↓	↑

7. The **repo rate**. It is the borrowing fee paid by a stock borrower of the underlying shares. The higher the repo rate, the lower the forward price. As a result, the higher the repo rate, the lower the price of the call and the higher the value of a put.

	Call	Put
Repo rate increases	↓	↑
Repo rate decreases	↑	↓

The following table summarizes the impact on the value of a call and a put on a specific stock of an increase in the specified variable, assuming everything else is equal. It can be observed that changes in time to expiration and volatility have similar effects on the call and put values, while changes to the other factors affect call and put values in an opposite way.

Variable increased	Effect in call value	Effect in put value
Spot price	↑	↓
Strike price	↓	↑
Time to expiration	↑	↑
Implied volatility	↑	↑
Dividend	↓	↑
Interest rate	↑	↓
Repo	↓	↑

1.4.7 Historical Volatility vs. Implied Volatility

Historical volatility, or **realized volatility**, is the annualized standard deviation of the logarithm of price returns of an underlying over a specific period of time. It measures the historical variations of the underlying price over a certain time. It is retrospective, based on historical data, commonly using the underlying closing prices. It is expressed as an annualized percentage.

Implied volatility is the expected future realized volatility of the underlying during the life of the option. It is expressed as an annualized percentage.

The historical volatility is calculated as follows:

$$\text{Historical volatility} = \sigma_H = 100 \times \sqrt{\frac{252 \times \sum_{i=1}^{N}\left(Ln\frac{P_i}{P_{i-1}}\right)^2}{N}}$$

where:

Ln is the natural logarithm.

P_i and P_{i-1} are the official levels of the underlying on respectively the *i*th and *i*–1th observation days. In most cases the official level is the daily closing price.

N is the number of days that, as of the trade date, are expected to be scheduled trading days for the period from, but excluding the observation start date to, and including, the observation end date.

Observation day is each trading day during the observation period.

Observation period is the period from, but excluding, the observation start date to, but excluding the observation end date.

As an example, let us take the stock prices of a stock during a month to calculate the historical volatility performing the following steps:

1. Calculate the daily lognormal returns.
2. Square each return to capture size, but not sign.
3. Sum the squared returns over the period.
4. Annualize by the 252 trading days per year.

5. Divide by the number of observations.
6. Take the square root to convert variance to volatility.
7. Multiply by 100 to express it as a percentage.

Day	Stock price	$Ln(P_i/P_{i-1})$	$[Ln(P_i/P_{i-1})]^2$
1	123		
2	117	−0.05001	0.002501
3	114	−0.02598	0.000675
4	111	−0.02667	0.000711
5	113	0.017858	0.000319
6	116	0.026202	0.000687
7	119	0.025533	0.000652
8	112	−0.06062	0.003675
9	118	0.052186	0.002723
10	123	0.0415	0.001722
11	117	−0.05001	0.002501
12	119	0.01695	0.000287
13	120	0.008368	0.000070
14	119	−0.00837	0.000070
15	124	0.041158	0.001694
16	125	0.008032	0.0000645
17	123	−0.01613	0.00026
18	122	−0.00816	0.0000666
19	121	−0.00823	0.0000677
20	120	−0.0083	0.0000689
		Sum	0.018816

The sum of the squared returns over the period was 0.018816. The annualization of this figure was 4.741632 (= 0.018816 × 252). The adjustment of the annualized figure by dividing by the number of observations was 0.2371 (= 4.741632/20). The historical volatility in percentage terms was 23.71% (= 0.2371 × 100).

1.4.8 Put–Call Parity

The prices of European-style calls and puts on the same stock, with the same strike and the same time to expiration, are related by an expression termed "**put–call parity**" as follows:

$$S + P = PV(K) + C + PV(Dividends) + PV(Repo)$$

where S is the stock's spot price, P is the put price, $PV(K)$ is the present value of the exercise price, C is the call price, $PV(Dividends)$ is the present value of the expected dividends and $PV(Repo)$ is the present value of the stock borrowing fee.

The relationship can be understood by considering two portfolios; the first is comprised of the stock and the put option, and the second is comprised of the call and cash equal to the present value of the exercise price.

- If at expiry the stock price is above the strike, the put will not be exercised and the first portfolio would be worth the stock price at expiry. In the second portfolio, the call will be exercised, receiving the underlying stock in exchange for cash worth the strike. As a result, the second portfolio would be worth the stock price at expiry.

- If at expiry the stock price is below the strike, the put will be exercised, receiving cash worth the strike and delivering the underlying stock. As a result, the first portfolio would be worth the strike at expiry. In the second portfolio, the call will not be exercised and the cash would be worth the strike. As a result, the second portfolio would be worth the strike at expiry.

At expiry, both portfolios are worth the greater of the stock price and the strike price. As both portfolios are worth the same at expiry, then at inception of the strategy they must be worth the same too.

1.4.9   Options' Sensitivities, the "Greeks"

The essential risk measures of an option value are known as the "Greeks". An option sensitivity to each variable is measured by taking the partial derivative of the option value with respect to that particular variable. Option traders measure option Greeks in order to risk manage their option positions. In this subsection I will briefly cover the four so-called "first-order" Greeks and "gamma", which is a second-order Greek (see table below). A first-order Greek represents a first-order derivative of the option value with respect to a specific variable.

Variable	Symbol	Measures option sensitivity to
Delta	Δ	Change in underlying price
Vega	ν	Change in volatility
Gamma	Γ	Change in delta
Theta	None	Change in time to expiration
Rho	None	Change in interest rates

Delta

An option delta indicates the theoretical change in an option price with respect to changes in the price of the underlying stock. When the stock price changes by a small amount, the option price changes by the delta multiplied by that amount. The delta is commonly expressed as a percentage, measuring the change in an option price for a 1% change in the underlying stock price.

Figure 1.25 shows the delta of a European call on IBM stock with a strike price of USD 180, a time to expiration of 6 months, an interest rate of 4%, a dividend yield of 2% and a volatility of 30%, for different levels of IBM's stock price. It can be observed that the delta of a call option is always positive, as the call price increases when the underlying stock price rises. The graph shows that at USD 176 (a stock price quite close to the strike price), the delta of the call option is 50%. If the stock price moves up by USD 1 to USD 177, the call option would see its value increase by approximately USD 0.50 (= USD 1 × 50%).

Figure 1.26 shows the delta of a European put on IBM stock with a strike price of USD 180, a time to expiration of 6 months, an interest rate of 4%, a dividend yield of 2% and a volatility of 30%, for different levels of IBM's stock price. It can be observed that the delta of a put option is always negative as a rise in the underlying stock price would cause the put value to decrease. In other words, the put price increases when the underlying falls.

The absolute value of the delta can be loosely interpreted as an approximate measure of the probability that an option will expire in-the-money. If an option is very deep in-the-money, and therefore has a very high probability of being in-the-money at expiry, the absolute value of the delta will be close to 100%. If an option is very deep out-of-the-money, it has a low

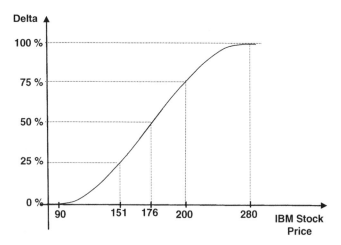

Figure 1.25   Delta of a European call as a function of IBM's stock price.

probability of being in-the-money at expiry, and therefore the absolute value of its delta will be close to zero. At-the-money options have a delta close to 50%, meaning roughly a 50% probability of being exercised at expiry.

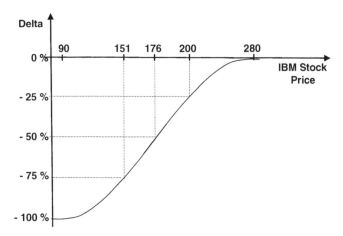

Figure 1.26   Delta of a European put as a function of IBM's stock price.

Relationship between call and put deltas

Given a call and put option on the same underlying, strike price and time to expiration, the sum of the absolute values of the delta of each option is always 100%. Therefore, if the delta for an option is known, one can compute the delta of an option with the same strike price, underlying and maturity but opposite right by subtracting 100% from the known value. For example, if the delta of a call is 35% then one can compute the delta of the corresponding put with the same strike price as $35\% - 100\% = -65\%$.

$$\text{Call delta} + \text{Absolute value(Put delta)} = 100\%$$

Vega

Vega measures the sensitivity of an option value to small changes in the implied volatility of the underlying. Note that vega is not actually the name of any Greek letter. Vega is typically expressed as the amount of money, per underlying share, the option value will gain or lose as volatility rises or falls by 1%. Vega can be an important Greek to monitor for an option trader, especially in volatile markets since some of the value of option strategies can be particularly sensitive to changes in volatility.

Vega increases as time to expiration increases. Vega is usually larger for at-the-money options. Vega generally increases with implied volatility, assuming everything else is equal.

Gamma

It was observed in the delta section that delta is a non-linear function. This is due to gamma. Gamma measures the sensitivity of an option delta to small changes in the underlying stock price. When a trader seeks to establish an effective delta-hedge for an option, he/she may also seek to neutralize the option gamma, as this will ensure that the hedge will be effective over a wider range of underlying price movements. Deep in-the-money or deep out-of-the-money options tend to have low gamma for both calls and puts. The value of gamma is higher for at-the-money, short-dated options. For example, in our 6-month call option on IBM at USD 180 stock price, the gamma of the option is 1.85%. Therefore, for a 1% upward move in IBM's stock price, the option delta will increase by 1.85%.

Theta

Theta measures the sensitivity of the option value to small changes in the time remaining to expiration. Theta is usually defined as the change in the value of an option for a one-day decrease in the time to expiration. Theta is always negative for both call and put options. The decrease in the value of calls and puts as time passes is known as time decay. Theta is non-linear, meaning that its value decreases faster as the option approaches maturity. For at-the-money options, where the value of the underlying is close to the strike price, the time decay increases as the option approaches expiration. For in-the-money and out-of-the-money options, where the underlying is not close to the strike price, the time decay is more linear.

Rho

Rho measures the sensitivity of the option value to small changes in the applicable interest rate. The changes in option prices for changes in interest rates are relatively small. For this reason, rho is the least used of the first-order Greeks. Rho is positive for call options and negative for put options.

1.4.10 Delta Hedging

As covered earlier, delta measures the sensitivity of an option value to small changes in the share price of the underlying stock. An option trading desk managing the position in an option is usually not interested in being exposed to directional movements in the underlying stock. The desk role is to profit from changes in implied and realized volatility. The trading desk will typically delta-hedge the option position so that the overall delta is zero. In this way a position in an option has less exposure to directional movements in the underlying stock, leaving exposure to changes in implied and realized volatility. Because the option delta changes with market conditions and time to expiry, the hedge needs to be adjusted continuously. Delta hedging is the term given to the process of ensuring that an option position has little or no exposure to the movements of the underlying stock price.

1.4.11 Offsetting Dividend Risk

When pricing a call or a put option, a string of expected dividends has to be assumed. Sometimes it is difficult to forecast the expected dividends, and banks may be unwilling to take dividend risk unless a very conservative dividend forecast is assumed.

Adjustments to Strike and Notional

An alternative is to assume a string of expected dividends, and adjust the option terms for any deviation of the realized dividends relative to the forecasted dividends. For long-term options on single stocks, it is a good way to improve their pricing. It means that the client, and not the bank, is taking the dividend risk. Commonly, the strike and notional are adjusted on the ex-dividend date for any deviation of the paid dividends relative to the assumed dividends, as follows:

Adjusted strike = Strike × Adjustment factor
Adjusted number of options = Number of options/Adjustment factor
Adjustment factor = (Record share price − Dividend deviation)/Record share price
Dividend deviation = Gross dividend − Assumed dividend

The "Record share price" is typically the closing share price on the day immediately preceding the ex-dividend date. Therefore, if the underlying stock distributes a gross dividend larger than the assumed dividend, the strike would be adjusted downwards, while the number of shares would be adjusted upwards.

Payment of the Dividend Adjusted for the Delta

Sometimes the counterparties to an option agree on a specific dividend string but, in case of a deviation of real dividends relative to assumed dividends, they prefer not to adjust the terms of the option. This could be the case of a transaction that involves a financing backed by a stock and a put to protect the value of the stock. A downwards adjustment of the put strike would probably imply the adjustment to the terms of the financing, usually a cumbersome task.

An alternative to adjusting the terms of the option is to make a payment that compensates the dividend deviation. The compensation amount is calculated as:

Compensation amount = Delta × Number of options × Dividend deviation

where:

Dividend deviation = Realized gross dividend − Assumed dividend

The delta is the delta of the option on the dividend record date (i.e., the trading day prior to the ex-dividend date). The delta of an option is not an absolutely transparent figure, depending on the model used. The delta is usually calculated by the bank at its sole discretion, but the other counterparty may challenge the calculation.

As an example, let us assume that the parties to an option agreed on a EUR 0.20 dividend for a specific semiannual period, and that during this period the distributed gross dividend was EUR 0.30. Let us assume further that the option is a call on 10 million shares and that the delta on the closing of the record date was 40%. The compensation amount would be calculated as follows:

$$\text{Compensation amount} = 40\% \times (10 \text{ million options}) \times (0.30 - 0.20) = \text{EUR } 400{,}000$$

Now we need to decide which counterparty to the option is required to pay this amount to the other party. Let us assume that the buyer – e.g., the bank – of the call option delta-hedges its position. The buyer would need to be short 4 million shares (= 40% delta × 10 million options). In other words, the buyer of the call would need to borrow 4 million shares of the underlying stock. On the dividend payment date, and under the stock borrowing/lending agreement, the bank would be required to pay EUR 1.2 million (= 0.30 dividend × 4 million borrowed shares) to the stock lender. However, the bank assumed that it was going to pay only EUR 0.8 million (= 0.20 dividend × 4 million borrowed shares) when it priced the option at its inception. As a result, the bank would need to receive EUR 400,000 from the other party to the option. Therefore, if the compensation amount is positive (i.e., a distributed dividend greater than the assumed dividend), this amount should be received by the call option buyer – the bank in this example – from the call option seller – the client in this example. Conversely, if the compensation amount is negative (i.e., a distributed dividend lower than the assumed dividend), the call option buyer must pay to the option seller the absolute value of the compensation amount.

In the case of a put option, the compensation amount is calculated in a similar way. However, if the compensation amount is positive (i.e., a distributed dividend greater than the assumed dividend), this amount should be paid by the put option buyer to the put option seller. Conversely, if the compensation amount is negative (i.e., a distributed dividend lower than the assumed dividend), the put option seller must pay to the option buyer the absolute value of the compensation amount. The following table summarizes the compensation amount payer/receiver for each type of option:

Dividend deviation	Call option – compensation amount payer	Put option – compensation amount payer
Distributed dividend > Assumed dividend	Option seller	Option buyer
Distributed dividend < Assumed dividend	Option buyer	Option seller

1.4.12 Adjustments to Option Terms Due to Other Corporate Actions

Corporate actions, such as a rights issue, a stock split, a bonus issue, etc., affect the price of an option if the terms of the option are not adjusted. As a result, option terms are adjusted to mitigate the effect of these corporate actions. As an example, I will go through the adjustments to be made in case of a rights issue.

Adjustment to Option Terms as a Result of a Rights Issue

In a rights issue, the price of the existing shares automatically adjusts downwards on the ex-date to take into account the discount offered to subscribe for the new shares. As a result, when a company has a rights issue an adjustment is made on the rights issue ex-date to the option strikes and notionals to appropriately reflect the impact of the rights. The adjustment is only made if PC > PS (see below for the definitions of these two variables). The adjustment factor is calculated as follows:

$$\text{Adjustment factor} = (\text{NE} \times \text{PC} + \text{NN} \times \text{PS})/[(\text{NE} + \text{NN}) \times \text{PC}]$$

where:

NE is the number of existing shares
NN is the number of new shares
PC is the cum-rights price
PS is the subscription price

Instead of using the number of existing and new shares, it is easier to use the numbers of the issue terms. For example, assume 4 per 9 rights issue. Thus, NE = 9 and NN = 4. Let us assume that PC = 31.4 and PS = 12.0. Therefore:

Adjustment factor = $(9 \times 31.4 + 4 \times 12.0)/[(9 + 4) \times 31.4] = 0.989897$
Adjusted strike = Strike × Adjustment factor
Adjusted number of options = Number of options/Adjustment factor

In this adjustment formula it is assumed that the new shares are entitled to any future dividend. However, sometimes the new shares are not entitled to an already declared dividend. In this case the dividend is added to the subscription price when calculating the adjustment factor. The formula then becomes:

$$\text{Adjustment factor} = [\text{NE} \times \text{PC} + \text{NN} \times (\text{PS} + \text{DIV})]/[(\text{NE} + \text{NN}) \times \text{PC}]$$

where:

DIV is the declared dividend per share.

1.4.13 Volatility Smile

An option premium is a function, among other variables, of the implied volatility of an underlying stock associated with a certain tenor and strike. The theoretical value of the option is derived through a theoretical pricing model such as the Black–Scholes option pricing model. One of the key assumptions of the Black–Scholes model is that the stock price follows a geometric Brownian motion with constant volatility. In other words, for a certain tenor, the model assumes that the implied volatilities of all the strikes are identical. However, in real markets implied volatility is far from constant. The volatility smile is a graph of the implied volatility of an option versus its strike, for a given tenor. It typically describes a smile-shaped curve.

The shape indicates the market belief that large movements in stock price occur with a higher probability than a theoretical option pricing model would predict, making out-of-the-money options more valuable. Figure 1.27 shows the volatility smile curve for IBM options with a 3-month time to expiration, as of 4 August 2010. It can be observed that the implied volatility in this example was lowest for 110% strikes and increased as strikes were set further. In the

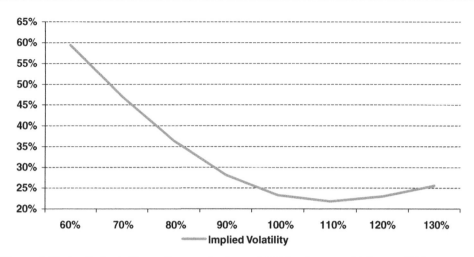

Figure 1.27   Implied volatility smile curve for 3-month IBM options, as of 4 August 2010.

equity markets the volatility smile curve is commonly not symmetrical; the volatility of low strikes is larger than for high strikes. A significant decline in a stock price typically triggers additional sales, therefore increasing the probability of a large drop, while a significant rise in the share price usually does not induce as much additional purchases.

Risk Reversal and the Skew

Skew measures the difference between the implied volatilities of a call and a put with the same delta. As we saw earlier, the implied volatility of a put option is usually larger than the implied volatility of a call option with the same delta. It means that out-of-the-money put options have a higher probability of finishing in-the-money compared with an out-of-the-money call with the same delta.

A risk reversal is the most common way to take a position in the implied volatility skew of a certain stock. A risk reversal is an option strategy that involves buying a call and selling a put, or selling a call and buying a put, with the same delta, on the same underlying and with the same expiration date. The most common risk-reversal transaction consists of trading a put and a call with a 25% delta each. For example, an investor that believes the 3-month 25% delta skew is too large (i.e., the implied volatility of the 25% delta put is too large relative to the implied volatility of the 25% delta call) will sell a 25% delta put and buy a 25% delta call, both with a 3-month expiry.

1.4.14   Implied Volatility Term Structure

The term structure of the implied volatility is a curve depicting the differing implied volatilities of at-the-money options on the same underlying with differing maturities. The scope of the curve indicates expected changes in the option market expectations for volatility over the short and long term. For example, if the market begins to expect an increase in implied volatility of a stock in the near term, the implied volatility of 1-month and 3-month options will rise

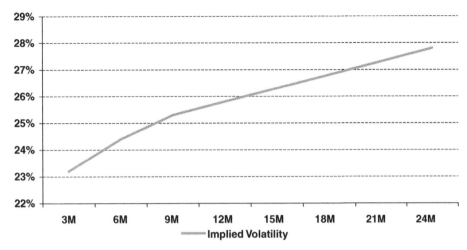

Figure 1.28 Implied volatility term structure for at-the-money options on IBM.

relative to longer-term options. If expectations are that volatility will not rise beyond a few months, the term structure might be flatter for longer-dated options. Expectations of higher near-term implied volatility will cause the term structure differential between 3-month and 1-year implied volatility to decrease. Figure 1.28 depicts IBM's term structure of volatilities as of 4 August 2010. The market expected volatilities of at-the-money options on IBM to rise in the medium term.

1.4.15 Composite and Quanto Options

First, let us assume that a USD-based investor buys a **standard call option** on Microsoft stock with a strike of K. If the stock price of Microsoft is S at expiry, the option payout at expiry would be:

$$\text{Payout} = \text{Number of options} \times \text{Max}(S - K, 0)$$

The stock price of Microsoft is denominated in USD. The option payout is also calculated in USD.

Let us assume now that a EUR-based investor buys a **composite call option** on Microsoft stock. The payout of the composite call would be:

$$\text{Payout} = \text{Number of options} \times \text{Max}(S/\text{FX}_T - K/\text{FX}_0, 0)$$

where FX_0 is the USD/EUR exchange rate prevailing at inception (to be more precise, at the time when the strike price is set) and FX_T is the USD/EUR exchange rate prevailing at expiry (to be more precise, at the time when the settlement price is calculated). The stock price of Microsoft is denominated in USD. The composite option payout is calculated in EUR. The investor is exposed to the movement of the USD/EUR exchange rate. If FX_T is lower than FX_0, the investor would benefit from a favorable FX movement.

Let us assume now that a EUR-based investor buys a **quanto call option** on Microsoft stock. The payout of the quanto call would be:

$$\text{Payout} = \text{Number of options} \times \text{Max}(S/\text{FX}_0 - K/\text{FX}_0, 0)$$

where FX_0 is the USD/EUR exchange rate prevailing at inception (to be more precise, at the time when the strike price is set). The stock price of Microsoft is denominated in USD. The quanto option payout is calculated in EUR. It can be seen that there is no FX_T in the formula. Thus, the investor is not exposed to the USD/EUR exchange rate.

1.5 DIVIDEND SWAPS

Dividend swaps are OTC derivatives that allow investors to purchase or sell the dividends paid over a specified period by a stock, a basket of stocks or an index or a combination thereof.

1.5.1 Dividend Swaps

For a given underlying, a dividend swap is the exchange, at a given maturity or periodically, of a fixed and a floating payment (see Figure 1.29). The long dividend swap counterparty will pay a fixed payment, representing the current estimated market value of dividends, and receive a floating payment, representing the distributed dividends over the period considered.

At the end of each period the fixed and floating payments are netted, resulting in the following payoff to be settled between the two parties:

$$\text{Settlement amount} = \text{Floating amount} - \text{Fixed amount}$$

The floating amount is the sum of the dividends actually paid by the underlying over the period considered.

The fixed amount is an amount set forth at the inception of the contract. It represents the expected dividends over the period considered.

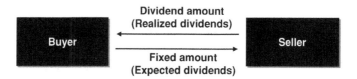

Figure 1.29 Dividend swap overview.

1.5.2 Applications of Dividend Swaps

Dividend swaps allow an investor to hedge positions involving uncertainty of dividend receipts/ payments and to express views on the future levels of dividend payments.

Hedging

Investment banks with a large activity in equity derivative products to retail and institutional investors experience large exposures to dividends. The exposure stems from the short positions in the calls embedded in capital guaranteed equity-linked products and the long positions in the puts embedded in reverse convertibles. Together, those positions create a short forward position that has to be hedged by buying the underlying stocks which pay an unknown amount of dividends into the future. To hedge their exposure, investment banks sell dividend swaps.

An investor may want to lock in the dividends to be received from an investment in a specific stock. This is commonly the case of investors who are financing the investment. Dividends may be used to meet the debt interest payments. A decline in dividends may jeopardize an investor's capacity to meet his/her debt commitments. To hedge this exposure the investor sells a dividend swap.

Convertible bond buyers are also natural users of dividend swaps. Often convertibles are long term with little or no dividend protection. Convertible bond investors are generally short dividend risk, that is, higher than expected dividends on the underlying stock may reduce the convertible bond value. The dividend sensitivity is relatively more pronounced for convertibles with high delta and long time to maturity. This is because to delta-hedge the embedded call option a convertible bond investor needs to sell a number of shares of the underlying stock such that the overall delta remains zero. Commonly, the investor needs to borrow the shares to be sold, and therefore pay the lender an amount equivalent to the dividends distributed to the borrowed shares. An increase in the dividend means that the investor is required to pay a higher than anticipated amount of dividends to the stock lender. Therefore, convertible bond investors are natural buyers of dividend swaps.

Profiting from Directional Views

An investor may want to profit from a specific view on dividends paid by a stock or an index without holding the underlying. For example, an investor can buy dividends outright if he/she feels current implied dividend levels for a particular period are too low. Dividends are arguably the most tangible measure of the economic fundamentals of companies. Companies signal their confidence about the future by raising their dividends, while companies in difficulties are forced to cut their dividends. Unlike stocks, dividends are correlated more to fundamentals because dividends are less exposed to market risk.

Profiting from Relative Value Views

An investor may want to profit from the relative value between one stream of dividend payments and another. For example, an investor can play a steepening of the dividend term structure by buying a longer dated dividend swap and selling a shorter dated one.

Diversification

An investor may want diversification in his/her bond–equity portfolio and simultaneously improve its risk–return profile. Dividends constitute an investment that is different from investing in bonds or directly in equities. Changes in dividend growth are more gradual than stock market movements. They take longer to rise/fall in bullish/bearish markets. As a result, dividends tend to exhibit lower volatility than cash equities.

1.5.3   Risks

The potential loss for the counterparty being long the dividend swap is limited to the fixed amount paid and would occur when the underlying pays no dividend. The potential loss for the counterparty being short the dividend swap is in theory unlimited.

Because dividend swaps are OTC instruments, a default by a counterparty to the dividend swap may originate a loss to the other party.

1.5.4   Main Dates in a Dividend Distribution

When referring to dividends, there are several dates that we need to be familiar with.

The **declaration date** is the date the company's board of directors approve the size of the dividend to be proposed for approval at the next AGM (i.e., a shareholders' annual general meeting). Usually the shareholders of the company approve this recommended dividend at the AGM. Then, on a later date, the company's board of directors approves the record and payment dates.

The **record date** is the date on which an investor has to be registered as a shareholder to be granted the dividend.

The definition of the **ex-dividend date** depends on the country where the stock exchange is located, being referred to either the trade date or the settlement date:

- For US and UK stocks, for example, the ex-dividend date is the first date on which the stock will be traded without entitlement to receive the dividends. Therefore, the ex-dividend date is the day that is two exchange business days immediately prior to the record date. At the market open on the ex-dividend date, the stock trades "excluding the dividend" or "ex-dividend". Before the ex-dividend date the stock is said to be "cum-dividend" (i.e., it has entitlement to the dividend).
- For EUR denominated stocks, for example, the ex-dividend date is the first date the stock settles without entitlement to receive the dividends. Therefore, the ex-dividend date is the exchange business day immediately following the record date.

The **payment date** is the date on which the dividend is received by the shareholder.

As an example, let us assume that IBM announced a cash dividend on 18 May 20X1. The record date was 8 June 20X1. The ex-dividend date was then 6 June 20X1. In the US stock market it takes three exchange business days for a trade to settle (i.e., when the shares are delivered to the stock buyer and the proceeds are received by the stock seller). Any IBM purchasing trades settling on or before 8 June 20X1 (the record date) will be entitled to receive the dividend. Therefore, an investor buying IBM shares prior to 6 June 20X1 will be entitled to receive the dividend. For example, an investor entering into a stock purchase on 5 June 20X1 will have the trade settled on 8 June 20X1, thus being entitled to receive the dividend. A purchase trade entered into on 6 June 20X1, the ex-dividend date, would be settled on 9 June 20X1 (after the record date) and, therefore, will not be entitled to receive the dividend.

1.5.5   Case Study: Single-stock Dividend Swap

Let's assume that on 31 December 20X0 Zurich Bank thinks that XYZ Corp.'s implied dividend levels for 20X1 are too conservative. XYZ already cut its dividend in 20X0, and the market is still very negative regarding XYZ's upcoming dividends. Zurich Bank thinks that XYZ's fundamentals are strong and it will be able to distribute higher cash dividends in the near future. As a result, Zurich Bank buys a dividend swap from Gigabank with the following terms:

Dividend Swap on a Single Stock – Main Terms	
Fixed amount payer (i.e., the buyer)	Zurich Bank
Dividend amount payer (i.e., the seller)	Gigabank
Trade date	31-December-20X0
Effective date	31-December-20X0
Termination date	31-December-20X2
Underlying stock	XYZ Corp. common stock (ordinary shares)
Exchange	Euronext
Related exchange	Eurex
Number of shares	10 million
Fixed strike	EUR 0.85, per stock
Fixed amount per dividend period	EUR 8.5 million (= Number of shares × Fixed strike)
Dividend amount per dividend period	Number of shares $\times \sum_{t=1}^{T} (d_t)$
Declared cash dividend percentage	100%
Declared cash equivalent dividend percentage	100%
Dividend periods	From 31-Dec-20X0 to 31-Dec-20X1, and from 1-Jan-20X2 to 31-Dec-20X2
Settlement amount payment date	One currency business day following the end date of the relevant dividend period
Settlement currency	EUR
Calculation agent	Gigabank

where:

Underlying is the stock or index whose dividends are being bought or sold.

Fixed strike is an amount set forth at the inception of the transaction, which can be interpreted as the implied dividend for one share during a dividend period.

Fixed amount is the product of (i) the number of shares and (ii) the fixed strike.

Dividend period(s) or valuation period(s) are the period(s) within which paid dividends will qualify. Commonly, a dividend period comprises a calendar year.

Settlement amount payment date(s) is the date(s) on which the payoff is settled. Settlement typically occurs one business day after each period ends. At each settlement date, amounts are netted and the settlement amount is computed. If the settlement amount is positive, the seller pays the buyer the settlement amount. If the settlement amount is negative, the buyer pays the seller the absolute value of the settlement amount:

$$\text{Settlement amount} = \text{Dividend amount} - \text{Fixed amount}$$

Dividend amount or distributed amount is the sum of all the dividends paid by the underlying during the dividend period. The dividend amount is calculated as the product of (i) the number of shares and (ii) the sum of all the d_t dividends distributed to one share during the dividend period:

$$\text{Dividend amount} = \text{Number of shares} \times \sum_{t=1}^{T} (d_t)$$

t means each weekday in the relevant dividend period, and T is the total number of weekdays in the relevant dividend period.

Number of shares is the underlying quantity upon which payment obligations are computed. It can be viewed as the amount to be paid for a one-point difference between the fixed amount and the dividend paid per share.

Qualifying dividend d_t. In respect of the underlying stock and each day t in the relevant dividend period: (i) if an ex-dividend date falls on such day, an amount equal to the "relevant dividend"; or (ii) otherwise zero. Distributed dividends are generally defined as a percentage (100% in our case) of the ordinary cash or stock dividends declared in the currency of the company's announcement. Dividends are considered before any applicable withholding tax and disregarding any tax credit. Stock dividends are included at the equivalent cash amount. Note that dividends are not reinvested in the money markets. Dividends are neither compounded nor capitalized.

Relevant dividend. In respect of the underlying stock and each day t in a dividend period: (a) the "declared cash dividend"; and/or (b) the "declared cash equivalent dividend", excluding any dividends in relation to which the related primary exchange adjusts the derivatives contracts that include the underlying.

Declared cash dividend. In respect of a relevant dividend, an amount per share as declared by the issuer where the ex-dividend date falls on such day t, before the withholding or deduction of taxes at source by or on behalf of any applicable authority having power to tax in respect of such dividend, and shall exclude: (a) any imputation or other credits, refunds or deductions granted by an applicable authority; and (b) any taxes, credits, refunds or benefits imposed, withheld, assessed or levied on the credits referred to in (a) above.

Declared cash equivalent dividend. In respect of a relevant dividend, an amount per share being the cash value of any stock dividend (whether or not such stock dividend comprises of shares that are not the common shares of the issuer) declared by the issuer where the ex-dividend date falls on such day t (or, if no cash value is declared by the relevant issuer, the cash value of such stock dividend as determined by the calculation agent, calculated by reference to the opening of such common shares on the ex-dividend date applicable to that stock dividend).

If holders of record may elect between receiving a declared cash dividend or a declared cash equivalent dividend, the dividend is deemed to be a declared cash dividend.

Where any relevant dividend is declared in a currency other than the settlement currency, then the calculation agent shall convert such relevant dividend into the settlement currency at the rate declared by the issuer, where any such rate is available or, if no such rate is available, at a rate determined by the calculation agent.

Ex-dividend date. In respect of a relevant dividend, the date that the share is scheduled to trade ex-dividend on the primary exchange or quotation system for such share.

Termination date is the date on which the contract ends.

In our example, the first dividend period started on 31 December 20X0 and ended on 31 December 20X1. Let us assume that XYZ distributed the following dividends around those dates:

Dividend number	Ex-dividend date	Terms	XYZ opening price on ex-dividend date	Derivatives adjustment on related exchange?
1	30-Dec-X0	EUR 0.30 cash	NA	No
2	1-Apr-X1	EUR 0.55 cash	NA	No
3	1-Jul-X1	1 new share for each 50 shares	EUR 20.00	No
4	1-Oct-X1	1 new share for each 30 shares	EUR 21.00	Yes
5	1-Nov-X1	EUR 1.20 cash	NA	Yes

In order to check if a dividend constitutes a "qualifying dividend", we have to check (i) if the ex-dividend date falls within the dividend period and (ii) if the terms of the derivatives (usually futures and options) on the underlying stock that trade on the related primary exchange are not adjusted.

Companies sometimes pay special or extraordinary dividends, which are usually excluded from the calculation of the qualifying dividends. In order to avoid arguing whether a specific dividend constitutes a qualifying dividend, contracts follow the related exchange rules. Dividends that cause an adjustment to derivatives on the same underlying (the designated contract) by the related primary exchange are not included. Therefore:

- Dividend 1 is not a qualifying dividend because its ex-dividend date is prior to the considered dividend period.
- Dividend 2 is a qualifying dividend because its ex-dividend date is within the considered dividend period and it does not cause an adjustment to the derivatives trading in the related primary exchange on XYZ Corp. Therefore, the "declared cash dividend" is EUR 0.55 and it will be taken into account when computing the dividend amount.
- Dividend 3 is a qualifying dividend because its ex-dividend date is within the considered dividend period and it does not cause an adjustment to the derivatives trading in the related primary exchange on XYZ Corp. It is a scrip dividend. For each existing share, the shareholder of XYZ received 1/50 shares. It is assumed that this 1/50 share is sold at the opening of the market on the ex-dividend date. XYZ shares were trading at that moment at EUR 20.00. Therefore, the "declared cash equivalent dividend" amount is EUR 0.40 (= 20/50).
- Dividend 4 is not a qualifying dividend because it causes an adjustment to the derivatives trading in the related primary exchange on XYZ Corp.
- Dividend 5 is not a qualifying dividend because it causes an adjustment to the derivatives trading in the related primary exchange on XYZ Corp.

As a consequence, the sum of the qualifying dividends is EUR 0.95 (= 0.55 + 0.40). The dividend amount for the period would be calculated as:

Dividend amount = Number of shares × Sum of qualifying dividends
Dividend amount = 10 million × 0.95 = EUR 9.5 million

The fixed amount was EUR 8.5 million. Thus, the settlement amount was EUR 1 million (= 9.5 million – 8.5 million). Because the settlement amount was positive, the fixed amount payer – Zurich Bank – received from the dividend amount payer – Gigabank – the EUR 1 million settlement amount on the settlement amount payment date – 1 January 20X2. Remember that there was a second dividend period that I will not cover as the mechanics to calculate the settlement amount are identical.

1.5.6 Case Study: Index Dividend Swap

Index dividend swaps give exposure to the dividends distributed by the stocks that are members of the index during a specific period. The mechanics of an index dividend swap are very similar to a single stock dividend swap. The only difference is a notably more complex computation of the actual dividends. As an example, let us assume that on 31 December 20X0 Zurich Bank thinks that EuroStoxx 50 implied dividend levels for 20X1 and 20X2 are too low. In 20X0 there has been a deep recession that has obliged auto and construction companies to skip dividends. Thus, banks' trading desks have been forced to sell their losing large long dividend positions. Zurich Bank thinks that as a result of the widespread unwinding of trades, the market dividend levels for the EuroStoxx 50 are discounting an unprecedented dividend cut for 20X1 and 20X2. As a result, Zurich Bank buys a two-year dividend swap on the EuroStoxx 50 from Gigabank with the following terms:

Dividend Swap on an Index – Main Terms	
Fixed amount payer (i.e., the buyer)	Zurich Bank
Dividend amount payer (i.e., the seller)	Gigabank
Trade date	31-December-20X0
Effective date	31-December-20X0
Termination date	31-December-20X2
Underlying index	EuroStoxx 50
Exchange	Euronext
Related exchange	Eurex
Number of baskets	100,000 (for avoidance of doubt, the number of baskets is in EUR and 10,000 contracts of EUR 10 tick value each)
Fixed strike	120 index points, per basket
Fixed amount per dividend period	EUR 12 million (= Number of baskets × Fixed strike)
Dividend amount per dividend period	Number of baskets $\times \sum_{t=1}^{T} \sum_{i=1}^{N} \left(\frac{n_{i,t} \times d_{i,t}}{D_t} \right)$
Declared cash dividend percentage	100%
Declared cash equivalent dividend percentage	100%
Dividend periods	From 31-Dec-20X0 to 31-Dec-20X1, and from 1-Jan-20X2 to 31-Dec-20X2
Settlement amount payment date	One currency business day following the end date of the relevant dividend period
Settlement currency	EUR
Calculation agent	Gigabank

The settlement amount is calculated as:

$$\text{Settlement amount} = \text{Dividend amount} - \text{Fixed amount}$$

The dividend amount is calculated as follows:

1. The total dividends paid by each company member of the index during the period considered are computed.
2. All the dividends calculated in (1) are summed up to arrive at a figure for the total dividends paid out on the index.
3. The amount calculated in (2) is divided by the index divisor to arrive at the dividends paid in index points.
4. The figure calculated in (3) is multiplied by the number of baskets.

More precisely, the dividend amount is calculated as follows:

$$\text{Dividend amount} = \text{Number of baskets} \times \sum_{t=1}^{T} \sum_{i=1}^{N} \left(\frac{n_{i,t} \times d_{i,t}}{D_t} \right)$$

where:

Number of baskets is the predetermined number of index points. It can be viewed as the amount to be paid for a one-point difference between the fixed amount and the dividend paid, weighted according the index.

t means each weekday in the relevant dividend period.

i means, in respect of each day t, each share that is comprised in the index on such day.

$n_{i,t}$ means, in respect of each share i and day t, the number of free-floating shares relating to such share comprised in the index, as calculated and published by the index sponsor on such day t.

The qualifying dividend $d_{i,t}$ means, in respect of each share i and day t: (i) if an ex-dividend date falls on such day, an amount equal to the relevant dividend; or (ii) otherwise zero.

D_i means, in respect of each day t, the official index divisor, as calculated and published by the index sponsor in respect of such share i and such day t.

Official index divisor is the value, calculated by the index sponsor, necessary to ensure that the numerical value of the index remains unchanged after a change in the composition of the index. The value of the index after any change in the composition is divided by the official index divisor to ensure that the value of the index returns to its normalized value.

Relevant dividend means, in respect of each share i and day t in a dividend period: (a) the "declared cash dividend percentage" specified in the transaction terms of any declared cash dividend; and/or (b) the "declared cash equivalent percentage" specified in the relevant transaction terms of any declared cash equivalent dividend, excluding any dividends in relation to which the index sponsor makes an adjustment to the index. Where the index sponsor has adjusted the index for part of a dividend, this relevant dividend provision applies only to the unadjusted part.

Declared cash dividend means, in respect of a relevant dividend of share i, an amount per share i as declared by the issuer of such share i where the ex-dividend date falls on such day t, before the withholding or deduction of taxes at source by or on behalf of any applicable authority having power to tax in respect of such dividend, and shall exclude: (a) any imputation or other credits, refunds or deductions granted by an applicable authority; and (b) any taxes, credits, refunds or benefits imposed, withheld, assessed or levied on the credits referred to in (a) above.

Declared cash equivalent dividend means, in respect of a relevant dividend of share i, an amount per share i being the cash value of any stock dividend (whether or not such stock dividend comprises of shares that are not the common shares of the issuer) declared by the issuer of such share i where the ex-dividend date falls on such day t (or, if no cash value is declared by the relevant issuer, the cash value of such stock dividend as determined by the calculation agent, calculated by reference to the opening of such common shares on the ex-dividend date applicable to that stock dividend).

If holders of record of share i may elect between receiving a declared cash dividend or a declared cash equivalent dividend, the dividend is deemed to be a declared cash dividend.

Where any relevant dividend is declared in a currency other than the "settlement currency", then the calculation agent shall convert such relevant dividend into the settlement currency at the rate declared by the issuer where any such rate is available or, if no such rate is available, at a rate determined by the calculation agent.

Ex-dividend date means, in respect of a relevant dividend, the date that share i is scheduled to trade ex-dividend on the primary exchange or quotation system for such share i.

Termination date is the date on which the contract ends.

Let us assume that the actual dividends paid by the stocks that are members of the EuroStoxx 50 index from 31 December 20X0 to 31 December 20X1 (the first dividend period) were 180 index points:

The dividend amount would be 18 million ($= 100{,}000 \times 180$)
The fixed amount was 12 million ($= 100{,}000 \times 120$)
The settlement amount would be EUR 6 million ($= 18$ million $- 12$ million)

As a consequence, the dividend swap buyer (Zurich Bank) received EUR 6 million one currency business day after 31 December 20X1.

1.5.7 Pricing Implied Dividends

The implied dividend of a stock can be calculated by using the put–call parity formula (as explained earlier in this chapter):

$$\text{Stock} + \text{Put} = \text{PV(Strike)} + \text{Call} + \text{PV(Dividends)} + \text{PV(Repo)}$$

where "PV" is the present value.
Solving for the dividends:

$$\text{PV(Dividends)} = \text{Stock} + \text{Put} - \text{Call} - \text{PV(Strike)} - \text{PV(Repo)}$$

1.6 VARIANCE SWAPS AND VOLATILITY SWAPS

Variance and volatility swaps give "pure" exposure to volatility. Volatility can also be traded using options, for example by trading a straddle, but an investment in a variance/volatility swap can be more efficient as it requires little re-hedging, unlike a gamma hedging option position. Another benefit of variance and volatility swaps is their zero upfront premium.

Variance swaps are OTC derivatives that allow investors to purchase or sell the realized variance, defined as the square of future realized volatility, over a specified period by a stock or an index or a combination thereof.

Volatility swaps are OTC derivatives that allow investors to purchase or sell the realized volatility over a specified period by a stock or an index or a combination thereof.

1.6.1 Variance Swaps Product Description

The holder of a EUR denominated variance swap at expiration receives a EUR "variance amount" for every point by which the stock realized variance has exceeded an expected predetermined variance amount. No premium is paid upfront to enter into the variance swap. For a given underlying, a variance swap is the exchange, at a given maturity or periodically, of a fixed and a floating amount (see Figure 1.30). At maturity, or at the end of each period, the fixed and the floating payments are netted between the two parties:

$$\text{Settlement amount} = \text{Floating amount} - \text{Fixed amount}$$

The floating amount represents the underling realized variance over the period:

$$\text{Floating amount} = \text{Variance amount} \times \text{Realized volatility}^2$$

The fixed amount represents the underlying expected variance over the period:

$$\text{Fixed amount} = \text{Variance amount} \times \text{Volatility strike}^2$$

As a result, the settlement amount can be computed as:

$$\text{Settlement amount} = \text{Variance amount} \times (\text{Realized volatility}^2 - \text{Volatility strike}^2)$$

If the settlement amount, also called the **equity amount**, is positive the seller pays the buyer the settlement amount. Conversely, if the settlement amount is negative the buyer pays the seller the absolute value of the settlement amount.

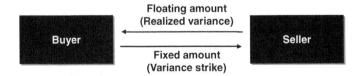

Figure 1.30 Variance swap flows.

Definitions

Realized volatility[2] is the realized stock variance (quoted in annual terms) over the life of the contract, expressed in percentage.

Volatility strike[2], also called **variance strike price**, is the delivery price for variance that makes the swap have zero value.

Variance amount, also called variance units, is the notional amount of the swap per unit of currency per annualized volatility point squared.

Termination date is the date on which the settlement amount is paid. It is usually three scheduled trading days after the observation end date.

As an example, let us assume that ABC believes that the market is estimating a too low level of future variance of XYZ's stock price over the next year. As a result, ABC enters into the following variance swap with Gigabank:

Variance Swap – Main Terms	
Buyer	ABC
Seller	Gigabank
Trade date	30-December-20X0
Termination date	5-January-20X2
Underlying	XYZ Corp
Observation start date	2-January-20X2
Observation end date	2-January-20X3
Variance amount	5,000
Volatility strike	25
Settlement date	Three exchange business days after the observation end date

In our example, if the realized volatility over the period was 30%, the buyer – ABC – would receive from the seller – Gigabank – a settlement amount equal to EUR 1,375,000, calculated as follows:

$$\text{Floating amount} = \text{Variance amount} \times \text{Realized volatility}^2$$
$$= 5,000 \times 30^2 = \text{EUR } 4,500,000$$
$$\text{Fixed amount} = \text{Variance amount} \times \text{Volatility strike}^2$$
$$= 5,000 \times 25^2 = \text{EUR } 3,125,000$$
$$\text{Settlement amount} = \text{EUR } 4,500,000 - 3,125,000 = 1,375,000$$

Conversely, if the realized volatility over the period was 15%, the buyer – ABC – would pay to the seller – Gigabank – the absolute value of the settlement amount (i.e., EUR 2,000,000), calculated as follows:

$$\text{Floating amount} = \text{Variance amount} \times \text{Realized volatility}^2$$
$$= 5,000 \times 15^2 = \text{EUR } 1,125,000$$
$$\text{Fixed amount} = \text{Variance amount} \times \text{Volatility strike}^2$$
$$= 5,000 \times 25^2 = \text{EUR } 3,125,000$$
$$\text{Settlement amount} = \text{EUR } 1,125,000 - 3,125,000 = -2,000,000$$

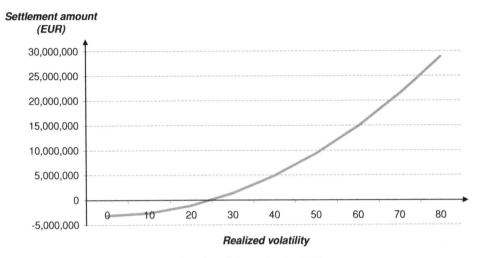

Figure 1.31   Settlement amount as a function of the realized volatility.

Figure 1.31 shows the settlement amount as a function of the realized volatility. The graph highlights the convexity profile of the settlement amount, providing an advantage to the buyer. In other words, for a large movement of the realized volatility, the buyer will benefit more from being right than he/she will lose from being wrong.

1.6.2 Calculation of the Realized Volatility and the Realized Variance

The formula to calculate the realized volatility or variance is defined at the beginning of the contract. The realized volatility σ_R is the annualized standard deviation of a stock's return during a period, expressed in percentage. A common formula is the following:

$$\text{Realized volatility} = \sigma_R = 100 \times \sqrt{\frac{252 \times \sum_{i=1}^{N} \left(Ln \frac{P_i}{P_{i-1}} \right)^2}{\text{Expected } N}}$$

This formula assumes that the stock price follows a log-normal distribution, one of the assumptions of the Black–Scholes model. It is important to note that stock prices in the formula are not adjusted for dividends. A stock with a high dividend yield may seem to be more volatile than a low dividend yielding stock.

Definitions

Ln is the natural logarithm.

P_i and P_{i-1} are the official levels of the underlying on respectively the ith and i–1th observation days. In most cases the official level is the daily closing price of the underlying.

N is the actual number of realized trading days for the period from, but excluding the observation start date to, and including, the observation end date.

252 is the **annualization factor**. Usually, it is assumed to be 252 trading days per year.

Expected N is the number of days that, as the trade date, are expected to be scheduled trading days for the period from, but excluding the observation start date to, and including, the observation end date. In other words, "expected N" is the number of pre-agreed observation days.

Observation day is each trading day during the observation period.

Observation period is the period from, but excluding, the observation start date to, but excluding, the observation end date.

The **realized variance** is calculated as:

$$\text{Realized variance} = (\text{Realized volatility})^2$$

1.6.3 Volatility Swaps Product Description

The holder of a EUR denominated volatility swap at expiration receives the EUR "volatility amount" for every point by which the stock realized volatility has exceeded an expected predetermined volatility amount. No premium is paid upfront to enter into the volatility swap. For a given underlying, a volatility swap is the exchange, at a given maturity or periodically, of a fixed and a floating amount (see Figure 1.32). At maturity, or at the end of each period, the fixed and the floating payments are netted between the two parties:

$$\text{Settlement amount} = \text{Floating amount} - \text{Fixed amount}$$

The floating amount represents the underlying realized volatility over the period:

$$\text{Floating amount} = \text{Volatility amount} \times \text{Realized volatility}$$

The fixed amount represents the underlying expected volatility over the period:

$$\text{Fixed amount} = \text{Volatility amount} \times \text{Volatility strike}$$

As a result, the settlement amount can be computed as:

$$\text{Settlement amount} = \text{Volatility amount} \times (\text{Realized volatility} - \text{Volatility strike})$$

If the settlement amount, also called the **equity amount**, is positive the seller pays the buyer the settlement amount. Conversely, if the settlement amount is negative the buyer pays the seller the absolute value of the settlement amount.

Volatility amount, also called **volatility units**, is the notional amount of the swap per unit of currency per annualized volatility.

For definitions of the other terms, please refer to the variance swap product description.

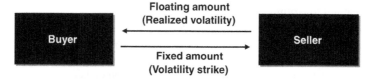

Figure 1.32   Volatility swap flows.

1.6.4   Volatility Swaps vs. Variance Swaps

Although options market participants talk about volatility, it is variance, or volatility squared, that has more fundamental theoretical significance. This is so because the correct way to value a swap is to value the portfolio that replicates it and the swap that can be replicated most reliably is a variance swap. A variance swap is a forward contract on annualized variance, the square of the realized volatility.

The payoff of a variance swap is convex in volatility, as illustrated in Figure 1.31. This means that an investor who is long a variance swap (i.e., receiving realized variance) will benefit from a larger amount if he/she is right than if he/she is wrong, for the same movement in volatility. This bias has a cost reflected in a slightly higher strike than the "fair" volatility. Thus, volatility swaps are a cheaper investment as a buyer, as Volatility swap$_{price}$ < Variance swap$_{price}$.

Similarly, volatility swaps have a better risk profile as a seller, as Volatility swap$_{convexity}$ < Variance swap$_{convexity}$.

An interesting property of variance swaps is their additivity. For example, the sum of a 3-month variance and a 9-month variance in 3 months is equal to a 12-month variance.

	Variance swaps	Volatility swaps
Pure volatility exposure	$\checkmark$	$\checkmark$
Positive convexity	$\checkmark$	
Implied/realized additivity	$\checkmark$	

1.6.5   Applications of Variance and Volatility Swaps

Variance and volatility swaps allow an investor to hedge positions involving uncertainty of volatility and to express views on future levels of volatility. A stock volatility is the simplest measure of its riskiness. Although volatility can be traded with options, volatility swaps provide a much more direct method.

Hedging against Volatility Movements

A portfolio of equity derivatives hedged with positions in the underlying stocks leaves exposure to realized volatility, which can be hedged by taking a position in variance or volatility swaps.

Also, risk arbitrageurs often take positions which assume that the spread between the stock prices of two companies planning to merge will narrow. If overall market volatility increases, the merger may become less likely and the spread may widen. By buying a volatility swap, an arbitrageur can put in place a proxy hedge.

Directional Views on Volatility

Variance and volatility swaps provide pure exposure to volatility. Volatility has several characteristics that make trading attractive. It is likely to grow when uncertainty and risk increase. As with interest rates, volatilities appear to revert to the mean; high volatilities will eventually decrease, low ones will likely rise. If an investor thinks current volatility is low, for the right price he/she might want to take a position that profits if volatility increases. For example, if an investor foresees a rapid decline in financial turmoil after a specific crisis, a short position in volatility might be appropriate.

Trading the Spread between Realized and Implied Volatility

Variance/volatility swaps allow an investor to capture the premium between implied and realized volatility. For example, let us assume that an investor buys a variance/volatility swap in a period in which stock prices are experiencing large moves while the implied volatility is much lower. The investor will benefit from a favorable carry associated with being long volatility.

Relative Value Views on Future Volatility

An investor who wants to take a view on the future levels of stock or index volatility can go long or short a future realized volatility. Forward trades are interesting because the forward volatility term structure tends to flatten for longer forward start dates. Because variance is additive, an investor can obtain a perfect exposure to forward implied volatility. For example, an investor can be long future realized volatility by buying a longer dated variance swap and selling a shorter dated one.

Trading Correlation (Dispersion Trades)

An investor may be looking to buy correlation by taking a long position on an index variance/volatility and a short position in the variance/volatility of the index components. Commonly, only the most liquid stocks are chosen among the index components and each variance/volatility swap notional is adjusted to match the same volatility sensitivity as the index.

Diversification

An investor may want diversification in his/her bond–equity portfolio and simultaneously improve its risk–return profile. Equity volatility constitutes an investment that is different from investing in bonds or directly in equities. Volatility is often negatively correlated with a stock or an index level, and tends to stay high after large downward moves in the market. Investing in a variance/volatility swap can bring diversification to a portfolio.

2

Equity Capital Markets Products

The objective of this chapter is to provide a good understanding of equity capital markets products such as rights issues and accelerated book-buildings. Convertibles and mandatory convertibles are covered in Chapter 3. A second aim is to help bank professionals to understand the main products provided by the bank equity capital markets (ECM) team. The ECM team specializes in the origination and execution of equity capital markets transactions.

2.1 MAIN EQUITY CAPITAL MARKETS PRODUCTS

This section briefly describes the main equity capital markets products.

2.1.1 Capital Increase Products

In challenging economic environments even fundamentally sound companies experience capital structure pressures. Stringent covenants and operating performance challenges oblige them to raise capital. Companies are generally reluctant to issue new equity because it is notably more expensive than debt. However, from time to time companies need to raise capital to finance acquisitions, to finance further growth or to lower leverage. Capital increase products aim at placing new shares of the company with institutional and/or retail investors. There are a number of alternatives for raising equity capital, but no set rules for identifying the optimal one. The cycle in which the company is, has a large influence on the capital increase product chosen, as shown in Figure 2.1. The main capital increase products are initial public offerings, rights issues, accelerated book-buildings (ABB) and hybrid issues.

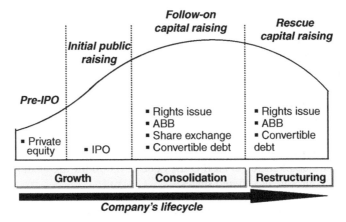

Figure 2.1 Capital increase products during a company's lifecycle.

Pre-emptive vs. Non-pre-emptive Capital Increase

A pre-emptive capital increase is an issue of new shares with subscription rights for current shareholders. Existing shareholders remain protected from dilution risk as they have a proportional take-up right.

A non-pre-emptive capital increase is an issue of new shares without subscription rights for current shareholders. Existing shareholders are exposed to dilution.

2.1.2   Secondary Placement Products

Core shareholders sometimes need to sell their investment in a company. In these transactions the company does not receive the proceeds of the placement. Two of the main secondary placement products are IPOs and ABBs. In an IPO, shares of a previously unlisted company are offered to stock market investors. After the IPO the company shares publicly trade on the stock market. Typically the sellers into an IPO are the company founders and/or private equity firms looking to cash in their original investment. In an ABB, shareholders holding a significant block of shares sell it to investors in a quick placement transaction.

2.1.3   Equity-linked Products

Sometimes companies want to monetize their stake in other companies without selling the stake issuing equity-linked products, such as mandatory exchangeable and exchangeable bonds. If the company issues equity-linked products, the instruments are called mandatory convertible and convertible bonds. Equity-linked instruments are covered in Chapter 3.

2.2   INITIAL PUBLIC OFFERINGS

2.2.1   Product Description

Initial public offerings (IPOs) are a product for privately owned companies aiming to list their shares on a public stock market (i.e., in an exchange). In an IPO, new and/or existing shares are offered to institutional investors, retail investors and to the company's employees. A listing enables the company to attract capital and realize its growth ambitions, while providing liquidity for its shareholders. For example, a private equity firm may have acquired a company via a leveraged buy-out (LBO). After years of partially repaying the debt, the private equity firm may decide to crystallize its investment by going public. Another example would be a private company's founders selling to the market part of their holdings to diversify their wealth. A third example would be a company selling new shares to fund its expansion plans. A final example would be a holding entity selling to the market part of its privately owned subsidiary to finance expansion plan requirements. IPOs provide investors the opportunity to diversify and invest in a company that was previously unavailable to them. The IPO process is also called a "**going public**" process.

Generally, the sale of shares in an IPO uses one of the following methods to establish an offer price and to allocate the offered shares:

- In a book-building process, also called the "traditional" method, the offer price is decided by the participating banks in conjunction with the offeror (i.e., the seller of the shares) based on the interest from institutional investors and the expected behavior of the shares once the trading for these shares starts. The allotment of the offered shares among the institutional investors is at the discretion of the participating banks based on multiple factors. Therefore, once the offer price is set, investors who bid at least that price may not be awarded shares in the offering.

- In a Dutch auction process, the offer price and the allotment of shares are determined automatically. The offeror sets the total number of shares being offered and sometimes a potential price range. Institutional and retail investors then submit a conditional order for the quantity of shares they wish to receive and the highest price they would be willing to pay. The offeror allocates the shares, starting with the highest bidder, until it has allocated all the shares being offered. The offer price is then set at the lowest bid it accepts. The price all awarded bidders pay is the offer price, even if they had bid higher. Therefore, once the offer price is set, investors who bid at least that price know that they are awarded shares in the offering.

Primary vs. Secondary Offerings vs. Follow-on Offering

In a **primary offering**, a company issues new shares. The number of shares outstanding increases. The proceeds go to the company. A **follow-on offering** is an issuance of stock subsequent to a company's IPO.

In a **secondary offering**, some shareholders offer existing listed shares. The proceeds go to the selling shareholders, not to the company. The number of shares outstanding does not change.

Some IPOs combine a primary offering and a secondary offering. For example, Google's IPO included both a sell-down by existing shareholders and a capital-raising by the company.

2.2.2 Benefits of Going Public

Going public can bring many benefits for a company, for example:

1. An easier future access of the company to the debt and equity markets through future new issues of convertible debt and equity.
2. A potential future use of stock as currency for expansion, facilitating acquisitions.
3. A possibility of better attracting and motivating key employees by offering them stock or stock options.
4. A lead to more disciplined management practices.
5. An adherence to corporate governance rules.
6. An increase of the company awareness and prestige in the market.

2.2.3 Drawbacks of Going Public

Going public also has drawbacks, for example:

1. The potential short-term focus of management decisions aimed at meeting or exceeding quarterly market expectations.
2. Access to the company's information by its competitors, suppliers and customers.
3. Scrutiny by shareholders and equity research analysts.
4. Vulnerability to hostile takeovers.
5. The increase in administrative expenses incurred as a result of the additional reporting requirements to the regulators and the market.

Figure 2.2   Phases of the IPO process.

2.2.4 The IPO Process

Going public through an IPO is a unique and challenging process. The process of taking a company public takes between three and five months, during which a considerable amount of management time and attention is required. The IPO process is a complex situation for the company's organization, involving many parties and requiring rigorous time management. The IPO process can be divided into four phases, as shown in Figure 2.2.

The process starts with the preparation of the company for the IPO. The second phase entails the preparation of the offering to be marketed. In a third phase the offering is marketed to institutional and retail investors. In a final phase the offering is placed with the new shareholders.

In order to gain a comprehensive picture of the mechanics of an IPO, each of the main tasks in each phase is covered in detail next, in chronological order. However, it is important to understand that several of the tasks involved need to be implemented concurrently.

2.2.5 Phase 1: Preparation of the Company

After probably years of internal debating, the private company's shareholders finally make the decision to take the company public. In a first phase the company needs to take the steps to get it ready to launch the IPO. The steps to be followed in this stage are typically:

1. The company's board of directors approve the IPO.
2. The company/selling shareholders appoint the **global coordinators**, the legal advisors, the communication agency, the printers and the roadshow consultants. Also the company auditors are brought in to work on the offering. The global coordinators are selected according to their strength in certain areas, as shown in Figure 2.3. In large IPOs, the company/selling

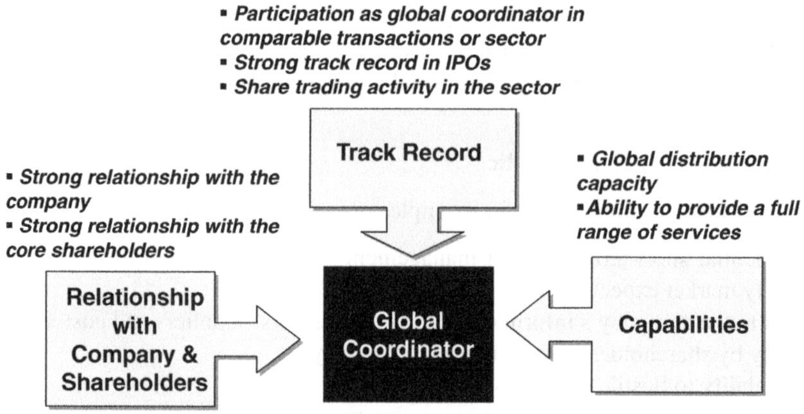

- *Participation as global coordinator in comparable transactions or sector*
- *Strong track record in IPOs*
- *Share trading activity in the sector*

- *Strong relationship with the company*
- *Strong relationship with the core shareholders*

Track Record

- *Global distribution capacity*
- *Ability to provide a full range of services*

Relationship with Company & Shareholders   **Global Coordinator**   **Capabilities**

Figure 2.3   Selection of global coordinators.

shareholders appoint also a "**financial advisor**" that advises on the offering. It is common that the financial adviser becomes one of the global coordinators. The fees taken from acting as a global coordinator are often used to subsidize being undertaken as a financial advisor. The table below outlines the main tasks of the other advisors:

Advisor	Main tasks
Offeror's legal counsel	Advice from a legal perspective on the overall structuring of the transaction Draft offering documentation Due diligence and legal opinion process Review underwriting and lock-up agreements
Underwriters' legal counsel	Advice from a legal perspective on the overall structuring of the transaction Review offering documentation Due diligence and legal opinion process Draft underwriting and lock-up agreements
Auditors	Accounting due diligence Review of the financial information included in the offering documents Provide comfort letter to offeror/underwriters
Communication agency	Design of communications plan Advertising campaign planning and execution
Printers	Printing and publishing services including distribution of documentation
Roadshow consultants	Organization of roadshow logistics

3. The advisors review the corporate organization to fit it with listed companies. The company, with the help of the legal advisors, adapts its legal status, shareholder agreements and company bylaws to meet the regulatory and legal requirements of listed companies. The auditors review the financial accounts to identify potential issues for the offering documents. Also the auditors check that accounting systems are in place for ongoing post-IPO quarterly reporting.
4. The global coordinators propose a preliminary size of the offering based on their expectation of demand and their estimates of a free float necessary to generate adequate aftermarket liquidity.

2.2.6 Phase 2: Preparation of the Offering

In a second stage, different groups are established to prepare all the elements that will be used later in the marketing stage. The steps to be followed are typically:

1. The project structure is established by the global coordinators and the company/selling shareholders. The project is split into different working groups, each taking care of a specific part of the project. Each group is responsible for specific tasks. Typically, seven working groups are defined, as illustrated in Figure 2.4. The working groups are interdependent, as at times a working group will require input from other working groups. The project is headed by the project coordination group and supervised by the steering committee.

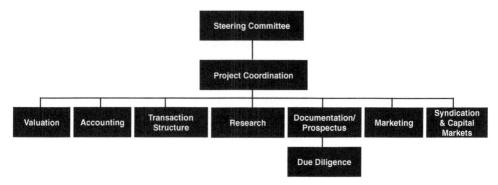

Figure 2.4 Project structure.

2. The preliminary **offering structure** is devised by the transaction structure group. This is a preliminary formulation. The final structure would be set after the pre-marketing stage. The main issues to be addressed are:
   - The total size of the IPO and its corresponding free float. The size should generate sufficient interest from investors, encourage coverage by equity research analysts post-IPO, and provide liquidity. The size of the offering has an effect on the offer price. In a small issue the offer price achieved may be low as investors become reluctant to participate and research coverage would be limited. In too large an issue, the offer price achieved may be low as investors become reluctant to participate due to a potential overhang of selling orders post-IPO. There is an intermediate zone in which the offer price is optimal, as depicted in Figure 2.5.
   - The size of the institutional tranche.
   - The size of the retail tranche. Retail investors act as a "safety net" as they are less sensitive to the offer price. The potential drawbacks to the inclusion of a retail tranche are: (i) if retail demand is insufficient, the size of the retail tranche cannot be reduced once the underwriting agreement has been signed, reducing the flexibility of the tranches; (ii) it requires a separate marketing documentation and the market regulator may require additional information; and (iii) a retail marketing campaign is required, increasing the transaction costs.

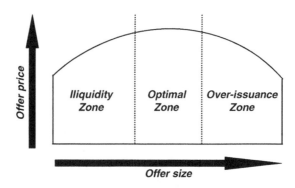

Figure 2.5 Offer price as a function of the offer size.

- The stock exchanges in which the shares will be listed.
- The fee structure.
- The lock-up agreements with the company, major shareholders and directors.

The Fee Structure

The syndicate members' remuneration is based on fees. Each IPO is likely to have a different fee structure. The objective of the fee structure is to give each syndicate participant a moderate fixed stake in the transaction, leaving most of their potential compensation in the form of upside that they can only earn if they perform well in generating orders. By way of an example, let's use the following fee structure:

	Percentage of offer size	Percentage of total fees
Management fee, divided into:	0.55%	20%
Global coordinators/bookrunners praecipium 50%		
Management fee 50%		
Underwriting fee	0.55%	20%
Sales commission, divided into:	1.65%	60%
Institutional placement 90%		
Retail placement 10%		
Total	**2.75%**	**100%**

The total level of fees is called the "**gross spread**". In this IPO, the gross spread amounted to 2.75% of the offering value. The gross spread was divided into:

- A **management fee**. This is a fee received for managing the transaction. In our example, the management fee represents 0.55% of the offering value, or 20% of the gross spread. In this example, half of the management fee is established as praecipium, equally divided among the global coordinators/bookrunners, and half as management fee, divided among lead/co-managers pro-rata to their underwriting commitments
- An **underwriting fee**. This is a fee received for bearing the risk of underwriting and the cost of aftermarket stabilization. This fee is divided among the underwriters, pro-rata to their underwriting commitments. In our example the underwriting fee represents 0.55% of the offering value, or 20% of the gross spread.
- A **selling commission**, also called "**selling concession**". This fee compensates and motivates the selling forces of the syndicate banks for their selling effort. In our example the selling commission represents 1.65% of the offering value, or 60% of the gross spread. The selling commission is divided between the banks placing the institutional tranche (90% of the commission, in our example) and the banks placing the retail tranche (10% of the commission, in our example). The selling commission to the banks placing the institutional tranche is allocated among the banks on the basis of designations, by orders directed to be allocated. In other words, each allocated institutional investor designates the sales commission to their manager of choice based on their assessment of the quality of service offered by each bank. This arrangement provides a direct correlation between marketing effort and compensation, motivating the syndicate banks to use their full

resources in the marketing effort. This compensation is usually capped to the global coordinators/bookrunners to provide added incentive to the rest of the syndicate banks.

Sometimes, in addition to the gross spread, there is an **incentive fee**. It tries to incentive participating banks to perform. This fee is payable at the sole discretion of the company/selling shareholders. The incentive fee is usually a small part of the overall fees, commonly less than 0.5% of the offering size. Although in most IPOs the incentive fee is available to all the banks of the syndicate group, in some IPOs only the global coordinators/bookrunners are entitled to receive it. Even though the payment of the incentive fee is discretionary, it is typically paid if some pre-agreed objectives are met, for example:

- The overall success of the IPO.
- The offer price being within a specific range.
- The conclusion of the IPO before a specific deadline.
- The selling effort of the banks.
- And/or, the reception of the IPO in the market.

3. The **offering timetable** is defined. The timetable states the start and end dates of each key task of the IPO.
4. A **due diligence** of the company is performed. All business lines and management of the company are analyzed in order to detect potential risks for investors. The due diligence is performed in three main areas: business, legal and accounting/financial. There is a special focus on certain issues, such as key contracts with customers and suppliers, labour contracts, environmental litigation and related party transactions. The due diligence process is led by the underwriters' legal counsel with a full collaboration from the company, its legal counsel, the legal counsel of the selling shareholders and the company auditors. The due diligence is crucial to value the company and to build up the equity story. It is important that all material aspects are disclosed to investors in the "risk factors" section of the prospectus to avoid potential demands and litigation from investors in the IPO.
5. A **theoretical valuation** of the company is estimated, which will be used as the basis for deciding the price range included in the analyst presentation. The valuation is provided by the valuation working group. The valuation is prepared in accordance with more than one methodology and takes into account other factors such as trends, expected demand and research analysts' views, as shown in Figure 2.6. The valuation is a recommendation of fair price, not a fairness opinion.
6. **Legal documentation**, both domestic and international.
7. **Selection of syndicate and underwriters**.

Selection of Syndicate and Underwriters

The placement syndicate is the group of banks that will be responsible for marketing and selling the offer to institutional and retail investors. Most of the banks participating in the syndicate also underwrite the deal. The company/selling shareholders enter into an underwriting agreement with the underwriters. Subject to the terms and conditions of the underwriting agreement, the company/selling shareholders agree to sell to the underwriters, and each underwriter severally agrees to purchase, all the shares being offered at a price equal to the offering price less the fees. The underwriting agreement also provides that if any underwriter defaults, the purchase commitments of the non-defaulting underwriters may also be increased or the offering may be terminated.

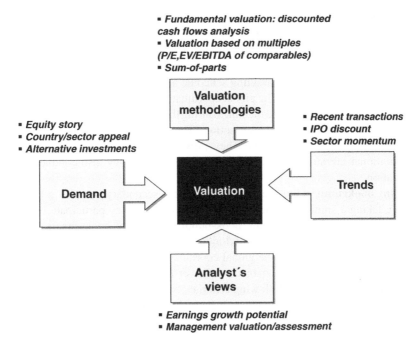

Figure 2.6 Inputs to a company valuation.

A successful execution requires a perfect coordination between all the banks syndicating the deal. The roles of the banks participating in an offering are grouped into different tiers depending on their degree of responsibility in placing the offering. The main groups in an offering are the following (see Figure 2.7):

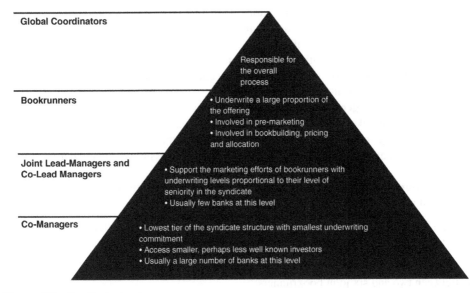

Figure 2.7 Syndicate structure.

- The **global coordinators** are the banks that run the deal. A large deal is usually placed in several countries. They are responsible for overseeing the entire offering and coordinating the underwriting and placing activities of the rest of the banks participating in the offering. They assist with the preparation of the offering, provide the most significant research publication, arrange the pre-marketing schedule and provide advice on the price range for publication in the prospectus. The global coordinators arrange and coordinate presentations, conference calls and one-on-one meetings during the offering with key institutional accounts to facilitate the success of the transaction. The global coordinators lead the syndicate group and contribute most orders. They provide continuous feedback to the company on institutional investors' attitude towards the offering. They also conduct the post-IPO stabilization.

- The **joint bookrunners** are the banks that have a secondary but also a key role in the offering, taking a significant underwriting commitment. They participate, with the global coordinators, in the pre-marketing, book-building (the joint bookrunners provide a substantial amount of orders), pricing and allocation of the offering. The joint bookrunners also publish equity research. The global coordinators and the joint bookrunners syndicate a part of the offering with other banks to lower their risk. Typically the selection of the bookrunners is based on the following criteria:

  (i) Their relevant underwriting experience, including their presence in relevant offerings in the industry, their valuation record, their number of sales professionals, geographical location and ranking, and their number of participations in large offerings.

  (ii) Their trading and distribution capacity, including the volume of trading of other stocks and their trading market share of industry peers.

  (iii) Their ability to act as bookrunner, including their previous experience as bookrunner and their reputation to work well with other banks.

  (iv) Their relationship with the company and relevant shareholders.

  (v) Their relationship with the global coordinators.

  (vi) The quality of their research, including the size of their research team, their ranking in research and their industry knowledge.

- The **joint co-bookrunners** and the **joint lead managers** have a middle tier role. They are usually a few banks. They are invited into the process after the preparation phase is finished. They have some influence in the syndicate and may contribute some orders. Usually, these are banks with a strong presence in specific countries and are chosen to enhance the distribution of the offering in those countries. They participate in the roadshow and usually publish equity research.

- The **co-lead managers** and the **co-managers** have a junior role in the offering. They are appointed to take some underwriting risk. They have limited influence in the offering decisions. Frequently, no distribution is expected from these banks. The co-lead managers and the co-managers focus on generating niche orders, possibly from smaller institutional investors.

- The **sub-underwriters** are commonly not part of the syndicate. They are appointed after the deal is launched to share underwriting risk.

The number of banks in a syndicate depends on the size of the offering and whether it includes a retail tranche. For large IPOs a typical syndicate structure includes:

- Two to three global coordinators.
- Between two and six joint bookrunners.

- Around three joint co-bookrunners/co-lead managers.
- A substantial number of co-lead managers/co-managers.

2.2.7   Phase 3: Marketing of the Offering

1. The **analyst presentation** is prepared and pitched to equity research analysts. The analyst presentation takes place several weeks prior to the pre-marketing. Each attendee must sign a confidentiality agreement as price-sensitive information is disclosed. The analyst presentation is the first public communication of the offering. It is a base document for equity analysts to write their pre-deal research reports. All the information included in the analyst presentation must be included in the prospectus. Commonly, four key topics are covered in the presentation. Firstly, an overview of the transaction is included. Secondly, the equity story is presented. Thirdly, an overview of the business is provided. Finally, an overview of the financial statements is provided. The most important part is the **equity story**. The equity story must simultaneously convey a "true message" of the company and make that image attractive to investors. The equity story:
   - Emphasizes the main selling points of the company in order to center investor focus.
   - Communicates the company's main strategic business lines.
   - Identifies the company strengths and sector appeal. It stresses future growth areas without placing attention on past events or excessively technical issues. It emphasizes recent contracts awarded and new products developed.
   - Identifies problematic areas for competitors in the past, preparing preventive responses.
   - Stresses the company's financial strategy, apart from the operating and main targets. Especially relevant are the dividend policy and the target capital structure.
2. The analysts produce the **pre-deal research** reports based on the analyst presentation right after this presentation takes place. Then the pre-deal research reports are reviewed and published. A limited number of copies are distributed to qualified investors. A **blackout period** commences upon publication of the pre-deal research reports and lasts until a specific number of business days, typically 40, after completion of the offer.
3. A preliminary price range for pre-marketing is set based on analyst consensus. Its aim is to check the appetite of investors intervening in the pre-marketing process.

Marketing to Investors

The marketing to institutional investors is a three-stage process, as highlighted in Figure 2.8. Firstly, a few selected investors are approached in what is called the pre-marketing stage. Secondly, all the targeted institutional investors are marketed in a roadshow. Finally, investors are approached during the book-building period to take their bids.

Retail investors are accessed through publicity campaigns and directly by the retail branches of their banks.

4. If the offering is originated outside the USA, a **pre-marketing** of the offering is executed. In the USA, pre-marketing of an offering is not allowed before its prospectus is approved by the regulator (the SEC). Outside the USA, a pre-marketing of the offering and an investor education takes place before the prospectus is produced. Pre-marketing is an important part of the offering. It can be particularly valuable for the flotation of companies where it is hard to judge investor appetite and for issuers that do not want to go below

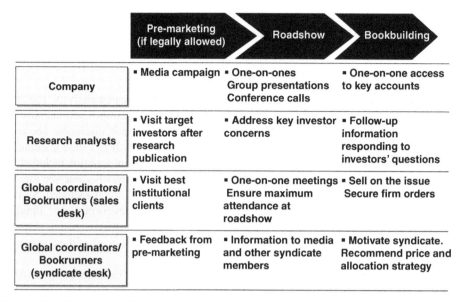

	Pre-marketing (if legally allowed)	Roadshow	Bookbuilding
Company	▪ Media campaign	▪ One-on-ones Group presentations Conference calls	▪ One-on-one access to key accounts
Research analysts	▪ Visit target investors after research publication	▪ Address key investor concerns	▪ Follow-up information responding to investors' questions
Global coordinators/ Bookrunners (sales desk)	▪ Visit best institutional clients	▪ One-on-one meetings Ensure maximum attendance at roadshow	▪ Sell on the issue Secure firm orders
Global coordinators/ Bookrunners (syndicate desk)	▪ Feedback from pre-marketing	▪ Information to media and other syndicate members	▪ Motivate syndicate. Recommend price and allocation strategy

Figure 2.8   Milestones of the marketing strategy to institutional investors.

a particular price level. Commonly, pre-marketing falls into two categories called "**pilot fishing**" and "**anchor marketing**". In a pilot fishing, a few trusted potential investors are reached by the bookrunners to gather a preliminary investor sentiment to check how the market is likely to respond to an issue. An anchor marketing consists in syndicate research analysts marketing the transaction with selected investors to collect feedback.

5. The **preliminary prospectus offering price range** is set, based on the pre-marketing feedback.
6. The **final offering structure** is determined by the company/selling shareholders in conjunction with the global coordinators/bookrunners, based on the pre-marketing feedback. It includes the final size and the likely division between the retail and the institutional tranches. The final offering structure is published in the preliminary prospectus.
7. The **offering circular** and a **preliminary prospectus**, also called "**red herring**", are prepared and submitted to the regulator. Afterwards, these two documents are published, usually when the roadshow starts. The offering circular is the actual disclosure document given to investors. Every IPO legally requires a prospectus. The prospectus is the definitive sale document and must contain all material information on the company. In theory, the prospectus is the investors' major source of information to base their investment decision regarding the offering. The contents of the prospectus are set out by the listing authorities responsible for the stock exchanges on which the stock is to be listed. A final version of the prospectus containing the final offer price will be filed later.
8. The **roadshow** takes place.

The Roadshow

Immediately after the publication of the preliminary prospectus, senior management of the company, representatives of the global coordinators/bookrunners and the communication agency undertake a tour of institutional investors to promote the offering. The roadshow typically takes between one and two weeks. It offers a key opportunity to management to present the equity story of the company and the investment opportunity to institutional investors. The roadshow is conducted simultaneously by two or three teams, one covering the United States, another covering Europe and sometimes a third team covering Asia. Sometimes the teams combine to pitch certain key investors. The senior management of the company has to be well prepared to answer all sorts of questions from well-informed investors. Prior to the event, investors typically have taken a careful look at the preliminary prospectus and at the analysts' research. There are three different types of events with investors on the roadshow:

- **Group presentations** allow the company to articulate its equity story to a good number, sometimes more than a hundred, of institutional investors. The presentations are generally conducted during a meal.
- **One-on-one meetings** are typically held with key investors in cities throughout the continent covered. The investors invited to the meetings are capable of placing very large orders, and are expected to generate the majority of the quality orders. The one-on-one meetings are arranged with a single or a small group of portfolio managers and buyside analysts. The meetings give participating investors the opportunity to question management on key issues of concern.
- **Conference calls** are conducted on an as-needed basis with selected investors who cannot attend the group presentations and one-on-one meetings. They can be organized as group calls as well as one-on-one calls.

9. The **book-building** of the institutional tranche takes place during a period called the "**offer period**" or "**book-building period**". The offer period is the limited time during which investors can bid for shares. The offer period starts on the same day as the roadshow and typically lasts around three weeks. There might be two offer periods, one for the institutional investors and another for the retail investors. During the offer period, the placing syndicate solicits non-binding indications of interest from institutional investors. Such indications consist of a number of shares each institutional investor is interested in acquiring at various price levels. Sometimes investors provide a number of shares and the maximum price (i.e., a limit price) they are willing to pay for the shares. The indications are generally modest in the first week of the roadshow, with the largest number of orders coming in the two days prior to the end of the offer period. At the end of the book-building period the demand from all institutional investors is aggregated into a single book managed by the global bookrunners.

10. Retail offering. Retail buy orders are received by the banks participating in the retail offering.

2.2.8   Phase 4: Placement of the Offering

1. The **offer price** is set after the book-building process is finished and demand exceeds supply. Remember that the offer price has been fine-tuned during the whole process, as shown in Figure 2.9. During the preparation for the offering, a broad "theoretical" price range was set. In the case of non-US companies a preliminary range for the pre-marketing is set, based on the consensus pricing in the analysts' pre-deal research, to check the preliminary appetite of investors. After the feedback is received from key investors, the price range, also called the "**red herring**", that will be included in the preliminary prospectus is established. Lastly,

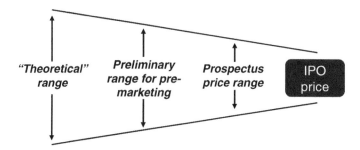

Figure 2.9 Offering price evolution.

after the book-building process is finalized, the final offering price is set. The offering price is not set according to any explicit rule, but rather based on the syndicate's interpretation of investors' indications of interest during the offer period and their perception on the likely aftermarket performance. The global coordinators/bookrunners generally establish the price at a level at which demand exceeds the number of shares offered. The goals are to optimize response to the domestic and international demands, and at the same time, create a "healthy" aftermarket.
2. The **final version of the prospectus** is filed with the regulator, published and distributed to the investors. This final prospectus includes the offer price.
3. The **allocation** of the shares to the institutional bidders and to the retail investors takes place. The allocation is performed at the syndicate's discretion.

Allocation Mechanics

Once the offer price has been set, the shares have to be allocated to the institutional and retail investors. Sometimes the shares allocated to institutional and retail are not matched by their respective demands, making it necessary to allocate shares from one tranche to the other. A placing lower than the total demand stimulates negotiation in the secondary market. Normally, not all institutional investors' bids are treated equally. Instead, institutional investors' allocations are based on a couple of factors aimed at ensuring healthy aftermarket share behavior.

The first factor is the **investor's profile**. This includes analyzing, among others, the following information regarding the investor:

- Sector/country investment history.
- IPO investment history (the allocation would try to avoid speculative investors and to benefit long-term investors).
- Frequency of participation in other IPOs.
- Size of indication of interest.
- Interest shown at roadshow events.
- Willingness to buy in the secondary market.

The second factor is the **investor's order profile**. This includes analyzing, among others, the following information regarding each order:

- Bid price.
- Size of the order.

- Price sensitivity (the allocation would favor less price-sensitive investors).
- Timing of indication of interest (the allocation would favor earlier investors).

The retail investors' allocation policy is usually an automatic process once the number of shares to be allocated to retail investors has been decided.

4. The stock starts trading in what is called the "**aftermarket**" trading. The global coordinators/bookrunners stabilize the share price and decide whether to exercise the greenshoe. The global coordinators/bookrunners are allowed to stabilize the share price within a period of commonly 30 days from the first day of trading, following specific rules set by the regulator. The global coordinators/bookrunners ensure liquidity in the market and support the share price in the event of technical weakness. As a result, the global coordinators/bookrunners commit capital in order to make a market in the stock.

Greenshoe or Overallotment Option

The "**greenshoe**" or "**overallotment**" option is used to create aftermarket support for the shares. It is usually a 30-day option granted after the listing to the global coordinators/bookrunners to purchase additional shares from the company/selling shareholders at the offer price. The greenshoe typically represents 10–15% of the offer size.

The greenshoe allows the global coordinators/bookrunners to create a protected "short" position, which will enhance the aftermarket support of the shares. During the allocation process, the global coordinators/bookrunners often allocate more than 100% of the shares offered, creating a short position. This short position is covered by the greenshoe option. Figure 2.10 summarizes the decision-making process followed by the banks as holders of the greenshoe option, assuming an option representing 15% of the offering.

- If the global coordinators/bookrunners expect aftermarket demand for the stock to be strong, they will typically allocate 115% of the issue, with the expectation that they will exercise the greenshoe option. If they are right (i.e., the stock price has a strong performance in the aftermarket), the banks will buy the shares from the company/selling shareholders through the greenshoe. The bought shares will, in turn, be delivered to

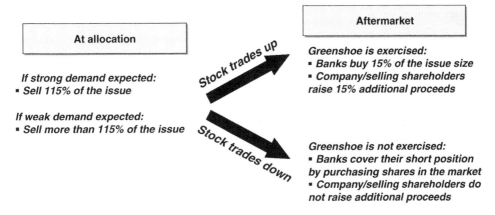

Figure 2.10   Strategy related to the greenshoe option.

the overallocated investors. As a result, the company/selling shareholders raise 15% additional proceeds.
- If the global coordinators/bookrunners expect aftermarket demand to be weak, they will try to allocate more than 115% of the issue. The shares exceeding the greenshoe option represent a "naked short" position in the stock, entirely at the risk of the global coordinators/bookrunners. If they are right (i.e., the stock price has a weak performance in the aftermarket), the banks will not exercise the greenshoe option, buying the shares directly in the market instead. The bought shares will, in turn, be delivered to the over-allocated investors. This buying provides support to the stock price. The company/selling shareholders do not raise additional proceeds.
5. The equity analysts of the global coordinators/bookrunners initiate research of the company 40 days after the offering and maintain ongoing coverage.

Lock-up Period

In most IPOs there is a lock-up period for the company, selling shareholders and key management. This period usually lasts between 4 and 12 months, starting immediately after the offering.

The Investor Relations Team

After the IPO, the company will need to proactively market the company to investors. The investor relations team is the link between the investors and the company. The main aim of the team is to allow the company to present its story to the market on a frequent and consistent basis. The team responds to queries from institutional and individual investors who own the company's shares. The team is also in charge of submitting periodic financial information to the regulators and main information agencies. In addition, the investor relations team organizes marketing events to keep analysts and investors abreast of corporate events. These events are mainly quarterly earnings conference calls, results roadshows and one-on-one meetings with key investors. In addition, the investor relations team keeps the company's top managers abreast of market developments, breaking news, trading activity, movements of the stock price, and investors' concerns and recommendations. The team is very small, commonly less than ten professionals. The head of the team should have direct access to the company's top management.

2.2.9 Key Success Factors Affecting an IPO

1. Choose the correct timing. Identify a window of opportunity:
   - Sector in favor with investors.
   - IPO market robust.
   - Stock market rallying.
   - Funds flowing into the equity market.
   - Country in favor with investors.
2. Choose the appropriate offering structure to access the market successfully while achieving the company's objectives:
   - Appropriate issue size.

- Attractive offer price.
- List only in value-added exchanges.

3. Choose capable banks and advisors:
   - Choose global coordinators/bookrunners based upon their distribution/research capabilities.
   - Select advisors with a proven track record in IPOs.
4. Execute a successful marketing strategy:
   - Differentiate the company from competitors.
   - Reinforce the leading characteristics of the company.
   - Ensure high-quality research in conjunction with highly regarded industry research.
   - Provide focused pre-deal research and intensive pre-marketing.
   - Prepare management thoroughly for the roadshow.
   - Access the most appropriate stable shareholder base.
   - Tailor marketing program to investor targeting strategy.
5. Implement a well-supported aftermarket performance:
   - Favor long-term investors in the allocation process.
   - Choose stabilization banks based upon aftermarket activity/perception.
   - Provide strong stabilization and aftermarket trading support.

2.2.10 Key Risk Factors Affecting an IPO

The following table summarizes the main challenges faced by an IPO and how to overcome them:

Phase	Risk	Effect	How to prevent/face them
Preparation of the offering	Selection of too many global coordinators/ bookrunners	• Risk of lack of interest in the process • Unnecessary tension • Lack of quality in the analysis • Distribution among investors with reduced knowledge of the equity story	• Selection of an appropriate number of global coordinators and an adequate syndicate structure
	Listing in too many exchanges	• Unnecessary multiplication of prospectuses	• Selection of an appropriate number of exchanges
Marketing of the offering	Valuation	• Too high offering price: limited demand could trigger a drop in aftermarket share price. Syndicate could be incapable of distributing the shares • Too low offering price: excessive demand could trigger a sharp rise in aftermarket share price without benefiting the company/selling shareholders	• Appropriate positioning • Adjust the price during the IPO process according to the perception of the market during the marketing phase • Identify and address all potential investor concerns

Phase	Risk	Effect	How to prevent/face them
	Unexpected events	• Market decline during the IPO process • Relevant changes in the management of the company • Unexpected event affecting the company/sector	• Select the appropriate market window
	Probable events	• Delays receiving the necessary approvals from the market regulator	• Allow the process calendar to face potential delays
Placement of the offering	Flowback	• Disposal of the shares by the subscribers of the offer at the time just after the IPO • Disposal of shares in the secondary market not offered in the IPO	• Allocate the shares to appropriate investors • Lock-up period of 180 days by the company and the selling shareholders and of at least 180 days by the management team

2.2.11 Case Study: Visa's IPO

As an example, let us review one of the largest IPOs in US history. In 2008, during difficult market conditions, Visa Inc. aimed to list on the New York Stock Exchange in a landmark offering to global investors. Visa Inc. operated the world's largest retail electronic payments network in the world. It had the largest number of branded credit and debit cards in circulation. Visa facilitated global commerce through the transfer of value and information among financial institutions, merchants, consumers, businesses and government entities. Visa provided financial institutions, its primary customers, with product platforms encompassing consumer credit, debit, prepaid and commercial payments. VisaNet, its secure, centralized, global processing platform, enabled Visa to provide financial institutions and merchants with a wide range of product platforms, transaction processing and related value-added services.

On 11 October 2006, Visa announced that some of its businesses would be merged and become a publicly traded company. Under the IPO restructuring, Visa Canada, Visa International and Visa USA were merged into the new public company, Visa Inc. Visa's Western Europe operation became a separate company, owned by its member banks that will also have a minority stake in Visa Inc.

On 3 October 2007, Visa completed its corporate restructuring with the formation of Visa Inc. The new company was the first step towards Visa's IPO. The second step came on 9 November 2007, when the new Visa Inc. submitted its USD 10 billion IPO filing with the US Securities and Exchange Commission and publicly announced the deal. JP Morgan and Goldman Sachs acted as global coordinators. The principal shareholders of Visa Inc. prior to the IPO were:

• JP Morgan Chase: 23.3%
• Visa Europe: 19.6%
• Bank of America: 11.5%

- National City: 8.0%
- Citigroup: 5.5%
- US Bancorp: 5.1%
- Wells Fargo: 5.1%

On 25 February 2008, Visa announced it would go ahead with the IPO. Besides the two global coordinators, another six banks were selected to participate in the deal as bookrunners. The law firm Davis Polk & Wardwell served as counsel to the underwriters, while the law firm White & Case LLP served as counsel to Visa Inc. The accounting/financial advisor was the company auditor, KPMG. The underwriters had a 30-day greenshoe option to purchase up to 40.6 million additional shares, 10% of the initial offering size, to cover any overallotments.

In total, 45 investment banks were selected to participate in the deal in several capacities, most notably as underwriters. The eight global coordinators/bookrunners underwrote 85.7% of the offering. Thus, only 14.3% of the offering was underwritten by the remaining 37 banks. The following table summarizes the underwriting commitments by the global coordinators/bookrunners:

Bank	Underwriting commitment (shares)	Percentage of total
Goldman Sachs	102.7 million	25.3%
JP Morgan	102.7 million	25.3%
UBS	30.4 million	7.5%
Bank of America	27.9 million	6.9%
Wachovia	26.3 million	6.5%
Citigroup	20.1 million	5.0%
HSBC	18.6 million	4.6%
Merrill Lynch	18.6 million	4.6%
Total	**347.3 million**	**85.7%**

The IPO roadshow comprised three teams traveling across three continents to visit 10 countries and 24 cities. There were 36 group investor meetings across the United States, Europe, the Middle East and Asia for a total of over 1,700 investors.

On 18 March 2008 the IPO took place. Visa sold 406 million shares at USD 44 per share (USD 2 above the high end of the expected USD 37–42 pricing range), raising USD 17.9 billion before fees in the largest initial public offering in US history at that time. The gross spread amounted to 2.80% of the deal value. The following table summarizes the main data of Visa Inc.'s IPO:

Visa Inc. IPO – Main Terms	
Common stock offered	406,000,000 shares of class A common stock
Greenshoe	40,600,000 shares (10% of the initial offering size)
Global coordinators/ bookrunners	Global coordinators/bookrunners: JP Morgan and Goldman Sachs Rest of bookrunners: Bank of America, Citigroup, HSBC, Merrill Lynch, UBS and Wachovia Securities
Total banks in syndicate	45 banks (8 bookrunners, 15 lead managers and 22 co-managers)

Visa Inc. IPO – Main Terms	
Counsel to the underwriters	Davis Polk & Wardwell
Counsel to the offeror	White & Case LLP
Initial price range	USD 37–42 (midpoint USD 39.50)
Offer price	USD 44.00
Deal value (excl. greenshoe)	USD 17,864,000,000
Deal value (incl. greenshoe)	USD 19,650,400,000
Disclosed gross spread	2.80% of deal value (45% selling concession, 27.5% management fees and 27.5% underwriting fees), or USD 550.2 million (including greenshoe)
Total proceeds after fees	USD
Trade date	19 March 2008

On 20 March 2008, the IPO underwriters exercised their overallotment option, purchasing an additional 40.6 million shares, bringing Visa's total IPO share count to 446.6 million, and bringing the total proceeds to USD 19.7 billion, before fees. The gross spread totaled USD 550.2 million, or 2.80% of the deal value. The offerors also incurred other expenses, including registration, filing and listing fees, printing fees and legal and accounting expenses, totaling USD 45.5 million.

The shares began trading on 19 March 2008 on the New York Stock Exchange under the ticker symbol "V". At the opening, the shares were trading at USD 59.50, 35% higher than the offering price. The delivery of the shares took place on 25 March 2008. There was a 180-day lock-up provision, expiring on 14 September 2008. Figure 2.11 summarizes the deal main dates.

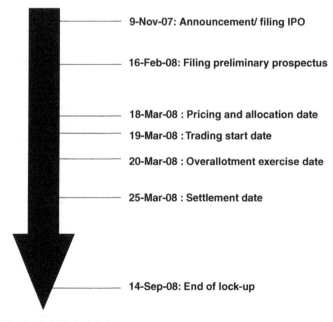

9-Nov-07: Announcement/ filing IPO

16-Feb-08: Filing preliminary prospectus

18-Mar-08 : Pricing and allocation date

19-Mar-08 : Trading start date

20-Mar-08 : Overallotment exercise date

25-Mar-08 : Settlement date

14-Sep-08: End of lock-up

Figure 2.11   Visa Inc.'s IPO deal dates.

2.3 CASE STUDY: GOOGLE'S DUTCH AUCTION IPO

In the previous section, a real example of a book-building method IPO was covered. In this section, a real example of a Dutch auction method IPO is covered. Few companies have chosen this method to go public.

Unlike the standard method, whereby offer prices are set by the global coordinators/bookrunners using a negotiated book-building process, in a Dutch auction method the offer price is set automatically based on the bids received. The Dutch method got its name from the famous Dutch tulip bulb mania that occurred in the Netherlands in the 17th century. In a Dutch auction process, the offeror (i.e., the seller of the shares) sets the total number of shares being offered and sometimes a potential price range. Investors then submit a conditional order for the quantity of shares they wish to receive and the highest price they are willing to pay. The offeror allocates the shares, starting with the highest bidder, until it has allocated all the shares being offered. The offer price is then set at the lowest bid it accepts. Therefore, the price all awarded bidders pay is the offer price, even if they had bid higher. If there are more bids than shares available, allotment is on a pro-rata basis among the bidders with smaller bids. As a result, once the offer price is set, investors who bid at least that price know that they are awarded shares in the offering.

The Dutch auction process was employed by Google to price and distribute its IPO. Critics charge that, in two respects, it was not a pure Dutch auction. First, after the bidding started, Google reduced the total number of shares being offered and also reduced the target offer price range to USD 85–95 from USD 108–135. Second, Dutch auctions are supposed to have a fixed number of shares and Google cut the size of the offering by 24%, giving successful bidders only 76% of the shares they requested. The following table summarizes the main data of Google's IPO (see also Figure 2.12):

Google IPO – Main Terms	
Common stock offered	19,605,053 shares of common stock
Greenshoe	2,940,758 shares (15% of the initial offering size)
Deal shares (incl. greenshoe)	22,545,811
Lead managers	Credit Suisse and Morgan Stanley
Total banks in syndicate	10 banks (2 lead managers and 8 co-managers)
Counsel to the underwriters	Simpson Thatcher & Bartlett
Counsel to the offeror	Wilson Sonsini Goodrich & Rosati
Auditor	Ernst & Young
Initial price range	USD 108–135. Changed later to USD 85–95
Offer price	USD 85.00
Deal value (excl. greenshoe)	USD 1,666,429,505
Deal value (incl. greenshoe)	USD 1,916,393,935
Disclosed gross spread	2.80% of deal value (0% selling concession, 70% management fees and 30% underwriting fees), or USD 53.7 million (including greenshoe)
Total proceeds after fees	USD 1,862.7 million
Trade date	19 August 2004

The initial target price range given by Google was USD 108–135. Based on the weak demand from investors, Google's target price range was changed to USD 85–95. At the end, Google set the offering price to USD 85, the lower price of the range, in the face of a deteriorating stock market and the skepticism from institutional investors.

Figure 2.12   Google's IPO deal dates.

On 20 August 2004, the underwriters exercised their greenshoe, acquiring an additional 2.9 million shares. As a result, the offerors raised USD 1.86 billion after paying a gross spread of 2.80% of the deal.

The underwriting commitment of the syndicate is shown in the following table:

Bank	Underwriting commitment (shares)	Percentage of total
Credit Suisse	7.1 million	36.2%
Morgan Stanley	7.1 million	36.2%
Goldman Sachs	1.2 million	6.1%
Allen & Co.	1.1 million	5.6%
Lehman Brothers	1.0 million	5.1%
Citigroup	0.8 million	4.1%
JP Morgan	0.5 million	2.6%
UBS	0.4 million	2.0%
WR Hambrecht	0.3 million	1.5%
Thomas Weisel	0.1 million	0.5%
Total	**19.6 million**	**100%**

A Dutch auction has several advantages over a book-building IPO:

- The offer price and the allotment of shares are established in a transparent way.
- It enables retail investors to participate in the pricing of the offering.
- It enables retail investors to have the same chance of buying shares as institutional investors.

- It is in theory cheaper. Lower fees are paid to the participating banks as their role is smaller. However, if we compare the gross spread paid to Visa Inc.'s IPO with the gross spread of Google's IPO we can see that they were similar.
- In theory, it reduces the volatility of the stock price in the aftermarket. The price is in theory a mechanism that results in an efficient price that perfectly equates supply and demand.

But also, a Dutch auction has several disadvantages over a book-building IPO:

- The outcome is more uncertain. The absence of a pre-marketing to key institutional investors to assess demand results in a much less precise preliminary price range. If demand is not there, it is discovered during the auction period, obliging the offeror to reduce the offering size late in the process. Even though Google's IPO generated great investor awareness due to its global name recognition, the offeror was forced to lower the price range due to a lack of demand at the original price range.
- Institutional investors may be less willing to invest due to the potentially less rigorous research efforts by the participating banks. Institutional investors may also become skeptical of companies using this process.
- Banks with outstanding IPO placement capabilities may be reluctant to participate due to their potentially minimized role in a Dutch auction IPO and their diminished control over the process.
- Participating banks may be less willing to allocate research and sales resources to an IPO in which their role is less relevant.
- The offer may be mispriced. The primary focus in Dutch auction IPOs is the retail investors. These investors may often lack the ability to set a bid price based on the stock's fundamentals, rather than purely on familiarity or general name recognition. Many academics argue that Google's Dutch auction method resulted in a mispriced offering because the offer price was USD 85 and it opened at USD 100, reflecting a 17.6% increase. This increase was substantially larger than similar IPOs executed in 2004. I disagree with such a conclusion, as Google name recognition was notably stronger than their peers. As we saw in the previous section, Visa Inc.'s IPO used the traditional book-building method and its shares opened 35% higher than the offering price. It is impossible to estimate what would have been the increase at the opening were a Dutch auction process to have been followed by Visa Inc.

2.4 RIGHTS ISSUES (OR RIGHTS OFFERINGS)

2.4.1 Product Description

A **rights issue**, also known as a **rights offering**, is the most common way to increase ordinary capital. A rights offering is a method for a listed company to raise additional funds, not by increasing debt, but by asking shareholders to invest more in the company. In a rights issue, existing shareholders are given the right to subscribe for a specific number of new shares in proportion to their existing shareholdings, at a specified price during a specified period.

Typically, once the company decides to launch a rights issue, a roadshow is organized in which the company's top management presents the objective and the general terms of the issue. Afterwards, unless the board of directors has authorization to raise capital, an extraordinary general meeting (EGM) takes place to vote on the rights issue. If the issue is approved, the company works with the placing banks to establish the final terms of the issue.

Once the final terms of the rights issue are decided, these are announced to the market. Commonly, registered shareholders at a date called the record date become qualifying shareholders, being entitled to subscribe for the rights issue. As a result, at the closing of the record date each qualifying shareholder receives one subscription right for each existing share owned.

After the record date, the qualifying shareholders need to decide whether or not to exercise their rights during a period called the subscription period. The subscription rights' holders have the following four alternatives:

1. Exercise, also known as to "take up", the subscription rights to subscribe for new shares of the company. Holders choosing to exercise their subscription rights do so by paying the subscription price. If a shareholder chooses to exercise all his/her subscription rights, the proportion of his/her ownership of the company after the rights issue will be the same as it was before the rights issue.
2. Refrain from participating in the rights issue by selling the rights in the stock market and receive the net proceeds of the sale in cash. The price the rights holder receives for his/her rights will depend on the market price for the rights at the relevant time. Be aware that the market price for rights is different from the subscription price. If a shareholder decides to sell all his/her subscription rights, the number of shares he/she holds will stay the same but the proportion of the total number of shares that he/she holds will be lower following completion of the rights issue (i.e., his/her stakeholding in the company will be diluted).
3. Buy additional subscription rights and subscribe for more shares.
4. Do nothing by letting the subscription rights lapse (i.e., expire). This alternative does not make financial sense as it is like throwing money away. Note that the subscription rights have an economic value, especially if the stock price exceeds the subscription price. As a result, the shareholder is always better off electing alternative (2) than this alternative.

Sometimes the shareholder can apply for shares without subscription rights. New shares which are not subscribed for with subscription rights can be offered to investors. Applications to subscribe for new shares without subscription rights can be submitted by any investor. Commonly, shareholders who have subscribed for shares by virtue of subscription rights are prioritized in the allocation of these new shares. The shareholder is however not guaranteed allocation of new shares.

The company pays underwriting and advisory fees to the placing and underwriting banks. The fees are a function, among other things, of the discount, the size of the issue, the duration of the underwriting and the volatility of the stock.

2.4.2 Main Definitions of a Rights Issue

Cum-rights price is the closing price of the stock on the record date.

Ex-rights date, also known as the "**ex-date**", is the first day the stock trades without the right to receive the subscription rights. It is the trading day immediately following the record date. At the market open on the ex-rights date, the stock trades "excluding the right".

Existing shares are the shares outstanding before the rights issue.

Expiration date is the last day of the subscription period. In other words, it is the last day that the subscription rights can be exercised. After the expiration date, those rights not yet subscribed will expire worthless unless the company provides for a mechanism to sell them in the market after the expiration date.

Qualifying shareholder, also called "**eligible shareholder**", means each shareholder entitled to a subscription right.

Record date is the date on which an investor has to be registered as a shareholder to be granted subscription rights. It should be noted that it takes several business days (typically three) after the acquisition of shares until the registration is effected. The registration is completed with the settlement of the shares.

Subscription period is the period during which subscription for new shares can be made by paying the subscription price. The subscription period typically begins on the ex-rights day. During the subscription period the company shareholders need to decide whether or not to exercise their subscription rights.

Subscription price, also known as the "**offer price**" or the "**rights price**", means the price at which the new shares would be issued. In other words, the subscription price is the price at which the shareholders can purchase each new share. The subscription price is generally at a discount to the current stock price as an incentive to exercise the rights.

Subscription right is a financial instrument that entitles the holder to subscribe for a certain number of new shares at a defined subscription price.

Terms are the number of new shares that a shareholder is entitled to for each number of old shares. For example, an 11 per 20 rights issue means that each 20 existing shares entitle the holder to 11 new shares.

TERP (theoretical ex-rights price), also known as "**adjusted price**", is the theoretical price of the stock on the ex-rights date.

Trade period is the period during which the subscription rights can be traded in the stock market. Commonly, the trade period coincides with the subscription period.

Underwriters are the entities, commonly banks, that guarantee a minimum amount of capital to be raised through the rights issue. Typical terms of an underwriting require the underwriters to subscribe to any subscription rights offered to, but not exercised by, shareholders.

2.4.3 Advantages and Weaknesses of a Rights Issue

A rights offering features a number of advantages:

1. It is an effective way of raising a substantial amount of new capital. For very large capital-raising efforts, a rights issue may be the only feasible alternative available.
2. All existing shareholders are invited to participate.
3. It is relatively quick to implement once the rights issue is approved by the shareholders and the relevant regulators. Typically, the subscription period takes two weeks.
4. The amount to be raised can be guaranteed. A rights issue can be fully underwritten by a syndicate of banks or otherwise guaranteed by a third party. However, even if the rights issue is fully underwritten, there is a remote risk that no new capital is raised after all. Commonly, underwriters have the right to terminate the underwriting contract if there is a material change in the circumstances of the company or in overall market conditions.

A rights offering features a number of weaknesses:

1. There is the risk of an unsuccessful rights offering if the market price of the offered shares falls below the subscription price. For this reason, rights offerings are generally conducted at a discount to the pre-offer market prices.

2. The announcement of a rights offering of this size would cause downward pressure on the stock price, and thus would increase the uncertainty mentioned in (1). To the extent that the typically negative market reaction to a stock offering causes an issue to be underpriced, such underpricing dilutes the value of current shareholders not subscribing for the new shares.

3. The issuer may have to offer a substantial number of shares in a weak market environment. For shareholders who do not exercise their rights, this may mean a substantial dilution.

4. The legal requirements can be substantial. Often a rights offering is structured as a public offering in several jurisdictions to allow as many shareholders as possible to participate in the offering. In this connection, the issuer needs to prepare a prospectus and have the same approved by the competent regulatory authorities in several countries. The time required to prepare and seek approval for a rights offering will significantly delay the issuance of new shares, not providing enough flexibility in case of unforeseen events or market disruptions. Additionally, a rights issue generally requires shareholder approval at an EGM.

5. The underwriting and advisory fees to be paid by the company to the participating banks can be substantial. The fees are a direct cost to the issuer and therefore to shareholders.

6. The sale of the rights by shareholders that decide not to exercise their subscription rights may trigger a tax liability.

2.4.4   Rights Offerings Success Factors

The main success factors of a rights offering are the following:

1. Backing by existing major shareholders. Partial backstops by major shareholders.
2. A strong case of use of proceeds.
3. Issue size in relation to market capitalization, liquidity.
4. Equity research recommendations.

2.4.5   Calculation of the TERP

The price of the existing shares automatically adjusts downwards on the ex-date to allow for the discount of the subscription price. The decrease of the stock price reflects the fact that the increased capital and reserves have been distributed over a larger number of shares. It does not represent a loss to shareholders or a cost to the company. The TERP, the theoretical ex-rights price, is the theoretical price of the stock on the ex-rights date. The TERP is calculated as follows:

$$TERP = (NE \times PA + NN \times PS)/(NE + NN)$$

where:

NE = the number of existing shares
NN = the number of new shares
PA = the stock closing price on the day immediately preceding the rights issue announce-
    ment date
PS = the subscription price

In this formula it is assumed that the new shares are entitled to any future dividend. However, sometimes the new shares are not entitled to an already declared dividend. In this case the dividend is added to the subscription price when calculating the TERP. The formula then becomes:

$$TERP = [NE \times PA + NN \times (PS + DIV)]/(NE + NN)$$

where:

DIV = the declared dividend per share

2.4.6   Case Study: ING's EUR 7.5 billion Rights Issue

On 26 October 2009, the Dutch bank ING announced its plans to raise EUR 7.5 billion via a rights issue. The issue was authorized by the EGM of ING shareholders on 25 November 2009. The two main decisions ING had to make before launching the rights issue were the proceeds to be raised from the issue and the discount to the TERP.

Sensitivity Analysis of the Discount to TERP

The subscription price is generally at a discount to the current stock price. The main reason is to make the offer relatively attractive to shareholders and encourage them either to exercise their rights or sell them so the share issue is "fully subscribed". The price discount also acts as a safeguard should the market price of the company shares fall before the issue is completed. If the market share price were to fall below the rights issue price, the issue would not have much chance of being a success, since shareholders could buy the shares cheaper in the market than by exercising their subscription rights. The discount is measured comparing the subscription price with the TERP. The following table shows the discount to TERP and the number of new shares to be issued as a function of the subscription price, assuming a EUR 8.92 closing price of ING shares prior to the announcement. The subscription price determines the number of new shares to be issued. It can be seen that the lower the subscription price the larger the discount to TERP and the larger the number of new shares to be issued.

Sensitivity Analysis – Discount to TERP						
Subscription price	3	4	5	6	7	A
Existing shares (million)	2,063.15	2,063.15	2,063.15	2,063.15	2,063.15	B
Proceeds to be raised (EUR million)	7,498.07	7,498.07	7,498.07	7,498.07	7,498.07	C
New shares to be issued (million)	2,499.36	1,874.52	1,499.61	1,249.68	1,071.15	D = C/A
Total shares after rights issue (million)	4,562.50	3,937.67	3,562.76	3,312.83	3,134.30	E = B + D
Closing price prior to announcement	8.92	8.92	8.92	8.92	8.92	F
TERP	5.68	6.58	7.27	7.82	8.26	G = (B × F + D × A)/E
Discount to TERP	47%	39%	31%	23%	15%	H = 1 – A/G

In a rights offering, the discount is irrelevant to existing shareholders. The deeper the discount the higher the rights value will be, and a shareholder's net worth is the same, assuming they take up their rights in full. There is no economic dilution as long as the existing shareholder either subscribes for new shares or sells the subscription rights.

Final Terms of ING's Rights Issue

On 27 November 2009 existing holders of common shares of ING Groep N.V. were offered rights entitling them to subscribe for new ordinary shares with the following terms:

ING Rights Issue – Final Terms

Issuer	ING Groep N.V.
Announcement date	27-November-2009
Record date	27-November-2009
Ex-date	30-November-2009
Expiration date	15-December-2009
Subscription period	From, and including, the ex-date to, and including, the expiration date
Trading period	Same as the subscription period
Subscription price	EUR 4.24
Cum-rights price	EUR 8.53
Stock price on the day prior to the announcement	EUR 8.92
Existing number of shares	2,063,147,968
Terms	6 per 7
Total shares offered	1,768,412,544
Amount to be raised	EUR 7,498.069 million
Adjustment factor	0.767878
Rank	Pari passu
Global coordinators and bookrunners	Goldman Sachs, ING Bank and JP Morgan
Underwriting	Fully underwritten by Goldman Sachs, JP Morgan and a group of other banks

The rights issue was a 6 for 7 rights issue of 1,768,412,544 new shares at an issue price of EUR 4.24 (the subscription price) through the granting of subscription rights to ING shareholders pro rata to their shareholdings. Each share held at the closing of 27 November 2009 (the record date) entitled its holder to one subscription right. Eligible rights holders could subscribe for 6 new shares for every 7 subscription rights that they held. The subscription rights could be exercised or traded from the opening of 30 November 2009 up to 15 December 2009 (the subscription and trading periods). The new shares were fully fungible and ranked pari passu with the existing shares.

Calculation of the TERP

As seen earlier, the TERP is calculated as:

$$TERP = (NE \times PA + NN \times PS)/(NE + NN)$$

where:

NE = the number of existing shares
NN = the number of new shares
PA = the closing price on the trading day immediately preceding the announcement of the
    final terms of the rights issue. EUR 8.92 in our case
PS = the subscription price. EUR 4.24 in our case

Instead of using the number of existing and new shares, it is easier to use the figures in the issue terms. In our case the terms were 6 per 7. Thus, NE = 7, NN = 6, PA = 8.92 and PS = 4.24. Therefore, the TERP was EUR 6.76:

$$\text{TERP} = (\text{NE} \times \text{PA} + \text{NN} \times \text{PS})/(\text{NE} + \text{NN})$$
$$= (7 \times 8.92 + 6 \times 4.24)/(7 + 6) = \text{EUR } 6.76$$

The subscription price of EUR 4.24 corresponded to an implied discount of 37.3% (= 1 − 4.24/6.76) to the TERP.

Calculation of the Rights' Theoretical Value

Theoretically, the value of the subscription rights associated with a share is equal to the difference between the TERP and the subscription price. In our case:

$$\text{Theoretical rights value} = \text{TERP} - \text{subscription price}$$
$$= 6.76 - 4.24 = \text{EUR } 2.52$$

Adjustment to Stock Historical Prices

The price of the existing shares automatically adjusts downward on the ex-date to take into account the discount offered to subscribe for the new shares. For example, imagine that you were an ING shareholder on the record date, when the shares were trading at EUR 8.53 (the cum-rights price). In theory, the next day the shares would be trading at EUR 6.76 (the TERP). In theory your portfolio lost 21% in one day (= 1 − 6.76/8.53), but the company is worth the same. This makes no sense.

As a result, when a company implements a rights issue, an adjustment is made to historical prices prior to the ex-date to appropriately reflect the impact of the rights. The adjustment allows investors to compare historical pricing with current pricing. The adjustment is only made if PC > PS (see below for the definitions of these two variables). The adjustment factor in ING's rights issue was calculated as follows:

$$\text{Adjustment factor} = (\text{NE} \times \text{PC} + \text{NN} \times \text{PS})/[(\text{NE} + \text{NN}) \times \text{PC}]$$

where:

NE = the number of existing shares
NN = the number of new shares

PC = the cum-rights price
PS = the subscription price

Instead of using the number of existing and new shares, it is easier to use the numbers of the issue terms. In our case the terms were 6 per 7. Thus, NE = 7, NN = 6, PC = 8.53 and PS = 4.24. Therefore:

$$\text{Adjustment factor} = (7 \times 8.53 + 6 \times 4.24)/[(7 + 6) \times 8.53]$$
$$= 0.767878$$

As a result, all the historical prices prior to the ex-date were adjusted by multiplying the historical price by the adjustment factor as shown in the following table:

Date	Closing price before adjustment	Closing price after adjustment
25-Nov-09	9.619	7.3862
26-Nov-09	8.916	6.8464
27-Nov-09	8.53	6.55
30-Nov-09	6.204	Not adjusted

Adjustment Factor and Not Entitlement to Dividends

In this adjustment formula it is assumed that the new shares are entitled to any future dividend. However, sometimes the new shares are not entitled to an already declared dividend. In this case the dividend is added to the subscription price when calculating the adjustment factor. The formula then becomes:

$$\text{Adjustment factor} = [(NE \times PC + NN \times (PS + DIV)]/[(NE + NN) \times PC]$$

where:

DIV = the declared dividend per share

Adjustment to Historical Dividends

In a similar way to the historical prices adjustment, historical dividends are adjusted to take into account the rights issue. Assume that the last dividend prior to the rights issue was EUR 0.26 per share. Remember that the adjustment factor was 0.767878. The adjustment to be performed to all historical dividends was:

$$\text{Adjusted dividend} = \text{Unadjusted dividend} \times \text{Adjustment factor}$$

In our example, the EUR 0.26 dividend was adjusted to EUR 0.20 (= 0.26 × 0.767878). The lower dividend simply reflects the increase in the number of shares due to the rights issue. If, for example, during the year following the rights issue ING distributes a EUR 0.20 cash dividend, this would not represent a reduction in ING's dividend distribution policy. Similarly, maintaining the dividend per share after the rights issue at EUR 0.26 represents an increase in dividend distribution policy.

Alternative Interpretation of a Rights Issue: Issue + Scrip Dividend

An alternative way to interpret a rights issue is to split it into two transactions, as follows:

1. ING's capital was first increased by EUR 7,498.07 million via a rights issue at the then prevailing market price. Through this issue, ING issued 879.02 million shares at EUR 8.53. After this transaction there were 2,960.17 million shares outstanding, and the TERP remained unchanged at EUR 8.53.
2. The company distributed a scrip dividend of 889.39 million shares (= 1,768.41 – 879.02). This was equivalent to a 1-for-3.32831 scrip dividend.

The adjustment factor represents the scrip dividend of the rights issue 0.768 [= 3.32831/ (3.32831 + 1)].

2.5 RIGHTS ISSUES OF CONVERTIBLE BONDS

Rights issues of assets other than common stock are relatively uncommon. In this section, a rights issue is analyzed where shareholders are given the right to subscribe to a convertible bond.

2.5.1 Case Study: Banco Popolare Rights Issue of a Convertible Bond

In 2010, Banco Popolare was the largest Italian cooperative bank by number of branches and the fifth largest Italian bank by total assets. On 30 January 2010, the shareholders of Banco Popolare approved in an extraordinary shareholders meeting the issuance of new convertible bonds with pre-emption rights to existing shareholders and holders of the 2000–2010 4.75% subordinated convertible bond. The transaction was aimed at reinforcing the bank's capital ratios. In addition, the issue allowed Banco Popolare to manage the timing of the sale of some non-strategic assets in a more flexible way. The transaction was structured as a rights issue of convertible bonds:

- The subscription terms for existing shareholders were one subscription right per share and one bond for every four subscription rights. Therefore, the rights issue terms were 1 for 4. A total of 640,149,751 rights were issued to existing shareholders.
- The subscription terms for the existing convertible bond holders were one subscription right per 2010 4.75% bond and 43 bonds for every 400 subscription rights. A total of 18,387,505 rights were issued to existing convertible bond holders.

The final terms for the new convertible bond were announced on 25 February 2010. The convertible bond had a notional of EUR 996.4 million, a 4-year maturity, a 4.75% coupon and an initial conversion premium of 34%. The following table shows the main terms of the convertible bond:

Banco Popolare Convertible Bond – Main Terms

Issuer	Banco Popolare Societá Cooperativa
Securities	Bonds convertible into ordinary shares of the issuer
Underlying shares	Ordinary shares of Banco Popolare
Status of the bonds	Senior unsecured
Notional	EUR 996.4 million
Nominal value of each denomination	EUR 6.25
Conversion ratio	1 share per bond
Issue date	24-March-2010
Settlement and listing date	31-March-2010
Maturity date	24-March-2014 (4 years)
Initial conversion premium	34%
Coupon	4.75%, paid annually (Act/365)
Issue price	100% of the nominal value
Redemption price	100% of the nominal value, subject to the early redemption option. The redemption amount could be paid in cash and/or in shares, at the issuer's option
Conversion period	At any time after 18 months from the issue date
Bond holder put	None
Dividend protection	Bond holders were protected against any dividends paid exceeding the threshold of: – €0.10 paid in 2010 and 2011 – €0.15 per year thereafter. Dividends above those levels led to an adjustment of the conversion ratio
Lock-up	90 days for the issuer
Joint lead managers and joint bookrunners	BNP Paribas and Mediobanca
Listing	Milan MTA

Press Release by Banco Popolare on 25 February 2010

". . . The convertible bonds have been designed bearing primarily Banco Popolare's shareholding structure in mind, with the intention of offering a type of investment of interest to our shareholders, in keeping with our objective to stand close to our market territory and its economic fabric. The convertible bond issue is aimed at bringing benefits to Banco Popolare by strengthening its capital base, in order to provide an increasing support to the lending activities in favour of local businesses, and to shore up the Group's Core Tier 1 ratio expected to stand stably above 7% . . ."

Key Dates of the Transaction

The rights could be traded during two and a half weeks starting on 1 March 2010. The holders of the rights could exercise their rights during three and a half weeks starting also on 1 March 2010. Figure 2.13 highlights the main dates of the transaction.

Offering Results

At the end of the subscription period on 24 March 2010, a total of 160,128,993 bonds were subscribed, accounting for 98.84% of total bonds offered, corresponding to EUR 984.8 million. In particular, the following rights were left unexercised:

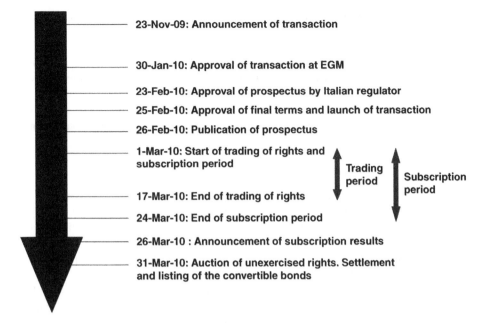

Figure 2.13   Key dates of Banco Popolare rights issue.

- 7,252,516 option rights associated with common shares (out of a total of 640,149,751 rights issued).
- 669,200 option rights associated with the 4.75% 2000–2010 convertible bonds (out of a total of 18,387,505 rights issued).

The remaining 1,885,068 bonds unsubscribed, corresponding to approximately EUR 11.6 million, were offered and sold in an auction on the Italian Stock Exchange on 31 March 2010. As a result, the final take-up after the auction was 100% of the issue.

Why Banco Popolare Issued the Convertible Bond

The new convertible bonds had a soft mandatory conversion clause ("early redemption option") after 18 months at the issuer option and at a 10% premium. The early redemption option allowed Banco Popolare to potentially reinforce the bank's capital ratios after the initial 18 months of the life of the convertible. After 18 months from the issue date, Banco Popolare could exercise the early redemption option, as follows:

- If the share price was below the conversion price, Banco Popolare would pay 110% of the nominal value of the bonds in cash and/or shares, at the issuer's option only.
- If the share price was above the conversion price, Banco Popolare would pay in shares only the value of the underlying shares plus 10% of the nominal value of the bonds.

Therefore, if Banco Popolare needed to strengthen its regulatory capital before maturity and after the initial 18 months, the bank had the option to call the bond and reimburse investors with newly issued shares that were worth 110% of the nominal value of the bond.

Additionally, at bond maturity the bank could increase its regulatory capital, even if the conversion right was out-of-the-money, as follows:

- If the convertible bond expired out-of-the-money, Banco Popolare would reimburse the nominal value of the bond with newly issued shares, where the value of the shares corresponded to 100% of the nominal value of the bond.
- If the convertible bond expired in-the-money, the bond holders would require Banco Popolare to convert the bond into newly issued shares, in accordance with the conversion price.

Main Drawback of the Transaction

The main drawback of the convertible bond issuance was the potential issuance of a large number of shares, were Banco Popolare to redeem the convertible bond in a notably weak market environment. The convertible bond could be early redeemed through the issuance of a variable number of shares so that the aggregate value of the newly issued shares equalled 110% of the redemption amount. In theory, this would mean that upon a sharp decline of the stock price, the potential number of shares could grow dramatically.

For example, let us assume that Banco Popolare was required by the Bank of Italy to increase its regulatory capital and that Banco Popolare decided to terminate the convertible bond early. Banco Popolare would need to repay 110% of the notional amount, or EUR 1,096.0 million (1.10 × EUR 996.4 million) in shares. Let us assume that the then prevailing stock price was EUR 2.50. Therefore, Banco Popolare would need to issue 438.4 million shares (= 1,096.0 million/2.50).

The best way to solve this drawback would have been to include a cap mechanism to the number of shares which could be issued. A cap in the number of shares to be issued would have meant a floor on the stock price at which the bond could be redeemed in shares. Under a cap mechanism, the convertible bond holders bear the risk of shares being below the floor. In other words, under a cap mechanism the bond holders are effectively selling a put on the shares to the convertible bond issuer. As a result, bond holders would have required a higher coupon to be compensated for their short put position.

2.6 ACCELERATED BOOK-BUILDINGS

2.6.1 Product Description

An **accelerated book-building** (**ABB**) and its variations (block trade, ABB with backstop) allow an investor to sell a block of stock quickly. The short placement period gives the seller confidence in the selling price to be obtained. An accelerated book-building may be done for either companies that have already gone public looking to issue additional shares to raise capital or shareholders looking to sell their stock position. Also, ABBs provide investors with the opportunity to buy the stock at a discount. There are three major ABB products:

1. An **ABB** transaction allows the quick disposal of a block of stock without any pre-agreed price guarantee. Under an ABB, the selling party mandates a bank or a group of banks to place a block of stock on a best effort basis. The book-building usually takes place after the market closes. Investors are requested to provide an interest in terms of number of shares and purchase price. The prices bid are sorted from highest to lowest. The block of shares is

then allocated, starting with the highest price bid and then downwards until all the shares are allocated. The allocation takes place before the market opens.

2. A **bought deal** or **block trade** grants a selling entity a quick disposal of a block of shares at a pre-agreed price. The banks leading the offering undertake to buy the block at an agreed price, generally lower than the stock market price. Once the agreement has been signed, the banks immediately place the stock with institutional investors. Time is the essence for the success of the placement, given the risk of a change in the stock price. The stock is placed quickly. Commonly, investors are asked to commit to the offer on the same day. Sometimes, the placement may be extended over an additional day due to the different time zones of the countries where the stock is being placed.

3. An **ABB with backstop** transaction is a combination of the previous two types of transaction. The banks leading the offering guarantee the selling entity a minimum price, for a fee. The block is then placed on a best effort basis with institutional investors. The block is placed at the greater of the average price obtained from the institutional investors and the minimum guaranteed price.

Hereafter, I will refer to these three products under the common name of ABBs.

2.6.2 Advantages and Weaknesses of an ABB

An ABB features a number of advantages:

1. It is an effective way of placing a block of shares immediately. Most ABBs are executed within 24 hours.
2. It can quickly take advantage of a temporary opportunity in the stock market.
3. The seller is not exposed to a price fall after the disposal is priced.
4. In the case of a capital-raising ABB, it does not require a prospectus.
5. In the case of a capital-raising ABB, it commonly does not require shareholder approval at an EGM.

An ABB features a number of weaknesses:

1. The stock is placed at a discount to the prevailing market price.
2. Size can be limited. A large block of an illiquid stock or in a weak market environment may not be placed at a reasonable price.
3. In the case of a capital-raising ABB, the stock is placed without pre-emption rights for existing shareholders. It means that existing shareholders are not invited to the ABB unless they are already a large shareholder in the company.

2.6.3 Estimating the Discount

The discount to the prevailing stock market price is the most relevant parameter in an ABB. The discount compensates the placing bank for the risk run in a bought deal. The bank managing a block trade bears the risk of placing the block with investors at a price lower than its acquisition price from the seller. The discount is a function, among other variables, of:

1. The stock market momentum.
2. The size of the block relative to the number of trading days (i.e., relative to the average daily volume of the stock).

3. The total size of the block.
4. The total size of the block relative to the stock free float.
5. The total size of the block relative to the market capitalization of the stock.

2.6.4   Case Study: IPIC's Disposal of 11.8% of Barclays

In 2008, in the middle of a global credit crisis, Barclays bypassed existing shareholders when it raised capital to comply with new capital requirements. Instead of selling new stock to the British government, Barclays agreed in October 2008 to sell GBP 2.8 billion of mandatorily convertible stock and GBP 3 billion of preferred stock to International Petroleum Investment Company of Abu Dhabi (IPIC), Qatar Holding LLC and Challenger Universal Ltd, an investment vehicle set up by Qatar.

From October 2008 until May 2009, Barclays shares gained 54%. IPIC held 9.75% mandatorily convertible notes due 30 September 2009 of Barclays. IPIC intended to dispose of the ordinary shares of Barclays, for which the mandatorily convertible notes were exchangeable by means of an accelerated book-build. IPIC exercised the notes to satisfy its obligations under the book-build. IPIC appointed Credit Suisse for the disposal. Credit Suisse acted as sole bookrunner and commenced the book-building on 2 June 2009. Credit Suisse was able to place the massive 11.8% stake in Barclays at 265 pence each share, a discount of 16% to the previous closing price of 316 pence. In the opening, Barclays shares dropped to 264.75 pence, just slightly below the 265 pence placing price. IPIC continued to hold warrants for 758.4 million Barclays shares that could be exercised at 197.8 pence.

IPIC Disposal of Barclays Stock through an ABB – Main Terms	
Seller	International Petroleum Investment Company of Abu Dhabi (IPIC)
Shares	Barclays plc
Number of shares	1,304.836 million
Percentage of share capital sold	11.8%
Disposal method	Accelerated book-building
Trading date	2-June-2009
Settlement date	5-June-2009
Placing price	GBP pence 265
Placing amount	GBP 3,457.815 million
Discount to previous closing price	16%
Fees	Not disclosed
Lead manager	Credit Suisse

2.7   AT THE MARKET OFFERINGS

2.7.1   Product Description

In an "at the market" (ATM) offering, blocks of stock are broken into smaller chunks and sold from time to time at the prevailing market price. Unlike a traditional ABB offering, in which all shares are sold at once to a group of investors, ATM sales dribble into the market over the course of days, weeks or even months. The method is especially useful for price-sensitive stocks or very large share sales, because unleashing a large block of shares in one day can seriously depress a stock price. The bank managing the sale is paid in per-share trading commissions rather than through a percentage underwriting fee. Usually the stock price falls on the announcement of the transaction to anticipate the upcoming sales orders.

2.7.2 Case Study: US Treasury Placement of Citigroup Shares

On 26 April 2010 the United States Department of the Treasury hired Morgan Stanley to manage the sale of part of its 27% stake in Citigroup. The US Treasury acquired the shares of Citigroup in connection with Citigroup's participation in the Troubled Asset Relief Program (TARP). TARP was established pursuant to the Emergency Economic Stabilization Act of 2008, which was enacted into law on 3 October 2008 in response to the financial crisis. On 28 October 2008, Citigroup issued to the US Treasury USD 25 billion of its perpetual preferred stock as part of the TARP Capital Purchase Program. This perpetual preferred stock was exchanged for shares of common stock in July 2009. As a result, on 26 April 2010 the US Treasury owned 7.69 billion shares of Citigroup. Additionally, the US Treasury held warrants to purchase 465.1 million shares of common stock issued by Citigroup, subject to adjustment from time to time, and USD 2.23 billion aggregate liquidation preference of trust preferred securities issued by a Citigroup trust. All these capital instruments were issued by Citigroup in exchange for USD 45 billion of aid.

On 26 April 2010, the US Treasury, Morgan Stanley and Citigroup entered into an agreement, under which the US Treasury could offer and sell up to 7.69 billion shares of common stock from time to time through Morgan Stanley as sales agent or as principal. The agented sale of shares was to be made by means of ordinary brokers' transactions, in block transactions or as otherwise agreed with the US Treasury. The US Treasury could also enter into a separate agreement to sell shares of common stock to Morgan Stanley as principal at a price agreed at the time of sale. Citigroup would not receive any proceeds from the stock sale.

Morgan Stanley agreed to sell, on behalf of the US Treasury, shares of common stock subject to the terms and conditions of the agreement among Citigroup, the US Treasury and Morgan Stanley on a daily basis or as otherwise agreed upon by the US Treasury and Morgan Stanley. The US Treasury devised a plan in 2010 of pre-arranged written trading strategies to help insulate officials from politically driven claims that they mistimed the market and got too little profit from the sales. The manner, amount and timing of the sales under any such plan were dependent upon a number of factors. The US Treasury would provide instructions, in accordance with the plan, to Morgan Stanley with respect to the manner of distribution of the shares. Morgan Stanley agreed to use its commercially reasonable efforts to sell the shares following the instructions.

The US Treasury divided its stake into blocks, instructing Morgan Stanley to sell one block at a time. The US Treasury approved an initial sale of a block of 1.5 billion shares, representing more than 19% of its total stake. The US Treasury gave Morgan Stanley the authority to sell a second block of shares once the initial 1.5 billion shares were sold. The US Treasury received the gross proceeds of the sale of shares for which Morgan Stanley acted as sales agent or principal without deduction of any commissions or fees. Once all the blocks were sold, the US Treasury received about USD 32 billion.

Citigroup agreed to reimburse the US Treasury for all discounts, selling commissions, stock transfer taxes and transaction fees incurred in connection with the sale. Morgan Stanley was paid in per-share trading commissions rather than through a percentage underwriting fee. Each month, Morgan Stanley received from the US Treasury a commission of USD 0.003 per share sold by Morgan Stanley using electronic trading systems and USD 0.0175 per share sold by Morgan Stanley using other means. That was a steep discount from the three cents to four cents a share that brokers normally charged for similar trades at that time. Morgan Stanley also received a one-time USD 500,000 administrative fee. In total, Morgan Stanley received approximately USD 82 million in commissions.

3

Convertible Bonds and Mandatory Convertible Bonds

This chapter examines the major characteristics of convertible bonds and mandatory convertible bonds. It covers the terminology, structures and price behavior of these instruments, as well as issuer and investor motivations. Also in this chapter, contingent convertibles – FRESHES, CASHES and ECNs – are covered in detail. Several real case studies are included: a convertible bond issued by the German corporate Infineon, a mandatory convertible bond issued by UBS, a FRESH issued by Fortis Bank, a CASHES issued by Unicredit and an ECN issued by Lloyds.

3.1 INTRODUCTION TO CONVERTIBLE BONDS

3.1.1 What are Convertible Bonds?

Convertible bonds are instruments which give the holder the right to "convert" a bond into a fixed number of the issuer's common stock (i.e., ordinary shares) at a specified price. Convertible bonds have both common stock and straight bond features. Like common stock, convertible bond holders benefit from an appreciation of the issuer common stock. Like straight bonds (i.e., non-convertible bonds), convertible bonds can have cash redemption at maturity and fixed coupon payments. In this way, convertible bonds reflect a combination of the benefits of stocks and those of bonds (see Figure 3.1).

	Equity Upside	Downside Protection
Common Shares	✓	X
Straight Bonds	X	✓
Convertible Bonds	✓	✓

Figure 3.1 Comparing a convertible bond with common shares and a straight bond.

Commonly, convertible bonds tend to pay lower coupons than straight bonds because their holders also participate in the underlying stock appreciation. However, convertible bonds can be tailored to meet an issuer's specific coupon requirements. For example, a convertible bond can be structured to look more like a bond with a high coupon and a high conversion premium, or more like equity, with a low coupon and a low conversion premium. The higher the coupon, the lower the probability of being converted into shares. The lower the conversion price, the higher the probability of being converted into shares. Thus, the higher the probability of conversion, the more equity-like the instrument behaves and the less straight debt-like the instrument behaves (see Figure 3.2).

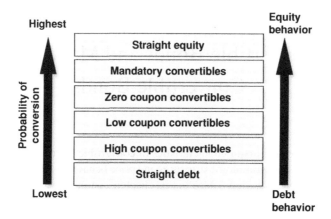

Figure 3.2 Equity vs. debt behavior for different convertible bonds.

From an issuer point of view, issuing a convertible has the following advantages relative to issuing common shares:

- If conversion takes place, shares are issued at a premium to the underlying share price on issue date.
- Normally less potential impact on share price.
- Preserves capacity to issue straight equity, as investor base is typically different.
- Generally less sensitivity to "use of proceeds" question.
- Dividend and voting rights are maintained until conversion (in exchangeable bonds).

Similarly, issuing a convertible has the following advantages relative to issuing straight debt:

- Cash coupon payments are lower (for low coupon convertibles).
- Preserves capacity to issue additional debt, as investor base is typically different.
- Usually fewer covenants are required.

3.1.2   Convertible vs. Exchangeable Bonds – Exchange Property

An exchangeable bond is similar to a convertible bond except that exercise by the holder results in conversion into the shares of another company rather than the shares of the issuer itself. Most of the characteristics described in this chapter for convertibles apply also to exchangeable bonds.

Exchange Property

A major difference between convertible and exchangeable bonds lies in the need to own the underlying stock. In a convertible bond and upon conversion, an issuer can issue new shares. Therefore, bond holders of a convertible bond know that the issuer can always meet the conversion requirements if the company has prior approval from shareholders. In an exchangeable bond and upon conversion, bond holders are only certain that their conversion will be met if the issuer owns the underlying stock. That is why in an exchangeable the underlying stock is called the "**exchange property**". The terms and conditions of an exchangeable include provisions that secure the use of the exchange property only to meet the exercises under the exchangeable.

3.2 WHO BUYS CONVERTIBLE BONDS?

Convertibles appeal to a broad range of investors with different risk profiles and investment criteria. For example, straight equity fund managers may find convertibles that offer a better risk–reward profile than the underlying shares. The main investors in convertible bonds are dedicated convertible funds and hedge funds.

Dedicated Convertible Funds

Funds fully dedicated to convertibles are one of the two main investors in convertible bonds. These funds buy convertibles primarily attracted by their upside opportunities with limited downside. For these types of fund, the most important factor influencing their decision is the issuer equity story. Other elements that these funds take into account are the pricing, the liquidity and the relative value of the issue. Their investment horizon is medium to long-term.

Hedge Funds

Hedge funds are the other main investors in convertible bonds. Unlike dedicated convertible funds, hedge funds are less focused on the issuer fundamental story. Although hedge fund convertible strategies vary widely, commonly hedge funds are attracted to convertibles because of arbitrage opportunities in these bonds. The term "convertible arbitrage" refers to the trading strategy of identifying convertibles which are not efficiently priced by the market in comparison to prices of other related instruments. Typically, these funds aim to exploit a lower than priced realized volatility. Hedge funds will usually buy an undervalued convertible bond and immunize its sensitivity to variations in the underlying share price at all times. This mitigation strategy is called delta-neutral hedging. The strategy implies selling short a portion of the underlying shares. The portion of the underlying shares to be short takes into account the probability of the convertible being exercised. As a consequence, sufficient borrow of the underlying shares is critical for these types of fund.

Equity Funds

Equity funds have historically used convertibles when they are an attractive alternative to straight equity. For example, in difficult market environments equity funds use convertibles as a defensive strategy to smooth out portfolio volatility. In principle, they invest in convertibles that offer both upside performance similar to the equity and downside protection should the underlying share decline. For these types of fund, the most important factor influencing their decision is the issuer equity story.

Equity Income Funds

These funds are cross-over income-oriented funds that look at convertibles as an alternative to straight equity. Their investment horizon is medium to long-term. For these funds an attractive equity exposure to the underlying stock is crucial and equity research and analysis is important.

High Yield Funds

These funds look at convertibles as an alternative to fixed-income investments. Their investment horizon is medium to long. For high yield funds an attractive coupon is crucial. Credit analysis is an important part of their decision-making process.

3.3 CONVERTIBLE BONDS: THE ISSUER PERSPECTIVE

Many different explanations have been put forward for why entities issue convertibles. My belief is that there is not one all-embracing reason. I identify five main types of motivation for issuing convertibles:

1. Entities that want to reduce their average cost of capital. Convertible bonds pay a lower coupon than straight debt.
2. Entities that need to raise cash and have already exhausted, or want to preserve, their access to the straight bond market. By tapping the convertible market, entities diversify their investor base.
3. Entities that want to access the convertible market in particular. The convertible market may experience a big appetite for convertibles, allowing entities to issue them at very attractive terms.
4. Entities that believe that their shares are overvalued by the market. If the shares drop as the entity expects, at maturity the convertible will not be converted. The final effect is equivalent to the entity having issued a straight bond but with a notably lower coupon.
5. Entities that are unrated and do not want to pay a large credit spread when raising new funding. When investing in a new bond, straight bond investors require a credit spread which is a function of the rating of the issuer. Unrated issues are often heavily penalized by institutional bond investors. However, convertible bond investors often make their investment decision based on the implied volatility priced in the convertible, giving less importance to the issuer's rating.

Other advantages for an issuer of a convertible bond are the following:

- If convertibles are converted, the issue of new stock will reinforce the equity base of the issuer.
- Upon conversion, stock is placed at a premium to the stock price prevailing on issue date. Therefore, relative to a common stock issuance, the issuer raises a larger amount of proceeds from the same amount of shares.
- Dividends and voting rights are maintained until conversion, if the issuer holds the underlying shares in an exchangeable bond.
- Limited covenants are included, usually limited to negative pledge and cross default. Commonly, no constraints are included regarding acquisitions or significant changes in the business.
- Documentation is usually very limited.

- Roadshows or other detailed communications are unnecessary.
- Execution is relatively quick. A convertible usually requires a preparation period before launch of two to three weeks only. The placement of the convertible bonds takes a few hours, reducing the exposure to market risk. It also enables the issuer to take quick advantage of favorable market windows, for example convertibles' high redemption levels, low convertible issuance levels and convertible funds awash with liquidity.
- No effect on basic earnings per share (EPS).

The main disadvantage for an issuer of a convertible bond is the potential dilution for existing shareholders, although less than in the case of a rights issue. Dilution can be avoided if the convertible terms include a "cash option" clause (to be explained later). Another disadvantage for an issuer of a convertible bond is its effect in diluted EPS, as its calculation assumes that the convertible bond will be converted.

3.4   CASE STUDY: INFINEON'S CONVERTIBLE BOND

3.4.1   Main Terms of Infineon's Convertible Bond

In order to become familiar with the terms of a convertible bond, let us describe the main terms of a convertible bond issued in 2009 by the German corporate Infineon Technologies. The terms of the convertible are outlined in the table below:

Infineon's Convertible Bond Terms	
Issuer	Infineon Technologies Holding B.V., a wholly owned subsidiary of Infineon Technologies A.G.
Notional amount	EUR 195.6 million
Redemption amount	100% of notional amount
Denomination	EUR 50,000
Issue date	26-May-2009
Maturity	26-May-2014
Underlying stock	Infineon Technologies A.G.'s common stock
Issue price	92.80%
Coupon	7.50%, semiannual Act/Act
Conversion price	EUR 2.61
Underlying number of shares	74.9 million ($=$ 195.6 million/2.61)
Conversion ratio	19,157.088
Conversion premium	25%
Share price at issue	EUR 2.09
Lockout period	From issue date to 24 August 2009
Hard no call	From issue date to 25 November 2011
Soft call	From 26 November 2011. Stock price must equal or exceed 150% of the conversion price (EUR 3.915) for 15 days out of 30 consecutive business days

Issuer is the entity that has the obligation to meet the contractual terms of the convertible bond.

Notional amount, or **nominal amount**, or **principal amount**, is the amount on which the issuer pays interest. The notional of Infineon's convertible was EUR 195.6 million.

Redemption amount is the amount received by the holder at maturity, if the bond is not converted. The redemption amount is expressed as a percentage of the notional amount. Commonly this percentage is 100%, or in other words, the bond is redeemed at par.

Denomination is the minimum portion of the notional amount that can be purchased. In Infineon's convertible an investor could buy only multiples of EUR 50,000.

Issue date is the date the convertible was first offered into the market.

Maturity date is the date on which the issuer must redeem the bonds for their redemption amount. Infineon's convertible matured in 5 years from the issue date.

Issue price is the price paid for the convertible by the holders when it was issued. The Infineon convertible was issued at 92.8% of the nominal amount, which means that the issue proceeds amounted to EUR 181.5 million (195.6 million × 92.80%).

Coupons are the interest payments on the bond. These can be paid either quarterly, semi-annually or annually. Commonly, this amount is fixed for the life of the bond. Infineon's convertible paid a fixed coupon set at 7.50% per annum, payable semiannually in arrears. The issue date is used as the interest accrual date for the first coupon period.

3.4.2 Conversion Price, Ratio, Premium and Lockout Period

A convertible gives the holder an option to convert the bonds into shares of the issuer at a specified price, the **conversion price**. The conversion price of Infineon's convertible was set at EUR 2.61. In other words, the conversion price is the price at which shares are effectively "bought" on conversion. At maturity, the bond holder will decide whether to convert the bond based on the following:

- If the share price is greater than the conversion price, the shares to be received are worth more than the redemption amount. As a result, the holder will prefer to convert the bond into shares.
- If the share price is equal to or lower than the conversion price, the shares to be received are worth less than, or equal to, the redemption amount. As a result, the holder will prefer to receive the redemption cash amount.

   Conversion ratio is the number of shares into which each bond denomination is convertible. The conversion ratio remains fixed throughout the life of the convertible bond, although it will usually be adjusted for stock splits, special dividends or other dilutive events, and "reset clauses". The conversion ratio is equal to the denomination divided by the conversion price. The conversion ratio of Infineon's convertible was 19,157.088 shares (= 50,000/2.61), meaning that an investor holding EUR 50,000 of bonds would convert to 19,157 shares.

$$\text{Conversion Ratio} = \frac{\text{Denomination}}{\text{Conversion Price}}$$

   Conversion premium is the percentage premium of the conversion price above the share price on issue date. In Infineon's convertible the conversion premium was 25%, meaning that Infineon's share price had to appreciate by at least 25% from its value at the convertible's inception to be worth exercising the conversion right.

   Lockout period is a clause that prevents the holder from exercising the conversion right during this period. In Infineon's convertible, the bond holders could not convert the bond into shares prior to 24 August 2009.

3.4.3 Hard No Call Period, Hard Call and Soft Call Options

Most convertible bonds are issued with a **call right**, that gives the issuer the right, but not the obligation, to force the bond holders to redeem the bond before its maturity date. Usually the call can be exercised by providing a notice period. An issuer can call a convertible bond to take advantage of refinancing the bond at cheaper levels (which can reduce financing expense) or to force bond holders to convert debt into equity (which can reduce debt levels). Upon the bond being called, the holder has the right to choose between (i) redemption at the call price (par or at accreted value) in cash and (ii) conversion into shares. As the call right may cap the equity upside by reducing the time value of the conversion right, the inclusion of a call right will tend to diminish the value of a convertible bond. Thus, a call right constitutes a disadvantage for the holder and a plus for the issuer. Callable convertible bonds usually include hard no call and soft call protections.

> **Hard no call period** is the period during which the bond cannot be called under any circumstances. In the Infineon convertible the hard call period started on issue date and ended on 25 November 2011. As a result, the holders had more than two years to benefit from a rise in Infineon's share price without being worried about the bond being called.
> **Call period** is the period during which the bond can be called. The call right is typically a soft call right:
>> **Soft call** is a call right that is subject to the share price being above a certain level, called the **trigger** or the **call hurdle**. The trigger is expressed as a percentage of the conversion price. In the case of Infineon's convertible, the trigger level was set at 150% of the conversion price. As a result, if the bond was called by the issuer the holders were guaranteed at least a 50% return. If the issuer elects to redeem early a convertible with a soft call protection, the terms of the bond commonly contain a clause whereby there is an automatic exercise of the conversion right. To prevent abnormal trading patterns triggering a provisional call, most convertible bonds require the share price to trade above the trigger price for a number of days before the provisional call is activated. In the case of Infineon's convertible, the shares had to trade at or above the trigger level for at least 15 days out of 30 consecutive business days. As a result of the trigger level being well above the conversion price, the holders will choose to convert to shares. Therefore, by exercising its call right, the issuer forces the conversion into shares. Before exercising its call right, the issuer must provide a call notice period (e.g., 30 days).
>> **Hard call** is a call right that is not subject to any trigger.

Figure 3.3 shows a simulated path of Infineon's share price. Five periods have been chosen to explain the mechanics of the convertible's soft call clause:

- In period 1, Infineon could not exercise its call right. Although the soft call trigger was surpassed during a substantial number of days, the bond could not be called as it was in its hard no call period.
- In period 2, Infineon could not exercise its call right. Although the hard no call period had elapsed, the number of days that Infineon's share price was trading above the trigger was zero (i.e., less than 15 days) during the previous 30 consecutive business days.
- In period 3, Infineon could not exercise its call right. Although the soft call trigger was surpassed and the bond was in its soft call period, the bond could not be called as the number of days that Infineon's share price was trading above the trigger was less than 15 days during the previous 30 consecutive business days.

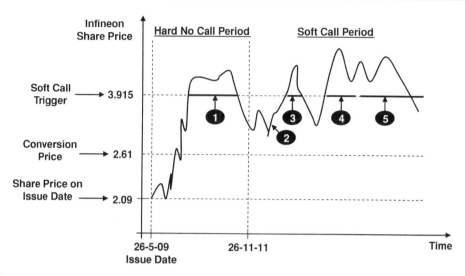

Figure 3.3   Simulation of call right scenarios.

- In period 4, Infineon could not exercise its call right for the same reasons mentioned for period 3.
- In period 5, Infineon could exercise its call right. The soft call trigger was surpassed, the bond was in its soft call period and the number of days that Infineon's share price was trading above the trigger was more than 15 days during the previous 30 consecutive business days.

3.4.4   Put Rights

A **put right** is a feature giving the holder the right, but not the obligation, to sell back the bond to the issuer. It helps the holder to get rid of the bond under adverse market conditions such as flat stock prices, rising issuer credit spreads and rising interest rates. Thus, a put right constitutes a disadvantage for the issuer and a plus for the holder. Most puttable convertibles can be put back to the issuer at par for cash.

The inclusion of puts can substantially reduce the cost of financing. The issuer can pay a lower coupon and/or obtain a higher conversion price than in non-puttable convertibles. Commonly, put rights can only be exercised at specific dates. For example, a seven-year convertible bond may have a put right exercisable on the third and fifth anniversary of the bond life. If the exercise of the put option is likely, the issuer will face a potential refinancing risk at the put date.

In assessing whether or not to ask for redemption on a put date, bond holders will compare the fair value of the convertible with the redemption price on this date:

- If the fair value of the convertible is greater than the redemption price (100%), bond holders will not ask for redemption. This situation may occur when the stock price trades above the conversion price or close to the conversion price. The exercise of the put right is not optimal because, by exercising the put, the bond holder would give up the time value of the conversion option.

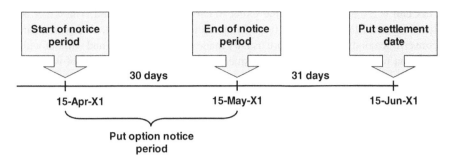

Figure 3.4 Put right relevant dates.

- If the fair value of the convertible is lower than the redemption price (100%), bond holders will ask for redemption. This situation may occur when the stock price trades well below the conversion price, and/or when the credit spread of the issuer has widened notably since the bond was issued.
- If the fair value of the convertible is equal to the redemption price (100%), bond holders are theoretically indifferent between exercising the put option and keeping the convertible.

In order to highlight how the put right exercise works in practice, let us assume that the terms of a convertible bond include a put right that allows the bond holder to redeem the bond early on 15 June 20X1 (the "put settlement date"). The terms of the put right (see Figure 3.4) state that the put right can be exercised by the bond holder providing there is a "put option notice" during the "put notice period". The put option notice period starts on the day that is 61 calendar days prior to the put settlement date (i.e., on 15 April 20X1) and ends on the day that is 31 calendar days prior to the put settlement date (i.e., on 15 May 20X1).

A bond holder seeking to exercise his/her put right must complete a "put option notice" and deliver it to the bond agent during the put notice period. Once the bond holder has tendered the notice, it can only be withdrawn with the consent of the issuer. On 15 June 20X1, the put settlement date, the exercised bonds become immediately due and payable.

3.4.5   Additional Clauses: Cash Option, Cash Top-up, Lock-up Period, Tax Call

A **cash option** is a feature enabling the issuer, at its sole discretion, to deliver to the bond holders that have chosen to convert the bond a cash amount reflecting the then prevailing value of the underlying stock, instead of delivering the underlying stock. The cash equivalent value is determined on the basis of the average closing stock price during a number of days (e.g., five) following the issuer decision to elect the cash option. This clause allows the issuer to avoid dilution upon conversion.

A **cash top-up** is a feature enabling the issuer to deliver shares at maturity whatever the stock price performance, even if the stock trades below the conversion price. Usually if the conversion price is not reached, additional cash compensation is added to the share delivery. The cash top-up feature provides the issuer with certainty regarding the underlying shares disposal.

A **lock-up period** is the period during which no entities of the issuer's group can sell shares and/or enter into equity-linked instruments based on the underlying stock.

A **tax call** is a feature enabling the issuer to early redeem the bond. The issuer is usually incorporated under the laws of tax favorable jurisdiction. As a result, all payments in respect of a convertible bond by the issuer are usually made free and clear of, and without withholding or deduction for, any taxes, duties, assessments or governmental charges of whatever nature imposed, levied, collected, withheld or assessed by the issuer jurisdiction authorities. In the event the issuer has to pay additional amounts, so its payments compensate for such withholding or deductions, the issuer can request early redemption of the convertible bonds. However, bond holders typically have the option to elect their bond to not be redeemed, but no such additional amounts will be paid.

3.4.6 Value of a Convertible Bond at Maturity

At maturity and in absence of the issuer being bankrupt, a convertible bond is worth the larger of (i) its cash redemption amount and (ii) the market value of the shares into which it is convertible, as shown in Figure 3.5 for Infineon's convertible.

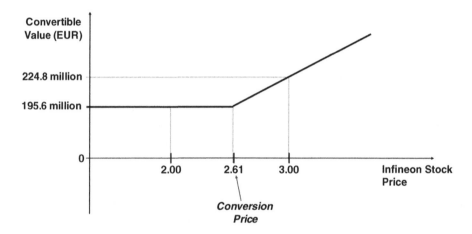

Figure 3.5   Theoretical price of Infineon's convertible bond at maturity.

3.4.7 Value of a Convertible Bond during its Life

A convertible bond can be split into two components (see Figure 3.6): a bond part and an option part. The bond part represents the coupon payments and the potential redemption in cash at par. The option part represents the right to exchange the bond for a fixed number of shares. The total value of the convertible is the sum of the value of these two components.

- The bond value is the present value of the coupons and principal due on the debt component. It represents the value floor of the convertible bond, assuming that the option component is worthless. The main factors influencing the value of the bond component are the bond coupon, the market level of the credit spread of the issuer, the bond maturity and the market level of interest rates.
- The option value is the value of the bond holder's call right embedded in the convertible bond. The strike price of the option is the conversion price. The main factors influencing

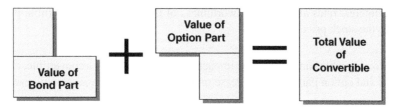

Figure 3.6   Components of a convertible bond valuation.

the option value are the conversion price, the underlying stock market price, the implied volatility of the underlying stock, the expected dividends, the repo rate, the bond maturity and the market level of interest rates.

During its life, the value of a convertible bond has the profile depicted in Figure 3.7. The graph shows the value of a convertible bond as a function of the underlying share price. We can split the graph into four different areas:

- A **distressed** area. In this area the stock price is very low. The issuer is in distress and the market is discounting with a significant probability that the issuer will be unable to repay the notional amount at maturity. The value of the convertible is below the bond floor.
- An **out-of-the-money** area. In this area the stock price is notably lower than the conversion price and as a result the probability of the convertible being exercised is quite low. The convertible behaves like a straight bond. Its price becomes more dependent on interest rates and the creditworthiness of the issuer and less on stock price. Thus, the bond trades close to its bond floor price.
- An **at-the-money** area. In this area the stock price is close to the conversion price. The convertible behaves like a mix of a straight bond and a stock.
- An **in-the-money** area. In this area the stock price is well above the conversion price. The convertible behaves like a stock. Its value becomes more dependent on the stock price and

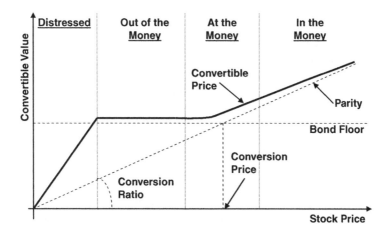

Figure 3.7   Theoretical price of a convertible bond.

less on interest rates and the creditworthiness of the issuer. The convertible price is quite close to the stock price.

The following table summarizes the impact on the total value of a convertible, and the value of its bond and option parts, of an increase in the specified variable, assuming everything else is equal:

	Bond part	Option part	Total Value
Increase convertible bond coupon	↑	NA	↑
Increase in stock price	NA	↑	↑
Increase conversion price/premium	NA	↓	↓
Increase underlying stock volatility	NA	↑	↑
Increase maturity	↓	↑	↓
Increase underlying stock dividend	NA	↓	↓
Increase credit spread	↓	NA	↓
Increase market interest rates	↓	↑	↓
Increase call hurdle	↑	↑	↑

There are other factors with a qualitative nature that may also affect the value of a convertible bond, for example:

- The underlying equity story.
- The convertible market overall strength.
- The issuer sector performance.

3.5 DELTA SHARE REPURCHASE STRATEGY

Hedge funds take a long position on a convertible and take a short position in the underlying common stock. Hedge funds will not short 100% of the underlying shares, but rather the percentage of the total amount that immunizes their position to movements of the underlying stock price. This percentage is referred to as the "delta" (in Chapter 1 the reader can find a detailed explanation of the delta concept). As a result of the stock sale, at issuance the underlying common stock price may experience a downward pressure.

In order to offset this downward pressure, an issuer can use part of the proceeds of a new convertible bond issue to repurchase the "delta" shares (i.e., the investors' short positions), as shown in Figure 3.8. Delta shares bought back at issue are taken out of the outstanding share count, resulting in an immediate and permanent accretive effect. For example, let us assume that the initial delta of Infineon's convertible was 28% and that 50% of the bond holders were going to short the underlying stock at issuance. Infineon would have acquired 14% of the underlying stock, or 10.49 million shares (= 14% × 74.91 million). Because the stock was trading at EUR 2.09 on issue date, Infineon would have spent EUR 21.92 million (= 10.49 million × 2.09). Infineon would then need to decide what to do with the treasury shares acquired, whether to sell them gradually onto the market or to keep them until a potential conversion of the bond.

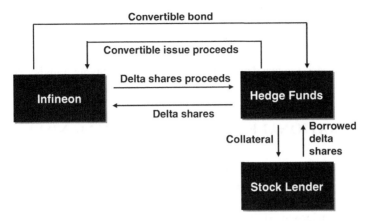

Figure 3.8   Delta share repurchase strategy for Infineon's convertible.

3.6   MANDATORY CONVERTIBLE BONDS

A mandatory convertible is an equity-linked instrument that performs mostly like common shares but has a higher income stream. These issues are mandatorily convertible (hence the name), at maturity or upon redemption, into common shares, irrespective of the price at which the shares are trading. The coupon at issue is usually higher than the current dividend yield of the underlying common stock.

3.7   RATIONALE FOR ISSUING MANDATORY CONVERTIBLES

Many different arguments have been put forward for why entities issue mandatory convertibles. My belief is that there is not one all-embracing reason. I identify six main types of motivation for issuing mandatory convertibles:

1. Entities that need to raise capital while delaying equity dilution until later. Although some mandatory convertible structures are treated as a liability from an accounting perspective, they generally count partially/totally as capital to rating agencies and regulators. These are entities that are notably leveraged and need to lower their debt-to-equity ratio. These entities could raise new shares through an accelerated book-building or a rights issue, but these two alternatives imply an immediate dilution to the entities' core shareholders, obliging them to acquire additional shares to avoid dilution. A mandatory convertible avoids dilution until its conversion date.
2. Entities that want to raise capital but want to avoid the generally substantial share price impact of a large accelerated book-building or a rights issue.
3. Entities that need to raise cash and have already exhausted, or want to preserve, their access to the straight bond market. By tapping the convertible market, entities diversify their investor base.
4. Entities that want to raise capital but want to tap a different investor base, not cannibalizing their existing shareholder base.
5. Entities that want to access the convertible market in particular. The convertible market may experience a big appetite for mandatory convertibles, allowing entities to issue them at very attractive terms.

6. Entities that believe their shares are overvalued by the market. If the shares drop as the entity expects, at maturity the convertible will be converted into shares at a higher than market price.

The main drawback for mandatory convertible issuers is paying a higher coupon than on straight non-convertible debt.

3.8 RATIONALE FOR INVESTING IN MANDATORY CONVERTIBLES

An investment in a mandatory convertible is a yield-enhanced investment in the underlying shares. As such, a mandatory offers no downside protection to an investor apart from the higher yield. A mandatory convertible presents the following advantages compared with an investment in the underlying shares:

- The investor receives a coupon that exceeds the dividend payments distributed to the underlying securities. However, the higher yield comes at a price: the investor is obliged to exchange the convertible for shares at a premium to the share price at issuance.
- The investor may be more protected in case the issuer files a bankruptcy petition before the final conversion date. The level of subordination of the convertible holders relative to the other claimants, whether the underlying note was senior or subordinated, prior to conversion date depends on the legal terms of the convertible. Commonly, if an issuer becomes insolvent prior to the convertible bond maturity, the contract terminates and the investors have no obligation to settle on the equity purchase. The notes, however, remain outstanding and participate as debt of the bankrupt debtor for recovery along with other senior subordinated or junior subordinated notes of the issuer, depending on the specific terms of the note.

The following is a disadvantage compared with an investment in the underlying shares:

- The investor may receive shares upon conversion at a premium relative to the share price at issuance. This is the case for most fixed parity mandatory convertibles.

3.9 FIXED PARITY MANDATORY CONVERTIBLES

A fixed parity mandatory convertible is a bond mandatorily convertible at maturity into stock at a fixed conversion ratio. Thus, investors receive a fixed number of shares at maturity. The conversion ratio is fixed through the life of the bond. The bonds are issued at a premium to the initial value of the underlying shares (typically 10–20%), compensated for by a coupon providing investors with a yield pick-up. From an investor's perspective, a fixed parity mandatory convertible functions like a high-yielding investment in the underlying equity.

3.9.1 Case Study: Banco Santander's Fixed Parity Mandatory Convertible

This case walks through the mechanics of fixed parity mandatory convertibles, using a real-life example: a fixed parity mandatory convertible issued by Banco Santander in 2007. The mandatory had the following terms:

Banco Santander's Mandatory Convertible Bond Terms

Issue date	4-October-2007
Issuer	Santander Emisora 150, S.A.U. (100% owned and guaranteed by Banco Santander S.A.)
Issue proceeds	EUR 7 billion
Notional	EUR 7 billion
Maturity date	4-October-2012 (5 years)
Coupon	7.30% until 4-October-2008, and Euribor plus 2.75% thereafter until the maturity date
Conversion price	EUR 16.04 per share (a 20% premium relative to the EUR 13.37 stock price on issue date)
Number of shares upon conversion	436,408,978 shares
Conversion by holder	Holders can convert early on 4-October-2009, 2010 and 2011, and must mandatorily convert on 4-October-2012

In a very general sense, the structure can be looked at as a yield-enhanced investment in common shares from which the investor trades away part of the underlying shares' upside in return for a higher coupon.

Figure 3.9 shows the number of shares to be received upon conversion by the investors in Banco Santander's mandatory convertible bond. This number is fixed to 436,408,978 shares, independently of Banco Santander's stock price at conversion.

From an issuer point of view, a fixed parity convertible bond has the following advantages:

• The stock is issued at a premium upon conversion.
• The instrument is considered as equity by the rating agencies.
• The instrument is accounted for as equity, except the coupons.
• The coupons are commonly tax deductible.

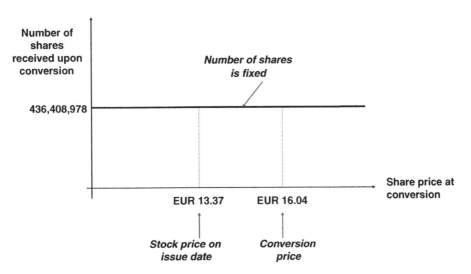

Figure 3.9 Number of shares delivered by Banco Santander upon conversion.

From an issuer point of view, a fixed parity convertible bond has the following drawbacks:

- Coupons are higher than the coupons of comparable straight debt.
- On issue date, the stock price of the underlying may experience a sharp fall as a result of investors selling the underlying to initially delta-hedge their positions. The delta of the instrument is 100%. As a result, investors immunizing their investment to changes in the underlying stock price need to sell all their underlying shares in the stock market.

3.10   VARIABLE PARITY MANDATORY CONVERTIBLES

Variable parity mandatory convertibles are securities which are mandatorily convertible into common stock at maturity and have no fixed conversion price. The number of shares received upon conversion will depend on the common stock price at maturity. The most common variable parity mandatory structure is called DECS. This type of mandatory structure is described in the following section.

3.11   DIVIDEND ENHANCED CONVERTIBLE SECURITIES

DECS stands for "Dividend Enhanced Convertible Securities" or "Dividend Enhanced Convertible Stock" or "Debt Exchangeable for Common Stock". It is the most common mandatory convertible structure. Although used to denote the same type of mandatory convertibles, there has been a hodgepodge of names. The names that fall under this category include PIES, DECS SAILS, ACES, PRIDES, TAPS, PEPS, EPICS, TIMES, MARCS, MEDS and some of the STRYPES. The instrument has full downside similar to holding common shares, a dead zone between the lower and the upper conversion price, and partial upside above the upper conversion price.

3.11.1   Conversion Mechanics of a DECS

In a very general sense, the structure can be looked at purely as a yield-enhanced investment in common shares from which the investor trades away part of the underlying shares' upside in return for a higher coupon. In other words, the security is like an investment in the underlying shares plus a sale of a call spread on the shares. From the issuer point of view, it is like a forward sale of the shares plus the purchase of a call spread.

In order to describe the conversion mechanism of a DECS, let us assume that a company called ABC Corp. issues the following DECS:

ABC DECS Terms	
Instrument type	DECS
Issuer	ABC Corp.
Notional	EUR 1 billion
Underlying shares	ABC Corp. common shares
Maturity date	3 years
Coupon	8%, paid annually
Share price on issue date	EUR 100
Lower conversion price	EUR 100 (100% of the share price on issue date)
Upper conversion price	EUR 120 (120% of the share price on issue date)

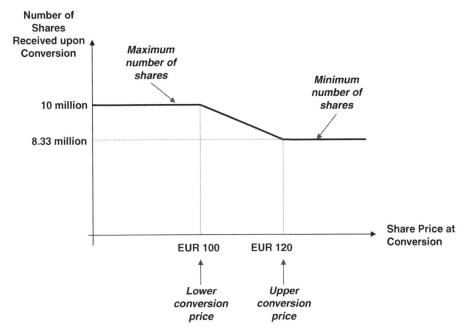

Figure 3.10   DECS number of shares to be received upon conversion.

At maturity, the DECS mandatorily converts into a number of shares that is a function of ABC's stock price at maturity. The conversion premium has a different meaning for a DECS than for a fixed parity mandatory convertible. The conversion price of a DECS varies according to the level of the underlying stock price at the date of conversion, being limited by the lower and upper conversion prices. The lower conversion price is usually the stock price prevailing at issuance. The upper conversion price is set at a premium to the stock price at issue, 20% in our example. Therefore, the number of shares received by the bond holder upon conversion depends on the price of the underlying stock upon conversion. Figure 3.10 shows the payoff structure in terms of common shares received by the DECS investors. If ABC's stock price has declined below the EUR 100 lower conversion price, typically the issue price, investors receive the maximum number of shares.

Maximum number of shares = DECS notional/Minimum conversion price
Maximum number of shares = EUR 1 billion/EUR 100 = 10 million shares

If ABC's stock price at maturity is between the lower conversion price and the upper conversion price, then investors receive shares worth the DECS notional:

Shares received = DECS notional/Share price at conversion
Shares received = EUR 1 billion/Share price at conversion

If ABC's stock price at maturity is above the upper conversion price (i.e., the upper strike price), investors receive the minimum number of shares:

Minimum number of shares = DECS notional/Maximum conversion price
Minimum number of shares = EUR 1 billion/EUR 120 = 8.33 million shares

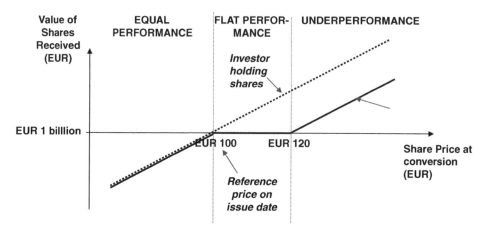

Figure 3.11   DECS's value of converted shares from an investor point of view.

3.11.2   Anatomy of a DECS

Let us analyze the DECS from an investor point of view using our previous example. Let us assume that the whole issue was acquired by one investor and that he/she holds the DECS until maturity. The investor would be investing EUR 1 billion in the DECS on issue date, receiving the 8% coupon during the life of the bond, getting the underlying shares upon conversion and selling the shares immediately after conversion. The value of the investment at maturity has the profile depicted in Figure 3.11. The graph shows the value of the investment at maturity as a function of the underlying share price at maturity, ignoring the DECS coupon. The graph also shows a EUR 1 billion investment in the underlying stock (i.e., an investment in 10 million shares), ignoring dividends. We can split the graph into three different areas:

- An **equal performance** area, in which the investment in the DECS resembles an investment in the underlying shares. In this area the share price at maturity is below the lower conversion price (or the share price at issuance). Upon the DECS conversion, the investor would be receiving 10 million shares. These shares will then be sold in the market, generating a loss. Ignoring the coupon, the investment would be equivalent to having invested in 10 million shares from the beginning. However, the investor received an 8% coupon, probably a much higher yield than the underlying shares dividend. Therefore all things taken into account, the investor was better off investing in the DECS rather than buying the underlying shares.
- A **flat** area, in which the investment in the DECS resembles no investment at all (or to be precise, an investment in a non-convertible bond). In this area, the share price at maturity is between the lower and upper conversion prices. Let us assume that the shares are trading at EUR 110 at maturity. Upon conversion, the investor receives 9,090,909 shares (= EUR 1 billion/110). The investor would then sell the shares in the market, receiving EUR 1 billion (= 9,090,909 shares × 110). Therefore, the investor receives an amount equal to his original investment, so it is like the investor had not invested in the DECS. However, during the life of the DECS the investor received the 8% coupon. Thus, all things being taken into account,

it is like an investment in a straight bond that pays an 8% coupon. Ignoring coupons and dividends, the investor would have been better off investing in the underlying shares rather than investing in the DECS.

- An **underperformance** area, in which the investment in the DECS resembles an investment in the shares acquired at the upper conversion price. In this area, the share price at maturity is above the upper conversion price. Let us assume that the shares are trading at EUR 150 at maturity. Upon conversion, the investor receives 8,333,333 shares (= EUR 1 billion/120). The investor would then sell the shares in the market, receiving approximately EUR 1.25 billion (= 8,333,333 shares × 150), realizing a EUR 250 million [= 8,333,333 shares × (150 – 120)] profit. Therefore, the investment in the DECS is like an investment in 8,333,333 shares acquired at EUR 120. The investor would have been better off investing directly in the underlying shares: the investor would have invested in 10 million shares at EUR 100, realizing a EUR 500 million [= 10 million shares × (150 – 100)] profit. However, we also need to take into consideration the DECS's 8% coupon relative to the stock dividends, which would have diminished the underperformance.

3.11.3 Embedded Derivatives in a DECS

From an issuer's point of view, the DECS mandatory can be viewed as a forward sale of the maximum number of shares plus the purchase of a call spread (see Figure 3.12), plus a string of coupon payments. The option premium from the purchase of the call spread is then paid to the investor in the form of higher coupon payments. Therefore, the present value of the yield pick-up (the amount by which the DECS yield exceeds the yield of a same maturity non-convertible debt from the same issuer) equals the premium of the call spread.

The call spread can be split into a purchased call with a lower strike and a sold call with a higher strike and lower number of options. DECS typically set the lower conversion price at the level of the common shares price at the time of issuance, which is the price at which the purchased call in the call spread is struck (i.e., the lower strike). At issuance, the mandatory

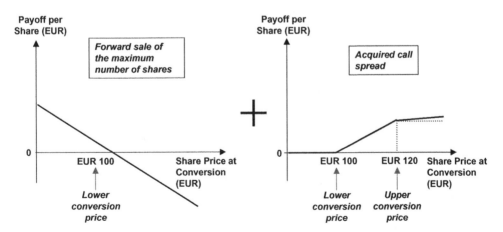

Figure 3.12 DECS embedded derivatives.

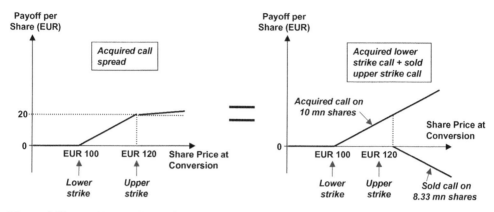

Figure 3.13   DECS embedded call spread.

is priced with a so-called conversion premium, which refers to the strike price of the sold call option (the upper strike). In our example, the lower strike price was set at EUR 100 and the upper strike price was set at 120. Therefore, ABC Corp. was long (i.e., purchased) a call with strike EUR 100 on 10 million shares and was short (i.e., sold) a call with strike EUR 120 on 8.33 million shares, as shown in Figure 3.13.

From an investor point of view, the DECS mandatory can be viewed as containing one forward purchase of the maximum number of shares and the sale of a call spread that partially limits equity upside. In exchange for the loss of a portion of the shares' upside, the investor receives a high periodic coupon.

3.11.4   Pricing a DECS

Previously, we saw that a DECS mandatory can be viewed as a forward sale of the maximum number of shares plus the purchase of a call spread plus a string of coupon payments. The sum of the present value of each component has to equal zero. Therefore:

$$PV(\text{Forward sale}) + \text{Call spread premium} - PV(\text{Coupon string}) = 0$$

3.12   CASE STUDY: UBS's DECS

This case walks through the mechanics of variable parity mandatory convertibles, using a real-life example of a DECS.

On 9 December 2007, UBS entered into a binding agreement with the Government of Singapore Investment Corporation Pte Ltd and an investor from the Middle East to issue mandatory convertible notes (MCN) with a face value of CHF 13 billion, subject to the approval of a capital increase by an EGM of UBS shareholders. At the EGM held on 27 February 2008, UBS's shareholders approved a conditional capital increase to issue up to 277,750,000 new shares to satisfy the conversion into UBS shares of the MCN.

On 5 March 2008, the Swiss bank UBS issued the MCN with a face value of CHF 13 billion. The terms of the MCN are outlined in the following table:

UBS's Mandatory Convertible Bond Terms

Issuer	UBS Convertible Securities (Jersey) Ltd
Notional	CHF 13 billion
Issue date	5-March-2008
Maturity date	5-March-2010 (i.e., 2 years from issue date)
	Potential early termination possible under certain circumstances)
Coupon	9% of notional, payable annually each 5th March
Reference price	CHF 51.48
	The reference price was set as the average of (i) and (ii) but not more than 10% higher or lower than (i):
	(i) closing price on 7-December-2007: CHF 57.2
	(ii) volume-weighted average price over three days before the EGM
Final price	Share price at maturity
Minimum conversion price	CHF 51.48 (100% of the reference price)
Maximum conversion price	CHF 60.23 (117% of the reference price)
Conversion at maturity	The mandatory convertible notes will be redeemed via conversion into a number of UBS shares, according to the following schedule:
	If final price is at or below the minimum conversion price:
	Notional/Minimum conversion price
	If final price is above the minimum conversion price and below the maximum conversion price:
	Notional/Final price
	If final price is at or above the maximum conversion price:
	Notional/Maximum conversion price
Voluntary early conversion by the holder	The holder can convert the MCN early, starting six months following the payment date and ending on 20th trading day prior to the maturity date
Anti-dilution provisions	If UBS A.G. issues new capital and the issue price of the new shares is below 95% of the market price, the conversion price would have to be adjusted for the value of the subscription rights. As a result, both the minimum and the maximum conversion price would be adjusted downwards
	If UBS A.G. issues new capital in excess of CHF 5 billion at a share price below the minimum conversion price, a reduction of the maximum conversion price would be triggered. If the new shares are issued at an offering price below CHF 44, the conversion price would be fixed at the level of the minimum conversion price and the maximum conversion price would fall away

---

If the MCN was converted at maturity, it would be converted for UBS shares at a price, called the "conversion price", linked to the prevailing market price of UBS shares on conversion date. The total amount of shares that the MCN holders would receive would then be calculated by dividing CHF 13 billion by the conversion price. The conversion price was set within a range of CHF 51.48 (the minimum conversion price) and CHF 60.23 (the maximum conversion price). There are basically three different scenarios for conversion at maturity (see Figure 3.14):

- If the prevailing share price was at or above the maximum conversion price – CHF 60.23 – the conversion price would be CHF 60.23. In this case the MCN holders would receive 215,839,283 shares (= 13 billion/60.23), the minimum number of shares.

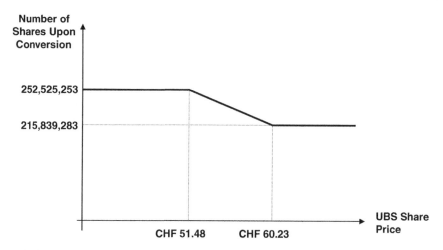

Figure 3.14   UBS's DECS shares delivered upon conversion.

- If the prevailing share price was below CHF 60.23 and above the minimum conversion price – CHF 51.48 – the conversion price would be the prevailing share price. In this case the MCN holders would receive a number of shares calculated as 13 billion/share price.
- If the prevailing share price was at or below CHF 51.48, the conversion price would be CHF 51.48. In this case the MCN holders would receive 252,525,253 shares (= 13 billion/51.48), the maximum number of shares.

Through the lifetime of the MCN, the holders would receive an annual coupon of 9% of the nominal.

3.13   SPECIAL CLAUSES IN CONVERTIBLES

3.13.1   Dividend Protection Clauses

Each time a dividend is distributed to the underlying stock of a convertible/exchangeable bond, its bond holders are penalized for any excess of this actual dividend relative to the dividend assumed when the convertible was priced. As a result, convertible/exchangeable bonds commonly include dividend protection clauses. Compensations to the bond holders due to dividend protection mechanisms can be made in the form of cash, which will prevent any further dilution, or via an adjustment of the conversion ratio/price, which may be more appealing to the rating agencies. A dividend protection clause can take several forms:

- A **dividend pass-through** mechanism, in which all ordinary and extraordinary dividends, in cash or in kind, distributed to the underlying are being passed directly to the bond holders proportionately to their bond holding. The inclusion of a dividend pass-through mechanism results in a lower fixed coupon because during the life of the investment the bond holders are expected to receive the dividends in addition to the coupons. The compensation to the bond holders can be executed either through a payment in cash – via an additional coupon – or through an adjustment to the conversion ratio.
- A **dividend threshold** mechanism, in which any excess ordinary and extraordinary dividends distributed to the underlying relative to an assumed string of dividends are passed to

the bond holders. At inception, a discrete chain of dividends is assumed and used to price the convertible. Any distributions to the underlying shares in excess of this pre-defined dividend chain threshold are passed to the bond holders either in cash or through an adjustment of the conversion ratio.

- A combination of dividend pass-through and dividend threshold mechanisms.

Dividend pass-through mechanisms are uncommon in convertible or mandatory convertible bonds. Even if the issuer of these bonds holds all the underlying shares in its balance sheet, it is not going to receive dividends on these shares because issuers do not distribute dividends to its treasury shares. As a result, any compensation paid to the bond holders through a dividend pass-through mechanism would require the issuer to pay it out of its own cash resources, penalizing the issuer.

Dividend threshold mechanisms are commonly included. At issuance, the chain of discrete dividends assumed is usually based on analysts' consensus estimates for the underlying stock. The assumed chain of discrete dividends is disclosed in the terms and conditions of the convertible/exchangeable.

Under both dividend pass-through mechanisms and dividend threshold mechanisms in convertible bonds, it is unlikely that the dividend compensation is implemented through a cash payment to the bond holders because it would require the computation of the delta of the conversion right, a parameter not directly observable in the market. Therefore, most dividend compensations in convertible bonds take place as an adjustment to the conversion ratio, and hence to the conversion price. This is not the case in mandatory convertible bonds, especially in fixed parity mandatory convertibles, that have a delta of 100% (or close to 100%). Thus, in mandatory convertible bonds, a transparent dividend compensation in cash may be implemented.

Sometimes, the dividend compensation passed to the bond holders contains a discount relative to the theoretical dividend compensation. This is often the case in dividend pass-through mechanisms. For example, an issuer of an exchangeable bond may suffer a withholding tax when receiving dividends on the underlying shares. In order to avoid being exposed to a dividend risk, the issuer may include a discount to the theoretical compensation. This discount takes into account the taxes levied on the actual dividends.

3.13.2 Coupon Deferral Clauses

One of the motivations for issuers of convertible or mandatory convertible bonds is to increase the equity credit from rating agencies. In order to increase equity recognition, convertibles sometimes include coupon deferral clauses. These clauses allow an issuer to defer its convertible coupon payments. A deferral is not elected at complete discretion of the issuer, but subject to a set of restrictions, for example:

- The issuer not having announced dividends to its common stock.
- The issuer not receiving bank/insurance regulator approval (for banks and insurance companies).
- The issuer not having bought back or redeemed any of its own stock.
- The issuer not having paid back or paid interest on any convertible securities ranking pari passu to the convertible bond.

Coupon deferral clauses can be structured in the following ways:

- Accumulation of deferred coupons, payable at the earlier of issuer call, takeover event and maturity.
- Acceleration of conversion into the maximum number of shares in the event of default on a coupon payment.
- Payment of the coupon in shares.

3.13.3   Call Option Make-whole Clauses

Sometimes mandatory convertibles include a **make-whole** clause that protects the bond holders in the event of early exercise of the issuer call option. Most make-whole clauses are defined as one of the following two definitions:

- The investor receives a given number of unpaid coupons in one lump sum. This is the most common way to define a make-whole clause. Remember that a mandatory convertible pays a coupon higher than a coupon of comparable straight debt. An early termination of the mandatory convertible implies that the bond holders will not receive the remaining high coupons. A make-whole amount corresponds to the prepayment of the remaining coupons, which the issuer is obliged to pay in case of an early termination of the instrument as a result of the issuer's own actions. In such an event, the issuer is required to make an additional payment that is derived from a formula based either on the present value or the sum of the remaining coupon payments, including any deferred payments.
- The investor gets back the time value that the conversion option had at issuance. For example, if a bond holder paid par for a convertible bond, the time value of the conversion represented 15% of the bond total value at issuance, the bond is called and the bond holder decides to convert, the bond holder would receive the underlying stock plus an extra 15% of the bond issue price.

3.13.4   Change-of-control Make-whole Clauses

Sometimes non-mandatory convertibles include a clause that protects the bond holders in the event of a takeover. If the stock holders of a convertible's underlying stock receive a cash offer for their shares, the stock price suddenly rises to the level of the offer and thereafter the stock price remains stable unless another offer is received. As a result, convertible bond holders can suffer substantial losses because the time value of the conversion option suddenly and completely disappears.

In June 2004 Mandalay Resort stock holders received a cash offer from MGM. Mandalay Resort's convertible did not include a cash takeover protection and their bond holders logged staggering losses. Hedge funds took a long position in the convertible and shorted the common stock. These hedge funds lost money on the short position and did not recover that on the long position because the convertible price did not increase in lock step with the common stock.

A **takeover make-whole** provision, also called **cash change-of-control make-whole** clause, is meant to compensate convertible bond holders for the sudden negation of the remaining option value. A **takeover make-whole** provision is usually triggered in the event the issuer is acquired in a transaction that includes more than a specific percentage, for example 10%, in cash. In such an event, the issuer is required to make an additional payment to the bond holders. Therefore, the cost is absorbed by the acquirer.

3.13.5   Clean-up Call Clauses

Often the terms of a convertible bond include a clause, a **clean-up call** clause, that allows an issuer to redeem the remaining bonds at any time. This right can only be exercised if a percentage of the bonds have already been redeemed, converted/exchanged into stock or repurchased. This percentage is usually set at a high level such as 85–90%. This right can only be exercised for all, but not some only, of the bonds outstanding. The issuer has to provide a minimum number of days' notice, 45 days for example.

3.13.6   Net Share Settlement Clauses

In order to reduce the dilutive effect upon conversion of the bond, a "**net share settlement**" clause may be included in the terms and conditions of a convertible bond. This clause allows a gradual dilution when the stock price exceeds the conversion price. A net share settlement clause lets an issuer of a convertible bond settle up to the convertible's principal amount in cash and pay the conversion option's in-the-money amount in shares. Since the principal amount is redeemed for cash, an issuer will have to refinance the debt upon a call.

The number of shares to be delivered upon conversion is a function of the stock price upon conversion, as follows:

$$\text{Number of shares} = [(\text{Stock price} - \text{Conversion price}) \times \text{Conversion shares}]/\text{Stock price}$$

In the case of Infineon's convertible:

$$\text{Number of shares} = [(\text{Stock price} - 2.61) \times 74.9 \text{ million}]/\text{Stock price}$$

The underlying stock will have to appreciate considerably before the actual shares issued begin to approach the nominal shares underlying the convertible issue. Figure 3.15 shows, for Infineon's convertible, the number of shares to be delivered by Infineon were the net-share settlement clause included in the terms of the bond. For example, with Infineon shares trading at EUR 4.50 upon conversion, 172% of the conversion price, Infineon would need to deliver 31.5 million shares. This number is notably lower than the 74.9 million shares to be delivered were the net-share clause not included in the terms of the bond.

3.14   CONTINGENT CONVERTIBLES: FRESHES, CASHES AND ECNS

The inclusion of structured conversion clauses permits a wide range of structural possibilities to meet issuer needs or investor demand. Contingent convertible bonds, also called "CoCos", are bonds that are mandatorily convertible into common stock in a certain prescribed circumstance, called the triggering event. CoCos begin their life as straight bonds, and absent their triggering event, will behave as such until maturity. CoCos were very popular in the United States because unlike regular convertible bonds their potential dilution was not included in the computation of the diluted number of shares (i.e., CoCos were not included in the diluted earnings per share computation), until conversion. A change in the US accounting standards eliminated the favorable treatment of CoCos relative to regular convertible bonds and, as a consequence, their issuance dried up.

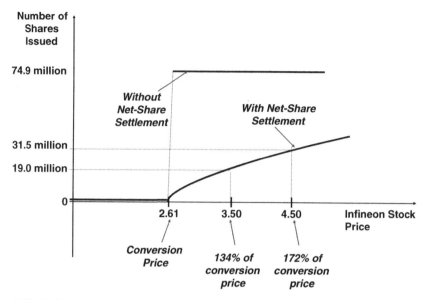

Figure 3.15 Infineon's convertible: shares to be delivered under net-share settlement.

Following the credit crisis of 2007–2008, CoCos became an interesting instrument to enhance bank regulatory capital. Several issues took place in Europe under different names, like FRESH, CASHES and ECN bonds. This section examines three contingent convertible instruments – FRESH, CASHES and ECN. A different type of contingent instrument, the SCN, is described briefly at the end of the section.

FRESH and CASHES are undated highly subordinated mandatory convertible bonds that convert into common stock only after the stock price rises sharply. These instruments do not include a possibility of redemption in cash. Thus, FRESH and CASHES have characteristics of both perpetual bonds and mandatory convertibles, being treated as debt by the tax authorities and as equity by the banking regulators. The bond holders only have a pledge on the underlying shares and can opt to convert their bonds for a fixed number of shares.

ECNs are dated or undated bonds that convert into common stock if the issuer bank regulatory capital falls below a predefined threshold.

3.14.1   Case Study: Fortis's FRESH Instrument

On 7 May 2002, the Belgian/Dutch bank Fortis issued a FRESH (Floating Rate Equity-linked Subordinated Hybrid) instrument through its Luxembourg-domiciled subsidiary Fortfinlux S.A. Fortis used this subsidiary because at that time under Belgian law options with an expiry date of more than 10 years were not permissible. FRESH, a name given by JP Morgan, is essentially a floating rate perpetual bond that mandatorily converts into shares under certain conditions. The instrument represented a combination of four characteristics, including an undated maturity, no redemption in cash, a floating rate coupon and an automatic, as well as optional, exchange into Fortis shares. The issue was intended to strengthen Fortis's solvency, as for regulatory purposes the FRESH was treated as part of Tier 1 capital. The following table summarizes the FRESH bond terms:

Fortis's FRESH Bond Terms	
Issuer	Fortfinlux S.A.
Co-obligors	The parent companies of Fortfinlux S.A.: Fortis S.A./N.V. and Fortis N.V., jointly and severally
Instrument	Floating rate equity-linked subordinated hybrid (FRESH) bond
ISIN code	XS0147484074
Rank	Below all debt and preference shares, but senior to ordinary shares
Issue date	7-May-2002
Notional amount	EUR 1.25 billion
Underlying shares	39.7 million Fortis S.A./N.V. shares
Maturity	Perpetual, subject to acceleration call and exchange right
Coupon	Euribor 3M + 1.35%, paid quarterly each 7th February, May, August and November
Coupon payment	Coupon normally paid in cash, but can be paid in shares to a value of 103% of the cash coupon if (1) no common stock dividend is paid; (2) the common dividend for a fiscal year represents a yield of less than 0.5%; or (3) there is a default on senior-ranking debt
Exchange price	EUR 31.50
Conversion premium	30% premium over the price of Fortis shares on issue date (EUR 24.23)
Issuer call	None
Acceleration call	The bond will automatically be converted if, at any time after the seventh anniversary of the issue date, Fortis stock for 20 consecutive trading days is equal to or greater than 150% of the conversion price (i.e., EUR 47.25)
Issuer put	None
Exercise right by bond holders	At any time from 40 days after the date of issuance, investors have the option to exchange the instruments for Fortis shares at the conversion price
Stock settlement coupon	To be covered later

The FRESH bond was undated and carried a cash coupon of 3-month Euribor plus 1.35% payable quarterly in arrears. The exchange price, EUR 31.50, was set at a 30% premium above the price of Fortis stock on issue date. The FRESH bond was guaranteed by Fortis S.A./N.V. and Fortis N.V., jointly and severally. At any time starting 40 days after the issue, holders of the FRESH bond had the right to exchange the FRESH for Fortis common stock at the exchange price. Furthermore, all the outstanding FRESH bond would be automatically exchanged into Fortis shares if, at any time after the seventh anniversary of the issue date, Fortis stock price traded at or above EUR 47.125, which was equal to 150% of the exchange price, for 20 consecutive trading days. Coupons relating to the FRESH bond ranked junior to any indebtedness or obligation, including preference shares, of the co-obligors, and senior to any common stock of the co-obligors, including the Fortis common stock. The sole recourse of the FRESH bond holders against any of the co-obligors was the underlying shares on which a right of pledge was granted for the benefit of the bond holders.

Concurrently with the issuance of FRESH bonds, Fortis issued 39.68 million new shares for market value (EUR 962 million) to JP Morgan. The shares were subsequently purchased by the issuer – Fortfinlux – and pledged to the collateral agent – JP Morgan – for the benefit of the bond holders.

Simultaneously, Fortis entered into a total return swap with the issuer, giving Fortis the right to the value of the underlying Fortis shares upon conversion, as well as to all future dividends paid on those Fortis shares.

The issue of the bond was intended to be classified as Tier 1 capital by the Belgian banking regulator and to maximize the equity treatment by the rating agencies. That is why the bond included features such as:

- Undated maturity.
- Mandatorily convertible into common stock.
- Subordinated ranking.
- Stock settlement coupon clause.
- No step-up call and put features.

The first main characteristic of the instrument was that it had no maturity date (i.e., was perpetual) and would remain outstanding until conversion.

The second main characteristic of the instrument was that its principal amount would not be paid in cash. The FRESH could be exchanged for Fortis shares at a price of EUR 31.50 per share at the discretion of the bond holder, at any time from the day that was 40 days after the issue date. From 7 May 2009, the bond would be automatically exchanged for Fortis shares at a price of EUR 31.50 per share if the price of the Fortis share was equal to or higher than EUR 47.25 on 20 consecutive trading days.

The third main characteristic of the bond was its subordinated ranking. The FRESH bond constituted direct and subordinated obligations of each Fortfinlux S.A., Fortis S.A./N.V. and Fortis N.V. as co-obligors, jointly and severally. The FRESH was subordinated to all other loans, subordinated loans and preference shares, but ranked senior to ordinary shares.

The sole recourse of the bond holders against any of the co-obligors was the 39.7 million underlying shares that were pledged by the issuer in favor of the bond holders. In other words, in the event of bankruptcy proceedings applicable to all of the co-obligors, the bond holders' sole right with respect to the principal amount of the FRESH bonds was the right to exchange their FRESH bonds for the underlying shares. Notwithstanding the foregoing, in the event of bankruptcy proceedings applicable to all of the co-obligors, the bond holders would continue to have claims for any past due coupons.

The fourth main characteristic of the bond was its stock settlement coupon feature. The bond paid a quarterly cash coupon of Euribor 3-month + 1.35% on the outstanding notional amount. All coupons which were payable during one year after the first announcement by Fortis stating an intention to propose that no dividend on the Fortis shares be declared – or that a dividend be declared that represented a dividend yield in any fiscal year lower than 0.5% – until the day first occurring after the first public announcement by Fortis that a dividend on the Fortis shares that equalled or exceeded in aggregate a 0.5% dividend yield, would be paid in stock (so-called "alternative coupon"). Note that on an annual basis and before Fortis's board of directors decided what dividend it would distribute, Fortis needed authorization from the Belgian bank regulator to distribute such dividend. Therefore, were Fortis solvency to be weak, the FRESH bond holders would be receiving shares rather than cash. The amount of shares would be such that their value represented 103% of the coupon. This obligation was, however, subject to the availability of sufficient authorized capital at the level of both co-obligors. Nonetheless, the co-obligors were contractually obliged to use all reasonable efforts to ensure that there was available at all times authorized capital equal to one year of "alternative coupons".

Any shortfall in the payment of an "alternative coupon" under the FRESH bond in the event of insufficient authorized capital was deferred (so-called "postponement event") until Fortis shareholders approved resolutions for a new authorized capital, at which time the shares would be issued at the then prevailing market price. On the expiry date of the "postponement event", Fortis would be obliged to utilize the remaining authorized capital to pay the "alternative coupon", and hence issue new shares, at the then current market price.

The final main characteristic of the bond was that it had no call and put rights. Neither Fortis nor the FRESH bond holders could redeem the bond early. However, bond holders could convert the bonds into shares. Therefore, the bond would remain outstanding until conversion.

Before this deal, the only proven way to achieve core Tier 1 capital was to issue shares or, in certain jurisdictions and under certain conditions, mandatory convertible bonds. The problem with such instruments was that dividends and, in most jurisdictions, interest coupons on mandatory convertible bonds were not tax-deductible. FRESH bonds solved this problem by combining the mandatory conversion feature, thus complying with banking regulatory capital guidelines and rating agencies' requirements, with no fixed maturity, thereby satisfying the tax authorities. The latter attached importance to the fact that the bonds may never be converted, and thus treated them as debt for tax purposes. As a result, Fortis was allowed to fully deduct the coupon payments.

A legal issue surrounded financial assistance and other capital protection laws in Belgium and Holland. The laws prevented a company from financially assisting the acquisition of its own shares by a third party. Thus, Fortis had to avoid binding itself or providing a guarantee on the bonds, because this could be seen as financially assisting the acquisition of its own shares.

3.14.2   Case Study: Unicredit's CASHES Instrument

By a resolution passed on 5 October 2008, Unicredit's board of directors approved a plan of measures aimed at strengthening Unicredit's capital in a total amount of EUR 3 billion through the issuance of 972 million new shares in a rights issue, and resolved to propose the capital increase to an EGM. Unicredit was Italy's largest bank in terms of assets. The resolution was approved by Unicredit's EGM on 14 November 2008 setting the rights issue offer price at EUR 3.083, equal to the price of the common stock of Unicredit at close of trading on 3 October 2008, which was the last trading day before the meeting of the bank's board of directors on 5 October 2008. The rights issue subscription period started on 5 January 2009 and ended on 23 January 2009. Due to the highly volatile stock market environment, Unicredit's stock price during the rights offering, around EUR 1.30, was notably below the offer price. As a result, most investors balked at buying shares in the rights offer. Only 4.6 million shares were subscribed under the rights issue (0.5% of the total). The unexercised options were later offered by Unicredit on the stock exchange during the period from 9 to 13 February 2009, but none of them were purchased.

The rights issue was fully underwritten by Mediobanca. In performance of the underwriting agreement and in order to ensure a good outcome for the capital increase, Mediobanca had the obligation to underwrite the number of newly issued shares corresponding to any rights remaining unexercised even after the offering of unexercised rights on the stock exchange. On 23 February 2009 Mediobanca subscribed for 967.6 million shares, for a countervalue of EUR 2.983 billion, corresponding to the rights that remained unsubscribed following the rights issue. On the basis of the underwriting agreement a CASHES (Convertible and Subordinated Hybrid Equity-linked Securities) instrument was issued, served by any shares not subscribed under the rights issue. The 967.6 million shares subscribed by Mediobanca were then used as underlying for the issuance of a CASHES bond. On 23 February 2009 Unicredit, through the transaction's fiduciary bank – Bank of New York Luxembourg – issued the CASHES instrument whose terms are summarized in the following table:

Unicredit's CASHES Bond Terms

Issuer	Bank of New York Luxembourg
Obligor	Unicredit S.p.A.
Instrument	Convertible and subordinated hybrid equity-linked securities (CASHES) bond
ISIN code	XS0413650218
Rank	Below all debt and preference shares, but senior to ordinary shares
Issue date	23-February-2009
Notional amount	EUR 2.983 billion
Underlying shares	967.6 million Unicredit shares
Maturity	15-December-2050, subject to acceleration call and exchange right
Coupon	Euribor 3-month plus 4.5%, paid quarterly
Coupon payment	Coupon paid in cash. The coupon will be paid if cash dividends are distributed in relation to Unicredit shares and if profits are shown in the consolidated financial statements for the preceding financial year. Any amount due on any coupon that is not paid, either in full or in part, for any given period is no longer due in any subsequent period
Conversion price	EUR 3.083
Conversion premium	237% (using a EUR 1.30 Unicredit's stock price on issue date)
Acceleration call	The bond will automatically be converted if, at any time after the seventh anniversary of the issue date, Unicredit's stock price for 40 consecutive days is equal to or greater than 150% of the conversion price (i.e., EUR 4.6245)
Exercise right by bond holders	At any time from 40 days after the date of issuance, investors have the option to exchange the instruments for Unicredit shares at the conversion price
Dividend protection	Bond holders would receive pro-rata any amount exceeding a dividend yield of Unicredit of 8%, to be calculated on the basis of the price of the shares recorded during the 30 business days preceding approval of the financial statements

The bond had a notional amount of EUR 3 billion and paid a quarterly coupon, paid in arrears, at a variable rate of Euribor 3-month plus 450 basis points. The coupon was paid if cash dividends were distributed in relation to Unicredit shares and if profits were shown in the consolidated financial statements for the preceding financial year. The coupon was not cumulative. Therefore, any amount due on any coupon that was not paid, either in full or in part, for any given period was no longer due in any subsequent period. Additionally, the CASHES bond holders would receive pro-rata any amount exceeding a dividend yield of Unicredit of 8%, to be calculated on the basis of the price of the shares recorded during the 30 business days preceding approval of the financial statements.

The CASHES had a 15 December 2050 maturity date and did not include the possibility of redemption in cash. However, it could be converted into Unicredit stock. The CASHES had a conversion price fixed at EUR 3.083. Conversion was possible, at the request of the bond holders, at any time starting at least 40 days from the issue date. Conversion would be automatic upon the occurrence of certain events, including the following:

- Following the seventh year after issue, the market price of Unicredit's common stock exceeded 150% of the conversion price (i.e., EUR 4.625, subject to any adjustments), for at least 20 days during any given period of 30 consecutive days.
- Unicredit's aggregate, consolidated or stand-alone capital requirement fell below 5% (or any other threshold set out in the applicable supervisory legislation for the purpose of absorbing losses in innovative capital instruments).
- Unicredit breached any of its payment obligations undertaken pursuant to the usufruct contract.
- Unicredit was/had been declared insolvent or was/had been in liquidation.
- The depositary bank was/had been declared insolvent or was/had been in liquidation.
- The maturity date had been reached.

The CASHES were mostly placed by Mediobanca among the main shareholders of Unicredit (Fondazione Cassa di Risparmio di Verona, Vicenza, Belluno e Ancona; Fondazione Cassa di Risparmio di Torino; Carimonte Holding S.p.A.; the Allianz Group and the Central Bank of Lybia). For them, the main attractiveness of the CASHES bond was its high coupon. The sole recourse of the CASHES bond holders against the obligor with respect to the notional amount was equal to the 967.6 million Unicredit shares that the depositary bank had pledged in favor of such holders.

For bank regulatory purposes, the CASHES bond was treated as part of Tier 1 capital. The CASHES constituted direct and senior obligation of Unicredit.

Building Blocks of the Transaction

The transaction had the following building blocks (see Figure 3.16):

1. Mediobanca subscribed for 967.6 million new shares of Unicredit, for a countervalue of EUR 2.983 billion.
2. Mediobanca transferred to a depositary bank – Mediobanca itself – 967.6 million Unicredit shares. The shares were used to service the issue of the CASHES instrument with a duration that corresponded to the remaining duration of the CASHES. Mediobanca received EUR 2.983 billion for the stock transfer. The role of the depositary bank was to hold the shares until the CASHES conversion and to enter into a series of agreements with the other parties to the transaction to transfer all the risks and rewards of the underlying shares.
3. Bank of New York Luxembourg (BoNY), the fiduciary bank, issued the CASHES and raised EUR 2.983 billion from investors.
4. BoNY, the fiduciary bank, entered into a pledge agreement with the depositary bank. Pursuant to this pledge agreement, BoNY posted as collateral the EUR 2.983 billion collected in the context of the issue of the CASHES, and the depositary bank pledged 967.6 million Unicredit shares – the exchange property – in favor of BoNY.
5. Unicredit and the depositary bank entered into an agreement of usufruct. Pursuant to the agreement, (i) the right to vote attaching to the CASHES underlying shares was suspended for the duration of the usufruct, and (ii) the right to receive dividends attached to the CASHES underlying shares was proportionally attributed to the other Unicredit shares. In this manner, the contractual framework governing the usufruct took into account a possible application by analogy of the legal framework governing treasury shares, specifically in reference to the right to vote and dividends. The usufruct, and therefore the ensuing sterilization

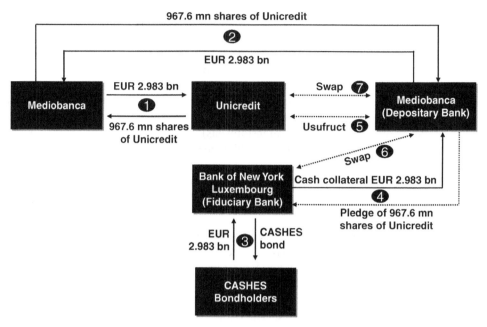

Figure 3.16   Overview of Unicredit's CASHES transaction.

of the right to vote and the right to receive dividends in relation to the CASHES underlying shares, would last until conversion of the CASHES or – in the event the CASHES bond was not converted – for a maximum period of 30 years (which is the maximum duration of usufruct in accordance with the Italian law). Starting from the thirtieth year, in absence of renewal of the agreement of usufruct (and in absence of conversion of the CASHES), Unicredit would have the right to receive from the depository bank an amount equal to the net dividends attached to the CASHES underlying shares, on the basis of the swap contract. As consideration for the right of usufruct, Unicredit undertook to pay to the depositary bank an annual usufruct fee, payable quarterly, equal to 3-month Euribor plus a spread of 450 basis points on the nominal value of the CASHES. Payment of the usufruct fee was expected to be due by Unicredit if cash dividends were distributed in relation to Unicredit shares and if profits were shown in the prior year's consolidated financial statements; which conditions were mirrored in the CASHES.

6. The fiduciary bank, BoNY, and the depositary bank entered into a swap under which the depositary bank would pay to BoNY a cash amount equal to the coupons/dividend protection payments of the CASHES.
7. Unicredit and the depositary bank entered into a swap under which Unicredit would pay to the depositary bank the dividend protection payments of the CASHES and any adjustments of the exchange property under the terms of the CASHES.

It would have been easier if BoNY also acted as depositary bank. The depositary bank would own shares representing 7% of Unicredit's share capital. Two elements prevented BoNY from becoming the depositary bank: (i) such an ownership of Unicredit would require the Bank of Italy's approval and (ii) the entity was not legally entitled to enter into the usufruct and swaps agreements required.

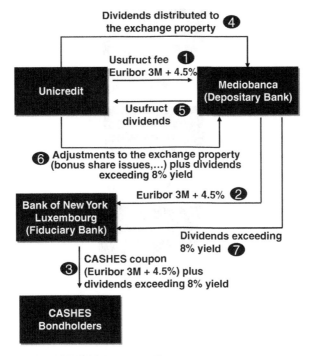

Figure 3.17   Flows during the life of the CASHES.

Flows During the Life of the CASHES

During the life of the transaction, the following flows would take place (see Figure 3.17):

1. Unicredit paid quarterly to the depositary bank the usufruct fee equal to 3-month Euribor plus a spread of 450 basis points on the nominal value of the CASHES. Payment of the usufruct fee was subject to Unicredit distributing cash dividends to its shareholders and reporting a profit in the prior year's consolidated financial statements.
2. The depositary bank paid quarterly to BoNY the amount it received under (1).
3. BoNY paid quarterly as coupon to the CASHES bond holders the amount it received under (2) and under (7). Therefore, BoNY's quarterly payments to the holders of the CASHES substantially corresponded to the payments due to Unicredit in accordance with the usufruct contract. Were Unicredit not to effect the payment it owned pursuant to the agreement of usufruct, BoNY would not pay the coupon to the holders of the CASHES.
4. The depositary bank received the dividends distributed to the underlying Unicredit shares.
5. The depositary bank paid to Unicredit, under the usufruct, the dividends it received under (4).
6. Unicredit paid to the depositary bank, under the swap, any amount exceeding a dividend yield of Unicredit of 8%, to be calculated on the basis of the price of the shares recorded during the 30 business days preceding approval of the financial statements. Also, Unicredit paid the depositary bank any other payments that required adjustment of the exchange property under the terms of the CASHES (bonus share issues, rights issues, etc.).
7. The depositary bank paid to BoNY, under the swap, any dividend amount exceeding a dividend yield of 8%.

Figure 3.18   Cash flows upon conversion of the CASHES.

Cash Flows upon Conversion of the CASHES

Each time a conversion took place, the following flows occurred (see Figure 3.18):

1. The depositary bank delivered to BoNY the exchange property corresponding to the converted bonds. The exchange property consisted of the remaining portion of the original 967.6 million shares of Unicredit plus any adjustments made to these shares as a consequence of corporate events (bonus shares issues, rights issues, etc.).
2. BoNY delivered to the CASHES bond holders the exchange property it received under (1).

Overall Position of the Depositary Bank

It can be seen from the flows analyzed earlier that the depositary bank was not exposed to any risks. The agreements it entered into with the different parties perfectly passed through any flows it received.

- No credit risk to Unicredit because any default by Unicredit would trigger the automatic conversion of the CASHES.
- No credit risk to BoNY as the shares pledged to BoNY by the depositary bank were fully collateralized.
- No market risk to Unicredit shares because they would be delivered to the CASHES bond holders upon conversion.
- No funded position because the acquisition of the shares at inception was financed by the cash collateral received from BoNY under the pledge agreement.
- No impact on its regulatory capital, due to all the previous reasons.

3.14.3   Case Study: Lloyds ECN

In December 2009, Lloyds Banking Group plc ("Lloyds") carried out a capital-raising program to avoid participating in a British government asset protection scheme. The program had an initial target size of GBP 21 billion to be raised through a GBP 13.5 billion rights issue and a GBP 7.5 billion offer to exchange subordinated bonds for ECNs (Enhanced Capital Notes). The ECNs were subordinated debt with maturities ranging from ten years to perpetual maturities. The unique feature of the ECNs was that their contingent conversion condition was not linked to Lloyds' common stock price reaching a certain level nor could they be converted at the discretion of the bond holders. The ECNs automatically converted into Lloyds' common stock if the Group's published consolidated core Tier 1 capital ratio fell to less than 5%. In contrast with FRESH and CASHES, investors would receive common stock at a time when both the capital ratios of the issuer and its stock price were diminished. The ECNs' conversion could add additional selling pressure caused by the former bond holders selling down their newly received stock holdings, accelerating the stock price decline. Another difference from FRESH and CASHES is that ECNs were not convertible into common stock at the option of the bond holder.

The following table shows the main terms of one of the ECNs issued by Lloyds:

Lloyds' ECN Bond Terms	
Issuer	LBG Capital No 1 plc
Guarantor	Lloyds Banking Group plc
Instrument	Enhanced capital notes (ECN) bond
ISIN code	XS0471767276
Rank	Subordinated
Issue date	15-December-2009
Notional amount	USD 1.26 billion
Maturity	Perpetual, subject to call right, redemption due to taxation and redemption for regulatory purposes
Coupon	8% to 15 June 2020; then USD Libor 3-month plus 6.405%, paid quarterly
Conversion price	GBP 0.592093
	The conversion price was calculated as the greater of (i) the VWAP of the stock for the five-day period ending on 17 November 2009 and (ii) 90% of the closing price on 17 November 2009
Call right	Callable at par by issuer on each coupon payment date, commencing on 15 June 2020, redemption due to taxation and redemption for regulatory purposes
Redemption due to taxation	On occurrence of a tax event
Redemption for regulatory purposes	On occurrence of a capital disqualification event
Mandatory conversion	Bond automatically converts into common stock at the conversion price if the Group's published consolidated core Tier 1 capital ratio falls below 5%
Exercise right by bond holders	None

ECNs' Redemption Rights

Lloyds could only redeem the perpetual ECNs early in the following two circumstances:

- A tax event had occurred and was continuing. A tax event was deemed to have occurred if (i) Lloyds was obliged to pay additional tax as a result of a change in UK tax law which could not be avoided by taking reasonable measures, or (ii) as a result of such change in tax law Lloyds would be entitled to (a) a tax deduction in respect of its financing expenses in relation to the ECNs or (b) have any loss resulting from such deduction taken into account when computing the group's tax liabilities, and in each case Lloyds could not avoid the event by taking reasonable measures.

• A capital disqualification event had taken place and was continuing. A capital disqualification event was deemed to have occurred if (i) at any time the ECNs no longer qualified for inclusion in the lower Tier 2 capital of Lloyds, or (ii) at any time the ECNs had ceased to be taken into account for purposes of any "stress test" applied by the British banking regulator in respect of the consolidated core Tier 1 ratio.

Attractiveness of the ECNs to Lloyds

The advantages of the ECNs issue were the following:

1. Concurrently with the ECNs issue, Lloyds launched a gigantic GBP 13.5 billion rights issue in a very difficult market. The ECNs allowed Lloyds to reduce the size of the rights offering.
2. The ECNs were designed to provide capital to Lloyds without being dilutive to shareholders at the time of their issue. The ECNs were eligible to be classified as lower Tier 2 capital. Because the bonds automatically converted if the Group's published consolidated core Tier 1 capital ratio fell below 5%, the ECNs also counted as core Tier 1 capital for the purposes of the British regulator's stress test framework when the stressed projection showed 5% core Tier 1, which was the trigger for conversion into common stock. Of course, the ECNs counted as core Tier 1 following conversion, thereby increasing Lloyds' core Tier 1 capital at such time.
3. The ECNs had embedded countercyclical features at an attractive cost. During the credit crisis of 2007–2008 many banks found themselves with insufficient capital to shield them against the downturn. The ECNs' countercyclical features stemmed from their ability to display loss-absorbing and equity-like qualities if Lloyds reached a low core Tier 1 capital. Lloyds could put in place countercyclical protection while having an attractive cost of capital in prosperous times.
4. The ECNs' coupon payments were tax deductible. In other words, the ECNs were treated as debt for tax purposes.
5. The ECNs were issued in exchange for some of Lloyds' upper Tier 2 capital instruments. The ECNs replaced instruments with high coupon and low regulatory bank capital content.

Attractiveness of the ECNs to Bond Holders

The attractiveness to the bond holders was the ECNs' high coupon. The coupons were set a large premium above the USD Libor interest rates or Lloyds' dividend yield. Our ECN paid a quarterly coupon of 8% to 15 June 2020 and thereafter USD Libor 3-month plus 6.405%.

Another interesting feature to the bond holders was that the ECNs' coupons contained non-discretionary payment provisions. Coupons on contingent convertible instruments are frequently deferrable and non-cumulative, or can be satisfied in common stock. Therefore, Lloyds' ECNs reduced the uncertainty regarding the coupon payments as Lloyds could not waive them. If Lloyds failed to make payment of an ECN coupon, the bond holders could institute legal proceedings against Lloyds to enforce such payment.

3.14.4   Case Study: Rabobank's SCN

This case highlights a version of contingent capital bonds issued by banks to increase their capacity to absorb losses in times of stress. In contrast with contingent convertible bonds, the SCNs are written down rather than being converted into common stock. In this case, the value of the SCN would be written down by 75% and the remaining 25% returned to investors if the issuer's core Tier 1 ratio breached 7%. This instrument is an interesting alternative for unlisted banks.

On 12 March 2010 Rabobank, an unlisted triple-A rated Dutch cooperative bank, issued a EUR 1.25 billion 10-year fixed rate Senior Contingent Note (SCN) issue, priced at an annual coupon of 6.875%. Since Rabobank was unlisted, it was not able to issue instruments that converted into common stock. Instead it issued an instrument that included a "write down" feature to be triggered if a trigger event occurred.

A trigger event occurred if, on any date (called an "initial trigger date") during the period from the issue date to a few days prior to the maturity date, the "equity capital ratio" of Rabobank was less than 7% (as certified by two members of Rabobank's executive board, on behalf of the executive board). Such trigger event had to continue on the date (called the "subsequent trigger test date") falling 20 business days after the initial trigger date to trigger the write-down feature, to allow Rabobank to take measures to restore the ratio.

If a trigger event occurred and was continuing on the relevant "subsequent trigger test date", then (i) the principal amount of the SCN automatically and permanently would be reduced to 25% of their original principal amount, and (ii) Rabobank immediately would redeem the SCN at 25% of the original principal amount together with any outstanding payments.

"Equity capital ratio" was defined as the ratio of the "equity capital" to the "risk-weighted assets", at such time calculated by the issuer on a consolidated basis. On issue date, the equity capital ratio of the Rabobank Group was 12.5%. Rabobank undertook to publish the equity capital ratio at least semiannually.

"Equity capital" was defined as the aggregate EUR amount of all instruments representing capital paid up or contributed to the Rabobank Group by its cooperative members and retained earnings of the Rabobank Group, at such time calculated by the issuer on a consolidated basis in accordance with the accounting standards applicable to the Rabobank Group at such time.

"Risk-weighted assets" were defined as the aggregate EUR amount of all risk-weighted assets of the Rabobank Group, calculated by the issuer on a consolidated basis in accordance with the rules and regulations of the Dutch Central Bank.

The offering was designed to ensure that Rabobank's core capital was strengthened in the very unlikely event that the bank's equity ratio was to fall below 7%. If the SCN principal amount was permanently reduced to 25% of its original principal amount, it would allow the bank to book a gain, enhancing its core Tier 1 capital.

The requirement that, following the trigger of the write-down feature, Rabobank had to redeem the SCN in cash could subject it to liquidity pressure. Rabobank would need to pay EUR 313 million (= 25% × 1.25 billion). Rabobank might need to either borrow or sell some of its assets. Due to the large fall in its core Tier 1 ratio, other banks could be unwilling to lend and any assets to be sold could be subject to liquidity difficulties.

From an investor point of view, the market value of the SCN could show substantial gaps. Because investors in the SCN would suffer a loss of a substantial proportion when the trigger event occurred, any indication that the equity capital ratio was trending toward the trigger event could have a large adverse effect on the market price of the SCN. More precisely, the SCN bond holders were exposed to the fluctuation in the equity capital ratio. As a result, the SCN bond holders were exposed to the variations in Rabobank's equity capital and risk-weighted assets. Because of the nature of the trigger event, it was very difficult to predict with any certainty when or if a write-down would occur, although Rabobank undertook to publish the equity capital ratio at least semiannually. For example, the basis of calculation of the risk-weighted assets could vary due to changes in the relevant rules and regulations of the Dutch Central Bank. Accordingly, trading behavior in respect of the SCN was very different from trading behavior associated with other types of hybrid bond.

However, Rabobank had a triple-A rating as it had always been amongst the most conservative banks in the world. By investing in the SCN bond holders expected Rabobank's unwavering commitment to prudence to continue for the following ten years.

4

Strategic Equity Transactions around Convertible/Exchangeable Bonds

This chapter examines strategic equity transactions built around convertible or exchangeable bonds. I will start by analyzing the structure around an exchangeable issued with a third-party guarantee. I will continue analyzing how Novartis issued a convertible bond through a third party to avoid a potential tax charge on its own shares. Then, I will analyze how Richemont crystallized gains in a convertible bond investment through warrants. Later, I will describe how Deutsche Bank monetized a stake with an exchangeable and a put option. Next I will analyze strategies to increase or decrease the likelihood of conversion with two cases: one from CSM and another from Microsoft. Next I will describe a transaction that allowed a double issuance of exchangeable bonds. I will continue with Cap Gemini's repurchase of conversion rights and repurchases of convertible bonds. Finally, I will give an example of pre-IPO convertible bonds.

4.1 ISSUING AN EXCHANGEABLE WITH A THIRD-PARTY GUARANTEE

4.1.1 Case Study: Controlinveste's Exchangeable Bonds on Portugal Telecom

Sometimes a private entity owns a substantial stake in a public company. A common thread of these private entities is the following: the founder and majority owner of a privately owned successful business acquires a significant stake in a publicly traded blue chip to diversify his/her assets. In a weak market environment, the owner wants to raise financing, but he/she is unwilling to sell the stake because its stock price is too low. One alternative is to raise financing by issuing an exchangeable bond on the stake, but the issuer will be a company which is not known to institutional investors, is unrated and is difficult to analyze. However, the owner and his/her companies are well known by a bank that has witnessed the expansion of the private entrepreneur's empire since its beginnings. One solution to raise financing is for the private entity to issue an exchangeable bond guaranteed by the bank. In order to cover the intricacies of exchangeable bonds guaranteed by third parties I will next dissect a real-life transaction.

In January 2010 Controlinveste International Finance ("the issuer") issued an exchangeable bond into shares of Portugal Telecom and guaranteed by Banco Comercial Portugues ("BCP"). Controlinveste was one of the largest media groups in Portugal, controlled by the entrepreneur Joaquim Oliveira. The exchangeable had the following main terms:

Controlinveste's Exchangeable Bond Terms

Issuer	Controlinveste International Finance, a wholly owned subsidiary of Controlinveste International
Guarantor	Banco Comercial Portugues S.A.
Rating	BBB+ by Standard and Poor's
Notional amount	EUR 224 million
Redemption amount	100% of notional amount
Denomination	EUR 50,000
Issue date	28-January-2010
Maturity	28-January-2015 (i.e., 5 years)
Underlying stock	Portugal Telecom, SGPS, S.A.
Issue price	100%
Coupon	3%, annual Act/Act
Exchange price	EUR 10.97
Underlying number of shares	20.42 million (= 224 million/10.97)
Exchange ratio	4,557.885 (= 50,000/10.97)
Exchange premium	35% above the share price at issue
Share price at issue	EUR 8.13
Exchange period	From 22-December-2014 until 7 days prior to the maturity date
Issuer call	None, except clean-up call and tax call
Extraordinary dividend protection	Protection for any cash dividend in excess of the threshold amount (defined below)
Bookrunners	Credit Suisse and Banco Comercial Portugues

4.1.2 Transaction Overview

For the sole purpose of issuing the exchangeable, Controlinveste International S.A.R.L. created Controlinveste International Finance ("the issuer"), a wholly owned SPV incorporated under Luxembourg laws. Controlinveste International was in turn a subsidiary of Controlinveste Communicacoes, SPGS, S.A., which was part of the Controlinveste group. On 27 January 2010, Controlinveste Communicacoes, SPGS, S.A., within a share capital increase through contributions in kind, transferred the ownership of 20.42 million shares of Portugal Telecom corresponding to 2.28% of Portugal Telecom's share capital to Controlinveste International S.A.R.L. ("Controlinveste International").

The structure of the transaction at inception had the following elements (see Figure 4.1):

1. On 28 January 2010, Controlinveste International sold, through a transaction executed over the counter, to the issuer 20.42 million shares of Portugal Telecom in exchange – the exchange property – for EUR 224 million.
2. Simultaneously, the issuer launched an exchangeable bond raising EUR 224 million, the offering size. The maturity of the exchangeable bond was five years. The bonds were issued at 100% of their notional amount and their coupon was 3% per annum, payable annually in arrears. The initial exchange price was set at EUR 10.97, representing a premium of 35% above the volume-weighted average price between launch and pricing.
3. The issuer entered into a dividend swap with Controlinveste International.
4. BCP, acting through its international Madeira branch, acted as guarantor and as custodian bank. BCP guaranteed the principal and coupons of the bond.

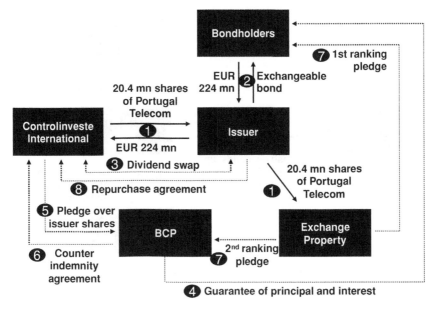

Figure 4.1   Overview of the transaction.

5. Controlinveste International granted a Luxembourg law pledge over 100% of the shares of the issuer to BCP.
6. Controlinveste International also entered into a "counter indemnity agreement" with BCP which gave BCP recourse to Controlinveste International in case payments were made under the guarantee.
7. The issuer granted a first-ranking pledge over the exchange property for the benefit of the bond holders and a second-ranking pledge for the benefit of the guarantor.
8. Controlinveste International and the issuer enter into a "repurchase agreement" that obliged, in case of redemption of the bond, Controlinveste International to reacquire the exchange property in exchange for the redemption amount and the last bond coupon.

4.1.3   Dividend Swap and Transaction Flows during the First Four Years

Under the exchangeable, the issuer had to pay a 3% coupon and its only source of income was the dividend payments distributed to the exchange property. As a result, the issuer was exposed every year to a dividend amount lower than the annual coupon payment. To mitigate this exposure, the issuer entered into a dividend swap with Controlinveste International. Under the terms of the dividend swap the issuer paid any cash dividends received by it in respect of the exchange property (except for any cash dividends paid on or after the fourth anniversary of the issue date). The dividend payments under the swap were limited (i) up to the threshold amount (as defined below) and (ii) up to an amount equivalent to the coupon payments on the bond in return for receiving payments matching the coupon payments of the bonds, except the last regular coupon amount due on the maturity date. In other words, as the issuer had to pass to the bond holders any dividend excess over the dividend yield threshold, this excess was kept by the issuer, and thus, was not paid under the dividend swap. The issuer also kept

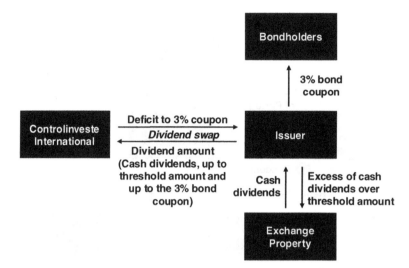

Figure 4.2   Issuer cash flows including the dividend swap, during the first four years.

any dividend amounts up to the 3% coupon. Therefore, under the dividend swap the issuer paid to Controlinveste International the dividend excess over the upcoming 3% coupons, up to the threshold amount. Also under the dividend swap, Controlinveste International paid to the issuer any deficits from the dividends kept by the issuer, so it could meet the 3% coupon payments and the extraordinary dividend protection payments.

Figure 4.2 depicts the issuer cash flows during the lifetime of the bond, except its last year.

Protection for any cash dividend in excess of the threshold amount was added to the exchange property during the first four years of the bond. The threshold amount was the product of (i) the arithmetic average of the daily VWAPs of the underlying stock over a period of five consecutive trading days including and ending on the dividend record date and (ii) the dividend threshold for the relevant financial year. The dividend yield threshold in respect of each financial year was:

- Financial year ending 31 December 2009: 7%.
- Financial year ending 31 December 2010: 7%.
- Financial year ending 31 December 2011: 7%.
- Financial year ending 31 December 2012: 5%.
- Financial year ending 31 December 2013: 5%.
- Financial year ending 31 December 2014: none.

The obligations of Controlinveste International under the dividend swap constituted unsubordinated and unsecured obligations of Controlinveste International ranking pari passu with all present and future unsecured and unsubordinated obligations of Controlinveste International.

Note that under the dividend swap, the issuer did not have to pay any "dividend amounts" on or after the fourth anniversary of the bond, and that Controlinveste International did not have to pay any "deficit amount" on the bond maturity date. The coupon payable on the maturity date was financed via the repurchase agreement (explained below) while any cash dividends received on or after the fourth anniversary of the bond were paid as dividend on the issuer's shares held by Controlinveste International.

If Controlinveste International did not pay the "deficit amount" on time for the issuer to pay the coupon, with the result that the full coupon was not paid by the issuer on the due date, the trustee would have demanded payment of the unpaid coupon amount from the guarantor under the guarantee and the guarantor would have been required to make payment of the relevant coupon amount within two business days following such demand.

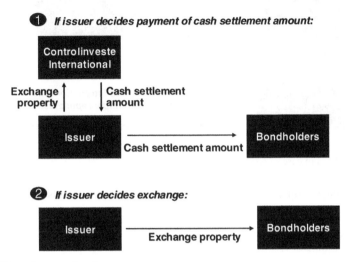

Figure 4.3   Flows in case of exchange.

4.1.4   Transaction Flows in Case of Exchanges or at Maturity

From 22 December 2014 and up to seven days prior to the maturity date, the bond holders could exercise their conversion right. If Portugal Telecom stock price was above the EUR 10.97 exchange price minus the per-share sum of the excess dividends above the threshold amounts (accumulated during the first four years), the bond holders would elect to exchange the bond for Portugal Telecom stock. The issuer then had the option to either deliver the exchange property or to pay a cash amount (see Figure 4.3). The cash amount represented the market value of the exchange property, including any accumulated excess amounts. The cash amount was calculated as the product of (i) the arithmetic average of the VWAP of the stock over five days starting on the fifth trading day after the relevant exchange date and (ii) the number of shares included in the exchange property.

Bond holders not exercising their exchange right received the final coupon and the redemption amount on the maturity date (see Figure 4.4). Pursuant to the repurchase agreement, Controlinveste International had the obligation to repurchase the exchange property for a cash amount equal to the sum of (i) the outstanding aggregate notional amount of the bond and (ii) the last coupon due on the maturity date. Controlinveste International had to pay to the issuer the cash amount on the third business day before the maturity date. If Controlinveste International failed to pay the cash amount on such date, BCP would have had to purchase the exchange property for the cash amount on the second business day immediately prior to the maturity date.

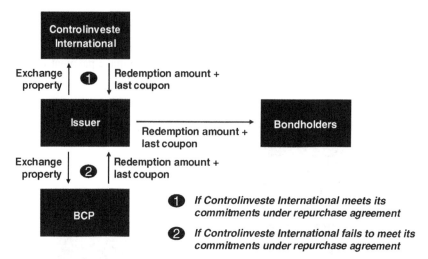

Figure 4.4   Flows in case of redemption.

4.1.5   Exchange Property Pledge and other Security Mechanisms

The exchange property initially comprised 20.42 million ordinary shares of Portugal Telecom. The exchange property was owned by the issuer. There were two pledges over the exchange property (see Figure 4.5):

- A first-ranking pledge in favor of the bond holders. This pledge made sure that upon conversion the bond holders would receive the underlying shares by preventing the issuer from selling the shares or using them for transactions other than the exchangeable during the exchangeable bond's life.
- A second-ranking pledge in favor of the guarantor. If the bond holders redeemed the bonds for cash, BCP guaranteed that the issuer would repay the bond holders. In case of the issuer becoming insolvent, BCP would be exposed to the issuer. To reduce this exposure, the exchange property was pledged on a secondary basis in favor of BCP. If the issuer did not meet its obligations upon the bond redemption, BCP would take ownership of the exchange property and would sell the shares to partially or totally mitigate BCP's exposure to the issuer.

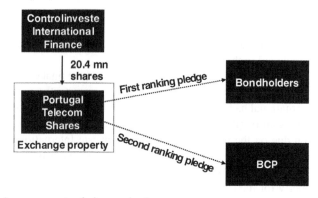

Figure 4.5   Exchange property pledge mechanism.

Because the issuer, Controlinveste International Finance, was an SPV, BCP needed an agreement – the counter indemnity agreement – to give it recourse to Controlinveste International in case payments were made under the guarantee.

4.1.6 Attractiveness of the Transaction to the Issuer and to BCP

The issuer took advantage of a strong demand for convertible/exchangeable instruments at the beginning of 2010. As a result, the issuer was able to obtain very favorable terms. Additionally, if the bond were exchanged for stock, the issuer would have effectively sold its stake at a 35% premium.

BCP, the guarantor, was able to reduce its overall exposure to Controlinveste. The proceeds of the exchangeable were used to partially repay debt owed to BCP. In this way, BCP replaced unsecured senior debt with senior debt backed by Portugal Telecom shares. This collateral was relatively liquid, allowing BCP to hedge its exposure, if wanted, by for example buying puts on Portugal Telecom. Additionally, BCP charged a fee for the guarantee.

4.2 ISSUING A CONVERTIBLE THROUGH A THIRD PARTY

4.2.1 Case Study: Novartis LEPOs and Put Options with Deutsche Bank

This case shows how Novartis entered into a structured transaction with Deutsche Bank to allow it to avoid paying a 53% withholding tax on 55 million treasury shares. The case also shows a way to structure the issuance of a convertible bond through a third party. Finally, the case highlights the implications of a zero-coupon feature on a convertible/exchangeable conversion price and the motivations for investors for investing in such bonds.

In December 2001, Novartis needed to use treasury shares as the underlying of an equity-linked transaction in order to avoid an unfavorable tax countdown. Under Swiss law, a company had to pay withholding tax of 53% if it held its own stock for more than six years. The treasury stock owned by Novartis was acquired in a previous CHF 4 billion buyback program that prevented Novartis from selling its treasury shares before the moment the withholding tax would trigger. However, the 53% withholding tax was not levied if a company reserved the stock for its use in an equity-linked transaction. The transaction helped Novartis to stop the tax clock for the time being.

One alternative for Novartis would have been to directly issue a convertible bond. The issuance of a convertible bond would have increased Novartis debt. However, being an AAA-rated company, Novartis was not keen to increase its leverage to solve a tax problem.

4.2.2 Transaction Overview

In December 2001, Novartis sold a total of 55 million 10-year call LEPO ("Low Exercise Price Options") options on Novartis shares, with an exercise price of CHF 0.01, to Deutsche Bank. Novartis received EUR 2.2 billion in proceeds (i.e., EUR 40 per LEPO). Simultaneously, Novartis sold a total of 55 million 9- and 10-year put options on Novartis shares to Deutsche Bank with an initial exercise price of EUR 51. Novartis received EUR 0.6 billion in proceeds (i.e., EUR 11 per put option). Overall, Novartis received EUR 2.8 billion from the sale of the two options.

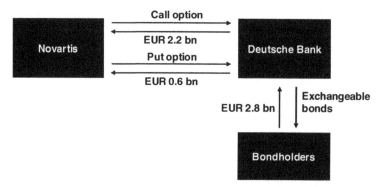

Figure 4.6   Transaction flows at inception.

The position was, in turn, resold by Deutsche Bank in the market through the issuance of two exchangeable bonds into Novartis stock. The exchangeable issuance allowed Deutsche Bank to offload most of its options exposure. The new offering consisted of two zero-coupon bonds that could be redeemed at a premium to their sale price. This deal was offered in two equally sized tranches of EUR 1.4 billion: one maturing in 2010 with a 3.125% effective yield and another maturing in 2011 with a 2.75% effective yield. Each bond came to the market with a 28.2% initial conversion premium. Figure 4.6 illustrates the transaction flows at inception. The following table summarizes the terms of the exchangeables:

Deutsche Bank's Exchangeable Bonds into Novartis	
Issuer	Deutsche Bank Finance N.V.
Guarantor	Deutsche Bank A.G.
Form of security	Bonds exchangeable into ordinary Novartis common stock
Size	Total size EUR 2.8 billion
	Tranche-2010: EUR 1.4 billion
	Tranche-2011: EUR 1.4 billion
Status	Senior, unsubordinated and unsecured
Maturity	Tranche-2010: 9 years (6-December-2010)
	Tranche-2011: 10 years (6-December-2011)
Issue price	100% of par (both tranches)
Coupon	Zero (both tranches)
Yield to maturity	Tranche-2010: 3.125% (annual)
	Tranche-2011: 2.75% (annual)
Redemption price	Tranche-2010: 131.9% of par (= EUR 1.8466 billion)
	Tranche-2011: 131.2% of par (= EUR 1.8368 billion)
Exchange price	EUR 51.00
Exchange premium	28.2% premium over the EUR 39.78 share price at pricing (both tranches)
Put features	Tranche-2010: Puttable in years 4 (at 113.1%) and 6 (at 120.28%)
	Tranche-2011: Puttable in years 3 (at 108.48%), 5 (at 114.53%) and 7 (at 120.91%)
Call features	Not callable for 3 years, thereafter callable at the accreted notional amount subject to the Novartis shares trading at 130% of the accreted notional amount

Deutsche Bank's Exchangeable Bonds into Novartis	
	Hard callable from year 5 (both tranches)
Use of proceeds	General corporate purposes
Other provisions	Issuer's cash-out option, takeover protection (at bond holders option put at 105% or substitution into new entity), anti-dilution protection, extraordinary dividend protection (3% threshold), no tax gross up, tax, legal, accounting and regulatory call at greater of market value and accreted principal amount, clean-up call (25%)

4.2.3 Deutsche Bank's Exposure to Novartis's Stock Price

Let us take a look at Deutsche Bank's flows at inception:

- Deutsche Bank bought a call with strike almost zero (CHF 0.01) on 55 million shares of Novartis. The bank paid EUR 40 per option, or a total of EUR 2.2 billion.
- Deutsche Bank bought a put with strike EUR 51 on 55 million shares of Novartis. The bank paid EUR 11 per option or a total of EUR 0.6 billion.
- Deutsche Bank issued the two exchangeable bonds, raising EUR 2.8 billion.

As a result, Deutsche Bank's cash position at inception was flat ($=-2.2$ billion -0.6 billion $+2.8$ billion).

In order to match the exchangeable bond redemption amounts, were the bond holders to exercise their bond put rights, the equity puts traded between Novartis and Deutsche Bank had an increasing strike profile:

- The 9-year put had an initial strike of EUR 51.00. The put could be exercised at the end of years 4 and 6, and at maturity. The put strike increased to EUR 57.68 in year 4 ($= 113.1\% \times 51$), EUR 61.34 in year 6 ($= 120.28\% \times 51$), and EUR 67.27 at maturity ($= 131.9\% \times 51$).
- The 10-year put had an initial strike of EUR 51.00. The put could be exercised at the end of years 3, 5 and 7, and at maturity. The put strike increased to EUR 55.32 ($= 108.48\% \times 51$) in year 3, EUR 58.41 ($= 114.53\% \times 51$) in year 5, EUR 61.66 ($= 120.91\% \times 51$) in year 7 and EUR 66.91 ($= 131.2\% \times 51$) at maturity.

Let us take a look at Deutsche Bank's flows at maturity, assuming both bonds were redeemed for cash at their respective maturities:

- Deutsche Bank would exercise the call, receiving 55 million shares of Novartis and paying to Novartis CHF 550,000 ($= 0.01 \times 55$ million). Due to its small size, I will ignore this payment in the upcoming calculations.
- Deutsche Bank would exercise the 9-year put, delivering 27.5 million ($= 55$ million/2) shares of Novartis and receiving from Novartis EUR 1.85 billion ($= 67.27 \times 27.5$ million).
- Deutsche Bank would exercise the 10-year put, delivering 27.5 million ($= 55$ million/2) shares of Novartis and receiving from Novartis EUR 1.84 billion ($= 66.91 \times 27.5$ million).
- Because the first bond redemption price was 131.9% of par, the first bond would be redeemed for EUR 1.85 billion ($= 131.9\% \times 1.4$ billion).
- Because the second bond redemption price was 131.2% of par, the second bond would be redeemed for EUR 1.84 billion ($= 131.2\% \times 1.4$ billion).

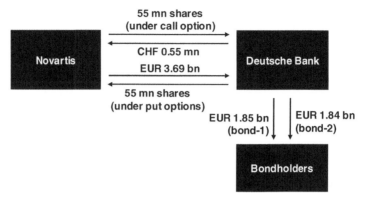

Figure 4.7   Transaction flows at maturity, assuming redemption.

As a result, Deutsche Bank's cash and stock positions at maturity in case of the bonds' redemption was flat (= 0 billion + 1.85 billion + 1.84 billion − 1.85 billion − 1.84 billion), as shown in Figure 4.7.

Let us take a look at Deutsche Bank's flows at maturity, assuming bonds were exchanged for Novartis shares at their respective maturities:

• Deutsche Bank would exercise the call, receiving 55 million shares of Novartis and paying to Novartis CHF 550,000 (= 0.01 × 55 million). Due to its small size, I will ignore this payment in the upcoming calculations.
• Deutsche Bank would not exercise the 9-year put.
• Deutsche Bank would not exercise the 10-year put.
• Upon exchange of the first bond, Deutsche Bank would deliver 22.5 million shares to the bond holders.
• Upon exchange of the second bond, Deutsche Bank would deliver 22.5 million shares to the bond holders.

As a result, Deutsche Bank's cash and stock positions at maturity were flat, ignoring the strike amount of the call option, as shown in Figure 4.8.

Therefore, in any scenario, Deutsche Bank's position was neutral. However, this outcome was true if Novartis did not fail to pay the strike amount of the puts upon their exercise.

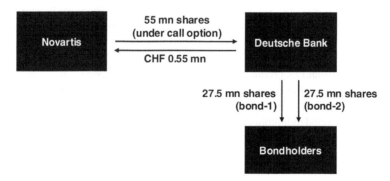

Figure 4.8   Transaction flows at maturity, assuming exchange.

Remember that under the puts Deutsche Bank had the right to sell the shares back to Novartis in exchange for the strike amount. So, if in any scenario Deutsche Bank did not profit, why did it enter into the trade? It was not publicly disclosed but most probably Deutsche Bank received a structuring fee from Novartis for putting in place the transaction. Also, by placing the bonds, Deutsche Bank's place in the convertible lead tables was enhanced, probably improving its chances of being mandated in other convertible deals.

4.2.4   Effect of Deutsche Bank's Zero-coupon Convertibles on the Exchange Price

Zero-coupon convertibles/exchangeables tend to be issued by companies with a high credit rating. In our case, Deutsche Bank's exchangeable did not pay a coupon. Deutsche Bank was rated AA by Standard and Poor's, a very strong credit rating. Instead, the bonds could be redeemed at a premium to their face value, if not exchanged into stock. Zero-coupon convertibles/exchangeables have no current yield. The yield to maturity (or to each put date) is achieved by means of either (i) an issue price at a discount to par and a redemption price at par, or (ii) an issue price at par and a redemption price at a premium to par. In our case, Deutsche Bank exchangeable bonds included the second alternative.

Let us take a look at Deutsche Bank's 2011 exchangeable. The bond was exchangeable into 27.5 million shares of Novartis (= EUR 1.4 billion/EUR 51.00). At maturity, the bond could be redeemed for EUR 1.8368 billion (i.e., 131.2% of par). The effective yield to maturity of the bond was 2.75% $[= 131.2\%^{(1/10)} - 1]$.

The redemption of the bond at a premium meant that at maturity Novartis's stock price had to trade above EUR 66.79 (= EUR 1.8368 billion/27.5 million shares) – the effective exchange price – to elicit bond holders to exchange. The effective exchange price was 31% larger than the initial EUR 51.00 exchange price. Thus, by exchanging the bond into a fixed number of shares, the zero-coupon profile caused the effective exchange price to rise, as shown in Figure 4.9. The graph also shows that the return on the bond remained constant unless the stock price rose a long way.

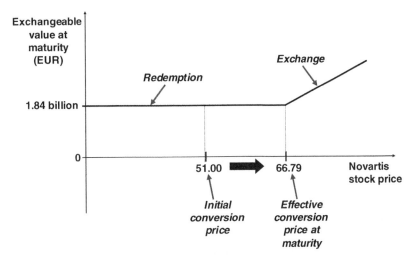

Figure 4.9   Payoff diagram of Deutsche Bank's zero-coupon 10-year exchangeable.

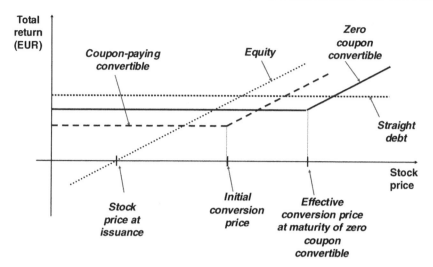

Figure 4.10   Comparison of a zero-coupon convertible total return with other instruments.

4.2.5   Attractiveness of Deutsche Bank's Zero-coupon Exchangeables to Investors

Due to the substantial difference between the conversion price based on the issue price and the conversion price based on the final redemption price, Deutsche Bank's exchangeable bonds were attractive for investors looking for upside equity exposure but with a very large fixed income component. However, for investors looking for a large equity component the bond was notably less attractive. Figure 4.10 compares the total return of a zero-coupon convertible/exchangeable with the total return of a direct investment in equity, a straight bond and a coupon paying convertible/exchangeable. It can be seen that the inclusion of the zero-coupon feature made the bond behave more like a straight bond and less like a direct equity investment.

4.2.6   Advantages to Novartis and Relevance of a Call Right

The transaction had several advantages to Novartis:

- It allowed Novartis to avoid paying a 53% withholding tax on the 55 million treasury shares.
- Under Swiss GAAP, the transaction had a very favorable accounting treatment. It allowed Novartis to account for the transaction as equity, as share premium, a total of EUR 2.8 billion. Novartis accounted for the option premium associated with the call and the put options as an increase in share premium at fair value less related issuance costs.
- It allowed Novartis to avoid accounting for the transaction as debt, protecting its AAA credit rating.

The introduction of a new rule by the US GAAP over the treatment of hedging practices and the adoption of IFRS rules rendered the transaction unattractive. For example, under IFRS the increasing strike profile of the puts obliged Novartis to account for them as derivative instruments instead of as a capital instrument. From 2005, Novartis's profit or loss statement was exposed to changes in the put fair value, notably increasing the volatility of its profit or loss statement. As a result, Novartis redeemed in advance these equity instruments on 26 June 2003. This case also highlights the importance of a call mechanism in a convertible/exchangeable. This bond was not callable for 3 years (i.e., until December 2004). Consequently, the bond could not be called in 2003 and Novartis had to repurchase the exchangeable in the market, paying a significant premium to elicit bond holders to sell their bonds.

4.3 CRYSTALLIZING A GAIN IN A CONVERTIBLE INVESTMENT THROUGH WARRANTS

4.3.1 Case Study: Richemont Warrants Issue on Back of Convertible Preference Shares

This case analyzes how Richemont, a Swiss luxury goods group owning a portfolio of leading international brands including Cartier, Montblanc and Dunhill, effectively crystallized the profit embedded in a subsidiary's holding of a convertible preferred stock through the issue of call warrants exercisable into common stock of British American Tobacco (BAT).

In December 2002 R&R Holdings S.A. (R&R), a Luxembourg-domiciled subsidiary of Richemont, was BAT's largest stock holder. BAT was one of the world's leading tobacco groups. Richemont held 66.7% of R&R and the remaining 33.3% of R&R was owned by Remgro Limited, a South African-listed company. R&R acquired its stock holding in June 1999 upon the merger of BAT and R&R's subsidiary Rothmans International B.V. At the time of the merger, BAT issued to R&R common stock and convertible redeemable preferred stock that equated to approximately 35% of the fully diluted issued common stock of BAT, 25% in ordinary shares and 10% in convertible preferred stock. R&R's voting rights were limited to a maximum of 25% under the terms of the standstill agreement with BAT. Under the terms of the merger agreement between Richemont, Remgro and BAT, the preferred stock could convert into 120.9 million shares of BAT at GBP 6.75 per share, as shown in the following table:

BAT Convertible Preferred Stock	
Issuer	British American Tobacco
Buyer	R&R Holdings S.A.
Issue date	7-June-1999
Instrument	Convertible preference shares
Underlying stock	British American Tobacco ordinary shares
Notional amount	GBP 816 million
Number of shares	120.9 million
Conversion price	GBP 6.75
Maturity	7-June-2004
Exercise date	28-May-2004
Redemption price	100% of notional amount
Other	The preference shares will automatically convert to ordinary shares in BAT if they are sold to the market prior to maturity

The preferred stock would automatically convert into common stock of BAT on a one-for-one basis on any sale of R&R to a third party. Otherwise, the preferred stock would be converted into BAT stock at GBP 6.75 per share on 7 June 2004.

Richemont announced in December 2002 that its subsidiary R&R was to offer 120.9 million secured European-style warrants exercisable at the option of the warrant holder into BAT common stock.

4.3.2 Warrants' Terms

In December 2002 R&R offered 120.9 million secured European-style warrants exercisable at the option of the warrant holder into common stock of BAT. A warrant is an option that is listed on a stock exchange. The warrants' expiration date was 28 May 2004, coinciding with the exercise date of the convertible preferred stock, and their strike was GBP 6.75 per warrant.

R&R Warrants on BAT	
Issuer	R&R Holding S.A.
Announcement date	11-December-2002
Stock	BAT ordinary shares
Warrant type	Call
Style	European
Number of warrants	120.9 million
Exercise price	GBP 6.75
Reference price	GBP 5.98
Conversion premium	12.9%
Exercise date	28-May-2004
Settlement date	7-June-2004
Premium per warrant	GBP 0.3428
Total premium	GBP 41.45 million
Listing	Luxembourg Stock Exchange
Settlement type	Physical delivery

On 28 May 2004, all the holders of the warrants exercised their rights, causing R&R's effective interest in BAT to decline to 18.6%. R&R subsequently exchanged its entire holding of preferred stock for BAT stock. In addition, R&R retained all of its original 25% holding of common stock in BAT.

4.3.3 Analysis of R&R's Position

The issuance of the call warrants realized the value of the conversion rights embedded in the terms of the preferred stock. In June 2004, R&R was to receive GBP 816 million either upon exercise of the warrants by warrant holders or through the redemption of the preferred stock by BAT (see Figure 4.11). The share of these proceeds, either through the disposal or the redemption, attributable to Richemont was to amount to GBP 544 million ($= 816$ million $\times$ 66.7%).

If BAT's stock price on 28 May 2004 was lower than or equal to GBP 6.75, R&R would receive GBP 816 million in cash:

- R&R would not convert the preferred stock, receiving from BAT GBP 816 million in cash.
- The warrant holders would not exercise their warrants. The warrants would expire worthless.

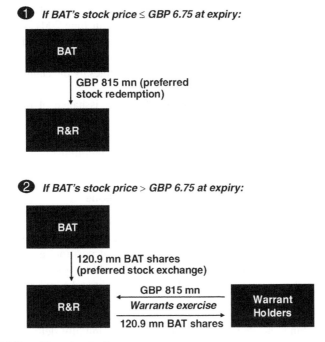

Figure 4.11 R&R position at maturity.

If BAT's stock price on 28 May 2004 was greater than GBP 6.75, R&R would exercise the preferred stock exercise right:

- R&R would convert the preferred stock, receiving from BAT 120.9 million shares of BAT.
- The warrant holders would exercise their warrants, paying GBP 816 million (= 120.9 million × 6.75) to R&R in exchange for 120.9 million shares of BAT.

Additionally, R&R raised GBP 41.45 million from the issuance of the warrants just after 11 December 2002. Thus, in total R&R received GBP 857.45 million (= 816 million + 41.45 million). The share of these proceeds from the disposal or redemption attributable to Richemont totalled GBP 572 million (= 857.45 million × 66.7%).

4.3.4   Main Benefits to Richemont of the Warrants Issue

The main benefits to Richemont (and to R&R) of the transaction were the following:

- It helped R&R to lock in the value of R&R's preferred stock stake. The combination of the preferred stock and the warrants guaranteed that R&R received GBP 816 million at their maturity.
- Richemont booked a EUR 301 million gain. Before the warrants issue, Richemont accounted for the preferred stock as an equity interest. The issue of the warrants irrevocably committed R&R to dispose of the balance of the preferred stock for GBP 816 million, either as a consequence of the exercise of the warrants or through the redemption of the preferred stock by BAT. Reflecting the fixed nature of the proceeds from the overall position, Richemont

accounted for the preferred stock as a debt rather than as an equity interest, carrying it at the discounted present value of the GBP 816 million in June 2004 plus the present value of the preferred stock dividend payments. Richemont also recognized the valuation of the conversion rights embedded within the preferred stock as a liability. The change in fair value of the conversion rights was fully offset at all times by the change in fair value of the warrants.

- R&R received GBP 41.45 million in cash from the issuance of the warrants (i.e., the warrants' premium).
- R&R crystallized the time value of the preferred stock embedded conversion right. The time value was GBP 41.45 million (i.e., the warrants' premium).

4.3.5   Effect on BAT's Stock Price of the Warrants Issue

Hedge funds investing in the warrants needed to sell BAT shares on issue date to initially delta-hedge their position. The initial delta of the warrants was approximately 30%. If all warrant investors were to maintain a delta-neutral initial position, a total of 36 million (= 120.9 million warrants × 30% delta) shares of BAT would be sold on issue date. In order to successfully place the warrants, R&R/Richemont needed to take into account two important facts:

- Firstly, hedge funds needed to borrow the shares to initially delta-hedge their position. Usually the issuer would lend the shares. In our case, R&R directly held 302 million shares of BAT, so it could lend 36 million shares to the hedge funds to accommodate their shorting needs.
- Secondly, the sale of the shares could have a large impact on BAT's stock price. The daily average trading volume of BAT stock was approximately 10 million shares. An uncontrolled sale of 36 million shares could have created a substantial stock overhang, negatively affecting BAT's stock price. In order to avoid a stock overhang, a block trade was organized by the banks managing the issue. They offered to acquire the shares at a 3.4% discount to the stock previous closing price. As a result, BAT's stock price on 11 December 2002 was unaffected by the transaction, closing at GBP 6.20 while the previous day it closed at GBP 6.19.

4.4   MONETIZING A STAKE WITH AN EXCHANGEABLE PLUS A PUT

4.4.1   Case Study: Deutsche Bank's Exchangeable into Brisa

The two most common ways to implement a future disposal of a stake are by entering into an equity derivative (a forward or an equity swap) or by issuing a mandatory convertible. If these two alternatives are not sufficiently attractive, there are other ways to implement it. This case shows how Deutsche Bank acquired a stake in Brisa, the largest Portuguese toll road operator, from the Portuguese State and how Deutsche Bank hedged its exposure by (i) issuing an exchangeable bond into the stake and (ii) buying a put from Brisa. One interesting characteristic of the transaction was that it not only mitigated Deutsche Bank's

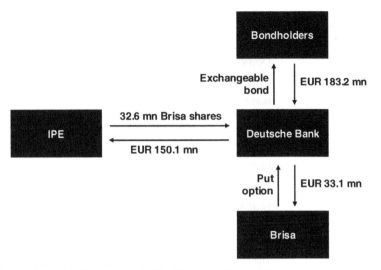

Figure 4.12 Building blocks of Deutsche Bank's transaction on Brisa.

market exposure to Brisa's stock price, but also mitigated Deutsche Bank's credit exposure to Brisa.

4.4.2   Transaction Overview

In November 2002, the Portuguese State-owned holding company Investimentos e Participacoes Empresariais, S.A. (IPE) was looking to sell its remaining 5.7% stake in Brisa comprising 32.6 million shares. IPE was set up in the 1970s to control companies that a revolutionary government seized. The Portuguese government was interested in selling this stake to help it keep its government debt level within the European Union limits. IPE was considering selling the stake through a block trade, but the discount required to place it was too large. In the meantime, Deutsche Bank proposed to IPE a transaction that could optimize such disposal. The transaction had three components (see Figure 4.12):

1. On 10 December 2002, IPE sold to Deutsche Bank its 5.7% stake in Brisa comprising 32.6 million shares. IPE received EUR 150.1 million. The price per share obtained by IPE was EUR 4.60, a small discount to Brisa's stock closing price on the previous day.
2. Simultaneously, Brisa sold to Deutsche Bank a five-year put option on 32.6 million shares of Brisa. The put had a EUR 5.62 strike. Brisa received a EUR 33.1 million premium. At expiry, Brisa could elect to settle the option either in cash or physically. Under the put Brisa would benefit from the appreciation of its stock price and would be exposed to its depreciation.
3. Concurrently with the two previous transactions, Deustche Bank issued a credit-linked bond exchangeable into Brisa stock. The underlying credit risk was to Brisa. The exchangeable bond had a five-year maturity and paid a quarterly coupon. The exchange price was EUR 5.62, coinciding with the strike of the put.

The terms of the exchangeable are outlined in the following table:

Deutsche Bank's Credit-linked Exchangeable Bond into Brisa

Issuer	Deutsche Bank A.G. London
Guarantor	Deutsche Bank A.G.
Issue date	10-December-2002
Settlement date	13-December-2002
Form of security	Bonds exchangeable into ordinary Brisa common stock
Notional amount	EUR 183.2 million
Status	Senior, unsubordinated and unsecured
Maturity	13-December-2007
Issue price	100% of par
Denominations	EUR 100,000
Coupon	Euribor 3-month – 50 bps, paid quarterly, Actual/360
Redemption price	100% of notional amount
Exchange price	EUR 5.62
Initial exchange premium	15%
Stock price at issuance	EUR 4.89
Exchange ratio	17,802.9 shares per denomination
Cash	The issuer shall be entitled upon exercise of the exchange right by a bond holder in lieu of delivery of all or a portion of the shares to pay to the bond holder a cash amount in EUR
Credit-linked clause	If a Brisa credit event occurs, for as long as such event continues, the issuer shall have no obligation to redeem the bond, whether at scheduled maturity or any date of early redemption, or make any interest payments, and interest shall cease to accrue on the bond
Brisa credit event	The occurrence of (i) any application for insolvency, bankruptcy or similar proceedings in respect of Brisa or any material subsidiary of Brisa or if Brisa or any material subsidiary of Brisa reaches an agreement with creditors in respect thereof or to suspend payments or otherwise suspend payments on its debts, (ii) any default or defaults, which continue after any applicable grace period, by Brisa or any material subsidiary of Brisa on payments in the aggregate amount of EUR 20 million or more (or the equivalent in one or more other currencies) in respect of financial indebtedness, or (iii) any default or defaults, which continue after any applicable grace period, by Brisa or any material subsidiary of Brisa in the aggregate amount of EUR 1 million or more owed to the issuer

4.4.3   Analysis of Deutsche Bank's Overall Position

The best way to understand Deutsche Bank's overall position under the transaction is to analyze its flows at maturity under two scenarios: (i) a first scenario in which the bond holders exercised the right to exchange the bond into Brisa shares, and (ii) a second scenario in which the bond is redeemed at its notional amount.

First Scenario at Maturity: Exchange

If, at maturity, Brisa's stock price was above the EUR 5.62 exchange price, the bond holders would exercise their right to exchange the bond into Brisa shares:

- Deutsche Bank would deliver 32.6 million shares of Brisa to the bond holders.
- Deutsche Bank would not exercise the put option.

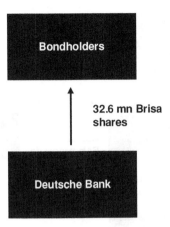

Figure 4.13   Deutsche Bank's flows upon exchange.

Thus, upon exchange, Deutsche Bank would deliver the stake acquired from IPE (see Figure 4.13). No cash would flow among the counterparties to the transaction.

Second Scenario at Maturity: Redemption

If, at maturity, Brisa's stock price was below or at the EUR 5.62 exchange price, the bond holders would not exercise their right to exchange the bond into Brisa shares and the bond would be redeemed. Deutsche Bank would exercise the put option. Brisa had the right to elect to settle the option either physically or in cash.

If Brisa elected physical settlement, the flows would be the following (see Figure 4.14):

- Deutsche Bank would pay the EUR 183.2 million redemption amount to the bond holders.

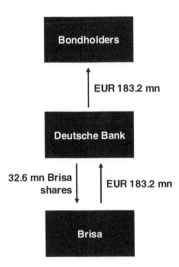

Figure 4.14   Deutsche Bank's flows in case of redemption and put option physically settled.

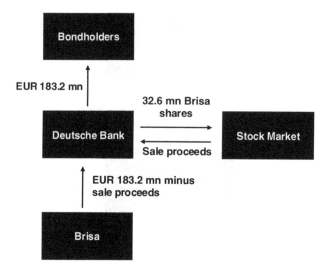

Figure 4.15   Deutsche Bank's flows in case of redemption and put option cash-settled.

• Deutsche Bank would exercise the put option. As Brisa elected physical delivery, Deutsche Bank would deliver to Brisa 32.6 million shares of Brisa and Deutsche Bank would receive from Brisa EUR 183.2 million.

If Brisa elected cash settlement, the flows would be the following (see Figure 4.15):

• Deutsche Bank would pay the EUR 183.2 million redemption amount to the bond holders.
• Deutsche Bank would sell the stake into the market.
• Deutsche Bank would exercise the put option. As Brisa elected cash settlement, Brisa would pay to Deutsche Bank the difference between (i) EUR 183.2 million and (ii) the proceeds from the disposal of the shares in the market.

It was crucial that the volume-weighted average price at which Deutsche Bank would sell its Brisa stake into the market had to coincide with the final price computed under the put option. Otherwise, Deutsche Bank would be exposed to Brisa's stock price as the sum of (i) proceeds from the sale into the market and (ii) the put settlement amount would not equal the bond redemption amount.

Thus, under a redemption scenario Deutsche Bank would sell the stake acquired from IPE either to Brisa under the put or onto the market. If the stake is sold to Brisa, Deutsche Bank would receive EUR 183.2 million from Brisa, and would use this amount to redeem the bond. If, on the other hand, the stake was sold into the market, Deutsche Bank would receive EUR 183.2 million from the combination of the sale into the market and the payoff from the put option, and would use this amount to redeem the bond.

Deutsche Bank's Credit Exposure to Brisa

We just saw that either on redemption or upon exchange, Deutsche Bank did not bear any exposure to Brisa's stock price. This conclusion was true only if Brisa was able to meet its commitments under the put. The put protected Deutsche Bank if, at maturity, the bond holders did not exchange the bond into stock and the stock price was below the exchange price. Let us assume that the bond was redeemed and that Deutsche Bank exercised the put when Brisa was insolvent. Under physical settlement Brisa would fail to pay to Deutsche Bank the EUR 183.2 million strike amount. It would oblige Deutsche Bank to sell the shares in the market and the sale proceeds most probably would be notably lower than the EUR 183.2 million it had to pay to the bond holders. Therefore, an insolvency of Brisa could create substantial losses to Deutsche Bank. To make things worse, there was a high correlation between a low Brisa stock price and Brisa becoming insolvent.

By structuring the exchangeable with a credit-linked feature, Deutsche Bank could mitigate its credit exposure to Brisa. The credit-linked feature of the exchangeable bond offered bond holders a synthetic credit exposure to Brisa. Following a credit event the coupon payments would be stopped and will not accrue. If at maturity Brisa was still insolvent, the bond would not be redeemed. Once all senior claims to Brisa were settled, the bond would be redeemed at its outstanding notional balance adjusted by a percentage – the recovery rate – that represented the percentage of each payment claim that an unsecured and senior creditor of Brisa would have received in respect of such claim in an insolvency, bankruptcy or similar proceeding with respect to Brisa.

4.5 INCREASING LIKELIHOOD OF CONVERSION WITH A CALL SPREAD

4.5.1 Case Study: Chartered Semiconductor's Call Spread with Goldman Sachs

This case shows how a company took advantage of its low stock price to synthetically reduce the conversion price of its existing convertible, as a result increasing the likelihood of issuance of new shares. The case also introduces the call spread strategy.

On 2 April 2001 Chartered Semiconductor Manufacturing (CSM), a Singapore-based technology company, issued a convertible bond with a notional amount of USD 575 million. The redemption price of the bond at maturity was 115.5% of its notional amount (USD 664.1 million). The bond paid a 2.5% coupon. The maturity of the bond was 2 April 2006 (i.e., a 5-year term). The bond was convertible into common stock of CSM at a conversion price of USD 3.09, representing a 33% initial conversion premium. Upon conversion, CSM would deliver 214.8 million new shares to the bond holders. CSM's stock price prevailing at issuance was USD 2.32. Although CSM's stock price was denominated in Singapore dollars, I am using its USD converted price because the convertible bond was denominated in USD. Also because the convertible bond original terms were adjusted to various corporate actions, I have adjusted its terms as of August 2004.

In August 2004, CSM's stock was trading at USD 0.62, well below the USD 2.32 price prevailing at issuance of the convertible bond. At that time, the USD 3.09 conversion price represented approximately a 400% (= 3.09/0.62 – 1) conversion premium. Because CSM core shareholders were already willing to assume the potential dilution resulting upon the bond's conversion, CSM was looking to benefit from an increase in the likelihood of the bond's conversion.

As a result, on 11 August 2004, CSM entered into a compo call spread transaction with Goldman Sachs, with the following terms:

CSM's Call Spread with Goldman Sachs	
Party A	Chartered Semiconductor Manufacturing (CSM)
Party B	Goldman Sachs
Intrument	Compo call spread
Trade date	11-August-2004
Shares	CSM ordinary shares
Number of options/shares	214.8 million
Lower strike call	
Lower strike call buyer	Party B (Goldman Sachs)
Lower strike call seller	Party A (CSM)
Lower strike price	USD 0.93
Settlement type	Cash settlement or physical settlement, at CSM election
Expiry date	From 2-January-2005 to 2-April-2006
Upper strike call	
Upper strike call buyer	Party A (CSM)
Upper strike call seller	Party B (Goldman Sachs)
Upper strike price	USD 3.09
Settlement type	Cash settlement
Expiry date	In coordination with the low strike call exercise
Overall premium	USD 40 million (assumed)
Soft call	To be covered later

CSM sold to Goldman Sachs a USD denominated compo call option on 214.8 million of its shares at a strike price of USD 0.93 per share (the lower strike price). Under the option, Goldman Sachs could purchase 214.8 million CSM shares at an agreed price of USD 0.93. This price represented a premium of 50% to CSM's closing share price on 11 August 2004. The number of shares under the call was equal to the number of shares that were originally planned for issuance under CSM's convertible bond. If the call option was exercised by Goldman Sachs, CSM could settle the option by issuing shares or paying cash to Goldman Sachs. The option was exercisable by Goldman Sachs from 2 January 2005 and expired on 2 April 2006, matching the maturity date of the convertible bond.

Simultaneously, CSM bought from Goldman Sachs a compo call option on 214.8 million of its shares at a strike price of USD 3.09 per share (the upper strike price). The option was cash-settled. By acquiring this call option, CSM effectively bought back the conversion option embedded in the convertible bond. Under the existing terms of the convertible bond, CSM expected the bond to be converted into shares by the bond holders if its share price reached USD 3.09.

4.5.2 Goldman Sachs's Overall Position

Goldman Sachs was long a call spread. A long call spread position was created by buying a call option and selling another call with a higher strike. Both calls were on the same underlying and had the same expiration date.

Goldman Sachs paid a USD 40 million premium for the call spread. This premium was paid upfront (i.e., in August 2004). At expiry there were three scenarios (see Figure 4.16):

• CSM's stock price trading below USD 0.93. Goldman Sachs would have lost the USD 40 million premium paid.

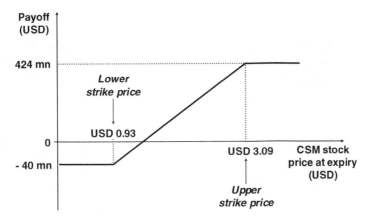

Figure 4.16 Goldman Sachs's overall payoff under the call spread.

- CSM's stock price trading at or above USD 0.93 and below USD 3.09. Goldman Sachs would exercise the lower strike price call but CSM would not exercise the upper strike price call. CSM could elect between settling the lower exercise price call in cash or in shares. Let us assume that CSM elected cash settlement and that CSM traded at USD 3.09, Goldman Sachs would receive from CSM an amount in cash between zero and USD 464 million [= 214.8 million × (3.09 − 0.93)]. Therefore, taking into account the USD 40 million premium paid at inception, the payoff to Goldman Sachs would be between a loss of USD 40 million and a gain of USD 424 million (= 464 million − 40 million).
- CSM's stock price at or above USD 3.09. Both Goldman Sachs and CSM would exercise their calls. Assuming that CSM elected cash settlement under the lower strike price call, Goldman Sachs would receive from CSM an amount in cash equal to: USD [214.8 × (CSM stock price − 0.93)] million. CSM would receive from Goldman Sachs an amount of cash equal to: USD [214.8 × (CSM stock price − 3.09)] million. The sum of these two amounts would result in CSM paying to Goldman Sachs 464 million. Therefore, taking into account the USD 40 million premium paid at inception, the payoff to Goldman Sachs would be a gain of USD 424 million (= 464 million − 40 million).

These calculations are a bit misleading because they do not take into account the cash flows timing differences. Remember that the call spread premium was paid in August 2004 and the option settlement amount was received between January 2005 and April 2006.

4.5.3 CSM's Overall Position

CSM had two positions, one due to its convertible bond issue and a second one due to the call spread. During the exercise period, from 2 January 2005 to 2 April 2006, there were three potential scenarios.

Scenario 1: CSM's Stock Price below USD 0.93

Under this scenario, CSM's flows at expiry will be the following:

- The bond holders will not convert the convertible bond. The bond would be redeemed, paying CSM USD 664.1 million to the bond holders.

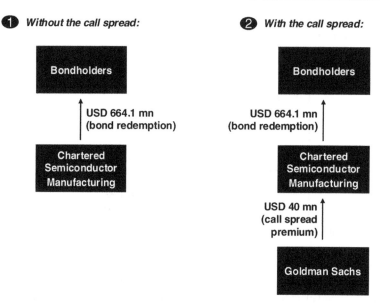

Figure 4.17   CSM's overall flows in scenario 1, without and with the call spread.

- Goldman Sachs will not exercise the lower strike call.
- CSM will not exercise the upper strike call.

As a result, CSM would not issue new shares and CSM would not receive or pay any additional cash through the call spread. However, CSM received a USD 40 million premium for entering into the call spread in August 2004. Figure 4.17 shows CSM's overall flows under this scenario without and with the call spread transaction. It can be seen that CSM was USD 40 million better off by entering into the call spread.

Scenario 2: CSM's Stock Price at or above USD 0.93 and below USD 3.09

CSM's flows under this scenario at expiry will be the following:

- The bond holders will not convert the convertible bond. The bond would be redeemed, paying CSM USD 664.1 million to the bond holders.
- Goldman Sachs will exercise the lower strike call. CSM would elect to settle the option by either:
  - (i) Physical settlement. CSM would deliver 214.8 million new shares and would receive USD 199.8 million (= 0.93 × 214.8 million).
  - (ii) Cash settlement. CSM would pay to Goldman Sachs a cash amount equal to the difference between the share price at the time of exercise and the lower strike price of USD 0.93 for the 214.8 million shares.
- CSM will not exercise the upper strike call.

If CSM elected physical settlement, CSM would issue 214.8 million new shares. CSM would receive almost USD 200 million cash through the call spread. This cash amount could be used for partial repayment of the convertible bond. In this case, CSM would receive this

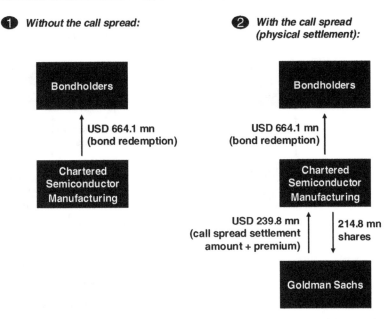

Figure 4.18   CSM's overall flows in scenario 2, physical settlement, without/with the call spread.

USD 199.8 million cash amount in addition to the USD 40 million received for entering into the call spread in August 2004. Physical settlement under the lower strike price call was the most logical choice. Figure 4.18 shows CSM's overall flows under this scenario without and with the call spread transaction, were CSM to elect physical settlement.

If CSM elected cash settlement, the amount of cash to be paid by CSM to Goldman Sachs would be a function of the then prevailing CSM's USD stock price:

$$\text{Cash amount} = (\text{USD stock price} - 0.93) \times 214.8 \text{ million new shares}$$

The maximum cash amount to be paid by CSM was USD 464.0 million [$= (3.09 - 0.93) \times$ 214.8 million] taking place when CSM's stock price was close to USD 3.09 at expiry.

Scenario 3: CSM's Stock Price at or above USD 3.09

CSM's flows under this scenario at expiry will be the following:

- The bond holders will convert the convertible bond. CSM will deliver 214.8 million new shares to the bond holders.
- Goldman Sachs will exercise the lower strike call. CSM would elect to settle the option by either:
- Physical settlement. CSM will deliver 214.8 million new shares, receiving USD 199.8 million ($= 0.93 \times 214.8$ million).
- Cash settlement. CSM will pay to Goldman Sachs a cash amount equal to the difference between the share price at the time of exercise and the lower strike price of USD 0.93 for the 214.8 million shares.

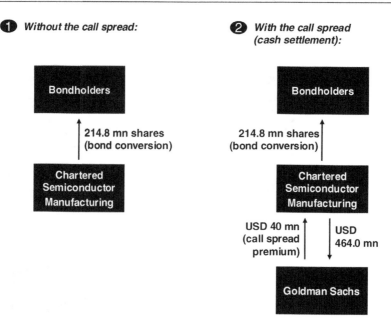

Figure 4.19   CSM's overall flows in scenario 3, cash settlement, without/with the call spread.

- CSM will exercise the upper strike call. CSM would receive from Goldman Sachs an amount equal to the difference between the share price at the time of exercise and the upper strike price of USD 3.09 for the 214.8 million shares.

If CSM elected physical settlement, CSM would issue 429.6 million (= 214.8 million × 2) new shares. CSM would receive almost USD 200 million cash through the lower strike call plus the appreciation of the shares above USD 3.09. This cash amount could be used for partial repayment of the convertible bond. In my view, it was unlikely that CSM would elect physical settlement unless it experienced refinancing difficulties or/and if it needed to strengthen its equity base. It would cause a much larger dilution to CSM's shareholders than originally planned.

More likely, CSM would elect cash settlement under the lower strike price call. If the shares were trading above USD 3.09, probably CSM prospects would be positive, not needing to further strengthen its equity base. CSM would deliver 214.8 million new shares to the bond holders and would pay USD 464.0 million [= 214.8 million × (3.09 – 0.93)] to Goldman Sachs. This cash amount equaled the difference between the upper strike price of USD 3.09 and the lower strike price of USD 0.93 for the 214.8 million shares. Figure 4.19 shows the flows for CSM were it to elect cash settlement under the lower strike price call.

4.5.4   Attractiveness of the Transaction to CSM

The main benefits to CSM were the following:

- The call spread transaction had the effect of reducing substantially the conversion price of the existing convertible bond, as shown in Figure 4.20. The low strike price was USD 0.93, representing a 50% (= 0.93/0.62 – 1) conversion premium on trade date. Therefore, the call

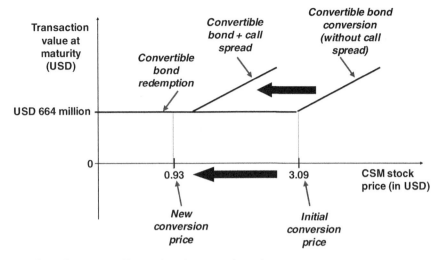

Figure 4.20   Effect of the call spread on the conversion price.

spread increased the likelihood of CSM issuing the shares originally planned for issuance upon conversion of the convertible bond. In other words, the call spread avoided additional dilution to shareholders beyond what was originally contemplated when the convertible bond was issued.

- If the lower strike price call was exercised, under the physical settlement alternative CSM would receive approximately USD 200 million, an amount that could be used to partially redeem the convertible bond.
- CSM received an upfront premium for the call spread. The amount of the premium received by CSM was not disclosed, but I guess it was approximately USD 40 million.

4.5.5   Additional Remarks

Net share settlement

In order to provide more flexibility to CSM regarding the number of shares to be issued under the transaction, it would have been interesting to include a third settlement method in the terms and conditions of the lower strike price call.

We just saw that in the third scenario, CSM's stock price being at or above USD 3.09, upon exercise of the lower strike price call CSM had to choose between:

- Electing cash settlement. It would imply the payment to Goldman Sachs of USD 464.0 million if CSM elected cash settlement and the issuance of 214.8 million shares to the bond holders. This election would mean the payment of a notably large cash amount.
- Electing physical settlement. It would imply the issuance of 429.6 million shares to the bond holders and to Goldman Sachs in exchange for approximately USD 200 million. This election would mean the issuance of a much larger than planned number of shares.

It would have been interesting to add a third settlement alternative for CSM to the lower strike price call terms and conditions, a combination of cash settlement and net share settlement. For

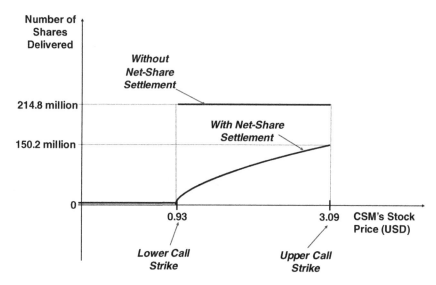

Figure 4.21   Number of shares to be delivered under net share settlement.

example, if CSM elected this third settlement alternative, net share settlement, the settlement would have the following two parts:

- A first part, a settlement in shares representing the option payoff due to the stock price appreciation between the lower and the upper strike prices.
- A second part, a settlement in cash representing the option payoff due to the stock price appreciation beyond the upper strike price. This second part would be completely offset by the payoff of the upper strike price call.

The number of shares to be delivered under the first part, the net share settlement, would be a function of the stock price upon conversion, as follows (see Figure 4.21):

Number of shares = [(3.09 − 0.93) × 214.8 million shares]/USD stock price
Number of shares = 464.0 million/USD stock price

The maximum number of shares to be delivered to Goldman Sachs would be 150.2 million shares (= 464.0 million/3.09), taking place when CSM's stock price reached exactly USD 3.09. This number of shares is significantly lower than the 214.8 million shares that CSM had to deliver were it to elect physical settlement under the lower strike price call.

Soft call

Because the call spread transaction was contractually separate from the convertible bond, it did not affect the terms and conditions of the bond. However, the terms and conditions of the call spread had to mimic the put and call rights embedded in the convertible bond. For example, the convertible bond had a "soft call" feature.

The soft call feature allowed CSM to elect for early termination of the call spread if its share price rose and remained above USD 1.17 for a defined period of time. The price represented 125% of the lower strike price.

4.6 DECREASING LIKELIHOOD OF CONVERSION WITH A CALL SPREAD

4.6.1 Case Study: Microsoft's Convertible Plus Call Spread

This case shows how a company synthetically increased the conversion price in a convertible bond with a call spread, as a result reducing the likelihood of issuance of new shares. On 15 June 2010, Microsoft issued a USD 1.25 billion zero-coupon convertible bond. The bond had a 3-year maturity and was convertible into Microsoft stock at USD 33.40, representing a premium of 33% above Microsoft's stock price at issuance. The following table summarizes the convertible bond terms:

Microsoft's Convertible Bond	
Issuer	Microsoft Corp.
Issue date	15-June-2010
Notional amount	USD 1.25 billion
Maturity	15-June-2013 (3 years)
Issue price	100% of par
Coupon	0%
Redemption price	100% of notional amount
Exchange price	USD 33.40 (a 33% premium)
Underlying shares	37.4 million shares of Microsoft

Concurrent with the issuance of the bonds, Microsoft entered into a cash-settled call spread (a "call spread overlay") with several banks. Under the terms of the call spread overlay:

- Microsoft purchased a call option on its own stock with strike USD 33.40, equal to the initial conversion price of the convertible bond. The underlying shares to the call option were 37.4 million, equal to the full number of shares underlying the convertible bond.
- Microsoft sold a call option on its own stock with strike USD 37.16, or 48% above Microsoft's stock price on trade date (EUR 25.11). The underlying shares to the call option were 37.4 million.

The call spread transaction was intended to reduce the potential dilution upon conversion of the convertible bond (see Figure 4.22). The call spread had the economic effect of increasing the conversion price of the convertible bond to that of the call spread upper strike (i.e., USD 37.16).

4.7 DOUBLE ISSUANCE OF EXCHANGEABLE BONDS

4.7.1 Case Study: ABC'S Double Exchangeable

This case shows how a company can take advantage of a share price well below the exchange price of an existing exchangeable to issue a second exchangeable. Let us assume that on

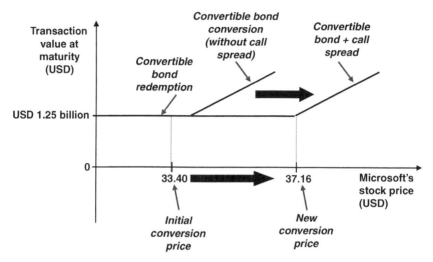

Figure 4.22   Effect of the call spread on the overall conversion price.

1 June 20X1, ABC issued an exchangeable bond (the "first exchangeable bond") into XYZ stock with the following terms:

ABC's First Exchangeable Bond into XYZ	
Issuer	ABC Corp.
Issue date	1-June-20X1
Notional amount	EUR 1 billion
Maturity	1-June-20X6 (5 years)
Issue price	100% of par
Coupon	2% semiannual 30/360
Redemption price	100% of notional amount
Exchange price	EUR 10.00
Underlying shares	100 million shares of XYZ

After the issue date, XYZ's stock price has gradually fallen, reaching EUR 3.50 at the end of June 20X2. Since then, the shares have recovered and reached EUR 5.00 on 1 December 20X3. On this date, ABC believed that it was unlikely that the shares would recover to the EUR 10.00 exchange price and that the share price would be depressed for the next few years.

ABC first considered buying back the existing exchangeable and issuing a new one. This alternative faced three major hurdles from ABC's viewpoint:

- ABC would have to pay a substantial premium to repurchase a large size.
- ABC would redeem a large borrowing (EUR 1 billion) in which it was paying a very attractive financing cost (only 2%).
- A new exchangeable issue would raise much lower financing.

Therefore, ABC discarded this alternative. Instead, ABC decided to issue a new exchangeable (the "second exchangeable bond") with the following terms:

ABC's Second Exchangeable Bond into XYZ	
Issuer	ABC Corp.
Issue date	1-December-20X3
Notional amount	EUR 600 million
Maturity	1 June 20X6 (2.5 years)
Issue price	100% of par
Coupon	3% semiannual 30/360
Redemption price	If at maturity XYZ shares trade below, or at, the exchange price: 100% of the notional amount (i.e., EUR 600 million)
	If at maturity XYZ shares trade above the capped share price: 166.67% of the notional amount (i.e., EUR 1 billion)
Automatic exchange	If XYZ shares trade below, or at, the capped share price and above the exchange price at maturity: the bonds would automatically exchange for XYZ shares at the exchange price per share
Exchange price	EUR 6.00 (a 20% premium to XYZ's share price at issuance)
Capped share price	EUR 10.00 (the first exchangeable bond's exchange price)
Underlying shares	100 million shares of XYZ

The issue of the second exchangeable allowed ABC to raise EUR 600 million and to pay a low coupon. This second bond also increased the likelihood of disposal of the XYZ shares. The second exchangeable included some unique features:

- The number of shares underlying both exchangeable bonds were identical, 100 million XYZ shares. It meant that the XYZ shares could not be pledged to the second exchangeable as they were already pledged to the first one. As a result and upon default of ABC, the second exchangeable bond holders did not have any collateral to reduce their exposure to ABC. ABC could have set up a secondary pledge in favor of the second exchangeable bond holders, but this secondary pledge would probably need the acceptance of the first exchangeable bond holders, an approval not easy to obtain.
- The second exchangeable had a EUR 10.00 capped share price, the exchange price of the first exchangeable bond, causing the potential benefit of its bond holders to be limited to 66.67% of their initial investment. As a result, the overall exchange price upon exchange of any of the two exchangeable bonds was lowered to EUR 6.00. Figure 4.23 shows that the combination of the exchange right of both bonds was equivalent to an exchange right at EUR 6.00.

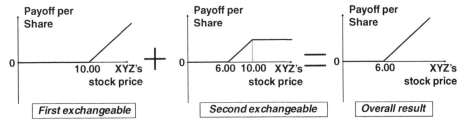

Figure 4.23 Per share profit for the bond holders of both exchangeables, ignoring coupons.

At maturity, three scenarios were possible:

- If XYZ shares traded below, or at, EUR 6.00. ABC would redeem in cash the first and the second exchangeables, paying EUR 1 billion and EUR 600 million respectively.
- If XYZ traded above EUR 6.00 but below, or at, EUR 10.00. ABC would redeem the first exchangeable, paying EUR 1 billion. ABC would deliver 100 million XYZ shares under the second exchangeable.
- If XYZ traded above EUR 10.00. ABC would deliver 100 million XYZ shares under the first exchangeable. ABC would redeem the second exchangeable paying EUR 1 billion.

The terms of the second exchangeable bond had to take into account any early redemption rights under the first exchangeable. Let us assume that the first exchangeable had a soft call that allowed ABC to redeem the bond if XYZ's stock price exceeded 150% of the exchange price (i.e., EUR 15.00). The second exchangeable had also to include an early redemption clause. In this case, ABC had to include a soft call in the second exchangeable allowing it to redeem early if XYZ's stock price exceeded EUR 15.00. Of course, early redemption would require ABC to pay EUR 1 billion (i.e., 166.67% of the notional amount) to the bond holders.

Advantages and Weaknesses of the Strategy

The advantages of the strategy were the following:

- ABC was able to raise new financing at a low cost.
- ABC did not need to pledge additional shares to issue the second exchangeable.
- ABC did not need to buy back the existing exchangeable bond.
- ABC participated in an appreciation of XYZ's share price up to the second exchangeable's exchange price.
- ABC increased the likelihood of disposal of the XYZ shares.
- ABC retained ownership of the stake, maintaining the voting rights and receiving the dividends.

The weaknesses of the strategy were the following:

- ABC reduced its participation in a potential appreciation of the underlying shares.
- The second exchangeable's bond holders did not have the underlying shares pledged in their favor. The absence of an exchange property would cause the bond holders to be unsecured, although ranked senior, in case of ABC becoming insolvent.
- The structured characteristic of the second exchangeable may make a public placement difficult. There are two reasons for this: (i) the underlying shares could not be pledged to the second exchangeable and (ii) the capped exchange price was an unusual feature. If the second exchangeable bond was privately placed with the bank arranging the transaction and it kept the bond in its books: (i) it needed to borrow a substantial amount of XYZ stock to delta-hedge its position and (ii) it would face a large credit exposure to ABC.

4.8   BUYING BACK CONVERSION RIGHTS

4.8.1   Case Study: Cap Gemini's Repurchase of Conversion Right from Société Générale

This case shows how a company took advantage of a share price well below the exchange price of an existing convertible to buy back the embedded conversion right. This buyback allowed

Cap Gemini to issue a second convertible without substantially increasing the potential dilution upon conversion.

In June 2003, Cap Gemini, a French provider of IT consulting and services, issued a convertible bond. The total amount of the issue was EUR 460 million, initially convertible into 9 million Cap Gemini shares at an initial conversion price of EUR 51 per share. The bond paid an interest of 2.50% per year. The bond could be converted at any time from 11 August 2003 until 20 December 2009. The bond would be redeemed in full on 1 January 2010 in cash at par. The following table summarizes the convertible bond terms:

Cap Gemini's Convertible Bond	
Issuer	Cap Gemini
Issue date	24-June-2003
Settlement date	2-July-2003
Notional amount	EUR 460 million
Maturity	1-January-2010 (6.5 years)
Issue price	100% of par
Coupon	2.50%
Redemption price	100% of notional amount
Conversion price	EUR 51.00 (a 70% premium to the EUR 30.00 stock price at issuance)
Underlying shares	9 million shares of Cap Gemini
Soft call	From 2-July-2007. Stock price must equal or exceed 125% of the conversion price

In June 2005, Cap Gemini's stock was trading at EUR 26.00. Therefore, the conversion price represented a 96% (= 51.00/26.00 − 1) premium to the then prevailing stock price. The implied volatilities of Cap Gemini options had been constantly decreasing over the last several months. The implied volatility of options with expiry January 2010 and strike 196% was trading around 24%, at similar levels to the implied volatility originally used to price the convertible bond.

Cap Gemini took advantage of the low stock price and the attractive implied volatility levels to neutralize in full the potential dilutive impact of the convertible bond. In order to buy back the conversion right embedded in the convertible bond, Cap Gemini bought from Société Générale a call option on 9 million Cap Gemini shares, equal to the number of shares underlying the convertible bond, with the following terms:

Call Option – Main Terms	
Buyer	Cap Gemini
Seller	Société Générale
Notional amount	EUR 234 million
Expiry date	1-January-2010 (6.5 years)
Premium	EUR 16 million (6.8% of the notional amount, or EUR 1.78 per share)
Initial price	EUR 26.00
Exercise price	EUR 51.00
Underlying shares	9 million shares of Cap Gemini

The buyback of the conversion right of the existing convertible provided Cap Gemini with a great advantage. It could issue a new convertible without substantially increasing the potential

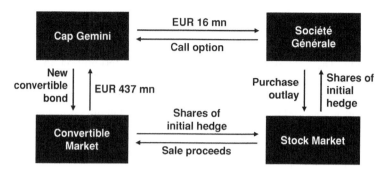

Figure 4.24   Initial flows of Cap Gemini's convertible strategy.

dilution upon conversion. Thus, Cap Gemini also took advantage of the strong demand for convertibles to issue a new convertible bond. The new bond had a EUR 37.00 conversion price, a maturity on 1 January 2012, 11.8 million underlying shares and a EUR 437 million notional amount. Part of these proceeds was used to pay the premium of the call option.

The buyback of the conversion right of the existing convertible and the concurrent issuance of the new convertible also had the advantage of reducing the initial impact on Cap Gemini's share price. The convertible bond holders needed to sell Cap Gemini shares to initially delta-hedge their position. Société Générale, the call option seller, had to buy Cap Gemini shares to initially delta-hedge its position. As a result, part of the two executions offset each other, reducing the impact on Cap Gemini's stock price (see Figure 4.24).

Advantages and Weaknesses of the Strategy

The advantages of the strategy were the following:

- Cap Gemini neutralized in full the dilution upon potential conversion of the bond, without buying back the existing exchangeable bond.
- Cap Gemini issued a new convertible bond, without substantially increasing potential dilution upon conversion.
- Cap Gemini was able to repurchase the embedded option at an attractive price, taking advantage of the stock price fall since issuance and of attractive volatility levels.
- The bank selling the call option had to buy a significant number of shares of Cap Gemini to initially delta-hedge its position, providing a support to Cap Gemini's stock price.

The weaknesses of the strategy were the following:

- Cap Gemini had to pay a EUR 16 million premium.
- Cap Gemini stopped benefiting from a potential further decline of its stock price.

Special Clauses

The call option had to take into account the convertible's dividend protection clause. Commonly, convertible bond holders are protected against dividends representing a dividend yield in excess of a certain percentage in any given year. An adjustment of the conversion ratio is then performed for the portion exceeding the predetermined dividend yield percentage.

Therefore, the call option had to include an adjustment mechanism such that the conversion ratio and the call exercise price remained identical over their term. In our case, Cap Gemini's convertible bond holders were protected against yearly distributions exceeding a 5% dividend yield. Thus, the call option needed to incorporate a similar mechanism.

The convertible bond included a soft call option. Under this option, Cap Gemini could redeem, from 2 July 2007 and until 20 December 2009, the outstanding bond at an early redemption price equal to par plus accrued interest, if Cap Gemini's stock price traded, at least on 20 trading days during the 40 trading days immediately preceding the date of publication of a notice relating to such early redemption, above 125% of such early redemption price. Upon early redemption, the bond holders could elect the redemption to be either in cash or converted into Cap Gemini shares. Usually the terms of the acquired call do not include a clause mirroring a convertible bond's soft call rights. Cap Gemini could do the following:

- If Cap Gemini believed that it would exercise the soft call right when entitled to, it could acquire an American-style call option. An American call option would allow Cap Gemini to exercise the call at any time.
- Otherwise, Cap Gemini could acquire a European-style call option. It meant that if Cap Gemini exercised it soft call right under the convertible it had to sell back the call option to the bank. Normally, it would work out because the total value of the option would exceed its intrinsic value. Therefore, the payout above the redemption price under the convertible bond could be covered by the proceeds from selling back the call option.

Another clause that needed to be carefully taken into account was the settlement type. Again, the call had to maintain the same flexibility that the issuer had under the convertible bond. In our case, Cap Gemini only allowed for delivery of the underlying shares upon conversion. As a result, the call option could only be physically settled upon exercise.

Any other clauses that could cause divergences between the conversion right and the call option features also had to be carefully taken into consideration. For example, any early redemption right (i.e., a put right) at the option of the bond holders. In Cap Gemini's convertible, bond holders could request the early redemption of all or part of their bonds in the event of a change of control of the company. The call option had to include a similar mechanism for early exercise.

4.9 BUYING BACK CONVERTIBLE/EXCHANGEABLE BONDS

4.9.1 Case Study: TUI's Convertible Bond

During the financial crisis of 2007–2008, a good number of market disruptions created unusual opportunities to buy back existing convertible and exchangeable bonds at fire sale prices:

- Stock prices plummeted sharply, reducing the value of the conversion/exchange rights embedded in the bonds.
- Convertible bond funds and hedge funds witnessed a record high number of redemptions as investors tried to obtain cash and to stop their losses, forcing these funds to sell their assets.
- Capital markets and investors became more risk averse, requiring sky high spreads to finance corporates. As a result, the existing convertible/exchangeable coupons became unattractive.

Figure 4.25   Market price of TUI's 2.50% September 2012 convertible bond.

TUI A.G., the German tourism and logistic services company, could have bought back its 2.75% September 2012 convertible bond at half its issue price in October 2008, in March 2009 and in July 2009 (see Figure 4.25).

Equity Swap Alternative

The main problem with this strategy is that when the exceptionally attractive opportunity to buy back a convertible/exchangeable occurred, the company was also likely to experience a difficult situation. The company was probably devoting its energies to refinancing maturing debt and to lengthening the maturity of its existing debt. Raising additional financing just to take advantage of an unusual opportunity may not be the company's main priority.

One solution for the company was to enter into an equity swap on the convertible/exchangeable bond. As an example, let us assume that on 28 October 2008 TUI was willing to acquire EUR 200 million notional of its convertible bond at 50% price (i.e., EUR 100 million market value) and entered into a cash-settled equity swap on its convertible with Gigabank. The maturity of the equity swap was 1.5 years (i.e., 28 April 2010).

Flows of the Transaction

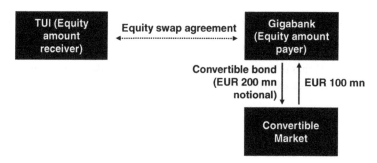

Figure 4.26   Flows on trade date.

The flows of the transaction on the trade date were as follows (see Figure 4.26):

- TUI and Gigabank entered into the cash-settled total return equity swap on EUR 200 million notional of the convertible bond. The initial price was set at 50% of its par price, or EUR 100 million (the equity swap notional).
- Gigabank bought a EUR 200 million notional of the convertible bond, paying EUR 100 million (plus accrued interest), so the bank initially hedged its position.

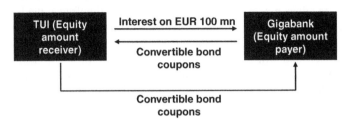

Figure 4.27   Flows during the life of the equity swap.

The flows of the transaction during the life of the equity swap were as follows (see Figure 4.27):

- TUI paid an interest, the floating amount, to Gigabank based on the EUR 100 million equity swap notional.
- Gigabank paid to TUI an amount equivalent to the coupon Gigabank received through the underlying convertible bond. This amount was paid on the convertible bond's coupon payment date.

At the equity swap maturity (i.e., 28 April 2010), the convertible bond was trading at 90%. Therefore, the equity swap underlying convertible bond was worth EUR 180 million. The flows of the transaction at maturity were as follows (see Figure 4.28):

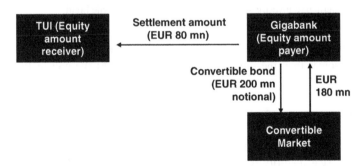

Figure 4.28   Flows on the settlement date of the equity swap.

- Gigabank unwound its hedge, selling a EUR 200 million notional of the convertible bond, receiving EUR 180 million (plus accrued interest) in the market.
- TUI and Gigabank settled the equity swap after calculating the settlement amount, taking into account the EUR 100 million equity swap notional. The settlement amount was EUR 80 million (= 180 million – 100 million).

4.10 PRE-IPO CONVERTIBLE BONDS

Structures around convertibles can provide an interesting financing alternative to companies expecting their own IPO to take place. The structure covered in this section allows a company to pre-place a convertible bond ahead of an IPO. The company issues a bond that will conditionally become convertible, dependent upon whether or not an IPO occurs (the "triggering event"). If the IPO does not occur within a predetermined timeframe, the bond is simply redeemed at favorable terms for the investor, giving an extra yield above the company's straight debt. However, if the event does occur, the bond will become convertible on predefined terms.

The convertible bond will be priced based on variables known in advance, such as the company's credit spreads and the market interest rates. However, there are two other variables needed to price the convertible bond, the implied volatility and the assumed dividends, whose estimation is notably challenging. Unless investors in the pre-IPO convertible bond are given a put right, they may require a too conservative level on these two variables. As a consequence, these types of bond include a put right that gives the bond holders the right to put the bond back to the company, should they not want the convertible at the time of the triggering event.

As an example, let us assume that the yield on the company's one-year straight debt is 5%. Let us assume further that a convertible bond starting in 1 year and with a 3-year term, with a conversion premium of 20%, is estimated to pay a coupon of 2%. If the market remains unchanged and the IPO of the company takes within 1 year, an investor could invest in a 1-year bond receiving a 5% yield and then, at its maturity, invest in a 3-year convertible bond receiving a 2% coupon (see Figure 4.29).

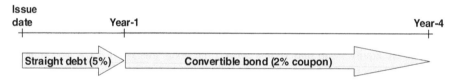

Figure 4.29 Alternative investor strategy to the pre-IPO convertible bond.

Alternatively, the company could be issuing a bond that pays a coupon of 4% during the first year (1% lower than the yield of comparable debt). At the end of the first year (see Figure 4.30):

- If the IPO did not occur, the bond redeemed at a yield of 6% (1% higher than the yield of comparable debt).
- If the IPO did occur, the bond became a convertible bond with a conversion premium of 20% and a 3-year maturity. The coupon of the convertible bond was 3% (1% higher than the coupon of a similar convertible bond). If the investor did not want to remain invested in the convertible bond, he/she could put the bond back at par to the company, realizing a yield of 4%.

From an investor's perspective:

- If the IPO did not occur, the transaction provided an enhanced yield. The resulting yield to maturity was 1% higher than the yield of comparable straight debt.

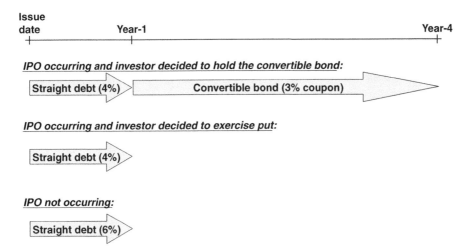

Figure 4.30   Investment yield under the different scenarios of the pre-IPO convertible bond.

- If the IPO did occur, the transaction provided a very attractively valued convertible, paying a coupon 1% higher than the coupon of comparable convertible debt. If at the end of the first year, the investor did not deem the convertible terms to be sufficiently attractive, he/she could have the bond redeemed, but then his/her 1-year investment would have realized a yield 1% lower than the yield of comparable straight debt.

From the company's perspective:

- The company was able to raise finance, tapping the convertible bond market.
- By launching the bond, the issuer sent out a very strong signal that it was expecting the IPO to occur.
- The company was exposed to an IPO not occurring. Upon this event, it would have incurred a financial expense higher than its cost of straight debt.

5

Hedging and Yield Enhancing Strategic Stakes

This chapter and the next one examine the management of strategic stakes. A strategic stake, also called a "concentrated stock position", is a substantial equity position in a stock, usually taken with a long-term view. Strategic equity transactions can be implemented to enhance the acquisition, hedge, yield enhancement and disposal of a stake. In this chapter I will focus on the hedging and yield enhancement of strategic stakes. I will assume that the reader is already familiar with equity options, otherwise, I strongly recommend the reader to carefully read Chapter 1.

5.1 HEDGING A STRATEGIC STAKE

An investor owning a strategic stake is exposed to a decrease in its value. The simplest way to mitigate an exposure to the downside of a stock price is to sell the stake. However, an investor is often unable or unwilling to sell the stake. For example, an investor may have a strong commercial relationship with the company or may believe that the stock has attractive future prospects, or may want to avoid a substantial tax bill. This section covers the main strategies to protect a strategic stake.

Common Background Information

Let's assume that on 1 June 20X1, ABC Corporation (ABC) owned 40 million shares of XYZ. On that date XYZ stock was trading at EUR 10.00, and thus, the stake was worth EUR 400 million. ABC was worried about a potential large fall in XYZ's stock price. Figure 5.1 highlights the value of the stake as a function of XYZ's stock price. ABC was looking to protect the value of the stake in 12 months' time but it was not willing to sell its stake unless the stock price experienced a substantial rise.

5.1.1 Hedging with a Put Option

The simplest way to hedge ABC's position, without selling the stake, was to buy a put option on XYZ. The purchase of a put option could provide ABC protection against downward stock price movements below the put's strike price. During the life of the put, ABC continued to participate in any stock appreciation. The put option compensated ABC for any fall in XYZ's stock price below the strike price. The maximum potential loss for ABC was the premium paid.

  The two main parameters that ABC had to determine were the put expiration date and its strike price. ABC chose a 12-month expiry date (i.e., 1 June 20X2) because it wanted to hedge

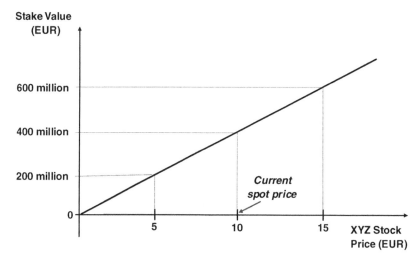

Figure 5.1   Value of ABC's stake in XYZ as a function of its stock price.

the value of the stake in 12 months' time. The selection of the strike price very much depended on ABC's risk aversion, its view on the stock price and the premium amount it was willing to pay for the hedge. ABC received from Gigabank quotes of 12-month European puts on XYZ stock for different strikes, as shown in the following table. Remember that the premium of an option is usually quoted as a percentage of its notional amount.

Put strike	Implied volatility	Premium
100%	24.4%	8.5%
90%	28.0%	5.5%
80%	33.2%	3.9%
70%	39.8%	2.9%
60%	47.5%	2.3%

Other option terms that ABC needed to define included:

- The type of option – European or American. A European option can only be exercised at expiration. An American option can be exercised at any time during the life of the option. ABC chose a European type of option because it was interested in hedging the value of the stake only at expiry.
- The type of settlement – cash or physical. ABC was not looking to sell the shares at expiry, and as a result, chose cash settlement only.

ABC decided to buy the 90% strike put. The 100% put was too expensive. Also, ABC was not willing to be exposed to a loss larger than 16%. Taking into account its 5.5% premium, the 90% put implied a maximum loss of 15.5% (= 100% – 90% + 5.5%), occurring if the shares traded at 90% at expiry. The main terms of the put option were the following:

Cash-settled Put Option – Main Terms

Buyer	ABC Corp.
Seller	Gigabank
Option type	Put
Trade date	1-June-20X1
Expiration date	1-June-20X2
Option style	European
Shares	XYZ
Number of options	40 million (one share per option)
Strike price	EUR 9.00 (90% of the spot price)
Spot price	EUR 10.00
Premium	5.5% of the notional amount, or
	EUR 22 million (i.e., EUR 0.55 per share)
Premium payment date	3-June-20X1
Notional amount	Number of options × Spot price
	EUR 400 million
Settlement price	The closing price of the shares on the valuation date
Settlement method	Cash settlement
Cash settlement amount	The maximum of:
	(i) Number of options × (Strike price – Settlement price), and
	(ii) Zero
Cash settlement payment date	4-June-20X2

ABC paid a 5.5% premium on 3 June 20X1. The notional amount was EUR 400 million (= 40 million × 10.00), equal to the product of (i) the number of options and (ii) the spot price. Therefore, the premium was EUR 22 million (= 5.5% × 400 million), or EUR 0.55 per share (= 5.5% × 10.00).

At expiry, there were two scenarios:

- If XYZ's stock price was greater than or equal to the put strike price, the option would expire worthless.
- If XYZ's stock price was lower than the put strike price, ABC would receive from Gigabank a cash amount equal to the number of options × (strike price – settlement price). For example, if XYZ's stock price at expiry was EUR 7.00, ABC would receive EUR 80 million [= 40 million × (9.00 – 7.00)].

Figure 5.2 depicts ABC's payoff under the put as a function of XYZ's stock price at expiry, taking into account the settlement amount and the EUR 22 million upfront premium and ignoring timing differences. Therefore, the payoff was calculated as: EUR 40 million × Max(strike price – settlement price, 0) – EUR 22 million.

Advantages and Weaknesses of the Strategy

The advantages of the strategy were the following:

- At expiration, ABC had full downside protection below the put strike price.
- ABC retained ownership of the stake, maintaining the voting rights and receiving the dividends.
- ABC participated in full in a potential appreciation of the stake.

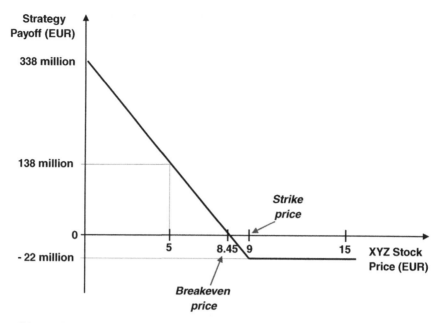

Figure 5.2 ABC's payoff under the put as a function of XYZ's stock price at expiry.

The weaknesses of the strategy were the following:

- ABC paid an upfront premium.
- ABC was exposed to the difference between the stock price prevailing at inception and the put strike price.
- In order to delta-hedge its position, the seller of the option (i.e., Gigabank) needed to borrow the stock in order to maintain a short position in the underlying stock over the term of the transaction.

5.1.2   Hedging with a Put Spread

Let us assume that ABC was interested in buying the 90% put, but found the 5.5% premium too expensive. Let us assume further that ABC had the view that XYZ stock price would not be falling substantially. As a result, ABC considered buying the 90% put and selling a lower strike put, both with a 12-month expiry. The purchase (sale) of a put while simultaneously selling (buying) another put on the same underlying is called a put spread. After studying different alternatives, ABC entered into a 90%/70% put spread strategy, by buying a 90% put and selling a 70% put.

A 90%/70% put spread meant that the stake was protected once it had fallen by 10% (i.e., fallen through the 90% strike) and would continue to be protected thereafter as long as XYZ's stock price did not decline by more than 30% (i.e., fall through the 70% strike).

The following table summarizes the terms of the put spread (the rest of the terms were identical to the 90% put terms specified in the previous subsection):

Cash-settled Put Spread – Main Terms	
Upper strike price	EUR 9.00 (i.e., 90% of the initial price)
Lower strike price	EUR 7.00 (i.e., 70% of the initial price)
Upper strike put buyer	ABC Corp.
Lower strike put buyer	Gigabank
Premium	3.0% of the notional amount, or
	EUR 12 million (i.e., EUR 0.3 per share)

ABC paid a 3% premium on 3 June 20X1. The notional amount was EUR 400 million (= 40 million × 10.00), equal to the product of (i) the number of options and (ii) the spot price. Therefore, the premium was EUR 12 million (= 3% × 400 million), or EUR 0.3 per share (= 3% × 10.00).

At expiry there were three scenarios:

- If XYZ's stock price was greater than, or equal to, the EUR 9.00 upper strike price, both puts would expire worthless.
- If XYZ's stock price was lower than the EUR 9.00 upper strike price and greater than the EUR 7.00 lower strike price, ABC would receive from Gigabank a cash amount equal to the number of options × (upper strike price – settlement price). For example, if XYZ's stock price at expiry was EUR 8.00, ABC would receive EUR 40 million [= 40 million × (9.00 – 8.00)].
- If XYZ's stock price was lower than, or equal to, the EUR 7.00 lower strike price, ABC would receive EUR 80 million [= 40 million × (9.00 – 7.00)] from Gigabank.

Figure 5.3 depicts ABC's payoff under the put spread as a function of XYZ's stock price at expiry, taking into account the settlement amount and the EUR 12 million upfront premium and ignoring timing differences. The payoff was calculated as: EUR 40 million × [Max(upper strike price – settlement price, 0) – Max(lower strike price – settlement price, 0)] – EUR 12 million.

A put spread can take advantage of a steep skew. When the skew is large, the implied volatility of the lower strike put is notably larger than the implied volatility of the upper strike put. As a result, the lower strike put is sold at an attractive premium relative to that of the upper strike.

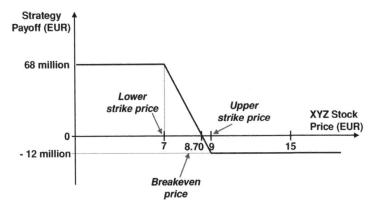

Figure 5.3   ABC's payoff under the put spread as a function of XYZ's stock price at expiry.

Advantages and Weaknesses of the Strategy

The advantages of the strategy were the following:

- At expiration, ABC had downside protection below the upper strike price.
- ABC retained ownership of the stake, maintaining the voting rights and receiving the dividends.
- ABC participated in full in an appreciation of the stake.
- The premium paid was significantly lower than the premium to be paid under the single put hedging strategy.

The weaknesses of the strategy were the following:

- ABC paid an upfront premium.
- ABC was exposed to the difference between the stock price prevailing at inception and the upper strike price.
- ABC's downside protection was limited below the lower strike price.
- In order to delta-hedge its position, the seller of the upper strike put option (i.e., Gigabank) needed to borrow the stock in order to maintain a short position in the underlying stock over the term of the transaction.

5.1.3 Hedging with a Collar

When protecting a stake with a put, a popular way of reducing the cost of the hedging strategy is to sell an out-of-the-money call. When the purchase of a put option is combined with the simultaneous sale of a call option, the strategy is known as a **collar**. The premium received by the sale of the call partially, or totally, reduces the premium to be paid for the put. Should an investor want a specific put, it is possible to find a call with a certain strike price such that the proceeds from the call sale finance completely the purchase of the put. A collar that does not require any overall premium payment (or receipt) is called a **zero-cost collar**.

Let us assume that ABC was interested in buying the 90% put but did not want to pay any premium for the downside protection. ABC then sold a call 108% to completely offset the cost of the put. With this zero-cost collar strategy, ABC protected for zero cost its downside exposure below 90% of the then prevailing stock price at the expense of capping any gains should the stock price rise by more than 8%. The following table summarizes the terms of the zero-cost collar (the rest of the terms were identical to the 90% put terms specified earlier):

Cash-settled Zero-cost Collar – Main Terms	
Put strike price	EUR 9.00 (i.e., 90% of the initial price)
Put buyer	ABC Corp.
Put cash settlement amount	The maximum of: (i) Number of options × (Put strike price – Settlement price), and (ii) Zero
Call strike price	EUR 10.80 (i.e., 108% of the initial price)
Call buyer	Gigabank
Call cash settlement amount	The maximum of: (i) Number of options × (Settlement price – Call strike price), and (ii) Zero
Overall premium	None

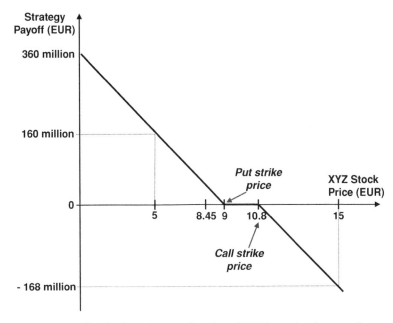

Figure 5.4   ABC's payoff under the collar as a function of XYZ's stock price at expiry.

At expiry there were three scenarios:

- If XYZ's stock price was greater than the EUR 10.80 call strike price, ABC would pay to Gigabank a cash amount equal to the number of options × (settlement price – call strike price). For example, if XYZ's stock price at expiry was EUR 12.00, ABC would pay to Gigabank EUR 48 million [= 40 million × (12.00 – 10.80)]. The put would expire worthless.
- If XYZ's stock price was lower than, or equal to, the EUR 10.80 call strike price and greater than, or equal to, the EUR 9.00 put strike price, both options would expire worthless.
- If XYZ's stock price was lower than the EUR 9.00 put strike price, ABC would receive from Gigabank a cash amount equal to the number of options × (put strike price – settlement price). For example, if XYZ's stock price at expiry was EUR 7.00, ABC would receive EUR 80 million [= 40 million × (9.00 – 7.00)].

Figure 5.4 depicts ABC's payoff under the zero-cost collar as a function of XYZ's stock price at expiry. The payoff was calculated as: EUR 40 million × [Max(put strike price – settlement price, 0) – Max(settlement price – call strike price, 0)]. The graph shows that by establishing the zero-cost collar, a minimum value and a maximum value were created around ABC's equity position until the expiry of the options. The minimum value was EUR 360 million (= 40 million × 9.00) and the maximum value was EUR 432 million (= 40 million × 10.80).

Advantages and Weaknesses of the Strategy

The advantages of the collar strategy were the following:

- At expiration, ABC had full downside protection below the EUR 9.00 put strike price.
- ABC retained ownership of the stake, maintaining the voting rights and receiving the dividends.

- ABC participated up to a certain level (EUR 10.80) in an appreciation of the stake.
- The premium paid was significantly lower (zero in our case) than the premium to be paid under either the single put or the put spread hedging strategies.

The weaknesses of the strategy were the following:

- ABC did not participate in XYZ's stock price appreciation above the EUR 10.80 call strike price.
- ABC was exposed to the difference between the EUR 10.00 stock price prevailing at inception and the EUR 9.00 put strike price.
- In order to delta-hedge its position, the seller of the option (i.e., Gigabank) needed to borrow the stock in order to maintain a short position in the underlying stock over the term of the transaction.

5.1.4   Hedging with a Put Spread Collar

The main problem with the zero-cost collar strategy is that it limits notably the participation in the upside of the stock. In our previous example, ABC sold a 108% call, not allowing it to participate beyond an 8% appreciation of the stock. One solution to increase the strike of the call is to combine a put spread with a call, in a zero-cost strategy. This strategy is called a zero-cost **put spread collar** strategy. Under this strategy, the premium received by the sale of the call totally offsets the premium to be paid for the put spread.

Let us assume that ABC was interested in buying the 90% put without paying a premium, but found the zero-cost collar strategy unattractive. Instead, ABC entered into a zero-cost put spread collar strategy in which ABC bought a 90% put, sold a 70% put and sold a 118% call. With this strategy, ABC protected for zero cost its downside exposure below 90%, and up to 70%, of the then prevailing stock price at the expense of capping any gains should the stock price rise by more than 18%. The following table summarizes the terms of the zero-cost put spread collar (the rest of the terms were identical to the 90% put terms specified in an earlier subsection):

Cash-settled Zero-cost Put Spread Collar – Main Terms	
Upper put strike price	EUR 9.00 (i.e., 90% of the initial price)
Upper put buyer	ABC Corp.
Upper put cash settlement amount	The maximum of: (i) Number of options × (Upper put strike price – Settlement price), and (ii) Zero
Lower put strike price	EUR 7.00 (i.e., 70% of the initial price)
Lower put buyer	Gigabank
Lower put cash settlement amount	The maximum of: (i) Number of options × (Lower put strike price – Settlement price), and (ii) Zero
Call strike price	EUR 11.80 (i.e., 118% of the initial price)
Call buyer	Gigabank
Call cash settlement amount	The maximum of: (i) Number of options × (Settlement price – Call strike price), and (ii) Zero
Overall premium	None

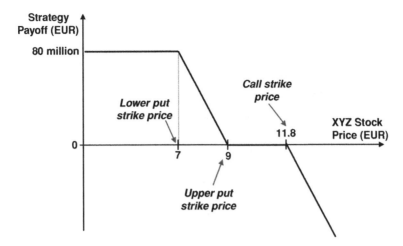

Figure 5.5   ABC's payoff under the put spread collar as a function of XYZ's stock price at expiry.

At expiry there were four scenarios:

- If XYZ's stock price was greater than the EUR 11.80 call strike price, ABC would pay to Gigabank a cash amount equal to the number of options × (settlement price – call strike price). For example, if XYZ's stock price at expiry was EUR 14.00, ABC would pay to Gigabank EUR 88 million [= 40 million × (14.00 – 11.80)]. The two puts would expire worthless.
- If XYZ's stock price was lower than, or equal to, the EUR 10.80 call strike price and greater than, or equal to, the EUR 9.00 upper put strike price, the three options would expire worthless.
- If XYZ's stock price was lower than the EUR 9.00 put strike price and greater than or equal to the EUR 7.00 lower strike price, ABC would receive from Gigabank a cash amount equal to the number of options × (upper put strike price – settlement price). For example, if XYZ's stock price at expiry was EUR 7.50, ABC would receive EUR 60 million [= 40 million × (9.00 – 7.50)]. Both the call and the lower strike put would expire worthless.
- If XYZ's stock price was lower than the EUR 7.00 lower strike price, ABC would receive EUR 80 million [= 40 million × (9.00 – 7.00)] from Gigabank as net compensation from the two puts. The call would expire worthless.

Figure 5.5 depicts ABC's payoff under the zero-cost put spread collar as a function of XYZ's stock price at expiry. The payoff was calculated as: EUR 40 million × [Max(upper put strike price – settlement price, 0) – Max(lower put strike price – settlement price, 0) – Max(settlement price – call strike price, 0)].

5.1.5   Hedging with a Fly Put Spread

Let us assume that ABC was interested in buying the 90% put and that it had the view that it was quite unlikely that XYZ's stock would fall below 70%. ABC considered that the 90%/70% put spread was providing an unnecessary protection below the 70% level. As an alternative, ABC entered into a fly put spread. A fly put spread, or butterfly put spread, extends the put spread concept further by limiting the protection obtained. In our case, a fly put spread strategy could be built as follows:

- ABC buys a 90% put (the upper strike put), on 40 million shares.
- ABC sells a 70% put (the middle strike put), on 80 million shares.
- ABC buys a 50% put (the lower strike put), on 40 million shares.

This strategy can also be designed as the combination of two put spreads:

- ABC buys a 90%/70% put spread, on 40 million shares.
- ABC sells a 70%/50% put spread, on 40 million shares.

ABC paid a 2.1% premium, or EUR 8.4 million (= 400 million × 2.1%), to enter into the fly put spread strategy. With this strategy, ABC protected for a modest premium its downside exposure below 90%, and up to 70% (of the then prevailing stock price) at the expense of gradually losing its protection were the stock to fall below 70%. Below 50%, ABC would have lost all its protection.

At expiry there were four scenarios:

- If XYZ's stock price was greater than, or equal to, the EUR 9.00 upper put strike price, the three options would expire worthless.
- If XYZ's stock price was lower than the EUR 9.00 upper put strike price and greater than, or equal to, the EUR 7.00 middle put strike price, ABC would receive from Gigabank a cash amount equal to the number of options × (upper put strike price – settlement price). For example, if XYZ's stock price at expiry was EUR 7.50, ABC would receive EUR 60 million [= 40 million × (9.00 – 7.50)]. Both the middle strike put and the lower strike put would expire worthless.
- If XYZ's stock price was lower than the EUR 7.00 middle put strike price and greater than, or equal to, the EUR 5.00 lower put strike price, ABC would receive from Gigabank a cash amount equal to the number of options × (upper put strike price – settlement price) – 2 × number of options × (middle put strike price – settlement price). For example, if XYZ's stock price at expiry was EUR 6.00, ABC would receive EUR 40 million [= 40 million × (9.00 – 6.00) – 80 million × (7.00 – 6.00)]. The lower strike put would expire worthless.
- If XYZ's stock price was lower than, or equal to, the EUR 5.00 lower put strike price the overall settlement amount would be zero.

Figure 5.6 depicts ABC's payoff under the fly put spread as a function of XYZ's stock price at expiry, taking into account the settlement amount and the upfront premium, and ignoring timing differences. The payoff was calculated as: EUR 40 million × [Max(upper put strike price – settlement price, 0) – 2 × Max(middle put strike price – settlement price, 0) + Max(lower put strike price – settlement price, 0)] – EUR 8.4 million.

Advantages and Weaknesses of the Strategy

The advantages of the strategy were the following:

- At expiration, ABC had full downside protection between the EUR 9.00 upper put strike price and the EUR 7.00 middle put strike price.
- ABC retained ownership of the stake, maintaining the voting rights and receiving the dividends.

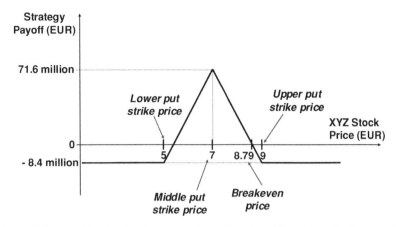

Figure 5.6   ABC's payoff under the fly put spread as a function of XYZ's stock price at expiry.

- ABC participated in full in an appreciation of the stake.
- The premium paid was significantly lower than the premium to be paid under the single put or the put spread hedging strategies.

The weaknesses of the strategy were the following:

- ABC paid an upfront premium.
- ABC was exposed to the difference between the EUR 10.00 stock price prevailing at inception and the EUR 9.00 upper put strike price.
- ABC's downside protection faded below the EUR 7.00 middle put strike price, being completely lost below the EUR 5.00 lower put strike price.
- In order to delta-hedge its position, the seller of the option, i.e., Gigabank, needed to borrow the stock in order to maintain a short position in the underlying stock over the term of the transaction.

5.1.6   Hedging with a Knock-out Put

A knock-out put takes the fly put spread or the put spread strategies to an extreme. If the share price closes below the knock-out barrier at expiry, the put expires worthless. In contrast, a put spread delivers a capped payout, the difference between the two put strike prices.

Let us assume that ABC entered into a knock-out put with a 90% strike price and a 70% knock-out barrier. ABC paid a 1.9% premium, or EUR 7.6 million (= 400 million × 1.9%), to buy the knock-out put. With this strategy, ABC protected for a modest premium its downside exposure below 90%, and up to 70% (of the then prevailing stock price) at the expense of losing its protection were the stock price to fall below 70% at expiry.

At expiry there were three scenarios:

- If XYZ's stock price was greater than, or equal to, the EUR 9.00 put strike price, the knock-out put option would expire worthless.
- If XYZ's stock price was lower than the EUR 9.00 strike price and greater than, or equal to, the EUR 7.00 knock-out barrier, ABC would receive from Gigabank a cash amount equal to the number of options × (put strike price − settlement price). For example, if XYZ's

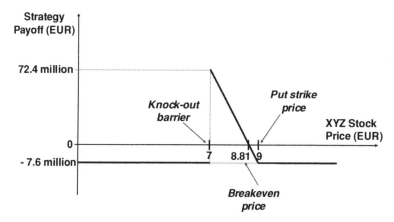

Figure 5.7   ABC's payoff under the knock-out put as a function of XYZ's stock price at expiry.

stock price at expiry was EUR 7.50, ABC would receive EUR 60 million [= 40 million ×
(9.00 − 7.50)].
- If XYZ's stock price was lower than the EUR 7.00 knock-out barrier, the put option would
expire worthless.

Figure 5.7 depicts ABC's payoff under the knock-out put as a function of XYZ's stock
price at expiry, taking into account the settlement amount and the EUR 7.6 million upfront
premium, and ignoring timing differences. The payoff was calculated as either: (i) if the
settlement price was above or at the knock-out barrier, the payoff was EUR 40 million ×
[Max(strike price − settlement price, 0)] − EUR 7.6 million, or (ii) otherwise, the payoff was
minus EUR 7.6 million.

Advantages and Weaknesses of the Strategy

The advantages of the strategy were the following:

- At expiration, ABC had full downside protection between the EUR 9.00 strike price and
the EUR 7.00 knock-out barrier.
- ABC retained ownership of the stake, maintaining the voting rights and receiving the
dividends.
- ABC participated in full in an appreciation of the stake.
- The premium paid was significantly lower than that of a single put and the put spread
hedging strategies.

The weaknesses of the strategy were the following:

- ABC paid an upfront premium.
- ABC was exposed to the difference between the EUR 10.00 stock price prevailing at
inception and the EUR 9.00 strike price.
- ABC's downside protection disappeared below the EUR 7.00 knock-out barrier.

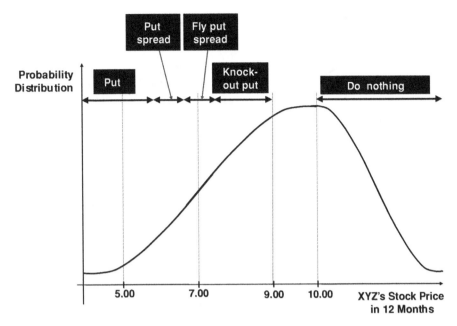

Figure 5.8   Suggested hedging strategy based on XYZ's stock price expectations at maturity.

- In order to delta-hedge its position, the seller of the option, i.e., Gigabank, needed to borrow the stock in order to maintain a short position in the underlying stock over the term of the transaction.

5.1.7 Summary of Main Hedging Strategies

The strategies just covered are the most common hedging strategies. Each company has overriding objectives and challenges, and correctly identifying those forms an integral element to the success of a hedging strategy. In Figure 5.8, I have tried to select the optimal hedging strategy, as a function of ABC's expectations regarding XYZ's stock price in 12 months. It can be seen that the probability distribution of XYZ's stock price is not symmetrical due to the volatility skew (i.e., implied volatilities for puts being notably greater than volatilities for calls).

5.1.8 Hedging with Ladder Puts

A ladder option is an option that locks in gains once the underlying reaches predetermined price levels or "rungs". A ladder put locks in a minimum payout if the underlying falls below a rung before expiry. This feature may be valuable for entities that want to buy a put to limit losses when the stake share price declines, but want to avoid the frustration of seeing the share price recover later. An important advantage of ladder puts versus a standard put is that the former provides better mark-to-market protection against an early market decline because some of its payout may get locked in at intrinsic value before expiry.

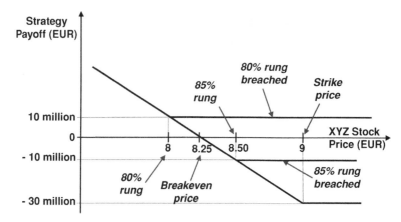

Figure 5.9   ABC's payoff under the ladder put as a function of XYZ's stock price at expiry.

Let us assume that ABC bought a ladder put on 40 million XYZ shares, with a 90% strike (EUR 9.00) and a 12-month expiry. The ladder had two rungs, one at 85% (EUR 8.50) and another at 80% (EUR 8.00). ABC paid 7.5%, or EUR 30 million ($=$ 400 million $\times$ 7.5%), for the ladder put. The payoff of the ladder put, ignoring its premium, would be at least the payoff of a standard put.

- If XYZ stock price reached 85% (EUR 8.50) at any time during the life of the put, the settlement amount would be locked in to be at least EUR 20 million [$=$ 40 million $\times$ (9.00 – 8.50)].
- If XYZ stock price reached 80% (EUR 8.00) at any time during the life of the put, the settlement amount would be locked in to be at least EUR 40 million [$=$ 40 million $\times$ (9.00 – 8.00)].

Figure 5.9 shows the ladder put payoff as a function of XYZ's stock price at expiry, taking into account the settlement amount and the EUR 30 million upfront premium, and ignoring timing differences. The settlement amount was calculated as EUR 40 million $\times$ Max(put strike – settlement price, 0), with a minimum of EUR 20 million (or EUR 40 million) if the 85% (or the 80%) rung was reached during the life of the option.

Advantages and Weaknesses of the Strategy

The advantages of the ladder put strategy were the following:

- At expiration, ABC had full downside protection below the EUR 9.00 put strike price.
- ABC locked in gains each time a rung was reached.
- ABC retained ownership of the stake, maintaining the voting rights and receiving the dividends.
- ABC participated in full in an appreciation of the stake.

The weaknesses of the strategy were the following:

- ABC paid an upfront premium.
- The premium paid was significantly larger than that of a standard put.

- ABC was exposed to the difference between the EUR 10.00 stock price prevailing at inception and the EUR 9.00 strike price.
- In order to delta-hedge its position, the seller of the option, i.e., Gigabank, needed to borrow the stock in order to maintain a short position in the underlying stock over the term of the transaction.

5.1.9 Hedging with Variable Premium and Variable Expiry Timer Puts

During periods in which the implied volatility of the stock to be hedged is unusually high, a more structured hedging strategy might make sense: a hedge with timer puts. There are two types of timer puts: (i) timer puts with variable premium and (ii) timer puts with variable expiry.

As an example, let us assume that the stock market in general is experiencing an unprecedented level of implied volatilities. As a result, 12-month 90% puts on XYZ are priced using a 50% implied volatility (a volatility much larger than XYZ's 30% 12-month average historical volatility), resulting in a EUR 35 million premium. Let us assume further that ABC believed that the realized volatility of such an option would be much lower than the implied volatility the market was pricing. Instead of acquiring the standard put option, ABC decided to purchase a timer put.

Timer Puts with Variable Premium

A timer put with variable premium is similar to a standard put except that the premium paid upfront is adjusted at expiry to take into account the realized volatility of the underlying stock during the life of the option.

Let us assume that ABC bought from Gigabank a 12-month, 90% strike timer put with variable premium. ABC paid a EUR 35 million premium at inception to Gigabank due to a pricing using a 50% implied volatility. This premium would be adjusted at expiry, to take into account the realized volatility of XYZ's stock during the 12-month life of the put. The terms of the timer put were identical to those of the 12-month, 90% strike, standard put covered earlier in this chapter, except that two new terms called "rebate" and "realized volatility" were added to the terms and conditions of the put. The "rebate" term was defined as follows:

- Rebate: Two currency business days after the exercise date, the "rebate payer" shall pay to the "rebate receiver" the "rebate amount", as shown in the following table (the rebate amount will be linearly interpolated using the two closest realized volatility levels):

Realized volatility	Rebate amount (EUR)	Rebate amount payer	Rebate amount receiver
≥ 70%	14 million	ABC	Gigabank
60%	7 million	ABC	Gigabank
50%	Zero	—	—
40%	7 million	Gigabank	ABC
≤ 30%	14 million	Gigabank	ABC

For example, if the realized volatility during the 12-month life of the option was 30%, ABC would receive a EUR 14 million rebate. Taking into account the initial EUR 35 million premium and ignoring the time value of money, ABC would have paid a EUR 21 million

(= 35 million − 14 million) total premium for the put option. Using a different example, if the realized volatility was 60%, ABC would pay a EUR 7 million rebate. Taking into account the initial EUR 35 million premium and ignoring the time value of money, ABC would have paid a EUR 42 million (= 35 million + 7 million) total premium for the put option. Therefore, ABC was exposed to the realized volatility of XYZ's stock.

Realized Volatility Calculation

The formula to calculate the realized volatility is defined at inception of the trade. The realized volatility σ_R is the annualized standard deviation of a stock's returns during a period, expressed in percentage. A common formula is the following:

$$\text{Realized volatility} = \sigma_R = 100 \times \sqrt{\frac{252 \times \sum_{i=1}^{N} \left(Ln \frac{P_i}{P_{i-1}} \right)^2}{\text{Expected } N}}$$

where:

> Ln is the natural logarithm.
> P_i and P_{i-1} are the official levels of the underlying on respectively the ith and $i-1$th observation days. In most cases the official level is the daily closing price of the underlying. In our case, the underlying was XYZ stock and the official level was the closing price.
> N is the actual number of realized trading days for the period from, but excluding the observation start date to, and including, the observation end date. In our case, there were 252 trading days during the timer put's life.
> 252 is the **annualization factor**. Usually it is assumed 252 trading days per year.
> **Expected N** is the number of days that, as the trade date, are expected to be scheduled trading days for the period from, but excluding the observation start date to, and including, the observation end date. In other words, "expected N" is the number of agreed observation days. In our case, there were 252 trading days during the timer put's life.
> **Observation day** is each trading day during the observation period.
> **Observation period** is the period from, but excluding, the observation start date to, but excluding, the observation end date.

Timer Puts with Variable Expiry

A less popular strategy when hedging a strategic stake is to buy a timer put with variable expiry. The terms of a timer put are identical to those of a standard put except that the timer put's expiration date is unknown on the trade date. The realized volatility of the underlying is used to determine the expiry of the option, as opposed to this being set at trade inception for a standard option.

Let us assume that ABC bought from Gigabank a timer put with variable expiry. ABC paid a EUR 22 million premium at inception to Gigabank. This premium would *not* be adjusted at expiry. Instead, the expiry date was unknown at inception, being set once a realized 30% volatility of XYZ's stock was "consumed". The terms of the timer put were identical to those of the 12-month, 90% strike, standard put covered earlier in this chapter, except that two new terms called "expiration date" and "realized volatility" would be added to the terms and conditions of the put. These terms were defined as follows:

- Expiration date: The first trading date that the realized volatility is greater than, or equal to, 30%.
- Realized volatility (the terms P_i and P_{i-1} were defined earlier for the timer puts with variable premium):

$$\text{Realized volatility} = \sigma_R = 100 \times \sqrt{\frac{252 \times \sum_{i=1}^{N} \left(Ln\frac{P_i}{P_{i-1}} \right)^2}{N}}$$

where:

> N is number of trading days from, but excluding, the observation start date to, and including, the current observation day.
>
> **Observation day** is each trading day during the period from, but excluding, the trade date to, but including, the date on which the expiration date is set.

ABC expected the 12-month realized volatility to be 30%. If ABC was right, the option would expire in 12 months. If XYZ showed a more volatile pattern since the trade date, the life of the option would be shorter than 12 months. Conversely, if it showed a less volatile pattern, the life of the option would be longer than 12 months.

In my view a timer put with variable premium makes more sense than a timer put with variable expiry, as ABC knows at inception that it will be protected during the next 12 months. Nevertheless, a timer put with variable expiry should not be completely discarded as a useful hedging strategy, especially if ABC wants to spend a certain limited premium. If the realized volatility is consumed much quicker than expected, for example during 9 months, probably it is because XYZ's stock price has fallen sharply. At the 9-month expiry, ABC can decide what to do next: whether to sell the stake, enter into a 3-month forward or buy a new 3-month put.

5.1.10 Hedging with Pay-later Puts

A pay-later put is a put option that is paid for only if the stock price declines. Thus, there is no upfront premium and the buyer pays for the protection only as the protection is needed. At inception the buyer of the option gets a standard put option for free. However, the buyer pays immediately a fixed amount once the underlying stock price falls below predetermined price levels or "rungs". This feature may be valuable for entities that want to buy a put to limit losses, but that want to avoid the frustration of paying for a protection that was not needed during the life of the option. However, it is possible that all the rungs are breached and the protection turns out to be more expensive than a standard put. It is also possible that all the rungs are breached during the life, making the buyer pay a substantial premium, and that at the end the protection was not needed because the stock price ended up above the strike price.

As an example, let us assume that ABC was interested in buying a 90% European put with 1-year expiry on 40 million shares of XYZ to consolidate the recent strong performance of XYZ stock. Remember from an earlier example that a standard put was worth a EUR 22 million premium (i.e., 5.5%). Because the stock market was strong, ABC thought that it was quite

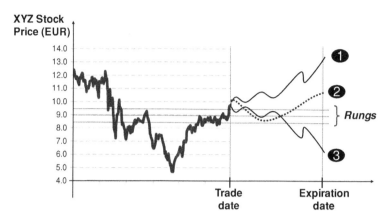

Figure 5.10   Sample scenarios of XYZ's stock price.

likely that the protection would turn out to be useless. However, ABC was convinced that if XYZ stock price reversed it would reverse sharply. As a result, ABC bought a pay-later put with three rungs, at the 95%, 90% and 85% levels. The breach of any of these three rungs would oblige ABC to pay a EUR 12 million premium (i.e., 3%) immediately. Regarding the cost of the protection, four scenarios were possible:

- If no rungs were breached during the life of the option, the cost would be zero. This cost would look very favorable relative to the EUR 22 million premium of the standard put.
- If only the 95% rung was breached during the life of the option, the cost would be EUR 12 million. This cost would look notably favorable relative to the EUR 22 million premium of the standard put.
- If only the 95% and 90% rungs were breached during the life of the option, the cost would be EUR 24 million. This cost would look similar to the EUR 22 million premium of the standard put.
- If all the rungs were breached during the life of the option, the cost would be EUR 36 million. This cost would look notably unfavorable relative to the EUR 22 million premium of the standard put.

As an example, let us assume three scenarios of future performance of XYZ's stock price (see Figure 5.10):

- Under the first scenario, XYZ's stock price continued its rally. ABC did not pay any premium for the put because no rungs were breached during the life of the option. As a result, ABC got a 90% put for free.
- Under the second scenario, XYZ's stock price suffered a temporary correction, ending above its initial level. ABC paid a EUR 24 million premium because two rungs were breached during the life of the option. The protection was not needed at the end.
- Under the third scenario, XYZ's stock price suffered a sharp correction, ending well below its initial level. ABC paid a EUR 36 million premium because all three rungs were breached during the life of the option. The protection was needed. However, ABC would have paid a notably lower premium (EUR 22 million) by buying a standard put option.

Ignoring the premium, the payoff of the pay-later option at expiry was identical to that of a standard put option. Therefore, at expiry, there were two scenarios:

- If XYZ's stock price was greater than or equal to the 90% put strike price, the option would expire worthless.
- If XYZ's stock price was lower than the 90% put strike price, ABC would receive from Gigabank a cash amount equal to the number of options × (strike price – settlement price). For example, if XYZ's stock price at expiry was EUR 7.00, ABC would receive EUR 80 million [= 40 million × (9.00 – 7.00)].

Advantages and Weaknesses of the Strategy

The advantages of the pay-later strategy were the following:

- At expiration, ABC had full downside protection below the put strike price.
- In a bullish or moderately bearish performance of XYZ's stock price, the pay-later premium was notably lower than that of a standard put.
- ABC retained ownership of the stake, maintaining the voting rights and receiving the dividends.
- ABC participated in full in an appreciation of the stake.

The weaknesses of the pay-later strategy were the following:

- In a temporary or more permanent bearish performance of XYZ's stock price, the pay-later premium was notably greater than that of a standard put.
- ABC was exposed to the difference between the stock price prevailing at inception and the put strike price.
- In order to delta-hedge its position, the seller of the option needed to borrow the stock in order to maintain a short position in the underlying stock over the term of the transaction.

5.2 YIELD ENHANCEMENT OF A STRATEGIC STAKE

In this section I will briefly cover different strategies to generate additional income on a strategic stake.

5.2.1 Lending the Stock

An investor can obtain an additional income by lending the strategic stake without taking any major additional risk. By lending the stock, the investor receives a fee, called the **borrowing fee**. As seen in Chapter 1, the stock can be lent on an open basis or on a guaranteed basis. A stock lent on an open basis can be terminated early by any of the two parties at any time, while a stock lent on a guaranteed basis cannot be terminated early before maturity.

The lending fee is quoted on an annual basis and calculated on a daily basis. For very liquid stocks, the lending fee can be small (e.g., 10 bps). However, there are situations in which the lending fee can be substantial (e.g., 5%), like the following:

- There is a stock-for-stock hostile tender offer. Arbitrageurs with a view that the offer will succeed would be selling the stock of the acquirer and buying the stock of the buyer. To sell the stock of the acquirer, the arbitrageurs would need to borrow the stock.

- The stock fundamentals are very weak, attracting hedge funds willing to short a stock. However, there is no stock lending market in that stock.
- An investment bank is trying to offer a derivatives hedge position to a client on a stock, but there is no stock lending market in that stock.

5.2.2 Selling Part of the Upside with a Call

A popular way to increase the yield on a strategic stake is to sell a call on the stake, a strategy called "covered call writing". The investor would receive a premium for providing the call buyer with the right to acquire the underlying shares at the call strike price. By receiving a premium, the investor is being compensated for the possibility of selling the stock at a determined price in the future.

Let us assume that ABC owns 40 million shares of XYZ stock, which is currently trading at EUR 10.00 per share. Therefore, the stake is worth EUR 400 million. ABC wants to generate additional income and is willing to sell the stake if the stock appreciates by 15% in 12 months' time. ABC sells a 12-month European call with a strike price of EUR 11.50. ABC receives a 4%, or EUR 16 million (= 400 million × 4%), upfront premium. The following table describes the main terms of the call option:

Cash-settled Call Option – Main Terms	
Buyer	Gigabank
Seller	ABC Corp.
Option type	Call
Trade date	1-June-20X1
Expiration date	1-June-20X2
Option style	European
Shares	XYZ
Number of options	40 million (one share per option)
Strike price	EUR 11.50 (115% of the spot price)
Spot price	EUR 10.00
Premium	4% of the notional amount, or
	EUR 16 million (i.e., EUR 0.40 per share)
Premium payment date	3-June-20X1
Notional amount	Number of options × Spot price
	EUR 400 million
Settlement price	The closing price of the shares on the valuation date
Settlement method	Cash or physical settlement, to be elected by the option seller (ABC Corp.) five business days prior to the expiration date
Cash settlement amount	The maximum of:
	(i) Number of options × (Settlement price – Strike price), and
	(ii) Zero
Cash settlement payment date	4-June-20X2

One interesting feature of the call option was that it could be cash settled or physically settled, at ABC's election. This feature provided ABC flexibility to not have to sell the stake if the call was exercised by Gigabank. For example, if the option was slightly in-the-money at expiry, ABC would prefer to choose cash settlement, paying the modest settlement amount and keeping the stake. However, if the option was very deep-in-the-money and, thus, the settlement amount very large, ABC would prefer to choose physical settlement, delivering the shares.

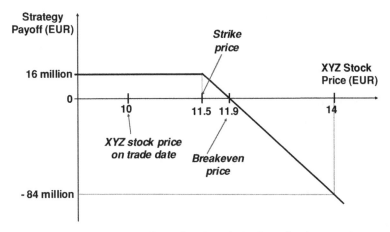

Figure 5.11   ABC's payoff under the call as a function of XYZ's stock price at expiry.

At expiry, there were two scenarios:

- If XYZ's stock price was greater than the EUR 11.50 call strike price, ABC would choose between cash and physical settlement. In case of physical settlement, ABC would deliver to Gigabank 40 million shares of XYZ in exchange for EUR 460 million (= 40 million × 11.50) – the strike amount. In case of cash settlement, ABC would pay to Gigabank a cash amount equal to the number of options × (settlement price – strike price). For example, if XYZ's stock price at expiry was EUR 13.00, ABC would pay to Gigabank EUR 60 million [= 40 million × (13.00 – 11.50)].
- If XYZ's stock price was lower than, or equal to, the EUR 11.50 call strike price, the option would expire worthless. If XYZ stock increased in price moderately, below the EUR 11.50 strike price, ABC would have the best scenario. ABC would benefit from the price appreciation and the received premium.

Figure 5.11 depicts ABC's payoff under the call as a function of XYZ's stock price at expiry, taking into account the settlement amount and the EUR 16 million upfront premium and ignoring timing differences. Therefore, the payoff was calculated as: EUR 16 million – EUR 40 million × Max(settlement price – strike price, 0).

Advantages and Weaknesses of the Strategy

The advantages of the strategy are the following:

- Investor receives an upfront premium.
- Investor benefits from a stock price appreciation up to the call strike price.
- Investor retains ownership of the stake, maintaining the voting rights and receiving the dividends.

The weaknesses of the strategy are the following:

- Investor does not participate in the stock price appreciation above the call strike price.
- Investor does not get any downside protection. However, the upfront premium can be viewed as a cushion against a drop in the stake's value.

- To meet the option settlement, the investor should not sell the stake during the life of the call, unless he/she terminates the call early, which can be costly.
- In order to delta-hedge its position, the buyer of the call option needs to borrow the stock in order to maintain a short position in the underlying stock over the term of the transaction.

5.2.3 Monetization of Dividend Optionality

Sometimes, when distributing a dividend, a listed company gives shareholders the right to choose between receiving cash (a cash dividend) and receiving stock (a scrip dividend). Sometimes the number of shares underlying the scrip dividend is calculated incorporating a discount to the then prevailing share price. This discount is included to incentivize the election of the scrip dividend alternative. If the election period is large enough, the election right may contain an embedded value that can be monetized.

As an example, let us assume that on 1 September 20X1, ABC owns 40 million shares (the "number of shares") of XYZ. Let us assume that XYZ would be distributing a dividend on 16 December 20X1. XYZ would give, until 4 December 20X1, the right to its shareholders to choose between a cash dividend and a scrip dividend.

- In case a cash dividend is chosen, XYZ would pay a gross dividend per share of EUR 0.20 (the "gross dividend"), net of a 15% withholding tax (the "withholding tax"), on 16 December 20X1.
- In case of a scrip dividend, the number of shares to be received per share would be calculated by dividing (i) 0.20 by (ii) the conversion price. The conversion price would be calculated by multiplying (i) 90% (i.e., a 10% discount) by (ii) the average opening price of XYZ stock during the striking period (the "reference price"). The striking period would be the period from, and including, 14 September 20X1 to, and including, 11 October 20X1.

Because ABC always elects to receive a cash dividend, it is willing to sell the option embedded in the dividend election. For example, ABC would be selling a call on XYZ stock on 1 September 20X1 to Gigabank with the following terms:

Physically-settled Call Option – Main Terms	
Buyer	Gigabank
Seller	ABC Corp.
Option type	Call
Trade date	1-September-20X1
Expiration date	4-December-20X1
Option style	European
Shares	XYZ
Number of options	To be described below (one share per option)
Strike price	To be described below
Premium	To be described below
Premium payment date	13-October-20X1
Settlement method	Physical settlement
Settlement date	16-December-20X1

The definition of the number of options, the strike price and the premium describes the process described next. On 11 October 20X1, the reference price would be calculated as the average opening price of XYZ stock during the striking period. Let us assume that the reference price was 11.00. The conversion price would then be calculated as 90% of the reference price:

$$\text{Conversion price} = 90\% \times \text{Reference price}$$
$$= 90\% \times 11.00 = \text{EUR } 9.90$$

The number of shares to be received by ABC as a dividend, were it to elect a scrip dividend, would be calculated as follows:

$$\text{Number of dividend shares} = \text{Number of shares} \times (\text{Gross cash dividend/Reference price})$$
$$\times (1 - \text{Withholding tax})$$
$$\text{Number of dividend shares} = 40 \text{ million} \times (0.20/9.90) \times (1 - 15\%) = 686{,}869 \text{ shares}$$

The number of options of the call would be the number of dividend shares, thus, 686,869 options.

The strike price of the call would be the conversion price, therefore, EUR 9.90.

Gigabank was willing to pay the intrinsic value of the call. Therefore, the premium was calculated as:

$$\text{Premium} = \text{Number of options} \times (\text{Reference price} - \text{Strike price})$$
$$\text{Premium} = 686{,}869 \times (11.00 - 9.90) = \text{EUR } 755{,}556$$

Regarding the call option, there would be two scenarios at expiry (4-December-20X1):

- If XYZ's stock price was greater than the EUR 9.90 call strike price, Gigabank would exercise the call. ABC would deliver to Gigabank 686,869 shares of XYZ in exchange for EUR 6.8 million (= 686,869 × 9.90) – the strike amount.
- If XYZ's stock price was lower than, or equal to, the EUR 9.90 call strike price, the option would expire worthless.

Next I am going to explain the mechanics of the transaction by analyzing the different steps of the transaction, combining the flows of the dividend election right and the call.

Steps at **inception** (1 September 20X1):

- ABC sells the call to Gigabank. The strike price, the number of options and the premium are unknown on trade date.

Steps on the **reference price fixing date** (11 October 20X1):

- The scrip dividend terms are fixed.
- The call strike price, the number of options and the premium are fixed. Gigabank pays the premium on 13 October 20X1.

Steps on **expiration date** (4 December 20X1) (two different scenarios could occur):

1. If XYZ's stock price was lower than, or equal to, the EUR 9.90 call strike price, ABC would be receiving EUR 6.8 million:
   - Gigabank would not exercise the call.
   - ABC will elect cash settlement. As a result, ABC would receive a EUR 6.8 million [= 40 million × 0.20 × (1 – 15%)] cash dividend.

2. If XYZ's stock price was greater than the EUR 9.90 call strike price, ABC would be receiving EUR 6.8 million:
   - Gigabank would exercise the call. ABC would deliver to Gigabank 686,869 shares of XYZ in exchange for EUR 6.8 million ($= 686,869 \times 9.90$) – the strike amount.
   - ABC would elect scrip dividend, receiving 686,869 shares from XYZ.

As a result, in any scenario, ABC would be receiving EUR 6.8 million and EUR 755,556 (i.e., the call premium). Therefore, ABC would be better off by implementing this strategy than by choosing a cash-only dividend. However, bear in mind that ABC may be levied corporate taxes on the premium received.

5.2.4 Reduction of Dividend Withholding Taxes with a Stock Lending Strategy

Frequently, investors are levied a withholding tax when receiving a dividend from the issuer of the strategic stake. In general, investors would be subject to one of the following situations:

- The investor is not levied any withholding tax.
- The investor is levied a withholding tax and is able to recover it at a later stage.
- The investor is levied a withholding tax and is able to use it against a tax base.
- The investor is levied a withholding tax and is unable to recover it.

The last situation is typical of foreign investors domiciled in tax haven jurisdictions. Let us assume that ABC owned 40 million of XYZ shares and that when a dividend is distributed to these shares ABC is levied a 15% withholding tax and is unable to recover it. Let us assume further that in three weeks, XYZ would be distributing a EUR 0.20 gross dividend per share. Thus, the gross dividend to be distributed to the 40 million XYZ shares would be EUR 8,000,000 ($= 40$ million $\times 0.20$). Taking into account the 15% withholding tax, ABC would be receiving EUR 6,800,000 [$= 8$ million $\times (1 - 15\%)$].

Let us assume that Gigabank had a domestic presence in XYZ's jurisdiction and was able to receive a dividend on XYZ shares without being levied any taxes. A potential strategy for ABC would be to temporarily "transfer ownership" of the shares to Gigabank, and have the bank receive the dividend tax-free. Commonly, the temporary transfer of ownership is done in one of two ways:

- To enter into a stock lending transaction.
- To enter into a converse transaction.

Stock Lending Strategy

The implementation of a stock lending transaction is the simplest way to reduce the tax effects on dividends. However, some banks may be reluctant to enter into this type of trade with the only purpose of exploiting a tax arbitrage situation because the tax authorities may question the tax treatment of the transaction. Let us assume that Gigabank and ABC entered into a stock lending transaction with the following steps:

- Two weeks before the ex-dividend date, ABC lent its 40 million XYZ shares to Gigabank. Ownership was transferred to Gigabank. Because, on the dividend record date, Gigabank was the owner of the shares, it was entitled to receive the upcoming dividend.

- On dividend payment date Gigabank received the EUR 8 million dividend, free of any taxes.
- Also on dividend payment date Gigabank paid ABC a manufactured dividend of EUR 7.3 million.
- Two weeks after dividend payment date, Gigabank returned the stock and paid a EUR 100,000 fee.

As a result, ABC received a total of EUR 7.4 million (= 7.3 million + 0.1 mn) under the transaction. This amount represented 600,000 more than the EUR 6.8 million net dividend ABC would have received if it had not entered into the transaction. However, this transaction would probably require ABC and Gigabank to disclose the transfer of ownership (the 40 million shares could represent a substantial percentage of XYZ's share capital), potentially alerting the tax authorities about the existence of a tax arbitrage transaction.

5.2.5   Reduction of Dividend Withholding Taxes with a Converse Strategy

A converse strategy is a bit more robust than the previous stock lending transaction. Remember that a converse is the combination of a long (short) position in a European call and a simultaneous short (long) position in a European put, with the same terms. Let us assume that besides the assumptions mentioned in the stock lending transaction, XYZ's stock was trading at EUR 10.00. The converse transaction was implemented as follows:

- Two weeks before the ex-dividend date, ABC sold 40 million XYZ shares to Gigabank. ABC received EUR 400 million (= 40 million × 10.00). Ownership was then transferred to Gigabank. Because, on the dividend record date, Gigabank was the owner of the shares, it was entitled to receive the upcoming dividend. Simultaneously, ABC and Gigabank entered into a zero-cost converse. Under the converse, ABC purchased a European call and sold a European put. The strike of both options was 10.185. The expiration date of the options was two weeks after the dividend payment date.
- On dividend payment date Gigabank received the EUR 8 million dividend, free of any taxes.
- At expiry, i.e., two weeks after dividend payment date, either ABC exercised the call or Gigabank exercised the put. As a result, ABC bought back the 40 million XYZ shares, receiving EUR 407.4 million (= 40 million × 10.185).

Thus, ABC received a total of EUR 7.4 million (= 407.4 million − 400 million) under the transaction. This amount represented 600,000 more than the EUR 6.8 million net dividend it would have received if it had not entered into the transaction. Although this transaction would probably require ABC and Gigabank to disclose the transfer of ownership (remember that the 40 million shares could represent a significant percentage of XYZ's share capital), it was under an initial sale and a later purchase being potentially friendlier than a pure stock lending trade. A weakness of this converse trade was the large credit risk exposure that Gigabank had to ABC because of the EUR 400 million initial payment. However, this exposure was collateralized by the XYZ shares. A way to avoid this credit exposure was to have ABC post the EUR 400 million received at inception as cash collateral to the converse transaction.

6

Disposal of Strategic Stakes

The sale of a strategic stake is not a straightforward matter. Typically the number of shares to be sold represents a large multiple of the stock's average daily volume. Therefore, an immediate and direct sale of the stake onto the market by the investor can have a large negative impact on the stock price, reducing the disposal proceeds. This chapter examines the most common selling strategies.

There is no such thing as the perfect disposal strategy. Each strategy has its strengths and weaknesses. What was the optimal strategy can only be determined "a posteriori", i.e., once it is possible to see the actual stock price behavior during the relevant period. However, "a priori" it makes sense to determine the objectives of the disposal and then try to design a strategy that could meet these objectives.

6.1 MOST COMMON DISPOSAL STRATEGIES

There are many disposal strategies. In general, the various disposal strategies can be grouped into the following three categories (see Figure 6.1):

- **Deterministic disposal strategies**. In these transactions, the number of shares to be sold and the selling price are known at the strategy's inception. These strategies include immediate disposal strategies such as accelerated book-building placements and secondary public offerings, and deferred disposal strategies such as the issuance of mandatory exchangeables.
- **Enhanced disposal strategies**. By implementing these transactions, investors try to sell the stake either at their own entire discretion, at a premium or in a transparent way. In these strategies, the sale price and/or the number of shares to be sold is unknown in advance. These strategies include sale of calls, issuance of exchangeable bonds, execution of range accruals and execution of VWAP-linked instruments.
- **Derecognition strategies**. The main motivation behind these strategies is not to sell the stake but to derecognize it for accounting and/or tax purposes. These strategies include combinations of equity swaps and calls, and/or combinations of equity forwards and calls.

Next, I will describe these strategies in detail using a case study. These strategies can be combined to better achieve disposal objectives.

6.1.1 Case Study Assumptions

Let us assume that on 1 June 20X0, ABC Corp. owned 40 million shares of XYZ Corp. The shares were trading at EUR 10.00. ABC was looking to sell the stake. XYZ's average daily volume during the last six months was 4 million shares. Other relevant assumptions were:

- The block was worth EUR 400 million.
- The block represented 10% of XYZ's market capitalization.

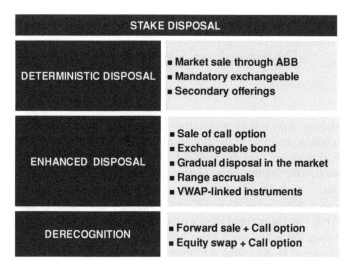

Figure 6.1   Main disposal strategies.

- The block represented 10 average trading day volumes (ADTV).
- The block represented 15% of XYZ's free float.

6.1.2   Market Dribbling Out or Gradual Sale

One of the most common disposal strategies of a large block is a market dribble-out. This strategy encompasses selling the shares onto the open market in small lots that will not be likely to affect the stock price significantly. As a general rule, a disposal on one day of a number of shares representing more than 20% of the stock's average daily volume is likely to affect the stock price. In our case, ABC decided to not exceed 20% of the daily volume. Because XYZ's average daily volume during the last six months was 4 million shares, under the dribbling-out strategy ABC would be selling approximately 0.8 million (= 4 million × 20%) shares each day. The sale of 40 million shares was then expected to take approximately 50 trading days (i.e., more than two months).

The advantages of this strategy were the following:

- ABC had complete control of the disposal process. If during the execution of the sale XYZ's stock price fell notably, ABC could stop it and resume it later once the market conditions improved.
- ABC could benefit from a future positive behavior of XYZ's stock price.
- There were no fees to be paid to investment banks, other than the usual brokerage commissions.
- There were no discounts to each day's market price of XYZ stock.

The disadvantages of this strategy were the following:

- There was a great uncertainty regarding the disposal price. During 50 trading days, XYZ's stock price could move notably. It could fall and not recover later, making ABC miss attractive price levels.

- ABC needed to devote resources to implement the execution. At least one person was required to follow the stock price and to give the orders to ABC's stockbrokers.
- If the disposal was executed in a weak market environment, the officers making the decision may be subject to criticism from other top management.

6.2 DETERMINISTIC DISPOSAL STRATEGIES

In this section I will cover the main strategies to dispose of a strategic stake. A common thread of these strategies is that ABC will be able to dispose of its stake in its entirety and to know at inception the disposal price. That is why I call these disposal strategies "deterministic".

6.2.1 ABB – Block Trade

The most common disposal strategy is an **accelerated book-building process (ABB)**. This strategy ensures a full disposal of the stake through a quick execution. The placement usually takes place after the closing of a specific day and before the next day's opening of the stock market. In Chapter 2 the reader can find a detailed description of an ABB. In a nutshell, an ABB is the placement of a block of shares with institutional investors, with the help of an investment bank. If the investment bank guarantees a minimum price, the ABB is called an **ABB with backstop**. If the block is sold directly to the investment bank at a pre-agreed price, the ABB is called a **bought deal** or a **block trade**.

In our case, ABC decided that the best alternative was a block trade. ABC wanted to sell the stock overnight and to agree on a price before the process was implemented. The price was set at a discount to the closing market share price. Therefore, ABC contacted Gigabank, to obtain an indication regarding the discount.

Discount Estimation by Gigabank

Were Gigabank to acquire the XYZ block from ABC at the pre-agreed price, it would need to place the block with institutional investors. Thus, in order to provide ABC with a quote, Gigabank had to estimate what discount to the previous closing price institutional investors would require to buy a large number of shares of XYZ. To assess this discount, Gigabank looked at the discount at which other comparable placements took place:

- The **stock market momentum**. The stock market was experiencing a mild positive performance. It was expected that this positive momentum could last several days. As a result, Gigabank did not include any negative adjustment to the discount due to the stock market momentum.
- The **size of the block relative to XYZ's average daily volume**. The block represented 10 trading days. This number was not large compared with other ABBs. Figure 6.2 shows the discounts at which other ABBs were placed during the last 12 months as a function of their number of trading days. It can be seen that blocks representing 10 trading days were placed at a 3% discount.
- The **total size of the block**. The block was worth EUR 400 million. This size was quite large compared with that of most ABBs placed during the last 12 months. Following a similar analysis to the one followed previously, similar-sized ABBs were placed at a 5% discount.

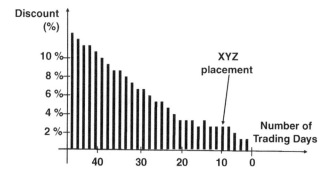

Figure 6.2   Discount of comparable ABBs as a function to their number of trading days.

- The **total size of the block relative to the stock free float**. The block represented 15% of XYZ's free float. This size was quite modest compared with that of most ABBs placed during the last 12 months. Following a similar analysis to the one followed previously, similar-sized ABBs were placed at a 4.5% discount.
- The **total size of the block relative to the market capitalization of the stock**. The block represented 10% of XYZ's market capitalization. This number was quite in line with the average size of the other ABBs. Following a similar analysis to the one followed previously, similar-sized ABBs were placed at a 3.8% discount.

Taking into account all the previous comparisons, Gigabank decided to quote a 4% discount to ABC. Let us assume that ABC found the discount reasonable, and mandated Gigabank to place the block before the opening of the market. Because the closing price of XYZ's stock was EUR 10.00, ABC sold the stake to Gigabank at EUR 9.60 (= 10.00 × 96%). As a result, in three trading days ABC received EUR 384 million (= 40 million × 9.60).

Advantages and Weaknesses of the Block Trade Strategy

The advantages of the block trade strategy were the following:

- The disposal was executed immediately, after the closing and before the opening of a trading day.
- ABC received the disposal proceeds immediately.
- ABC was not exposed to a price fall after the disposal was priced.
- It quickly took advantage of a temporary opportunity in the stock market.

The disadvantages of the block trade strategy were the following:

- The stock was placed at a significant discount to the prevailing market price.
- ABC could not benefit from a future positive behavior of XYZ's stock price.
- Although not relevant in our case, sometimes a placement at a reasonable discount may not be possible if the size of the block is large or if the market environment is weak.
- ABC did not keep the voting rights and did not receive the dividends to the shares after the transaction.

When the block size is a substantial number of trading days it is worth coupling an ABB transaction with a placement with strategic shareholders and other long-term financial investors. Such strategic placement may be a direct sale of shares and/or a sale of put (which is an engagement to buy shares).

6.2.2 Mandatory Exchangeable Bond

Another disposal alternative for ABC was to issue a mandatory exchangeable bond on 40 million XYZ shares. As we saw in Chapter 3, a mandatory exchangeable bond is a bond mandatorily convertible at maturity into a fixed or variable number of shares of the underlying stock. Gigabank proposed ABC the issuance of a 3-year fixed parity exchangeable bond with the following terms:

ABC's Mandatory Exchangeable Bond Terms	
Issuer	ABC Corp.
Notional amount	EUR 460 million
Issue date	1-June-20X0
Maturity	1-June-20X3
Underlying stock	XYZ common stock
Issue price	100%
Coupon	7%, semiannual Act/Act
Exchange price	EUR 11.50 (a 15% premium to the EUR 10.00 share price at issue)
Underlying number of shares	40 million
Exchange period	From issue date to maturity date
Dividend protection	Protection for any cash dividend in excess of a threshold amount
Issuer call	None, except a 10% clean-up call and tax call

Advantages and Weaknesses of the Strategy

The advantages of this strategy were the following:

- The disposal pricing was determined at inception.
- ABC received the disposal proceeds immediately.
- ABC kept the voting rights (of the unlent shares) and received the dividends during the life of the exchangeable.
- Upon exchange, the shares were placed at a premium.
- ABC was not exposed to a price fall after the disposal was priced.
- It quickly took advantage of a temporary opportunity in the equity-linked market.

The disadvantages of this strategy were the following:

- ABC had to pay coupon larger than in comparable straight debt.
- ABC could not benefit from a future positive behavior of XYZ's stock price.
- ABC had to lend most of the stake to the exchangeable investors so they could hedge their exposure to XYZ's stock price. ABC did not have the voting rights associated with the lent shares.

6.2.3 Indirect Issue of an Exchangeable Bond

Another way to dispose of a stake is to sell it to an investment bank. The investment bank can issue an exchangeable bond. The feasibility of this strategy is dependent on finding a third

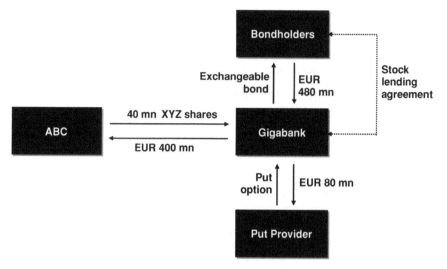

Figure 6.3   Building blocks of an indirect issue of an exchangeable bond.

party (the "put provider") willing to sell to the investment bank a put on the underlying shares of the exchangeable (see Figure 6.3). The put is needed so that at maturity, if the exchangeable is not exercised, the investment bank is able to sell its stake to the put provider. The put provider may end up holding the exchangeable bond's underlying shares at its maturity in case of no exchange. Usually, the put provider would be either the issuer of the shares (XYZ in our case) or a core shareholder of XYZ. This strategy was covered in detail in Chapter 4, in a case study on Deutsche Bank's exchangeable into Brisa.

Advantages and Weaknesses of the Strategy

The advantages of this strategy were the following:

- The disposal pricing was determined immediately.
- ABC received the disposal proceeds immediately.
- ABC was not exposed to a price fall after the disposal was priced.
- It quickly took advantage of a temporary opportunity in the equity-linked market.

    The disadvantages of this strategy were the following:

- Gigabank had to find a third party willing to sell a put option on the stake.
- ABC could not benefit from a future positive behavior of XYZ's stock price.
- ABC did not keep the voting rights and did not receive the dividends to the shares after the transaction.

6.3 ENHANCED DISPOSAL STRATEGIES

In the previous section I covered the main "deterministic" strategies to dispose of a strategic stake. A common thread of these strategies was that ABC was able to dispose of its stake entirely and was also able to know at inception the disposal price. In this section I will cover disposal strategies that try to enhance a specific feature of the sale. That is why I call these strategies "enhanced" disposal strategies. A majority of the enhanced disposal strategies try to obtain a better disposal price than that of a deterministic strategy, but there could be other enhancement motivations.

6.3.1 Direct Issue of an Exchangeable Bond

A typical way to enhance the disposal price of a sale of a stake is to issue an exchangeable bond. As we saw in Chapter 3, an exchangeable bond gives the holder the right to exchange the bond for a number of shares of the underlying stock. Let us assume that Gigabank contacted ABC to propose a transaction that took advantage of a strong demand for exchangeables. Gigabank proposed ABC the issuance of a 3-year bond exchangeable into 40 million shares of XYZ with a 20% premium. Let us assume that ABC approved the strategy because it allowed it to sell the stake at an attractive premium. The exchangeable had the following main terms:

ABC's Exchangeable Bond Terms	
Issuer	ABC Corp.
Notional amount	EUR 480 million
Redemption amount	100% of notional amount
Issue date	1-June-20X0
Maturity	1-June-20X3 (i.e., 3 years)
Underlying stock	XYZ common stock
Issue price	100%
Coupon	3%, semiannual Act/Act
Exchange price	EUR 12.00 (a 20% premium to the EUR 10.00 share price at issue)
Underlying number of shares	40 million
Exchange period	From issue date to maturity date
Dividend protection	Protection for any cash dividend in excess of a threshold amount
Issuer call	None, except a 10% clean-up call and tax call

At maturity, or upon early exchange, there would be two scenarios:

1. If XYZ's stock price was at, or below, the EUR 12.00 exchange price:
   - The bond holders would request the redemption of the bond, receiving in cash its redemption value (100% of the EUR 480 million notional amount).
   - ABC would keep its stake, not meeting its objective of selling its XYZ stake. However, ABC raised EUR 480 million for three years at a low cost.
2. If XYZ's stock price was above the EUR 12.00 exchange price:
   - The bond holders would exercise their exchange right. Upon exchange, the exchangeable investors would receive 40 million XYZ shares.
   - ABC would have sold all its XYZ's stake, meeting its objective of selling its entire XYZ stake at a premium. The sale took place at a 20% premium to the stock price at inception. Therefore, ABC obtained EUR 480 million.

Advantages and Weaknesses of the Strategy

The advantages of this strategy were the following:

- ABC could benefit from a future positive behavior of XYZ's stock price up to the EUR 12.00 exchange price.
- ABC quickly took advantage of a temporary opportunity in the equity-linked market.
- ABC raised EUR 480 million financing at an advantageous cost. The 3% coupon was notably lower than the yield of 3-year straight debt issued by ABC.
- ABC kept the voting rights associated with the unlent shares and received the dividends.

The disadvantages of this strategy were the following:

- ABC had no certainty regarding the sale of the stake. The disposal only took place if XYZ's stock price was above the EUR 12.00 exchange price.
- ABC was exposed to a future price fall of XYZ's stock price. If at maturity XYZ's stock price was below its EUR 10.00 level at inception, XYZ would still own the stake and it would be worth less than its initial EUR 400 million value.
- ABC had to lend part of the stake to the exchangeable investors so they could delta-hedge their position.
- ABC did not have the voting rights associated with the lent shares.

6.3.2   Sale of a Call Option

An alternative available to ABC was to sell a call option on 40 million shares of XYZ. This alternative is similar to the issuance of an exchangeable in that it allows an investor to sell the stake at a premium. Let us assume that the demand for exchangeable bonds was subdued and that ABC liked the idea of selling the stake at a premium.

The main limitation of this strategy is the feasible size. The investment bank acquiring the call usually manages the option risks. The main limitation in terms of size is caused by the hedge of the gamma risk at expiry. Gamma measures the variation of the delta for a 1% change in the stock price. Remember that the delta at expiry is either 100% or zero. If the delta is 100% (i.e., the stock price is above the strike price, the option is in-the-money just prior to expiry), it requires the bank long the call to short 100% of the underlying shares. If the delta is zero (i.e., the option is at-the-money or out-of-the-money just prior to expiry), it requires the bank to not have any position in the underlying stock. Imagine that shortly before expiry the call was out-of-the-money and that the stock price moved, causing the option to suddenly be in-the-money. Rapidly, the bank would need to sell all the underlying shares onto the market. If the number of shares was very substantial, the sale could largely affect the shares' stock price, causing the bank to sell the shares at a price much lower than expected. As a result, if the number of underlying shares is large relative to the stock's average daily volume, the bank could be incurring a large loss at maturity.

Let us assume that Gigabank was willing to trade options on XYZ a number of shares not exceeding five daily trading days. Because the block represented 10 trading days, Gigabank could only buy call options on 20 million XYZ shares, representing half of the stake. The terms of the call option were:

Physically Settled Call Option – Main Terms	
Buyer	Gigabank
Seller	ABC Corp.
Option type	Call
Trade date	1-June-20X0
Expiration date	1-June-20X1 (1 year)
Option style	European
Shares	XYZ common stock
Number of options	20 million
Strike price	EUR 12.00 (120% of the EUR 10.00 stock price on trade date)
Premium	EUR 8 million (4% of the option notional amount)
Notional amount	EUR 200 million (= 20 million × 10.00)
Premium payment date	3-June-20X0
Settlement method	Physical settlement
Settlement date	4-June-20X1

At expiry (i.e., one year after trade date), there would be two scenarios:

1. If XYZ's stock price was at, or below, the EUR 12.00 strike price:
   - The call option would not be exercised.
   - ABC would keep its stake, not meeting its objective of selling its XYZ stake. However, ABC received a EUR 8 million upfront premium.
2. If XYZ's stock price was above the EUR 12.00 strike price:
   - The call option would be exercised. ABC would sell half of its stake at a 20% premium, or EUR 12.00 per share and receive EUR 240 million (= 20 million × 12.00).
   - Additionally, ABC received a EUR 8 million upfront premium.

Advantages and Weaknesses of the Strategy

The advantages of this strategy were the following:

- ABC could benefit from a future positive behavior of XYZ's stock price up to the EUR 12.00 strike price.
- ABC received a EUR 8 million upfront premium.
- ABC kept the voting rights associated with the unlent shares and received the dividends.

The disadvantages of this strategy were the following:

- ABC had no certainty regarding the sale of the stake. The disposal only took place if XYZ's stock price was above the EUR 12.00 strike price.
- ABC could only implement this strategy for half of its stake (i.e., 20 million shares). ABC needed to put in place another disposal strategy for the other half of the stake.
- ABC was exposed to a future price fall of XYZ's stock price. If at maturity XYZ's stock price was below its EUR 10.00 level at inception, XYZ would still own half of the stake and it would be worth less than its initial EUR 200 million value.
- ABC had to lend part of the stake to Gigabank so it could delta-hedge its position.
- ABC did not have the voting rights associated with the lent shares.

6.3.3 One-speed Range Accrual

In the following subsections, I will cover a popular way to sell a stake at a premium. Range accrual instruments allow the daily sale of shares at a premium to the stock price prevailing at the strategy's inception. There are many versions of this strategy. I will review next the one-speed range accrual instrument.

An alternative available to ABC was to enter into a range accrual with one speed. As an example, let us assume that ABC enters into the following one-speed range accrual:

One-speed Range Accrual – Main Terms	
Buyer	Gigabank
Seller	ABC Corp.
Option type	Range accrual
Trade date	1-June-20X0
Start date	7-June-20X0
Maturity date	7-June-20X1 (1 year)
Shares	XYZ common stock
Maximum number of shares	20 million
Initial price	The volume-weighted average sale price per share at which the buyer (Gigabank) puts in place its initial hedge
Strike price	EUR 10.80 (108% of the EUR 10.00 initial price)
Barrier	EUR 9.20 (92% of the EUR 10.00 initial price)
Premium	None
Accrual periods	Each monthly period from, and including, the start date to, and including, the maturity date
Number of shares	For each accrual period: 80,000 × Number of days
Number of days	The number of trading days during the monthly period that the closing price of the shares is greater than, or equal to, the barrier
Settlement method	Physical settlement
	The buyer shall acquire from the seller the number of shares at a price per share equal to the strike price
Settlement date	Three exchange business days immediately following the end of the corresponding monthly period

The different steps of the transaction during its life are the following (see Figure 6.4):

- On trade date, ABC and Gigabank agreed on the terms of the range accrual. The strike price and the barrier were defined as a percentage, 108% and 92% respectively, of the initial price. Although ABC owned 40 million shares of XYZ, the range accrual could only be done for 20 million shares to make the transaction "risk manageable" to Gigabank. Thus, the transaction could only be implemented for 50% of ABC's stake in XYZ.
- Starting on the trade date (1 June 20X0), Gigabank put in place its initial hedge by selling a number of XYZ shares in the market. Gigabank needed to borrow a number of shares. Because the stock lending market for XYZ stock was too illiquid, ABC lent the corresponding shares to Gigabank so it could implement its initial hedge. Gigabank finished the initial hedge execution on the start date (7 June 20X0). The initial price, EUR 10.00, was the volume-weighted average price at which Gigabank sold the necessary shares to establish its initial hedge. As a result, on trade date the strike price and the barrier were respectively set at EUR 10.80 (108%) and 9.20 (92%).

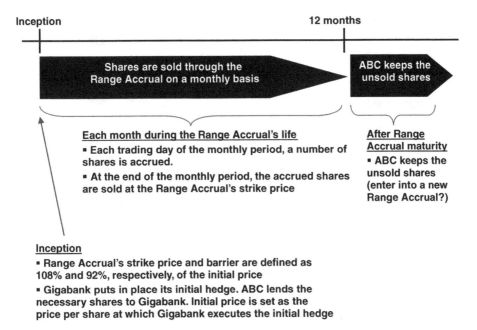

Figure 6.4   One-speed range accrual, steps of the transaction during its life.

The one-speed accrual allowed ABC to sell shares of XYZ at EUR 10.80, an 8% premium to the initial price. The maximum number of shares that ABC could end up selling was 20 million. Assuming 250 trading days over the 1-year term of the transaction, each trading day ABC could accrue a maximum of 80,000 shares (= 20 million/250).

The 12-month term of the transaction was divided into 12 monthly periods (the "accrual periods"). On each trading day of the accrual period, the number of shares accruing that day was a function of the closing price of XYZ's stock on that day (see Figure 6.5):

- If the stock closing price was greater than, or equal to, the EUR 9.20 barrier, 80,000 shares accrued that day.
- If the stock closing price was lower than the EUR 9.20 barrier, no shares accrued that day.

Three exchange business days following the end of the monthly accrual period (the "settlement date"), ABC sold to Gigabank the aggregate of the accrued shares (the "number of shares") during the monthly accrual period. The shares were sold by ABC at EUR 10.80

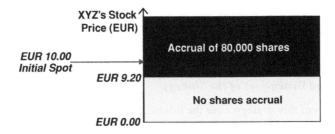

Figure 6.5   One-speed range accrual, daily accrual mechanism.

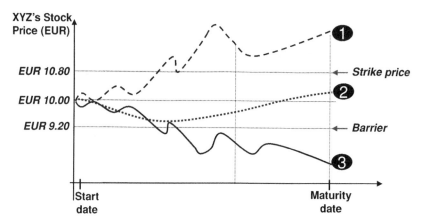

Figure 6.6   One-speed range accrual, simulated scenarios of XYZ's stock price behavior.

per share. For example, if during a monthly accrual period, the number of days was 15, the number of shares was 1.2 million (= 15 × 80,000). As a result, ABC sold 1.2 million shares at EUR 10.80 to Gigabank at the end of the monthly accrual period.

At maturity, any outstanding shares borrowed by Gigabank were returned to ABC. ABC still owned any shares not accrued during the life of the range accrual.

In order to highlight the strengths and weaknesses of the strategy, let us assume three different price behaviors of XYZ's stock price during the life of the instrument (see Figure 6.6):

- Under the first scenario, XYZ's stock price experienced a strong rally. Because the stock price always traded above the EUR 9.20 barrier, all the 20 million shares accrued, and therefore sold, over the term of the instrument. However, ABC was not entirely satisfied with the range accrual strategy because it sold the shares at EUR 10.80. It is true that this price was an 8% premium to the initial price. However, without entering into the instrument ABC could have obtained a higher selling price.
- Under the second scenario, XYZ's stock price experienced a movement without an overall bullish or bearish trend. Because the stock price always traded above the EUR 9.20 barrier, all the 20 million shares accrued, and therefore sold, over the term of the instrument. ABC was very satisfied with the range accrual performance because it was able to sell the shares at EUR 10.80, while the stock traded below this level during all the life of the instrument.
- Under the third scenario, XYZ's stock price experienced a strong correction. Excluding the first few months, the stock traded below the EUR 9.20 barrier. As a result only 5 million shares accrued, and therefore sold, over the term of the instrument. ABC was very satisfied with the range accrual performance because it was able to sell the shares at EUR 10.80, while the stock traded well below this level during most of the 12-month term. At the end of the instrument's life ABC still owned the 15 million unaccrued shares.

Advantages and Weaknesses of the Strategy

The advantages of this strategy were the following:

- ABC sold the accrued shares at a premium to the initial price.
- ABC benefited from each day that the stock price traded between the EUR 9.20 barrier and the EUR 10.80 strike price.

- ABC paid no premium to enter into the transaction.
- ABC kept the voting rights associated with the unlent XYZ shares and received the dividends.
- ABC had complete flexibility to pursue other strategies on the unaccrued shares.

The disadvantages of this strategy were the following:

- ABC had no certainty regarding the number of shares to be sold. The disposal only took place if XYZ's stock price was above the EUR 9.20 barrier. XYZ ended up owning all the unaccrued shares.
- ABC could only implement this strategy for half of its stake (i.e., 20 million shares). ABC needed to put in place another disposal strategy for the other half of its stake.
- ABC did not benefit from a stock price above the EUR 10.80 strike price.
- ABC was exposed to a future price fall of XYZ's stock price below the EUR 9.20 barrier.
- ABC had to lend part of the stake to Gigabank so it could delta-hedge its position. ABC did not have the voting rights associated with the lent shares.
- The range accrual was accounted for as a derivative. The instrument needed to be fair valued through the income statement at each reporting date.

Building Blocks

From ABC's viewpoint, the one-speed range accrual was built by combining a purchased knock-out put and a short call. Each trading day over the term of the range accrual, a combination of these two options expired on such day, as follows (see Figure 6.7):

- ABC sold a string of call options with strike price EUR 10.80 on 80,000 XYZ shares. There was a call for each trading day of the 12-month period (i.e., 250 calls). In other words, only one call expired on each day of the 12-month period.
- ABC bought a string of put options with strike price EUR 10.80 on 80,000 XYZ shares. There was a put for each trading day of the 12-month period (i.e., 250 puts). In other words, only one put expired on each day of the 12-month period. Each put ceased to exist if, on its expiry date, XYZ's stock price was below the EUR 9.20 barrier. Therefore, this option was a knock-out put.

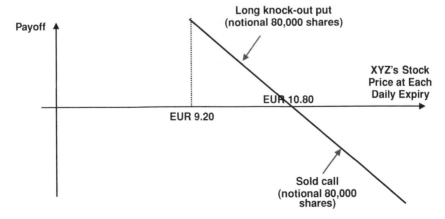

Figure 6.7   One-speed range accrual, building blocks of the transaction.

6.3.4 Double-speed Range Accrual

A variation available to ABC was to enter into a range accrual with double speed. The first objective was to increase the sale price (i.e., the strike price) from EUR 10.80 to EUR 11.50. Therefore, any shares sold through the range accrual instrument were sold at a 15% premium to the initial price. A second objective was to expand the ranges in which shares accrued. Under the one-speed range accrual, XYZ's stock price had to trade above EUR 9.20 to accrue shares on an observation day. Under the two-speed range accrual, XYZ's stock price had to trade above EUR 8.50 to accrue shares on an observation day. However, these two objectives were achieved in exchange for including a middle range in which just 40,000 shares accrued on a daily basis.

The mechanics of the double-speed range accrual are similar to the one-speed range accrual. The only difference lies in the daily accrual mechanism. As we saw earlier, the 12-month term of the transaction was divided into 12 monthly periods (the "accrual periods"). On each trading day of the accrual period, the number of shares accruing that day was a function of the closing price of XYZ's stock on such day (see Figure 6.8):

- If the stock closing price was greater than the EUR 11.50 strike price, 80,000 shares accrued that day.
- If the stock closing price was greater than, or equal to, the EUR 8.50 barrier and lower than, or equal to, the EUR 11.50 strike price, 40,000 shares accrued that day.
- If the stock closing price was lower than the EUR 8.50 barrier, no shares accrued that day.

At the end of each monthly period, the accrued shares were sold by ABC to Gigabank at EUR 11.50 (i.e., the strike price).

Comparison with the One-speed Range Accrual

If we compare the two-speed range accrual with the one-speed range accrual, the performance of one strategy relative to the other depends on XYZ's stock price behavior:

- In a strong stock market from the start, the two-speed range accrual is likely to outperform. Although a similar number of shares would be sold through both instruments, the accrued

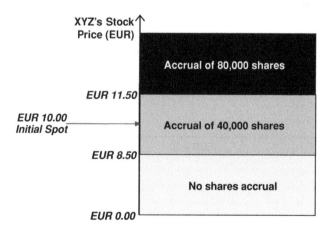

Figure 6.8 Two-speed range accrual, daily accrual mechanism.

shares under the two-speed range accrual would be sold at EUR 11.50 instead of at EUR 10.80.

- In moderately positive, or moderately negative, stock market behaviors, the one-speed range accrual is likely to outperform. A much larger number of shares is likely to accrue under the one-speed range accrual. The fact that the shares are sold at a lower price than in the two-speed version will be more than compensated by the larger number of shares sold.
- In a notably weak market from the beginning, the two-speed range accrual is likely to outperform as it will take longer to reach the barrier level.

Building Blocks

From ABC's viewpoint, the two-speed range accrual was built by combining, on a daily basis, a purchased knock-out put and a short call. Each trading day over the term of the range accrual, a combination expired on such day, as follows (see Figure 6.9):

- ABC sold a string of call options with strike price EUR 11.50 on 80,000 XYZ shares. There was a call for each trading day of the 12-month period (i.e., 250 calls). In other words, only one call expired on each day of the 12-month period.
- ABC bought a string of put options with strike EUR 11.50 on 40,000 XYZ shares. There was a put for each trading day of the 12-month period (i.e., 250 puts). In other words, only one put expired on each day of the 12-month period. Each put ceased to exist if on its expiry date, XYZ's stock price was below the EUR 8.50 barrier. Therefore, this option was a knock-out put.

6.3.5 Double-speed Range Accrual with Final Call

Another popular version of the range accrual instrument is a range accrual with a final call. Let us take the previous section's two-speed range accrual. This range accrual had a barrier set at EUR 8.50 and a strike price at EUR 11.50 (a 15% premium to the initial price). By including the sale of a call and maintaining the barrier unchanged, the strike price could be set at EUR 11.80 (an 18% premium to the initial price). The call gave Gigabank the right, but not

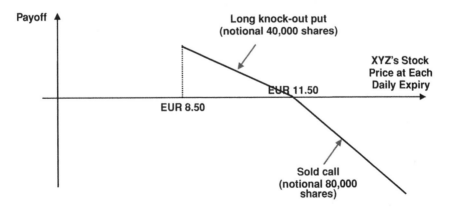

Figure 6.9 Two-speed range accrual, building blocks of the transaction.

the obligation, to buy at maturity at the strike price all the unaccrued (and thus unsold) shares during the 12-month tenor of the instrument.

As an example, let us assume that out of the maximum 20 million shares, ABC sold 8 million shares through the accrual process during its 12-month duration. At maturity, Gigabank had the right to buy 12 million (= 20 million − 8 million) shares at EUR 11.80. Therefore:

- If at maturity XYZ's stock price was greater than EUR 11.80, Gigabank would exercise the call and ABC would sell to the bank 12 million shares at EUR 11.80. ABC would then have sold all its 20 million XYZ shares.
- If at maturity XYZ's stock price was lower than, or equal to, EUR 11.80, Gigabank would not exercise the call. Then, ABC would still own 12 million XYZ shares.

The improvement in the strike price caused by the inclusion of the call, from a 15% premium to an 18% premium, was not very large. Why didn't it result in a larger strike price? This was because a stock price at maturity well above the EUR 11.80 strike price would likely mean that the daily accrual mechanism accrued 80,000 shares for many days. Therefore, if the call was exercised at maturity, the number of unaccrued shares would likely be low.

The improvement in the strike price was not for free. By selling the final call option, ABC lost the flexibility of selling the unaccrued shares during the life of the instrument. ABC had to wait until maturity to know if it would be left with any unsold shares.

6.3.6   Double-speed Range Accrual with Deduction

Another popular version of the range accrual instrument is a range accrual with a deduction feature. Let us take the two-speed range accrual. This range accrual had a barrier set at EUR 8.50 and a strike price at EUR 11.50 (a 15% premium to the initial price). Better terms can be achieved if already accrued shares can be "unaccrued" again. The following two-speed accrual improves the strike price to EUR 11.80 (i.e., an 18% premium to the initial price). As we saw earlier, the 12-month term of the transaction was divided into 12 monthly periods (the "accrual periods"). On each trading day of the accrual period, the number of shares accruing that day was a function of the closing price of XYZ's stock on such day (see Figure 6.10):

- If the stock closing price was greater than the EUR 11.80 strike price, 80,000 shares accrued that day.
- If the stock closing price was greater than, or equal to, the EUR 8.50 barrier and lower than, or equal to, the EUR 11.80 strike price, 40,000 shares accrued that day.
- If the stock closing price was lower than the EUR 8.50 barrier, no shares accrued that day. A maximum of 80,000 shares will be deducted from the month-to-date total number of accrued shares.

At the end of each monthly period, the accrued shares were sold by ABC to Gigabank at EUR 11.80 (i.e., the strike price). This alternative is notably speculative, as a drop during a month can wipe out the already month-to-date accrued shares.

6.3.7   Double-speed Range Accrual with Knock-out

Another version of the range accrual instrument is a range accrual with a knock-out feature. Let us take the two-speed range accrual. This range accrual had a barrier set at EUR 8.50 and a

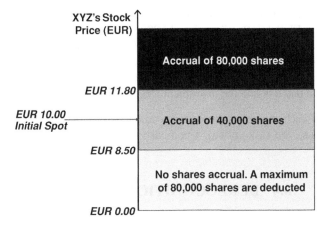

Figure 6.10 Two-speed range accrual with deduction, daily accrual mechanism.

strike price at EUR 11.50 (a 15% premium to the initial price). Better terms can be achieved if the range accrual terminates early when a barrier is reached. The following two-speed accrual improves the strike price to EUR 11.60 (i.e., a 16% premium to the initial price), but includes a knock-out barrier at EUR 8.00. If, on any observation day, XYZ stock is trading at or below EUR 8.00, the range accrual terminates and the accrued shares are sold. As we saw earlier, the 12-month term of the transaction was divided into 12 monthly periods (the "accrual periods"). On each trading day of the accrual period, the number of shares accruing that day was a function of the closing price of XYZ's stock on such day (see Figure 6.11):

- If the stock closing price was greater than the EUR 11.60 strike price, 80,000 shares accrued that day.

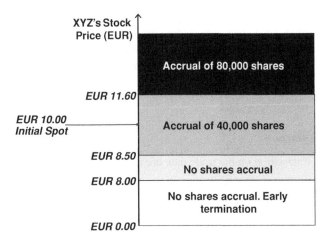

Figure 6.11 Two-speed range accrual with barrier, daily accrual mechanism.

- If the stock closing price was greater than, or equal to, the EUR 8.50 barrier and lower than, or equal to, the EUR 11.60 strike price, 40,000 shares accrued that day.
- If the stock closing price was lower than the EUR 8.50 barrier and greater than the EUR 8.00 knock-out barrier, no shares accrued that day.
- If the stock closing price was lower than, or equal to, the EUR 8.00 knock-out barrier, no shares accrued that day and the instrument terminated early.

At the end of each monthly period, the accrued shares were sold by ABC to Gigabank at EUR 11.60 (i.e., the strike price). Upon early termination, the accrued shares would be settled.

6.4 DERECOGNITION STRATEGIES

In this section I will cover the main strategies to immediately derecognize a strategic stake. A company might be interested in accelerating derecognition of a strategic stake for many different reasons, such as:

- The company is obliged to sell the stake for legal reasons. The company has just merged with another company, a competitor of XYZ, and the competition authorities have required the disposal of the strategic stake.
- The company holds substantial unrealized capital gains on a strategic stake, and is willing to recognize these capital gains immediately to improve reported earnings.
- The company wants to disclose to the market that it has sold a stake, but wants to keep its participation in the stake's performance.
- The company already sold part of a strategic stake, claiming a special capital tax treatment. Any additional disposals of the stake not implemented during the same tax year cannot be subject to the same capital gains tax advantageous treatment.

6.4.1 Sale + Cash-settled Equity Swap

A popular strategy to accelerate the disposal of a stake while maintaining its economic exposure is to combine the sale with a cash-settled equity swap. Let us assume that ABC holds 40 million shares of XYZ, and that the shares are trading at EUR 10.00. ABC is obliged to sell the stake to meet the requirements set by the antitrust authorities, but believes that the current EUR 10.00 stock price is too low. ABC decides to sell the stake and enter into a cash-settled equity swap in which ABC would be the equity amount receiver. The maturity of the equity swap is one year.

Flows of the Transaction

The flows of the transaction on the trade date are as follows (see Figure 6.12):

- ABC and Gigabank enter into the cash-settled total return equity swap on 40 million shares of XYZ. The initial price is set at EUR 10.00.
- ABC sells the 40 million XYZ shares to Gigabank, so the bank initially hedges its position. Thus, ABC receives EUR 400 million.
- ABC and Gigabank disclose the sale and purchase of the stake, respectively. ABC meets the requirements of the antitrust authorities.

Figure 6.12   Flows on trade date.

The flows of the transaction during the life of the equity swap are as follows (see Figure 6.13):

- ABC pays an interest, the floating amount, to Gigabank based on the EUR 400 million equity swap notional.
- Gigabank pays to ABC an amount, the dividend amount, equivalent to the dividends distributed to the underlying XYZ shares. This amount is paid on the same date the dividends are paid by XYZ to its shareholders.

Figure 6.13   Flows during the life of the equity swap.

The flows of the transaction at maturity (i.e., on the settlement date of the equity swap) are as follows (see Figure 6.14):

- Gigabank unwinds its hedge by selling 40 million shares of XYZ onto the market.
- ABC and Gigabank settle the equity swap after calculating the settlement amount.

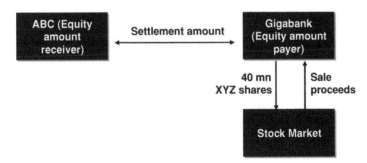

Figure 6.14   Flows on the settlement date of the equity swap.

Before approaching maturity, ABC would assess if XYZ's stock price was attractive enough. If the price was still unattractive, most probably ABC would request the extension of the equity swap maturity, probably for another year.

At maturity (i.e., on the equity swap valuation date), the settlement amount would be calculated as:

$$\text{Settlement amount} = \text{Number of shares} \times (\text{Settlement price} - \text{Initial price})$$
$$\text{Settlement amount} = \text{EUR 40 million} \times (\text{Settlement price} - 10.00)$$

The settlement price is the price at which Gigabank unwinds its hedge position (i.e., the sale price of the 40 million XYZ shares onto the market) at maturity.

- If the settlement amount was positive, the equity amount payer – Gigabank – would pay to the equity amount receiver – ABC – the settlement amount. For example, if the settlement price was EUR 13.00, ABC would receive from Gigabank EUR 120 million [= 40 million × (13.00 – 10.00)].
- If the settlement amount was negative, the equity amount receiver – ABC – would pay to the equity amount payer – Gigabank – the absolute value of the settlement amount. For example, if the settlement price was EUR 8.00, Gigabank would receive from ABC EUR 80 million [= Absolute value of 40 million × (8.00 – 10.00)].

Advantages and Weaknesses of the Strategy

The advantages of this strategy were the following:

- The transaction could be implemented very quickly, without a need to find third-party investors. Therefore, it allowed immediate disposal and a subsequent search/negotiation with potentially interested investors.
- The transaction could be implemented for a large size. Thus, ABC could dispose of the whole stake in one shot.
- ABC could benefit from a rising stock price during the equity swap term. ABC could dispose of the stake in a weak stock market environment, but benefit from a potential rebound later on.
- ABC still received the dividends distributed to the underlying shares.
- ABC paid no premium to enter into the transaction.

The disadvantages of this strategy were the following:

- ABC remained exposed to a falling stock price during the equity swap term.
- ABC did not have the voting rights associated with the underlying shares.
- Derecognition was not achieved. I will comment on this subject next.

Final Comments

The main objective of the transaction was for ABC to end the ownership of the voting rights associated with the strategic stake. The sale of the stake to Gigabank at inception meant that Gigabank was the owner of the voting rights pertaining to the stake from that date. The terms of the transaction had to be carefully designed in order to avoid any suspicion of ABC and Gigabank acting in concert. In Chapter 7, there is a case (Telefonica's offer to Portugal Telecom) that covers this subject.

The equity swap transaction did not try to achieve any specific accounting treatment. The way it was designed most probably could not achieve derecognition because ABC kept all the economic benefits and costs associated with an ownership of the stake. Usually derecognition is achieved by stopping to receive (pay) one of the benefits (costs). For example, Gigabank could keep the dividend instead of passing it through to ABC. A common shortcoming when derecognition is achieved is that the equity swap could thereafter be treated as a purely speculative instrument, being fair valued at each balance sheet date with changes in fair value reported in the income statement. In this case, the equity swap could cause ABC to report a more volatile income statement.

The equity swap could also be structured to optimize the timing of the disposal from a tax standpoint. Usually, the tax treatment follows the accounting treatment. Therefore, the taxation of a disposal commonly takes place when derecognition is achieved from an accounting standpoint.

6.4.2 Physically Settled Equity Swap + Call Option

A popular strategy to accelerate the disposal of a stake while maintaining the economic exposure to a strategic stake is to combine a physically settled equity swap with a cash-settled call option. The main advantage of this alternative is that it may achieve derecognition while maintaining the ownership of the stake.

Let us assume that ABC holds 40 million shares of XYZ, and that the shares are trading at EUR 10.00. ABC is looking to derecognize the stake to be able to immediately recognize a capital gain, but believes that the current EUR 10.00 stock price is too low. Also ABC wants to retain the stake's voting rights. To achieve these objectives, ABC enters into the following transaction: (i) ABC keeps the stake; (ii) ABC enters into a physically settled equity swap with Gigabank, in which ABC would be the equity amount payer; and (iii) ABC buys a cash-settled deep-in-the-money call from Gigabank. The maturity of the equity swap and the call is one year.

Flows of the Transaction

The flows of the transaction on trade date are as follows:

- ABC and Gigabank enter into a physically settled total return equity swap on 40 million shares of XYZ with Gigabank. The initial price is set at EUR 10.00. The maturity of the swap is 1 year. At maturity, Gigabank will sell 40 million shares of XYZ to Gigabank at EUR 10.00 per share. ABC will pay to Gigabank the dividends distributed to the underlying shares. Gigabank will pay a quarterly interest to ABC.
- ABC buys from Gigabank a cash-settled call on 40 million XYZ shares with a strike of EUR 6.00 (i.e., a 60% strike). The expiry of the call is 1 year. ABC pays a EUR 172 million (i.e., EUR 4.30 per share) premium. The initial delta of the option is 85%, or 34 million shares (= 85% × 40 million).
- Gigabank borrows from ABC 6 million XYZ shares (to be explained next), so the bank initially hedges its position.

Let us take a look at Gigabank's initial delta position (see Chapter 1 for a description of the delta concept). Under the equity swap, Gigabank had to sell 40 million shares as its delta was −100%. Under the call, Gigabank had to buy 34 million (= 85% × 40 million) shares, as its delta was 85%. As a result, Gigabank had to sell 6 million shares (40 million – 34 million). In order to sell these shares, Gigabank had to borrow the same number of shares from ABC (or from the market).

The flows of the transaction during the life of the equity swap and the call are as follows:

- Gigabank pays an interest, the floating amount, to ABC based on the EUR 400 million equity swap notional.

- ABC pays to Gigabank an amount, the dividend amount, equivalent to the dividends distributed to the underlying 40 million XYZ shares. This amount is paid on the same date the dividends are paid by XYZ to its shareholders.
- Gigabank pays to ABC the dividends and a borrowing fee on the borrowed 6 million shares.

The flows of the transaction at maturity of the equity swap (or at expiry of the call) are as follows:

- Under the equity swap, ABC delivers 40 million XYZ shares to Gigabank and receives EUR 400 million.
- ABC exercises the call if XYZ's stock price is greater than the EUR 6.00 strike, receiving the settlement amount. If XYZ's stock price is lower than, or equal to, the EUR 6.00 strike, the call expires worthless. The settlement amount is calculated as 40 million × Max[(settlement price – strike price), 0].

Gigabank's Position under the Transaction

Let us analyze Gigabank's position under the transaction, ignoring the equity swap's interest and dividend flows:

- Under the equity swap, Gigabank had a long position in the 40 million underlying shares at EUR 10.00 (the equity swap initial price). Therefore, it benefited from XYZ's stock price being above EUR 10.00 and was exposed to a stock price below EUR 10.00.
- Under the call, Gigabank was exposed to a share price above the call strike (EUR 6.00). Gigabank received a EUR 4.3 per share premium.

As a result, Gigabank was short a put with strike EUR 6.00 (see Figure 6.15). It received a EUR 0.3 premium.

Advantages and Weaknesses of the Strategy

The advantages of this strategy were the following:

- The transaction allowed immediate derecognition of the stake. Some auditors may question the accounting derecognition because the combination of the equity swap and the call option was similar to owning the shares for a stock price above EUR 6.00. In such a situation, the

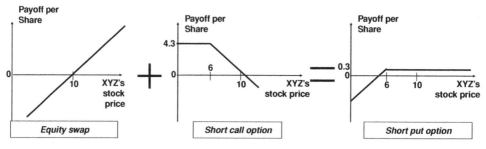

Figure 6.15   Gigabank's overall position under the transaction.

strike of the call may need to be higher (e.g., at EUR 8.00) to make it less similar to a long position in the underlying shares.

- The transaction could be implemented for a large size. In our case, ABC could derecognize the whole stake in one shot. This is not always true. Under the transaction, Gigabank was, in effect, short a put, limiting the potential size it could trade.
- ABC could benefit from a rising stock price during the transaction term. ABC could derecognize the stake in a weak stock market environment, but benefit from a potential rebound later on.
- ABC was not exposed to a share price below the strike of the call.
- ABC kept the voting rights associated with the underlying unlent shares.

The disadvantages of this strategy were the following:

- ABC did not keep the dividends distributed to the underlying shares.
- ABC paid a substantial premium to acquire the call. ABC probably needed to raise financing.
- ABC remained exposed to a falling stock price, up to the call strike.

6.5 COMBINATION OF ABB AND A CALL OPTION/EXCHANGEABLE

The combination of an accelerated book-building and a call option (or an exchangeable bond) enables investors to partially dispose of a strategic stake, minimizing the negative impact on the stock price caused by the disposal. In a real case, I will cover the technicalities of such a strategy.

6.5.1 Case Study: Germany's Disposal of Fraport with JP Morgan's Collaboration

This transaction shows a real-life example of a transaction in which an investor sold its strategic stake via an accelerated book-building (ABB) trade and the sale of a call. The sale of a call was mirrored by the issuance of an exchangeable bond.

Background Information

In 2005, Germany's finances were under strain as near-record unemployment boosted welfare payments and weak domestic growth saddled tax income. The budget deficit as a proportion of gross domestic product exceeded the European Union's 3% limit every year during the last three years. The large deficit forced the German government to sell assets to cut debt and reduce interest payments. The objectives were to quickly reduce its budget deficit, which the Bundesbank described as "extraordinarily critical", and to safeguard its AAA rating. S&P, the credit rating agency, threatened to cut Germany's AAA rating unless Germany improved its public finances. Germany had the highest debt levels, as a percentage of GDP, among the sovereigns – holding an AAA credit rating.

In October 2005, the German government was planning the privatization of its remaining 18.25% stake, or 16.6 million shares, in Fraport A.G., the operator of the Frankfurt Airport. Frankfurt Airport was Europe's second busiest airport after London's Heathrow Airport. Fraport A.G. had a market cap of approximately EUR 3.5 billion. Therefore, the 18.25% stake was worth approximately EUR 640 million.

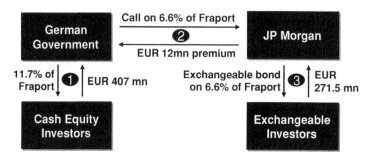

Figure 6.16   German government's disposal of Fraport.

The objectives of the German government were:

- To dispose of the whole stake in one transaction.
- To maximize the disposal price.
- To quickly execute the transaction.
- To minimize the downward pressure on Fraport's stock price.

The easiest and quickest way to sell the stake was through an accelerated book-building placement (an "ABB"). However, the stake represented a large number of Fraport's average daily volume. An ABB for the whole size required such a large discount that it became unattractive.

To achieve most of these objectives, the German government decided that the best solution was to dispose of the stake via the combination of two transactions, to be executed simultaneously:

- An ABB.
- An issuance of an exchangeable bond.

However, because the German government was not allowed to issue the exchangeable bond directly for Maastricht budgetary reasons, it had to rely on a third party – JP Morgan – to issue an exchangeable. As a result, instead of issuing an exchangeable directly, the German government sold a call option to JP Morgan. In turn, JP Morgan then used the call option to issue an exchangeable bond. Figure 6.16 depicts the strategy building blocks:

1. The German government sold 64% of its Fraport's stake, or 11.7% of Fraport's share capital, via an ABB, raising EUR 407 million.
2. The German government sold a 17-month call option to JP Morgan on 36% of the stake, or 6.6% of Fraport's share capital. The German government received a EUR 12 million premium for the call option.
3. JP Morgan issued an exchangeable bond mirroring the terms of the call option bought from the German government. JP Morgan raised EUR 271.5 million through the sale of the exchangeable bond.

The Accelerated Book-build

The German government's first step was the disposal of 64% of the total stake (i.e., 11.7% of Fraport's share capital) in an ABB with institutional investors and with Lufthansa. JP Morgan and Morgan Stanley managed the direct sale of stock. The 10.6 million shares of Fraport were sold at EUR 38.40 price per share, a 4% discount to prior-day Fraport's closing stock price. Therefore, Germany raised a total of EUR 407 million.

A large portion of the ABB was placed with Deutsche Lufthansa A.G. ("Lufthansa"), Europe's second largest airline at that time. Lufthansa acquired 4.95% of Fraport, or 4.5 million shares. Lufthansa spent EUR 173 million. The airline bought the holding to take a seat on Fraport's supervisory board, in order to play a role in the airport's decision-making. Fraport planned to expand Frankfurt's airport with a new terminal and a new runaway. About 60% of Lufthansa's passengers flew through Frankfurt, and the airport accounted for roughly half of its take-offs and landings.

The sale left the German state of Hesse and the city of Frankfurt as the largest shareholders in Fraport, owning 50% of the company. At that time Hesse and Frankfurt had no plan to buy or sell shares in Fraport because of a 10-year lock-up they agreed to at Fraport's IPO in June 2001.

The Sale of a Call

The German government sold a call with a 113% strike on 6.6% of Fraport's share capital. The overall premium received by the German government was not disclosed, but I assume it was 5% of the notional, or EUR 12 million. The option had a 17-month expiry, and allowed for physical settlement only. The following table summarizes the call main terms:

Physically Settled Call Option – Main Terms	
Buyer	JP Morgan
Seller	The German government
Option type	Call
Trade date	26-October-2005
Expiration date	7-March-2007 (i.e., 17 months)
Option style	American. Option could be exercised from 1-March-2007 up to expiration date
Shares	Fraport A.G.
Number of options	6 million
Strike price	EUR 45.25 (113% of the EUR 40.04 stock's closing price on previous day
Premium	EUR 12 million (5% of the option notional amount)
Notional amount	EUR 240.2 million (= 6 million × 40.04)
Premium payment date	28-October-2005
Settlement method	Physical settlement
Settlement date	Three exchange business days from 26-October-2005

The Exchangeable Bond

Concurrently with the previous two transactions, JP Morgan issued a zero-coupon bond exchangeable for Fraport stock. JP Morgan issued the exchangeable bond in order to hedge its exposure to Fraport's stock price under the call option it bought from the German government. The exchangeable had a 17-month maturity, a notional amount of EUR 271.5 million and an exchange price of EUR 45.25, or 13% above the closing price on the day prior to its issuance. The following table summarizes the exchangeable main terms:

JP Morgan's Exchangeable Bond Terms

Issuer	JP Morgan Bank Luxembourg S.A.
Notional amount	EUR 271.5 million
Redemption amount	100% of notional amount
Issue date	26-October-2005
Maturity	12-March-2007
Underlying stock	Fraport A.G.
Issue price	100.15%
Coupon	Zero
Exchange price	EUR 45.25
Underlying number of shares	6 million (= 271.5 million/45.25)
Exchange premium	13% above the stock closing price on previous trading day (the share price)
Closing stock price on previous trading day	EUR 40.04
Exchange period	From 1-March-2007 to 7-March-2007
Issuer call	None, except clean-up call and tax call

Scenarios at Maturity

At maturity of the exchangeable bond (to be precise, during the last week of the exchangeable's life), there were two scenarios:

1. If Fraport's stock price was at, or below, the EUR 45.25 exchange price:
   - The bond holders would request the redemption of the bond, receiving in cash the bond's redemption value (100% of the notional amount).
   - JP Morgan would not exercise the call option.
   - The German government would keep 6.6% of Fraport's share capital, not meeting its objective of selling its whole Fraport's stake. However, the German government received the EUR 12 million premium at inception.
2. If Fraport's stock price was above the EUR 45.25 exchange price:
   - The bond holders would exercise their exchange right. Upon exchange, the exchangeable investors would receive 6 million Fraport shares.
   - JP Morgan would exercise the call, receiving 6 million Fraport shares from the German government and paying EUR 271.5 million (= 6 million × 45.25).
   - The German government would have sold all its Fraport's stake, meeting its objective. The sale corresponding to the call option would have been at a 13% premium, receiving EUR 271.5 million. Additionally, the German government received a EUR 12 million premium at inception. In this scenario, its decision to enter into the call agreement would prove a notably better strategy than the ABB alternative. Through the ABB, assuming unrealistically the same price for the whole stake, the German government would have received EUR 230.4 (= 6 million shares × 38.40). Therefore, under the call strategy it was better off by EUR 53.1 million (= 271.5 million + 12.0 million − 230.4 million).

The low conversion premium − 13% − allowed for a high probability of conversion. The bond had a zero-coupon feature, to perfectly mirror the call option terms. In other words, the bond paid a zero coupon to make sure that if the call was exercised, the exchangeable would in theory be exercised too. The call 5% premium was in theory the present value of the yield of straight bonds issued by JP Morgan with the same tenor.

Advantages and Weaknesses of the Transaction

The advantages of the transaction to the German government were:

- The whole transaction was executed simultaneously.
- The ABB discount price was lower compared with a sole ABB.
- The call option allowed for a potential future disposal at a premium.
- It kept the voting rights and received the dividends on the shares underlying the call option.
- It diversified the investor base by targeting both cash equity and equity-linked investors with limited overlap.
- It took advantage of a strong demand in the cash equity and equity-linked markets.
- It benefited from an attractive price of Fraport stock.

The weaknesses of the transaction to the German government were:

- There was no certainty regarding the disposal of the shares underlying the call option.
- There was a negative impact on Fraport's stock price. However, it was significantly less negative than in a sole ABB transaction.

7

Strategic Equity Derivatives in Mergers and Acquisitions

This chapter examines examples of entities that have used equity derivatives in an M&A situation. In some circumstances the use of equity derivatives has greatly impacted corporate control contests. In this chapter I have tried to analyze the most common uses of equity derivatives in M&A situations by covering real cases. As we will see, in M&A there is no such thing as the perfect strategic equity derivatives solution for a specific situation. The interpretation of securities laws for a specific equity derivatives transaction is quite subjective. Regulators often have differing interpretations regarding the same transaction. To make it more challenging, securities regulations change over time and differ from country to country. However, I think it is useful to learn from past experiences to devise more robust M&A strategies.

Numerous are the motivations behind the use of equity derivatives in M&A situations. A common thread would be an insurgent shareholder and/or a potential bidder accumulating a block of stock to gain shareholder approval for his/her proposals. The temptation to buy a pre-offer block is very strong because it may help the insurgent shareholder and/or potential bidder to lock in attractive share acquisition prices, to increase voting rights, to avoid disclosure requirements and/or to avoid public offer requirements. There are other motivations for using equity derivatives, more unusual – for example, securing a block of shares during a standstill period.

Locking in Acquisition Prices

When an acquirer's intentions become public knowledge, the target company's stock price will rise significantly to incorporate the offer price and the likelihood of a deal being consummated. Therefore, a potential acquirer has a strong incentive to buy as much stock as possible prior to an offer to lock in pre-offer acquisition prices.

Moreover, in an active merger market a third party may join the contest, making a more attractive counter-offer for the target company. In this situation the original potential acquirer could find itself a loser in a bidding war, having to pay expensive legal and investment banking advisory fees. Acquiring stock in the market at pre-offer prices may offset the incurred expenses and may even provide the losing bidder with a net profit on the transaction.

A public offer is usually financed with a bridge loan, which would later be replaced by a mix of syndicated loans and public bonds. Often when the acquirer has made the decision to purchase a pre-offer block, the bridge financing has not been agreed yet. Strategic equity derivatives may help to acquire a pre-offer block without a substantial financial commitment.

Increasing Voting Rights

A sizable block of a target company stock can also provide valuable leverage in an eventually contested shareholders' meeting (i.e., a **proxy contest**). For example, by acquiring a large block of the target company's stock, a bidder can launch an accelerated proxy fight. Fundamentally, a proxy contest is defined by a date and set of proposals to be voted in an extraordinary general (shareholders') meeting (an "EGM"). An EGM date formally determines when shareholders will gather to vote on the various proposals. The term "proxy" is used because many shareholders – rather than attending the meeting in person – vote in absentia, granting a right, or proxy, to someone else who then votes the shares. A shareholder will generally give its proxy either to the management or the insurgent, depending on which side the shareholder favors.

Typically, there are four main forms of proxy contests:

- Contests for seats on the board of directors of the target. An insurgent shareholder may use this means to replace opposing directors. The directors can normally count on a certain percentage of votes to support their position. Some of these votes might be through management's own stock holdings.
- Contests to clear the way for a tender offer. Many modern takeover defenses, such as the poison pill, can only be removed through a shareholder vote.
- Contests to approve a merger or acquisition. The target directors may oppose a merger and an insurgent shareholder may be in favor.
- Contests to approve changes in the target company strategic plans. For example, an insurgent shareholder may seek the disposal of a strategic asset with the proceeds paid to shareholders by means of a special dividend. Another common situation would be an insurgent shareholder seeking the approval of an aggressive buyback program.

The bidder can benefit from the voting power associated with the shares it owns. Such voting power can prove critical at various stages of a fight for control. By entering into equity derivatives transactions, an insurgent investor may obtain additional voting rights, helping him/her:

- To increase the likelihood of approval/rejection of resolutions voted in an AGM/EGM.
- To be able to call an EGM. For example, a 10% shareholding may entitle an investor to call a shareholders' meeting. This threshold is usually defined in the company articles of association (i.e., the certificate of association or bylaws).
- To be able to submit resolutions to an AGM/EGM.

Avoiding Disclosure Requirements

Disclosure and regulatory approval requirements can be a barrier to secret pre-announcement accumulation. Equity derivatives may help to gain de facto control over a substantial amount of the target's shares before the transaction is disclosed or regulator approval is obtained, circumventing the restrictions to a direct acquisition. These restrictions can take different forms:

- Disclosure requirements of a significant shareholding in public (i.e., listed) companies. These requirements try to make the market aware of an interest in a company in excess of a specified limit, to avoid takeover abuses. The stock market regulator, and often the target company, must be notified of the direct or indirect acquisition or disposal of a "qualifying holding". A qualified holding is a holding which represents at least a certain percentage (e.g., 5%) of the share capital or voting rights of a listed company.
- Regulatory approvals before the acquisition of a stake. For example, the acquisition of substantial shareholdings in banks and insurance institutions will, in most countries, require a notification to, or consent of, the relevant banking/insurance regulatory authority. The

regulator, generally, has several months to oppose the intended transaction if, "in view of the need to ensure sound and prudent management" of the target, it is not satisfied as to the suitability of the purchaser.
- Antitrust authorities may require approval before the acquisition of a stake. For example, an antitrust authority may take months before assessing whether an M&A transaction can create or strengthen a dominant position as a result of which competition would be significantly and lastingly eliminated or reduced.

Avoiding Mandatory Offer Requirements

Equity derivatives may avoid mandatory takeover bids if the relevant thresholds are exceeded. The acquisition of a shareholding above certain thresholds may trigger a requirement for a public offer for a part of the company. Typically, if a shareholder has more than 50% of the voting rights of a listed company, he/she is required to make a mandatory takeover bid for all the outstanding shares. In some countries, the ownership of more than 30% of the share capital of a company may trigger a partial takeover bid. Equity derivatives may help to gain de facto control over a substantial amount of the target's shares without triggering a mandatory offer.

7.1 KEEPING VOTING RIGHTS IN PROXY CONTESTS

The first type of M&A situations analyzed in this chapter involves keeping the voting rights in a proxy contest. As we saw earlier, a proxy contest is a voting process in which a single shareholder or a group of shareholders require a company to make a certain decision through the use of the mechanism of corporate voting.

7.1.1 Case Study: Montalban Partners' Disposal of Gold International

This transaction shows a fictional example of how a single shareholder may attempt to use his/her voting rights to garner support for the disposal of a subsidiary. It is common that a shareholder cannot vote any resolution on any relationship between the company and the shareholder, not pertaining to the company's bylaws. This case shows how a shareholder parked its voting rights in a proxy contest and the potential legal implications for the participating parties.

In January 20X0, Montalban Partners – a private equity firm – was interested in selling its fully owned subsidiary – Gold International – to Precious Metals Inc. for USD 3 billion. Montalban Partners was Precious Metals' largest shareholder, owning 10% of its common stock (see Figure 7.1). The offer was going to be voted in an EGM to take place on 15 February 20X0. Precious Metals board of directors strongly opposed the offer.

Ahead of the EGM, Montalban Partners decided to enter into a derivative in order to transfer its voting rights to another other shareholder. Thus, Montalban Partners entered into a cash-settled equity swap and direct sale with a bank – Gigabank – (see Figure 7.2). The notional of the equity swap represented 10% of Precious Metals. Gigabank had to buy Precious Metals shares to hedge its market exposure under the equity swap. Thus, Gigabank put in place its hedge by acquiring 10% of the share capital of Precious Metals from Montalban Partners. The equity swap included a clause allowing Gigabank vote at its complete own discretion and to ignore any voting recommendations from Montalban Partners.

Right after entering into the equity swap, Montalban Partners in a regulatory filing informed Precious Metals' stock market regulator that it no longer held a stake in Precious Metals.

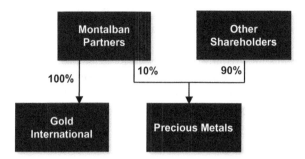

Figure 7.1   Montalban Partners' strategic stakes.

Simultaneously, Gigabank disclosed that it held a 10% stake in Precious Metals. Following this announcement, Precious Metals board of directors moved to bar Gigabank from voting, arguing that Montalban Partners and Gigabank had a conflict of interest. According to the stock market law, a shareholder could not vote on issues involving a "relation", existing or to be created, between the company and that shareholder. Montalban Partners argued that it had no agreement with Gigabank on how it will vote.

On 15 February 20X0, the acquisition offer was submitted for approval to Precious Metals' EGM. 60% of the submitted votes voted in favour and 40% against it.

Designing the Transaction

When designing the transaction, the participating parties have to carefully take into account the following issues:

Firstly, the equity swap confirmation has to be written in such a way as to avoid any suspicion of the parties acting in concert. The confirmations had to state that Gigabank would be voting independently. As an example, the confirmation of the equity swap between the company (i.e., Montalban Partners in our case) and the bank can include the following representation: "Gigabank will freely exercise, in its entire discretion, in any general shareholders' meeting of Precious Metals, the voting rights attributable to all the shares of the Precious Metals that it may hold at all times in order to hedge the transaction".

It is advisable to go even further by adding to the representation that the company will not instruct the bank to exercise in any general shareholders' meeting of the Precious Metals the voting rights attributable to all the shares of the Precious Metals that the bank may hold at all times to hedge the transaction. Moreover, in the event that the bank receives any instruction

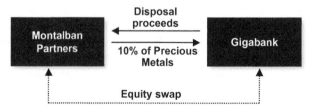

Figure 7.2   Equity swap transaction.

from the company that affects the exercise of such voting rights, the bank will ignore any such instruction.

Secondly, in implementing this sort of transaction, the parties have to assess what are their disclosure requirements. Montalban Partners had to disclose the sale of its stake. The optimal scenario would have been the bank not disclosing its stake in Precious Metals. However, Gigabank was obliged to disclose at inception of the transaction its 10% stake in Precious Metals because according to the stock market regulations any shareholder had to disclose an ownership exceeding the 5% and each multiple of 5% thresholds. That meant that placing more than 5% with a bank would make the market aware of the sale of the stock to the bank. In our case Montalban Partners could have entered into two equity swaps with two banks, each on 4.99% of Precious Metals share capital, and in theory these banks could have avoided a disclosure obligation because their percentage of the underlying stock did not exceed 5% of the voting rights.

Usually derivatives do not need to be disclosed unless they lead to a change in the attribution of voting rights. In our case, Montalban Partners was not required to disclose the execution of the equity swap because it only allowed for cash settlement.

In some jurisdictions, all transactions entailing a transfer of voting rights, or of attributed voting rights, involving a member of the board might need to be disclosed, even though their size represent less than the legal disclosure thresholds.

Conclusions

In my view, transactions aimed at keeping voting rights in a proxy contest are likely to backfire. Although the sound design of the equity swap agreement in regard to the voting rights of the underlying shares prevented the derivative parties from being sued by other Precious Metals shareholders or its board of directors, there was a substantial reputational risk. If the transaction was detected by, for example, Precious Metals board of directors (remember that it opposed the transaction) it was very likely that they would try to have the stock market regulator rule that Montalban Partners still controlled 10% of Precious Metals' voting rights even after it sold its stake. If such claim was confirmed by the stock market regulator, the EGM's chairman would prevent Gigabank from voting at the EGM. A public relations fight may endure and other previously indifferent shareholders might vote against the proposal.

What about Gigabank's position? Gigabank made an attractive profit consisting in the floating amount spread that accrued over the life of the equity swap. The bank was not exposed to market risk, being otherwise exposed to Montalban Partners's credit risk. However, participation in M&A related strategic equity derivatives is a two sided sword. On one hand, Gigabank enhanced its relationship with Montalban Partners, being uniquely positioned to participate in other future highly confidential transactions with the company. On the other hand, Gigabank worsened its position to attract future business from Precious Metals, unless this company's board of directors were replaced.

7.2 SUBMITTING RESOLUTIONS TO AN AGM

The second type of M&A situation analyzed in this chapter involves using strategic equity instruments to increase voting rights with the objective of being able to submit proposals to an AGM and increase the likelihood of approval of these proposals.

7.2.1 Case Study: Laxey's Stock Lending Transaction

This case shows how a hedge fund entered into a stock lending transaction to increase its influence in the decision-making of a company. The stock lending transaction allowed the fund to obtain a substantial stake in a company and to include its own proposals in the company's AGM agenda.

In April 2002, Laxey Partners Ltd ("Laxey"), a closely held British fund, owned 2% of the third largest British real estate company, British Land plc. British Land shares were trading at a discount of about 30% to its net asset value. Other real estate companies were taking the opportunity to acquire back some of their own stock. At that time, British Land's chairman – John Riblat – said that although buybacks were not generally in the board's agenda, the company could consider such a transaction if it couldn't foresee other attractive investment opportunities.

Laxey wanted British Land to offer shareholders the chance to vote on a share buyback plan. Laxey proposed that British Land buy 10% of its outstanding shares for a minimum 700 pence per share if, in the four weeks prior to the end of the first six months of the fiscal year and the full fiscal year, its shares traded at a discount in excess of an average 15% of its net asset value. Laxey also wanted the company to propose the potential purchase of an additional 20% of its shares every year. Laxey proposed the two resolutions to be put to the 2002 annual general meeting (AGM) to take place in July 2002. Laxey added a third resolution requesting British Land to hire advisers to help manage property investments.

Just prior to the AGM, Laxey raised its stake in British Land to 9% by borrowing shares to gain voting rights. Shares on loan generally cannot be voted by their lender unless the shares are recalled. Stock borrowers, on the other hand, can vote the borrowed shares.

On 16 July 2002, British Land's AGM took place and its shareholders voted against Laxey's three resolutions.

The Stock Borrowing Transaction – Flows at Inception

At inception, the following processes took place (as shown in Figure 7.3):

- The securities lending and borrowing agreement was agreed and signed by Laxey and the stock lender on 7% of British Land's share capital.
- The 7% of British Land's share capital was transferred from the lender custody account to the Laxey's custody account. Legal title passed to Laxey, so it could disclose its ownership and vote the stock.
- Collateral was posted by Laxey, to reduce the lender's credit exposure to Laxey. Commonly, the stock borrower has to post cash or other liquid securities. The market value of the collateral posted was probably 105% of the market value of the stock borrowed.

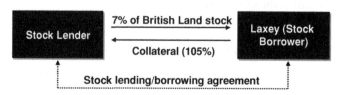

Figure 7.3 Stock lending/borrowing flows at inception.

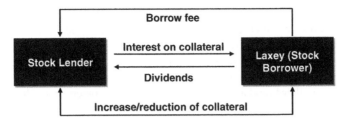

Figure 7.4   Stock lending/borrowing flows during the life of the agreement.

The Stock Borrowing Transaction – Flows during its Life

During the life of the stock lending and borrowing agreement, the following processes took place (as shown in Figure 7.4):

- Laxey paid the borrowing fee to the lender.
- The lender paid interest to Laxey on the cash collateral. The interest was calculated on a daily basis.
- Laxey paid to the lender an amount equivalent to the dividends distributed to the borrowed shares – a manufactured dividend.
- Collateral was readjusted on a daily basis, so the market value of the collateral posted was 105% of the market value of the stock borrowed.

The Stock Borrowing Transaction – Flows at Maturity or upon Early Termination

At maturity of the agreement, or upon early termination, the following processes took place (as shown in Figure 7.5):

- The stock was returned from Laxey's custody account to the lender's custody account.
- Posted collateral was returned by the lender to Laxey.

Other Comments

The use of stock lending transactions is a legal and cost-efficient way to increase voting rights in a shareholders' meeting. However, this strategy faces several constraints.

First, the building of a position is not trivial as it is often difficult to borrow a large number of shares. This is especially the case if the potential gains of having resolutions approved or rejected are substantial and powerful hedge funds and arbitrageurs enter the fray. Hedge funds may borrow the shares to benefit from a potential large fall in the company's stock price if a resolution is approved (or rejected). In the case of proxy fights, in which a takeover is voted, an active presence of arbitrageurs may make it difficult to borrow a substantial number of

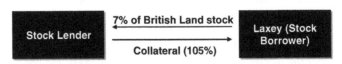

Figure 7.5   Stock lending/borrowing flows at maturity (or early termination).

shares. In a stock-for-stock merger, arbitrageurs typically buy the target's shares and sell short the acquirer's shares. In our case, Laxey could only build a 9% stake, a position that proved insufficient to change the voting results.

Second, a stock borrowing transaction may require substantial resources to implement. Laxey had to post collateral to the stock lenders, to reduce their credit exposure to Laxey, in the form of cash or other liquid assets. Sometimes stock borrowers do not have such resources available.

Third, if a stock borrowing strategy is unveiled, the credibility of the shareholder behind the strategy may be undermined. Under this strategy a shareholder does not bear the economic risks and benefits of holding the borrowed shares. In our case, British Land's board exposed Laxey's strategy, giving the impression that Laxey was a pure speculator without any interest in the long-term success of the company.

Finally, a majority of the stock lenders can recall the lent shares at any time. The stock borrower may be required to return the stock before the shareholders' voting takes place, obliging the stock borrower to replace the recalled shares.

7.3 INCREASING LIKELIHOOD OF SUCCESS OF A MERGER ARBITRAGE POSITION

In this section I will cover a real case in which a hedge fund's merger arbitrage position was enhanced by the use of derivatives. In a way the case covered in this section is similar to the previous two cases because all of them used derivatives to increase voting rights in a proxy contest.

7.3.1 Case Study: Perry's Equity Swaps with Bear Stearns and Goldman Sachs

This case shows how a hedge fund increased its likelihood of profiting from a merger arbitrage position linked to the Mylan–King merger, by entering into an equity derivatives transaction with Bear Stearns and Goldman Sachs.

In order to increase the likelihood of consummation of the Mylan–King merger, Perry purchased Mylan shares in order to vote the shares in favor of the merger. At the same time, in order to avoid the economic risk of owning Mylan shares, Perry entered into a series of equity swaps designed to fully hedge its financial exposure to Mylan's stock price.

Merger Arbitrage

A merger arbitrageur tries to profit from a stock-for-stock merger by entering into the so-called risk–arbitrage spread trade. A risk–arbitrage spread trade is a transaction designed to take advantage of an arbitrage spread opportunity. An arbitrage spread opportunity is created when, as a result of a merger announcement, the stock of the acquiring company ("the acquirer") trades at a higher adjusted price than the shares of the company it seeks to purchase ("the target"). The adjusted price refers to the stock price of the acquirer adjusted for how many shares of the acquirer the target's shares will convert to in the stock-for-stock merger. This pre-completion spread between the adjusted price of the acquirer's shares and the price of the target's shares reflects market uncertainty about deal consummation, i.e., whether the premium offered to the target company will be realized. Thus, the pre-completion spread widens if there are indications that the merger will not be completed. Conversely, the pre-completion spread narrows as confidence grows that the merger will be completed.

A risk–arbitrage spread trade is established by acquiring shares of the target and selling short a corresponding number of shares of the acquirer. When the merger is completed, the shares of the target become shares of the acquirer, and these shares can be used by the arbitrageur to cover its short sales of the acquirer's stock. If the merger is not completed, no profit is realized from the risk–arbitrage spread and a substantial loss may result.

Chronology of the Transaction

Perry, a New York-based investment adviser, had invested in King intermittently from October 2001. Beginning in March 2004, Perry had built a significant position in King. On 23 July 2004, Perry had accumulated a total of 4.34 million shares of King at an average cost of USD 15.08 per share. Because King's share price declined between March and July 2004, Perry sustained a paper loss of USD 20.4 million.

On 26 July 2004 Mylan, an American manufacturer of generic pharmaceutical products, announced an agreement to acquire King, an established brand-name pharmaceutical company. The agreement provided that King shareholders would receive 0.9 shares of Mylan common stock for each outstanding share of King stock. Pursuant to the terms of the agreement, consummation of the merger was subject to the approval of both Mylan and King shareholders. On the day of the merger announcement, King's stock price went up almost 25% and Perry could have sold its King shares then and recouped a portion of its trading losses.

Following the merger announcement, Perry tried to maximize its profits by converting its long position in King in a risk–arbitrage spread trade through the short sale of a corresponding number of Mylan shares. In the five days immediately following the merger announcement, Perry sold short 3.8 million shares of Mylan and adjusted its King position in order to establish its risk–arbitrage spread position, the profitability of which was contingent upon a successful completion of the merger. If the merger had been completed at that time, Perry's existing risk–arbitrage spread position would have resulted in a gain to Perry of approximately USD 14.4 million, offsetting much of its paper loss on King. Perry also continued to increase its King position, such that as of the close of business on 13 August 2004, Perry held 5.2 million shares of King, representing 2.1% of King's share capital.

On 18 August 2004, a prominent activist investor and certain entities he controlled (collectively, the "activist investor") received approval from the relevant authority, the Federal Trade Commission, to purchase between USD 100 million and USD 500 million worth of Mylan shares, representing between 2.4% and 11.9% of Mylan's share capital. On 7 September 2004 the activist investor disclosed that it had acquired 6.8% of Mylan's stock and that it opposed the Mylan–King merger and intended to solicit proxies against it. The activist investor filing signaled that winning Mylan shareholder approval of the merger would be difficult and the market reacted swiftly. Between 7 September 2004 and 17 September 2004 the activist investor increased his position to 8.9% of Mylan's stock. As a consequence, the risk–arbitrage spread widened by 59%, from USD 3.26 to USD 5.19. The risk–arbitrage spread reflected market uncertainty as to whether the merger would succeed in the face of the activist investor's opposition, particularly given that there was no indication that any other large Mylan shareholder supported the merger. If the activist investor succeeded in blocking the merger, Perry would lose its anticipated profit from its risk–arbitrage spread trade.

Following the activist investor's disclosure of his position, Perry began exploring various ways of acquiring Mylan voting rights without economic risk and without public disclosure. Perry wanted to obtain Mylan stock in order to vote in favor of the merger and thereby counter the activist investor's votes, but did not want to take on the economic risk of owning Mylan shares. In addition, because Perry wanted to profit from a wider risk–arbitrage spread, Perry did not want the market to be aware that Perry was building a position to vote in favor of the merger. Had the market known that he was acquiring Mylan shares sufficient to offset the activist investor's position, the spread would have narrowed to reflect the increased likelihood that the merger would be completed, thereby reducing Perry's potential profits on its risk–arbitrage spread trades. As a result, Perry researched possible mechanisms to purchase or transfer Mylan stock without making the market aware of his intentions and eliminating Perry's economic exposure to Mylan's stock. Perry had never before engaged in a similar strategy.

Starting on 8 September 2004 and ending on 24 September 2004, Perry acquired 26.6 million shares, or 9.9% of Mylan's share capital, to vote in favor of the Mylan–King merger and to counter the activist investor's opposition. Perry purchased 5.6 million of these Mylan shares in regular open-market transactions, all of which shares were offset by short sales Perry had already in Mylan. Although an investor typically would cover a short position and close out the short (and stop paying financing fees to the bank through whom it was executing the short), Perry kept both positions open – long Mylan and short Mylan – thereby paying financing fees to its prime brokers for its existing short position while retaining the right to vote the shares purchased to cover the short.

Perry acquired the remaining 21 million shares of Mylan from, and engaged in a series of equity swap transactions with, two banks – Bear Stearns and Goldman Sachs – that gave Perry voting rights to Mylan shares while eliminating Perry's economic risk of holding the shares.

On 19 November 2004, the activist investor announced that he intended to make a USD 20 per share tender offer for Mylan. Shortly thereafter, at the end of the day on 22 November 2004, a news article was published that speculated that Perry and other hedge funds had taken positions in Mylan to vote in favor of the merger and capture the significant risk–arbitrage spread, without having any economic interest in the company or exposure to Mylan's stock price.

On 23 November 2004, Perry consulted with counsel at a law firm, who opined that Perry should disclose its position in light of the activist investor's tender offer. The law firm opined that because of the tender offer, Perry now could be said to hold its Mylan shares with the purpose or effect of changing or influencing the control of Mylan. On 29 November 2004, Perry disclosed its Mylan position, more than two months after Perry had acquired more than 5% of Mylan shares.

The Mylan–King merger was not completed for reasons unrelated to the above described trading. On 8 December 2004, King announced that it would have to restate earnings for 2002, 2003 and the first six months of 2004. On 27 February 2005, Mylan and King announced that they had mutually agreed to terminate the proposed merger because they were "not able to agree upon terms for a revised transaction".

Anatomy of the Transaction

The transaction through which Perry obtained voting rights on 21 million shares of Mylan had three different parts, as shown in Figure 7.6.

Firstly, Bear Stearns and Goldman Sachs borrowed 21 million Mylan shares from the stock lending market. The banks posted collateral to the stock lenders. The transfer of the shares

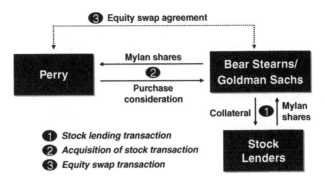

Figure 7.6 Building blocks of Perry's transaction on Mylan.

from the stock lenders who previously owned them to the banks were not reported to the market as a whole, keeping the stock lending transaction hidden from the market.

Secondly, the two banks sold to Perry 21 million shares of Mylan stock. Perry took several steps to ensure that the purchase transactions would be hidden from the market. The acquisition was executed in blocks of 1 million to 2 million shares, which Perry purchased in foreign markets or in the New York Stock Exchange (NYSE) after hours. At that time, NYSE over-the-counter trades made between 6:30 p.m. and midnight were reported to the relevant exchange on the next trading day and marked "as of". Trades reported in this way were not disseminated to the market as a whole. By contrast, trades that took place during regular business hours were immediately publicly disseminated. By structuring the transaction in this way, these trades were not reported by any volume-reporting or other public dissemination services, even though on many days Perry's share purchases eclipsed the total volume of all Mylan shares reported to have been purchased through all reporting exchanges. Thus other market participants were unaware that Perry was obtaining a very large voting interest in Mylan that could be used to counter the activist investor's opposition to the merger.

Thirdly, at the same time as it was acquiring its long position in Mylan through short sales by the banks, Perry was executing cash-settled equity swap agreements with the banks tied to the underlying Mylan shares Perry was purchasing from the banks. Through the cash-settled equity swaps Perry agreed to reimburse the banks for the difference between the price at which the banks short sold the Mylan shares to Perry and the market price at the time the transaction was unwound. If the market price at that time was lower, the banks agreed to reimburse Perry for the difference between the price Perry paid for the stock and the market price at the time the transaction was unwound. Conversely, if the market price at that time was higher, Perry agreed to reimburse the banks for the difference between the market price at the time the transaction was unwound and the price Perry paid for the stock.

The cash-settled equity swap agreements effectively eliminated any economic risk Perry had from owning, and the banks from short selling, Mylan shares. As a result of the combination of the purchase/sale of stock and the equity swap transactions, neither Perry nor the banks were at risk of any movement in the price of Mylan stock.

- Because the banks sold the Mylan shares to Perry, they were short the stock. Therefore, the banks were at risk if the price of Mylan stock was up at the time the banks needed to cover their short positions. Under the equity swaps, the banks benefited from a rise and were exposed to a fall in Mylan's stock price. Thus, the combination of the stock sale and the equity swaps mitigated the bank's market risk to Mylan stock.

- At the same time, Perry – which was long the 21 million shares – was at risk if the price of Mylan stock was down, and benefited if Mylan's stock price was up, at the time Perry wished to unwind its position. Under the equity swaps, Perry benefited from a fall and was exposed to a rise in Mylan's stock price. Thus, the combination of the stock sale and the equity swaps mitigated Perry's market risk to Mylan stock.

Additional Comments

The main drawback of this type of transaction is the substantial resources needed to implement it. However, in this case Perry was able to acquire its 9.9% stake in Mylan without making a significant financial outlay. Perry financed its purchase of Mylan stock through an extension of its existing margin line of credit at its prime broker. For each purchase of Mylan stock, in the three days between trade date and settlement date, Perry drew upon its margin account to have enough cash deposited into its cash account to satisfy payment for the long position. The funds were then transferred to the banks by the settlement date. In total, Perry paid less than USD 7.2 million to its prime broker to finance the purchase of the 26.6 million Mylan shares, worth approximately USD 492 million. Perry also earned interest on its short positions and on the collateral it gave to the banks for the equity swaps. As a result, accounting for all of Perry's costs and also the interest it earned on its various positions, Perry paid only USD 5.76 million to acquire voting rights to almost 10% of Mylan's shares.

In my view, it would have been easier just to implement a stock borrowing transaction between the two banks and Perry. However, as we saw in an earlier case, the main drawback of a stock borrowing is that Perry could be seen as an "unreal" shareholder, undermining the credibility of its position.

Perry unlawfully failed to disclose its position when it exceeded the 5% ownership threshold. US securities law required any person who has acquired beneficial ownership of more than 5% of the voting class of equity securities to report such acquisition within 10 days after such acquisition. However, as an alternative, the rules allow the use of short-form disclosure statements with differing timing requirements under certain conditions. Under this alternative, certain qualified institutional investors may file a short-form statement within 45 days after the end of the calendar year in which they made the triggering acquisition, so long as the institutional investor acquired the securities "in the ordinary course of his business and not with the purpose nor with the effect of changing or influencing the control of the issuer, nor in connection with or as a participant in any transaction having such purpose or effect". Perry claimed that it was eligible to file a short-form statement within 45 days after the end of the calendar year because it acquired the shares in the ordinary course of business and not with a view toward, or as part of a plan having the purpose or effect of, changing or influencing control of Mylan. Perry claimed that the deal was a reverse triangular merger, with a subsidiary of Mylan merging into King, and that there would be no change in the Mylan board as a result of the merger. The SEC claimed that Perry was not entitled to defer filing and instituted legal proceedings to impose remedial sanctions against Perry. In the end, Perry paid USD 150,000 to the SEC to settle the accusations and, as a result, the SEC ceased the proceedings.

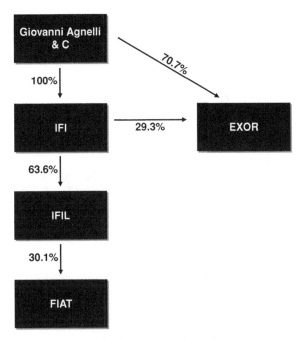

Figure 7.7   Legal structure of Agnelli family's ownership of Fiat.

7.4   AVOIDING MANDATORY OFFER RULES

7.4.1   Case Study: Agnelli Family Equity Swap with Merrill Lynch

This case provides a real-life example of a transaction aimed at avoiding future dilution without triggering a full mandatory offer. The Agnelli family, the founders of Fiat Group S.p.a. ("Fiat"), controlled Fiat through a cascade of companies (see Figure 7.7). Fiat was one of the largest car and truck manufacturers in Europe. Giovanni Agnelli & C, a privately held partnership, owned 100% of the investment company IFI, as well as another holding company called Exor Group. IFI owned 63.6% of the listed company IFIL, which in turn owned 30.1% of Fiat. IFIL was the largest shareholder of Fiat.

In October 2002, Fiat signed a EUR 3 billion mandatory convertible facility with a consortium of banks for the purpose of providing it with the financial resources to implement a restructuring plan. The facility had a term of three years, expiring on 10 October 2005. Fiat could elect to repay the facility in cash at any time prior to maturity on condition that its credit rating remained at least equal to the investment grade level. Any residual liability for principal would be repaid with common stock of Fiat, which the lending banks agreed to underwrite and offer pre-emptively to all shareholders. The conversion price of the facility would be the average of EUR 15.5 and the average stock price of Fiat in the last three or six months, depending on the case, preceding the repayment date.

In April 2005, after Fiat's poor performance, it was becoming clearer that the mandatory convertible facility would not be repaid, and thus, would be converted into Fiat's common stock. If the banks converted their facility into Fiat shares on 20 September 2005, they would

Figure 7.8   Fiat's stock price from April-01 to April-05.

get 24% of Fiat's share capital, diluting IFIL's ownership to 23%. IFIL was interested in keeping its stake at 30%. In principle, IFIL had two alternatives:

- To wait until 20 September 2005 to acquire an additional 7% of Fiat, being exposed to a future higher stock price.
- To acquire the 7% immediately, taking advantage of the then depressed Fiat's stock price (see Figure 7.8). However, this alternative would cause IFIL to exceed the 30% statutory threshold to launch a mandatory offer in cash for the remaining stock of Fiat. A mandatory full bid would require a huge investment, an unrealistic commitment even for the Agnelli family.

The Agnelli family opted for the first alternative, but hedged its exposure to a future higher stock price of Fiat by making its Luxembourg-based subsidiary Exor Group enter into a cash-settled total return equity swap with Merrill Lynch ("Merrill"). As a result, on 26 April 2005 Exor and Merrill entered into an equity swap with the following terms:

Exor's Cash-settled Total Return Equity Swap Terms	
Party A	Exor Group
Party B	Merrill Lynch
Trade date	26-April-2005
Termination date	26-October-2008
Early termination	Party A may partially or totally terminate the transaction early at any time by providing a termination notice to Party B
Underlying currency	EUR
Equity amount part	
Equity amount payer	Party B (Merrill Lynch)
Equity amount receiver	Party A (Exor Group)
Shares	Fiat common shares
Cash settlement	Applicable
Number of shares	90 million
Initial price	The volume-weighted average at which Party B puts in place its initial hedge. The initial price was set at EUR 5.50

Exor's Cash-settled Total Return Equity Swap Terms

Equity notional amount	EUR 495 million
	Number of shares × Initial price
Settlement price	The volume-weighted average at which Party B unwinds its hedge of the transaction during the month ("the final period") following a termination notice. Party B can extend such final period at its own discretion to assure a smooth execution of its hedge unwind
Settlement date	Three trading days after the last day of the final period
Floating amount part	
Floating amount payer	Party A (Exor)
Notional amount	The equity notional amount
Payment dates	At the end of each quarter
Floating rate option	EUR-Euribor
Designated maturity	3 months
Spread	Plus 50 bps (0.50%)
Floating rate day count fraction	Actual/360
Dividend amount	
Dividend amount	100% of the paid amount
Dividend payer	Party B (Merrill Lynch)
Dividend receiver	Party A (Exor)
Dividend period	The period commencing on, and including, the third scheduled trading day preceding the effective date and ending on, and including, the valuation date
Dividend payment date	The date of the payment of the dividend by the issuer of the shares
Independent amount	Party A shall post on the trade date EUR 10 million, and at all times shall post a EUR cash amount equal to 10% of the equity notional amount

The underlying number of Fiat shares of the equity swap was 90 million, representing 7% of Fiat's voting capital. The equity swap only allowed for cash settlement. Exor paid quarterly Euribor 3-month plus 0.50% on a notional of EUR 495 million. Exor posted a EUR 10 million collateral on trade date and gradually increased this amount, in coordination with Merrill's implementation of its initial hedge, to equal 10% of the equity swap notional. As a result, after the initial hedging period Exor posted EUR 49.5 million cash collateral to Merrill. In order to hedge the transaction, Merrill gradually acquired 90 million Fiat shares in the market in the period between 26 April and 7 June at an average price of EUR 5.50. This price became the initial price.

The same day, 26 April 2005, Fiat announced that it would not repay the USD 3 billion mandatory convertible facility, therefore obliging the facility lenders to automatically convert the facility into stock in September 2005.

On 15 September 2005, Exor and Merrill agreed to modify the terms of the equity swap to allow Exor to elect between cash and physical settlement for up to 82.25 million shares. The remaining 7.75 million shares continued to allow only for cash settlement. The physical settlement feature required disclosure of the equity swap to the Italian stock market regulator. Besides the equity swap disclosure, Merrill disclosed its 7% stake in Fiat.

In September 2005, the mandatory convertible facility was extinguished by its conversion to Fiat's common stock. The conversion took place on 20 September 2005. As a result, Fiat issued 291.8 million shares at a price of EUR 10.28.

On 20 September 2005, simultaneously to the execution of the facility's conversion, Exor gave notice for the partial early termination of the equity swap for 82.25 million shares, opting for physical settlement. As a result, Exor received 82.25 million shares of Fiat from Merrill in exchange for EUR 461 million. Exor paid EUR 5.60 per share, the EUR 5.50 initial price plus EUR 0.10 of interest and broken funding costs. Concurrently, Exor sold the 82.25 million shares to IFIL at a price of EUR 6.50 per share. As a result, Exor realized a significant capital gain of EUR 74 million. Exor continued to have exposure to a residual 7.75 million Fiat shares through the remaining equity swap.

The transaction triggered an investigation by the Italian stock market regulator. Three issues were investigated: (i) if the transaction breached Italy's mandatory bid rules; (ii) if the transaction should have been disclosed at inception; and (iii) if the profit generated by the sale of the shares by Exor to IFIL was legal. Let us discuss these issues next.

Mandatory Bid

The transaction legally avoided a mandatory bid if the parties could prove that they were not acting in concert. In my view, it could help to justify the absence of joint exercise of the political rights if Merrill Lynch did not make available to Exor the voting rights associated with the 90 million underlying shares, or if the equity swap terms included a clause preventing Merrill from voting. The Italian stock market regulator ruled that no breach of the Italian mandatory bid rules occurred.

Disclosure of the Transaction

A second issue was the need to disclose the equity swap on its trade date. The cash-settlement feature made the transaction more robust from a legal standpoint. According to the Italian law, the cash settlement feature avoided the need to disclose the transaction. However, at the beginning Merrill did not disclose that it owned 7% of Fiat. By 7 June 2005, Merrill exceeded the 5% Italian legal threshold and it should have disclosed this fact.

The amendment to the equity swap to allow for physical settlement obliged the parties to disclosure equity swap. A big question remains if the change to the equity swap terms was planned from the start. If so, the temporary cash-settlement feature would have been a subterfuge to avoid informing the market. The existence of the equity swap was very relevant because it would have hinted to the market about the upcoming conversion of the mandatory convertible facility.

In my view the difference between cash settlement and physical settlement is rather subtle. In both cases, Merrill would need to sell 90 million Fiat shares to unwind its hedge.

- In a physically settled equity swap, Merrill would sell the shares directly to Exor.
- In a cash-settled equity swap, Merrill would sell the shares onto the market. However, Exor could always acquire the 90 million shares through the stock exchange in coordination with Merrill's sale.

Therefore, under a cash-settled equity swap Exor could have acquired the underlying shares without taking a large price risk.

The Italian stock market regulator found Exor guilty of market manipulation, ruling that Exor should have disclosed the position in Fiat. It fined IFIL and Giovanni Agnelli & C

EUR 7.5 million, and fined and suspended two directors from serving on boards of public companies.

Market Abuse

The sale by Exor of the 82.25 million Fiat shares to IFIL also raised some legal questions. Exor sold the shares to IFIL at EUR 6.50, a price notably higher than its EUR 5.50 acquisition price. IFIL's minority shareholders wondered whether this transaction amounted to a diversion of their funds to the Agnellis. Exor argued that the EUR 6.50 execution price was the result of a negotiation between Exor and IFIL and that the price took into consideration the size of the block and the average VWAP of Fiat's stock during the previous three and six months (EUR 6.90 and EUR 6.10 per share). The board of directors of IFIL obtained a fairness opinion that confirmed the adequacy of the EUR 6.50 price.

7.5   INCREASING LIKELIHOOD OF SUCCESS OF A TAKEOVER

7.5.1   Case Study: Unipol's Takeover of BNL and Call/Put Combination with Deutsche Bank

This case provides a real-life example of an equity derivatives transaction aimed at increasing the likelihood of a merger taking place. The case also shows how derivatives can secure the acquisition price of a stake before obtaining authorization to acquire it.

In April 2005 BBVA, Spain's second largest bank, announced its interest in acquiring full control of Banca Nazionale del Lavoro S.p.A. (BNL). BBVA already controlled 15% of BNL's ordinary share capital. BBVA offered EUR 2.72 for each BNL share. The offer soon appeared to have hit strong opposition when the governor of the Bank of Italy (BoI), Antonio Fazio, was openly opposed to the offer and when a group of BNL's core investors declared their refusal to sell their 25% stake in BNL to BBVA. As the different parties searched for a compromise, a new suitor, Unipol Assicurazioni S.p.A (Unipol), appeared.

At the end of the first half of 2005, within the limits authorized by the BoI, Unipol held 9.95% of BNL's ordinary share capital, consisting of a direct holding of 155 million shares, or 5.12%, whilst the remaining 4.83%, or 146,320,000 shares, were acquired through its subsidiary Aurora Assicurazioni.

On 1 July 2005, Unipol and Deutsche Bank entered into a converse transaction on 75.5 million shares of BNL. Under the converse Unipol acquired a European call and sold to Deutsche Bank an American put, both with strike price EUR 2.9173 per share and expiry date 18 July 2005.

On 15 July BoI authorized Unipol to raise its shareholding in the ordinary share capital of BNL to 14.99%. On 17 July Unipol's board of directors authorized its chairman and vice-chairman to continue the negotiations underway with top international and Italian banks, financial operators and other partners aimed at achieving potential business and/or company partnerships.

On 18 July 2005, Deutsche Bank exercised its put and Unipol acquired the underlying 75.5 million shares of BNL at EUR 2.9173 per share. Also on 18 July 2005, Unipol acquired from Bayerische Hypo und Vereinsbank A.G. and from Dresdner Bank 50 million and 25 million shares of BNL respectively. In total, Unipol acquired 150.5 million BNL shares for a total counter value of EUR 437.8 million. On conclusion of these acquisitions, Unipol held 14.92%

of BNL's ordinary share capital. As it was deemed to be significant under Italian stock market law, BNL disclosed the stake to the Italian stock market regulator CONSOB.

On 18 July 2005 Unipol signed with a group of core shareholders of BNL, all grouped under the name "pact members", a shareholders' agreement ("the shareholders' agreement") including a consultation and block agreement, relating to the shareholdings owned by Unipol and the pact members in BNL, amounting to 30.86% of the BNL share capital. The shareholders' agreement was intended to enable Unipol and the other partners to lump their BNL holdings together, in order to identify common company and business strategies that would boost BNL operational capabilities. The shareholders' agreement included a lock-up period on the BNL shareholdings conferred by the pact members, in which they committed to not transferring the syndicated shares until the 30th day following the closing of the offer, and the granting to Unipol of the right of pre-emption, an option right for Unipol to purchase from the pact members either totally or partially their BNL shares at EUR 2.70 per share on the 30th day following the closing of the offer, the terms and conditions for the launching of the mandatory tender offer and the commitment not to take part in the BBVA public exchange offer. Unipol, moreover, granted some of the pact members the right to sell to Unipol the BNL ordinary shares held by them in the event of some specific conditions.

Concomitantly, Unipol signed with Credit Suisse First Boston (CSFB) an agreement ("the CSFB agreement") relating to: (i) the procedures to be followed in the event of transfer of the BNL shareholding owned by CSFB; (ii) the pursuit of commonly shared commercial and financial plans; and (iii) the terms and conditions for the launching of the mandatory tender offer. Furthermore, Unipol signed a separate agreement with CSFB regulating a call option for Unipol and a put option for CSFB, both with a strike price of EUR 2.70 per share, of CSFB's shareholding in BNL, representing 4.18% of BNL's ordinary share capital, and which could be raised up to 4.50%. These options could be exercised subject to some specific conditions.

Concurrently with the signing of the shareholders' agreement and the CSFB agreement, Unipol also subscribed agreements with other parties ("the other parties") which, inter alia, granted Unipol the right to purchase at EUR 2.70 per share the BNL shares held by them, representing in all 6.6% of the BNL share capital, and also establish the reciprocal assumption of further commitments, such as a lock-up period, the prohibition on the purchase of further BNL shares and the commitment not to take part in the offer launched by the BBVA. Unipol, moreover, granted some of the other parties the right to sell to Unipol the BNL ordinary shares held by them in the event of some specific conditions.

The signing of these agreements by Unipol, the pact members, CSFB and the other parties implied the joint obligation of these parties to launch a tender offer on the totality of the BNL ordinary shares, representing 59.24% of BNL's ordinary share capital. This joint commitment was to be economically fulfilled solely by Unipol, which would uphold all related costs, including the payment of the amount due for the BNL shares involved in the offer, thus keeping indemnified the pact members, CSFB and the other parties from these obligations. Unipol agreed to pay each shareholder adhering to the offer the cash amount of EUR 2.70 for each share. This unitary amount, calculated taking into account the price of the exercise of the call/put options also, was above the minimum price derived from the application of the criteria of the Italian takeover law in so far as Unipol decided to pay out a premium of 5.7%. To those taking part in the offer, such a price represented a premium equal to 25.4% of the daily arithmetic weighted average of the official quotations of BNL ordinary shares over the previous 12 months or a premium of 0.4% on the closing price of ordinary shares on 15 July 2005. Subject to obtaining the authorizations prescribed by the then current regulations, the offer was expected to be launched in September 2005. In the event of full completion of the offer, Unipol would own up to around 64.83% of the fully diluted ordinary share capital of BNL. At the time of the offer, Unipol's market value was less than half that of BNL.

In theory, the total counter value of the public tender offer was EUR 4.96 billion. In practical terms, Unipol anticipated that the maximum expenditure would drop to a figure of no more than EUR 4.53 billion, with the Deutsche Bank and Credit Suisse First Boston shareholdings in BNL not included as part of the mandatory public tender offer (accounting for 4.88% and 0.31% of the ordinary share capital respectively), since they were the subject of option call contracts in favor of Unipol. In addition, assuming that the Banca Popolare dell'Emilia Romagna shareholding in BNL (amounting to approximately 3.87% of BNL's ordinary share capital) could be deemed to be stable, consequently it was not expected that it would accept the bid. In this case the actual maximum expenditure anticipated by Unipol would drop still further to a total of EUR 4.2 billion.

Also on 18 July 2005, Unipol subscribed with Deutsche Bank A.G. London ("Deutsche Bank") two converse agreements on a total of 151.157 million BNL shares, or 4.99% of the BNL share capital. Deutsche Bank, furthermore, committed itself not to sell or tender BNL shares involved in the derivative agreements to BBVA's takeover bid. The agreement did not prevent Deutsche Bank from entering into other transactions linked to BNL shares as part of its normal banking activity. The two agreements included a clause in which Deutsche Bank committed itself not to take part in the offer launched by the BBVA. Unlike the rest of the terms of the two transactions, this clause was not disclosed to avoid the impression that Deutsche Bank was not considered as acting in concert in Unipol's tender offer.

- Under the first converse, which Unipol called "the sport hedge", Unipol purchased from Deutsche Bank an American call option, with a strike price of EUR 2.70 per share, to be exercised during a period of six months starting on the termination date of the offer, and Deutsche Bank purchased from Unipol a European put option which would expire at the earliest of (i) the exercise date of the call option and (ii) the third anniversary of its trade date. The put option had a strike price of EUR 2.70 to be adjusted upwards to take into account the time value of money and to be adjusted downwards by any dividend distributed to the underlying shares. Both options were on 65.281 million shares, or 2.15% of BNL's ordinary share capital, and had a strike price of EUR 2.70 per share.
- Under the second converse, which Unipol called "the put & call hedge", Unipol purchased from Deutsche Bank a European call option, with a strike price of EUR 2.70 per share, to be exercised on 18 January 2006, and Deutsche Bank purchased from Unipol a European put option which would expire at the earliest of (i) the exercise date of the call option and (ii) the third anniversary of its trade date. The put option had a strike price of EUR 2.70 to be adjusted upwards to take into account the time value of money and to be adjusted downwards by any dividend distributed to the underlying shares. Both options were on 85.876 million shares, or 2.84% of BNL's ordinary share capital, and had a strike price of EUR 2.70 per share.

On 22 July 2005, BBVA withdrew its offer for BNL.

On 4 August the request for authorization to acquire a controlling stake in BNL was submitted to the BoI, and on 8 August the request for authorization to acquire full control of BNL Vita S.p.A., BNL's insurance subsidiary, was submitted to the Italian insurance regulator ISVAP. On 16 August a communication containing the essential elements of the public tender offer and the draft offer document was submitted to CONSOB, in accordance with Italian law. At the same time a press release with the essential elements of the mandatory public tender offer was issued.

On 12 August 2005, Unipol acquired from Deutsche Bank an American put, which Unipol called "the contingent put" that gave Unipol the right to sell to Deutsche Bank a number of shares of BNL equal to the difference, if positive, between (i) the number of shares tendered and (ii) the difference between the total number of shares object of the offer and 65,281,000 shares. The option could be exercised during the 15 calendar days following the closing of the offer.

On 29 August an EGM of Unipol authorized the board of directors to increase Unipol's share capital by up to EUR 2.6 billion. The EGM also passed the motion to cease indicating the nominal value of the shares and to amend the company's by-laws accordingly. In this respect it should be mentioned that on 12 August 2005 the holding company Finsoe paid EUR 896 million on account for the future capital increase and that subscription to the remaining amount would be guaranteed by an underwriting bank syndicate consisting of leading Italian and foreign banks. The capital increase was intended to partially finance the mandatory public tender offer. Another objective of the capital increase was to strengthen Unipol's equity in order to keep equity ratios in line with the relevant laws and regulations. The capital increase was expected to be carried out in the fourth quarter of 2005. The offer was also to be financed by Unipol issuing subordinated debenture loans and/or other sources of long-term funding for a maximum of EUR 1.4 billion and releasing own funds, mainly through asset disposals, amounting to approximately EUR 0.8 billion.

On 31 August CONSOB approved the publication of the offer document relating to the mandatory public tender offer for BNL shares.

On 6 September 2005, Italy's antitrust authority resolved not to open a preliminary investigation into the operation to acquire control of BNL by Unipol, since it did not create or strengthen a dominant position as a result of which competition would be significantly and lastingly eliminated or reduced. The antitrust authority also approved the wording of a communication to be sent to the Bank of Italy containing its opinion on the impact the operation in question would have on banking markets, specifying that it "did not significantly affect markets involving bank deposits and lending".

On 12 September 2005 the board of directors of Unipol, availing itself of the powers conferred by the EGM of 29 August 2005, resolved to propose to shareholders a share capital increase of up to EUR 2.6 through a rights issue.

On 15 October Deutsche Bank bought 40,000 BNL shares for EUR 2.755 per share related to a trading activity unrelated to the offer.

On 21 October 2005, BNL rejected Unipol's takeover offer. BNL did not consider Unipol's offer price to be fair.

On 2 November 2005, Unipol announced the successful conclusion of its right issue, raising EUR 2.58 million.

On 3 November 2005, Unipol and Deutsche Bank modified the terms of the puts part of the "spot hedge" and the "put & call hedge" agreements to include the possibility of cash settlement election by Unipol. This change was aimed at reducing Unipol's financial commitment were Deutsche Bank to exercise any of its puts.

On 19 December Antonio Fazio, the governor of the Bank of Italy, stepped down after his conduct in the battle for BNL and in other takeover fights came under investigation by the European Commission. Mario Dragui became the new governor.

On 23 December 2005, CONSOB deemed the options contracts between Unipol and Deutsche Bank to be shareholders' agreements and that, as a result of these agreements and the fact that in the middle of October Deutsche Bank had acquired more BNL shares at EUR 2.755 per share, the bid price should have been increased to EUR 2.755 per share. As a result, CONSOB forced Unipol to increase the offer to match the price it paid to other investors.

On 28 December 2005, Unipol raised its offer for BNL by 2% to EUR 2.755. This increase implied that Unipol would spend EUR 84 million more, a small impact. That increased the size of the offer to EUR 5 billion from EUR 4.9 billion.

On 10 January 2006, Unipol's bid was rejected by the Bank of Italy, ending the insurer's six-month attempt to take over BNL. The Bank of Italy stated that the conditions for complying with the requirements of prudence relating to the capital adequacy required for the acquisition of the control of BNL to be authorized had not been met. It definitively confirmed this opinion on 3 February 2006.

On 4 February 2006, Unipol's board of directors approved an agreement with the French bank BNP Paribas, to sell the BNL shares held by it and by its financial partners. This agreement, which could not be implemented until the required authorizations were received, provided for payment of EUR 2.925 per share. The sale resulted in a total capital gain for Unipol of approximately EUR 81 million, which enabled most of the costs incurred in launching the bid to be offset and the put options on BNL shares held by the principal financial partners in the operation to be terminated.

Conclusions

This case highlights how Unipol increased its chances of success with its offer for BNL by entering into two equity converse transactions with CSFB and Deutsche Bank, prior to raising the offer financing. At the end the Bank of Italy did not approve the takeover, but otherwise the converses would have notably helped Unipol to achieve its objective.

One interesting fact of the transaction was that Unipol had to improve the offer as a result of Deutsche Bank's tiny purchase of shares in the market during the offer period. This could have been a very costly mistake. According to CONSOB, Deustche Bank's undisclosed written commitment to not tender any BNL shares related to the converses limited the transfer of shares and was considered as acting in concert in Unipol's tender offer. The fact that the commitment was not disclosed greatly weakened Deutsche Bank's reply to CONSOB because it gave the impression that Deutsche Bank and Unipol were interested in hiding this parasocial agreement. In my view, its undisclosure did not make sense. The transaction was not substantially different from the disclosed converse transaction signed between Unipol and CSFB.

8
Stock Options Plans Hedging

This chapter briefly describes the main stock-based compensation plans. These plans include all arrangements by which employees receive shares of stock or other equity instruments of the employer or the employer incurs liabilities to employees in amounts based on the price of the employer's stock. I will start by describing the main plans. I will continue by reviewing the IFRS accounting for these plans. A good understanding of the accounting for stock-based plans is crucial in order to implement a sound hedging strategy. Next, I will examine the most common hedging strategies for hedging stock options plans, including some innovative strategies to reduce the cost of hedging these plans. Finally, I will discuss HSBC's share performance award, a highly structured share plan.

8.1 MAIN EQUITY-BASED COMPENSATION PLANS

Equity-based compensations plans are a tool to further align employee interests with those of the company's shareholders by enhancing further the link between pay and long-term performance. These compensation plans are typically discretionary, providing flexibility to reward particular achievements or exceptional performance. As a result, most compensation plans are granted to senior key talent who are actively leading the drive to achieve sustained profitability at the company and who are expected to contribute most significantly to its long-term future and economic success.

8.1.1 Main Equity-based Compensation Plans

In this section I will briefly cover the major share-based compensation plans. Continuously, human resources consulting firms are developing new types of plan. Additionally, changes in tax regimes usually bring new types of plan. However, most plans can be classified under one of the following categories.

Stock Options Plans

An employee stock options plan (ESOP) represents the right awarded to certain employees to purchase a number of common shares of the company at a pre-agreed exercise price, commonly subject to certain conditions. The exercise price is usually set at the market price of the underlying shares on the date of grant or an average of the stock price during a period up to the date of grant.

Stock Appreciation Rights

A stock appreciation right (SAR) plan provides eligible employees of the company with the right to receive cash equal to the appreciation of the company's common shares over a pre-established strike price. Therefore, a SAR is a cash-settled ESOP.

Share Plans

There are many variations to share plans. In general, employees of the company either voluntarily buy shares of the company in advantageous terms, or are granted a number of shares for free.

The most common design of a share plan, the so-called "equity plus plan" or "leverage share savings plan", is a voluntary plan that gives eligible employees the opportunity to purchase shares of the company at the stock price on the purchase date and generally receive at no additional cost a number of shares (e.g., two shares) for each share purchased, up to a maximum annual limit, after a certain vesting period of several years (e.g., three). Commonly, the free shares to be received are forfeitable in certain circumstances.

Another typical design of a share plan is a voluntary plan, the so-called "discounted purchase plan", that gives eligible employees the opportunity to purchase shares of the company at a discount to the stock price on the purchase date. Shares purchased under the share plan are restricted from sale during a certain period (e.g., three years) from the time of purchase.

As mentioned earlier, there are all sorts of variations to the two previous designs. At the end of this chapter, the share plan awarded by HSBC is covered, which in my view is one of the most complex I have seen.

Employee Stock Ownership Plans

An employee stock ownership plan (trust ESOP) is a retirement plan in which the company contributes its stock to a trust for the benefit of the company's employees. This type of plan should not be confused with employee stock options plans, also called ESOPs, which we saw earlier. The structures of trust ESOPS vary, but typically they are arrangements whereby a trust is set up by the company to acquire shares in the company for the benefit of the employees. Therefore, in a trust ESOP, its beneficiaries do not hold the stock directly (i.e., beneficiaries do not actually buy shares). Instead, the company contributes its own shares to the trust (i.e., the plan), contributes cash to buy its own stock, or, quite commonly, the plan borrows money from the company to buy stock. The structure of the plan is designed to benefit from significant tax advantages for the company, the employees and the sellers. Employees gradually vest in their accounts and receive their benefits when they leave the company (although there may be distributions prior to that). Hereinafter, I will use the term ESOP to refer to stock options plans only.

8.1.2 Terminology of Stock Option Plans and SARs

There are specific terms of stock option plans and SARs. The main terms are the following:

Beneficiary is the award recipient.

Grant date (see Figure 8.1) is the date at which the entity and the beneficiary agree to the share-based payment arrangement, being when the entity and the counterparty have a shared understanding of the terms and conditions of the arrangement. If that agreement is subject to an approval process (for example, by shareholders), the grant date is the date when that approval is obtained.

Vesting conditions are the conditions that must be satisfied for the beneficiary to become entitled to receive the award. Vesting conditions include service conditions, which require the other party to complete a specified period of service, and performance conditions,

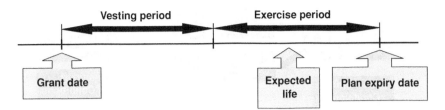

Figure 8.1 ESOP/SAR main dates.

which require specified performance targets to be met (such as a specified increase in the entity's profit over a specified period of time). Vesting conditions are either:

- Market conditions.
- Non-market conditions.

Vesting period (see Figure 8.1) is the waiting period under an equity-based incentive plan that must expire before the beneficiary becomes irrevocably entitled to the options involved. The beneficiary cannot sell or exercise unvested stock options. Vesting usually continues after termination of employment in cases such as redundancy or retirement. Vesting is commonly accelerated if the recipient's termination of employment is due to death or disability.

Exercise period (see Figure 8.1) is the period in which the beneficiaries may exercise their rights. Commonly, the exercise period starts just after the end of the vesting period.

Exercise price is the price at which the beneficiary can acquire the award underlying shares in the case of a stock options plan. In the case of a SAR, the exercise price refers to the price over which the appreciation of the shares would be calculated, and therefore, paid to the beneficiary.

Expected life is the best estimate as to when the beneficiaries are likely to exercise their options. In order to estimate the expected life, the company takes into account the vesting period, the past history of beneficiaries exercise, the price of the underlying stock relative to its historical averages, the employee's level within the organization and the underlying stock expected volatility.

Forfeiture of options rights is the potential cancellation of an award during the vesting period. An award, or portions of it, may be subject to forfeiture in certain circumstances. For example, an award may be forfeited if the recipient voluntarily terminates employment before the end of the relevant vesting period, or if the beneficiary is involved in certain harmful acts, such as breaches of legal, regulatory and compliance standards.

Dividends distributed to the underlying shares: Commonly, the beneficiary is not entitled to receive dividends before the settlement of the award.

8.2 IFRS ACCOUNTING FOR EQUITY-BASED COMPENSATION PLANS

This section reviews the accounting under IFRS for equity-based plans. The accounting standard that guides the recognition of share-based payments is IFRS 2 "Share-based Payment". IFRS 2 defines a share-based payment as a transaction in which the entity receives or acquires goods and services either as consideration for its equity instruments or by incurring liabilities for amounts based on the price of the entity's shares or other equity instruments of the entity.

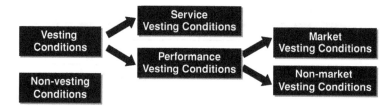

Figure 8.2   IFRS share-based award conditions.

The accounting requirements for the share-based payment depend on how the transaction will be settled:

- The issuance/delivery of equity (stock options plans, share purchase plans).
- The delivery of cash (SARs), or the issuance/delivery of equity with a cash alternative.

Frequently, an option right may only be exercised if specific performance targets, called conditions, are met during the vesting period (see Figure 8.2).

IFRS 2 groups all conditions between non-vesting conditions and vesting conditions:

- **Non-vesting conditions** are conditions that determine whether the company receives the services that entitle the counterparty to the share-based payment. If a non-vesting condition is not met, the company is not receiving the "work" that entitles a beneficiary to the share-based payment. For example, a company may grant stock options to a board member on the condition that the member does not compete with the company during the vesting period. If the board member leaves to work for a competitor during the vesting period, the award is terminated. Another example of a non-vesting condition, for share plans, would be a requirement for the employee to make investments in the company shares.
- **Vesting conditions** are conditions other than non-vesting conditions.

Under IFRS 2, vesting conditions are divided into service and performance vesting conditions:

- **Service vesting conditions** are conditions that if not achieved result in forfeiture, such as the beneficiary's employment during the vesting period.
- **Performance vesting conditions** are vesting conditions other than service conditions.

Under IFRS 2, performance vesting targets are divided into market and non-market vesting conditions:

- **A market vesting condition** is defined by IFRS 2 as "a condition upon which the exercise price, vesting or exercisability of an equity instrument depends that is related to the market price of the entity's equity instruments, such as attaining a specified share price or a specified amount of intrinsic value of a share option, or achieving a specified target that is based on the market price of the entity's equity instruments relative to an index of market prices of equity instruments of other entities". In summary, a market vesting condition is linked to the equity markets.
- **A non-market vesting condition** is a performance vesting condition other than a market condition. For example, an award may be exercised only if a certain earnings-per-share is met, or a certain EBITDA growth is achieved.

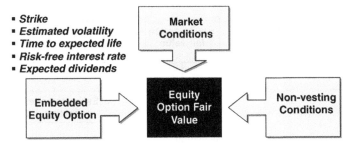

Figure 8.3 Equity option fair value estimation.

8.2.1 Accounting for Stock Options Plans

As we saw earlier, stock options plans can only be settled by delivering shares to the beneficiary. The settlement exclusively in shares establishes the rules for the plan's recognition, as follows.

Accounting Entries on Grant Date

On grant date, the fair value of the "equity option" is estimated. An important ingredient of this estimate is the fair value of the equity option embedded in the award (see Figure 8.3), which is determined using an option-pricing model, typically the Black–Scholes model. The model takes into account the stock price at the grant date, the exercise price, the expected life of the option, the volatility of the underlying stock, the expected dividends on it and the risk-free interest rate over the expected life of the option.

- The expected life of the option is estimated using various behavioral assumptions, for example, exercise patterns of similar plans.
- Market vesting conditions and non-vesting conditions are taken into account when estimating the fair value of the equity instruments granted.
- Non-market vesting conditions and service conditions are not taken into account.

No accounting entries take place on grant date.

Accounting Entries at Each Reporting Date during the Life of the Award

At each reporting date, the total compensation expense associated with the award is calculated (see Figure 8.4). The expense is measured by adjusting the fair value of the equity option that was calculated on grant date for the expected likelihood of meeting the non-market vesting and service conditions. For example, if there is an 80% chance of achieving the non-market vesting and service conditions, the number of options is adjusted by multiplying the options' fair value by 80%. Consequently, the compensation expense takes into account the expected number of options that are expected to vest. One of the ingredients of this adjustment is the estimation of the forfeiture rate for service conditions. Based on historical data of employees' turnover, the company estimates the percentage of the beneficiaries that will leave the company before the vesting period lapses.

The total compensation expense is evenly allocated over the expected life of the award. For example, let us assume that a company reports its financial statements on an annual basis. If at the first reporting date the total compensation is estimated to be EUR 16 million and the

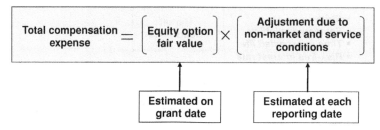

Figure 8.4   ESOP personnel expense calculation.

vesting period of the award is four years, the yearly compensation expense to be recognized on this date would be EUR 4 million (= 16 million/4). The compensation expense allocated to the first year would be charged to the income statement and a corresponding increase in equity would be recognized, as follows:

Personnel expense (P&L)	4,000,000		
		ESOP reserve (equity)	4,000,000

At each subsequent reporting date, the adjustment due to non-market and ser-vice vesting conditions is re-estimated. Using our previous example, let us assume that the total compensation is revised at the second yearly reporting date to EUR 20 million from EUR 16 million. The yearly compensation expense to be allocated over the four-year vesting period becomes EUR 5 million (= 20 million/4). The compensation expense allocated to the second yearly period would be as follows:

Personnel expense (P&L)	5,000,000		
		ESOP reserve (equity)	5,000,000

Also, on the second reporting date an adjustment has to be made if the total compensation expense is revised due to changes in the estimation of the number of equity instruments expected to vest. This adjustment brings the already recognized compensation expense in line with the new total compensation estimate. As the company already recognized EUR 4 million expense at the first yearly reporting date, the company would need to make a EUR 1 million (= 5 million – 4 million) adjustment to bring it in line with the new EUR 5 million yearly compensation expense, as follows:

Personnel expense (P&L)	1,000,000		
		ESOP reserve (equity)	1,000,000

The accounting recognition at the remaining reporting dates is similar to the recognition outlined for the second yearly reporting date. Therefore, on a cumulative basis, no amount is recognized if the equity instruments granted do not vest because of a failure to satisfy non-market or service vesting conditions.

However, if an ESOP achieves the non-market and the service conditions but does not achieve the market or non-vesting conditions, the amount recognized in the ESOP reserve and as compensation expense is not reversed.

Accounting Entries at Settlement or at Expiry

At maturity of the ESOP or upon its exercise, the balance of the ESOP reserve is recycled to another account of the shareholders' equity section. There are two scenarios we need to consider: (i) all (or part of) the plan options expire unexercised and (ii) all (or part of) the plan options are exercised.

Let us assume that all the beneficiaries behave identically and that by its maturity the ESOP has not been exercised. Let us assume that the ESOP reserve shows a balance of EUR 20 million. Therefore, a compensation expense of EUR 20 million should already have been recognized during the ESOP's expected life. It would be illogical to leave a balance on the ESOP reserve which relates to an ESOP that no longer exists. Therefore, the balance of the ESOP reserve is recycled to other account(s) of the shareholders' equity section. The credit is usually taken to retained earnings but there is nothing to prohibit it from being credited to a separate equity reserve. The accounting entries in our example would be the following:

ESOP reserve (equity)	20,000,000		
		Retained earnings (equity)	20,000,000

Upon exercise of the ESOP, there would also be a recycle within the shareholders' equity section, but it has to be implemented in accordance with the action taken by the company. Upon exercise of the ESOP, the company has two alternatives: (i) to issue new shares or (ii) to deliver treasury shares.

Conclusions

If the non-market vesting conditions and the service conditions are satisfied while the ESOP's market and non-vesting conditions are met, the personnel expense is not reversed, and the total expense ends up increasing shareholders' equity, even if the ESOP expires unexercised. Thus, if an ESOP has a market vesting condition or a non-vesting condition, the company might still recognize an expense even if that condition is not attained and the option does not vest.

By contrast, an ESOP subject only to a non-market vesting condition does not result in an expense if the condition is not met.

8.2.2 Accounting for Stock Appreciation Rights

As mentioned earlier, SARs plans – if exercised – are settled by paying to the beneficiary the intrinsic value of the underlying option in cash. The accounting recognition of cash-settled awards is covered next. The accounting recognition for awards in which either the beneficiary or the company can choose between settling the award in cash or in shares follows a similar procedure, except that if the physical settlement is elected on exercise date there is an additional accounting entry to recognize the delivery of the shares.

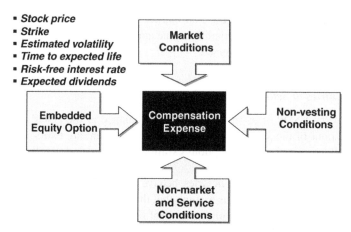

Figure 8.5   SAR personnel expense calculation.

Required Actions on Grant Date

On grant date, no actions take place.

Accounting Entries at Each Reporting Date during the Life of the Award

At each reporting date, the total compensation expense associated with the award is calculated (see Figure 8.5). The expense is measured by fair valuing the embedded equity option and adjusting it for the likelihood of achievement of all the vesting (market, non-market and service) and non-vesting conditions.

The total compensation expense is evenly allocated over the expected life of the award. For example, let us assume that a company reports its financial statements on an annual basis. If, at the first reporting date, the total compensation is estimated to be EUR 16 million and the expected life of the award is four years, the yearly compensation expense to be recognized on this date would be EUR 4 million (= 16 million/4). The compensation expense allocated to the first year would be charged to the income statement and a corresponding increase in liabilities would be recognized, as follows:

Personnel expense (P&L)	4,000,000		
		SAR award (liabilities)	4,000,000

At each subsequent reporting date, the compensation expense would be re-estimated. Using our previous example, let us assume that the total compensation is revised at the second yearly reporting date to EUR 20 million from EUR 16 million. The yearly compensation expense to be allocated over the four-year expected life of the award becomes EUR 5 million (= 20 million/4). The compensation expense allocated to the second yearly period would be as follows:

Personnel expense (P&L)	5,000,000		
		SAR award (liabilities)	5,000,000

Also, on the second reporting date an adjustment has to be made if the total compensation expense is revised due to changes in the estimation of the number of equity instruments expected to vest. This adjustment brings the already recognized compensation expense in line with the new total compensation estimate. As the company already recognized EUR 4 million expense at the first yearly reporting date, the company would need to make a EUR 1 million (= 5 million – 4 million) adjustment to bring it in line with the new EUR 5 million yearly compensation expense, as follows:

Personnel expense (P&L)	1,000,000		
		SAR award (liabilities)	1,000,000

The accounting recognition at the remaining reporting dates is similar to the recognition outlined for the second yearly reporting date. Therefore, on a cumulative basis, no amount is recognized if the equity instruments granted do not vest because of a failure to satisfy market and/or non-market vesting conditions.

8.3   CASE STUDY: ABC'S ESOP AND SAR

8.3.1   Main Terms of ABC's ESOP and SAR

In order to illustrate the hedging and accounting of stock options plans and SARs, let us look at an example. Let us assume that ABC, a European company, on 1 January 20X1 granted two share-based plans, an ESOP and a SAR, with identical terms (except the settlement mode) to its top management. The main terms of the ESOP were the following (see Figure 8.6):

- Grant date: 1 January 20X1.
- Number of options: 2 million per plan (or 4 million options in total).
- Number of beneficiaries: 50.
- Exercise price: EUR 50.00 (ABC's stock price on grant date).
- Vesting period: From 1 January 20X1 to 31 December 20X3 (i.e., 3 years duration).
- Exercise period: At any time from 1 January 20X4 to 31 December 20X4.
- Settlement: Upon exercise, beneficiaries will receive one share per option and pay the strike amount (i.e., the number of options times the strike price).

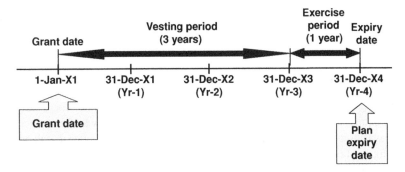

Figure 8.6   ABC's ESOP/SAR main dates.

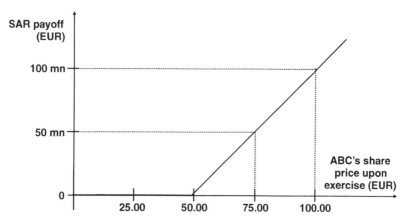

Figure 8.7   ABC's SAR payoff as a function of the average price upon exercise.

- Market vesting conditions: ABC's stock total return, including dividends, has to outperform the EuroStoxx50 index.
- Service conditions: Each grant is conditional upon the beneficiary remaining in service over the vesting period.
- Non-market vesting conditions: Each grant is conditional upon ABC's EBITDA achieving a 10% annual growth rate during the vesting period.

Under the ESOP, if a beneficiary exercised his/her options, he/she would pay the exercise amount (i.e., the EUR 50.00 strike times the number of options exercised) and receive the options' underlying ABC shares. The ESOP had a three-year vesting period. After completion of the vesting period, each beneficiary could exercise his/her vested options during the year commencing on the end date of the vesting period, subject to the achievement of three vesting conditions: (i) that ABC's stock price outperformed the European most liquid stock index; (ii) that the beneficiary remained an employee during the vesting period; and (iii) that during the vesting period ABC's EBITDA grew at least 10% annually.

Under the SAR, the mechanics were the same except its payoff upon exercise. If a beneficiary exercised his/her options, he/she would receive in cash the intrinsic value of the options. The intrinsic value of the options was defined as the difference between the value of ABC's stock at expiry and the EUR 50.00 award exercise price, for the number of options the beneficiary had exercised. Figure 8.7 depicts the SAR payoff as a function of the average stock price upon exercise.

8.3.2   Accounting for ABC's ESOP

In this section I will cover how ABC's ESOP plan was accounted for. In summary, the embedded equity stock option (including the market conditions) was fair valued only when the ESOP was granted. The compensation expense was calculated at each balance sheet date by adjusting the fair value of the embedded equity option for the likelihood of achievement of the non-market and service conditions. The total fair value was recognized as a personnel expense spread over the vesting period of the plan and an equity reserve.

Actions Required on Grant Date

On grant date, ABC estimated the fair value of the equity option, ignoring the non-market and service vesting conditions, but taking into account the non-vesting conditions (in this case there were no non-vesting conditions). Based on historical data, ABC estimated that on average the beneficiaries would exercise the fair value of the option at the end of the first six months of the exercise period (i.e., 3.5 years after the grant date). Thus, the best estimation of the expected life of the award was 3.5 years. The fair value of the equity option was calculated by pricing a call option on ABC stock with a strike of EUR 50.00 (i.e., at-the-money), an expiry of 3.5 years, a volatility equal to the implied volatility for such options on ABC stock and a 2% expected dividend yield of ABC stock during its life. The option valuation also included the market vesting condition (the outperformance of the EuroStoxx50 index), assuming a 60% correlation between ABC's stock price and the index. ABC used the Monte Carlo simulation method to estimate the fair value of this option, coming up with a EUR 21 million fair value. Beware that the fair value of the option did not include any estimates regarding the non-market and service conditions.

No accounting entries took place on grant date.

Accounting Entries at Each Reporting Date during the Life of the Award

At each reporting date, the total compensation expense associated with the award was calculated (see Figure 8.8). The expense was measured by adjusting the equity option fair value (that was calculated on the grant date) for the expected likelihood of meeting the non-market and service vesting conditions. Consequently, the compensation expense took into account the expected number of options that were expected to vest. Based on historical data of employees' turnover, ABC estimated the percentage of the beneficiaries expected to leave the company before the vesting period lapsed. Also, ABC estimated the likelihood of ABC's EBITDA achieving a 10% annual growth rate during the vesting period.

The total compensation (i.e., personnel) expense was evenly allocated over the three-year vesting period of the award. The following table shows the personnel expense at each reporting date, assuming that ABC reported its financial statements on an annual basis.

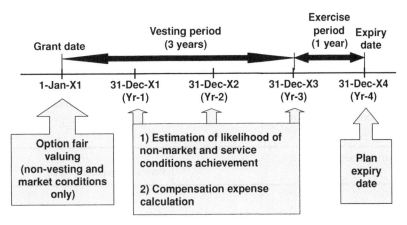

Figure 8.8 ABC's ESOP personnel expense calculation dates.

Date	Equity option fair value (EUR million)	Adjustment due to non-market conditions	Total personnel expense (EUR million)	Period personnel expense (EUR million)	Adjustments to previous entries (EUR million)
31-Dec-X1	21.0	80%	16.8	5.6	—
31-Dec-X2	21.0[1]	70%[2]	14.7[3]	4.9[4]	<0.7>[5]
31-Dec-X3	21.0	75%	15.8	5.3	0.8[6]

(1) Calculated at grant date, and fixed during the life of the award.
(2) Estimated on each reporting date.
(3) (1) × (2) = 21 million × 70%.
(4) (3)/three accounting periods = 14.7 million/3.
(5) 4.9 million − 5.6 million.
(6) (5.3 million × 2) − (4.9 million × 2).

On 31 December 20X1, ABC estimated the expected likelihood of meeting the non-market vesting conditions to be 80%. A EUR 16.8 million total compensation expense was calculated by multiplying the 80% estimation by the EUR 21 million equity option fair value. The compensation expense allocated to the first year was charged to the income statement and a corresponding increase in equity was recognized, as follows (amounts in EUR million):

Personnel expense (P&L)	5.6		
		ESOP reserve (equity)	5.6

On 31 December 20X2, the expected likelihood of meeting the non-market and service vesting conditions was re-estimated to be 70%. A EUR 14.7 million total compensation expense was calculated by multiplying the 70% estimation by the EUR 21 million equity option fair value. The compensation expense allocated to the second year was charged to the income statement and a corresponding increase in equity was recognized, as follows (amounts in EUR million):

Personnel expense (P&L)	4.9		
		ESOP reserve (equity)	4.9

Also on 31 December 20X2, a EUR 0.7 million adjustment to the compensation expense was implemented as the new annual expense was EUR 4.9 million while the personnel expense recognized on 31 December 20X1 was EUR 5.6 million. The adjustment was recorded as follows (amounts in EUR million):

ESOP reserve (equity)	0.7		
		Personnel expense (P&L)	0.7

Following the same reasoning, and using the numbers in the table above, the accounting entries on 31 December 20X3 were the following (amounts in EUR million):

Personnel expense (P&L)	5.3		
		ESOP reserve (equity)	5.3

Personnel expense (P&L)	0.8		
		ESOP reserve (equity)	0.8

Accounting Entries upon Exercise or Unexercised Expiry

At maturity of an ESOP or upon its exercise, the balance of the ESOP reserve was recycled to another account of the shareholders' equity section. There are two scenarios to consider: (i) all (or part of) the plan options expired unexercised and (ii) all (or part of) the plan options were exercised.

In order to describe the accounting entries under the first scenario, let us assume that under ABC's ESOP all the beneficiaries behaved identically and upon the ESOP expiration on 31 December 20X4 it was not exercised. The ESOP reserve showed a balance of EUR 15.8 million. Therefore, a compensation expense of EUR 15.8 million had been recognized during the ESOP's vesting period. It would have been illogical to leave a balance on the ESOP reserve which related to an ESOP that no longer existed. Therefore, the balance of the ESOP reserve was recycled to other account(s) of the shareholders' equity section. The credit was taken to retained earnings but it could have been credited to a separate equity reserve. The accounting entries were the following (amounts in EUR million):

ESOP reserve (equity)	15.8		
		Retained earnings (equity)	15.8

Under the second scenario, exercise of the ESOP, there was also a recycle within the shareholders' equity section, but the accounts affected depended on the action taken by the company. Upon exercise of the ESOP, the company had two alternatives: (i) to issue new shares or (ii) to deliver treasury shares.

Let us assume that the ESOP was exercised simultaneously by all the beneficiaries at the end of the fourth year and that ABC issued 2 million new shares, with a nominal value of EUR 2 million. Upon exercise of the ESOP the beneficiaries paid the EUR 100 million (= 2 million × 50.00) strike amount and received the new shares. The accounting entries were the following (amounts in EUR million):

Cash (assets)	100		
ESOP reserve (equity)	15.8		
		Common stock (equity)	2
		Additional paid-in capital (equity)	98
		Retained earnings (equity)	15.8

If the company delivered treasury shares, the accounting entries were the following (amounts in EUR million), assuming that the treasury shares delivered were originally recognized at EUR 15 million:

Cash (assets)	100		
ESOP reserve (equity)	15.8		
		Treasury shares (equity)	15
		Additional paid-in capital (equity)	85
		Retained earnings (equity)	15.8

Conclusions

If, at the end of the vesting period, the non-market condition (i.e., ABC's EBITDA 10% growth) was not achieved, a reversal of the ESOP's personnel expense already recognized would have taken place. Thus, on a cumulative basis no amount of personnel expense is recognized if the equity instruments granted do not vest because of a failure to satisfy non-market vesting conditions or service conditions.

If the non-market vesting conditions and the service conditions were satisfied while an ESOP's market and non-vesting conditions (in our case there were no non-vesting conditions) were met, the personnel expense would not be reversed, and the total expense would end up increasing shareholders' equity, even if the ESOP expired unexercised. Thus, if an ESOP has a market vesting condition or a non-vesting condition, the company might still recognize an expense even if that condition is not attained and the option does not vest.

From the grant date ABC knew the maximum amount of compensation expense that it could end up recognizing in P&L. This maximum amount was the fair value of the equity option on grant date (i.e., EUR 21 million).

8.3.3   Accounting for ABC's SAR

In this subsection I will cover how ABC's SAR plan was accounted for. In summary, the whole award was fair valued periodically at each balance sheet date. The fair value was recognized as a personnel expense spread over the life of the plan and a liability.

Actions Required on Grant Date

No actions and no accounting entries took place on grant date.

Accounting Entries at Each Reporting Date during the Life of the Award

At each reporting date, the total compensation expense associated with the award was calculated (see Figure 8.9) by estimating the fair value of the embedded equity option expense and adjusting it for the expected likelihood of meeting the non-market and service vesting conditions. Consequently, the compensation expense took into account the expected number of options that were expected to vest.

The total compensation (i.e., personnel) expense was evenly allocated over the three-year vesting period. The following table shows the personnel expense at each reporting date, assuming that ABC reported its financial statements on an annual basis.

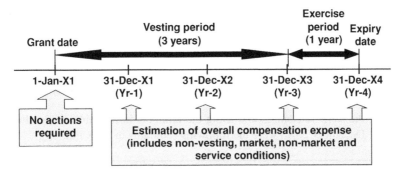

Figure 8.9   ABC's SAR personnel expense calculation dates.

Date	Equity option fair value (EUR million)	Adjustment due to non-market conditions	Total personnel expense (EUR million)	Period personnel expense (EUR million)	Adjustments to previous entries (EUR million)
31-Dec-X1	20.0	80%	16.0	5.3	—
31-Dec-X2	26.0[1]	70%[1]	18.2[2]	6.1[3]	0.8[4]
31-Dec-X3	29.0	75%	21.8	7.3	2.4[5]

(1) Calculated at each reporting date.
(2) 26.0 million × 70%.
(3) (2)/three accounting periods = 18.2 million/3, assuming a 3-year vesting period.
(4) 6.1 million – 5.3 million.
(5) (7.3 million × 2) – (6.1 million × 2), assuming a 3-year expected life.

On 31 December 20X1, ABC estimated both (i) the fair value of the embedded equity option (EUR 20 million) and (ii) the expected likelihood of meeting the non-market and service vesting conditions (80%). A EUR 16 million total compensation expense was calculated by multiplying the 80% estimation by the EUR 20 million equity option fair value. The compensation expense allocated to the first year was charged to the income statement and a corresponding increase in liabilities was recognized, as follows (amounts in EUR million):

Personnel expense (P&L)	5.3		
		SAR award (liabilities)	5.3

Repeating the process executed on the previous reporting date, on 31 December 20X2 ABC estimated a EUR 18.2 million compensation expense. Of this expense, EUR 6.1 million was allocated to the second year, being charged to the income statement and to liabilities, as follows (amounts in EUR million):

Personnel expense (P&L)	6.1		
		SAR award (liabilities)	6.1

Also on 31 December 20X2, a EUR 0.8 million adjustment to the compensation expense was implemented as the new annual expense was EUR 6.1 million while the personnel expense recognized on 31 December 20X1 was EUR 5.3 million. The adjustment was recorded as follows (amounts in EUR million):

Personnel expense (P&L)	0.8		
		SAR award (liabilities)	0.8

Following the same reasoning, and using the numbers in the table above, the accounting entries on 31 December 20X3 were the following (amounts in EUR million):

Personnel expense (P&L)	7.3		
		SAR award (liabilities)	7.3
Personnel expense (P&L)	2.4		
		SAR award (liabilities)	2.4

Accounting Entries upon Exercise or Unexercised Expiry

Let us assume that no beneficiaries exercised their rights prior to the SAR's expiry date. Let us assume further that at expiry, on 31 December 20X4, all the beneficiaries behaved identically. Then, there are two scenarios to consider: (i) all the SAR options expired unexercised and (ii) all the plan options were exercised.

Under the first scenario, the SAR lapsed fully unexercised. Thus, the SAR's fair value was zero. At the previous reporting dates a total EUR 21.8 million compensation expense was recognized. Therefore, this compensation expense had to be reversed on 31 December 20X4. The accounting entries were the following (amounts in EUR million):

SAR award (liabilities)	21.8		
		Personnel expense (P&L)	21.8

Under the second scenario, the SAR was fully exercised. Let us assume that on 31 December 20X4 ABC's share price was EUR 68. The SAR's fair value was EUR 36 million [$= 2$ million $\times$ $(68 - 50)$]. As ABC had already recognized a total EUR 21.8 million compensation expense, an additional EUR 14.2 million ($= 36$ million $- 21.8$ million) expense was recognized, as follows (amounts in EUR million):

Personnel expense (P&L)	14.2		
		SAR award (liabilities)	14.2

Additionally, the EUR 36 million cash award payment to the beneficiaries was recognized as follows (amounts in EUR million):

SAR award (liabilities)	36		
		Cash (assets)	36

Conclusions

At each reporting date ABC had to fair value the SAR award. It had several implications:

- ABC's income statement was exposed to a rising stock price, potentially increasing its volatility.
- Overall, ABC did not have to recognize a compensation expense were the SAR to expire worthless.
- On grant date ABC did not know the maximum amount of compensation expense that it could end up recognizing in P&L. Similarly on grant date, ABC did not know the amount of cash it would need to meet the SAR award.

8.4   MAIN ESOP/SAR HEDGING STRATEGIES

In this section I will cover the main strategies (see Figure 8.10) to hedge ESOPs and SARs, using ABC's share awards.

8.4.1   Underlying Risks in ESOPs and SARs

One not unusual hedging strategy is to do nothing. ABC would be exposed to the risk inherent in the plans. The risks in an ESOP and in a SAR differ due to their accounting and settlement differences. Thus, hedging strategies for an ESOP may not work for a SAR, and vice versa.

Risks in an ESOP

ABC was not exposed to equity market risk. Remember that from an accounting perspective, under the ESOP the equity option is estimated at grant date. During the expected life of the award, the equity option is not fair valued. Only the expectations of meeting the non-market conditions are reassessed at each reporting date. Therefore, ABC's P&L was not exposed to changes in ABC's stock price or changes in the likelihood of meeting the market conditions (i.e., ABC stock had to outperform the EuroStoxx50 index). In other words, ABC's P&L was not exposed to equity risk. While ABC'S P&L was exposed to non-market risks, its hedge is usually not feasible.

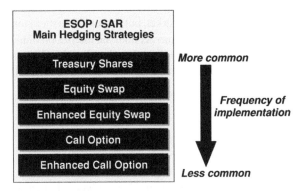

Figure 8.10   ESOP/SAR main hedging strategies.

ABC was exposed to dilution risk. If the ESOP ended up being exercised, ABC would need to deliver shares to the beneficiaries. Probably these shares would be newly issued, increasing the number of shares outstanding and, thus, diluting existing shareholders. However, the dilution risk was limited. New shares would be issued at EUR 50.00 per share.

Risks in a SAR

ABC was exposed to market risk. Remember that from an accounting perspective, under ESOP the equity option is fair valued at each reporting date. Therefore, ABC's P&L was exposed to changes in ABC's stock price or changes in the likelihood of meeting the market conditions (i.e., ABC stock had to outperform the EuroStoxx50 index).

ABC's P&L was exposed to the achievement of the non-market Conditions too. However, hedging these risks is usually not feasible.

ABC was also exposed to liquidity risk. Upon exercise, ABC would need to pay cash to the beneficiaries. A large amount of cash may require ABC to use precious liquidity resources or/and to raise financing.

ABC was not exposed to dilution risk as upon exercise no shares would be delivered to the beneficiaries.

8.4.2   Hedging with Treasury Shares

Hedging with treasury shares is, in my experience, the most common way to hedge ESOPs or SARs. In order to fully hedge the ESOP/SAR with treasury shares, on 1 January 20X1 ABC would need to acquire 4 million shares (2 million shares per plan) in the market, investing EUR 200 million. The treasury shares would be held in its balance sheet in coordination with the unexercised stock options. Each time that a beneficiary exercises his/her option rights:

- Related to the SAR, ABC would sell in the market the shares corresponding to the exercised options at the then prevailing share price. ABC would pay the beneficiary the intrinsic value of the exercised stock options.
- Related to the ESOP, ABC would deliver the shares to the beneficiary in exchange for the exercise amount.

At maturity of the plan, ABC would need to decide what to do with the remaining shares. In theory, ABC would sell the shares in the market, but it could keep them for future ESOPs/SARs.

This strategy can be optimized to take into account the likelihood of meeting the non-market conditions and the market conditions not directly related to ABC's stock price. As a result, ABC would acquire a number of shares equivalent to the number of the plans' options expected to vest.

Strengths of the Strategy

The strategy has the following strengths:

- If the plan options are exercised, ABC would have effectively met the settlement commitments under both plans.

- Ignoring the financing costs related to the treasury shares, this hedging alternative is cheaper than hedging with calls if the plans are exercised. If the stock options are exercised, ABC would have saved the call premium, which can be substantial.
- The initial acquisition of the shares may have a positive effect on ABC's stock price.
- The hedge is not revalued during the life of the plan. Thus, there is a parallel accounting treatment in equity of the ESOP's embedded equity option and the treasury shares.

Weaknesses of the Strategy

The strategy has the following drawbacks:

- The acquisition of treasury shares uses resources from the company. ABC might need to raise financing to fund the own shares acquisition.
- The acquisition of treasury shares has a negative impact on the debt-to-equity ratio. Treasury shares are deducted from equity, increasing ABC's leverage.
- The hedge is not revalued. This is a weakness only for SARs. The SAR plan would be revalued periodically while the hedge will not be. As a result, ABC would experience a mismatch in P&L.
- At maturity of the plan the shares hedging unexercised options are not needed any more. ABC might sell the shares in the market at a price below acquisition price, permanently reducing equity.
- ABC does not receive the treasury shares dividends, as it cannot distribute dividends to its own shares.
- The acquisition of treasury shares may affect ABC's flexibility in managing its treasury shares. Legally, companies have a maximum limit (e.g., 10%) that sets the maximum percentage of voting capital that they can hold in own shares. Buying a substantial amount of treasury shares may bring the company close to the legal limit, restricting potential acquisition of more shares.
- Although the shares acquired to hedge a plan in theory should remain in the company's balance sheet until expiration, there is a potential temptation to manage these shares like the rest of the treasury shares. Some companies manage their holdings of treasury shares dynamically, to alleviate potential disruptions in stock market trading. For example, a company may acquire treasury shares to provide liquidity when there is a large selling order in the market and sell them later when its stock shows an undesirable strength.

8.4.3 Hedging with Equity Swaps

One relatively common hedging strategy is to enter into an equity swap. Due to their significantly different effects, I will separate the analysis for each type of plan.

Hedging an ESOP with an Equity Swap

Let us assume that ABC hedged its ESOP plan with an equity swap. The strategy is in a way similar to a combination of a financing and an acquisition of treasury shares. Let us assume that ABC entered into a total return equity swap with the following terms:

- Trade date: 1 January 20X1 (the plan's grant date).
- Termination date: 31 December 20X4.

- Number of shares: 2 million (the ESOP's number of options).
- Shares: ABC's common stock.
- Initial price: EUR 50.00 (ABC's stock price on trade date).
- Initial equity notional amount: EUR 100 million.
- Equity amount receiver: ABC.
- ABC can partially/totally terminate the equity swap early, at any time from 1 January 20X3 to 31 December 20X4.
- ABC pays quarterly Euribor-3m plus 150 bps on the equity notional amount.
- ABC receives 100% of the gross dividends paid to the underlying shares.
- Settlement: physical settlement only.

The strategy is executed as follows:

1. ABC enters into the equity swap on the plan's grant date. No upfront premium is paid.
2. During the life of the equity swap, ABC pays the equity swap floating amount, Euribor plus 150 basis points on the equity swap notional. The equity swap notional is initially EUR 100 million, and would be adjusted to take into account the swap partial early terminations.
3. During the life of the equity swap, ABC receives any dividends distributed to the underlying shares.
4. Upon exercise of the plans, ABC would partially early terminate a number of shares of the equity swap equivalent to the number of options exercised under the plan. For example, if 200,000 options are exercised by the ESOP beneficiaries, ABC would early terminate 200,000 shares of the equity swap. Under the equity swap, ABC would pay EUR 10 million ($= 0.2$ million $\times 50$) and receive 200,000 own shares. These shares would be delivered to the beneficiaries in exchange for a EUR 10 million payment.
5. If, at the end of the vesting period, the non-market conditions have not been achieved, ABC has two alternatives: either to maintain the equity swap until its maturity or to totally early terminate it. In any case, ABC would end up buying 50 million own shares and paying EUR 100 million. ABC would then need to decide whether to hold the treasury shares for future share-based plans or to sell them in the market.
6. If, at expiry of the ESOP, there are options that remain unexercised, ABC would buy through the equity swap the remaining shares and pay EUR 50 per share. ABC would then need to decide what to do with the own shares: whether to hold them for future share-based plans or to sell them onto the market.

The equity swap would be treated for accounting purposes as an equity instrument. The initial accounting entry under IFRS would be (amounts in EUR millions) the following, assuming that EUR 86 million is the present value of the EUR 100 million equity notional:

Derivatives on own shares (equity)	86		
		Equity swap (liabilities)	86

The equity swap would not be fair valued during its life. As a result, the equity swap does not add volatility to the income statement as both the plan (ignoring service conditions) and the equity swap do not require fair valuing after the grant date. However, a liability would be recognized, increasing ABC's leverage metrics.

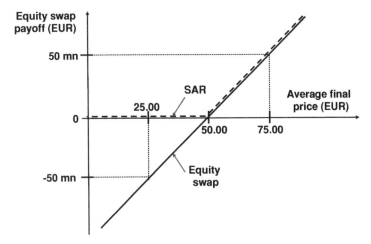

Figure 8.11 Equity swap settlement amount.

Hedging a SAR with an Equity Swap

Let us assume that ABC hedged its SAR plan with an equity swap. The terms would be identical to the equity swap traded to hedge the ESOP, except its settlement terms. This equity swap allowed for cash settlement only. Therefore, at each partial early termination and/or at maturity:

- ABC would receive, if ABC's stock price is greater than EUR 50.00:

$$\text{Number of shares terminated} \times (\text{Stock price} - 50.00)$$

- ABC would pay, if ABC's stock price is lower than EUR 50.00:

$$\text{Number of shares terminated} \times (50.00 - \text{Stock price})$$

Figure 8.11 shows the equity swap settlement amount as a function of the average final price. It can be seen that if the average final price was greater than EUR 50.00, and ignoring the SAR's service conditions, ABC would have perfectly hedged its commitment under the SAR. However, if the average final price was lower than EUR 50.00, ABC could lose a substantial amount.

The strategy is executed as follows:

1. ABC enters into the equity swap on the plan's grant date. No upfront premium is paid.
2. During the life of the equity swap, ABC pays the equity swap floating amount, Euribor plus 150 basis points on the equity swap notional. The equity swap notional is initially EUR 100 million, and would be adjusted to take into account the swap partial early terminations.
3. During the life of the equity swap, ABC receives any dividends distributed to the underlying shares.
4. Upon exercise of the plans, ABC would partially early terminate a number of shares of the equity swap equal to the number of options exercised under the plan. For example, if 200,000 options are exercised by the SAR beneficiaries, ABC would early terminate

200,000 shares of the equity swap. Assuming a EUR 60 ABC's stock price at the time of the exercises, under the equity swap, ABC would receive a EUR 2 million [= 0.2 million × (60 – 50)] settlement amount. This amount would be paid in turn to the SAR beneficiaries.

5. If, at the end of the vesting period, the non-market conditions have not been achieved, ABC has two alternatives: either to maintain the equity swap or to totally early terminate it. In order to avoid further exposure to ABC's stock price, ABC would probably early terminate it. ABC would either (i) receive the appreciation of the underlying shares above EUR 50, or (ii) pay the depreciation of the underlying shares below EUR 50.

6. If, at expiry of the ESOP, there are options that remain unexercised, the equity swap would terminate. ABC would either (i) receive the appreciation of the remaining underlying shares above EUR 50, or (ii) pay the depreciation of the remaining underlying shares below EUR 50.

The equity swap would be treated for accounting purposes as a derivative. It is unlikely that ABC would be able to apply hedge accounting as the payoffs of the SAR (a call option) and the equity swap were very different when ABC's stock price was below EUR 50.00. As a result, the equity swap would be fair valued through P&L at each reporting date. Remember that the SAR would also be fair valued at each reporting date, but the change in fair value would be allocated over the vesting period. Therefore:

- If ABC's share price is greater than 50.00, the change in fair value of the SAR and the equity swap would be similar (ignoring the time value of the equity option underlying the SAR and the adjustments due to the service condition). However, there would be an accounting mismatch in P&L, as the whole change in fair value of the swap would be recognized in P&L while one-third of the change in fair value of the SAR would be recognized in P&L.
- If ABC's share price is lower than 50.00, the change in fair value of the equity swap would be notably different from that of the SAR. To make things worse, only one-third of the change in fair value of the SAR would be recognized in P&L. As a result, a substantial mismatch in P&L could result, potentially increasing the volatility of ABC's income statement.

In summary, this hedging strategy could end up creating substantial distortions in ABC's financial statements. In the next subsection I will cover a more friendly variation of the equity swap.

Strengths of the Strategy

The strategy has the following strengths:

- If the plan options were exercised, ABC would have effectively met the settlement commitments under both plans.
- ABC was not using cash resources, in contrast to a hedge with treasury shares.
- Ignoring the financing costs related to the equity swap, this hedging alternative was cheaper than hedging with calls if the plans were exercised. If the awards' options were exercised, ABC would have saved the call premium, which was substantial.
- The bank counterparty to the equity swap needed to buy the underlying shares in the market at inception. This initial acquisition had a positive effect on ABC's stock price.
- Regarding the ESOP, the hedge was not revalued during the life of the plan. Thus, there was a similar accounting treatment in equity of the ESOP's embedded equity option and the treasury shares.

Weaknesses of the Strategy

The strategy has the following drawbacks:

- If the plans were unexercised because ABC shares were trading below EUR 50.00, ABC would either end up with unwanted treasury shares (in case of the ESOP) or with a loss (in case of the SAR).
- Regarding the SAR, if the shares were trading below EUR 50.00, there could be a substantial increase in the volatility of ABC's income statement due to the accounting recognition mismatch in P&L between the equity swap and the SAR.
- Regarding the ESOP, the equity swap had a double-negative effect on ABC's leverage metrics – for example, on its debt-to-equity ratio. On the one hand, there was a liability recognized from inception. On the other hand, there was an equity entry that reduced the balance of the shareholders' equity section of ABC's balance sheet.
- The equity swap consumed credit lines with its counterparty, reducing its flexibility to deal with this party.
- In some jurisdictions, an equity swap may be treated as treasury shares from a legal perspective. This may affect ABC's flexibility in managing its treasury shares, as they are usually subject to a maximum legal limit.

8.4.4   Hedging a SAR with an Enhanced Equity Swap

As we saw in the previous subsection, hedging a SAR with an equity swap can create substantial distortions in ABC's financial statements, especially in P&L. In this subsection I will cover a more friendly variation of the equity swap.

A long position in an equity swap can be viewed as the combination of a purchased call option and a sold put option, with a strike equal to the reference price (see Figure 8.12).

In our case, ABC would buy a call option and sell a put option with the following common terms to hedge the SAR:

- Trade date: 1 January 20X1 (the plan's grant date).
- Counterparties: ABC and Gigabank.
- Number of options: 2 million.
- Shares: ABC's common stock.
- Exercise price: EUR 50.00 (ABC's stock price on trade date).
- Exercise period: At any time from 1 January 20X3 to 31 December 20X4.

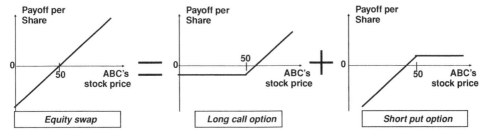

Figure 8.12   Split of an equity swap into a call option and a put option.

- Partial exercise: The buyer can partially/totally exercise the options during the exercise period.
- Settlement: Cash settlement only.
- Additional condition: The option can only be exercised if ABC's stock total return (i.e., including dividend reinvestment) has outperformed the EuroStoxx50 index from trade date to 31 December 20X2.
- Upfront premium: EUR 21 million (i.e., 21% of ABC's stock price on trade date), to be paid two currency business days following the trade date.
- Dividends: Gigabank will pay ABC an amount equal to the delta times the gross dividends distributed to the underlying shares.

Now, from an accounting point of view, ABC could apply hedge accounting for the call option. As a result, the change in the fair value of the SAR (excluding the effect of the service conditions) and that of the call option, after being both allocated to the vesting period, would cancel each other in P&L. The put would be recognized as a speculative derivative, and therefore, the full change in its fair value would be recognized in P&L. This way, the accounting mismatch between the SAR and its hedge would be caused only by the put. For example, if the put became deeper out-of-the-money, the accounting mismatch would gradually disappear.

8.4.5   Hedging with Standard Call Options

One relatively uncommon hedging strategy is to acquire from a bank a call option that perfectly mirrors the equity option embedded in an ESOP/SAR plan. Therefore, ABC would buy call options with the following terms:

- Trade date: 1 January 20X1 (the plan's grant date).
- Number of options: 4 million (2 million per plan).
- Buyer: ABC.
- Shares: ABC's common stock.
- Exercise price: EUR 50.00 (ABC's stock price on trade date).
- Exercise period: At any time from 1 January 20X3 to 31 December 20X4.
- Partial exercise: ABC can partially/totally exercise the options during the exercise period.
- Settlement: For 2 million options (i.e., those hedging the ESOP), physical settlement only. For the remaining 2 million options (i.e., those hedging the SAR), cash settlement only.
- Additional condition: The options could only be exercised if ABC's stock total return (i.e., including dividend reinvestment) has outperformed the EuroStoxx50 index from trade date to 31 December 20X2.
- Upfront premium: EUR 42 million (i.e., 21% of ABC's stock price on trade date), to be paid two currency business days following the trade date.

The strategy is executed as follows:

1. ABC buys the call options on the plan's grant date, paying a EUR 42 million premium two currency business days following the trade date.
2. Upon exercise of the plans, ABC would exercise a number of call options equivalent to the number of options exercised under the plan. For example, if 200,000 options are exercised by the ESOP beneficiaries, ABC would exercise 200,000 physically settled call options, paying EUR 10 million (= 0.2 million × 50) and receiving 200,000 own shares. These shares would be delivered to the beneficiaries in exchange for a EUR 10 million payment.

If, for example, there are 200,000 options exercised by the SAR plan beneficiaries when ABC's stock is trading at EUR 60, ABC would exercise 200,000 cash-settled call options, receiving EUR 2 million [= 0.2 million × (60 − 50)]. ABC in turn would pay EUR 2 million to the SAR beneficiaries.

3. If, at the end of the vesting period, the non-market conditions have not been achieved, ABC would sell the options in the market.
4. If, at expiry of the plans, there are options that remain unexercised, ABC would exercise the corresponding call options if they are in-the-money.

As we can see, the exercises under the plans are perfectly hedged by the call options exercises. From an accounting point of view:

- Due to their physical settlement term, the call options hedging the ESOP plan would be recognized in equity and no fair valuing during their life would be required. Therefore, the hedge would have no impact in P&L. Remember, however, that the potential effects on P&L volatility due to non-market vesting conditions remain unchanged.
- Regarding the call options hedging the SAR plan, ABC would need to apply hedge accounting in order to minimize any mismatch with the plan's accounting recognition. Therefore, the hedge would eliminate the plan's impact in P&L due to market vesting conditions. Remember, however, that the potential effects on P&L volatility due to non-market vesting conditions remain unchanged.

Strengths of the Strategy

The strategy has the following strengths:

- If the plan options are exercised, ABC would have effectively met the settlement commitments under both plans.
- ABC is not exposed to a share price lower than the strike price.
- In the case of the SAR, the hedge eliminates the plan's P&L impact due to market conditions as ABC is able to apply hedge accounting.
- The accounting treatment of the hedge is similar to that of the plans, not creating accounting distortions.
- The implementation of the hedge may have a positive effect on ABC's stock price as the bank supplying the call options needs to acquire ABC shares in the market at inception.
- ABC may sell the options at the end of the vesting period if the non-market conditions are not achieved. The sale would effectively reduce the hedge cost.

Weaknesses of the Strategy

The strategy has the following drawbacks:

- ABC needs to pay a substantial premium upfront, as the ESOP/SAR have long-term maturities, using resources from the company. ABC might need to raise financing to fund the premium. However, the premium is notably lower than the initial outflow when hedging the plans with treasury shares.
- The acquisition of a call has a negative impact on the debt-to-equity ratio. The premium is deducted from equity, increasing ABC's leverage. However, the effect on leverage is notably lower than the effect when hedging the plans with treasury shares.

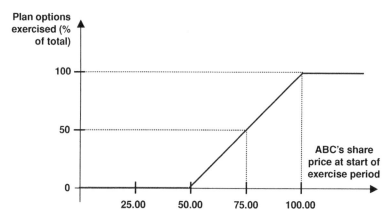

Figure 8.13 Expected beneficiaries' early exercise pattern as a function of ABC's stock price.

8.4.6   Hedging with Auto Call Options

The main weakness of hedging a plan with a call option is the premium to be paid. As ESOPs/SARs have typically long-term expiries, a call option on a highly volatile stock can be prohibitively expensive. Optimally, the ESOP/SAR beneficiaries would exercise their options at the end of the expiry date (assuming no large special dividends are distributed to the underlying shares). However, if an ESOP/SAR beneficiary is exercised before the award final expiry date, this obliges the sponsoring company to exercise its hedging call option early, foregoing the call option's time value. Let us assume that ABC looked at past patterns of beneficiary exercise behavior and estimated that the percentage of the ESOP/SAR options that would be exercised at the start of the exercise period followed a straight line, as shown in Figure 8.13.

One way to lower the premium of a hedging call option is to incorporate the expected beneficiaries' early exercise pattern in the terms of the option. This option is often referred to as an "auto call option" or a "call option with an automatic early exercise". The terms of the auto call would be identical to those of the call detailed earlier, except that one new term would be included. The term would be defined as follows:

- Automatic early exercise: If, on the first date of the exercise period, ABC's stock closing price (X) is greater than EUR 50.00, the following number of options will be exercised on this date:

  Lower of (i) the outstanding "Number of options" and (ii) the initial "Number of options"
  $\times[(X - 50.00)/50.00]$

If the exercise period is long (e.g., 3 years), an auto call option can be notably cheaper than a standard option. Of course, ABC would be running the risk that the beneficiaries do not behave as planned.

8.4.7   Hedging with Timer Call Options

Imagine that ABC was looking at hedging its plans with a call option at a time during which volatilities were sky high. When quoting the call option, banks were pricing a 50% implied volatility (a volatility much larger than ABC's 30% long-term historical volatility), resulting in a EUR 35 million premium per plan. ABC believed that the realized volatility of such an option would be much lower than the implied volatility the market was pricing. Instead of acquiring the standard call option, ABC decided to purchase a timer call (see Chapter 5 for a description of timer puts). The terms of the timer call would be identical to those of the standard call, except that one new term would be included. The term would be defined as follows:

- Rebate = two currency business days after the first exercise date. The "rebate payer" will pay to the "rebate receiver" the "rebate amount", as shown in the following table (the rebate amount will be linearly interpolated using the two closest realized volatility levels):

Realized volatility	Rebate amount (EUR)	Rebate amount payer	Rebate amount receiver
≥ 70%	14 million	ABC	Gigabank
60%	7 million	ABC	Gigabank
50%	Zero	—	—
40%	7 million	Gigabank	ABC
≤ 30%	14 million	Gigabank	ABC

Therefore, if the realized volatility (see the timer puts description in Chapter 5 for the definition of realized volatility) from trade date up to the first exercise period was 30%, ABC would receive a EUR 14 million rebate. Taking into account the initial EUR 35 million premium and ignoring the time value of money, ABC would have paid EUR 21 million (= 35 million – 14 million) for the option. On the contrary, if the realized volatility was 60%, ABC would pay a EUR 7 million rebate. Taking into account the initial EUR 35 million premium and ignoring the time value of money, ABC would have paid EUR 42 million (= 35 million + 7 million).

8.5 HSBC'S PERFORMANCE SHARE PLAN

In this section I will review a highly structured share plan awarded by HSBC. Similar plans were awarded by UBS and Banco Santander. The hedging of this type of plan is very complex, and I will explain why.

8.5.1 Terms of HSBC's Performance Share Plan

In 2007 HSBC awarded a deferred share-based variable remuneration which was payable in shares of the bank. The plan had a 3-year term. The award was divided into two parts. The number of shares to be delivered under the first half was defined by comparing HSBC's total shareholder return (TSR) with that of a benchmark group of 28 financial institutions. The number of shares to be delivered under the second half was subject to achieving a target earnings per share (EPS). The plan also included service vesting conditions, such as the beneficiary being employed during the vesting period.

- **Total shareholder return (TSR)** measured the total return of a stock, i.e. both the dividend yield and the capital appreciation of the share price. TSR was calculated by assuming that

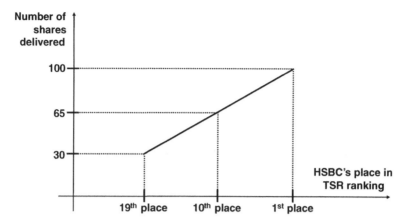

Figure 8.14   Number of shares delivered to the beneficiary.

(a) someone bought the share at the start of the vesting period, (b) any dividends received on the share had been used to buy more shares when received, and (c) the shares (plus dividend shares) were sold at the end of the vesting period. For example, if no dividends were paid and the share price increased from CU100 to CU107 after one year, the TSR would be 7%.

At the date of grant, a peer group of 28 banks was selected among the members of the Dow Jones Banks Titans 30, an index comprising the top 30 companies by market capitalization in the banking sector. Also, on grant date, a maximum number of shares were established for each beneficiary. One half of the award was subject to the TSR measure and the other half was subject to an EPS target. I will hereafter only consider the TSR element of the award, to focus the analysis.

At the end of the vesting period, the TSR of each bank (including HSBC) during the vesting period was calculated. The TSRs were ranked from first to last. The shares assigned to the TSR measure were released to the beneficiary on a sliding scale from 30% to 100% in accordance with HSBC's position among the group of benchmark financial institutions, providing that HSBC's place in the ranking was not below the top 19th TSR. Figure 8.14 depicts the number of shares delivered to a beneficiary, assuming 100 shares were initially awarded to the beneficiary. Therefore, the beneficiary received the maximum of shares only if HSBC fared first in the TSR ranking.

8.5.2 Accounting for the Plan

The accounting for the plan followed the rules we covered earlier for the ESOP. In this case, the TSR ranking profile was a market condition, as all the variables were related to a financial market. Thus, at the date of grant HSBC estimated the fair value of the embedded option using the Monte Carlo method, incorporating the TSR performance target. This fair value was not remeasured during the vesting period.

At each reporting date, the likelihood of achievement of the service conditions was estimated. The personnel costs were calculated by multiplying the fair value of the equity option by this estimation. The personnel costs were allocated over the vesting period, with a credit to equity.

At the end of the vesting period, HSBC issued new shares to meet the award. The equity recognized during the vesting period was then recycled to the "common stock" and "additional paid-in capital" accounts.

8.5.3 Hedging the Plan

The hedging of the plan is quite complex. Let us assume that to hedge the position HSBC buys the underlying equity option from Gigabank. Gigabank would then need to dynamically hedge its position. This option is an outperformance option; the more banking stocks that HSBC shares outperform, the larger the number of shares that Gigabank would need to deliver to HSBC. On trade date:

- Gigabank bought shares of HSBC.
- Gigabank sold shares of the 28 benchmark financial institutions. Therefore, Gigabank needed to borrow shares of the 28 stocks for 3 years. Fortunately, this group of banks was large and liquid, with an active stock lending market.
- Gigabank had to estimate the volatility of each stock and the correlation between each pair of stocks (including HSBC).
- Gigabank needed to hedge the FX risk. Most of the 28 benchmark banking stocks were denominated in a currency other than GBP. Gigabank sold the foreign currencies and acquired GBP.

The main challenge of hedging this option was to manage the discontinuity around the 19th place in the ranking. Imagine that the option approached its expiry date (i.e., 3 years after its trade date) and HSBC's position in the ranking moved from the 20th to the 19th place. Suddenly, the number of shares to be delivered varied from zero to 30% of the maximum. The hedge would jump in accordance with the shares to be delivered, making Gigabank acquire 30% of the maximum HSBC shares. If HSBC's stock moved back to the 20th place in the ranking, Gigabank would need to sell back the shares onto the market. Due to this large gap, Gigabank could incur substantial losses when buying and subsequently selling. As a result, Gigabank charged HSBC a premium that took into account this risk.

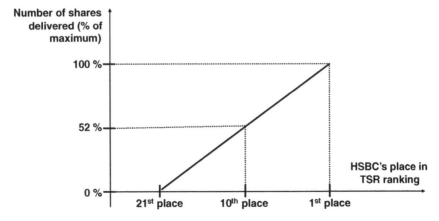

Figure 8.15   Number of shares delivered to the beneficiary.

What HSBC should have done is to design a plan with a friendlier hedging profile. For example, as shown in Figure 8.15, it could eliminate the discontinuity by extending the straight line to reach a point at which no shares are delivered. Gigabank would have priced the option more aggressively. Also, the fair value of the plan's equity option would have diminished, lowering the compensation cost to be recognized.

Another drawback of the plan is the mismatch created in P&L if HSBC hedged the plan with the mirror option from Gigabank. Remember that HSBC did not fair value the plan's underlying equity option at each reporting date. Due to the potential delivery of shares at maturity, the counter-entry to the personnel expense was an equity entry. The only changes in compensation expense were due to changes in the expectations of attainment of the service conditions, typically a small variation. However, the change in fair value of the mirror option from Gigabank was recognized in the P&L, as HSBC was not able to apply hedge accounting. As a result, there was a recognition mismatch in P&L, potentially increasing the volatility of HSBC's income statement.

This strategy can be improved by taking into account the likelihood of meeting the service conditions. As a result, ABC would acquire from Gigabank a number of options equivalent to the number of plan options expected to vest.

Alternative Hedging Strategy

The acquisition of such a highly structured option can be very expensive. One alternative would be to hedge the plan with treasury shares. On grant date, ABC would acquire a number of treasury shares equal to the number of the plans' options expected to vest. ABC would then adjust the number of treasury shares to incorporate any changes in its expectation regarding the vesting of the plan options.

9

Equity Financings

This chapter provides a detailed understanding of the mechanics of equity financings. Equity financings are indebtedness transactions collateralized by shares. Typically, corporates, financial institutions and high net worth individuals use equity financings to raise cash off the back of their equity stakes as an alternative funding source outside the traditional debt and equity capital markets. There are multiple ways of implementing an equity financing. In the following sections I will cover the most common equity financing structures.

9.1 CASE STUDY: EQUITY COLLATERALIZED BOND

One common way of implementing an equity financing is to issue a bond collateralized by an equity stake. In order to study the different elements of a structured bond collateralized by shares, let us assume a fictional transaction. In 20X1 the ABC Group, one of the Middle East's largest privately owned financial/industrial conglomerates with interests primarily in oil, gas and banking, as well as other investments, approached Gigabank to raise financing secured by part of its stake in XYZ Petroleum ("XYZ").

ABC Group operated through a series of fully owned holding companies, each with specific industrial focus. One of these holding companies was Oil Holding, which held the oil and gas investments of the ABC Group. Oil Holding owned 30% of XYZ's share capital. XYZ was a publicly quoted company.

On 1 June 20X1, Gigabank arranged a USD 300 million structured equity financing for Oil Holding via the issuance of a bond. The bond was issued by a special purpose entity (see Figure 9.1), Oil SPE, fully owned by Oil Holding. Oil SPE had no assets or activities other than (i) to hold ABC's stake in XYZ and (ii) to provide a loan to its parent Oil Holding. The aim of the financing was to make an intra-group loan to Oil Holding for the purpose of acquiring other oil and gas assets to be retained within the group.

9.1.1 Bond Terms

The bond was secured by XYZ shares, guaranteed by Oil Holding, issued to Gigabank solely and subject to cash margining. The main terms of the bond are outlined in the table below:

Oil SPE's Bond Terms	
Issuer	Oil SPE, a wholly owned subsidiary of Oil Holding
Guarantor	Oil Holding
Notional amount	USD 300 million
Redemption amount	100% of notional amount
Issue date	1-June-20X1
Maturity	1-June-20X4 (3 years)
Coupon	USD Libor 3m + spread, paid quarterly Spread: +250 bps
Collateral	46.15 million shares of XYZ (20% of XYZ's share capital). Pledge over the collateral

Oil SPE's Bond Terms

Collateral value on issue date	USD 461.5 million (i.e., USD 10.00 per share)
Initial LTV	65%
Call right	The issuer has the right to call in whole or in part the bond on or after the 18-month anniversary of the issue, subject to a payment of 1% of the notional prepaid
Trustee	Securities Trust Services
Collateral agent	Gigabank
Cash collateral agent	Gigabank
Escrow agent	Gigabank
Calculation agent	Gigabank
Margining	Cash margining applies (see below)
Early termination events	Deal specific (see below)
Events of default	Customary plus deal specific (see below)

9.1.2   Main Documents of the Financing

The documents that formalize an equity financing transaction vary from one financing to another. In this case, the documents of the Oil SPE transaction were the following.

The cash collateral agreement created a charge in respect of any cash margin pledged pursuant to the collateral agreement and in respect of the account in which it was held. The cash collateral assignment assigned the contents of the cash margin account to the cash collateral agent for the benefit of the bond holders. The parties to the cash collateral agreement were the cash collateral agent and the issuer.

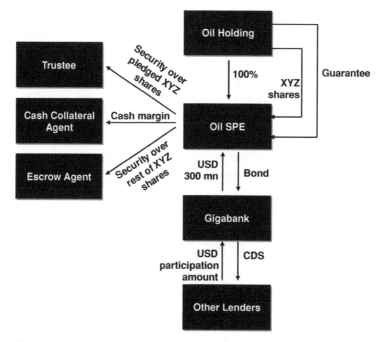

Figure 9.1   Transaction structure.

The collateral and pledge agreement allowed the collateral agent to declare collateral events of default in certain circumstances. The agreement also specified the posting of cash margin. The pledgor pledged to the collateral agent a security interest in and to, and a lien upon and right of setoff against, all the pledgor's right, title and interest in and to the collateral. The financing's security was on the XYZ shares in the collateral account. The parties to the collateral agreement were the pledgor, the depositary, the collateral agent and the trustee.

The credit default swaps (CDS) formalized the participation of the lenders other than Gigabank in the financing, being agreed between each lender and Gigabank. The exposure of a lender under the CDS represented a synthetic exposure to the bond.

The escrow agreement served to lock up the issuer's XYZ shares that were not part of the collateral agreement. Remember that Oil Holding had 30% of XYZ, while the financing was backed by 20% of XYZ's share capital. Issuer's XYZ shares in excess of the securities pledged to the collateral account were placed in escrow and held by the escrow agent. This prevented XYZ shares that were not part of the financing collateral from coming onto the market until after the financing collateral had been foreclosed, if required. Any XYZ shares acquired by the issuer after entering into the financing transaction were also placed in escrow for as long as the bond was outstanding. It should be noted that the bond's security was on the shares in the collateral account and the cash in the cash margin account, not on the shares in the escrow account. The escrow agreement was signed by the issuer, the guarantor, the escrow agent and the calculation agent.

The guarantee set out the terms of the parent company Oil Holding's guarantee.

The indenture set out the terms and conditions of the issued bond, including the guarantee from the guarantor. In addition, it set out certain events of default that may lead to the bond becoming immediately due and payable. The indenture also set out certain early termination events that, though not events of default, could lead to the bond becoming due and payable. The parties to the indenture were the issuer, the guarantor, the trustee and the calculation agent.

In our case, the bond was wholly subscribed by Gigabank (the "purchaser"). **The subscription agreement** set out the issuance of the bond by the issuer and the subscription of the bond by the purchaser. It contained certain conditions precedent to closing. The parties to the purchase agreement were the issuer, the guarantor and the purchaser.

9.1.3 Parties to an Equity Financing

In an equity financing there are several parties involved. In most financings several of the roles are performed by the bank arranging the financing.

The borrower is the entity receiving the proceeds of the financing. In our transaction, Oil SPE was the borrower.

The calculation agent, Gigabank, determined the bond coupons, performed the margin calculations and checked that no early termination events were triggered. The calculation agent was also responsible for computing the outstanding bond notional together with the accrued interest and any other amounts due in respect of the bond upon occurrence of an early termination event or a credit event.

The cash collateral agent retained responsibility for administering all the margin calls payments/releases for the life of the transaction and their related interest payments to the borrower. In our case, the cash collateral agent was Gigabank.

The collateral agent retained responsibility for administering all the movements of shares held in the collateral account. Any movements of these shares required prior consent from the trustee. In our case, the collateral agent was Gigabank.

The escrow agent retained responsibility for administering all the transactions related to the shares held in the escrow account (i.e., the other XYZ shares not pledged for the benefit of the transaction). The escrow agent made sure that any action taken on these shares complied with the provisions set forth in the indenture agreement. Thus, any pledge or transfer of the shares held in the escrow account required prior approval of the escrow agent. In our case, the escrow agent was Gigabank.

The guarantor was the entity that agreed to be legally bound to meet the issuer obligations under the indenture if the issuer did not meet such commitments. Because the issuer was an SPE, the lenders required Oil SPE's parent (Oil Holding) to guarantee the financing. As a result, the bondholders could pursue a claim against Oil Holding if Oil SPE did not meet its obligations under the bond.

The lenders were the entities providing the equity financing. In our transaction, Gigabank was the main lender, facing the borrower directly via the bond. The other lenders did not face the borrower directly, but through credit default swaps.

The pledgor, Oil SPE, pledged to the collateral agent a security interest in and to, and a lien upon and right of setoff against, all the pledgor's right, title and interest in and to the collateral. The pledgor had to warrant and represent good title to the shares which were free from liens and encumbrances or prior pledge with full authority to transfer the shares as collateral security. The pledgor was subject to certain covenants, as we will see later in this section.

During the term thereof and as long as there was no default, the pledgor had full rights to vote the pledged shares and was entitled to all dividends income, except that stock dividends would be pledged. In the event a stock dividend or further issue of stock by the issuer of the XYZ shares, the pledgor had to pledge these shares as additional collateral for the debt. Upon payment of the debt, the pledged shares would be returned to the pledgor and the pledge agreement would be terminated. Upon default the pledgor would pay all reasonable attorneys' fees and cost of collections.

The trustee held title to the pledged shares for the benefit of the bondholders. The trustee made sure that any action taken on the collateral complied with the provisions set forth in the indenture agreement. Thus, any release or foreclosure of the collateral required prior approval of the trustee. In our case, the trustee was Securities Trust Services. Gigabank could not be the trustee due to conflicts of interest.

9.1.4 Accounts in an Equity Financing

An equity financing requires the opening of several accounts. Some accounts are cash accounts and some accounts are stock custody accounts. In our financing, the main accounts were the following:

The cash margin account held the cash margin posted by the issuer. This account was pledged to the bond holders.

The bond evidenced a secured claim against the issuer and the guarantor. **The collateral account** held the shares that were pledged to secure the bonds. At the beginning of the transaction, Oil SPE opened a collateral account with Gigabank, the collateral agent. Once the account was opened, Oil SPE transferred the collateral shares to the account. Oil SPE provided a security charge (i.e., a pledge) over the collateral account and its contents to the trustee representing the bond holders. The collateral account held 46.15 million shares of XYZ, representing 20% of its share capital.

The financing's security was on the shares in the collateral account. The issuer held its remainder XYZ shares in **the escrow account**, opened in its name. The escrow account mechanism ensured that the issuer's shares in XYZ were locked up and could not come to the market until after foreclosure on the shares in the collateral account. In some equity financings there is no escrow account, giving the borrower absolute freedom to use any unpledged shares.

9.1.5   Credit Enhancement Tools

Security Mechanism

The security mechanism was comprised of the shares collateralizing the transaction and the cash pledged. The bond was secured by 46.15 million shares of XYZ (20% of its share capital). The collateral was held in the collateral account. Under the collateral agreement, the pledgor granted unto the collateral agent a security interest in and to, and a lien upon and right of set-off against, all the pledgor's right, title and interest in and to, the pledged items. The collateral agent acted as agent for the trustee and, inter alia, would realize the pledged shares upon default. The cash pledged pursuant to the cash margin call mechanism (see below) was also part of the bond collateral.

Margin Call Mechanism

The main objective of the margin call mechanism was to preserve the loan to value (LTV) of the financing. On each trading day during the life of the bond, the closing price of XYZ stock was observed and the transaction LTV was calculated.

Loan to Value (LTV)

The loan to value was the ratio, expressed as a percentage, of (i) the drawn amount less the cash collateral, divided by (ii) the market value of the secured collateral.

$$LTV = \frac{\text{Drawn amount} - \text{Cash collateral}}{\text{Market value of secured collateral}}$$

In some transactions, the issuer is required to post an initial margin. Consequently, any initial margin has to be included in the cash collateral component of the LTV formula. In our transaction, there was no initial collateral and the initial LTV at time of issuance was 65%. The main levels of the cash margining mechanism were:

- LTV margin level: 70%
- LTV reset level: 65%
- LTV release level: 60%

The LTV was computed on each trading day of the stock (the "valuation date"). The market value of the collateral (i.e., the pledged shares) was calculated using the closing price of the stock on the preceding valuation date.

- If, on a valuation day, the LTV was greater than the LTV margin level (70%), the calculation agent gave written notice to the issuer requiring the issuer to post cash in USD as collateral so that the LTV was restored to the LTV reset level (65%). Where this notice was given by 9 a.m. New York time on any valuation day, such cash had to be received by 2 p.m. New York time on the business day immediately succeeding such day.
- Where the LTV was less than, or equal to, the LTV release level (60%) for a period of three consecutive valuation days, the collateral agent would on request by the issuer be required to release cash to the issuer so that the LTV was equal to or less than the LTV reset level (65%). Only cash margin previously posted by the issuer plus interest thereon could be returned.

As an example, let us assume that XYZ's stock price had the following behavior during the first eight valuation days:

Valuation day	XYZ's share price (USD)	Drawn amount (USD million)	Cash collateral (USD million)	Market value of collateral (USD million)[1]	LTV[2]	Cash to be posted (USD million)[3]
Inception	10.00	300	0	461.50	65%	–
1	9.00	300	0	415.35	72%	30.0
2	8.00	300	30.0	369.20	73%	30.0
3	9.20	300	60.0	424.58	57%	0[4]
4	9.30	300	60.0	429.20	56%	0[4]
5	9.10	300	60.0	419.97	57%	<33.0>
6	8.50	300	27.0	392.28	70%	0
7	7.90	300	27.0	364.59	75%	36.0
8	7.50	300	63.0	346.13	68%	0

(1) The market value of the collateral was calculated as: 46.15 million shares multiplied by XYZ's share price.
(2) The LTV was calculated as: (Drawn amount – Cash collateral)/(Market value of collateral).
(3) The cash to be posted was calculated as: [Drawn amount – Cash collateral – (LTV reset level × Market value of collateral)] = (300 million – Cash collateral – 65% × Market value of collateral).
(4) On valuation days 3 and 4, the LTV was below the 60% LTV release level. However, cash collateral could not be released because there had to be three consecutive trading days below the LTV reset level to allow a cash collateral release. As a result, on valuation day 5 USD 33 million cash was released.

In some financings, the borrower is allowed to post additional shares of XYZ up to a certain level. For example, upon the first margin call only, the issuer may post additional shares. Thereafter, margin calls have to be met in cash only. This was not the case in our transaction.

9.1.6 Early Termination Events

An equity financing may include certain early termination events (also called "acceleration events") that, through not events of default, may lead to the financing becoming due and payable. Upon early termination, the calculation agent would compute the outstanding bond notional together with the accrued interest and any other amounts due in respect of the bond. In this section, I will cover the early termination events most commonly included in equity financings.

Stock Trigger Event

One common early termination event is a "stock trigger event". This event occurs if the calculation agent determines that an intra-day price per share is equal to or less than a predetermined level (typically 50%) of the initial price at any time during the trading session. The intra-day price per share is defined as "the official price per share quoted on the exchange or, if no such price is available, the price per share as determined by the calculation agent in good faith and in reasonable manner".

A stock trigger event protects the lenders from a potential situation in which the stock has lost substantial value (e.g., 50%) and it is likely to accelerate its share price fall because the company's fundamentals have been severely and permanently impaired. The borrower up to now has met the margin calls, but a continuing fall may endanger its power to meet additional margin calls. Therefore, besides protecting the lenders, a stock trigger event may provide investment discipline to the borrower, giving it an incentive to exit the investment before it is too late.

LTV Trigger Event

The LTV trigger event tries to protect the lenders from gaps in the stock price. At transaction inception an LTV trigger level is set, for example at 75%. If, at any time – including intra-day prices – the LTV is greater than the LTV trigger level (75%), it constitutes an "early termination event".

Rating Trigger Event

The lenders may have the right to terminate the transaction early upon occurrence of a rating trigger event. This right can be exercised if the borrower's long-term credit rating is downgraded below a predetermined threshold by one of the major rating agencies – S&P, Moody's or Fitch – or ceases to have a rating. For example, a rating trigger event may occur if:

- The credit rating of the borrower is downgraded to BBB–/Baa3 or below by either Standard & Poor's Rating Services or any successor thereof or Moody's Investors Service or any successor thereof.
- Or, the borrower ceases to have a public credit rating with Standard & Poor's or Moody's.

Covenants

An early termination event occurs if the calculation agent determines that the issuer failed to observe or perform a specific covenant, if not remedied after a pre-specified number of days from the date of occurrence of such event. Covenants are the part of a financing agreement where lenders give the borrower and/or the guarantor a set of rules explicitly stating what the borrower and/or the guarantor must do or not do as an entity to remain in compliance with the financing agreement. Types of covenant include:

- **Financial covenants** impose certain financial requirements on the borrower. These typically include measurements of: (a) minimum earnings or cash flow, measured by ratios such as cash flow to interest, debt service and fixed charges; (b) maximum leverage, tested through debt coverage; and/or (c) adequate liquidity, as seen by a current or quick ratio. In addition, the covenants may stipulate a minimum tangible net worth or maximum level of investment in capital expenditures. Financial covenants are sometimes referred to as maintenance covenants originating from the borrower's obligation to maintain these financial levels and ratios.

- **Affirmative covenants** stipulate actions that the borrower must make, such as pay debt service, pay taxes and maintain insurance.
- **Negative covenants** prohibit certain actions of the borrower, such as combining with other companies, selling certain assets, making acquisitions, or taking on additional debt.

In our transaction, the bond primarily contained "negative covenants" that limited Oil Holding's (and Oil SPE's) ability to, among other things: (i) incur additional debt or issue certain preferred shares; (ii) pay dividends on or make other distributions in respect of its capital stock or make other restricted payments; (iii) make certain investments; (iv) sell certain assets; and (v) create or permit to exist dividend and/or payment restrictions affecting its restricted subsidiaries. For example, there was a negative covenant capping debt within the issuer. Under the transaction, the issuer was obliged to not exceed an aggregate outstanding notional amount of indebtedness of USD 500 million, other than permitted subordinated borrowing. Within this cap, the bond used USD 300 million. Therefore, any additional financing (a "permitted financing transaction") could not exceed USD 200 million.

A permitted financing transaction was one secured by the assets in the escrow account. In our case, there were restrictions in place to protect the position of the bond holders. Any additional indebtedness had to comply with the following requirements:

- It could only be secured by assets in the escrow account.
- It would cross default the bond.
- It was subject to a 30-day standstill upon default. In other words, a third-party pledge in a permitted financing transaction had to agree to not foreclose on the escrow assets within 30 days of an event leading to an early termination of the permitted financing transaction (that would cross default the bond). This standstill allowed a clear market from disposing of the shares in the bond's collateral account.
- It had to involve Gigabank as calculation agent.

Additionally, in our transaction the calculation agent could allow the issuer to raise subordinated debt. A permitted subordinated indebtedness was defined as indebtedness owed by the issuer to the guarantor or any affiliate of the issuer or the guarantor that was contractually subordinated, to the reasonable satisfaction of the calculation agent. The indenture set out several restrictions to the aggregate amount of permitted subordinated indebtedness that could be raised. This amount could not exceed at any time the sum of (1) cash margin at such time, (2) the aggregate of all amounts that became due under the bond at such time, and (3) USD 1 million to be used for the reasonable administration expenses of the issuer. The permitted subordinated indebtedness documentation had to be to the calculation agent's satisfaction.

Upon the issuer's failure to observe or perform these covenants, the trustee would declare the bond immediately due and payable, if not remedied after 90 days from the date of notice of default.

Other Early Termination Events

A transaction may include other early termination events to protect the bond holders. For example, an early termination of the bond may occur on:

- The ADTV (Average Daily Trading Volume) of the pledged shares, tested over a specific number of days, falling below a certain threshold level. In our transaction, the collateral represented 30 full ADTVs. A sharp fall in XYZ's ADTV would imply a larger than expected period to sell the collateral, upon default, increasing the risk of losses.

- Nationalization of XYZ.
- Delisting of XYZ shares.
- Cross default or cross acceleration to the issuer's or the guarantor's indebtedness or event of default, subject to a USD 10 million threshold and a cure period of 20 business days.
- Any legal proceeding instituted or other event occurred that called into question the binding effect of the issuer under the indenture or collateral agreement.
- Any legal proceeding resulted in a final judgment to dispose of the shares held in the escrow account.
- The guarantee held in a judicial proceeding to be unenforceable or not in full force or effect.
- A final judgment against the issuer or the guarantor unsatisfied for 20 business days, but, with respect to the guarantor only, only where the amount is lower than USD 10 million.
- An early termination of any permitted financing transaction.
- Involuntary and voluntary bankruptcy or insolvency of the issuer or the guarantor.
- A stock market disruption for more than a pre-specified number of consecutive days.
- A mandatory bid triggered in relation to the XYZ shares. In our case, Oil Holding owned 30% of XYZ. If Oil Holding exceeded a 30% ownership it would be obliged to make an offer for 100% of the XYZ. An offer for the remaining shares could significantly affect the risk profile of the transaction.

Grace or Cure Periods

Some of the early termination events have a cure period, also called a "grace period". A grace period is a period during which the issuer and/or guarantor are given the chance to remedy an early termination event, before triggering an early termination of the indebtedness. Commonly, there is a 20 business day cure period for early termination events, although some cure periods are longer and other events do not have a cure period. Furthermore, in certain circumstances the cure period runs until the event becomes effective.

Make-whole Amount

In some financings, the amount due and payable by the issuer upon occurrence of an early termination event includes a make-whole amount. The make-whole amount is the present value of the aggregate of all payments representing the financing spread that would have been paid by the issuer as per the scheduled terms of the bond from the date of default to its scheduled maturity. In our case, the financing spread was 250 basis points.

9.1.7 Events of Default

Our indenture contained several events of default. Upon occurrence of an event of default, the trustee would be required to declare the bond immediately due. Usually, there is a grace period (a "cure period") during which the borrower can remedy the situation. If the default continues beyond the cured period, the trustee would declare the event of default.

Failure to Comply with Payment of Interest and Principal

In our transaction an event of default would occur if the issuer defaulted in payment of the bond's interest or principal.

Failure to Comply with Margin Calls

In our case, an event of default would occur if adequate cash was not provided as margin on its due date, unless the failure to pay was caused by administrative or technical error or the banking system experienced difficulties and the issuer had already provided a SWIFT confirmation from the issuer's correspondent bank for USD to confirm the sending of funds, and payment was received within three business days of its due date.

Failure to Comply with Collateral Requirements

Under the collateral agreement, the collateral agent would declare an event of default upon the occurrence of:

- Failure of the collateral account to contain at least 46.15 million shares of XYZ.
- Or, failure at any time of the security interests to constitute valid and perfected security interests in all of the collateral.

Liquidation Procedure

Upon occurrence of an event of default, the trustee would be required to declare the bond immediately due and payable. The following process, as defined in the indenture agreement, would then be executed:

- The calculation agent, Gigabank, would compute the outstanding bond notional together with the accrued interest and any other amounts due in respect of the bond.
- Following the trustee's approval, the collateral agent (Gigabank) would foreclose the 46.15 million shares of XYZ held in the collateral account. In some cases the shares in the collateral account exceed the threshold amount above which a mandatory bid would be triggered. Upon enforcement, Gigabank would own the pledged shares. The enforcement mechanism has to be designed to avoid a mandatory bid requirement for Gigabank.
- The collateral agent would be appointed as disposal agent and would liquidate the collateral selling it onto the market. Gigabank would probably seek to sell it quickly through an ABB.
- The cash collateral agent, Gigabank, would deliver any funds in the cash margin account to the collateral agent, also Gigabank in our case.

The proceeds of the liquidation of the collateral would be applied by the collateral agent in the following order of priorities (see Figure 9.2):

- First, the payment to the collateral agent and the cash collateral agent of the expenses of such sale or other realization, including reasonable compensation to each of the collateral agent and the cash collateral agent and its agents and counsel, and all expenses, liabilities and advances incurred or made by the collateral agent and the cash collateral agent in connection therewith, including brokerage fees in connection with the sale by the collateral agent of any pledged item (other than break funding costs).
- Second, the payment to the trustee of any costs and expenses incurred in connection with the event of default and such sale or other realization, including reasonable compensation to the trustee and its agents and counsel, and all documented expenses, liabilities and advances incurred or made by the trustee in connection therewith.

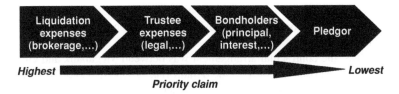

Figure 9.2 Liquidation proceeds' assignment process.

- Third, the payment to the trustee for distribution in accordance with the terms of the indenture, including for pro rata distribution to the bond holders of an amount equal to the principal, interest due and payable under the bond, and any make-whole amount due. The make-whole amount included the present value of the bond spread that would have been paid by the issuer as per the scheduled terms of the bond from the date of default.
- Finally, if all the obligations of the pledgor under the indenture have been fully discharged or sufficient funds have been set aside by the collateral agent at the request of the pledgor for the discharge thereof, any remaining proceeds would be released to the pledgor.

In the event of an under-recovery in respect to the bond following enforcement, the collateral agent could try to dispose of the shares held in the escrow account not securing any permitted financing transactions, to satisfy a residual claim under the bond. However, under certain securities laws it is unlikely that these shares could be sold without restrictions, unlike the shares in the collateral account.

In the event of an under-recovery in respect of the bond following enforcement, the bond holders could pursue a claim against the issuer and the guarantor. The bond ranked pari passu with claims of other unsecured and unsubordinated creditors. Under the CDS, Gigabank would deliver the corresponding part of the bond to each CDS counterparty. The CDS counterparty would pay the bond notional amount minus the cash margin posted by the issuer minus the recovery amount realized from the liquidation of the share collateral.

9.1.8   Syndicating the Equity Financing with a Credit Default Swap

Once Oil Holding mandated Gigabank for the bond issuance, the bank tried to place part of the transaction with other lenders, primarily banks. This process is called syndication. Gigabank took the risk of taking a larger than expected participation in the financing, if other lenders lacked appetite for participating in the financing.

Other lenders could participate in the financing by either (i) acquiring part of the bond from Gigabank or (ii) entering into credit default swaps (CDSs) with Gigabank. In our transaction, Gigabank preferred the latter solution. Let us assume that another bank called Megabank was interested in participating in the financing. The main differences between syndicating a transaction via a bond or via a CDS were the following:

- Gigabank was the only entity facing Oil SPE. It gave the bank better visibility vis-à-vis the borrower. It also gave Gigabank more control to enforce the borrower obligations under the bond (e.g., the covenants).
- Gigabank did not need to list the bond.

- Megabank did not have to fund the transaction, as in a CDS there is no exchange of principals, unless Gigabank required cash collateral to be posted by Megabank to credit enhance the CDS.
- With the CDS, the contractual arrangement was between Megabank and Gigabank. Thus, Megabank was exposed not only to the default risk of Oil SPE and Oil Holding, but also to the ability of Gigabank to make good under the CDS. Therefore, a CDS increased Megabank's counterparty risk under the transaction. Similarly, if no collateral was posted by Megabank at the beginning of the transaction, Gigabank had a large counterparty risk exposure to Megabank if a credit event occurred.
- The sale of the risk by Megabank to a third party would be a bit more complicated through a CDS. Instead, if Megabank acquired part of the bond directly, it would be easier to sell it to third parties.

Megabank participated in the financing via a credit default swap where the reference obligation was the indenture for the bond and the reference entity was Oil SPE. Thus, the investors faced Gigabank, and Gigabank faced Oil SPE. Gigabank handled all the operational issues. Let us assume that Megabank took a USD 60 million risk piece. The main terms of the CDS with Megabank were:

Physically Settled Credit Default Swap	
Trade date	1-June-20X1
Floating rate payer ("Seller")	Megabank
Fixed rate payer ("Buyer")	Gigabank
Scheduled termination date	The earlier of:
	(i) The redemption date for the reference obligation, if the reference entity or the buyer exercises its right to terminate the reference obligation early, or
	(ii) 1-June-20X4
Reference obligation	The bond with notional amount USD 300 million issued by Oil SPE on 1 June 20X1 and guaranteed by Oil Holding
Reference obligation notional	USD 300 million, subject to reduction with effect from each day on which any payment of principal is made to the holders of the reference obligation in respect of the reference obligation (as a result of accelerated amortization, acceleration of payment obligations, redemption or otherwise)
Reference entity	Oil SPE
Reference price	100%
Calculation amount	20% multiplied by the reference obligation notional (representing USD 60 million of the reference obligation)
Fixed payments	
Fixed payments payer	Buyer (Gigabank)
Fixed payments	250 bps per annum Act/360, paid on a quarterly basis. Fixed amounts shall be payable in respect of the period from the last fixed rate payment date immediately preceding an event of default under the terms of the reference obligation to the date on which such event of default occurs
Floating payments	
Floating payments payer	Seller (Megabank)
Conditions to settlement	Credit event notice. Notifying party: the buyer.
	Notice of publicly available information: inapplicable

Physically Settled Credit Default Swap	
Credit events	(i) Failure to pay (grace period extension: applicable, payment required: USD 1)
	(ii) Obligation event of default (default requirement: USD 1)
Obligations	Obligation category: reference obligation only
Settlement terms	
Settlement method	Physical settlement
Amount payable by Seller	Calculation amount plus any accrued but unpaid interest up to and including the termination date on calculation amount minus the pro rata cash margin posted in respect of the reference obligation minus the pro rata recovery amount under the liquidation of the reference obligation's collateral
Delivery obligations	Delivery obligation category: reference obligation only
Calculation agent	Gigabank

Under the CDS, two scenarios could take place during its life:

- If no credit event occurred, i.e., no events of default have occurred under the bond, the buyer of the protection (Gigabank) would pay to the seller (Megabank) a regular premium of 250 basis points on a quarterly basis (see Figure 9.3). This amount is called the fixed payment amount.

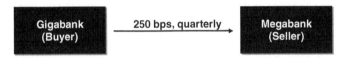

Figure 9.3   CDS pre-credit event flows.

- Following a credit event, i.e., an event of default has occurred under the bond, the protection buyer (Gigabank) would provide the seller (Megabank) 20% of the bond in return for a cash payment amounting to its corresponding notional amount (i.e., USD 60 million) minus the corresponding cash margin posted by the bond issuer minus the recovery amount under the liquidation of the collateral (see Figure 9.4). The protection buyer (Gigabank) would then stop paying the fixed amount. As a result, the seller (Megabank) would end up directly owning its corresponding part of the bond.

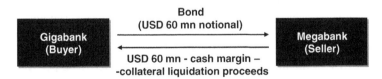

Figure 9.4   CDS flows if a credit event occurred.

9.1.9   Recourse vs. Non-recourse Equity Financings

The case just covered was a recourse equity financing. In general there are two types of equity financing: recourse and non-recourse equity:

- Upon default in a recourse financing, the lenders would seize the pledged collateral to meet the borrower obligations under the financing. If the realized value of the foreclosed collateral is lower than the amounts due under the financing, the lenders may pursue a claim against the borrower. Thus, the under-recovered amount would be claimed in conjunction with all other pari passu ranked claims against the borrower.
- Upon default in a non-recourse financing, the lenders would seize the pledged collateral to meet the borrower obligations under the financing. If the realized value of the foreclosed collateral is lower than the amounts due under the financing, the lenders may not pursue a claim against the borrower, thus realizing a loss. Therefore, the financing spread of a non-recourse financing is, in general, notably larger than that of a comparable recourse financing to compensate for the higher risk assumed by the lenders.

9.2 SALE + EQUITY SWAP

9.2.1 Transaction Description

One way to structure an equity financing is by combining a sale of stock and an equity swap. By entering into an equity swap, the borrower retains the stock dividends and its exposure to the stock price. The equity financing transaction is structured as follows:

1. A **stock sale** in which the investor sells the stock to the bank. Therefore, during the life of the transaction, the bank is the owner of the shares, receiving the dividends and having the stock voting rights.
2. A **total return equity swap** in which the investor receives during the life of the equity swap from the lending bank the dividends (called "manufactured dividends"), pays to the bank an interest and at maturity receives (pays) the positive (negative) performance of the stock. As a result, through the equity swap the borrower retains the economic exposure to the sold shares.

9.2.2 Equity Swap Terms

Let us assume the same inputs as in the previous case, primarily:

- On 1 June 20X1, Gigabank arranged a USD 300 million structured equity financing for a special purpose entity, Oil SPE, fully owned by Oil Holding. The term of the financing was 3 years. The spread of the financing was 250 basis points.
- The financing was secured by 46.15 million shares of XYZ, representing 20% of its share capital.
- The financing was guaranteed by Oil Holding.
- The initial LTV of the financing was 65%, based on a USD 10.00 per XYZ share at the beginning of the transaction.
- A margining mechanism (see previous case in this chapter).
- Early termination events and events of default (see previous case in this chapter).

The counterparties to the equity swap were Oil SPE and Gigabank. Although the maturity of the equity swap was 3 years, Oil SPE could terminate it early, either totally or partially, at any time. The main terms of the equity swap are shown in the following table (the parts not detailed will be covered later):

Total Return Equity Swap Terms

Party A	Oil SPE, guaranteed by Oil Holding
Party B	Gigabank
Trade date	29-May-20X1
Effective date	1-June-20X1
Final termination date	1-June-20X4 (i.e., 3 years after the effective date)
Termination date	A date occurring on the earlier of (i) the final termination date, (ii) the final early unwind date and (iii) the early termination date
Early unwind	Party A (Oil SPE) may terminate this transaction in full or in part on any exchange business day prior to the termination date, subject to a prepayment fee by giving four exchange business days' notice in writing to Party B (Gigabank) of the number of shares subject to such early unwind. Party A (Oil SPE) shall also specify to Party B (Gigabank) a new initial valuation date in respect of this early unwind
	If an early unwind occurs in respect of less than all of the number of shares, the terms of the transaction shall be adjusted accordingly
	If, following an early unwind, the number of shares becomes zero, the valuation date for such early unwind becomes the early unwind date
Underlying currency	USD
Initial exchange part	To be covered later
Equity amount part	To be covered later
Floating amount part	To be covered later
Dividend amount part	To be covered later
Interim exchange part	To be covered later
Other	To be covered later

Initial Exchange Part

The initial exchange part of the equity swap contained the sale by Oil SPE of 30 million XYZ shares to Gigabank in exchange for USD 300 million, the financing amount. The sale was settled on 1 June 20X1:

Total Return Equity Swap Terms – Initial Exchange Part

Initial exchange	
Initial exchange	On the effective date, Party A (Oil SPE) shall deliver to Party B (Gigabank) 30 million XYZ shares and Party B (Gigabank) shall pay to Party A (Oil SPE) an amount in USD equal to 300 million

Floating Amount Part

The floating amount part of the equity swap contained the interest to be paid periodically by Oil SPE during the life of the equity swap. This part represented the interest to be paid on the loaned USD 300 million. Oil SPE paid quarterly USD Libor 3-month plus 250 basis points, calculated initially on the USD 300 million notional. Every time a partial termination of the equity swap took place, Oil SPE paid interest thereafter on the outstanding notional amount:

Total Return Equity Swap Terms – Floating Amount Part

Floating amount part

Floating amount payer	Party A (Oil SPE)
Notional amount	The time-weighted average equity notional amount from, and including, the previous floating amount payment date to, and excluding, the floating amount payment date
Payment dates	At the end of each quarter
	The last payment day is the later of (i) the last physical settlement payment date and (ii) the last cash settlement payment date
Floating rate option	USD Libor fixed on the second local business day preceding the last floating amount payment date. The floating rate for the initial period would be determined two local business days prior to the effective date
Designated maturity	3 months
Spread	Plus 250 bps (2.50%)
Floating rate day count fraction	Actual/360

The dividend part

Remember that Oil SPE sold 30 million XYZ shares at the beginning. The shares were acquired by Gigabank. Consequently, Gigabank received directly from XYZ any dividends distributed to the 30 million XYZ shares. Under the equity swap dividend part, Gigabank passed the received dividends to Oil SPE. These dividends are called "manufactured dividends". Thus, the dividend part of the equity swap allowed Oil SPE to retain the dividends distributed to the equity swap underlying shares. The dividends paid were net of any withholding and other taxes levied at source. Therefore, if Oil SPE benefited from a more advantageous tax treatment than Gigabank in relation to XYZ dividends, this advantage was likely to be lost through the equity swap:

Total Return Equity Swap Terms – Dividend Part

Dividend amount part

Dividend amount	The result of (i) multiplied by (ii)
	(i) The dividend per share paid by the issuer to holders of record of a share, net of withholding or taxes at the source by or on behalf of any applicable authority having power to tax such a dividend and shall exclude any imputation or other credits, refunds or deductions granted by any applicable authority having power to tax in respect of such dividend and any taxes, credits, refunds or benefits imposed, withheld, assessed or levied thereon, in relation to which the date (the record date) by reference to which registered holders are identified as being entitled to a cash dividend payable in relation to such shares occurs during the dividend period
	(ii) The number of shares on such record date
Dividend payer	Party B (Gigabank)
Dividend receiver	Party A (Oil SPE)
Dividend period	The period commencing on, and including, the third scheduled trading day preceding the effective date and ending on, and including, the termination date
Dividend payment date	Two currency business days after the date of the payment of the dividend by the issuer of the shares to the holders of the shares in the market
Reinvestment of dividends	Not applicable

The Equity Amount Part

Oil SPE had the right to partially or totally unwind the transaction. On each early unwind, Oil SPE had to pay to Gigabank a 1% prepayment fee calculated on the unwind amount. The equity amount part of the equity swap contained the settlement process at each early unwind and at maturity of the transaction. Oil SPE could elect between cash and physical settlement. Generally, Oil SPE would elect physical settlement because this would imply recovering the 30 million shares (or the portion applicable to the early unwind) sold at inception and repaying the debt. However, were Oil SPE not interested in retaining the stake, it could elect cash settlement. Under a cash settlement, the shares underlying the unwind would be sold onto the market by Gigabank, and any excess (deficit) over the unwound amount would be paid by Gigabank (Oil SPE) to Oil SPE (Gigabank) in the form of a settlement amount:

Total Return Equity Swap Terms – Equity Amount Part

Equity amount part

Equity amount payer	Party B (Gigabank)
Equity amount receiver	Party A (Oil SPE)
Shares	XYZ common shares
Number of shares	30 million. The number of shares shall be reduced on each day during the unwind period by the number of shares that Party B has unwound its hedge position in respect of this transaction on such day
Initial price	USD 10.00
Equity notional amount	Number of shares × Initial price Initially USD 300 million
Final initial valuation date	The maturity date
Settlement method election	Applicable Electing party: Party A (Oil SPE) Settlement method election date: the day that is two exchange business days prior to the initial valuation date Default settlement method: cash settlement
Physical settlement	Applicable
Physical settlement payment date	The date that falls one settlement cycle following the initial valuation date
Cash settlement	Applicable
Settlement currency	USD
Final price	In respect of each valuation date, the volume-weighted average price per share (net of taxes and commissions) at which Party B (Gigabank) unwinds its hedge positions with respect to this transaction during the unwind period on such valuation date
Unwind period	A period commencing on, and including, the initial valuation date and consisting of the number of consecutive exchange business days that Party B (Gigabank) in consultation with Party A (Oil SPE) determines to be necessary to unwind its hedge position on a best effort basis with respect to this transaction Each day of the unwind period is deemed to be a valuation date
Cash settlement payment date	The date that falls one settlement cycle following the valuation date
Prepayment fee	An amount in USD calculated by the calculation agent (Gigabank) following the formula below: 1% × Early unwind amount Early unwind amount is the product of (a) the number of shares subject to such early unwind and (b) the initial price The prepayment fee shall be payable by Party A (Oil SPE) to Party B (Gigabank) on the physical settlement date or the last cash settlement payment date relating to the early unwind

Interim Exchange Part

The interim exchange part of the equity swap contained the margin call mechanism. Remember that the objective of this credit enhancement tool was to preserve the LTV of the equity financing. The functioning of the margin call mechanism was explained in the previous case study of this chapter. The interim exchange part also contained the additional 16.15 million XYZ shares that Oil SPE posted as collateral to the transaction, so the initial LTV was 65%:

Total Return Equity Swap Terms – Interim Exchange Part

Interim exchange

Party A interim exchange amount	If, on a collateral valuation date, the LTV ratio is greater than the LTV margin level (70%), Party A (Oil SPE) shall pay to Party B (Gigabank), on the first business day following such date, the required cash margin amount
Party B interim exchange amount	If, during three consecutive collateral valuation dates, the LTV ratio is lower than the LTV release level (65%), Party B (Gigabank) shall pay to Party A (Oil SPE), on the first business day following such date, the absolute value of the required cash margin amount
LTV ratio	In respect of each collateral valuation date, the number expressed as a percentage equal to (i) divided by (ii), with: (i) the result of (a) the equity notional amount minus (b) the cash collateral amount (ii) the market value of the shares
Required cash margin amount	In respect of each collateral valuation date, an amount in USD equal to: (i) the equity notional amount minus (ii) the cash collateral amount minus (iii) (a) the LTV reset level multiplied by (b) the market value of the shares
LTV margin level	70%
LTV reset level	65%
LTV release level	60%
Market value of the shares	In respect of each collateral valuation date, (i) multiplied by (ii), with: (i) the sum of (a) the number of shares and (b) the number of additional shares (ii) the closing price per share on the exchange on the exchange business day immediately preceding such collateral valuation date, as determined by the calculation agent
Exchange	New York Stock Exchange
Additional share collateral	On the effective date, Party A (Oil SPE) shall post 16.15 million shares (the "number of additional shares") of XYZ as collateral in favor of Party B (Gigabank) The additional share collateral would be released in accordance with the reduction in the number of shares
Collateral valuation dates	Each exchange business day from, and including, the effective date to, and including, the final initial valuation date
Cash collateral amount	From the effective date, an amount in USD equal to the aggregate Party A interim exchange amounts minus the aggregate Party B interim exchange amounts

---

Final Exchange

The final exchange part of the equity swap made sure that Gigabank returned to Oil SPE the cash margin posted at the end of the life of the transaction:

Total Return Equity Swap Terms – Final Exchange Part	
Final exchange	
Party B final exchange amount	On the physical settlement date or cash settlement date relating to the final initial valuation date, as appropriate, Party B (Gigabank) shall pay to Party A (Oil SPE) a USD amount equal to the cash collateral amount

Other Parts of the Equity Swap

The equity swap also included, among other terms, the early termination events and events of default that were described in the previous case study of this chapter. I have avoided repeating them for simplicity:

Total Return Equity Swap Terms – Other Parts	
Other	
Calculation agent	Gigabank
Early termination events	Deal specific (same as in the previous case)
Events of default	Customary plus deal specific (same as in the previous case)

9.2.3 Equity Swap Flows

At inception of the transaction the following steps took place simultaneously (see Figure 9.5):

1. Oil SPE and Gigabank entered into the total return equity swap. Through the equity swap Oil SPE kept the full economic exposure to the share price performance.
2. Oil SPE sold 30 million shares to Gigabank for a consideration equal to their market value (i.e., USD 300 million). This transaction was described in the initial exchange part of the equity swap. Thus, the financing amount, USD 300 million, was the share sale proceeds.
3. Oil SPE posted 16.15 million shares of XYZ as collateral in favor of Gigabank, in order to achieve an initial LTV of 65%.

During the life of the equity swap, the following flows were exchanged (see Figure 9.6):

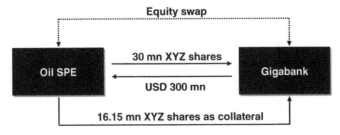

Figure 9.5 Flows at inception.

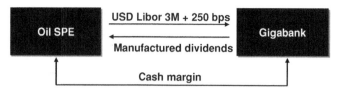

Figure 9.6   Flows during the equity swap life.

1. Periodically, Oil SPE paid to Gigabank the financing costs. On a quarterly basis, Oil SPE paid USD Libor 3m + 250 basis points on the equity swap notional. The equity swap notional was the outstanding financing amount. At inception, the equity swap notional was USD 300 million. Because Oil SPE could partially unwind the transaction early, the equity swap notional was adjusted upon each early unwind.
2. Gigabank paid to Oil SPE an amount equivalent to the dividends received on the underlying shares, each time a dividend was distributed to such shares. These flows are called "manufactured dividends".
3. The margining mechanism allowed Gigabank to call for cash margin if the LTV of the transaction surpassed the 70% LTV margin level. The margining mechanism also allowed for the release of previously posted cash margin if the LTV of the transaction was below the 60% LTV release level.
4. In this transaction, the posted cash margin was not remunerated. Otherwise, Gigabank would have paid the corresponding interest periodically.

At maturity and at each early unwind, Oil SPE could choose between physical and cash settlement. If Oil SPE was willing to buy back the shares, it would elect physical settlement. Conversely, if Oil SPE was unwilling to continue participating in XYZ's stock price behavior, it would elect cash settlement.

In case Oil SPE chose physical settlement, assuming for simplicity no early unwinds over the term of the transaction, the flows were the following (see Figure 9.7):

1. Gigabank would sell the shares back to Oil SPE against repayment of the equity notional amount. Gigabank would deliver 30 million shares of XYZ in exchange for USD 300 million. Thus, with this flow Oil SPE repaid the loan.
2. Any cash margin posted by Oil SPE and not previously released would be returned by Gigabank to Oil SPE.
3. Any remaining additional shares posted as collateral would be returned by Gigabank to Oil SPE. Thus, 16.15 million shares of XYZ were released.

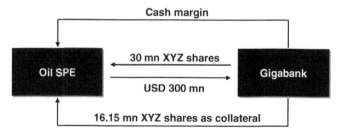

Figure 9.7   Flows at maturity of the equity swap, assuming physical settlement.

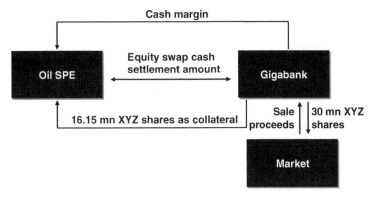

Figure 9.8   Flows at maturity of the equity swap, assuming cash settlement.

Alternatively, in case Oil SPE chose cash settlement, assuming no early unwinds over the term of the transaction, the flows were the following (see Figure 9.8):

1. Gigabank would sell the 30 million underlying shares onto the open market during the unwind period. During each day of the unwind period (each day, a valuation date), Gigabank would compute the volume-weighted average sale price, called the "final price".
2. Oil SPE would receive (pay) the positive (negative) performance of the underlying shares. The cash settlement amount would be computed as the product of (i) the number of shares sold on the valuation date and (ii) the difference between the final price and the initial price (i.e., the appreciation/depreciation of the final price relative to the USD 10.00 share price at which Gigabank acquired the underlying shares at inception). If the cash settlement amount was positive, Gigabank would pay such amount to Oil SPE. Otherwise, Oil SPE would pay the absolute value of the cash settlement amount to Gigabank.
3. Any cash margin posted by Oil SPE and not previously released would be returned by Gigabank to Oil SPE.
4. Any remaining shares posted as collateral would be returned by Gigabank to Oil SPE. Thus, 16.15 million shares of XYZ would be released.

9.2.4   Advantages and Weaknesses

There are several advantages of the "sale plus equity swap" strategy:

1. The investor raises cash by diversifying his/her sources of financing.
2. The investor maintains his/her economic exposure to the shares, including the dividend.
3. The investor benefits from a higher return on the investment due to the lower equity committed to the investment.
4. The investor can unwind the transaction early at any time.
5. The margin call mechanism may strengthen the investor's investment discipline.
6. The transaction consumes less counterparty credit lines than an alternative uncollateralized financing.
7. The terms of the equity swap are subject to the ISDA definitions, a robust legal framework.

There are several weaknesses of the "sale plus equity swap" strategy:

1. The investor is required to post additional collateral as the shares drop. As a result, in a weak stock market environment the investor may need to post precious liquidity at an unfavorable moment.
2. The investor sells the shares to the bank at inception and therefore he/she does not keep the voting rights. This weakness can be overcome by stating in the agreement that the bank would provide the investor with the attached voting rights at any AGM or EGM during the life of the equity swap.
3. The investor may not be able to retain any tax advantages related to the dividends. Frequently, investors holding a large stake in the stock benefit from an advantageous tax treatment on the dividends received. Through the sale plus equity swap solution, the investor receives a manufactured dividend that might be treated as financial income and taxed at the general corporate tax, if de-recognition is required.
4. The investor may be required to de-recognize the shares from his/her balance sheet as a result of the share sale at inception. If this is the case, the investor will be recognizing the capital gains or losses associated with this investment. However, due to the fact that the investor keeps all the economic exposure to the shares, in most accounting standards de-recognition may not be required and therefore this weakness may not exist.
5. The bank may be penalized from a regulatory capital perspective for holding the shares in its balance sheet. However, commonly banks are able to treat the combination of the share acquisition and the equity swap as a collateralized financing, a much better regulatory capital treatment.
6. The investor and the bank have to incur in the transaction costs/commissions associated with the sale/purchase of the shares.

9.3 PREPAID FORWARD + EQUITY SWAP + PLEDGE

9.3.1 Product Description

One way to raise cash without selling the shares is to combine several derivatives into a transaction that mirrors the flows of a loan as follows:

1. A **prepaid forward** transaction in which the investor is short a forward (i.e., commits to sell the shares to the lending bank at maturity at the then prevailing price) and receives the financing amount upfront in the form of a prepayment. At maturity, the forward is cash settled (i.e., no effective transfer of shares).
2. A **price return equity swap** transaction in which the investor receives (pays) the positive (negative) performance of the stock at maturity. This equity swap is a price return equity swap, and thus, the investor is exposed to the performance of the stock price only (i.e., dividends are excluded from the return computation).
3. A **pledge** transaction in which the investor pledges in favor of the lending bank a portfolio of stocks. Usually the issuer of the shares pledged is identical to the issuer of the underlying shares of the derivative transactions in (1) and (2). The market value of the shares pledged commonly exceeds the financing amount, to achieve an initial LTV.

9.3.2 Equity Derivatives Terms

Let us assume the same inputs as in the previous case, primarily:

- On 1 June 20X1, Gigabank arranged a USD 300 million structured equity financing for a special purpose entity, Oil SPE, fully owned by Oil Holding. The term of the financing was 3 years. The spread of the financing was 250 basis points.
- The financing was secured by 46.15 million shares of XYZ, representing 20% of its share capital.
- The financing was guaranteed by Oil Holding.
- The initial LTV of the financing was 65%, based on a USD 10.00 per XYZ share at the beginning of the transaction.
- A margining mechanism (see first case in this chapter).
- Early termination events and events of default (see first case in this chapter).

The counterparties to the prepaid forward and the equity swap were Oil SPE and Gigabank. Although the maturity of both equity derivatives was 3 years, Oil SPE could terminate them early, either totally or partially, at any time. Also, the transaction would terminate early upon occurrence of an early termination event. The main terms of the equity derivatives transactions are shown in the following table (the parts not detailed will be covered later):

Prepaid Forward and Equity Swap – Common Terms

Common terms	
Party A	Oil SPE, guaranteed by Oil Holding
Party B	Gigabank
Trade date	29-May-20X1
Effective date	1-June-20X1
Final termination date	1-June-20X4 (i.e., 3 years after the effective date)
Termination date	A date occurring on the earlier of (i) the final termination date, (ii) the final early unwind date and (iii) the early termination date
Early unwind	Party A (Oil SPE) may terminate this transaction in full or in part on any exchange business day prior to the termination date, subject to a prepayment fee by giving four exchange business days' notice in writing to Party B (Gigabank) of the number of shares subject to such early unwind. Party A (Oil SPE) shall also specify to Party B (Gigabank) a valuation date in respect of this early unwind. If an early unwind occurs in respect of less than all of the number of shares, the terms of the transaction shall be adjusted accordingly
	If, following an early unwind, the number of shares becomes zero, the valuation date for such early unwind becomes the final early unwind date
Shares	XYZ common shares
Exchange	New York Stock Exchange
Number of shares	30 million. The number of shares shall be reduced on each forward cash settlement date by the number of shares in respect of such early unwind
Initial price	USD 10.00
Underlying currency	USD
Calculation agent	Party B (Gigabank)
Prepaid forward part	To be covered later
Equity swap part	To be covered later
Other	To be covered later

Prepaid Forward Part

The prepaid forward carried out the payment of the USD 300 million financing amount to Oil SPE. This payment was defined in the "prepayment amount" term of the forward and paid on the effective date. The prepaid forward could only be cash settled. Every time that Oil SPE decided to unwind the transaction early, it had to provide a valuation date on which the early unwind became effective. At maturity, or at each early unwinding, Oil SPE partially or totally repaid the borrowed amount via the "forward cash settlement amount". This amount was the market value of the underlying shares at the exchange closing on the valuation date. The terms of the prepaid forward are shown in the following table:

Prepaid Forward Plus Equity Swap Terms – Prepaid Forward Part	
General terms	
Buyer	Party B (Gigabank)
Seller	Party A (Oil SPE)
Forward price	Initial price (i.e., EUR 10.00)
Prepayment	Applicable
Prepayment amount	USD 300 million
Prepayment amount payer	Party B (Gigabank)
Prepayment date	The effective date
Equity notional amount	Number of shares × Initial price
	Initially USD 300 million
Cash settlement	Applicable
Settlement currency	USD
Final price	In respect of each valuation date, the price per share at the valuation time
Final valuation date	The maturity date
Valuation time	The closing time on the exchange for its regular trading session
Forward cash settlement amount	Number of shares × Final price
Forward cash settlement amount payment date	The date that falls one settlement cycle following the valuation date
Forward cash settlement amount payer	Party A (Oil SPE)

In the prepaid forward plus equity swap strategy, unlike in the sale plus equity swap strategy, there is no need to define an unwind period because Gigabank does not have to dispose of any shares following an early unwind notice.

Equity Swap Part

Let us assume that Oil SPE did not unwind the transaction early and that at maturity the shares closed at USD 17.00. According to the terms of the prepaid forward, Oil SPE had to pay USD 510 million (= 30 million shares × 17.00), the "forward cash settlement amount". In contrast, Oil SPE only received USD 300 million at inception, the prepayment amount. Aiming to offset the difference between these two amounts of the prepaid forward, an equity swap was also part of the transaction. Let us review next each section of the equity swap part.

The Equity Amount Section of the Equity Swap

Oil SPE had the right to partially or totally unwind the transaction early, specifying in the early termination notice a valuation date on which the early unwind became effective. The equity amount part of the equity swap contained the equity swap settlement process at each early unwind, at an early termination and at the final termination of the transaction. Similarly to the prepaid forward part, at each valuation date the final price was calculated as the market value of the underlying shares at the exchange closing on the valuation date. At each early unwind, Oil SPE had to pay a 1% unwind fee calculated on the amount unwound. The terms of the equity amount section of the equity swap are shown in the following table:

Prepaid Forward Plus Equity Swap Terms – Equity Amount Section of the Equity Swap Part	
Equity amount part	
Equity amount payer	Party B (Gigabank)
Equity amount receiver	Party A (Oil SPE)
Equity notional amount	Number of shares × Initial price
	Initially USD 300 million
Settlement method election	Not applicable
Cash settlement	Applicable
Settlement currency	USD
Final price	In respect of each valuation date, the price per share at the valuation time
Final valuation date	The maturity date
Valuation time	The closing time on the exchange for its regular trading session
Cash settlement payment date	The date that falls one settlement cycle following the valuation date
Prepayment fee	An amount in USD calculated by the calculation agent (Gigabank) following the formula below:
	1% × Early unwind amount
	The early unwind amount is the product of (a) the number of shares subject to such early unwind and (b) the initial price
	The prepayment fee shall be payable by Party A (Oil SPE) to Party B (Gigabank) on the cash settlement payment date relating to the early unwind

Floating Amount Part

The floating amount part of the equity swap contained the interest to be paid periodically by Oil SPE during the life of the equity swap. This part represented the interest to be paid on the loaned USD 300 million. Oil SPE paid quarterly USD Libor 3-month plus 250 basis points, calculated initially on the USD 300 million notional. After a partial termination of the equity swap took place, Oil SPE paid interest on the outstanding notional amount only:

Prepaid Forward Plus Equity Swap Terms – Floating Amount Section of the Equity Swap Part	
Floating amount part	
Floating amount payer	Party A (Oil SPE)
Notional amount	The time-weighted average equity notional amount from, and including, the previous floating amount payment date to, and excluding, the floating amount payment date

Prepaid Forward Plus Equity Swap Terms – Floating Amount Section of the Equity Swap Part *(Cont)*	
Payment dates	At the end of each quarter
	The last payment day is the day that falls one settlement cycle following the final valuation date
Floating rate option	USD Libor fixed on the second local business day preceding the last floating amount payment date. The floating rate for the initial period would be determined two local business days prior to the effective date
Designated maturity	3 months
Spread	Plus 250 bps (2.50%)
Floating rate day count fraction	Actual/360

The Dividend Part

In contrast with the "sale plus equity swap" strategy, under the "prepaid forward plus equity swap plus pledge" strategy Oil SPE remained the owner of the underlying shares. Therefore, the equity swap did not have a dividend part as Oil SPE received directly the dividends distributed to the shares.

Interim Exchange Part

The interim exchange part of the equity swap contained the margin call mechanism. Remember that the objective of this credit enhancement tool was to preserve the LTV of the equity financing. The functioning of the margin call mechanism was explained in the first case study of this chapter. The terms of the interim exchange part of the equity swap were almost identical to that of the previous "sale plus equity swap" strategy:

Prepaid Forward Plus Equity Swap Terms – Interim Exchange Section of the Equity Swap Part	
Interim exchange	
Party A interim exchange amount	If, on a collateral valuation date, the LTV ratio is greater than the LTV margin level (70%), Party A (Oil SPE) shall pay to Party B (Gigabank), on the first business day following such date, the required cash margin amount
Party B interim exchange amount	If, during three consecutive collateral valuation dates, the LTV ratio is lower than the LTV release level (65%), Party B (Gigabank) shall pay to Party A (Oil SPE), on the first business day following such date, the absolute value of the required cash margin amount
LTV ratio	In respect of each collateral valuation date, the number expressed as a percentage equal to (i) divided by (ii), with:
	(i) (a) the equity notional amount minus (b) the cash collateral amount
	(ii) the market value of the pledged shares
Required cash margin amount	In respect of each collateral valuation date, an amount in USD equal to:
	(i) the equity notional amount minus
	(ii) the cash collateral amount minus
	(iii) (a) the LTV reset level multiplied by (b) the market value of the shares

Prepaid Forward Plus Equity Swap Terms – Interim Exchange Section of the Equity Swap Part

LTV margin level	70%
LTV reset level	65%
LTV release level	60%
Market value of the shares	In respect of each collateral valuation date, (i) multiplied by (ii): (i) the number of pledged shares (ii) the closing price per share on the exchange on the exchange business day immediately preceding such collateral valuation date, as determined by the calculation agent
Exchange	New York Stock Exchange
Share collateral	On the effective date, Party A (Oil SPE) shall pledge 46.15 million shares (the "number of pledged shares") of XYZ in favor of Party B (Gigabank) The share collateral would be released in accordance with the reduction in the number of shares
Collateral valuation dates	Each exchange business day from, and including, the effective date to, and including, the termination date
Cash collateral amount	From the effective date, an amount in USD equal to the aggregate Party A interim exchange amounts minus the aggregate Party B interim exchange amounts

Final Exchange

The final exchange part of the equity swap made sure that Gigabank would return to Oil SPE at maturity of the transaction the cash margin posted. The terms of the interim exchange part of the equity swap were very similar to those of the previous "sale plus equity swap" strategy:

Prepaid Forward Plus Equity Swap Terms – Final Exchange Section of the Equity Swap Part

Final exchange	
Party B final exchange amount	On the termination date, Party B (Gigabank) shall pay to Party A (Oil SPE) a USD amount equal to the cash collateral amount

Other Parts

The equity swap also included, among other terms, the early termination events and events of default that were described in the first case study of this chapter. I have avoided repeating them for simplicity:

Total Return Equity Swap Terms – Other Parts

Other	
Early termination events	Deal specific (same as in the "equity collateralized bond" case). The date that the early termination event is triggered becomes the early termination date
Events of default	Customary plus deal specific (same as in the "equity collateralized bond" case)

9.3.3 Transaction Flows

At inception of the transaction the following steps took place simultaneously (see Figure 9.9):

Figure 9.9 Flows at inception.

1. Oil SPE and Gigabank entered into a prepaid forward. Oil SPE received from Gigabank the financing amount through the prepaid forward. The consideration received, EUR 300 million, was a portion (65%) of the market value of the shares pledged at inception, to achieve the initial 65% LTV.
2. Oil SPE and Gigabank entered into a price return equity swap. Through the combination of the prepaid forward and the equity swap, Oil SPE kept the full economic exposure to XYZ's share price performance.
3. Oil SPE pledged 46.15 million XYZ shares in favor of Gigabank, securing the transaction.

During the life of the equity swap, the following flows were exchanged (see Figure 9.10):

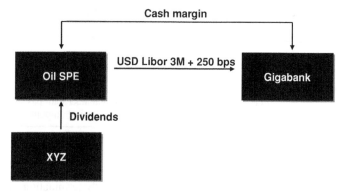

Figure 9.10 Flows during the life of the transaction.

1. Periodically, Oil SPE paid to Gigabank the financing costs. On a quarterly basis, Oil SPE paid USD Libor 3m + 250 basis points on the equity swap notional. The equity swap notional was the outstanding financing amount. At inception, the equity swap notional was USD 300 million. Because Oil SPE could partially unwind the transaction early, the equity swap notional was adjusted upon each early unwind.
2. The margining mechanism allowed Gigabank to call for cash margin if the LTV of the transaction surpassed the 70% LTV margin level. The margining mechanism also allowed for the release of previously posted cash margin if the LTV of the transaction was below the 60% LTV release level.

3. In this transaction, the posted cash margin was not remunerated. Otherwise, Gigabank would have paid the corresponding interest periodically.

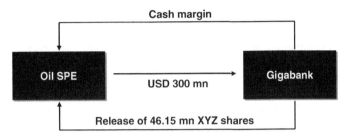

Figure 9.11   Flows at maturity of the transaction.

At maturity of the prepaid forward and the equity swap the following flows took place, assuming that no early unwinds took place during the life of the transaction (see Figure 9.11):

1. The prepaid forward was cash settled. As a result, Oil SPE paid to Gigabank the market value of the stock.
2. The equity swap was cash settled. Oil SPE received (paid) the positive (negative) performance of the 30 million XYZ shares relative to their USD 10.00 initial price. The net flow of (1) and (2) resulted in the USD 300 million financing amount being repaid by Oil SPE to Gigabank.
3. Any cash margin posted by Oil SPE and not previously released was returned by Gigabank to Oil SPE.
4. The 46.15 million XYZ shares originally pledged by Oil SPE were released by Gigabank.

As an example, let us assume that there were no early terminations and that at maturity XYZ's share price, the final price, was USD 8.00. Remember that the initial price of the shares was USD 10.00 and the initial number of shares was 30 million:

- Under the prepaid forward, the forward cash settlement amount was USD 240 million ($= 30$ million $\times$ 8.00), to be paid by Oil SPE to Gigabank.
- Under the equity swap, the absolute value of the cash settlement amount was USD 60 million [$= 30$ million $\times$ (10.00 – 8.00)], to be paid by Oil SPE to Gigabank.
- Therefore, the net amount paid by Oil SPE to Gigabank at maturity was USD 300 million ($= 240$ million $+ 60$ million), the financing amount.

Now, let us assume that at maturity XYZ's share price, the final price, was USD 14.00. Remember that the initial price of the shares was USD 10.00 and the number of shares was 30 million:

- Under the prepaid forward, the forward cash settlement amount was USD 420 million ($= 30$ million $\times$ 14.00), to be paid by Oil SPE to Gigabank.
- Under the equity swap, the cash settlement amount was USD 120 million [$= 30$ million $\times$ (14.00 – 8.00)], to be paid by Gigabank to Oil SPE.
- Therefore, the net amount paid by Oil SPE to Gigabank at maturity was USD 300 million ($= 420$ million $- 120$ million), the financing amount.

9.3.4 Advantages and Weaknesses

There are several advantages of the prepaid forward + equity swap solution:

1. The investor raises cash by diversifying his/her sources of financing.
2. The investor owns the stock and therefore keeps the voting rights.
3. The investor receives the dividends directly from the issuer of the stock. Thus, the investor is able to retain any tax advantages related to the dividends. Frequently, investors holding a large stake in the stock benefit from an advantageous tax treatment on the dividends received.
4. There is no sale of the stock, so no recognition of capital gains or losses associated with the equity financing takes place.
5. The investor can unwind the transaction early at any time.
6. The terms of the prepaid forward and the equity swap are subject to the ISDA definitions, a robust legal framework.
7. The transaction consumes less counterparty credit lines than an alternative uncollateralized financing.
8. The investor benefits from a higher return on the investment due to the lower equity committed to the investment.

There are several weaknesses of the prepaid forward + equity swap solution:

1. The investor is required to post additional collateral as the shares drop. As a result, in a weak stock market environment the investor may need to use precious liquidity at an unfavorable moment. However, the margin call mechanism may strengthen the investor's investment discipline.
2. The shares are pledged to secure the transaction. The formalization of the pledge may require the supervision of a notary, an additional cost.

9.4 REPO FINANCING

9.4.1 Product Description

One way to implement an equity financing is to enter into a repo financing. A repo is not a derivative because it is not treated as an independent asset whose value is derived from another asset. The repo financing structure allows the lender to buy the shares, having title to them, allowing its possession in the event of default. Thus, this solution circumvents issues surrounding enforcement of the pledge.

In our case the transaction would be implemented as follows:

1. On the effective date, 1 June 20X1, Oil SPE sells to Gigabank 46.15 million shares of XYZ for USD 300 million. Title to the shares is transferred from Oil SPE to Gigabank.
2. Periodically, Oil SPE paid to Gigabank on a quarterly basis. Oil SPE paid USD Libor 3m + 250 basis points on the repo notional. The repo notional was the outstanding financing amount. At inception, the repo notional was USD 300 million. Because Oil SPE could partially unwind the transaction early, the repo notional was adjusted upon each early unwind.
3. Gigabank paid to Oil SPE an amount equivalent to the dividends received on the underlying shares, each time a dividend was distributed to such shares.

4. During the life of the repo, Oil SPE posts cash collateral to Gigabank to replicate the margining mechanism.
5. At maturity, Oil SPE buys from Gigabank 46.15 million shares of XYZ for a redemption amount. Title to the shares is transferred back to Oil SPE. The redemption amount equates to the repo notional, initially USD 300 million.

One of the consequences of the transfer of title of the XYZ shares is that the voting rights attached to the shares are passed to Gigabank. Thus, the repo agreement should provide that Gigabank must exercise these voting rights in accordance with Oil SPE's directions.

One of the main advantages of the "repo" financing relative to other types of financing is that Gigabank can lend the shares in the stock lending market, obtaining an extra yield. Gigabank can share the lending fee with Oil SPE, resulting in a lower spread.

9.5 STOCK LOAN FINANCING

9.5.1 Product Description

One way to implement an equity financing is to enter into a stock loan agreement. The structure of a stock loan is very similar to that of a repo financing. A stock loan is a transaction in which securities are transferred by one party to another in return for an undertaking to redeliver equivalent securities (i.e., the same number of shares of the same issuer) at a future date. A stock loan is not a derivative because it is not treated as an independent asset whose value is derived from another asset. The mechanism is unlike a pledge, where title does not pass and further, under which the lender therefore has no right to borrow the shares. The stock lending structure allows the lender therefore:

1. To borrow the shares.
2. To have title to those shares, allowing its possession in the event of default. Thus, this solution circumvents issues surrounding enforcement of the pledge.

In our case the transaction would be implemented as follows:

1. On the effective date, 1 June 20X1, Gigabank borrows 46.15 million shares of XYZ from Oil SPE. Title to the shares is transferred from Oil SPE to Gigabank.
2. Also on the effective date, 1 June 20X1, Gigabank provides USD 300 million cash collateral to Oil SPE. Title to the cash collateral is also transferred and so can be used by Oil SPE for its own purposes.
3. During the life of the stock loan, Oil SPE pays to Gigabank quarterly interest (USD Libor + 250 basis points) on the cash collateral posted by Gigabank.
4. During the life of the stock loan, Gigabank pays to Oil SPE an amount equivalent to the dividends received on the borrowed 46.15 million shares of XYZ, each time a dividend was distributed to such shares.
5. During the life of the stock loan, the collateral posted by Gigabank is adjusted to replicate the margining mechanism.
6. At maturity, Oil SPE returned the outstanding cash collateral posted by Gigabank.
7. Also at maturity, Gigabank returned the borrowed 46.15 million shares of XYZ.

One of the consequences of the transfer of title of the XYZ shares is that the voting rights attached to the shares are passed to Gigabank. Thus, the stock loan agreement should provide that Gigabank must exercise these voting rights in accordance with Oil SPE's directions.

One of the main advantages of the "stock loan" financing relative to other types of financing is that Gigabank can lend the shares in the stock lending market, obtaining an extra yield. Gigabank can share the lending fee with Oil SPE, resulting in a lower spread.

9.6 PUT FINANCING

A risk-controlled way of raising financing on the back of an equity stake is for an investor to purchase a put option and, on the back of the put option, raise financing from a bank. The major weakness of both the previously covered equity financing strategies is the margin call mechanism. As the stock price drops, the borrower is required to post collateral commonly in cash. Another weakness of these equity financing strategies is that the LTV cannot be very high, to protect the lender. Because under a put financing the bank's financing is fully, or almost fully, protected, the amount of the loan can be set close to the strike of the put option, allowing a higher LTV than other strategies. Also, this strategy requires no cash margining. The main problem of the put financing strategy is that the borrower has to acquire the put, which can be very costly if the volatility of the underlying stock is high and/or the term of the financing is long.

9.6.1 Product Description

In order to describe the mechanics of a put financing, let us take our previous example in which Oil SPE was looking to raise financing collateralized by a pledge of 46.15 million XYZ shares, which were worth USD 461.50 million. Levels of 3-year European puts on XYZ shares were the following, assuming the 3-year USD swap rate at 4% and a dividend yield of 3%:

Strike	Strike (USD)	Volatility	Premium (%)	Premium (USD million)
100%	10.00	25%	14%	64.6
90%	9.00	28%	11%	50.8
80%	8.00	31%	9%	41.5
70%	7.00	34%	7%	32.3
60%	6.00	37%	5%	23.1

Let us assume that due to the almost full mitigation of the counterparty credit risk, the put financing spread was 120 basis points (instead of the 250 basis points spread in our previous cases). If Oil SPE would be paying the interest quarterly, and Gigabank believed that the highest level that USD Libor 3-month could reach was 10% during the next 3 years, the maximum exposure to Oil SPE due to the interest payments was 2.8% [= (10% + 1.2%)/4]. Thus, Gigabank was willing to finance Oil SPE at a level equal to the strike of the put minus 2.8%.

Let us assume further that Oil SPE was willing to buy the 90% put, paying USD 50.8 million. Gigabank would then be willing to provide financing for 87.2% (= 90% − 2.8%) of the value of the stock. Thus, Oil SPE raised USD 402.4 million (= 87.2% × 461.50 million). Because Oil SPE had to pay the put premium, the net amount raised was USD 351.6 million (= 402.4 million − 50.8 million).

The flows at inception were the following:

1. Oil SPE pledged 46.15 million XYZ shares in favor of Gigabank. Title remained with Oil SPE.
2. Oil SPE acquired from Gigabank a 3-year European put with strike price USD 9.00 (i.e., a 90% strike) and paid USD 50.8 million. At expiry, the option could be cash or physically settled, at Oil SPE's election.
3. Gigabank provided a USD 402.4 million loan to Oil SPE. The flows of (2) and (3) were netted, resulting in USD 351.6 million.
4. Gigabank borrowed a number of XYZ shares to initially delta-hedge the put option. Gigabank then sold the borrowed XYZ shares onto the open market.

The flows during the life of the transaction were the following:

1. Oil SPE paid to Gigabank USD Libor 3-month plus 120 basis points on the USD 402.4 million loan.
2. Oil SPE received directly from XYZ the dividends distributed to the 46.15 million XYZ shares.
3. Oil SPE did not post any cash margin.
4. Gigabank adjusted its delta-hedge, borrowing additional XYZ shares if needed.

At maturity, if XYZ's share price was greater than, or equal to, the USD 9.00 strike price, Oil SPE would not exercise the put. Oil SPE would repay the USD 402.4 million loan. To repay this amount, Oil SPE could sell a part of its XYZ shares onto the open market.

At maturity, if XYZ's share price was below the USD 9.00 strike price, the put would be exercised. Oil SPE could choose between physical and cash settlement:

- If Oil SPE chose physical settlement, Oil SPE would deliver to Gigabank the pledged 46.15 million XYZ shares, receiving the USD 415.4 million (= 46.15 million × 9.00) strike amount. Oil SPE would repay the USD 402.4 million loan. Gigabank would net the strike amount and the loan redemption amount, paying USD 13 million (= 415.4 million – 402.4 million) to Oil SPE.
- If Oil SPE chose cash settlement, Gigabank would sell the underlying shares onto the market, at an average share price (the final price). Oil SPE would receive the put cash settlement amount [i.e., 46.15 million shares × (9.00 – final price)]. Oil SPE would repay the USD 402.4 million loan. The put cash settlement amount would be netted with the loan redemption amount.

9.6.2   Advantages and Weaknesses

There are several advantages of the put financing strategy:

1. The LTV can be larger than in other equity financings. The LTV is set close to the level of the put strike.
2. The investor is not exposed to a share price decline below the put strike.
3. There are no margin calls.
4. The financing spread is lower than the spread of other equity financings, due to the absence of credit risk.
5. The investor does not cannibalize existing credit lines from the bank providing the financing.

6. It can be a cost-effective way to raise non-recourse financing. A put financing may be provided to an investor with a weak credit without requiring a guarantee from a stronger credit third party.

There are several weaknesses of the put financing strategy:

1. The investor has to pay the put option premium, which can be quite sizable if the tenor is long and/or the implied volatility of the stock is high.
2. The size of the equity financing is dependent on the notional of the put. The bank providing the put may be able to provide a put only for a very limited number of shares, causing the investor to be unable to raise the targeted financing.
3. The put provider, typically the lending bank, would need to borrow shares in the market to hedge its market risk. Often, stock borrowing is not available for large numbers of shares, limiting the size of the put. An alternative would be to make available for borrowing the shares pledged, losing the borrower the corresponding voting rights and receiving the corresponding manufactured dividends.

9.7 COLLARED FINANCING

The major weakness of the put financing is the substantial premium to be paid to purchase the put option. An alternative is to simultaneously sell a call option to reduce the overall premium. A financing that includes a call and a put is called a **collared financing**. The inclusion of the call limits the upside participation in the underlying equity stake. Nonetheless, the investment could still earn an attractive return due to the potential high leverage of the strategy. This strategy is particularly attractive to investors that are looking to put in place a highly leveraged investment in a stock with a high dividend yield.

9.7.1 Product Description

Let us assume that Oil SPE entered into an 80%/119% collared financing. Following the reasoning described in the previous "put financing" strategy, Gigabank was willing to provide a 3-year loan with an amount up to the put strike minus 2.8%. Therefore, the notional amount of the loan was USD 356.3 million [= 461.5 million × (80% − 2.8%)].
    The flows at inception were the following:

1. Oil SPE bought from Gigabank a 3-year European put option with strike 8.00 (i.e., 80% of the spot price) on 46.15 million XYZ shares. The premium of the put was USD 41.5 million. The option could be cash or physically settled, at Oil SPE's election.
2. Oil SPE sold to Gigabank a 3-year European call option with strike 11.90 (i.e., 119% of the spot price) and on 46.15 million XYZ shares. The premium of the call was also USD 41.5 million. The option could be cash or physically settled, at Oil SPE's election.
3. Oil SPE borrowed USD 356.3 million from Gigabank. Under the 3-year loan, Oil SPE has to pay USD Libor 3-month plus 120 basis points on a quarterly basis. There were no margin calls.
4. Oil SPE pledged 46.15 million XYZ shares in favor of Gigabank. Title remained with Oil SPE.
5. Gigabank borrowed a number of XYZ shares to initially hedge the transaction. Gigabank then sold the borrowed XYZ shares onto the open market.

The flows during the life of the transaction were the following:

1. Oil SPE paid to Gigabank USD Libor 3-month plus 120 basis points on the USD 356.3 million loan.
2. Oil SPE received directly from XYZ the dividends distributed to the unlent portion of the 46.15 million XYZ shares. Oil SPE received a manufactured dividend on the lent shares.
3. Oil SPE did not post any cash margin.
4. Gigabank adjusted its delta-hedge, borrowing any additional XYZ shares if needed.

At maturity, Oil SPE could choose between physical and cash settlement upon exercise of any of the two options. If Oil SPE elected physical settlement:

- If XYZ's share price was greater than the USD 11.90 call strike price, Oil SPE would deliver 46.15 million XYZ shares in exchange for USD 549.2 million ($= 46.15$ million $\times$ 11.90). Oil SPE would repay the USD 356.3 million loan. Both amounts would be netted, realizing Oil SPE a profit of USD 192.9 million ($= 549.2$ million $-$ 356.3 million). Gigabank would return the borrowed XYZ shares.
- If XYZ's share was lower than the USD 8.00 put strike price, Oil SPE would deliver to Gigabank the pledged 46.15 million XYZ shares, receiving USD 369.2 million ($= 46.15$ million $\times$ 8.00) strike amount. Oil SPE would repay the USD 356.3 million loan. Gigabank would net the strike amount and the loan redemption amount, paying USD 12.9 million ($= 369.2$ million $-$ 356.3 million) to Oil SPE. Gigabank would return the borrowed XYZ shares.

If Oil SPE elected cash settlement:

- If XYZ's share price was greater than the USD 11.90 call strike price, Oil SPE would pay to Gigabank the appreciation of the XYZ shares above the USD 11.90 call strike price. For example, if XYZ's stock price was USD 13.00, Oil SPE would pay to Gigabank USD 50.8 million [$= 46.15$ million $\times$ (13.00 $-$ 11.90)]. Also, Oil SPE would repay the USD 356.3 million loan. Gigabank would return the borrowed XYZ shares.
- If XYZ's share was lower than the USD 8.00 put strike price, Oil SPE would receive from Gigabank the depreciation of XYZ shares below the USD 8.00 put strike price. For example, if XYZ's stock price was USD 6.00, Oil SPE would receive from Gigabank USD 92.3 million [$= 46.15$ million $\times$ (8.00 $-$ 6.00)]. Also, Oil SPE would repay the USD 356.2 million loan. These two amounts would be netted. Gigabank would return the borrowed XYZ shares.

If no option were exercised because XYZ's share was lower than, or equal to, the USD 11.90 call strike price and greater than, or equal to, the USD 8.00 put strike price, Oil SPE would repay the USD 356.2 million loan. In theory, the delta of the collar in this scenario would be zero, so Gigabank already returned any borrowed XYZ shares.

9.7.2 Advantages and Weaknesses

There are several advantages of the collared financing strategy:

1. The LTV is typically larger than the LTV of other equity financings. The LTV is set close to the level of the put strike.

2. The investor does not have to pay a premium for the put. It is offset by the premium of the call.
3. The investor is not exposed to a share price decline below the put strike.
4. There are no margin calls.
5. The financing spread is lower than the spread of other equity financings, due to the absence of credit risk.
6. The investor does not cannibalize existing credit lines from the bank providing the financing.
7. It can be a cost-effective way to raise non-recourse financing. With a collared financing to an investor with a weak credit there is no need for a guarantee from a third party.

There are several weaknesses of the collared financing strategy:

1. The investor does not participate in the underlying stock appreciation above the call strike.
2. An early unwind of the transaction implies unwinding both options, which can result in the investor having to pay a sizable amount of option time value.
3. The size of the equity financing is dependent on the notional of the put (and therefore, the collar). The bank providing the collar may be able to provide a collar only for a very limited number of shares, leaving the investor unable to raise the targeted financing.
4. The collar provider, typically the lending bank, would need to borrow shares in the market to hedge its market risk. Often, stock borrowing is not available for large numbers of shares, limiting the size of the put. An alternative would be to make available for borrowing the shares pledged, losing the borrower the corresponding voting rights and receiving manufactured dividends.

9.8   REVOLVING MARGIN LOAN FACILITIES

The most common equity financing strategy is a **margin loan**, also called a **Lombard loan**. In this section I will walk through a margin loan. All the cases we covered previously in this chapter included term financings. In a term financing, the borrower draws down the full amount of the financing immediately and repays the loan at maturity (or at an early unwind). In our previous cases, Oil SPE already had the XYZ shares and drew the total financing amount at inception.

If an investor is looking to quickly benefit from a sudden and sharp fall of a stock, a term loan may not be the best solution as it typically takes several weeks to put in place, especially if it needs to be syndicated. An investor may prefer instead to have an available financing so he/she can quickly acquire a block of shares. This type of financing is called a **revolving credit facility**. In a revolving credit facility, the borrower can draw from the facility up to the full amount of the facility and, once the borrower repays, the limit is reset (hence the term revolving).

9.8.1   Case Study: Oil SPE's Revolving Margin Loan Facility

Let us assume that Oil SPE signed with Gigabank a revolving facility to finance up to USD 1 billion acquisitions in listed oil companies in Europe and the USA. The facility had a maturity of three years and could be drawn in multiple drawdowns of USD 10 million, with a minimum amount of USD 100 million per drawdown. The terms of the loan facility were as follows:

Oil SPE's Revolving Margin Loan Facility Terms	
Borrower	Oil SPE, a wholly owned subsidiary of Oil Holding
Guarantor	Oil Holding
Lender	Gigabank
Facility type	Secured revolving loan facility
Facility amount	USD 1 billion
Signing date	1-June-20X1
Ranking	The facility is a senior secured obligation of the borrower and the guarantor
Availability period	The period from and including the signing date to and excluding the final maturity
Final maturity	1-June-20X4 (i.e., 3 years from the signing date)
Revolving facility	Any part of the facility which is repaid is available to be re-borrowed during the availability period
Drawdowns	The borrower may draw down the facility amount in multiple drawdowns, subject to a minimum amount of USD 100 million per drawing, to be drawn in multiples of USD 10 million
Final repayment	Bullet repayment at the final maturity
Facility agent	Gigabank
Other terms	To be covered below

Let us take a look at the interest and fees to be paid by Oil SPE under the facility. The fees were the following:

- An **upfront fee** calculated on the facility amount. The upfront fee is commonly payable at funding and its size depends on the size and complexity of the deal. If the deal is syndicated, the distribution of the upfront fee is by tier in the syndicate. Allocation of the fee is a function of size of commitment, with the bookrunners receiving a larger proportion. In our case the upfront fee was 0.80% of the USD 1 billion facility amount.
- An **interest** of USD Libor 3-month plus 250 basis points, calculated on the drawn amount at the start of the quarterly interest period. Any drawdowns taking place during the quarterly period also accrued interest calculated using the interpolated USD Libor rate from the drawdown date to the end of the quarterly period plus the 250 basis points spread. Therefore, any amounts returned during the quarterly period were not deducted from the interest calculation.
- A **commitment fee** of 1% calculated on the unused portion of the facility during the quarterly period. To be consistent with the calculation of the interest, any drawdowns taking place during the quarterly period were also deducted from the calculation of the commitment fee from the drawdown date to the end of the quarterly interest period.
- In other financings there might also be an **administrative agent fee**, which is a pre-determined annual fee paid to the administrative agent or the bank that has the role of administering all of the interest and principal payments, and monitoring the loan post-issue.
- Also in other financings there might be a **structuring fee**, paid to the lead bank for structuring a complex facility.

Oil SPE's Revolving Margin Loan Facility Terms (Continuation)

Upfront fee	0.80% of the facility amount, to be paid on the signing date
Interest	USD Libor 3m + spread, paid quarterly, and calculated on the drawn amount at the beginning of the interest period
	Spread: + 250 bps
	In the event of any further drawing that occurs during an ongoing interest period, the interest period for such additional drawing shall be the period from such drawing to the end of such interest period and its interest rate shall be the relevant interpolated USD Libor rate
Commitment fee	An annual 1%, paid quarterly, calculated on the unutilized portion of the facility at the beginning of the interest period
	In the event of any further drawing that occurs during an ongoing interest period, the commitment fee for such additional drawing from the drawing date to the end of such interest period shall be deducted from the calculation of the commitment fee

Next, let us take a look at the facility's collateral. This was the most complex part of the financing terms. The transaction was secured by a combination of cash and common shares (the "secured collateral"). The borrower could change the composition of the secured collateral up to six times per quarter. Upon borrower default, the lender will seize the secured collateral and immediately liquidate it. The lender imposed some requirements on the composition of the collateral to facilitate its orderly and quick disposal. In our financing, limitations were set on any stock added to the secured collateral:

- Market capitalization: the stock had to have a market capitalization of at least USD 10 billion.
- Membership of a major stock index: the stock had to be a member of a major stock index.
- Diversification: the stock could not represent more than 20% of the collateral.
- Liquidity: the stock added could not represent more than three daily trading days.

In this financing, any stock added to the secured collateral had to comply with all the requirements. However, it allowed the added stock to miss either the diversification or the liquidity requirements.

Other financings may include other requirements, for example a maximum percentage of the share capital of the stock, to preclude an obligation to launch a public offer. Other restrictions may set a maximum percentage of the free float of the stock.

Oil SPE's Revolving Margin Loan Facility Terms (Continuation)

Reshuffle	The borrower has the right to change the composition (a "reshuffle") of the secured collateral at any time during the availability period, by providing a reshuffle notice to the facility agent. Any common shares added to the secured collateral shall take the form of eligible collateral
	The borrower cannot execute more than six reshuffles per interest period
Secured collateral	Secured collateral shall take the form of common shares as well as any cash collateral posted by the borrower, and must at all times be sufficient to meet the covenants and the margin requirements set out herein

Oil SPE's Revolving Margin Loan Facility Terms (Continuation)	
	Secured collateral shall be subject to legally enforceable security for the benefit of and in a form satisfactory to the facility agent and shall be held in a secured account with the custodian in a jurisdiction acceptable to the facility agent
Eligible collateral	Eligible collateral shall mean any common shares subject to the following requirements: (i) each issuer of the common shares should have a market capitalization of at least USD 10 billion equivalent on the day immediately preceding the date such equity security is added to the secured collateral; and (ii) each issuer of the common shares should be a member of the Bloomberg World Energy Index (Bloomberg code BWENRS) and of one of the following indices on the date such security is added to the secured collateral: Dow Jones EuroStoxx50 Index S&P 500 Index FTSE 100 Index Nikkei 225 Index Hang Seng Index and (iii) either the conditions (a) or (b): (a) the market value of the common shares of the same issuer shall not constitute more than 20% of the market value of the secured collateral on the date such security is added to the secured collateral (b) the number of shares of the same issuer shall not constitute more than three times the average daily trading volume of the shares, as determined by the facility agent, during the 90 exchange trading days preceding the date such security is added to the secured collateral.

A major problem with this financing was the requirement of any stock in the collateral to be in the oil and gas industry. This requirement could result in a high correlation between the stocks in the collateral pool. If one of the stocks had a very poor performance, it was likely that other stocks in the collateral pool also showed a weak performance, increasing the risk to the lender under the transaction. This requirement was included by the borrower to comply with its articles of association.

The transaction also had margining mechanisms and covenants. I am not going to repeat these protection mechanisms as their functioning was already covered in detail in this chapter's first case study.

10

Share Buybacks and Other Transactions on Treasury Shares

Corporate and financial institutions with strong balance sheets and significant cash flows are tasked with capital-allocation decisions that require their executives to choose from an array of investment alternatives. These alternatives include the investment in their current businesses, the acquisition of other businesses and the return of capital to shareholders. The return of capital to shareholders via dividend distributions was the almost exclusive course of action in the 1970s. Another alternative is the return of capital via share repurchases. This alternative gained ground through the next two decades, and eclipsed dividend distributions during the dotcom revolution of the late 1990s and early 2000s. Share repurchases reflect a company's confidence in its long-term growth and profitability. In this chapter I will focus on share repurchases, or share buybacks, analyzing the main strategies used by companies engaged in these programs.

A company can purchase its own shares provided that it is authorized to do so by its articles of association (i.e., bylaws) and complies with certain statutory formalities. It must be authorized by the company's shareholders by an ordinary resolution. The authority commonly specifies the maximum number of shares which may be purchased, the maximum and minimum prices which may be paid and the date on which the authority will expire.

Normally, shares which are purchased by the issuer are cancelled. However, a company is permitted to hold own shares, subject to its legal limit (e.g., 10% of the company's issued ordinary share capital).

10.1 OPEN MARKET REPURCHASE PROGRAMS

One of the most common methods in share buybacks is to buy shares directly on the open market. Normally, the company targets a period (e.g., 12 months) during which either a number of shares would be acquired or a total cash amount would be spent. Under an open market repurchase (OMR) strategy, the treasury department is responsible for the execution of the repurchase. On a daily basis, the treasury executives follow the company's share price and give purchase orders to a stockbroker. The company executives may accelerate the targeted repurchase of shares when the shares experience a weak performance and delay the repurchase of shares when the shares experience a strong performance. In choppy markets with no overall direction, this strategy can be very interesting. An OMR strategy can help treasury executives to become more familiar with the company's share behavior, as on a daily basis these executives will follow the stock price movements, better understanding the forces behind these movements.

An OMR strategy can also be helpful to improve the liquidity of the stock when there are notably more sellers than buyers. This is, for example, the case of a shareholder selling a large block of shares. The company can buy the block, avoiding a sharp drop in its stock price.

Similarly, when there is a large buying order on the market, the company can sell part of its own shares to avoid a large rise in its share price.

One of the major constraints of the OMR strategy is the impossibility of acquiring shares during blackout periods. These periods try to prevent the company and its executives from trading the company shares when sensitive information is known by the insiders but not yet by the market. For example, a blackout period may be set during the 20 days prior to an earnings release. Most blackout periods last at least 60 trading days per annum. It means that there are a substantial number of days that the company will not be able to take advantage of potential opportunities.

Another major weakness occurs in a strongly rising market. The executives involved in the OMR may prefer to delay the repurchases and wait for a potential upcoming correction. If the correction does not materialize, they may end up finally repurchasing the planned shares at a higher level, increasing the overall cost of the repurchase, besides causing unnecessary frustration and anxiety to the executives involved.

Market Abuse and Safe Harbours

Another major constraint of OMRs is that buy orders have to be executed in compliance with market abuse and safe harbour rules. Essentially market abuse rules try to avoid stock market manipulation. Regarding buybacks, the most relevant type of market abuse is effecting transactions or orders to trade, on own shares which give, or are likely to give, a false or misleading impression as to the supply of, or demand for, or as to the price of the company's stock, or to secure its price at an abnormal or artificial level. The primary purpose of safe harbour rules is to minimize market impact from a company's repurchases of own shares by limiting how, when, at what price and how many shares a company's common stock can be bought back. Safe harbour rules also protect a company from liability for market manipulation if the rules are followed when acquiring own shares. However, the mere fact that a buyback program does not fulfil the safe harbour requirements does not prevent a company from purchasing its own shares in the market. It can still do so in accordance with its buyback program as long its conduct does not amount to market abuse.

In some jurisdictions there are specific rules regarding buyback programs. For example, the EU has in place a regulation on buybacks and stabilization. Any purchase of own shares in accordance with these requirements will not constitute market abuse. This provides a safe harbor so far as market abuse is concerned.

Blackout Periods

In order to avoid abusing the market, most listed companies are prevented from purchasing own shares during blackout periods (also called "close periods"). The restrictions during blackout periods prevent a company from benefiting at the expense of stock market participants due to the possession of inside information. A blackout period usually starts one or two months preceding the announcement of preliminary and interim accounts, and ends on public disclosure of such accounts. Commonly, this restriction does not apply if the company has in place a buyback program managed by an independent third party which makes trading decisions in relation to the company's shares independently of, and uninfluenced by, the company.

Advantages and Weaknesses of an OMR Strategy

The advantages of an OMR strategy are the following:

- The company has complete flexibility to acquire the shares on the open market at its own discretion.
- The company benefits from a stock price decline.
- It helps treasury executives to become more familiar with the company's share behavior.
- It can help smooth imbalances in the trading of the company's stock. For example, the company can buy a block of shares offered by a shareholder, avoiding a sharp drop in its share price.
- The company avoids paying any premium for options or fees for delegated executions.

The disadvantages of an OMR strategy are the following:

- The company is exposed to a rising stock market. A steady climb in the stock price may substantially increase the cost of future share repurchases.
- The company has to devote resources to execute the shares repurchase.
- In most jurisdictions, the company cannot acquire own shares during blackout periods.
- Share purchases have to be carefully executed to comply with safe harbor rules.
- A bad timing of the execution, for example in an upward market followed by a sharply declining market, may cause the executives involved to be the subject of unfair criticism from shareholders.

10.2   ACCELERATED REPURCHASE PROGRAMS

From 2004, there has been a proliferation in the US of buyback programs executed under a strategy called accelerated stock repurchase (ASR). The main attraction of these programs is the rapid reduction of the number of shares outstanding. Next, I will analyze this type of transaction using a real case.

10.2.1   Case Study: Hewlett Packard's ASR with Merrill Lynch

In September 2004 Hewlett Packard (HP), the US electronics manufacturer, announced that it repurchased approximately USD 1.3 billion of its outstanding common stock. "HP has accelerated its share repurchases in recent quarters and today's announcement signals our intent to aggressively repurchase shares in the immediate future. We believe that at current price levels, HP shares represent an attractive investment", said Carly Fiorina, HP's chairman and chief executive officer. The major aim of HP's share repurchasing programs was to minimize shareholder value dilution due to the exercise of employee options. The shares were purchased from Merrill Lynch under an ASR. Let us take a look at the building blocks of this ASR transaction (see Figure 10.1):

1. On 19 September 2004, Merrill Lynch borrowed 71 million HP shares from the market in a string of stock lending transactions with several stock lenders. Merrill Lynch posted collateral.

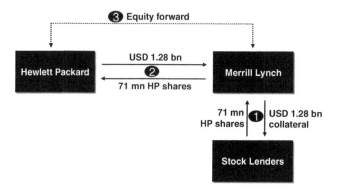

Figure 10.1   Building blocks of HP's ASR.

2. On 19 September 2004, HP acquired 71 million shares from Merrill Lynch at a fixed price – USD 18.00 – spending USD 1.28 billion. The shares were delivered all at once, enabling the company to subtract the number of repurchased shares from its share count, which had an immediate positive effect on its earnings per share.
3. Also on 19 September 2004, HP and Merrill Lynch entered into an equity forward on 71 million shares of HP. The forward would be maturing in six months' time (in reality, the forward was split into several tranches each maturing on a different date, but I am assuming a single maturity to simplify the analysis).
4. During the six months following 19 September 2004, Merrill Lynch acquired HP shares in the open market on a daily basis, trying to replicate the VWAP.
5. At maturity of the forward, HP settled the forward. The settlement price was the arithmetic average of HP's VWAP during the six-month tenor of the forward.

The Equity Forward

Prior to the forward maturity, HP could choose between cash and net share settlement. The settlement amount was calculated as:

Settlement amount = Number of shares × (Settlement price − Forward price)

Settlement amount = 71 million × (Settlement price − 18.00)

The settlement price was the arithmetic average of the daily VWAP of HP stock during the life of the forward.

In case of cash settlement, two scenarios were possible:

- If the settlement price was greater than the USD 18.00 forward price and HP chose cash settlement, HP paid the settlement amount to Merrill Lynch. For example, if the settlement price was USD 19.00, HP would pay USD 71 million [= 71 million × (19.00 − 18.00)].
- Conversely, if the settlement price was lower than the USD 18.00 forward price and HP chose cash settlement, HP received the absolute value of the settlement amount from Merrill Lynch. For example, if the settlement price was USD 16.00, HP would receive USD 142 million [= Absolute value (71 million) × (16.00 − 18.00)].

Normally, HP would be choosing the net share alternative if it preferred not to pay (or receive) cash from Merrill Lynch. The number of shares to be delivered (or received) by HP would be calculated as follows:

$$\text{Number of net shares} = \text{Settlement amount}/\text{Net share price}$$

- If HP had to deliver shares under the net share settlement alternative, HP and Merrill Lynch would agree on a period during which HP would be delivering shares to Merrill Lynch, and in turn, Merrill Lynch would sell these shares onto the open market. The execution will take place until the cumulative sale consideration equals the settlement amount. The net share price would then be the volume-weighted average selling price.
- Similarly, if Merrill Lynch had to deliver shares to HP under the net share settlement alternative, HP and Merrill Lynch would agree on a period during which Merrill Lynch would be buying shares in the market, and in turn, Merrill Lynch would deliver these shares to HP, until the cumulative sale consideration equals the settlement amount.

It can be inferred from the above that the combination of the purchase of shares at inception and the equity forward resulted in a repurchase price for HP equal to the arithmetic average of the daily VWAP of HP stock during the life of the forward.

Adjustments to Earnings per Share

The implementation of the ASR program immediately caused a decrease in the weighted-average number of shares assumed to be outstanding in calculating **basic earnings per share**. Because HP acquired the 71 million shares, this number of shares was immediately deducted from HP's shares outstanding.

During the life of the equity forward, an adjustment to the number of shares outstanding had to be performed when calculating the **diluted earnings per share**, to include the effects of a potential net share settlement of the equity forward, if such settlement was dilutive. In other words, if on a balance sheet date, the forward represented potential obligation to issue additional shares to Merrill Lynch, those additional shares had to be treated as issued and outstanding when calculating diluted earnings per share. To be dilutive, on the reporting date the arithmetic average of the VWAPs of HP stock since the forward inception had to be greater than the USD 18.00 forward price because under such a situation HP would have an additional obligation to deliver shares (under a net share settlement) to Merrill Lynch.

In our case, to simplify the analysis, we assumed that the equity forward had a sole 6-month maturity. Let us assume that on 31 December 2004, a financial reporting date, the arithmetic average of the VWAPs of HP stock since the forward inception was USD 19.00 and that HP's stock was trading at USD 20.00. If the forward were settled on that date and HP elected net share settlement, HP would deliver to Merrill Lynch 3.55 million [= 71 million $\times$ (19.00 − 18.00)/20.00] shares. As a consequence, HP had to take into account an additional 3.55 million shares when calculating the diluted earnings per share.

Advantages and Weaknesses of the ASR Strategy to HP

The advantages of HP's ASR strategy were the following:

- HP's share count was reduced immediately, improving earnings per share.

- HP benefited from a potential HP stock price decline subsequent to the ASR execution. The ASR locked in the average of the VWAPs of HP stock during the life of the forward.
- No premium was paid for options. The forward premium was zero.
- The forward contract was treated as an equity instrument under US GAAP. Any amounts (cash or shares) paid or received upon settlement of the contract were recorded directly in equity. Therefore, there was no income statement recognition. Beware that since 2004, US GAAP rules regarding the equity forward have varied.

The disadvantages of HP's ASR strategy were the following:

- HP was exposed to a potential stock price rise during the life of the equity forward.
- An aggressive purchase of stock by Merrill Lynch could put upward pressure on the stock price and therefore increase the actual repurchase price.
- The potential dilution, if any, calculated at each reporting date, reduced HP's diluted earnings per share.
- Merrill Lynch was not covered by the SEC's safe harbor provision at that time. The SEC ruled that ASRs and equity forwards were private transactions and not riskless principal trades effected on behalf of HP, and therefore, ineligible for the safe harbor provisions.

10.3   VWAP-LINKED REPURCHASE PROGRAMS

Under the OMR strategy, the company buys its own shares without a defined set of rules, resulting in a non-transparent repurchase price. Under the ASR strategy, the combination of the purchase of shares at inception and the equity forward resulted in a repurchase price for HP equal to the arithmetic average of the daily VWAP of HP stock during the life of the forward. However, this conclusion was not straightforward. VWAP-linked repurchase programs try to improve the transparency of buyback execution. The VWAP is a reliable and observable average price. It enables the company's stock holders to verify the quality of a share buyback program execution. A VWAP-linked strategy does not mean that the company loses all flexibility in acquiring shares; it can be complemented with opportunistic purchases via an OMR strategy during periods of a substantially weak stock price.

10.3.1   Execution on a Best Effort Basis

A way to implement a VWAP-linked repurchase strategy consists of the company delegating the execution to a stockbroker. The company and the broker would commonly agree on a number of shares to be acquired during a pre-agreed period. The broker then acquires shares on behalf of the company on a daily basis on the open market, trying to replicate the VWAP of such a day. The broker does not guarantee that the company would be buying the shares at the average of the daily VWAPs during the acquisition period. As a result, the company may be buying the shares during the acquisition period at a price higher or lower than the average VWAP.

The deviation between the realized purchase price and the average VWAP during the acquisition period is usually small because brokers usually use automatic execution programs that try to minimize these deviations. These programs also make sure that the execution complies with safe harbor rules. However, it causes substantial frustration and mistrust when a broker, day after day, reports to the company an acquisition price larger than the VWAP of such day.

It is not unusual that the company targets a cash amount to be spent instead of a number of shares to be acquired. The company and the broker would commonly agree on a daily amount of cash outlay to be spent during a pre-agreed period. The broker then acquires shares on behalf of the company on a daily basis on the open market, trying to replicate the VWAP of such day, spending the targeted cash amount. However, the achievement of the VWAP is not guaranteed by the broker. These types of execution have two major weaknesses:

- An execution based on a fixed cash amount is trickier for the broker than an execution based on a fixed number of shares. As a result, it is more difficult for the broker to achieve the daily VWAP.
- Even if the daily VWAP is achieved, the resulting average acquisition price will likely deviate from the arithmetic average of the daily VWAPs during the acquisition period. This likely deviation is due to the fact that the company acquires more shares when the stock price is low than when the stock price is high. As a result, when computing the arithmetic average of the VWAPs during a certain period, the shares acquired during a low price day will weight more than the shares acquired during a high price day, creating the earlier mentioned deviation. This weakness could largely be mitigated if the company targets a USD volume-weighted average VWAP instead of a simple arithmetic average VWAP.

10.3.2   Execution on a Guaranteed Basis

Another way to implement a VWAP-linked strategy is to have the executing broker to guarantee the average VWAP during the execution purchase period.

- In a transaction in which the number of shares to be acquired each day is pre-agreed, at the end of each trading day of the execution period the company will acquire the pre-agreed number of daily shares at the VWAP of such day.
- In a transaction in which the amount of cash to be spent each day is pre-agreed, at the end of each trading day of the execution period the company will acquire a number of shares at the VWAP of that day, such that the outlay equals the pre-agreed daily cash amount.

The broker then assumes the potential cost, or benefit, of any deviations of the realized acquisition price from the VWAP. As a compensation for bearing this risk, the company pays the broker a fee, for example 10 basis points (0.10%) of the total cash outlay.

10.3.3   Advantages and Weaknesses of a VWAP-linked Strategy

The advantages of a guaranteed VWAP-linked strategy are the following:

- The execution is transparent to all parties, including shareholders and research analysts, especially under guaranteed VWAP-linked strategies. This transparency avoids potential claims of poor execution from shareholders.
- The company benefits from a stock price decline.
- The company avoids paying any premium for options.
- The company usually delegates the execution to a stockbroker, avoiding devoting substantial internal resources to the repurchase program.
- Usually, the stockbroker can acquire shares during blackout periods. This is the case under irrevocable and non-discretionary buyback programs.

The disadvantages of a guaranteed VWAP-linked strategy are the following:

- It eliminates the company's flexibility to acquire the shares on the open market at its own discretion. However, a VWAP-linked strategy can be complemented with opportunistic purchases via an OMR strategy.
- The company is exposed to a rising stock market. A steady climb of the stock price may substantially increase the cost of future share repurchases.
- Share purchases have to be carefully executed to comply with safe harbor rules.
- The company usually has to pay a fee for the execution, especially under guaranteed VWAP strategies.

10.3.4   Execution at a Discounted VWAP

An interesting alternative is to enhance a guaranteed execution granting a right to the bank performing the execution. Usually, the right consists of the bank being able to terminate the share repurchase execution early on any trading day prior to the pre-agreed maximum maturity of the execution. For receiving this right, the bank would then compensate the company by assuring the acquisition of the shares at the average VWAP of the execution period minus a pre-agreed discount (e.g., 50 basis points). The amount of discount is dependent on, among other variables, the size of the transaction relative to the stock's average daily trading amount, the transaction's maximum maturity and the volatility of the stock. As an example, let us assume that the company targets a specific cash amount (the "notional amount"), to be spent under a VWAP-linked transaction with weekly settlements. The different steps of the transaction at inception would be the following:

1. The company determines the total cash amount to be spent under the transaction.
2. The company verifies that the transaction meets the authorizations given by the company shareholders and the company bylaws.
3. The company and a bank agree on the terms of the transaction:
   - The notional amount, the discount to the VWAP and the maximum execution period are agreed.
   - The maximum percentage of the daily volume for the executions. For example, that the daily purchases must never exceed 20% of the stock's average daily volume on the stock exchange, during the 20 trading days preceding the date of purchase.
   - Other restrictions may be included to ensure that the execution of the purchases complies with the company's bylaws and authorizations on own shares. For example, the company and the bank agree that the repurchase price in any one day may not exceed by more than 10%, or undercut by more than 20%, the arithmetic mean of the closing prices of the shares on the last three days of trading.
   - The agreement may provide for further restrictions to meet safe harbor rules. For example, the bank must not purchase the company shares at a price higher than the highest price of the last independent trade on the stock exchange and the highest current bid on the exchange.
   - Additionally, the agreement terms have to clearly state that the acquisition of the shares is irrevocable and non-discretionary, to allow the bank to acquire shares during blackout periods.

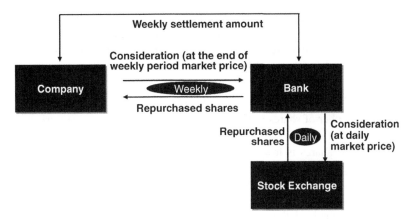

Figure 10.2   Discounted VWAP-linked transaction – weekly period flows.

4. The company deposits a pre-agreed cash amount at the beginning of the transaction. This amount approximates the expected outlay for a weekly purchase of shares. This advance is intended to reduce the bank's credit exposure to the company. Sometimes, when the company has a good credit rating, this deposit is void.

During each weekly period, the steps would be the following (see Figure 10.2):

1. On a daily basis, the bank acquires shares on the open market for its own account. The bank reports to the company the number of shares purchased that day, the VWAP and the cumulative amount of shares acquired since the beginning of the program. The company verifies that the purchases made that day do not exceed the pre-agreed restrictions (e.g., the maximum percentage limit of the daily volume).
2. At the end of the week, the company buys from the bank the shares the latter acquired during the week, at the arithmetic average of the VWAP of each trading day during the week (the "weekly average VWAP"). The company, commonly, is able to repurchase these shares during blackout periods. This acquisition is executed in two steps: first, the company buys the shares at the then prevailing share price (the "market price") through the stock exchange, and, second, both parties settle (the "weekly settlement amount") the difference between the market price and the weekly average VWAP. If the weekly settlement amount is positive, the bank will pay to the company the weekly settlement amount. Conversely, if the weekly settlement amount is negative, the company will pay to the bank the absolute value of the weekly settlement amount. The weekly settlement amount is calculated as follows, taking into account the number of shares repurchased by the company during the weekly period (the "weekly repurchased shares"):

$$\text{Weekly settlement amount} = \text{Weekly repurchased shares}$$
$$\times (\text{Market price} - \text{Weekly average VWAP})$$

The transaction ends once the pre-agreed total cash amount to be spent under the transaction has been reached. At the transaction's end date:

1. The bank notifies the end of the execution to the company.

2. The company and the bank calculate the arithmetic average of the daily VWAPs (the "final average VWAP") from the first day to the last day of execution.
3. The two parties also calculate the final repurchase price and the total number of shares to be repurchased by the company (the "number of shares"), as follows:

$$\text{Final repurchase price} = \text{Final average VWAP} \times (1 - \text{Discount})$$
$$\text{Number of shares} = (\text{Notional amount})/(\text{Final repurchase price})$$

4. If the number of shares is lower than the number of shares already repurchased by the company during the weekly periods, the company buys from the bank the additional shares at the then prevailing market price. Conversely, if the number of shares is greater than the number of shares already repurchased by the company during the weekly periods, the company sells to the bank the excess shares at the then prevailing market price.
5. The two parties also calculate the volume-weighted average price at which the company has repurchased the shares (the "average acquisition price") on a weekly basis during the life of the transaction.
6. The company and the bank settle an amount (the "settlement amount") so the acquisition price of the repurchased shares becomes the final average VWAP adjusted for the discount. If the settlement amount is positive, the company receives from the bank the settlement amount. Conversely, if the settlement amount is negative, the company pays to the bank the absolute value of the settlement amount. The settlement amount is calculated as follows:

$$\text{Settlement amount} = \text{Number of repurchased shares}$$
$$\times (\text{Average acquisition price} - \text{Final repurchase price})$$

7. The bank returns any initial deposit posted by the company. Often, the bank requires the company to post an initial deposit so it does not have to finance the weekly repurchases.

Final Comments

If the company is indifferent about the term of a share repurchase execution, this strategy can be interesting. The main attractiveness is not only the guaranteed execution but also the discount to the average VWAP obtained.

However, this transaction has several weaknesses relative to a normal guaranteed VWAP execution:

- There are limitations in terms of size. Very large buybacks relative to the stock's average daily volume will be priced with an unattractive discount because they provide little flexibility in shortening the execution's term.
- The bank has entire flexibility on the cash spent periodically (weekly in our example). A concentration of purchases in some weeks may require the company to pay a larger than expected cash amount for the shares.
- As the transaction is notably structured, its unwind can be costly. Sometimes, the company wants to terminate the transaction early because the shares are trading at an unattractively high price.

10.3.5   Execution at a Capped VWAP

An interesting alternative is to enhance a guaranteed execution by capping the average VWAP. The bank has the right to accelerate the completion of the share repurchase execution in exchange for providing the company with a cap on the average VWAP. Therefore, the company is guaranteed a maximum repurchase price. The cap level is pre-agreed at inception and is established as a percentage (e.g., 120%) of the initial price.

The steps are similar to the steps of the "discount to the VWAP" strategy. There are only two differences relative to the process previously outlined for the discounted VWAP strategy (see previous subsections):

- The bank needs to put in place an initial hedge, by buying a number of the company's shares in the market. The volume-weighted average price at which the bank acquires the shares corresponding to the initial hedge becomes the initial price. Once the initial price is known, the cap is then known. The company would represent that it is not in possession of any material non-public information during the initial hedging period used to determine the initial price.
- At the end of the execution the final price would be calculated as follows:

$$\text{Final price} = \text{Min(Cap level, Final average VWAP)}$$

As an example, let us assume that ABC, a US-based company, enters into an execution agreement with Gigabank. Under the agreement, ABC would end up buying USD 200 million worth of own shares. ABC's stock is trading at USD 10.00 at inception. Gigabank guarantees that the repurchase price would be the arithmetic average of ABC's VWAP during the execution period, subject to a maximum repurchase price of USD 12.00. Gigabank is required to execute the share repurchase during a maximum period of 9 months. Gigabank can accelerate the completion of the execution. To illustrate the mechanics of the strategy, I have assumed two scenarios:

1. ABC completes the execution after 6 months (see Figure 10.3). The arithmetic average of ABC's VWAPs during the 6 months was USD 14.20. Because the average VWAP was greater than the USD 12.00 maximum repurchase price, ABC then repurchased 16.67 million shares (= 200 million/12.00) at an average price of USD 12.00.

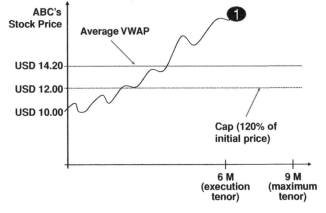

Figure 10.3   Capped VWAP-linked transaction – scenario one.

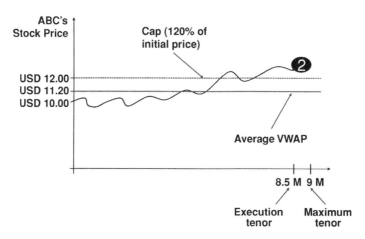

Figure 10.4   Capped VWAP-linked transaction – scenario two.

2. ABC completes the execution after 8.5 months (see Figure 10.4). The arithmetic average of ABC's stock VWAPs during the 8.5 months was USD 11.20. Because the average VWAP was lower than, or equal to, the USD 12.00 maximum repurchase price, ABC then repurchased 17.86 million shares (= 200 million/11.20) at an average price of USD 11.20.

Under the first scenario, ABC's decision to enter into the capped VWAP strategy was a great one. ABC repurchased 16.67 million shares. Without the cap, and assuming an execution matching the average VWAP, ABC would have repurchased 14.08 million (= 200 million/14.20) shares.

Under the second scenario, ABC would have been better off entering into a discounted VWAP strategy. Assume that the discount would have been 50 basis points. Under a discounted VWAP strategy, ABC would have repurchased 17.95 million [= 200 million/(11.20 × (1 − 0.50%)] shares. As we just saw, under the capped VWAP strategy, ABC acquired 17.86 million shares.

10.4 PREPAID COLLARED REPURCHASE PROGRAMS

The main weakness of the standard ASR analyzed earlier was that HP was exposed to an increase in its stock price. A stock price rise was likely given the fact that Merrill Lynch had to buy 71 million shares during the six-month life of the ASR and that HP also acquired a substantial amount of shares in the open market. Prepaid collared repurchase programs (PCRPs) try to mitigate this exposure by capping the VWAP over the time period that the transaction remains outstanding. To avoid the payment of an upfront premium, PCRPs also include a floor on the VWAP over the transaction term. In essence, a PCRP is a collared VWAP-linked transaction. In the PCRP that I am going to analyze next, the collar is applied to the average VWAP of each weekly period, instead of applying only to the overall average VWAP during the transaction term.

10.4.1 Case Study: Hewlett Packard's PCRP with BNP Paribas

On 14 February 2006, HP's board of directors authorized USD 4 billion for future repurchases of HP's outstanding shares of common stock. This buyback aimed to offset potential dilution under its employee stock option and share ownership plans. Instead of offsetting dilution upfront with an ASR, HP was more interested in offsetting dilution as it occurred. One alternative was to wait until dilution happened to offset it by repurchasing shares from the market that mirrored the number of options exercised. However, under this alternative HP was exposed to a rising stock price. If HP's stock price went up it would be buying shares at a rising price, incurring in a higher cost. To make things worse, the higher the stock price, the higher the number of stock options exercised by their beneficiaries. Other alternatives included the purchase of in-the-money calls or call spreads, but they required a substantial upfront premium. Instead, HP decided to enter into a collar-type structure, buying a string of calls and selling a string of puts, at no cost.

In March 2006, HP and BNP Paribas entered into a PCRP. HP called the deal a "prepaid variable repurchase" transaction on USD 1.716 billion. The PCRP allowed HP to cap the price paid per share and to impact shares outstanding evenly over time. The building blocks of the transaction at inception were the following:

1. HP paid BNP Paribas USD 1.716 billion upfront.
2. HP and BNP Paribas entered into the PCRP. The transaction had a one-year maturity. No shares were purchased by HP upfront.

On a weekly basis over the one-year term of the PCRP, and assuming 52 weeks over the one-year term:

1. BNP Paribas acquired shares on a daily basis during the weekly period, trying to replicate the VWAP of the day.
2. At the end of the weekly period, the average VWAP was calculated. The collared VWAP and the number of shares to be received by HP were then calculated as:

$$\text{Collared VWAP} = \text{Min}[\text{Max}(\text{average VWAP}, 24.60), 33.15]$$

$$\text{Number of shares} = \text{USD } 1.716 \text{ billion}/52/\text{Collared VWAP}$$

Therefore, the USD 1.716 billion paid by HP to BNP Paribas at the beginning of the transaction represented one million shares during 52 weeks at USD 33.15, the highest price per share HP had to pay under the agreement.

The PCRP Agreement

At inception of the PCRP, HP paid to BNP Paribas USD 1.716 billion. Under the PCRP, BNP Paribas agreed to deliver to HP between 1 million and 1.34 million HP shares every week over the course of a year. The exact number of shares to be repurchased was based upon the VWAP of HP's shares during each weekly settlement period, subject to the minimum and maximum price as well as regulatory limitations on the number of shares HP was permitted to repurchase. The minimum and maximum prices per share were USD 24.60 and USD 33.15, respectively. These prices were pre-agreed at inception of the transaction. As a result, the minimum and maximum number of shares HP could receive under the program was 52 million shares (i.e., one million shares per week) and 70 million shares (i.e., 1.34 million shares per week), respectively. HP decreased its shares outstanding each weekly settlement period as it physically received shares.

From an accounting point of view, HP initially recorded the USD 1.7 billion payment as a prepaid stock repurchase in the stock holders' equity section of its balance sheet, and in the cash flows from financing activities of its statement of cash flows. The prepaid funds were expended rateably over the term of the program.

Advantages and Weaknesses of the PCRP Strategy to HP

The advantages of HP's PCRP strategy were the following:

- HP was not exposed to a stock price above USD 33.15.
- HP did benefit from a stock price decline over the term of the PCRP down to USD 24.60.
- Share count was reduced gradually over the term of the PCRP, following more closely the timing of the dilution generated by the exercises of HP's stock option programs. This was one of the initial objectives of HP. However, it could be argued that for the stock it is better to have an upfront reduction in the number of shares outstanding, like the one generated by ASRs.
- No premium was paid for options.
- The PCRP was treated as an equity instrument under US GAAP. The upfront amount and any number of shares received upon the weekly settlements of the contract were recorded directly in equity. Therefore, there was no income statement recognition. Beware that US GAAP rules regarding the transaction may have varied.
- The implied volatilities of the puts HP sold were greater than the volatility of the calls it purchased through the collar.

The disadvantages of HP's PCRP strategy were the following:

- HP was exposed to a potential HP stock price rise over the term of the PCRP, up to USD 33.15.
- HP did not benefit from a stock price below USD 24.60.
- HP had to advance USD 1.716 billion to cover the future cost of the share repurchase.
- At inception, BNP Paribas had to buy a large number of HP shares to hedge its collar position, because the bank was long a string of puts and short a string of calls. This initial purchase gave an additional momentum to HP's stock price, potentially increasing the floor and the cap levels of the PCRP and the costs of future share repurchases.
- BNP Paribas was not covered by the SEC's safe harbor provision at that time. The SEC ruled that ASRs and equity forwards, and thus also PCRPs, were private transactions and not riskless principal trades effected on behalf of HP, and therefore, ineligible for the safe harbor provisions.

10.5 DEEP-IN-THE-MONEY CALL PURCHASE

As seen earlier, a company executing a buyback program is exposed to a rising stock price. Usually, companies target a cash amount to be spent in acquiring own shares under a buyback program. A rising stock price means that the company would end up buying a lower number of shares than expected. An alternative for a company is to buy call options on its own stock to mitigate this exposure. The call will hedge the company against a rise in its share price.

10.5.1 Case Study: ABC's Acquisition of a Deep-in-the-money Call Option

Let us assume that ABC targeted to repurchase USD 600 million of its outstanding common stock over the next 12 months and that ABC's stock price was trading at USD 10.00. Thus, ABC planned to spend USD 50 million (= 600 million/12) per month. ABC was worried that its stock price could rally during the next 12 months, causing it to acquire a number of shares lower than expected. In order to lock in a maximum price per share, ABC considered purchasing a call option.

At-the-money Call versus Deep-in-the-money Call

First, ABC considered buying a string of at-the-money calls (i.e., with strike price 100% of ABC's USD 10.00 initial stock price). ABC would enter into 12 calls, expiring at the end of each of the next 12 monthly periods. The underlying number of shares to each call option was 5 million (= 50 million/10.00). The options were physically settled. The overall premium was 8% of its notional amount, or USD 48 million (= 8% × 60 million × 10.00), or EUR 0.08 per share. Thus, ABC's stock price had to be at maturity above USD 10.80 [= 10.00 × (1 + 8%)] for this strategy to be profitable. The overall delta of this string of call options was 53%.

Next, ABC considered buying a string of deep-in-the-money calls with a strike price of USD 7.00 (i.e., 70% of ABC's USD 10.00 initial stock price). ABC would enter into 12 calls, expiring at the end of each of the next 12 monthly periods. The underlying number of shares to each call option was 5 million. The options were physically settled. The overall premium was 32% of its notional amount, or USD 192 million (= 32% × 60 million × 10.00). ABC's stock price had to be at maturity above USD 10.20 [= 10.00 × (70% + 32%)] for this strategy to be profitable. The overall delta of this option was 90%.

Let us compare the two call option strategies (see Figure 10.5):

- The breakeven stock price of the deep-in-the-money call alternative (USD 10.20) was lower than that of the at-the-money call alternative (USD 10.80). This was because the time value of the former alternative was only 2% (= 70% + 32% – 100%), while the time value of the latter was 8% (= 100% + 8% – 100%).
- The premium of the deep-in-the-money call alternative was much larger than that of the at-the-money call alternative. ABC had to pay a USD 192 million premium to acquire the deep-in-the-money call, while the premium of the at-the-money call was USD 48 million.
- As a result of the previous two elements, premiums and strikes, the deep-in-the-money call alternative outperformed the at-the-money call alternative when ABC's stock price was greater than USD 9.40. Conversely, the deep-in-the-money call alternative underperformed the at-the-money call alternative when ABC's stock price was lower than USD 9.40.
- The delta of the deep-in-the-money call alternative (90%) was much larger than the delta of the at-the-money call alternative (53%). To initially hedge its position, Gigabank needed to buy 54 million (= 60 million × 90%) ABC shares at inception of the deep-in-the-money call strategy. However, to initially hedge its position under the at-the-money call Gigabank needed to buy 31.8 million (= 60 million × 53%) ABC shares. Therefore, the implementation of the deep-in-the-money call strategy took longer than that of the at-the-money call strategy. Remember that the strike prices were set as a percentage of the

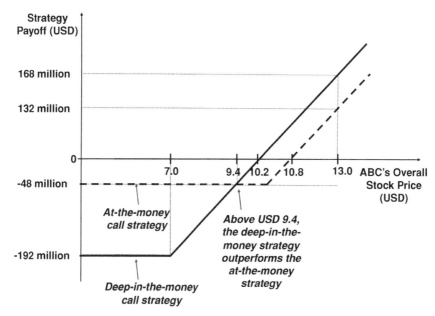

Figure 10.5 Payoff comparisons under the deep-in-the-money and at-the-money call strategies.

volume-weighted average price per share at which Gigabank acquired the shares necessary to implement its initial hedge. Consequently, ABC was exposed to a share price rise until Gigabank ended executing its initial hedge.

In my view, for cash-rich companies it makes sense to buy deep-in-the-money calls rather than at-the-money calls. As this was ABC's situation, it acquired the following string of calls:

Physically Settled Call Options – Main Terms	
Buyer	ABC Corp.
Seller	Gigabank
Option type	Call
Trade date	1-October-20X1
Expiration date	12 expiries. The 10th of each month starting on November 20X1 and ending on October 20X2
Option style	European
Shares	ABC Corp.
Number of options	5 million per expiry (i.e., 60 million in total)
Strike price	USD 7.00 (set as 70% of the initial price)
Initial price	The volume-weighted average price per share at which Gigabank acquires the shares necessary to implement its initial hedge. The initial price was set to USD 10.00
Total premium	USD 192 million (32% of the option notional amount)
Notional amount	USD 600 million (= 60 million × 10.00)
Premium payment date	12-October-20X1
Settlement method	Physical settlement only
Settlement date	Three exchange business days after the exercise date

At each expiry, there were two scenarios:

- If ABC's stock price was greater than the USD 7.00 strike price, ABC would exercise the call, buying 5 million own shares at USD 7.00 per share. ABC would spend USD 35 million (= 5 million × 7.00).
- If ABC's stock price was lower than, or equal to, the USD 7.00 strike price, ABC would not exercise the call. Instead, ABC would be buying in the market a number of shares equal to: USD 35 million/stock price. For example, if ABC's stock price was USD 6.00, ABC would purchase 5.83 million (= 35 million/6.00) shares. The shares would be acquired in the market at the then prevailing stock price.

One major problem with this strategy is that if a monthly call option was not exercised, ABC would be obliged to acquire the 5 million monthly shares in the market. If it was able to acquire the shares on the closing at the end of the monthly period, there was no risk for ABC. However, if the number of shares was substantial (a very frequent situation), ABC would need to buy the shares during the next several days after the call expiry date to avoid having a strong effect on its stock price. In this situation, ABC was exposed to a rising stock price until the 5 million shares were acquired in the market.

Advantages and Weaknesses of a Deep-in-the-money Call Purchase Strategy

The advantages of a deep-in-the-money call purchase strategy are the following:

- The company is not exposed to an increasing stock price.
- The company benefits from a stock price decline.
- By buying deep-in-the-money, the company avoids paying a large amount of time value. The total value of a deep-in-the-money call strategy is almost entirely comprised of its intrinsic value.
- The company sends the market a positive signal regarding its share price.

The disadvantages of a deep-in-the-money call purchase strategy are the following:

- The company has to pay a large upfront premium.
- The stock price must be greater than the strike price by the premium to breakeven.
- The company is subject to a risk between the average daily price and the monthly closing price, unless it is able to acquire all the monthly shares at the end of its related monthly period.
- The bank selling the option has to buy a large number of shares at inception, potentially giving additional upward momentum to the stock price. This may substantially increase the cost of future share repurchases.

10.6 ASIAN CALL PURCHASE

Let us assume that ABC did not have the resources to acquire a string of deep-in-the-money calls, and that it was considering the purchase of a string of at-the-money calls. As we saw in the previous section, the premium was substantial, USD 40 million. The objective of this strategy was to limit the repurchase price of its monthly buyback requirements over a year to EUR 10.00 per share (ignoring the premium). Although buying the string of at-the-money calls met ABC's objective, ABC was overprotected. For example, if one month ABC was paying EUR 12.00 and another month it was paying EUR 8.00, the average purchase price was EUR 10.00 [= (12.00 + 8.00)/2]. Under the string of calls, ABC would have paid EUR 9.00 [= (10.00 + 8.00)/2]. Thus, ABC was not worried about each month acquiring shares below EUR 10.00. Instead, ABC was worried about an overall repurchase price exceeding EUR 10.00.

An Asian call (an Asian average rate call) is a type of option where the payoff is computed taking into account the average of the underlying stock price during a period. For example, ABC could have entered into the following Asian call:

Cash-settled Asian Call Options – Main Terms

Buyer	ABC Corp.
Seller	Gigabank
Option type	Call
Trade date	1-October-20X1
Expiration date	10-October-20X2
Option style	Asian
Shares	ABC Corp.
Number of options	60 million
Strike price	USD 10.00 (set as 100% of the initial price)
Initial price	The volume-weighted average price per share at which Gigabank acquires the shares necessary to implement its initial hedge. The initial price was set to USD 10.00
Final price	The arithmetic average of the daily closing prices of the shares from 10-October-20X1 to 9-October-20X2 (both included). Only exchange business days would be included in the calculation
Total premium	USD 36 million (6% of the option notional amount)
Notional amount	USD 600 million (= 60 million shares × 10.00)
Premium payment date	12-October-20X1
Settlement method	Cash settlement only
Settlement date	Three exchange business days after the exercise date

---

The call would be settled in cash. The settlement amount was calculated as follows:

$$\text{Settlement amount} = \text{Number of shares} \times \text{Max(Final price} - \text{Strike price}, 0)$$

$$\text{Settlement amount} = 60 \text{ million} \times \text{Max(Final price} - 10.00, 0)$$

$$\text{Final price} = (\text{Closing price}_1 + \text{Closing price}_2 + \cdots + \text{Closing price}_{252})/252$$

The final price was computed as the arithmetic average of the closing prices of ABC stock during the annual period. As an example, let us assume that ABC's stock price behavior during the 12-month period was that depicted in Figure 10.6. The average closing price over the 12-month period was EUR 11.80. The settlement amount was then EUR 108 million [= 60 million × (11.80 – 10.00)].

The Asian call strategy had two strengths relative to the at-the-money standard call option strategy. Firstly, the premium was lower (USD 36 million vs. USD 48 million). Secondly, it allowed ABC to acquire the shares in the market on a daily basis. If it acquired 250,000

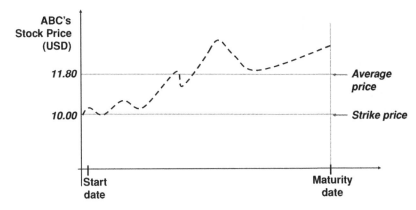

Figure 10.6   ABC's stock price behavior during the Asian call annual observation period.

($= 5$ million/20) shares in the market each trading day, assuming 20 trading days in the month, ABC was perfectly hedged with the Asian option.

10.7 PUBLICLY OFFERED REPURCHASE PROGRAMS

One way to implement a repurchase program in a very transparent manner is to acquire own shares via a **public repurchase offer**. Under this strategy all shareholders are given an identical opportunity to benefit from a buyback. The offer solicitation provides for a submission period, the number of shares the company intends to acquire, the offer price and other terms and conditions. The company may in its solicitation either state that:

- The purchase price is fixed.
- Or, the purchase price would be determined by way of an auction procedure. In this case, the company usually states a range within which offers may be submitted. Typically, the solicitation usually includes the possibility of adjusting the price range during the submission period if, after publication of the solicitation, offer and demand show important imbalances or if significant share price fluctuations occur during the submission period. Upon acceptance, the final purchase price will be determined from all the submitted sale offers.

If the number of company shares offered for sale exceeds the total volume of shares the company intended to acquire (i.e., the offer is oversubscribed), acceptance is commonly based on quotas. Furthermore, the company may provide for preferred acceptance of small lots of shares.

10.7.1   Case Study: Corporacion Dermoestetica's Public Offer to Acquire Own Shares

This case highlights how Corporacion Dermoestetica ("Dermoestetica"), a Spanish plastic-surgery provider, successfully completed its share buyback by offering to buy back own shares from all its shareholders.

In July 2009, Dermoestetica planned to acquire 47.4% of its shares at EUR 5.50 per share, a 74% premium to the stock closing price prior to the buyback announcement. The buyback would be implemented via a public cash offer to all Dermoestetica's shareholders. The buyback aimed to distribute part of Dermoestetica's sale proceeds of the British laser-eye provider Ultralase Ltd. Immediately following the announcement, Dermoestetica's stock price surged 46% to EUR 4.60.

In September 2009, the offer was accepted by 90% of the shareholders. Because the accepted sale orders exceeded the maximum number of shares to be repurchased, a pro rata adjustment factor of 52.9% was applied to the sale orders. In October 2009, the repurchased shares were amortized.

In practice, this transaction was equivalent, before any taxes were levied, to a special dividend. The decision to distribute excess cash via a share repurchase instead of a special dividend was due to the following:

- The company took advantage of a depressed stock price. Since its IPO at EUR 9.10 in July 2005, Dermoestetica's stock price had been declining. A purchase at EUR 5.50 signaled the market that the company viewed its stock price as notably cheap.
- The reduction in the number of shares outstanding meant that the company would distribute fewer ordinary dividends in the future, if the dividend policy was unchanged. Therefore, the company was able to save future cash resources.
- The earnings per share were greatly improved by the share buyback.
- The share buyback probably had a tax advantage for the selling shareholders. As I mentioned earlier, the selling shareholders probably realized a capital loss. A special dividend would probably have meant that Dermoestetica's retail shareholders would be levied a withholding tax.

10.8 PUBLIC OFFER OF PUT OPTIONS

One way to implement a repurchase program is to publicly offer a put option to all shareholders.

10.8.1 Case Study: Swisscom's Public Offer of Put Options

This case highlights how Swisscom, a Swiss telecommunications company, successfully completed its share buyback by issuing tradeable put options to all its shareholders. Following Swisscom's AGM in April 2006 approving a CHF 2.2 billion buyback program, the company's board of directors approved a public offering of put options to its shareholders. The proposed structure was intended to treat all shareholders equally by giving them a right to sell part of their shares to the company at a premium to the then prevailing stock price.

The put options were assigned to shareholders free of charge on 30 August 2006 with an exercise date of 13 September 2006. 23 put options entitled the bearer to sell two registered shares for CHF 450 gross or CHF 292.85 net per share (less 35% federal withholding tax on the difference between the share buyback price and the par value). The options were traded from 30 August to 12 September 2006 on the Swiss stock exchange. The options could be exercised on 13 September 2006. Alternatively, the put options could be sold on the exchange during their trading period. The following table highlights the key details of the offering:

Swisscom's Public Offer of Put Options – Main Terms	
Allocation of put options	One put option for each Swisscom share. The put options will automatically be booked to the custody accounts of Swisscom shareholders on 30 August 2006
Option trading	The put options may be freely traded for a period of 10 trading days starting 30 August 2006
Exercise ratio and strike price	If exercised, 23 put options entitle the holder to sell two Swisscom shares at a gross price of CHF 450 per share
Option type	European (can only be exercised at maturity)
Exercise of put options	13 September 2006, until 12.00 noon (CEST). Put options not exercised in time, and the rights associated with them, shall expire without compensation
Payment of the buyback price	If the put options are exercised, the net buyback price will be paid out on delivery of the corresponding number of Swisscom registered shares and put options on 18 September 2006
Listing of the put options	The put options are to be listed on 16 August 2006. They will be traded on the SWX Swiss Exchange from 30 August to 12 September 2006
Costs	The costs of allocating and exercising put options deposited with banks in Switzerland will be borne free of charge by Swisscom (but not the fees for the sale of options or the purchase of additional options)

Of the 56,718,561 put options issued, 56,541,107 or 99.69% were exercised. Swisscom thus bought back 4,916,618 of its own shares for the capital reduction, which was equivalent to 8% of voting rights and share capital recorded. The share buyback volume amounted to CHF 2.2 billion.

This solution was implemented because Swisscom's largest shareholder, the Swiss government, was looking to dispose of its stake. The structure used allowed it to sell part of its stake in a transparent manner. Before the buyback, the Swiss government owned 62.5% of Swisscom's share capital. Upon completion of the buyback, the Swiss government owned 53.9% of Swisscom's share capital.

10.9 PRIVATE SALE OF A PUT OPTION

An exotic way of implementing a repurchase of stock is to sell a put option to a bank. Let us assume that ABC sold a put option to Gigabank with the following terms:

Physically Settled Put Option – Main Terms	
Seller	ABC Corp.
Buyer	Gigabank
Option type	European put
Trade date	1-June-20X1
Expiration date	1-June-20X2
Shares	ABC Corp.
Number of options	20 million (one share per option)
Strike price	USD 10.00 (100% of the spot price)
Spot price	USD 10.00

Physically Settled Put Option – Main Terms (*Cont*)	
Premium	8% of the notional amount, or USD 16 million (i.e., USD 0.8 per share)
Premium payment date	3-June-20X1
Notional amount	USD 200 million (i.e., Number of options × Spot price)
Settlement method	Physical settlement
Cash settlement payment date	4-June-20X2

Shortly after inception, i.e., on 3 June 20X1, ABC received a USD 16 million premium from Gigabank. This premium represented USD 0.80 per share.

At expiry, on 1 June 20X2, two scenarios could occur:

- If XYZ's stock price was greater than or equal to the USD 10.00 strike price, the option would expire worthless. Overall ABC would have received the USD 16 million premium, enhancing other open market repurchases by USD 0.80.
- If XYZ's stock price was lower than the USD 10.00 strike price, ABC would receive from Gigabank 20 million shares in exchange for the payment of EUR 200 million. Taking into account the 0.80 per share upfront premium, ABC would have repurchased 20 million own shares at USD 9.20 each.

This is a very opportunistic strategy that can be used to complement other repurchase strategies. Otherwise, ABC may end up being exposed to a rising price without being able to repurchase the shares until the put's expiration date.

Advantages and Weaknesses of a Put Sale Strategy

The advantages of a put sale strategy are the following:

- The company receives a large upfront premium.
- Upon disclosure, the company conveys a positive view on its stock price.

The disadvantages of a put sale strategy are the following:

- The company is exposed to an increasing stock price.
- The company does not benefit from a stock price decline.
- The bank buying the put option has to buy a large number of shares at inception, potentially giving additional upward momentum to the stock price. This may substantially increase the cost of future share repurchases.

10.10 ACQUISITION OF SHARES WITH A RANGE ACCRUAL

10.10.1 One-speed Range Accrual

In the following sections, I will cover a popular way to buy own shares at a discount. Range accrual instruments allow the daily purchase of shares at a discount to the stock price prevailing at the strategy's inception. There are many versions of this strategy. I will review next the one-speed range accrual instrument. The selling version was covered in Chapter 6.

Let us assume that ABC targeted to repurchase USD 600 million of its outstanding common stock over the next 12 months and that ABC's stock price was trading at USD 10.00. ABC was interested in acquiring shares at a discount, and as a result, entered into the following one-speed range accrual:

One-speed Range Accrual – Main Terms

Buyer	ABC Corp.
Seller	Gigabank
Option type	Range accrual
Trade date	1-June-20X1
Start date	7-June-20X1
Maturity date	7-June-20X2 (1 year)
Shares	XYZ common stock
Maximum number of shares	65.2 million
Initial price	The volume-weighted average sale price per share at which the seller (Gigabank) puts in place its initial hedge
Strike price	USD 9.20 (92% of the EUR 10.00 initial price)
Barrier	USD 10.80 (108% of the EUR 10.00 initial price)
Premium	None
Accrual periods	Each monthly period from, and including, the start date to, and including, the maturity date
Number of shares	For each accrual period: 260,000 × Number of days
Number of days	The number of trading days during the monthly period that the closing price of the shares is lower than, or equal to, the barrier
Settlement method	Physical settlement
	The buyer shall acquire from the seller the number of shares at a price per share equal to the strike price
Settlement date	Three exchange business days immediately following the end of the corresponding monthly period

The different steps of the transaction during its life are the following (see Figure 10.7).

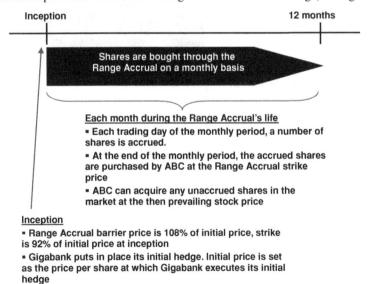

Figure 10.7 One-speed range accrual, steps of the transaction during its term.

On trade date, ABC and Gigabank agreed on the terms of the range accrual. The strike price and the barrier were defined as a percentage, 92% and 108% respectively, of the initial price. The maximum number of shares, 65.2 million, was determined by dividing (i) the buyback's USD 600 million target amount by (ii) the USD 9.20 strike price. The number of shares for each monthly accrual period was calculated by multiplying (i) 260,000 and (ii) the number of trading days during the monthly period that the closing price of the shares was lower than, or equal to, the barrier. The 260,000 figure represented the maximum number of shares that could accrue on a trading day and was determined by dividing (i) the 65.2 million shares by (ii) 250 trading days from start to maturity date.

Starting on the trade date (1 June 20X1), Gigabank put in place its initial hedge by buying a number of ABC shares in the market. Gigabank finished the initial hedge execution on the start date (7 June 20X1). The initial price, USD 10.00, was the volume-weighted average price at which Gigabank acquired the necessary ABC shares to establish its initial hedge. As a result, on trade date the strike price and the barrier were respectively set at USD 9.20 and USD 10.80.

The one-speed accrual allowed ABC to buy own shares at USD 9.20, an 8% discount to the initial price. The maximum number of shares that ABC could end up buying was 65.2 million. Assuming 250 trading days over the one-year term of the transaction, each trading day ABC could accrue a maximum of 260,000 shares.

The 12-month term of the transaction was divided into 12 monthly periods (the "accrual periods"). On each trading day of the accrual period, the number of shares accruing that day was a function of the closing price of ABC's stock on that day (see Figure 10.8):

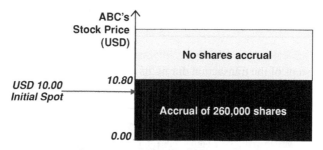

Figure 10.8 One-speed range accrual, daily accrual mechanism.

- If the stock closing price was lower than, or equal to, the USD 10.80 barrier, 260,000 shares accrued that day.
- If the stock closing price was greater than the USD 10.80 barrier, no shares accrued that day.

Three exchange business days following the end of the monthly accrual period (the "settlement date"), ABC purchased from Gigabank the aggregate of the accrued shares during the accrual period. The accrued shares were acquired at USD 9.20 per share.

In order to highlight the strengths and weaknesses of the strategy, let us assume three different price performances of ABC's stock price during the life of the instrument (see Figure 10.9):

- Under the first scenario, ABC's stock price experienced a strong rally. Excluding the first few months, the stock traded above the USD 10.80 strike. As a result, only 16 million shares were accrued, and therefore acquired, over the term of the instrument. ABC was relatively satisfied with the range accrual performance because it was able to buy the shares at

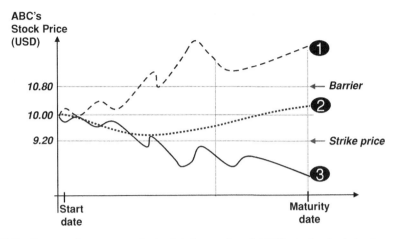

Figure 10.9   One-speed range accrual, simulated scenarios of ABC's stock price behavior.

USD 9.20, while the stock traded well above this level during most of its term. At the end of the instrument's life ABC only spent USD 147.2 million (= 16 million × 9.20), acquiring own shares. ABC spent the remaining USD 452.8 million (= 600 million – 147.2 million) acquiring shares in the market at the then prevailing stock price.

- Under the second scenario, ABC's stock price experienced a performance without an overall direction. Because ABC's stock price always traded below the USD 10.80 barrier, all the 65.2 million shares were accrued, and therefore acquired, over the term of the instrument. ABC was very satisfied with the range accrual performance because it was able to acquire the shares at USD 9.20, while the stock traded above this level during all the life of the instrument.
- Under the third scenario, XYZ's stock price experienced a strong correction. Because the stock price always traded below the USD 10.80 strike, all the 65.2 million shares were accrued, and therefore acquired, over the term of the instrument. However, ABC was not entirely satisfied with the range accrual strategy because it acquired the shares at USD 9.20. It is true that this price was an 8% discount to the initial price. However, without entering into the instrument ABC could have obtained a lower overall acquisition price in the market.

Advantages and Weaknesses of the Strategy

The advantages of this strategy were the following:

- ABC acquired the accrued shares at a discount to the initial price.
- ABC benefited from each day that the stock price traded between the USD 9.20 strike price and the USD 10.80 barrier.
- ABC had complete flexibility to pursue other strategies on the shares that were not accrued.

The disadvantages of this strategy were the following:

- ABC had no certainty regarding the number of shares to be acquired. Purchases took place only if ABC's stock price was below the USD 10.80 barrier.

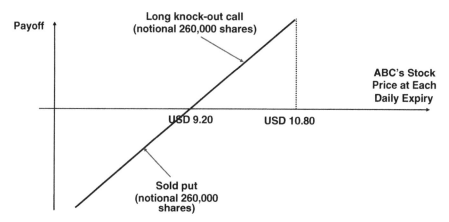

Figure 10.10 One-speed range accrual, building blocks of the transaction.

- ABC did not benefit from a stock price below the USD 9.20 strike price.
- ABC was exposed to a future rise of ABC's stock price.
- The range accrual was accounted for as a derivative. ABC fair valued the instrument through the income statement.
- This was not the case, but a range accrual may be feasible only for a limited number of shares. This limitation may require the company to implement another buyback strategy.

Building Blocks

From ABC's viewpoint, the one-speed range accrual was built by combining a purchased knock-out call and a short put. Each trading day over the term of the range accrual, a combination expired on such day, as follows (see Figure 10.10):

- ABC sold a string of put options with strike price USD 9.20 on 260,000 ABC shares. There was a put for each trading day of the 12-month period (i.e., 250 puts). In other words, only one put expired on each day of the 12-month period.
- ABC bought a string of call options with strike ABC 9.20 on 260,000 XYZ shares. There was a call for each trading day of the 12-month period (i.e., 250 calls). In other words, only one call expired on each day of the 12-month period. Each call ceased to exist if, on its expiry date, ABC's stock price was above the USD 10.80 barrier. Therefore, this option was a knock-out call.

10.10.2 Double-speed Range Accrual

A variation available to ABC was to enter into a range accrual with double speed. The first objective was to reduce the purchase price from USD 9.20 to EUR 8.50. Therefore, any shares sold through the double-speed range accrual instrument were sold at a 15% discount to the initial price. A second objective was to expand the ranges in which shares accrued. Under the one-speed range accrual, ABC's stock price had to trade below USD 10.80 to accrue some shares on an observation day. Under the two-speed range accrual, ABC's stock price had to trade above USD 11.50 to accrue some shares on an observation day. However, these two

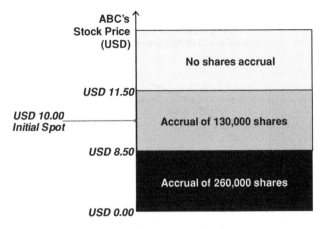

Figure 10.11 Two-speed range accrual, daily accrual mechanism.

objectives were achieved in exchange for including a middle range in which just 130,000 shares accrued.

The mechanics of the double-speed range accrual are similar to the one-speed range accrual. The only difference lies in the daily accrual mechanism. As we saw earlier, the 12-month term of the transaction was divided into 12 monthly periods (the "accrual periods"). On each trading day of the accrual period, the number of shares accruing that day was a function of the closing price of ABC's stock on that day (see Figure 10.11):

- If the stock closing price was lower than the USD 8.50 strike price, 260,000 shares accrued that day.
- If the stock closing price was lower than, or equal to, the EUR 11.50 barrier and greater than, or equal to, the USD 8.50 strike price, 130,000 shares accrued that day.
- If the stock closing price was greater than the USD 11.50 barrier, no shares accrued that day.

At the end of each monthly period, the accrued shares were bought by ABC from Gigabank at the USD 8.50 strike price.

Comparison to the One-speed Range Accrual

If we compare the two-speed range accrual with the one-speed range accrual, the performance of one strategy relative to the other depends on ABC's stock price behavior:

- In a very weak stock market from start, the two-speed range accrual is likely to outperform. Although a similar number of shares would be accrued under both instruments, however, the shares bought under the two-speed range accrual would be acquired at USD 8.50 instead of at USD 9.20.
- In moderately positive, or moderately negative, stock market behaviors, the one-speed range accrual is likely to outperform. A much larger number of shares are likely to accrue under the one-speed range accrual. The fact that the shares are bought at a higher price than in the two-speed version will be more than compensated by the larger number of shares bought.

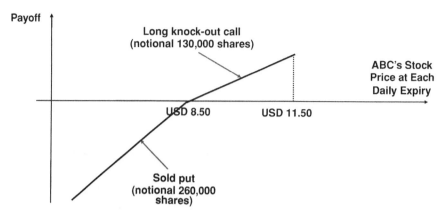

Figure 10.12   Two-speed range accrual, building blocks of the transaction.

- In a notably strong market from the beginning, the two-speed range accrual is likely to outperform as it will take longer to reach the barrier level.

Building Blocks

From ABC's viewpoint, the two-speed range accrual was built by combining a purchased knock-out call and a short put. Each trading day over the term of the range accrual, a combination expired on such day, as follows (see Figure 10.12):

- ABC sold a string of put options with strike price USD 8.50 on 260,000 ABC shares. There was a put for each trading day of the 12-month period (i.e., 250 puts). In other words, only one put expired on each day of the 12-month period.
- ABC bought a string of call options with strike ABC 8.50 on 130,000 XYZ shares. There was a call for each trading day of the 12-month period (i.e., 250 calls). In other words, only one call expired on each day of the 12-month period. Each call ceased to exist if, on its expiry date, ABC's stock price was above the USD 11.50 barrier. Therefore, this option was a knock-out call.

10.10.3   Double-speed Range Accrual with Final Put

Another popular version of the range accrual instrument is a range accrual with a final put. Let us take the previous section's two-speed range accrual. This range accrual had a strike price set at USD 8.50 (a 15% discount to the initial price) and a barrier at USD 11.50. By including the sale of a put and maintaining the barrier unchanged, the strike price could be set at USD 8.20 (an 18% discount to the initial price). The put gave Gigabank the right, but not the obligation, to sell at maturity at the strike price all the unaccrued (and thus unsold) shares during the 12-month tenor of the instrument.

 As an example, let us assume that out of the maximum 62.5 million shares, ABC bought 42.5 million shares through the accrual process during its 12-month duration. At maturity, Gigabank had the right to sell to ABC 20 million (= 62.5 million – 42.5 million) shares at USD 8.20. Therefore:

- If, at maturity, ABC's stock price was lower than USD 8.20, Gigabank would exercise the put and ABC would buy from the bank 20 million shares at USD 8.20. ABC would then have bought all its target 62.5 million ABC shares.
- If, at maturity, ABC's stock price was greater than, or equal to, USD 8.20, Gigabank would not exercise the call. Then, ABC would need to acquire 20 million own shares in the market.

The improvement in strike price caused by the inclusion of the put, from a 15% discount to an 18% discount, was not very large. Why didn't it result in a lower strike price? This was because a stock price at maturity well below the USD 9.20 strike price would likely mean that the daily accrual mechanism accrued 260,000 shares for many days. Therefore, if the put was exercised at maturity, the number of unaccrued shares would likely be low.

10.11   OTHER TRANSACTIONS ON TREASURY SHARES

10.11.1   Case Study: ABC's Restructuring of Call on Own Shares

In October 20X1 ABC, a European entity, was considering the exercise of a call option on its own shares that allowed for physical settlement only. The option type was American allowing ABC to exercise the call at any time. The call was purchased in February 20X1 by ABC from Weakbank to take advantage of its low share price. ABC paid a EUR 30 million premium. The call allowed ABC to acquire 70 million of its own shares, representing 7% of ABC's share capital. The expiration date of the American call was 15 April 20X3 and its strike price was EUR 5.00 per share.

In October 20X1, Weakbank's credit rating was downgraded several notches by Moody's and ABC was worried that Weakbank might not be able to meet its obligations under the call. An early exercise was considered, but ABC already owned 8% of its share capital, making the exercise of the call not feasible because it would cause ABC to exceed its 10% legal limit on treasury shares. ABC considered other alternatives, including:

1. To exercise Weakbank's call receiving the underlying shares in exchange for its strike amount, to immediately sell the purchased shares to a third bank and simultaneously to enter into a call option with this third bank with the same terms as the old call. This was the simplest solution. However, it would cause ABC to exceed the 10% legal limit on treasury shares, although temporarily. In most jurisdictions there is a period in which a company can exceed the maximum legal limit on treasury shares. In this case, ABC could not legally implement this solution. Besides, the size of the option was too large relative to ABC's stock daily average volume, making its risk management too risky.
2. To wait until 15 April 20X3, the call expiration date, to exercise the call. This alternative was not pursued because ABC was afraid that Weakbank could go bust.
3. To sell back the call option to Weakbank (i.e., to unwind the transaction). However, the quote received from Weakbank was unattractive as it wanted to avoid making any large cash payments.
4. To sell the call to a third party. ABC contacted Gigabank to explore this alternative. However, this alternative faced three major constraints that made it unfeasible:
   - The size of the option was too large relative to ABC's stock daily average volume, making its risk management too risky.

- The third party buyer would be exposed to Weakbank's credit risk unless the underlying ABC shares held by Weakbank could be pledged in favour of Gigabank.
5. To execute the strategy described next.

Transaction Implemented by ABC

ABC implemented a transaction split into the following components (see Figure 10.13):

1. ABC sold 5% of its share capital (50 million shares) to Gigabank. In exchange, ABC received from Gigabank the market value of the shares, or EUR 450 million (= 50 mn × 9.00). Gigabank was entitled to receive dividends and to exercise the voting rights attached to the shares.

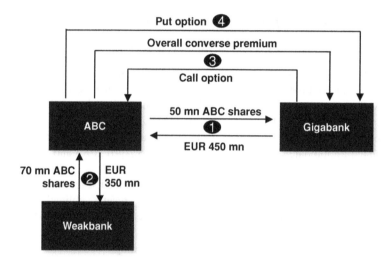

Figure 10.13 ABC's transaction on own shares, flows at inception.

2. ABC exercised Weakbank's call option. Consequently, ABC acquired 70 million ABC shares from Weakbank paying the EUR 350 million (= 70 mn × 5.00) strike amount. Therefore, ABC owned 10% of its share capital, the maximum legal.
3. ABC acquired from Gigabank an American call option on 50 million ABC shares with a strike price of EUR 9.00. The call expiration date was 15 April 20X3. The call could be exercised by ABC at any time up to its expiration date. Upon exercise, ABC could elect between cash and physical settlement.
4. ABC sold to Gigabank a European put on 50 million ABC shares with a strike price of EUR 9.00. The put expiration date was 15 April 20X3. The put option could only be exercised on the expiration date. However, the put would be automatically exercised if the call option was exercised by ABC. Upon exercise, ABC could elect between cash and physical settlement.

The combination of the call and the put described in 3) and 4) was a "converse", making sure that at least one of the two options would be exercised. ABC paid to Gigabank a EUR 10 million premium.

Flows upon Exercise

If on exercise date, ABC's share price were above the EUR 9.00 strike price, ABC would exercise the call. The put would automatically expire worthless. Remember that ABC could elect between cash and cash settlement.

- If ABC had the legal authorization to acquire the 50 million ABC shares, ABC would elect physical settlement. Consequently, ABC would acquire from Gigabank 50 million ABC shares and would pay to Gigabank EUR 450 million (= 50 million × 9.00). Therefore, ABC would have acquired 5% of its own share capital.
- If ABC did not have the legal authorization to acquire the 50 million own shares, it would elect cash settlement. Gigabank would then gradually sell the underlying 50 million ABC shares in the market. ABC would receive the difference between the disposal proceeds and the EUR 450 million strike amount. Due to the large period required for the shares disposal, it may cause the disposal proceeds to be lower than the EUR 450 million strike amount. In this case, ABC would pay to Gigabank the difference between those amounts.

If on exercise date ABC's share price were trading below the EUR 9.00 strike price, Gigabank would exercise the put. The call would expire worthless. In this case, ABC would elect between physical and cash settlement. The effects are identical to the two settlement scenarios analyzed when the call was exercised.

Therefore, if ABC elected physical settlement ABC would be acquiring 5% of its own capital at EUR 9.00 per share. If ABC elected cash settlement, ABC would be either receiving or paying the difference between the disposal proceeds and the strike amount.

ABC's Overall Position under the Transaction

From a credit risk point of view, ABC was exposed to Gigabank under the call. If upon exercise ABC's share price was above the EUR 9.00 strike price and ABC chose cash settlement, Gigabank would be required to pay the appreciation of the underlying shares above the EUR 450 million strike amount. ABC could have avoided being exposed to Gigabank by having the bank pledge the underlying shares to ABC. In this case, if Gigabank did not meet its obligations, ABC would take ownership of the pledged shares.

Also from a credit risk standpoint, ABC was exposed to Weakbank until the settlement of the call. This exposure lasted very shortly because ABC exercised Weakbank's call immediately.

From a market risk point of view, ABC was exposed under the put to a fall in its share price below the EUR 9.00 strike price. Conversely, ABC benefited under the call from a share price above the EUR 9.00 strike price. Therefore, ignoring upfront premiums, ABC's position was identical to having bought the underlying shares (see Figure 10.14). In other words, the position from a market risk viewpoint was equivalent to having partially exercised Weakbank's call for 50 million options.

From a cash point of view, ABC's position at inception was positive (see Figure 10.13). ABC paid EUR 350 million to Weakbank, ABC received EUR 450 million from the share sale to Gigabank and ABC paid a EUR 10 premium to Gigabank to enter into the converse. Therefore, combining the two share trades and the converse transaction ABC received EUR 90 million (= 450 mn − 350 mn − 10 mn) in cash.

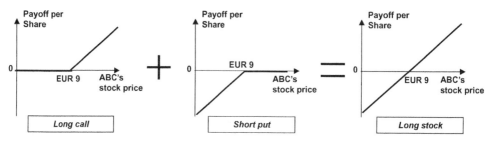

Figure 10.14   ABC's overall market risk position.

Gigabank' Overall Position under the Transaction

From a credit risk point of view Gigabank was exposed to ABC under the put. If upon exercise ABC's share price was below EUR 9.00 strike price and in case of cash settlement, ABC would be required to pay the depreciation of the underlying shares below the EUR 450 million strike amount. In case of physical settlement, ABC would be required to pay the EUR 450 million strike amount. Gigabank could have reduced its exposure to ABC by having the company post cash collateral to Gigabank. In this case, if ABC did not meet its obligations, Gigabank would take ownership of the cash collateral.

Gigabank could have mitigated the credit risk to ABC by structuring the transaction as a pre-paid forward whereby ABC would pay upfront the forward amount. This transaction is equivalent to a collateralized call and put combination in which ABC posts the whole strike amount as collateral to the transaction.

From a market risk point of view, Gigabank' position was neutral (see Figure 10.15). By owning the underlying shares, Gigabank was exposed to a fall in its share price below the EUR

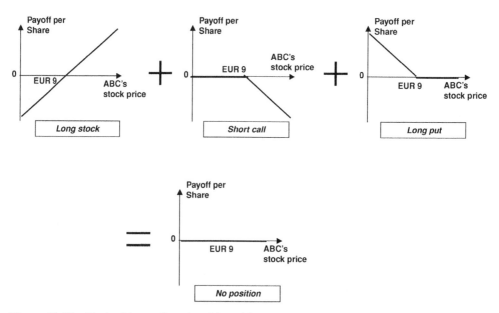

Figure 10.15   Gigabank' overall market risk position.

9.00 acquisition price and participated in the appreciation of the shares above EUR 9.00. This position was fully offset by its exposure to ABC's stock price under the combination of the sold call and the bought put. Under the call Gigabank was exposed to a stock price above the EUR 9.00 strike price. Under the put, Gigabank benefited from a stock price below the EUR 9.00 strike price. Therefore, overall Gigabank was not exposed to ABC's share price.

From a cash point of view, Gigabank's position at inception was negative (see Figure 10.13). By buying the converse underlying shares from ABC, Gigabank had to pay to ABC EUR 450 million. Gigabank received EUR 10 million linked to the converse. As a result, Gigabank had to finance EUR 440 million ($= 450$ mn $- 10$ mn).

Legal Considerations

Derivative transactions on treasury shares are a delicate matter. Before signing the agreements, Gigabank had to validate ABC's legal ability to enter into the transaction. To validate it, the transaction legal advisors had to review ABC's articles of association, the approved resolutions of ABC's AGMs/EGMs and the legal rules on treasury shares in ABC's jurisdiction.

Gigabank's initial acquisition of 50 million ABC shares at inception to hedge its market exposure under the converse made it the beneficial owner of the shares. As such, Gigabank was entitled to receive the dividends distributed to the shares and to vote the attached voting rights. However, Gigabank was not exposed to ABC's stock price. In contrast, ABC's overall position was equivalent to a holding of 150 million own shares (100 million shares directly and 50 million under the converse). If ABC held 150 million treasury shares, ABC's shareholders would be entitled to receive the pro rata share of the dividends that in theory corresponded to them and ABC would not be entitled to exercise their attached voting rights. Therefore, if ABC did not receive back from Gigabank any distributed dividends to the shares or if Gigabank exercised its voting rights in a non-neutral way, ABC's other shareholders could be at a disadvantage.

In order to have Gigabank paying back the dividends to ABC, several alternatives could be implemented:

- To have Gigabank to pay back to ABC any dividends received. Under this alternative Gigabank would pay to ABC an amount equal to the product of (i) the strategy delta, (ii) the number of shares and (iii) the dividend per share received by Gigabank. In this case, the strategy delta was 100% at all times;
- To adjust downwards the strikes of the call and the put for any dividends received by Gigabank, and to simultaneously adjust upwards the number of options; or
- To assume a dividend string during the life of the options and to adjust either downwards or upwards the strikes of the call and the put (and their number of options) for any deviation of the realized dividends relative to the assumed dividends. Under this alternative, the premium of the call to be paid by ABC at inception had to be take into account the present value of the assumed dividends.

In order to have Gigabank voting rights a neutral effect in any of ABC's AGMs or EGMs during the life of the transaction, two alternatives could be implemented:

- To not enable Gigabank to exercise its voting rights attached to the shares. In my view, this the most neutral position from a shareholder point of view, if there is enough quorum to vote a certain proposal brought to an AGM/EGM;

- To have Gigabank to do its outmost to participate at any AGM or EGM taking place during the life of the options and to exercise its voting right by voting in favour of the strategic corporate proposals (e.g., the disposal of an asset) submitted and recommended by ABC's board of directors except if Gigabank believed that it was clearly against the interest of the shareholders and voting in favour could trigger shareholder liability of Gigabank. For non strategic matters (e.g., the approval of ABC's financial statements), to have Gigabank to vote in favour or against the proposal at its own discretion. The parties would need to define what matters are considered to be strategic matters. In my view, under this alternative Gigabank may face a conflict of interest if an attractive resolution for the shareholders that has been previously rejected by the board of directors is voted. Gigabank could be afraid of jeopardizing a strong relationship if it votes in favour.

Another important legal element of the transaction was to restrict Gigabank from selling, except as provided for in the call and put agreements, or lending the shares during the life of the options unless an event of default was triggered. This restriction assured ABC that the shares would not be used by other market participants to implement short positions in the stock or to exercise the shares' voting rights.

In this type of transactions it is common to include a clause in the terms and conditions that protects each party from the other party not meeting its legal disclosure requirements. In this case, Gigabank had to disclose to the stock market regulator the ownership of 5% of ABC's share capital. Regarding ABC's disclosure of the converse, it is usually a grey area. In M&A situations, the parties usually try to avoid disclosing this sort of transactions. In our case, it made sense to disclose the converse transaction. Its disclosure would help investors and research analysts to obtain a better picture of ABC's prospects.

Accounting Considerations

ABC reported under IFRS rules. At inception, the transaction had a positive effect on ABC's equity but it also made ABC's income statement to be exposed to ABC's share price.

Before the transaction, ABC was long Weakbank's call on its own shares. Because the call only allowed for physical settlement, it was treated from an accounting perspective as an equity instrument. As such, the fair value of the option at its inception (i.e., its EUR 30 million premium) was recognized in equity, reducing ABC shareholders' equity. Additionally, ABC held 80 million own shares at a cost of EUR 560 million (assuming that ABC purchased those shares at an average acquisition price of EUR 7.00 per share), which reduced ABC's equity by this amount. Therefore, before the transaction ABC's equity presented a deduction of EUR 590 million (= 30 mn + 560 mn).

The effects of the transaction were the following:

- The sale of 50 million treasury shares to Gigabank at EUR 9.00 each, increased ABC's equity by EUR 450 million.
- The exercise of Weakbank's call released its original EUR 30 million deduction from equity. However, its exercise caused the acquisition of 70 million own shares at EUR 5.00 each, reducing ABC's equity by EUR 350 million. Thus, the overall negative effect on ABC's equity of the call exercise was a reduction in equity of EUR 320 million (= 350 mn − 30 mn).
- The converse allowed for the election between physical and cash settlement. This provision caused the converse to be treated as a derivative. Thus, ABC was obliged during the life of

the converse to fair value it and to recognize the change in fair value in the profit or loss statement. Any increase in the value of its own shares from the previous financial reporting date implied a gain, and conversely, any decrease in the value of its own shares from the previous measurement implied a loss.

As a result of the transaction, ABC released EUR 130 million ($= 450$ mn $- 320$ mn) from equity. However, the fair valuing of the converse through profit or loss could increase the volatility of ABC's income statement.

ABC could have avoided the recognition of the converse as a derivative if its options allowed for physical settlement only. This potential solution faced three constraints: (i) the combination of the two instruments could be legally characterized as treasury shares, (ii) ABC wanted to be able to cash settle the transaction in case it did not have the legal permission or the resources to buy back the underlying shares and (iii) from an IFRS point of view, it would require ABC to recognize a liability due to ABC's potential obligation to deliver cash were Gigabank to exercise the put.

10.11.2   Case Study: Gilead's Share Repurchase Program Financed with Convertible Bonds

This real-life case highlights how a company combined a share repurchase program with the issuance of two convertible bonds. The case also shows how Gilead entered into two call spread transactions to reduce the potential dilution of Gilead's common stock upon future conversion of the convertible bonds.

In May 2010 Gilead Sciences Inc. ("Gilead"), a US-based drug maker, announced that its board of directors had authorized a new USD 5 billion share repurchase program through the next three years (i.e., until May 2013), following the completion of a USD 1 billion share buyback program initiated in January 2010. In a statement, Gilead's chairman and chief executive officer, John Martin, said: "Gilead's board of directors and senior management team believe that the stock repurchase program announced today represents an appropriate and strategic use of the company's cash, while allowing sufficient flexibility for other expenditures going forward, including investments in research and development and licensing or partnership opportunities".

On 30 July 2010, Gilead issued a USD 1.1 billion principal amount convertible senior bond due 1 May 2014. The convertible bond had an initial conversion price of USD 45.04 per share (a 35% conversion premium over the USD 33.39 closing price of Gilead's stock on the day prior to the issue date). The bond paid a semiannual coupon of 1% and could be converted into 24.4 million shares of Gilead's common stock. Simultaneously, Gilead issued another USD 1.1 billion principal amount convertible senior bond, due 1 May 2016. The convertible bond had an initial conversion price of USD 45.41 per share (a 36% conversion premium). The bond paid a semiannual coupon of 1.625% and could be converted into 24.2 million shares of Gilead's common stock. Upon conversion, the bond holders of both convertibles would receive cash up to the principal amount, and any excess conversion value would be settled, at Gilead's election, in cash, common stock or a combination of cash and common stock. Gilead expected to use at least USD 1 billion of the net proceeds from the offerings to repurchase shares of its common stock. The remaining proceeds from the offering were added to Gilead's working capital and were used for general corporate purposes, including additional repurchases of its common stock, and repayment of Gilead's existing indebtedness. The total commission paid to the banks involved in the placement totaled USD 33 million.

In connection with the sale of the convertible bonds, Gilead entered into two call spread transactions with JP Morgan and Goldman Sachs to reduce the potential dilution of Gilead's common stock upon future conversion of the bonds. Gilead acquired the call options embedded in the convertible bonds and sold call warrants to the two investment banks. The bought call option associated with the 2014 convertible had 24.4 million underlying shares, an initial USD 45.04 strike price and a 1 May 2014 expiration date. The bought call option associated with the 2016 convertible had 24.2 million underlying shares, an initial USD 45.41 strike price and expiry in May 2016. The call warrants associated with the 2014 bond had an exercise price of USD 56.762, which was 70% higher than the USD 33.39 closing price of Gilead's stock on the day prior to the issue date, and covered 24.4 million shares. The call warrants associated with the 2016 bond had an exercise price of USD 60.102, which was 80% higher than the USD 33.39 closing price of Gilead's stock on the day prior to the issue date, and covered 24.2 million shares. Gilead paid for the purchased calls an aggregate amount of USD 311.8 million of the proceeds from the sale of the convertible bonds. Gilead received on aggregate a premium of USD 132.5 million from the sale of the warrants.

Figure 10.16 shows the building blocks of the transaction. It can be inferred that the total proceeds from the convertible bond issues and the call spreads were USD 1.988 billion (2,200 million – 312 million + 133 million – 33 million).

To show the flows at maturity, or upon early conversion, I will only cover the 2014 bond. The reasoning for the 2016 bond is similar. There were three potential scenarios:

1. If Gilead's stock price was lower than, or equal to, the USD 45.04 conversion price:
   • The bond holders would not exercise their conversion right. The convertible bond would be redeemed at par, requiring Gilead to pay USD 1.1 billion.
   • Both the purchased call and the sold call warrants would expire worthless.

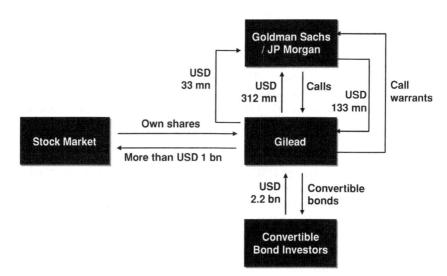

Figure 10.16   Building blocks of Gilead's transaction.

2. If Gilead's stock price was greater than the USD 45.04 conversion price and lower than, or equal to, the warrants' USD 56.762 strike price:
   - The bond holders would exercise their conversion right. Gilead would pay USD 1.1 billion plus the excess conversion value. Gilead would then choose between paying the conversion value in cash or in shares.
   - Gilead would exercise the purchased call. The call would be settled in an identical way to the settlement of the convertible's excess conversion value.
   - The sold call warrants would expire worthless.
3. If Gilead's stock price was greater than the warrants' USD 56.762 strike price:
   - The bond holders would exercise their conversion right. Gilead would pay USD 1.1 billion plus the excess conversion value. Gilead would then choose between paying the conversion value in cash or in shares.
   - Gilead would exercise the purchased call. The call would be settled in an identical way to the settlement of the convertible's excess conversion value.
   - The call warrants' holders would exercise their right.

Final Comments

The acquisition of own shares financed with the issuance of convertible debt is a quick way to leverage the capital structure of the company. In some jurisdictions, it can also be attractive from a tax viewpoint. Interest on the debt is usually tax deductible, while profits on own shares can be tax free in some countries.

In my view, the transaction had two main strengths. Firstly, it allowed Gilead to partially finance the share repurchase, with a low financial cost. Secondly, it allowed Gilead to lock in large profits if the warrants were exercised. As an example, let us assume that Gilead bought back own shares at an average price equal to the USD 33.39 stock price prevailing at inception. An exercise of the call warrants would imply selling the stock at 56.762 (or USD 60.102), a substantial profit. However, it would mean that Gilead had to keep in its balance sheet an equivalent number of shares.

The banks (Goldman Sachs and JP Morgan) selling the call spread needed to acquire shares in the market at inception of the transaction. This buying activity was partially offset by the initial selling from the convertible bond holders. However, if there was a net buying activity, Gilead had to be careful to avoid buying own shares while the two banks put in place their initial hedge. Otherwise, share price could be driven up unnecessarily.

11

Bank Regulatory Capital

This chapter provides a detailed understanding of the calculation of bank regulatory capital. Without such understanding, it would be difficult for a strategic equity practitioner to assess the merits or weaknesses of a specific transaction. At the time of writing this chapter, the Basel III framework had just been released and the regulatory treatment of some items was still undefined. Please refer to the full text of the proposal for further details. Strategic equity transactions can be devised to:

- Enhance the capital eligibility of financial instruments.
- Reduce the impact of deduction from capital of a specific item.
- And/or, reduce the capital consumption of a specific asset.

11.1 AN OVERVIEW OF BASEL III

11.1.1 Precedent Bank Regulatory Capital Accords

In this section I will cover a brief story of the Basel accords (see Figure 11.1). During the financial crises of the 1970s and 1980s, the large banks depleted their capital levels. In 1988, the Basel Supervisors Committee intended, through the Basel Accord, to establish capital requirements aimed at protecting depositors from undue bank and systemic risk. The Accord, Basel I, provided uniform definitions for capital as well as minimum capital adequacy levels based on the riskiness of assets (a minimum of 4% for Tier 1 capital, which was mainly equity less goodwill, and 8% for the sum of Tier 1 capital and Tier 2 capital). Basel I risk measurements related almost entirely to credit risk, perceived to be the main risk incurred by banks. Capital regulations under Basel I came into effect in December 1992, after development and consultations since 1988. Basel I was amended in 1996 to introduce capital requirements to address market risk in banks' trading books.

In 2004, banking regulators worked on a new version of the Basel accord, as Basel I was not sufficiently sensitive in measuring risk exposures. In July 2006, the Basel Committee on

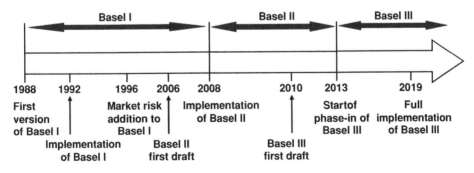

Figure 11.1 Bank regulatory capital accords.

Banking Supervision published the "International Convergence of Capital Measurement and Capital Standards", known as Basel II, which replaced Basel I. The supervisory objectives for Basel II were to (i) promote safety and soundness in the financial system and maintain a certain overall level of capital in the system, (ii) enhance competitive equality, (iii) constitute a more comprehensive approach to measuring risk exposures and (iv) focus on internationally active banks.

Basel II was built around three "pillars":

- **Pillar 1**, called "**Minimum Capital Requirements**", established the minimum amount of capital that a bank should have against its credit, market and operational risks. It provided the methodology for calculating the risk exposures in the assets of a bank's balance sheet (the "risk-weighted assets"). The capital ratio was calculated using the definition of regulatory capital and risk-weighted assets. In this chapter I will be focusing only on Pillar I.
- **Pillar 2**, called "**Supervisory Review and Evaluation Process**", involved both banks and regulators taking a view on whether a firm should hold additional capital against risks not covered in Pillar 1. Part of the Pillar 2 process was the "Internal Capital Adequacy Assessment Process" (ICAAP), which was the bank's self-assessment of risks not captured by Pillar 1.
- **Pillar 3**, called "**Market Discipline**", was related to market discipline and aimed to make firms more transparent by requiring them to disclosure specific, prescribed details of their risks, capital and risk management.

The unprecedented nature of the 2007–2008 financial crisis obliged the Basel Committee on Banking Supervision (BCBS) to propose an amendment to Basel II, commonly called Basel III. The new standards were to be implemented in 2013. At the heart of the new framework were more stringent capital requirements, as well as the introduction of liquidity rules.

The Capital Requirements Directive (CRD) implements Basel III in the EU and the national banking regulators then give effect to the CRD by including the requirements of the CRD in their own rulebooks. Beware that some changes to the general framework may be accepted by the CRD. The national regulators of the bank supervise it on a consolidated basis and therefore receive information on the capital adequacy of, and set capital requirements for, the bank as a whole. Individual banking subsidiaries are directly regulated by their local banking regulators, who set and monitor their capital adequacy requirements. In the United Kingdom, the banking regulator is the Financial Services Authority (FSA). In the United States, bank holding companies are regulated by the Board of Governors of the Federal Reserve System (the "Federal Reserve Board").

11.1.2   The Capital Ratio

For each category of regulatory capital (common equity, total Tier 1, Tier 2 capital) the Basel III accord sets a minimum requirement. In other words, for each category of regulatory capital the corresponding capital ratio of a bank has to be larger than, or equal to, a required minimum. The capital ratio is calculated as follows:

$$\text{Capital Ratio} = \frac{\text{Amount of capital}}{\text{Risk-weighted assets}} = \sigma_R = 100 \times \sqrt{\frac{252 \times \sum_{i=1}^{N} \left(Ln\frac{P_i}{P_{i-1}} \right)^2}{N}}$$

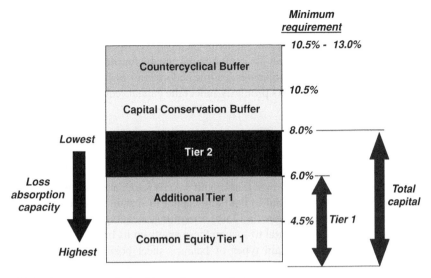

Figure 11.2   Components of a bank's regulatory capital.

11.1.3   Bank Regulatory Capital

According to Basel III, a bank's regulatory capital is divided into several categories or tiers of capital (see Figure 11.2): common equity Tier 1, additional Tier 1 capital, Tier 2 capital and two additional capital buffers. These categories try to group constituents of capital depending on their degree of permanence and loss absorbency.

Tier 1 capital is so-called because it is the best quality capital from the regulator's perspective. It includes (i) permanent shareholders' equity, referred to as **common equity Tier 1 capital**, and (ii) some instruments with ability to absorb losses, referred to as **additional Tier 1 capital**. Tier 1 capital is aimed at absorbing losses, helping banks to "**remain going concerns**" (i.e., to remain solvent). **Tier 2 capital**, a capital with less loss absorption capability, is aimed at providing loss absorption on a "**gone concern**" basis (i.e., in case of insolvency of the bank) to protect depositors. The sum of Tier 1 and Tier 2 capital is called "total capital".

In addition to Tier 1 and Tier 2 capital there are two other categories of capital. The **capital conservation buffer** is designed to provide banks with an extra source of capital to draw on during times of financial and/or economic stress. The **countercyclical buffer** is designed to protect the bank from periods of excess aggregate credit growth.

11.1.4   Risk-weighted Assets

The risk-weighted assets (RWAs) are a bank's assets and off-balance sheet items that carry credit, market, operational and/or non-counterparty risk:

- **Market risk RWAs** reflect the capital requirements of potential changes in the fair values of financial instruments in response to market movements inherent in both the balance sheet and the off-balance sheet items.

- **Credit risk RWAs** reflect the capital requirements for the possibility of a loss being incurred as the result of a borrower or counterparty failing to meet its financial obligations or as a result of deterioration in the credit quality of the borrower or counterparty.
- **Operational risk RWAs** reflect the capital requirements for the risk of loss resulting from inadequate or failed internal processes, people and systems or from external events.
- **Non-counterparty risk RWAs** primarily reflect the capital requirements for premises and equipment.

RWAs are computed by adjusting each asset and off-balance sheet item for risk in order to determine a bank's real exposure to potential losses. Some assets are assigned a higher risk than others. For example, government bonds with a AAA rating are assigned a 0% weighting, meaning that a bank does not need to hold any capital to sustain these assets on its balance sheet. The riskiest assets are assigned a 1250% weighting, meaning that a bank would need to hold a substantial amount of capital to sustain these assets on its balance sheet.

Figure 11.3 illustrates the main types of balance sheet position and off-balance sheet exposure that translate into market, credit, operational and non-counterparty risk RWAs of Credit Suisse under Basel II as of 2Q2010 (in CHF billion). RWAs totalled 233 billion, while the total assets on Credit Suisse's balance sheet totalled 1,138 billion.

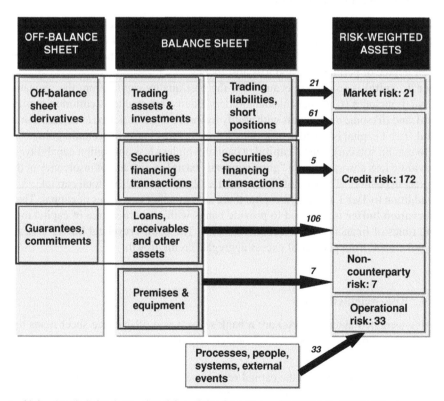

Figure 11.3   Credit Suisse's Basel II risk-weighted assets as of 2Q2010 (in CHF billion).

Banking Book vs. Trading Book

Banking operations are categorized as either banking book or trading book, and risk-weighted assets are determined accordingly. Each national regulator determines which assets are part of the trading and banking books. The regulatory definition of trading book and banking book assets generally parallels the definition of trading (i.e., assets at fair value through profit and loss) and non-trading assets under IFRS/US GAAP. However, due to specific differences between the regulatory and accounting framework, certain assets may be classified as trading book for market risk reporting purposes even though they are non-trading assets under IFRS/US GAAP. Conversely, a bank may also have assets that are assigned to the banking book even though they are trading assets under IFRS/US GAAP.

Banking book RWAs are measured by means of a hierarchy of risk weightings classified according to the nature of each asset and counterparty, taking into account any eligible collateral or guarantees. Banking book off-balance sheet items giving rise to credit, foreign exchange or interest rate risk are assigned weights appropriate to the category of the counterparty, taking into account any eligible collateral or guarantees.

Trading book RWAs are determined by taking into account market-related risks such as foreign exchange, interest rate and equity position risks and counterparty risk. Under Basel II the model used to determine the trading book RWAs was Value-at-Risk (VaR) based, with a multiplier applied by the regulator. Its output was typically for modest absolute RWA requirements. Figure 11.3 shows that Credit Suisse's RWAs for market risk were only CHF 21 billion, less than 10% of the bank's overall RWAs. The problems with this methodology were twofold: first, VaR is not a stress-loss predictor, so building a capital requirement (inherently the unexpected loss cushion) from VaR can run the risk of miscalibrating; second, the models and/or the multiplier were too optimistic, so large banks with large volatile trading books ended up holding too little regulatory capital against their trading books.

11.2   TIER 1 CAPITAL

The objective of Tier 1 capital is to absorb losses and help banks to remain going concerns (i.e., to prevent failures). There are two layers of Tier 1 capital:

- Common equity Tier 1 capital.
- Additional Tier 1 capital.

11.2.1   Common Equity Tier 1 Capital

The common equity component of Tier 1 capital, also referred to as "core Tier 1 capital" or "core equity capital", is considered the highest form of loss absorbing capital. It consists of common stock (i.e., common shares) plus reserves less some deductions. Other instruments can be included which are deemed fully equivalent to common stock in terms of their capital quality as regards loss absorption and do not possess features which could cause the condition of the bank to be weakened as a going concern during periods of market stress. For example, in the rare cases where a bank issued non-voting common shares, to be included in the common equity component of Tier 1 capital, they must be identical to voting common shares of the issuing bank in all respects except the absence of voting rights.

The criteria also apply to financial institutions, such as mutual, cooperative or saving banks, that do not issue common shares. Taking into account their specific constitution and legal

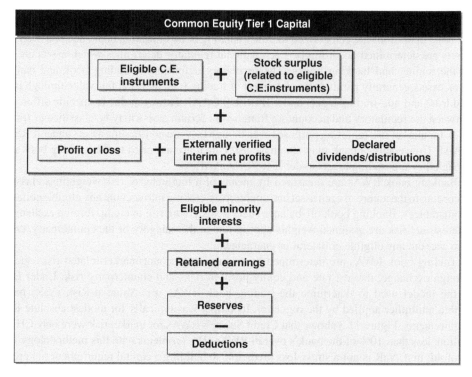

Figure 11.4 Major components in the calculation of common equity Tier 1 capital.

structure, the national supervisors apply the criteria preserving the quality of the instruments to be included in the common equity component of Tier 1 capital by requiring that the eligible instruments are deemed fully equivalent to common shares in terms of their capital quality as regards loss absorption and do not possess features which could cause the condition of the bank to be weakened as a going concern during periods of market stress.

Figure 11.4 illustrates the major components in the calculation of common equity Tier 1 capital.

Criteria Governing Instruments' Inclusion in the Common Equity Component of Tier 1

For an instrument to be included in the common equity capital, the predominant form of Tier 1 capital, it must meet all of the following criteria:

1. Represents the most subordinated claim in liquidation of the bank.
2. Entitled to a claim of the residual assets that is proportional with its share of issued capital, after all senior claims have been repaid in liquidation (i.e., has an unlimited and variable claim, not a fixed or capped claim).
3. Principal is perpetual and never repaid outside of liquidation (setting aside discretionary repurchases or other means of effectively reducing capital in a discretionary manner that is allowable under national law).

4. The bank does nothing to create an expectation at issuance that the instrument will be bought back, redeemed or cancelled nor do the statutory or contractual terms provide any feature which might give rise to such an expectation. This criterion does not oppose banks being market makers in their own shares.

5. Distributions (i.e., dividends and coupons) are paid out of distributable items (retained earnings included). The level of distributions is not in any way tied or linked to the amount paid in at issuance and is not subject to a cap (except to the extent that a bank is unable to pay distributions that exceed the level of distributable items).

6. There are no circumstances under which the distributions are obligatory. Non-payment is therefore not an event of default.

7. Distributions are paid only after all legal and contractual obligations have been met and payments on more senior capital instruments have been made. This means that there are no preferential distributions, including in respect of other elements classified as the highest quality issued capital.

8. It is the issued capital that takes the first and proportionately greatest share of any losses as they occur. Within the highest quality capital, each instrument absorbs losses on a going concern basis proportionately and pari passu with all the others.

9. The paid in amount is recognized as equity capital (i.e., not recognized as a liability) for determining balance sheet insolvency.

10. The paid-in amount is classified as equity under the relevant accounting standards.

11. It is directly issued and paid-up, and the bank cannot directly or indirectly have funded the purchase of the instrument.

12. The paid-in amount is neither secured nor covered by a guarantee of the issuer or related entity or subject to any other arrangement that legally or economically enhances the seniority of the claim.

13. It is only issued with the approval of the owners of the issuing bank, either given directly by the owners or, if permitted by applicable law, given by the board of directors or by other persons duly authorized by the owners.

14. It is clearly and separately disclosed on the bank's balance sheet.

Stock Surplus

Stock surplus (i.e., share premium) is only permitted to be included in the common equity component of Tier 1 if the shares giving rise to the stock surplus are also permitted to be included in the common equity component of Tier 1.

Banks should not be given credit in the common equity component of Tier 1 when they issue shares outside the common equity component of Tier 1 which have a low nominal value and high stock surplus. In this sense the proposal ensures that there is no loophole for including instruments other than common shares in the common equity component of Tier 1.

Minority Interests

Minority interests arise in many situations, for example the use of local partners or the partial flotation of locally incorporated subsidiaries. Under Basel III, minority interests are not fully eligible for inclusion in the common equity component of Tier 1 capital. Although minority interest absorbs losses within the subsidiary to which it relates, this exclusion is based on the premise that this capital is not fully available to support risks in the group as a whole, and that it may represent an interest in a subsidiary with little or no risk. Basel III requires the excess capital above the minimum capital requirement of a subsidiary that is a bank to be deducted in proportion to the minority interest share. This treatment is strictly available where all minority investments in the bank subsidiary solely represent genuine third-party common equity contributions to the subsidiary.

Minority interests arising from the issue of an instrument by a fully consolidated subsidiary of the bank may receive recognition in common equity Tier 1 only if:

- The instrument giving rise to the minority interest would, if issued by the bank, meet the criteria for classification as common equity Tier 1 capital.
- The subsidiary that issued the instrument is itself a bank. Any institution that is subject to the same minimum prudential standards and level of supervision as a bank may be considered a bank.
- And, the parent bank or affiliate has not entered into any arrangements to fund directly or indirectly minority investment in the subsidiary whether through an SPV or through another vehicle or arrangement.

The amount of minority interest meeting the criteria above that can be recognized is determined as follows:

- Total minority interests meeting the criteria above minus the amount of the surplus common equity Tier 1 of the subsidiary attributable to the minority shareholders.
- Surplus common equity Tier 1 of the subsidiary is calculated as the common equity Tier 1 of the subsidiary minus the lower of: (1) the minimum common equity Tier 1 requirement of the subsidiary plus the capital conservation buffer (i.e., 7.0% of risk-weighted assets) and (2) the portion of the consolidated minimum common equity Tier 1 requirement plus the capital conservation buffer (i.e., 7.0% of consolidated risk-weighted assets) that relates to the subsidiary.
- The amount of the surplus common equity Tier 1 that is attributable to the minority shareholders is calculated by multiplying the surplus common equity Tier 1 by the percentage of common equity Tier 1 that is held by minority shareholders.

In my view, the minority interest deduction reduces the incentive of banks to overcapitalize banking subsidiaries, which is against Basel III's spirit. It also creates an asymmetry between the numerator and the denominator of the capital ratio because Basel III ignores the excess capital of the subsidiary representing the minority interest at group level while the risk exposures related to this excess are fully recognized in the consolidated accounts (i.e., it does not deduct from total RWAs the quota corresponding to the excess capital related to the minority interest on the entity level).

Mandatory Convertibles and Contingent Capital Instruments

At the time this book was being written, the Basel III committee had not yet reviewed the role that contingent capital, convertible capital instruments and mandatory convertible instruments play in a regulatory capital framework.

Minimum Requirements

The minimum requirement for common equity capital is 4.5% of RWAs after the application of adjustments. However, when combined with the capital conservation buffer, the resulting common equity requirement is 7% of RWAs.

$$\text{Common Equity Capital Ratio} = \frac{\text{Common Equity capital}}{\text{Risk-weighted assets}} \geq 4.5\%$$

11.2.2   Additional Tier 1 Capital

Although the predominant form of Tier 1 capital must be common equity, Basel III allows instruments other than common shares to be included in another element of Tier 1 capital called "additional Tier 1" capital, also called "non-core Tier 1" capital or "contingent" capital, if they meet certain requirements. An instrument to be included in additional Tier 1 capital shall meet the following criteria:

1. It must help the bank avoid payment default through payments being discretionary.
2. It must help the bank avoid balance sheet insolvency by the instrument not contributing to liabilities exceeding assets if such a balance sheet test forms part of applicable national insolvency law.
3. And, it must be able to bear losses while the firm remains a going concern.

Criteria Governing Instruments' Inclusion in the Additional Tier 1 Capital Component

For an instrument to be included in additional Tier 1 capital, the supplementary form of Tier 1 capital, it must meet all of the following criteria:

1. Issued and paid-in.
2. Subordinated to depositors, general creditors and subordinated debt of the bank.
3. Is neither secured nor covered by a guarantee of the issuer or related entity or other arrangement that legally or economically enhances the seniority of the claim vis-à-vis bank creditors.
4. Is perpetual (i.e., there is no maturity date) and there are no step-ups or incentives to redeem.
5. May be callable at the initiative of the issuer only after a minimum of five years:
    (a) To exercise a call option a bank must receive prior supervisory approval; and
    (b) A bank must not do anything which creates an expectation that the call will be exercised; and
    (c) Banks must not exercise a call unless:
        (i) They, concurrently at the latest, replace the called instrument with capital of the same or better quality and the replacement of this capital is done at conditions which are sustainable for the income capacity of the bank; or
        (ii) The bank demonstrates that its capital position is well above the minimum capital requirements after the call option is exercised.
6. Any repayment of principal (e.g., through repurchase or redemption) must be with prior supervisory approval and banks should not assume or create market expectations that supervisory approval will be given.

7. Dividend/coupon discretion:
   (a) The bank must have full discretion at all times to cancel distributions/payments. Dividend pushers are prohibited. A dividend pusher is a requirement to make a dividend/coupon payment on the instrument if the bank has made a payment on another, typically more junior, instrument.
   (b) Cancellation of discretionary payments must not be an event of default.
   (c) Banks must have full access to cancelled payments to meet obligations as they fall due.
   (d) Cancellation of distributions/payments must not impose restrictions on the bank except in relation to distributions to common stock holders.
8. Dividends/coupons must be paid out of distributable items.
9. The instrument cannot have a credit-sensitive dividend feature, that is a dividend/coupon that is reset periodically based in whole or in part on the banking organization's current credit standing.
10. The instrument cannot contribute to liabilities exceeding assets if such a balance sheet test forms part of national insolvency law.
11. Instruments classified as liabilities must have principal loss absorption through either (i) conversion to common shares at an objective pre-specified trigger point or (ii) a write-down mechanism which allocates losses to the instrument at a pre-specified trigger point. The write-down will have the following effects:
    (a) To reduce the claim of the instrument in liquidation.
    (b) To reduce the amount repaid when a call is exercised.
    (c) To partially or fully reduce coupon/dividend payments on the instrument.
12. Neither the bank nor a related party over which the bank exercises control or significant influence can have purchased the instrument, nor can the bank directly or indirectly have funded the purchase of the instrument.
13. The instrument cannot have any features that hinder recapitalization, such as provisions that require the issuer to compensate investors if a new instrument is issued at a lower price during a specified time frame.
14. If the instrument is not issued out of an operating entity or the holding company in the consolidated group (e.g., a special purpose vehicle, "SPV"), proceeds must be immediately available without limitation to an operating entity or the holding company in the consolidated group in a form which meets or exceeds all of the other criteria for inclusion in additional Tier 1 capital.

Stock Surplus

Stock surplus (i.e., share premium) is only permitted to be included in the additional Tier 1 capital component if the instruments giving rise to the stock surplus are also permitted to be included in the additional Tier 1 capital component.

Minority Interests

Tier 1 capital instruments issued by a fully consolidated subsidiary of the bank to third-party investors (including minority interest amounts included in the calculation of common equity Tier 1 capital) may receive recognition in Tier 1 capital only if the instruments would, if issued by the bank, meet all of the criteria for classification as Tier 1 capital. The amount of this capital that will be recognized in Tier 1 will be calculated as follows:

- Total Tier 1 of the subsidiary issued to third parties minus the amount of the surplus Tier 1 of the subsidiary attributable to the third-party investors.
- Surplus Tier 1 of the subsidiary is calculated as the Tier 1 of the subsidiary minus the lower of: (1) the minimum Tier 1 requirement of the subsidiary plus the capital conservation buffer (i.e., 8.5% of risk-weighted assets) and (2) the portion of the consolidated minimum Tier 1 requirement plus the capital conservation buffer (i.e., 8.5% of consolidated risk-weighted assets) that relates to the subsidiary.
- The amount of the surplus Tier 1 that is attributable to the third-party investors is calculated by multiplying the surplus Tier 1 by the percentage of Tier 1 that is held by third-party investors.

The amount of this Tier 1 capital that is recognized in additional Tier 1 should exclude amounts already recognized in common equity Tier 1.

Deductions from Additional Tier 1 Capital

The following items must be deducted from additional Tier 1 capital:

- All of a bank's investments in its own eligible additional Tier 1 instruments, whether held directly or indirectly (unless already derecognized under the relevant accounting standards).
- Reciprocal cross holdings of Additional Tier 1 capital that are designed to artificially inflate the Additional Tier 1 capital position of a bank must be deducted in full. Banks must apply a "corresponding deduction approach" to such investments in the Additional Tier 1 capital of other banks, other financial institutions and insurance entities.

Calculation of Additional Tier 1 Capital

Figure 11.5 highlights the major components in the calculation of additional Tier 1 capital.

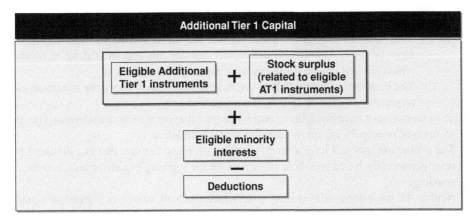

Figure 11.5   Major components in the calculation of additional Tier 1 capital.

Minimum Requirements

The minimum Tier 1 capital, which includes common equity capital and additional Tier 1 capital, requirement is 6% of RWAs. When combined with the capital conservation buffer, the resulting Tier 1 capital requirement is 8.5% of RWAs.

$$\text{Tier 1 Capital Ratio} = \frac{\text{Tier 1 capital}}{\text{Risk-weighted assets}} \geq 6\%$$

11.3   TIER 2 CAPITAL

The objective of Tier 2 is to provide loss absorption on a gone-concern basis. In other words, Tier 2 capital is intended to improve the position of depositors in case of insolvency of the bank. Based on this objective, there is a minimum set of criteria for an instrument to meet or exceed in order for it to be included in Tier 2 capital.

11.3.1   Criteria for Inclusion in Tier 2 Capital

1. Issued and paid-in.
2. Subordinated to depositors and general creditors of the bank.
3. Is neither secured nor covered by a guarantee of the issuer or related entity or other arrangement that legally or economically enhances the seniority of the claim vis-à-vis depositors and general bank creditors.
4. Maturity:
    (a) Minimum original maturity of at least five years.
    (b) Recognition in regulatory capital in the remaining five years before maturity is amortized on a straight-line basis.
    (c) There are no step-ups or other incentives to redeem.
5. May be callable at the initiative of the issuer only after a minimum of five years:
    (a) To exercise a call option a bank must receive prior supervisory approval; and
    (b) A bank must not do anything which creates an expectation that the call will be exercised; and
    (c) Banks must not exercise a call unless:
        (i) They, concurrently at the latest, replace the called instrument with capital of the same or better quality and the replacement of this capital is done at conditions which are sustainable for the income capacity of the bank; or
        (ii) The bank demonstrates that its capital position is well above the minimum capital requirements after the call option is exercised.
6. The investor must have no rights to accelerate the repayment of future scheduled payments (coupon or principal), except in bankruptcy and liquidation.
7. The instrument may not have a credit-sensitive dividend feature, that is a dividend that is reset periodically based in whole or in part on the banking organization's current credit standing.
8. Neither the bank nor a related party over which the bank exercises control or significant influence can have purchased, or directly or indirectly have funded the purchase of, the instrument.

9. If the instrument is not issued out of an operating entity or the holding company in the consolidated group (e.g., an SPV), proceeds must be immediately available without limitation to an operating entity or the holding company in the consolidated group in a form which meets or exceeds all of the other criteria for inclusion in Tier 2 capital. An operating entity is an entity set up to conduct business with clients with the intention of earning a profit in its own right.

Stock Surplus

Stock surplus (i.e., share premium) is only permitted to be included in the Tier 2 capital component if the instruments giving rise to the stock surplus are also permitted to be included in the Tier 2 capital component.

Minority Interests

Total capital instruments (i.e., Tier 1 and Tier 2 capital instruments) issued by a fully con-solidated subsidiary of the bank to third-party investors (including amounts included in the calculation of Tier 1 capital) may receive recognition in total capital only if the instruments would, if issued by the bank, meet all of the criteria for classification as Tier 1 or Tier 2 capital. The amount of this capital that will be recognized in consolidated total capital is calculated as follows:

- Total capital instruments of the subsidiary issued to third parties minus the amount of the surplus total capital of the subsidiary attributable to the third-party investors.
- Surplus total capital of the subsidiary is calculated as the total capital of the subsidiary minus the lower of: (1) the minimum total capital requirement of the subsidiary plus the capital conservation buffer (i.e., 10.5% of risk-weighted assets) and (2) the portion of the consolidated minimum total capital requirement plus the capital conservation buffer (i.e., 10.5% of consolidated risk-weighted assets) that relates to the subsidiary.
- The amount of the surplus total capital that is attributable to the third-party investors is calculated by multiplying the surplus total capital by the percentage of total capital that is held by third-party investors.

The amount of this total capital that is recognized in Tier 2 must exclude amounts recognized in common equity Tier 1 and amounts recognized in additional Tier 1.

Where capital has been issued to third parties out of an SPV, none of this capital can be included in common equity Tier 1. However, such capital can be included in consolidated additional Tier 1 or Tier 2 and treated as if the bank itself had issued the capital directly to the third parties only if it meets all the relevant entry criteria and the only asset of the SPV is its investment in the capital of the bank in a form that meets or exceeds all the relevant entry criteria (as required by criterion 14 for additional Tier 1 and criterion 9 for Tier 2). In cases where the capital has been issued to third parties through an SPV via a fully consolidated subsidiary of the bank, such capital may, subject to the requirements of this paragraph, be treated as if the subsidiary itself had issued it directly to the third parties and may be included in the bank's consolidated additional Tier 1 or Tier 2 in accordance with the treatment outlined for minority interests.

Additional Inclusions in Tier 2 Capital

The following items can be included in Tier 2 capital:

- For banks using the standardized approach to credit risk, provisions or loan-loss reserves held against future, presently unidentified losses. The inclusion is limited to a maximum of 1.25% of credit risk-weighted risk assets calculated under the standardized approach. Provisions ascribed to identify deterioration of particular assets or known liabilities, whether individual or grouped are excluded.
- Excess of total provisions over the total expected loss under the internal ratings-based (IRB) approach. The inclusion is limited to a maximum of 0.6% of credit risk-weighted risk assets calculated under the IRB approach. At national supervisor discretion, a limit lower than 0.6% may be applied.

Deductions from Tier 2 Capital

The following items must be deducted from additional Tier 1 capital:

- All of a bank's investments in its own eligible Tier 2 instruments, whether held directly or indirectly (unless already derecognized under the relevant accounting standards).
- Reciprocal cross holdings of Tier 2 capital that are designed to artificially inflate the Tier 2 capital position of a bank must be deducted in full. Banks must apply a "corresponding deduction approach" to such investments in the Tier 2 capital of other banks, other financial institutions and insurance entities.

Calculation of Tier 2 Capital

Figure 11.6 highlights the major components in the calculation of Tier 2 capital.

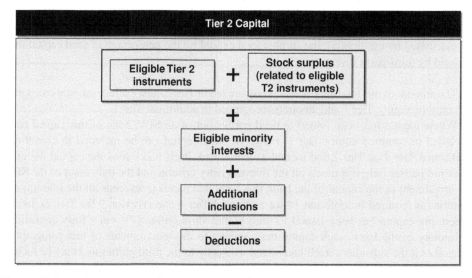

Figure 11.6   Major components in the calculation of Tier 2 capital.

Minimum Requirements

Total risk-based capital, which includes Tier 1 and Tier 2 capital, is 8% of RWAs. However, when combined with the capital conservation buffer, the resulting total risk-based capital requirement is 10.5% of RWAs.

$$\text{Total Capital Ratio} = \frac{\text{Total capital}}{\text{Risk-weighted assets}} \geq 8\%$$

11.3.2 Trigger Conditions for Hybrid Instruments

The terms and conditions of all non-common Tier 1 and Tier 2 instruments issued by an internationally active bank must have a provision that requires such instruments, at the option of the relevant authority, to either be written off or converted into common equity upon the occurrence of the trigger event unless:

- The governing jurisdiction of the bank has in place laws that (i) require such Tier 1 and Tier 2 instruments to be written off upon such event, or (ii) otherwise require such instruments to fully absorb losses before tax payers are exposed to loss.
- A peer group review confirms that the jurisdiction conforms with the previous clause.
- And, it is disclosed by the relevant regulator and by the issuing bank, in issuance documents going forward, that such instruments are subject to loss under clause (i).

Other conditions that have to be met are the following:

1. Any compensation paid to the instrument holders as a result of the write-off must be paid immediately in the form of common stock (or its equivalent in the case of non-joint stock companies).
2. The issuing bank must maintain at all times all prior authorization necessary to immediately issue the relevant number of shares specified in the instrument's terms and conditions should the trigger event occur.
3. The trigger event is the earlier of: (1) a decision that a write-off, without which the firm would become non-viable, is necessary, as determined by the relevant authority; and (2) the decision to make a public sector injection of capital, or equivalent support, without which the firm would have become non-viable, as determined by the relevant authority.
4. The issuance of any new shares as a result of the trigger event must occur prior to any public sector injection of capital so that the capital provided by the public sector is not diluted.
5. The relevant jurisdiction in determining the trigger event is the jurisdiction in which the capital is being given recognition for regulatory purposes. Therefore, where an issuing bank is part of a wider banking group and if the issuing bank wishes the instrument to be included in the consolidated group's capital in addition to its solo capital, the terms and conditions must specify an additional trigger event. This trigger event is the earlier of: (1) a decision that a write-off, without which the firm would become non-viable, is necessary, as determined by the relevant authority in the home jurisdiction; and (2) the decision to make a public sector injection of capital, or equivalent support, in the jurisdiction of the consolidated supervisor, without which the firm receiving the support would have become non-viable, as determined by the relevant authority in that jurisdiction.

6. Any common stock paid as compensation to the holders of the instrument must be common stock of either the issuing bank or of the parent company of the consolidated group (including any successor in resolution).

11.4   DEDUCTIONS FROM COMMON EQUITY TIER 1 CAPITAL

In order to ensure that capital is available to absorb losses, some adjustments are required to either (i) avoid double counting of capital or (ii) exclude elements of the equity section of a bank that are uncertain. The main regulatory capital deductions from common equity capital are the following:

- Goodwill and intangible assets (except mortgage servicing rights).
- Deferred tax assets that rely on future profitability.
- Cash flow hedge reserve.
- Shortfall of the stock of provisions to expected losses.
- Gain on sale related to securitization transactions.
- Cumulative gains and losses on own liabilities.
- Defined benefit pension assets and liabilities.
- Treasury stock.
- Reciprocal holdings in unconsolidated financial entities.
- Less than 10% holdings in unconsolidated financial entities.
- Significant holdings in unconsolidated financial entities.
- Combined deduction of significant investments in unconsolidated financial entities, MSRs and DTAs.

11.4.1   Goodwill and Other Intangible Assets (Except Mortgage Servicing Rights)

Basel III requires the deduction from common equity of goodwill and other intangibles, excluding mortgage servicing rights, including any goodwill included in the valuation of significant investments in the capital of banking, financial and insurance entities that are outside the scope of regulatory consolidation. The amount deducted should be net of any associated deferred tax liability which would be extinguished if the intangible asset becomes impaired or derecognized under the relevant accounting standards. Goodwill is created as part of a purchase price allocation. Basel III allows using IFRS in determining the level of intangible assets if national GAAP results in a wider range of assets being classified as intangible.

The proposed deduction addresses the high degree of uncertainty that intangible assets would have a positive realizable value in periods of stress or insolvency. Part of the reason for subtracting goodwill is to ensure acquisitive banks do not have an advantage over organically grown banks with the same real assets and liabilities.

11.4.2   Deferred Tax Assets

The treatment of deferred tax assets (DTAs) is quite complex. In this section I will try to briefly give a bit of color on why DTAs take place.

An Overview of DTAs According to IAS 12

According to IAS 12, DTAs can be classified as follows:

- DTAs resulting from timing differences. To be covered below.
- DTAs resulting from the carry forward of unused tax losses. This type of DTA represents a claim against tax authorities to reduce the tax on future profits due to net operating losses (NOLs). It arises where a bank incurs losses and there is insufficient other income against which the losses can be offset. IAS 12 requires that DTAs on unused tax losses may only be recognized to the extent that it is probable that future taxable profits will be available against which the unused tax losses can be utilized. Where a DTA arises from a NOL carried forward, the DTA has independent value and is not solely dependent on future profits from existing operations to be monetized. For example, simple additional equity from a legal entity perspective can be transferred to the jurisdiction to earn out the NOL, and a number of jurisdictions permit the transfer of the business to a new owner.
- DTAs resulting from the carry forward of unused tax credits. This type of DTA arises if the bank qualifies for tax credits, those tax credits have not been able to be applied to the taxes payable in the current period and the tax authorities permit a carry forward of such unused tax credits into future years. The accounting treatment is similar to DTAs resulting from the carry forward of unused tax losses. However, the tax credits may be subject to the satisfaction of specific requirements, and therefore, the recoverability testing of DTAs on unused tax credits is in most instances more difficult than for unused tax losses.
- DTAs representing current tax assets. These DTAs can result from a tax loss carry back or from a prepayment. They represent an existing claim against the fiscal authorities which is usually paid as soon as certain formal requirements are fulfilled (e.g., filing a tax return or an application).

A DTA resulting from timing differences (also referred to as "temporary differences") arises where there is a timing mismatch between the taxation of income/expense and the period in which the income/expense is recorded in the financial statements.

- A timing difference between accounting and tax systems arising from income being recognized for tax purposes before it is recognized for accounting purposes. This can arise from external or intra-group transactions. The DTA is in effect a prepayment to the tax authorities of an expense that will later be recognized for accounting purposes. One driver of this type of DTA is a prepaid interest.
- A timing difference between accounting and tax systems arising from expenses being recognized for accounting purposes before they are recognized for tax purposes. The position will automatically reverse through the passage of time. One driver of this type of DTA is the recognition of fair market value losses. In this case, the position will reverse either when the market value recovers or when the losses are crystallized for tax purposes. The existence of this type of DTA does not imply that the bank has incurred losses, instead it may represent a tax accounting concept designed to deal with differences in the timing of expense recognition between the financial statements and for tax purposes. For example, many tax systems only permit a deduction of loan-loss provisions upon actual realization of those losses; whereas the deduction for accounting arises at the time the provision is made. Another example of this type of DTA arises when a bank records an expense for deferred compensation in the financial statements over the vesting period (say, years 1 to 3) while this expense may not be deductible for tax purposes until the compensation is delivered

(say, year 4). In this case, a DTA would be recorded in years 1 to 3 in respect of the future tax deduction that would be available for the deferred compensation expense.

The tests for recognition of DTAs under IAS 12 are notably stringent. DTAs are only recognized to the extent that it is probable that sufficient taxable profit will be available against which unused tax credits and deductible temporary differences can be utilized. In particular, the accounting standard requires detailed profit projections to prove the ability to earn out the DTA. For example, in the case of an entity which has incurred losses, there is a high evidentiary hurdle to be overcome before DTAs can be recognized, even where there is a long or indefinite future period available for utilization of those tax losses.

Basel III Treatment of DTAs

Basel III makes a distinction between (i) deferred tax assets arising from timing differences, (ii) DTAs which rely on future profitability of the bank to be realized and (iii) DTAs which do not rely on the future profitability of the bank to be realized.

DTAs arising from timing differences receive limited recognition, subject to the threshold deduction treatment. Their recognition is capped at 10% of the bank's common equity Tier 1 capital, with an aggregate limit for DTAs, mortgage servicing rights and significant investments in unconsolidated financial entities of 15%. This combined deduction is covered later.

DTAs which rely on future profitability of the bank to be realized are fully deducted from common equity Tier 1 capital. Deferred tax assets may be netted with associated deferred tax liabilities (DTLs) only if the DTAs and DTLs relate to taxes levied by the same taxation authority and offsetting is permitted by the relevant taxation authority. The DTLs permitted to be netted against DTAs must exclude amounts that have been netted against the deduction of goodwill, intangibles and defined benefit pension assets, and must be allocated on a pro rata basis between DTAs subject to the threshold deduction treatment and DTAs that are to be deducted in full. This deduction requirement addresses the concern that undue reliance on these assets is not appropriate for prudential purposes, as they may provide no protection to depositors or governmental deposit insurance funds in insolvency and can be suddenly written off in a period of stress.

DTAs which do not rely on the future profitability of the bank to be realized are assigned the relevant sovereign risk weighting.

In reality, where a bank has been operating for a number of years, it will typically have a core level of timing differences which will continue in existence from year to year. This arises, in the case of deferred compensation for example, due to the DTA being reduced through share deliveries, while at the same time being increased as a result of new awards being expensed in the financial statements. Even a constantly profitable entity will typically have a core amount of DTAs arising from timing differences which will persist from year to year. This means that the bank would be constantly deducing these DTAs from common equity Tier 1.

11.4.3 Cash Flow Hedge Reserve

Under IAS 39/IFRS9 there is a component of the shareholders' equity section called the "cash flow hedge reserve". This component primarily includes the fair value of derivatives used to hedge assets, liabilities or future highly probable commitments.

Basel III requires the deduction of the positive and the addition of negative cash flow hedge reserve from the common equity component of Tier 1 where it relates to the hedging of items that are not fair valued on the balance sheet (including projected cash flows). This requirement tries to remove the element which gives rise to artificial volatility in shareholders' equity, as in this case the reserve only reflects one half of the picture, the fair value of the derivative but not the changes in fair value of the hedged future cash flow.

11.4.4   Shortfall of the Stock of Provisions to Expected Losses

Basel III requires a full deduction from the common equity component of Tier 1 capital of any shortfall of the stock of provisions to expected losses under the IRB approach. The full amount is deducted and is not reduced by any tax effects that could be expected to occur if provisions were to rise to the level of expected losses. This deduction is aimed at safeguarding a level playing field, avoiding that a bank with a low stock of provisions shows more Tier 1 capital, which could discourage banks from provisioning in excess of IRB's expected losses.

11.4.5   Gain-on-sale Related to Securitization Transactions

Basel III requires a full deduction from the common equity component of Tier 1 capital of any increase in equity capital resulting from a securitization transaction, such as that associated with expected future margin income (FMI) resulting in a gain-on-sale.

11.4.6   Gains and Losses on Fair Valued Own Liabilities due to Changes in Own Credit Risk

Basel III requires the deduction from common equity capital of all unrealized gains and losses that have resulted from changes in the fair value of liabilities that are due to changes in the bank's own credit risk.

11.4.7   Defined Benefit Pension Fund Assets and Liabilities

A defined benefit pension scheme is one where the level of pension payments that the employee will receive upon retirement are predefined – generally they are defined as a percentage of final salary, with that percentage depending on length of service. In most cases these schemes are "funded", i.e., pensioners receive their pension payments from a separate fund (often a trust) rather than directly from the company. The fund is built up over time with the employer, and in some cases the employee, making regular contributions to the fund over the employee's working life. In effect, with a defined benefit scheme the employer is taking the risk: the employee is entitled to a guaranteed pension income and the employer's contributions to the fund are likely to vary over time to reflect changing actuarial assumptions and investment performance.

Pension Assets

A pension fund is merely a collection of financial assets. Most pension funds invest in a mix of equities, bonds and other assets such as property or private equity. These assets can be valued either at market value (with the value of the fund fluctuating as markets rise and fall) or at actuarial values (normally based on the PV of expected future dividends).

Pension Liabilities

Banks operating defined benefit schemes have made a commitment to pay pensions to past and current employees. An employee's pension entitlement is typically based on a percentage of final salary multiplied by years of service. The actual amount paid out by the pension fund over time will therefore depend on salary levels, staff turnover, mortality rates, inflation rates and other assumptions. While some of these variables – such as pay increases – are under the employer's control, others – such as mortality rates and inflation – are clearly not.

Accounting Treatment under IAS 19 of Defined Benefit Plans

Under IAS 19, the net defined benefit liability is recorded in the statement of financial position as:

(a) The present value of the defined benefit obligation.
(b) Less the fair value of any plan assets.
(c) Taking into account any effect of the limit to the defined benefit asset, including any additional liability recognized for minimum funding requirements that relate to past service (together, the effect of the asset ceiling).

IAS 19 recognizes all changes in the value of the defined benefit obligation and in the value of plan assets in the financial statements in the period in which they occur. The changes in the net defined benefit liability (asset) are split into the following components:

• Service costs: recognized in P&L.
• Net interest income or expense: recognized in P&L as part of finance costs.
• Remeasurements of the net defined benefit liability (asset), including actuarial gains and losses: recognized in other comprehensive income (OCI).

Treatment under Basel III

Basel III applies no filter to net defined benefit pension fund liabilities. In other words, Basel III fully recognizes, as included on the balance sheet, liabilities arising from defined benefit pension funds in the calculation of the common equity component of Tier 1.

Additionally, Basel III requires the deduction of the value of each net defined benefit pension fund asset from the common equity component of Tier 1, net of any associated deferred tax liability which would be extinguished if the asset should become impaired or derecognized under the relevant accounting standards. Assets in the fund to which the bank has unrestricted and unfettered access can, with supervisory approval, offset the deduction. Such offsetting assets should be given the risk weight they would receive if they were owned directly by the bank.

The requirement for pension fund assets to be deducted from the common equity component of Tier 1 addresses the concern that assets arising from pension funds may not be capable of being withdrawn and used for the protection of depositors and other creditors of a bank, and thus, their only value stems from a reduction in future payments into the fund. Basel III allows for banks to reduce the deduction of the asset if they can address these concerns and show that the assets can be easily and promptly withdrawn from the fund. In my view, this deduction provides an incentive for banks to minimize the overfunding of pension funds or even accept underfunding, increasing pensions' risk.

11.4.8 Treasury Stock

In order to prevent capital arbitrage, Basel III requires the deduction from the common equity component of Tier 1 capital of direct and indirect holdings of own common shares, unless already derecognized under the relevant accounting standards. This also applies to shares held in the trading book. The objective of the deduction for holdings in own shares is to prevent double counting of a bank's capital. In addition:

- Any own stock which the bank could be contractually obliged to purchase should be deducted from its common equity Tier 1 capital.
- Basel III allows the netting of long positions in own shares with short positions, only if the short positions involve no counterparty risk.
- Banks should look through holdings of index securities to deduct exposures to own shares. In other words, if the bank stock happens to be a constituent of an index on which the bank has a long position, the bank has to deduct the part of the index position that corresponds to the bank stock. However, gross long positions in own shares resulting from holdings of index securities may be netted against short positions in own shares resulting from short positions in the same underlying index. In such cases the short positions may involve counterparty risk (which will be subject to the relevant counterparty credit risk charge).

Basel III considers it necessary to apply prudential filters to cash-settled derivatives on own shares.

I do not agree with the requirement to look through index securities, as own shares embedded in index securities do not reduce the risk-bearing capacity of a bank. The requirement, in my opinion, does not reflect the true risk position of these securities as they are mostly entered as part of the bank's market-making activities. A capital reduction of own shares embedded in an index security would put index member banks at a disadvantage to banks not represented in an index. Besides, the risk of such index trades is typically managed through banks' trading books and, as such, is subject to market risk capital requirements. Overlaying an additional deduction risks overstating capital requirements.

11.4.9 Reciprocal Stakes in Unconsolidated Financial Companies

All holdings of common equity capital which form part of a reciprocal cross holding agreement with unconsolidated financial companies (including insurance entities) or are investments in affiliated institutions (e.g., sister companies) are deducted in full from common equity capital on a corresponding basis.

11.4.10 Less than 10% Stakes in Unconsolidated Financial Companies

The regulatory adjustment described in this section applies to investments in the capital of banking, financial and insurance entities that are outside the scope of regulatory consolidation and where the bank does not own more than 10% of the issued common share capital of the entity. In addition:

- Investments include direct, indirect and synthetic holdings of capital instruments. Indirect holdings are exposures or parts of exposures that, if a direct holding loses its value, will result in a loss to the bank substantially equivalent to the loss in value of the direct holding. For example, banks should look through holdings of index securities to determine their underlying holdings of capital. If banks find it operationally burdensome to look through and monitor their exact exposure to the capital of other financial institutions as a result of their holdings of index securities, national authorities may permit banks, subject to prior supervisory approval, to use a conservative estimate.
- Holdings in both the banking book and trading book are to be included. Capital includes common stock and all other types of cash and synthetic capital instruments (e.g., subordinated debt). It is the net long position that is to be included (i.e., the gross long position net of short positions in the same underlying exposure where the maturity of the short position either matches the maturity of the long position or has a residual maturity of at least one year).
- Underwriting positions held for five working days or less can be excluded. Underwriting positions held for longer than five working days must be included.
- If the capital instrument for the entity in which the bank has invested does not meet the criteria for common equity Tier 1, additional Tier 1, or Tier 2 capital of the bank, the capital is to be considered common shares for the purposes of this regulatory adjustment. If the investment is issued out of a regulated financial entity and not included in regulatory capital in the relevant sector of the financial entity, it is not required to be deducted.
- National discretion applies to allow banks, with prior supervisory approval, to exclude temporarily certain investments where these have been made in the context of resolving or providing financial assistance to reorganize a distressed institution.

If the total of all holdings listed above in aggregate exceeds 10% of the bank's common equity (after applying all other regulatory adjustments in full listed prior to this one), then the amount above 10% is required to be deducted, applying a corresponding deduction approach. The same reasoning is followed to compute the deduction for Tier 1 capital and total capital by summing the total holdings of Tier 1 capital and total capital respectively. This means the deduction should be applied to the same component of capital for which the capital would qualify if it was issued by the bank itself. Accordingly, the amount to be deducted from common equity should be calculated as the total of all holdings which in aggregate exceed 10% of the bank's common equity (as per above) multiplied by the common equity holdings as a percentage of the total capital holdings. This would result in a common equity deduction which corresponds to the proportion of total capital holdings held in common equity. Similarly, the amount to be deducted from additional Tier 1 capital should be calculated as the total of all holdings which in aggregate exceed 10% of the bank's common equity (as per above) multiplied by the additional Tier 1 capital holdings as a percentage of the total capital holdings. The amount to be deducted from Tier 2 capital should be calculated as the total of all holdings which in aggregate exceed 10% of the bank's common equity (as per above) multiplied by the Tier 2 capital holdings as a percentage of the total capital holdings.

If, under the corresponding deduction approach, a bank is required to make a deduction from a particular tier of capital and it does not have enough of that tier of capital to satisfy that deduction, the shortfall will be deducted from the next higher tier of capital (e.g., if a bank does not have enough additional Tier 1 capital to satisfy the deduction, the shortfall will be deducted from common equity Tier 1).

Amounts below the threshold, which are not deducted, are risk weighted. Thus, instruments in the trading book are treated as per the market risk rules and instruments in the banking book should be treated as per the internal ratings-based approach or the standardized approach (as applicable). For the application of risk weighting the amount of the holdings must be allocated on a pro rata basis between those below and those above the threshold.

11.4.11   Significant Stakes in Unconsolidated Financial Companies

Banks use equity investments in other financial institutions to expand internationally, diversify their exposure to domestic markets and leverage local market expertise without the strategic and operational risks associated with acquisitions or building their own infrastructure in an unfamiliar market. Basel III allows a limited recognition of investments in financial sector entities, including insurance entities, which are outside the regulatory scope of consolidation to be deducted under certain conditions, to avoid double counting of capital. Full deduction of minority stakes in other financial institutions would have been overly punitive as it would have meant that these exposures had zero value in stressed going and gone-concern situations. Like any other investment, minority investments in other financial institutions can be sold to raise equity in a stressed scenario.

The regulatory adjustment described in this section applies to investments in the capital of banking, financial and insurance entities that are outside the scope of regulatory consolidation where the bank owns more than 10% of the issued common share capital of the issuing entity or where the entity is an affiliate of the bank. Investments in entities that are outside the scope of regulatory consolidation refer to investments in entities that have not been consolidated at all or have not been consolidated in such a way as to result in their assets being included in the calculation of consolidated risk-weighted assets of the group. An affiliate of a bank is defined as a company that controls, or is controlled by, or is under common control with, the bank. Control of a company is defined as (1) ownership, control, or holding with power to vote 20% or more of a class of voting securities of the company; or (2) consolidation of the company for financial reporting purposes. In addition:

- Investments include direct, indirect and synthetic holdings of capital instruments. For example, banks should look through holdings of index securities to determine their underlying holdings of capital. If banks find it operationally burdensome to look through and monitor their exact exposure to the capital of other financial institutions as a result of their holdings of index securities, national authorities may permit banks, subject to prior supervisory approval, to use a conservative estimate.
- Holdings in both the banking book and trading book are to be included. Capital includes common stock and all other types of cash and synthetic capital instruments (e.g., subordinated debt). It is the net long position that is to be included (i.e., the gross long position net of short positions in the same underlying exposure where the maturity of the short position either matches the maturity of the long position or has a residual maturity of at least one year).
- Underwriting positions held for five working days or less can be excluded. Underwriting positions held for longer than five working days must be included.
- If the capital instrument of the entity in which the bank has invested does not meet the criteria for common equity Tier 1, additional Tier 1, or Tier 2 capital of the bank, the capital

is to be considered common shares for the purposes of this regulatory adjustment. If the investment is issued out of a regulated financial entity and not included in regulatory capital in the relevant sector of the financial entity, it is not required to be deducted.

- National discretion applies to allow banks, with prior supervisory approval, to exclude temporarily certain investments where these have been made in the context of resolving or providing financial assistance to reorganize a distressed institution.

All investments included above that are not common shares must be fully deducted following a corresponding deduction approach. This means the deduction should be applied to the same tier of capital for which the capital would qualify if it was issued by the bank itself. If the bank is required to make a deduction from a particular tier of capital and it does not have enough of that tier of capital to satisfy that deduction, the shortfall will be deducted from the next higher tier of capital (e.g., if a bank does not have enough additional Tier 1 capital to satisfy the deduction, the shortfall will be deducted from common equity Tier 1).

Investments included above that are common shares will be subject to the threshold treatment described in the next section.

In my opinion, the need to look through indirect positions embedded in index securities is flawed. Many banks actively trade equities and index securities as part of their market-making activities, not to make strategic investments in other financial institutions. Furthermore, holdings of index positions do not create regulatory capital in a financial institution which is a member of the index. Hence, a capital deduction is not justified. Furthermore, a capital deduction of certain portions of an index product, which are hedged by a corresponding short position, results in an asymmetric risk position between the decomposed index product (capital deduction) and the hedge (RWA on that part of the hedge which refers to the capital deduction of the underlying asset). As a result, a fully hedged position is treated with a capital deduction and RWAs. Without the capital deduction, the net RWA on the fully hedged position is zero.

Also, there is no consistency with the treatment of unrealized gains on those participations. An increase in the market value of a participation in a financial entity may lead to a larger reduction from common equity.

11.4.12 Combined Deduction of Significant Investments in Unconsolidated Financial Entities, MSRs and DTAs

Instead of a full deduction, the following items may each receive limited recognition (see Figure 11.7) when calculating the common equity component of Tier 1, with recognition capped at 10% of the bank's common equity component (after applying all previous deductions):

- Significant investments (i.e., more than 10% of the issued share capital) in the common shares of unconsolidated financial institutions (including insurance activities).
- Mortgage servicing rights.
- DTAs arising from timing differences.

On 1 January 2013, a bank must deduct the amount by which the aggregate of the three items above exceeds 15% of its common equity component of Tier 1 (calculated prior to the deduction of these items but after application of all other regulatory adjustments applied in the calculation of common equity Tier 1). As of 1 January 2018, the calculation of the 15% limit will be subject to the following treatment: the amount of the three items that remains recognized after the application of all regulatory adjustments must not exceed 15% of the common equity Tier 1 capital, calculated after all regulatory adjustments.

Aggregate Deductions		
Significant investments (>10%) in the common shares of unconsolidated financial institutions	Recognition capped at 10% of Tier 1 Common Equity	Deduction of the amount by which the aggregate of the 3 items exceeds 15% of Tier 1 Common Equity
Mortgage servicing rights (MSRs)	Recognition capped at 10% of Tier 1 Common Equity	
Deferred tax assets arising from timing differences	Recognition capped at 10% of Tier 1 Common Equity	

Figure 11.7   Summary of aggregate deductions.

The amount of the three items not deducted in the calculation of common equity Tier 1 will be risk weighted at 250%.

Mortgage Servicing Rights

Mortgage servicing rights are financial assets associated with a set of legal documents. There is an active market for mortgage servicing and sale is possible on both a going and gone-concern basis. These assets are typically hedged for prepayment risk. Payments to mortgage services are the highest priority claim on interest distributions in a securitization structure.

11.4.13   Basel II 50/50 Deductions

In relation to certain assets, Basel II required deductions to be made 50% from Tier 1 and 50% from Tier 2, or gave banks the option of applying a 1250% risk weight. The 50:50 deductions complicated the definition of capital, particularly in the application of the limits. Basel III requires that these assets receive a 1250% risk weight. These assets include:

- Certain securitization exposures.
- Certain equity exposures under the PD/LGD approach.
- Non-payment/delivery on non-DvP and non-PvP transactions.
- Significant investments in commercial entities.

11.5   OTHER CAPITAL BUFFERS

The holding of capital buffers over regulatory minimum levels is a necessary and standard practice of well-run banks. Outside periods of stress, Basel III requires banks to hold buffers of capital above the regulatory minima. Basel III considers two types of capital buffer, the capital conservation buffer and the countercyclical buffer.

11.5.1   Capital Conservation Buffer

The capital conservation buffer is designed to provide banks with an extra source of capital that can be drawn on during times of financial and economic stress. The philosophy behind the capital conservation buffer is to create a capital cushion during "good times" that can absorb shocks in periods of stress.

The target capital conservation buffer is at 2.5% of RWAs and must consist of common equity Tier 1 instruments. While banks are allowed to draw on this buffer during periods of stress, the more of the buffer that is drawn by a bank (i.e., as the buffer is depleted), the greater the restrictions that will be imposed on it in respect of earnings distributions such as dividends, share buybacks and discretionary employee bonuses. Basel III imposes minimum capital conservation ratios for entering the range, as shown in the table below. For example, a bank with a CET1 capital ratio in the range of 5.125–5.75% is required to conserve 80% of its earnings in the subsequent financial year (i.e., pay out no more than 20% in terms of dividends, share buybacks and discretionary bonus payments). If the bank wants to make payments in excess of the constraints imposed by this regime, it would have the option of raising capital in the private sector equal to the amount above the constraint which it wishes to distribute. This would be discussed with the bank's supervisor as part of the capital planning process.

The common equity Tier 1 ratio includes amounts used to meet the 4.5% minimum common equity Tier 1 requirement, but excludes any additional common equity Tier 1 needed to meet the 6% Tier 1 and 8% total capital requirements. For example, a bank with 8% common equity Tier 1 and no additional Tier 1 or Tier 2 capital would meet all minimum capital requirements, but would have a zero conservation buffer and therefore be subject to the 100% constraint on capital distributions.

Common equity Tier 1 ratio	Minimum capital conservation ratio
4.5–5.125%	100%
>5.125–5.75%	80%
>5.75–6.375%	60%
>6.375–7.0%	40%
>7.0%	0%

Set out below are a number of other key aspects of the requirements.

- Elements subject to the restriction on distributions: Items considered to be distributions include dividends and share buybacks, discretionary payments on other Tier 1 capital instruments and discretionary bonus payments to staff. Payments that do not result in a depletion of common equity Tier 1, which may for example include certain scrip dividends, are not considered distributions.
- Definition of earnings: Earnings are defined as distributable profits calculated prior to the deduction of elements subject to the restriction on distributions. Earnings are calculated after the tax which would have been reported had none of the distributable items been paid. As such, any tax impacts of making such distributions are reversed out. Where a bank does not have positive earnings and has a common equity Tier 1 ratio less than 7%, it would be restricted from making positive net distributions.
- Solo or consolidated application: The framework should be applied at the consolidated level, i.e., restrictions would be imposed on distributions out of the consolidated group. National supervisors would have the option of applying the regime at the solo level to conserve resources in specific parts of the group.

- Additional supervisory discretion: Although the buffer must be capable of being drawn down, banks should not choose in normal times to operate in the buffer range simply to compete with other banks and win market share. To ensure that this does not happen, supervisors have the additional discretion to impose time limits on banks operating within the buffer range on a case-by-case basis. In any case, supervisors should ensure that the capital plans of banks seek to rebuild buffers over an appropriate timeframe.

The capital conservation buffer will be phased in between 1 January 2016 and year-end 2018, becoming fully effective on 1 January 2019. It will begin at 0.625% of RWAs on 1 January 2016 and increase each subsequent year by an additional 0.625%, to reach its final level of 2.5% of RWAs on 1 January 2019.

11.5.2 Countercyclical Buffer

In addition to the capital conservation buffer described above, Basel III also requires a countercyclical capital buffer, a range of 0–2.5% of common equity or other fully loss absorbing capital, which is implemented in accordance with national circumstances. Typically, downturns in the banking sector are preceded by periods of excessive growth. The purpose of the countercyclical buffer is to achieve the broader macroprudential goal of protecting the banking sector from periods of excess aggregate credit growth. For any given country, this buffer will only be in effect when there is excess credit growth that is resulting in a system-wide build-up of risk. The buffer can be drawn on by the banks during these periods of excess credit.

Basel III recommends that countries experiencing excessive credit growth consider accelerating the build-up of the capital conservation buffer and the countercyclical buffer. National authorities have the discretion to impose shorter transition periods and should do so where appropriate.

The countercyclical buffer regime consists of the following elements:

- National authorities will monitor credit growth and other indicators that may signal a build-up of system-wide risk and make assessments of whether credit growth is excessive and is leading to the build-up of system-wide risk. Based on this assessment they will put in place a countercyclical buffer requirement when circumstances warrant. This requirement will be released when system-wide risk crystallizes or dissipates.
- Internationally active banks will look at the geographic location of their private sector credit exposures and calculate their bank-specific countercyclical capital buffer requirement as a weighted average of the requirements that are being applied in jurisdictions to which they have credit exposures.
- The countercyclical buffer requirement to which a bank is subject will extend the size of the capital conservation buffer. Banks will be subject to restrictions on distributions if they do not meet the requirement.

Each Basel Committee member jurisdiction will identify an authority with the responsibility to make decisions on the size of the countercyclical capital buffer. If the relevant national authority judges a period of excess credit growth to be leading to the build-up of system-wide risk, they will consider, together with any other macroprudential tools at their disposal, putting in place a countercyclical buffer requirement. This will vary between zero and 2.5% of risk-weighted assets, depending on their judgment as to the extent of the build-up of system-wide risk.

Banks will be subject to a countercyclical buffer that varies between zero and 2.5% to total risk-weighted assets. The buffer that will apply to each bank will reflect the geographic composition of its portfolio of credit exposures. Banks must meet this buffer with common equity Tier 1 or other fully loss absorbing capital or be subject to the restrictions on distributions. As with the capital conservation buffer, the framework is applied at the consolidated level. In addition, national supervisors may apply the regime at the solo level to conserve resources in specific parts of the group. The table below shows the minimum capital conservation ratios a bank must meet at various levels of the common equity Tier 1 capital. The common equity Tier 1 ratio includes amounts used to meet the 4.5% minimum common equity Tier 1 requirement, but excludes any additional common equity Tier 1 needed to meet the 6% Tier 1 and 8% total capital requirements. For example, a bank with 8% common equity Tier 1 and no additional Tier 1 or Tier 2 capital would meet all minimum capital requirements, but would have a zero countercyclical buffer and therefore be subject to the 100% constraint on capital distributions.

Common equity Tier 1 ratio	Minimum capital conservation ratio (% of earnings)
Within 1st quartile of buffer	100%
Within 2nd quartile of buffer	80%
Within 3rd quartile of buffer	60%
Within 4th quartile of buffer	40%
Above top of buffer	0%

11.6 TRANSITIONAL ARRANGEMENTS

While applicable from 1 January 2013, Basel III would be implemented with a long phase-in period.

11.6.1 Transitional Period

Regarding regulatory deductions, the Basel Committee introduced a transitional period between 2014 and 2018 before the full deductibility. The regulatory adjustments would be fully deducted from common equity by 1 January 2018.

Phase-in arrangements (all dates are as of 1 January):

	2013	2014	2015	2016	2017	2018	2019
Common equity capital ratio	3.5%	4.0%	4.5%	4.5%	4.5%	4.5%	4.5%
Capital conservation buffer				0.625%	1.25%	1.875%	2.50%
Minimum common equity plus capital conservation ratio	3.5%	4.0%	4.5%	5.125%	5.75%	6.375%	7.0%
Phase-in deductions from CET1		20%	40%	60%	80%	100%	100%
Minimum Tier 1 capital	4.5%	5.5%	6.0%	6.0%	6.0%	6.0%	6.0%
Minimum total capital	8.0%	8.0%	8.0%	8.0%	8.0%	8.0%	8.0%
Minimum total capital plus conservation buffer	8.0%	8.0%	8.0%	8.0%	8.0%	8.0%	8.0%
Capital instruments that no longer qualify as non-core Tier 1 capital or Tier 2 capital	Phased out over 10-year horizon beginning 2013						

The regulatory adjustments (i.e., deductions and prudential filters), including amounts above the aggregate 15% limit for investments in financial institutions, mortgage servicing rights and deferred tax assets from timing differences, would be fully deducted from common equity by 1 January 2018. In particular, the regulatory adjustments will begin at 20% of the required deductions from common equity on 1 January 2014, 40% on 1 January 2015, 60% on 1 January 2016, 80% on 1 January 2017, and reach 100% on 1 January 2018. During this transition period, the remainder not deducted from common equity will continue to be subject to existing national treatments.

11.6.2   Capital Instruments Failing Criteria for Eligibility in Capital

Capital instruments that fail to meet the criteria for eligibility in equity capital, and that have been issued before July 2010.

Existing public sector capital injections will be grandfathered until 1 January 2018. Capital instruments that no longer qualify as non-common equity Tier 1 capital or Tier 2 capital will be phased out over a 10-year horizon beginning 1 January 2013. Fixing the base at the nominal amount of such instruments outstanding on 1 January 2013, their recognition will be capped at 90% from 1 January 2013, with the cap reducing by 10 percentage points in each subsequent year, as shown in the table below. In addition, instruments with an incentive to be redeemed will be phased out at their effective maturity date.

	2013	2014	...	2019	2020	2021	2022
Non-qualifying capital instruments	90% cap	80%	...	30%	20%	10%	0%

All capital instruments that do not meet the criteria for inclusion in common equity Tier 1 will be excluded from common equity Tier 1 beginning 2013. However, instruments meeting the following three conditions will be phased out over a period until 2022:

- They are issued by a non-joint stock company.
- They are treated as equity under the prevailing accounting standards.
- They receive unlimited recognition as part of Tier 1 capital under current national banking law.

11.7   LEVERAGE RATIO

One of the causes of the 2007–2008 financial crisis was the build-up of excessive balance sheet leverage in the banking system, despite meeting their capital requirements. It was only when the banks were forced by market conditions to reduce their leverage that the financial system increased the downward pressure on asset prices. This exacerbated the decline in bank capital. To prevent the excessive deleveraging from happening again, Basel III introduced a leverage ratio. This ratio was designed to put a cap on the build-up of leverage in the banking system as well as introducing additional safeguards against model risk and measurement errors. The leverage ratio is a simple, transparent, non-risk-weighted measure, calculated as an average over the quarter:

$$\text{Tier 1 Leverage Ratio} = \frac{\text{Tier 1 capital}}{\text{Average total restated balance sheet assets}} \geq 3\%$$

A key point is the calculation of restated balance sheet assets (referred to as "exposure" by Basel III). It should generally follow the accounting measure of the exposure.

- For on-balance sheet, non-derivative exposures are net of specific provisions and valuation adjustments (e.g., credit valuation adjustments).
- Physical or financial collateral, guarantees or credit risk mitigation purchased is not allowed to reduce on-balance sheet exposures.
- Netting of loans and deposits is not allowed.

On-balance sheet assets are included using the accounting recognition. In addition:

- Repurchase agreements, reverse repurchase agreements, security lending and borrowing, and margin lending transactions, where the value of the transactions depends on the market valuations and the transactions are often subject to margin agreements, are included using their accounting measure of exposure and the regulatory netting rules based on the Basel II framework (except the rules for cross-product netting).
- Derivatives, including credit derivatives, are included using (i) their accounting measure of exposure, plus (ii) an add-on for potential future exposure calculated according to the current exposure method as identified in the Basel II framework (this ensures that all derivatives are converted in a consistent manner to a "loan equivalent" amount) and (iii) the regulatory netting rules based on the Basel II framework (except the rules for cross-product netting).
- For off-balance sheet (OBS) items, banks use uniform 100% credit conversion factors (CCFs), except a 10% CCF to be applied to unconditionally cancellable OBS commitments. This requirement puts OBS items (e.g., liquidity facilities, unconditionally cancellable commitments, direct credit substitutes, acceptances, standby letters of credit, trade letters of credit, failed transactions and unsettled securities) in the same position as loans. In my view this requirement is overly conservative as significant amounts of off-balance sheet exposures are never drawn and indeed some are arguably not commitments, if unconditionally cancellable.
- Deductions from the measure of Tier 1 capital must also be deducted from balance sheet asset calculations.

The Basel Committee agreed to test a minimum Tier 1 leverage ratio of 3% during the period from 1 January 2013 until 1 January 2017 ("the parallel run period"). Based on the results of the parallel run period, any final adjustments would be carried out in the first half of 2017 with a view to migrating to a Pillar 1 treatment on 1 January 2018 based on appropriate review and calibration.

11.8 LIQUIDITY COVERAGE RATIO

Banks experienced severe liquidity problems during the 2007–2008 financial crisis, despite meeting their capital requirements. Basel III requires banks to hold a pool of highly liquid assets which is sufficient to maintain the forecasted net cash outflows over a 30-day period, under stress assumptions (see Figure 11.8). This requirement tries to improve a bank's resilience against potential short-term liquidity shortages. The ratio is calculated as follows:

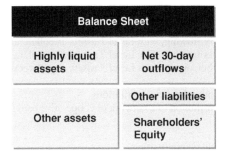

Figure 11.8 Liquidity coverage.

$$\text{Liquidity Coverage Ration (LCR)} = \frac{\text{Stock of highly liquid assets}}{\text{Net cash outflows over a 30-day time period}} \geq 100\%$$

Assets are considered "highly liquid" if they can be quickly converted into cash at almost no loss.

All assets in the liquidity pool must be managed as part of that pool and are subject to operational requirements. The assets must be available for the treasurer of the bank, unencumbered and freely available to group entities (see Basel III framework for a more detailed calculation of the liquidity coverage items).

Stock of highly liquid assets	Factor
Level 1 assets: Cash, central bank deposits, public sector, supranational securities with active repo market and with 0% risk weighting*	100%
Level 2 assets: Sovereign, central bank and PPE assets qualifying for 20% risk weighting. High-quality corporate and covered bonds with rating ≥ AA–	85%

*Including domestic sovereign debt for non-0% risk-weighted sovereigns, issued in foreign currency, to the extent that this currency matches the currency needs of the bank's operations in that jurisdiction.

Therefore, equities are not part of the high-quality liquid assets.
The denominator, "net cash outflows over a 30-day period", is calculated as follows:

$$\begin{array}{l} \text{Net cash outflows over a} \\ \text{30-day time period} \end{array} = \begin{array}{l} \text{Cash outflows over a} \\ \text{30-day time period} \\ \text{("cash outflows")} \end{array} - \begin{array}{l} \text{Minimum of (i) Cash inflows} \\ \text{over a 30-day time period} \\ \text{and (ii) 75\% of cash outflows} \end{array}$$

The list to calculate the cash outflows over a 30-day time period is quite extensive and I would prefer the reader to refer to the actual Basel III document.

The next table briefly summarizes the items to calculate the cash inflows and their associated available stable funding (ASF) factors.

Cash inflows over a 30-day stress period	Factor
Reverse repos and securities borrowing, with Level 1 assets as collateral	0%
Reverse repos and securities borrowing, with Level 2 assets as collateral	15%
Reverse repos and securities borrowing, with Level 3 assets as collateral	100%
Credit or liquidity facilities	0%
Operational deposits held at other financial institutions	0%
Deposits held at centralized institution of a network of cooperative banks	0% of the qualyifying deposits with the centralized institution
Amounts receivable from retail counterparties	50%
Amounts receivable from non-financial wholesale counterparties, from transactions other than those listed above	50%
Amounts receivable from financial institutions, from transactions other than those listed above	100%
Net derivative receivables	100%
Other contractual inflows (e.g., contractual payments from derivatives)	National supervisor discretion

The liquidity ratio would be effective in 2015 after an observation period.

11.9   NET STABLE FUNDING RATIO

Basel III requires a minimum amount of funding that is expected to be stable over a one-year time horizon based on liquidity risk factors assigned to assets and off-balance sheet exposures. This requirement provides incentives for banks to use stable sources to fund banks' balance sheets, off-balance sheet exposures and capital markets activities, therefore reducing the refinancing risks of a bank. The net stable funding ratio (NSFR) establishes the minimum amount of stable funding based on the liquidity characteristics of a bank's assets and activities over a more than one-year horizon. In other words, a bank must hold at least an amount of long-term (i.e., more than one year) funding equal to its long-term (i.e., more than one year) assets. The ratio is calculated as follows:

$$\text{Net Stable Funding Ratio (NSFR)} = \frac{\text{Available amout of stable funding}}{\text{Required amout of stable funding}} \geq 100\%$$

The numerator is calculated by summing a bank's liabilities, weighted by their degree of permanence. The next table briefly summarizes the specific liabilities and their associated required stable funding (RSF) factors.

Available amount of stable funding		Factor
Equity	Tier 1 and Tier 2 capital, other preferred stock and capital > 1 year	100%
Long-term funding	Long-term debt and deposits ≥ 1 year	100%
Stable deposits < 1 year	Retail customers and SMEs, according to LCR definition	90%
Less stable deposits < 1 year	Retail customers and SMEs, according to LCR definition	80%
Wholesale funding < 1 year	Non-financial corporates, central banks, supranationals and PSEs	50%
Other	All other liabilities and equity not included above	0%

Basel III considers that short-term deposits are rapidly gained, likely through high rates offered, and are treated as "less stable" by the guidelines. This is especially the case with wholesale deposits.

The denominator is calculated by summing a bank's assets, weighted by their degree of permanence. The next table briefly summarizes the specific assets and their associated RSF factors.

Required amount of stable funding		Factor
Fully liquid	Cash, short-term unsecured liquid instruments < 1 year, securities < 1 year, matched book positions (securities with exactly offsetting reverse repo), non-renewable loans to financials < 1 year	0%
Highly liquid	Sovereign, central bank, supranational debt with 0% risk weighting under Basel II standardized approach	5%
Very liquid	Unencumbered senior corporate and covered bonds ≥ 1 year, rated at least AA– Sovereign, central bank and PSE debt ≥ 1 year with 20% risk weighting	20%
Liquid	Unencumbered senior corporate and covered bonds ≥ 1 year, rated from A+ to A– Unencumbered listed equity securities Gold Corporate, sovereign, central bank and PSE loans < 1 year	50%
Less liquid	Unencumbered residential mortgages and other unencumbered loans (excluding loans to financial institutions ≥ 1 year with ≤ 35% risk weighting under Basel II standardized approach)	65%
Almost illiquid	Other retail and SME loans < 1 year	85%
Illiquid	All other assets	100%
Off-balance sheet positions	Undrawn amount of committed credit lines, liquidity facilities	5%
	Other contingent obligations	National supervisor discretion

The liquidity ratio will be effective in 2018 after an observation period.

11.10 CASE STUDY: CALCULATION OF MINORITY INTERESTS

In this section I will cover an example of how capital related to minority interests is allocated to the capital of the consolidated bank. This example is highly simplified, but provides an understanding of how a subsidiary contributes to the regulatory consolidated capital. Let us assume that Bank P is the parent bank, and that it has a sole subsidiary called Bank S. Figure 11.9 highlights the stand-alone balance sheets of each bank and the consolidated balance sheet (CET1: common equity Tier 1, AT1: additional Tier 1 and T2: Tier 2).

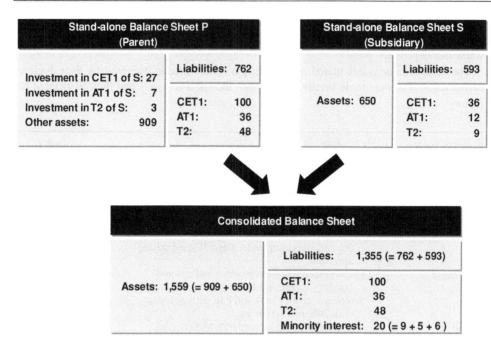

Figure 11.9   Bank P and Bank S, stand-alone and consolidated balance sheets.

Let us assume that Bank S's RWAs are 400. The first step is to calculate the minimum capital requirements for Bank S, including the capital conservation buffer. Bank S's surplus capital has been calculated for description purposes only:

Capital component	Minimum requirement (a)	RWAs (b)	Minimum requirement (c) = (a) × (b)	Bank S capital (d)	Bank S surplus (e) = (d) − (c)
CET1	6%	400	24	36	12
Total Tier 1	8.5%	400	34	48	14
Total capital	10.5%	400	42	57	15

The second step is to calculate the amount of the capital issued by Bank S to third parties that is included in the consolidated capital:

Capital component	Bank S capital (d)	Amount issued to third parties (g)	Bank S minimum requirement (c)	Amount included in consolidation (h) = (c) × (g)/(d)
CET1	36	9	24	6
Total Tier 1	48	14	34	10
Total capital	57	20	42	15

Thus, if we look at Bank S's total Tier 1 capital, we can see that only the minimum requirement attributed to third parties was included in the consolidated total Tier 1 capital (see Figure 11.10). In other words, the surplus total Tier 1 capital issued to third parties was excluded from consolidated total Tier 1 capital.

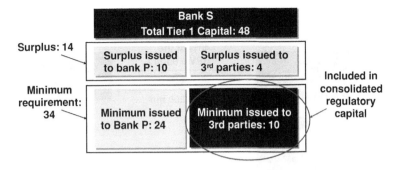

Figure 11.10 Bank S's total Tier 1 capital.

The third step is to calculate the components of Bank S's capital to be included in the consolidated regulatory capital [all data taken directly from column (h) in the previous table]:

$$CET1 = 6$$
$$AT1 = \text{Total Tier } 1 - CET1 = 10 - 6 = 4$$
$$T2 = \text{Total capital} - \text{Total Tier } 1 = 15 - 10 = 5$$

The last step is to calculate the consolidated regulatory capital:

Capital component	Bank P capital (i)	Added from Bank S (j)	Consolidated capital (k) = (i) + (j)
CET1	100	6	106
AT1	36	4	40
Tier 2	48	5	53

11.11 CASE STUDY: CREATING MINORITY INTERESTS

An interesting way to create capital under Basel II was to add minority interests that were not deducted from common equity Tier 1 capital. Although feasible under Basel II, the transaction described herein does not work under Basel III. However, I have included it to show an interesting strategic equity technique (see Figure 11.11).

Let us assume that a bank called SmallBank has a stake in a corporate, called ABC, worth EUR 500 million. The transaction is implemented along the following steps:

1. SmallBank creates an SPV. SmallBank provides the stake in ABC in exchange for the equity capital of the SPV. At this stage, SmallBank owns 100% of the SPV.
2. SmallBank sells 40% of the equity capital of the SPV to Gigabank in exchange for EUR 200 million. At this stage SmallBank owns 60% of the SPV.
3. Because, after implementing step (2), SmallBank has reduced its economic exposure from 100% to 60% to the ABC stake, SmallBank and Gigabank enter into an equity derivative. The derivative underlying shares are 40% of the ABC shares.

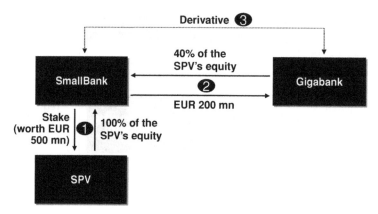

Figure 11.11   Creating non-deductible minority interests.

The strategy just covered is a very preliminary version of the transaction. It faces the following drawbacks:

1. The derivative will probably be booked in SmallBank's trading book. This means that SmallBank may be required to fair value the derivative through P&L, increasing the volatility of the P&L statement.
2. The derivative would be consuming capital as it bears market risk.
3. Gigabank would need to hedge its exposure to ABC's shares. To hedge its exposure, Gigabank would need to sell ABC shares in the market. Therefore, a sufficiently liquid stock lending market for ABC shares is required.

Figure 11.12 illustrates the consolidated balance sheet of SmallBank after implementing the transaction, ignoring the fair valuing of the derivative. The transaction generated EUR 200 million of minority interests.

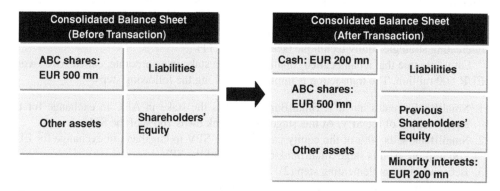

Figure 11.12   SmallBank's consolidated balance sheet, ignoring the derivative fair valuing.

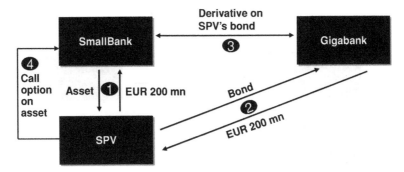

Figure 11.13   Reducing risk-weighting of an asset.

11.12   CASE STUDY: REDUCING RISK WEIGHTING

Let us assume that SmallBank has an asset in the banking book that has a high risk weighting (i.e., it highly consumes capital) that is worth EUR 200 million. The transaction is implemented along the following steps (see Figure 11.13):

1. SmallBank sells the asset to an ad-hoc SPV receiving EUR 200 million.
2. The SPV issues a bond to Gigabank with a face value of EUR 200 million.
3. SmallBank and Gigabank enter into a derivative on the SPV bond. The fair value of the derivative reflects the difference between the bond value and its EUR 200 million face value.
4. SmalBank buys from SPV a call option on the asset giving it the right to buy the asset for EUR 200 million.

At maturity of the derivative, the flows would be the following:

1. SmallBank exercises the call option, buying the asset and paying EUR 200 million.
2. The SPV redeems the bond, paying EUR 200 million to Gigabank.
3. The derivative on the SPV's bond is worth zero.

What if SmallBank does not exercise its call option? The SPV would then sell the asset onto the market. Let us assume that the proceeds of the disposal are EUR 150 million. The SPV would then redeem the bond, paying Gigabank EUR 150 million. Simultaneously, under the derivative SmallBank would pay to Gigabank EUR 50 million, corresponding to the difference between the bond EUR 200 million face value and its EUR 150 million market value.

As a result, SmallBank has switched an asset held in its banking book for a derivative held in its trading book. If the capital consumption of the derivative is much lower than that of the asset, SmallBank would maintain the same economic exposure to the asset but with a much lower risk weighting. The major drawback of this solution is that the derivative is marked-to-market through P&L, potentially increasing the volatility of SmallBank's P&L statement.

11.13   CASE STUDY: RELEASING COMMON EQUITY

Let us assume that in May 20X1 SmallBank has 30 million treasury shares, representing 2.4% of its share capital. These shares will be distributed to shareholders as a scrip dividend in July 20X1. The average acquisition price of these shares is EUR 6.00, therefore deducting

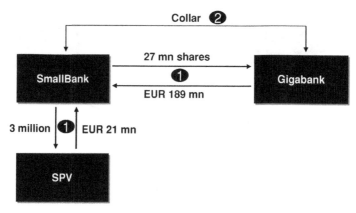

Figure 11.14   Releasing common equity capital.

the owners' equity section of SmallBank by EUR 180 million (= 30 million × 6.00). Let us assume further that SmallBank shares are trading at EUR 7.00. Thus, the shares have a market value of EUR 210 million (= 30 million × 7.00). The transaction is implemented along the following steps (see Figure 11.14):

1. SmallBank sells the treasury shares in two steps: 27 million shares to Gigabank so it can initially hedge the collar transaction and 3 million shares in the market. The proceeds for SmallBank are 210 million. In its stand-alone financial statements, SmallBank has to recognize a EUR 9 million [= (210 million – 180 million) × 30%] tax liability, assuming a 30% tax rate.
2. SmallBank and Gigabank enter into a collar. The change in fair value of the collar would be recognized in P&L. The collar had the following terms:
   • Underlying: SmallBank common stock
   • Number of options: 30 million
   • Settlement: cash settlement
   • Maturity: July 20X1 (just prior to the dividend distribution date), spread over several dates to reduce the gamma risk upon expiry
   • SmallBank buys a call with strike EUR 7.25
   • SmallBank sells a put with strike EUR 6.75
   • Premium: zero
   • Delta of the collar: 90% (i.e., 27 million shares)

At the end of June 20X1, SmallBank reported its regulatory capital ratios. Ignoring the change in fair value of the collar, SmallBank would have the following impacts in its common equity capital:

• The sale of the treasury shares would release EUR 210 million capital.
• The tax liability would reduce EUR 9 million from capital.

As a result, SmallBank has released EUR 201 million (= 210 million – 9 million) common equity capital.

At expiry, prior to July's dividend distribution, there are three scenarios:

- SmallBank's share price is greater than, or equal to, EUR 7.25. SmallBank exercises the call, receiving 30 million own shares and paying EUR 217.5 million (= 30 million × 7.25).
- SmallBank's share price is greater than EUR 6.75 and lower than EUR 7.25. Neither option is exercised. SmallBank buys 30 million own shares in the market.
- SmallBank's share price is lower than, or equal to, EUR 6.75. Gigabank exercises the put option, giving SmallBank 30 million shares and receiving EUR 202.5 million (= 30 million × 6.75).

Alternative with a Deep-in-the-money Call

The major drawback of the previous strategy was the P&L impact due to changes in the fair value of the collar. An alternative strategy uses a deep-in-the-money call rather than a collar. For example, let us assume that SmallBank bought a call with the following terms:

- Underlying: SmallBank common stock
- Number of options: 30 million
- Settlement: Physical settlement only
- Maturity: July 20X1 (just prior to the dividend distribution date), spread over several dates to reduce the gamma risk upon expiry
- SmallBank buys a call with strike EUR 5.60 (i.e., 80% of the then prevailing share price)
- Premium: EUR 1.54 (i.e., 22% of the then prevailing share price) per share, or a total of EUR 46.2 million
- Delta of the call: 90% (i.e., 27 million shares)

As the call could only be settled by SmallBank receiving the underlying shares, it was treated as an equity instrument, and therefore, no fair valuing was required after inception. The EUR 46.2 million premium was recognized in equity, reducing the amount of common equity capital. At the end of June 20X1, SmallBank reported its regulatory capital ratios. The transaction had the following impacts in its common equity capital:

- The sale of the treasury shares released EUR 210 million capital.
- The tax liability reduced capital by EUR 9 million.
- The purchase of the call reduced capital by EUR 46.2 million.

As a result, SmallBank released EUR 154.8 million (= 210 million − 9 million − 46.2 million) common equity capital by implementing this transaction.

11.14 CASE STUDY: REDUCING AN UNCONSOLIDATED FINANCIAL STAKE

Let us assume that SmallBank has a 13% stake in another bank, called RegionalBank. Under Basel III rules, SmallBank is heavily penalized if it holds a stake greater than 10% of the issued capital of RegionalBank. 3% of RegionalBank represents EUR 400 million. A potential transaction can be implemented along the following steps (see Figure 11.15):

1. SmallBank sells 3% of RegionalBank to Gigabank for EUR 400 million. Gigabank then becomes the owner of the stake and its related voting rights.
2. SmallBank buys a bond issued by Gigabank linked to the performance of a fund.

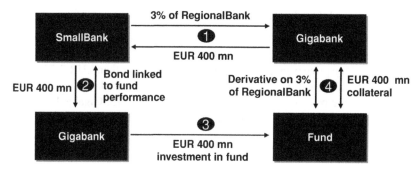

Figure 11.15   Reducing an unconsolidated financial stake.

3. Gigabank invests EUR 400 million in the fund underlying its bond. The fund is free to invest in equity derivatives and can post collateral.
4. The fund underlying Gigabank's bond is fully exposed to the performance to a 3% stake in RegionalBank. The derivative is fully collateralized with EUR 400 million cash posted in favor of Gigabank.

The main drawbacks of the transaction are as follows:

1. SmallBank would recognize a capital gain/loss upon disposal of the 3% stake.
2. SmallBank loses the voting rights on the disposed 3% stake. A usufruct transaction in which the voting rights are transferred to SmallBank can overcome this weakness. However, bank regulators could deem that SmallBank owns the 3% stake for regulatory purposes.
3. SmallBank has to trust that the fund performance mimics the behavior of a 3% stake in RegionalBank.
4. Gigabank may have to partially/totally deduct its 3% stake in RegionalBank from its common equity capital.
5. SmallBank auditors may require consolidation of the fund after a "look-through" approach to the bond.

11.15   CASE STUDY: COMMERZBANK'S CAPITAL STRUCTURE ENHANCEMENT WITH CREDIT SUISSE

On 13 January 2011, Commerzbank implemented a transaction to enhance its common equity Tier 1 capital. Under the new Basel III requirements, hybrid instruments could not contribute to a bank's common equity Tier 1 capital. Commerzbank exchanged hybrid instruments for cash and simultaneously new shares were issued, resulting in contribution in kind. The transaction was executed with Credit Suisse's collaboration and it comprised the following steps (see Figure 11.16):

1. Commerzbank issued 118 million new shares representing 10% of its share capital. The necessary resolutions were to be approved by Commerzbank's board of directors and the supervisory board on 21 January 2011.
2. A syndicate of banks led by Credit Suisse placed the new shares with institutional investors. The new shares were offered at a EUR 5.15–5.35 range (i.e., a discount of 9.5–6% relative to the EUR 5.69 previous day closing). The shares were finally placed at EUR 5.30 per

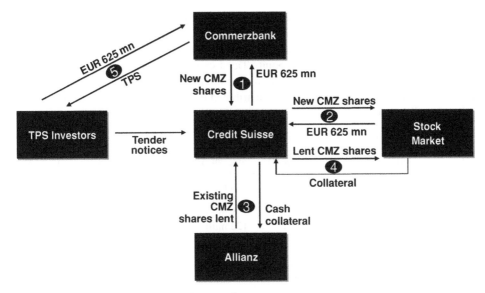

Figure 11.16   Commerzbank's capital transaction.

share (i.e., a 6.9% discount). Commerzbank shares fell 3.4% in the pre-market trading on 13 January 2011. The shares closed at EUR 5.355 on that day. As a result, Commerzbank raised EUR 625 million.

3. Allianz provided Credit Suisse with a stock lending facility of existing Commerzbank shares. Allianz had 10.3% of Commerzbank's share capital. Credit Suisse posted collateral.

4. The buyers of the new shares could borrow from Credit Suisse existing shares, so they were able to trade them before the new shares were delivered. The settlement of the new shares was expected to take place on 26 January 2011.

5. Credit Suisse invited investors to tender trust preferred securities (TPS) issued by companies of the Commerzbank group. Credit Suisse offered cash to the TPS investors, as shown in the table below. In order to participate in the tender offer, qualifying holders had to deliver a liquidation preference amount of TPS. The terms of the tender offer were the following:

TPS	Notional	Offer price	Tender amount (EUR)	Profit (EUR)	Order of priority
1	EUR 300 million	56.5%	170 million	130 million	1
2	EUR 300 million	48%	144 million	156 million	1
3	EUR 1 billion	71.5%	715 million	285 million	2
4	GBP 800 million	71.5%	686 million	273 million	2
5	EUR 600 million	57%	342 million	258 million	2
		Totals	2,057 million	1,102 million	

The transaction equalled a contribution in kind of a portion of the bank's TPS in exchange for the issue of new shares. Under Basel III the TPS would be eligible for additional Tier 1 capital, but not for common equity Tier 1 capital. The proceeds of the placement of the new shares determined the amount of TPS purchasable by the bank. As a result, a maximum of EUR 625 million of TPS was purchased. The allocation of the funds between the TPS was determined in accordance with the order of priority outlined in the table. TPS with the same rank in the order of priority were pro-rated equally.

The transaction had no significant impact on Commerzbank's Tier 1 capital ratio, but it resulted in an increase of its common equity Tier 1 capital. Let us assume that all the first two types of TPS were tendered for EUR 314 million (= 170 million + 144 million), and that the remaining EUR 311 million amount was distributed pro-rata to the remaining TPS, to fill the EUR 625 million target:

TPS	Notional	Tendered cash amount (EUR)	Accepted cash amount (EUR)	Notional tendered (EUR)	Profit (EUR)
1	EUR 300 million	170 million	170 million	300 million	130 million
2	EUR 300 million	144 million	144 million	300 million	156 million
3	EUR 1 billion	715 million	128 million	152 million	51 million
4	GBP 800 million	686 million	122 million	145 million	49 million
5	EUR 600 million	342 million	61 million	107 million	46 million
	Totals	2,057 million	625 million	1,004 million	432 million

The effect on common equity Tier 1 capital was an increase of EUR 1,057 million (= 625 million + 432 million), as follows:

• By issuing new shares, Commerzbank increased its common equity Tier 1 capital by EUR 625 million, the issue proceeds.
• By buying the TPS at a discount to their issue price, Commerzbank booked a gain of EUR 432 million.

The effect on additional Tier 1 capital was a reduction of EUR 1,004 million (see previous table). As a result, Tier 1 capital was almost unchanged, increasing by only 53 million (= 1,057 million − 1,004 million).

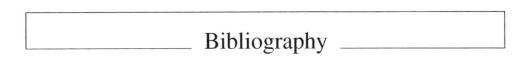

Bibliography

Basel Committee on Banking Supervision (2010) Basel III: A Global Regulatory Framework for More Resilient Banks and Banking Systems.

Basel Committee on Banking Supervision (2010) Guidance for National Authorities Operating the Countercyclical Capital Buffer.

International Accounting Standards Board (2010) IFRS 9 Hedge Accounting, Exposure Draft.

Ramirez, J. (2007) *Accounting for Derivatives*. John Wiley and Sons Ltd, Chichester, UK.

Index

ABB with backstops 98–9, 209–11
  see also accelerated book-buildings
ABBs *see* accelerated book-buildings
ABC double exchangeable case study 169–72
ABC restructuring of call on own shares case study 355–61
accelerated book-buildings (ABBs) 65–6, 98–100, 115, 207–8, 209–11, 229–33
  see also ABB with backstops; block trades
  advantages 99
  definition 65, 98–9, 209
  German disposal of Fraport with JP Morgan collaboration case study 229–33
  IPIC disposal of Barclays stock case study 100
  terms 100
  types 98–9
  weaknesses 99, 115
accelerated stock repurchase programs (ASRs), share buybacks 329–32, 339
acceleration events *see* early termination events
accounting considerations 257, 259–65, 266–73, 276, 284, 290–1, 332, 340, 369, 380, 381–3, 384
  see also IAS . . . ; IFRS . . . ; US GAAP . . .
acquisition prices, M&As 235
acquisition/sale price of shares, initial prices 15–16
actual days, equity swaps 9–26
additional Tier 1 capital 367, 373–6, 397–400, 405–6
  see also Basel III; Tier 1 . . .
  calculations 375–6, 406
  components 373–6, 377, 405
  deductions 375–6
  definition 367, 373
  inclusion criteria 373–4, 377, 405–6
  minimum requirements 376
  Tier 2 capital 375–6
additivity, variance swaps 63
administrative agent fees, revolving margin loan facilities 323–4
ADTVs 294–5
advisors, IPOs 68–87
affiliates 387–8
affirmative covenants, equity financings 294
'aftermarket' trading, IPOs 79–81
AGMs *see* annual general meetings
Agnelli family equity swap with Merrill Lynch case study 248–52

all dividends, dividends per basket calculations 20–1
Allen & Co. 86
Allianz 405–6
allocation of shares, IPOs 66–70, 78–87
American-style options 36, 231–3, 252–6
analyst presentations, IPOs 75–7
'anchor marketing' category, pre-marketing of the IPO offering 76
annual general meetings (AGMs) 235–6, 240–3, 308, 346–7
annualization factor 61–4, 196–7
antitrust authorities, M&As 237, 255–6
arbitrage 29, 105, 199–200, 204–5, 243–8
articles of association 236, 325, 327
ASF *see* available stable funding
Asian call purchases 343–5
ASRs *see* accelerated stock repurchase programs
asset managers, equity swaps 25–6
'at the market' offerings (ATMs), definition 100–2
at-the-money options 36–7, 43, 48–9, 113–14, 214–15, 267, 341–5
  see also intrinsic value . . .
ATMs *see* 'at the market' offerings
auditors 68–86, 228–9, 404
automatic exercise term (auto options) 31–2, 282
available stable funding (ASF) 395–7

balance sheets 266–73, 308, 327, 363, 364–9, 393–4, 395–400
Banco Popolare convertible bond rights issue case study 95–8
Banco Santander 116–18, 283
Bank of America 82–3
Bank of Italy (BoI) 252
Bank of New York (BoNY) 132–6
bank regulatory capital 97–8, 128–33, 137–40, 308, 365–406
  see also Basel . . . ; capital buffers; Tier . . .
  capital instruments failing capital eligibility criteria 393
  capital ratios 365, 366–7, 373, 376, 379, 390–2, 402–3
  case studies 397–406
  Commerzbank capital structure enhancement with Credit Suisse case study 404–6
  components 365–70
  concepts 365–406

bank regulatory capital (*Continued*)
  EU Capital Requirements Directive 366
  Federal Reserve System 366
  FSA 366
  hybrid instruments 379–80, 404–5
  leverage ratios 393–4
  liquidity coverage ratios 394–6
  minority interests 370–3, 374–5, 377–8, 397–400
  net stable funding ratios 396–7
  risk-weighted assets 365–6, 367–9, 373, 376, 398–401
  terminology 365–9
banking book operations 369, 386–7
bankruptcy petitions 116, 130, 196–7
banks 65, 72–88, 95–8, 128–33, 137–40, 237–48, 252–6,
  283–6, 308–20, 327–63, 365–406
  see also global coordinators; syndicates
  banking/trading-book operations 365, 369, 386–7,
    399–400
  financial crisis from 2007 393–4
  regulating bodies 366
Barclays 100
barrier options 191–9, 216–24, 348–55
Basel Accords 365–9
Basel I 365–6
Basel II 365–9, 389, 394, 399–400
  see also bank regulatory capital; Pillar . . . ;
    risk-weighted assets
Basel III 365–9, 371–2, 379–89, 397–406
  see also additional Tier 1 capital; bank regulatory
    capital
  capital conservation buffers 390–1, 398–400
  countercyclical buffers 391
  deductions from Tier 1 capital 380–93
  deferred tax assets 382, 388–9, 393
  defined benefit pension funds 384–5
  definition 365, 366
  hybrid instruments 379–80, 404–5
  implementation timescale 366, 392–3
  leverage ratios 393–4
  liquidity coverage ratios 394–6
  mandatory convertibles and contingent capital
    instruments 372
  minority interests 371–2, 397–400
  net stable funding ratios 396–7
  transitional arrangements 392–3
  unconsolidated financial companies 380, 385–9, 403–4
baskets of stocks 1–6, 18–26, 30–5, 56–8
BAT 153–6
BBVA 253–4
BCP, Controlinveste exchangeable bonds on Portugal
  Telecom case study 141–7
Bear Stearns 243–8
bearish views 1, 33–5, 51, 199
beneficiaries, equity-based compensation plans 258–86
best-effort execution basis, VWAP-linked repurchase
  programs 332–3
Black–Scholes options pricing model 38–40, 47–8,
  261–5
blackout periods 75–7, 328–9
block trades 98–9, 209–11
  see also accelerated book-buildings
BNL, Unipol takeover of BNL and call/put combination
  with Deutsche Bank 252–6

BNP Paribas 256, 339–40
boards of directors 68–84, 87–8, 236–56, 327,
  361–3
bonds 51, 64, 65, 66, 95–8, 103–40, 141–79, 229–33,
  248–9, 287–300, 313–14, 368, 395–7, 403–4
  see also convertible . . . ; exchangeable . . .
bonds collateralized by equity stakes 287–300, 313–14
  definition 287–8
  early termination events 292–5
bonus issues 46–7
book-building IPO process 66–7, 76, 77, 82–5, 87
bookrunners, IPOs 72–84
borrowing fees 4–6, 26–9, 41–2, 199–200, 228–9, 241–3,
  317–18
bought deals *see* block trades
breakeven prices, options 32–6, 183–5, 191, 201, 343
bridge loans, M&As 235
Brisa 141, 156–61
British Land plc 241–3
Brownian motion 47–8
bullish views 1, 25–6, 30–3, 51, 199
butterfly put spreads *see* fly put spreads
buybacks of conversion rights, Cap Gemini case study
  141, 172–5
buybacks of convertibles/exchangeables 141,
  175–7

calculation agents, equity financings 288–300,
  309–16
call options 30–51, 112–14, 121–4, 126–7, 148–79,
  186–9, 200–5, 207–8, 214–15, 216–33, 252–6,
  266–86, 340–63, 373–4, 376–7, 401–3
  see also collars; 'Greeks' (sensitivities); options . . .
  ABBs 229–33
  call/put deltas 43, 48
  covered call writing 200–2
  definition 30–1
  disposal of strategic stakes 207–8, 214–15, 229–33
  enhanced disposal of strategic stakes 207–8,
    214–15
  equity-based compensation plans 273, 278–83
  examples 30–3, 36–7, 42–4
  exchangeable bonds 229–33
  German disposal of Fraport with JP Morgan
    collaboration case study 229–33
  hedging 186–9, 278–83
  M&As 252–6
  make-whole clauses 126–7
  payoffs 32–3, 49–50, 162–3, 187, 200–1, 278–9,
    341–2
  put–call parity 41–2
  share buybacks 340–63
  strategic stakes 141, 161–70, 186–9, 200–5, 207–8,
    214–33
  terms 30–3, 46–7, 161–2, 173, 200, 202, 214–15, 231,
    252–6, 279–81, 283, 342–6, 403
  time value and intrinsic value 36–7, 283
  Unipol takeover of BNL and call/put combination with
    Deutsche Bank 252–6
call periods, convertible bonds 107–40
call rights 109–40, 152–3, 288–300
call spreads 141, 161–70, 361–3
Cap Gemini 141, 172–5

capital adequacy requirements 97–8, 128–33, 137–40, 308, 365–406
capital buffers 367, 376, 389–92
   see also capital conservation . . . ; countercyclical . . .
capital conservation buffers 367, 376, 389–93, 398–400
capital guaranteed equity-linked products 51
capital increase products 65–102, 107, 115–16, 123–7, 161–9, 173–4, 248–52, 273–4, 329–32, 339–40, 361–3
   see also accelerated book-buildings; equity capital market products; hybrid instruments; initial public offerings; rights issues
capital instruments failing capital eligibility criteria, bank regulatory capital 393
capital market products see equity capital market products
capital ratios 365, 366–7, 373, 376, 379, 390–2, 402–3
   see also bank regulatory capital; Basel . . . ; leverage . . . ; liquidity . . . ; net stable funding . . . ; risk-weighted assets; Tier 1 . . .
Capital Requirements Directive (CRD) 366
   see also Basel III
capital returns to shareholders 327, 346
   see also share buybacks
capital-allocation decisions 327–63
capped VWAP execution basis, VWAP-linked repurchase programs 337–8
cash collateral agents 288–300, 304–8, 313–16
cash flow hedge reserves, Tier 1 capital deductions 380, 382–3
cash margin accounts, equity financings 290–1, 312–16
cash option terms, convertible bonds 107, 111–12
cash settlement amounts, prepaid forwards plus equity swaps 310–16
cash top-ups, convertible bonds 111–12
cash-settled equity forwards 1–6
   see also equity forwards
cash-settled equity swaps 6–26, 207–8, 224–7, 249–52, 301–8, 314–16
   see also equity swaps
cash-settled options 30–50, 162–9, 182–4, 200–2, 280–3, 319, 320–2, 344–8, 385
   see also options
CASHES 103, 127–8, 131–6
CDSs see credit default swaps
change-of-control make-whole clauses, convertible bonds 126–7
Citigroup 83, 86, 101–2
clean-up call clauses, convertible bonds 127
close periods see blackout periods
closing prices, settlement prices of equity swaps 17
co-managers, IPO syndicates 73–87
CoCos see contingent convertibles
collared financing, equity financings 320–2
collars 186–9, 320–2, 338–40, 402–3
   see also call options; put options
   definition 186, 320
collateral 26–9, 114–15, 205, 241–8, 287–300, 313–16, 317–18, 324–5, 405–6
Commerzbank capital structure enhancement with Credit Suisse case study 404–6

commitment fees, revolving margin loan facilities 323–4
common stock 103–40, 153–6, 276–80, 324–5, 327–63, 365–406
   see also convertible bonds; equity . . . ; Tier 1 capital
communication agencies, IPOs 68–84
company lifecycles, equity capital market products 65–6
compensation amounts, offsetting dividend risks 45–6
compo equity swaps 21–3
composite options 49–50, 162–9
concentrated stock positions see strategic stakes
conference calls, IPO roadshows 76, 77
confirmation agreements 1–2, 6, 26–7
CONSOB 253–6
consolidated balance sheets, minority interests 397–400
contingent convertibles (CoCos) 103, 127–40
   see also CASHES; convertible bonds; ECNs; FRESHs; SCNs
Controlinveste exchangeable bonds on Portugal Telecom case study 141–7
converse transactions 204, 205, 252–6
conversion prices 103, 107–40, 166–9, 361–2
conversion ratios 107–40, 174–5
conversion rights, Cap Gemini case study 141, 172–5
convertible arbitrage, definition 105
convertible bonds 51, 65, 66, 95–8, 100, 103–40, 141–79, 248–52, 361–3, 379–80
   see also CASHES; contingent convertibles; ECNs; equity-linked products; FRESHs; mandatory . . .
   advantages 103–4, 106–7, 115–16, 117–18, 152–3
   Banco Popolare rights issue case study 95–8
   Basel III 372
   buybacks of conversion rights 141, 172–5
   buybacks of convertibles/exchangeables 141, 175–7
   buyer perspectives 105–6, 116, 118, 120–1, 138, 152–3, 178–9
   call option make-whole clauses 126–7
   call rights 109–40, 152–3
   call spreads 161–9, 361–3
   Cap Gemini repurchase of conversion rights case study 141, 172–5
   cash option terms 107, 111–12
   cash top-ups 111–12
   change-of-control make-whole clauses 126–7
   clean-up call clauses 127
   concepts 66, 103–40, 248–52, 361–3
   conversion premiums 103–4, 107–40, 148–79, 361–3
   coupon deferral clauses 125–6, 131
   coupons 103–40, 147, 151–3, 169, 177–9, 211–14, 361–3
   covenants 104, 106–7
   credit spreads 106, 114, 177–9
   CSM call spread with Goldman Sachs case study 141, 161–9
   definition 66, 103–5
   delta 114–15, 118
   dilution considerations 107, 115–16, 123–7, 161–9, 173–4, 361–3
   disadvantages 98, 107, 116, 118
   dividend protection clauses 124–5, 211–14
   dividend swaps 51
   equity swaps 156, 176–8
   exchangeable bonds 103–5

convertible bonds (*Continued*)
  fund types 105–6
  Gileads' share repurchase program financed with
    convertible bonds case study 361–3
  hedge funds 105–6, 114–15, 175–7
  implied volatility 106–7, 173–5
  Infineon case study 103, 107–15, 127–8
  issuer perspectives 106–7, 115–16, 117–19, 121–2,
    138, 147–53, 172–9
  likelihoods of conversion 141, 161–72
  liquidity 105–6, 107
  make-whole clauses 126–7
  Microsoft convertible plus call spread case study 141,
    169–70
  net share settlement clauses 127–8, 167–9
  Novartis LEPOs and put options with Deutsche Bank
    case study 141, 147–53
  pre-IPO convertible bonds 141, 178–9
  put rights 110–11, 175, 178–9
  reverse convertibles 51
  Richemont warrants issue on back of convertible
    preference shares case study 141, 153–6
  rights issues 95–8, 131–6, 248–9
  share buybacks 361–3
  soft call term 107–40, 162, 168–9
  special clauses 124–7, 174–5
  strategic equity transactions 141–79
  takeover make-whole clauses 126–7
  tax calls 111–12
  taxes 111–12, 363
  terms 95–6, 107–14, 116–17, 118–19, 123, 124–7,
    128–9, 132–3, 137, 169, 173, 174–5, 213
  third-party issues 141, 147–53
  TUI buyback convertible case study 141, 175–7
  types 103–5
  valuations 110–11, 112–14, 122, 177–9
  voting rights 103–4, 106–7, 153–6, 211
  warrants 141, 153–6, 362–3
  zero-coupon convertibles 104, 147, 151–3, 169, 231–3
convertible preference shares 141, 153–6
convexity 61, 63–4
Corporacion Dermoestetica's public offer to acquire own
  shares case study 345–6
corporate actions 46–7
  see also bonus issues; dividends; rights issues; stock
    splits
corporate governance 67
correlation trading, variance/volatility swaps 64
cost of carry, equity swaps 6–8
countercyclical buffers 367, 391–3
counterparty credit risk 28–9, 52, 318–19, 365–406
coupon deferral clauses, convertible bonds 125–6, 131
coupons 103–40, 142–79, 211–14, 232–3, 287–300,
    361–3
  see also interest payments
covenants 104, 106–7, 293–4, 325
covered call writing, yield enhancement of strategic
    stakes 200–2
credit conversion factors (CCFs) 394
credit default swaps (CDSs) 288–300
  see also credit events
credit derivatives 394
credit enhancement tools, equity financings 291–2

credit events 158–61, 288–300
  see also credit default swaps
credit ratings 106, 115, 130, 140, 142–3, 147–53,
    229–33, 248–9, 293–4, 368, 395–7
credit risk 28–9, 205, 240, 319, 355–61, 365–406
  see also bank regulatory capital; haircut uses
  definition 368
credit spreads, convertible bonds 106, 114, 177–9
Credit Suisse 86, 100, 142, 252–6, 368, 404–6
CSFB 253–6
  see also Credit Suisse
CSM call spread with Goldman Sachs case study 141,
    161–9
cum-rights price, definition 88
currencies 21–5, 285–6, 369
current ratios 293–4
custodian banks 142–7

dates in dividend distributions 52
day count fractions 5–6, 9–26, 249–52, 302–8,
    312–16
debt capital markets 26, 65–6, 67, 103–40, 287–325
  see also bonds
debt-to-equity ratios 115–16, 275, 279, 281, 293–4
declaration dates 52–8
declared cash dividends 20–1, 53–8
declared cash equivalent dividends 20–1, 53–8
DECS *see* dividend enhanced convertible securities
dedicated convertible funds 105–6
deep-in-the-money call purchases, share buybacks
    340–3
default events 288–300, 305, 313–16, 317–18
deferred tax assets (DTAs) 380–2, 388–9, 393
defined benefit pension funds 380, 383–5
delta 1, 42–8, 51, 105, 114–15, 118, 156, 174, 184–8,
    191, 193, 195, 199, 202, 214–15, 219, 227–9, 280,
    319
  see also gamma; risk reversals; skew
  definition 42–3
delta-hedging 1, 44–5, 51, 105, 118, 156, 174, 184–8,
    191, 193, 195, 199, 202, 214–15, 219, 319
  see also hedging
  definition 44–5
delta-neutral hedging 105, 156
denominations
  convertible bonds 107–40
  exchangeable bonds 142–79
depositary banks 131–6
derecognition strategies for the disposal of strategic
  stakes 207–8, 224–9, 308
  critique 226–7
  definition 207–8, 224
derivative instruments 1–64, 181–205, 219, 235–56,
    382–3, 385, 394, 400–1
  see also equity . . . ; forwards; futures . . . ; options;
    range accruals; swaps
  definition 316–17
deterministic disposal of strategic stakes 208–12
Deutsche Bank 141, 147–53, 156–61, 252–6
Deutsche Telekom (DTE) 2–4, 7–14
dilution 65, 88–98, 107, 115–16, 123–7, 161–9, 173–4,
    248–52, 273–4, 329–32, 339–40, 361–3
directional views 51, 63–4

disclosure requirements, M&As 235, 236–7, 247, 251–2, 256
discounted cash flows (DCFs), IPO valuations 73
discounted purchase share plans 258
discounted VWAP execution basis, VWAP-linked repurchase programs 334–6, 337–8
discounts 73, 91–5, 99–100, 209–11, 231–3, 258, 334–6, 337–8, 348–55
dispersion trades 64
  see also correlation . . .
disposal of strategic stakes 207–33
  see also strategic stakes
  ABBs 207–8, 209–11, 229–33
  call options 207–8, 214–15, 229–33
  cash-settled equity swaps 224–7
  concepts 207–33
  definition 207–8
  derecognition strategies 207–8, 224–9, 308
  deterministic disposal strategies 208–12
  double-speed range accruals 220–4
  double-speed range accruals with deductions 222–3
  double-speed range accruals with final call 221–2
  double-speed range accruals with knock-outs 222–4
  enhanced disposal strategies 207–8, 212–24
  equity swaps 207–8, 224–9
  exchangeable bonds 207–8, 211–12, 213–14, 229–33
  German disposal of Fraport with JP Morgan collaboration case study 229–33
  gradual sales 208–9
  indirect issues of exchangeable bonds 207–8, 211–12
  market dribble-outs 208–9
  one-speed range accruals 216–19, 220–1
  physically-settled equity swaps 227–9
  range accruals 207–8, 216–24
distressed convertible valuations 113–14
distributed amounts, dividend swaps 53–8
diversification 25–6, 51, 64, 66–7, 307, 316, 324–5, 387
  see also portfolios
dividend amount payers, dividend swaps 53–8
dividend amount per period, dividend swaps 53–8
dividend enhanced convertible securities (DECS) 118–24
  see also variable parity mandatory convertibles
  definition 118
dividend swaps 1, 50–8, 142–7
  see also swaps
  definition 50
  exchangeable bonds 142–7
  index dividend swaps 56–8
  terms 53, 56
dividend yields 42, 44, 61–4, 106, 115–40, 143–79, 181–205, 283–6, 318–19, 320–2
  see also rho
dividends 4–28, 38–41, 42, 44, 45–7, 50–8, 61–4, 91, 94–5, 103–40, 142–79, 181–205, 211–33, 249–52, 259–86, 300–8, 312–16, 318–22, 374
  amounts 6–26, 53–8, 144–7, 249–52, 301–8
  capital returns to shareholders 327, 346
  convertible bonds 103–40
  dates in distributions 52
  elections 202–4
  equity swaps 6–26, 249–52, 276–80, 300–8
  equity-based compensation plans 259–86

extraordinary (special) dividends 55
forward price calculations 4–6
implied dividends 52–3, 58
monetization of dividend optionality 202–4
offsetting dividend risks 45–7
options 38–41, 45–7, 318–22
pass-through mechanisms 124–5
per basket 18–21, 56–8
per share 91
periods 53–8
protection clauses 124–5, 142–7, 211–14
rights issues 91, 94–5
risk 45–7, 51
scrip dividends 11, 95, 202–4, 401–3
stock lending/borrowing transactions 26–9, 51, 204–5, 241–3, 300–8, 317–18, 320, 322
threshold mechanisms 124–5
double issuance of exchangeable bonds 141, 169–72
double-speed range accruals 220–4, 352–4
Dragui, Mario 255
drawn amounts, LTV 291–300
DTAs see deferred tax assets
due diligence 69–84
Dutch auctions, definition 67, 85–7
dynamic hedging 285–6

early termination events, equity financings 292–5, 305, 309–16
early unwind 301–8, 309–16, 322
earnings per share (EPS) 107, 260–1, 331–2
EBITDA 73, 260–1, 266–7, 270
ECM team see equity capital markets (ECM) team
ECNs 103, 127–8, 136–8
effective dates 9–26, 53–8, 301–8, 309–16
EGMs see extraordinary general meetings
eligible collateral, revolving margin loan facilities 324–5
eligible shareholders see qualifying shareholders
embedded options 50–1, 112–14, 121–4, 156, 162–9, 173–7, 202–4, 261–86, 362–3, 385
  see also convertible bonds
employee stock options plans (ESOPs) 257, 258–9, 262–86, 329–30
  see also stock options plans
  accounting entries 261–5, 266–73
  definition 257, 258
  terms 258, 265–6
employees, stock options plans 257–86, 329–30
enhanced disposal of strategic stakes 207–8, 212–24, 231–3
  definition 207–8, 212–13
  double-speed range accruals 220–4
  exchangeable bonds 213–14
  one-speed range accruals 216–19, 220–1
EPS see earnings per share
equity amount payers, equity swaps 6–26, 224–9, 249–52, 276–80, 302–8
equity amount receivers, equity swaps 6–26, 224–9, 249–52, 276–80, 302–8
equity amounts 6–26, 59–64, 224–9, 249–52, 276–80, 302–8, 311–16
  see also settlement amounts

equity capital market products 65–102, 103–40, 367, 369–73
  see also accelerated book-buildings; capital increase products; hybrid instruments; initial public offerings; rights issues
  company lifecycles 65–6
  overview 65–6
  types 65–6, 87–8, 103
equity capital markets (ECM) team 65
equity derivative instruments 1–64, 181–205, 235–56
  see also forwards; futures . . . ; options; swaps
  concepts 1–64
equity financings 287–325
  accounting entries 290–1
  bonds collateralized by equity stakes 287–300, 313–14
  case studies 287–300, 322–5
  CDSs 288–300
  collared financing 320–2
  collateral 287–300, 313–16, 317–18, 324–5
  concepts 287–325
  covenants 293–4, 325
  credit enhancement tools 291–2
  default events 288–300, 305, 313–16, 317–18
  definition 287
  early termination events 292–5, 305, 309–16
  equity swaps 300–16
  LTV 288–300, 304, 308–16, 318–22
  margin loans 322–5
  margining 288–308, 309–16, 318, 325
  parties 288–90
  prepaid forwards plus equity swaps 308–16
  put financing 318–22
  recourse/non-recourse types 299–300, 320
  repos 316–17
  sale plus equity swaps 300–8, 310, 313
  stock lending/borrowing transactions 317–18, 320–2
equity forwards 1–6, 156, 207–8, 308–16, 329–32, 340
  see also cash-settled . . . ; physically-settled . . .
  concepts 1–6, 308–16, 329–32
  definition 1–2
  examples 2–4, 308–16
  share buybacks 329–32, 340
  terms 2, 4, 309–13
  types 1–2
  US GAAP rules 332
equity funds, convertible bonds 105–6
equity income funds, convertible bonds 106
equity notional amounts 9–14, 17–26, 176–7, 227–9, 276–80, 302–8, 311–16
equity plus share plans 258
equity swaps 1, 6–26, 130, 142–7, 156, 176–8, 207–8, 224–9, 238–40, 243–52, 273–80, 300–16
  see also cash-settled . . . ; physically-settled . . . ; price return . . . ; swaps; total return . . .
  Agnelli family equity swap with Merrill Lynch case study 248–52
  asset managers 25–6
  compo equity swaps 21–3
  concepts 6–26, 224–9, 238–40, 243–52, 273–80

confirmation agreements 6
convertible bonds 156, 176–8
definition 6–7
derecognition strategies for the disposal of strategic stakes 207–8, 224–9, 308
disposal of strategic stakes 207–8, 224–9
diversification 25–6, 307, 316
equity financings 300–16
equity-based compensation plans 273–80
examples 7–14, 17–21, 238–40, 243–8
hedging 13–17, 23, 24–6, 239–40, 273–80
initial prices 9–12, 15–26, 225–9, 249–52, 276–80, 301–8, 309–16
M&As 238–40, 243–52
Perry's equity swaps with Bear Stearns and Goldman Sachs case study 243–8
prepaid forwards plus equity swaps 308–16
quanto equity swaps 23–5
sale plus equity swaps 300–8, 310, 313
settlement methods 6–26
stock indexes 1–6, 17–26
terms 9–13, 18, 21–2, 24, 249–50, 275–6, 300–8, 309–16
transaction flows 8–9, 13–14, 18–20, 22–3, 24–5, 224–9, 244–52, 305–8, 314–16
uses 25–6, 224–9, 238–40, 243–52, 273–80, 300–16
equity-based compensation plans 257–86, 329–30
  see also stock options plans
  accounting entries 261–5, 266–73, 284
  call options 273, 278–83
  case studies 265–83
  definition 257–9
  equity swaps 273–80
  fair values 261–2, 266–80, 284–6
  hedging 257, 273–83, 285–6
  HSBC share performance awards 257, 258, 283–6
  IFRS accounting 257, 259–65, 276
  risks 273–83
  taxes 257
  terminology 258–9
  terms 258–9, 265–6
  treasury shares 273–5, 278, 279, 281, 286
  types 257–9
equity-linked products 66, 103–40
  see also convertible bonds; mandatory convertibles
equity-story part of the analyst presentation, IPOs 75–7
Ernst & Young 86
escrow accounts, equity financings 291–4
escrow agents, bonds collateralized by equity stakes 288–300
escrow agreements, bonds collateralized by equity stakes 288–300
Eurex 2, 4, 53–8
Euribor 6, 9–14, 18–26, 129–32, 135–6, 158, 250–2, 276–80
Euronext 53–8
European Union (EU) 328, 366
European-style options 30–6, 41–3, 181–205, 214–15, 252–6, 318–22, 346–7
  see also options
  definition 36

Eurostoxx 50 index 17–21, 56–8, 265–83, 325
EV comparables, IPO valuations 73
ex-dividend dates 10–14, 39, 45–6, 52–8, 204–5,
    261–5
ex-rights date, definition 88
exchangeable bonds 103–5, 141–79, 207–8, 211–12,
    213–14, 229–33
    ABBs 229–33
    ABC double exchangeable case study 169–72
    buybacks of convertibles/exchangeables 141, 175–7
    call options 229–33
    Controlinveste exchangeable bonds on Portugal
        Telecom case study 141–7
    definition 103, 141–2
    deterministic disposal of strategic stakes 208,
        211–12
    Deutsche Bank exchangeable into Brisa case study
        141, 156–61
    disposal of strategic stakes 207–8, 211–12, 213–14,
        229–33
    dividend swaps 142–7
    double issuance 141, 169–72
    enhanced disposal of strategic stakes 213–14
    exchange property 105, 145–7, 151–3, 169–71,
        211–14, 231–3
    German disposal of Fraport with JP Morgan
        collaboration case study 229–33
    maturity 142–79, 211–14, 232–3
    Novartis LEPOs and put options with Deutsche Bank
        case study 141, 147–53
    premiums 142–79, 231–3
    put options 156–61
    regulators 230
    security mechanisms 146–7
    strategic equity transactions 141–79
    terms 141–2, 148–53, 158, 170–1, 211–12, 213,
        231–2
    third-party guarantees 141–7
    transaction flows 147–57, 158–61
    zero-coupon exchangeables 147, 151–3, 231–3
exercise of options 30–50, 265–86, 320–2
    see also American . . . ; European . . .
exercise periods, equity-based compensation plans
    259–86
exercise prices, equity-based compensation plans
    257–86
existing shares, rights issues 88–98
Exor 248–52
expected life terms, equity-based compensation plans
    259–86
expected losses, Tier 1 capital deductions 380, 383
expiration dates 30–50, 88–98, 181–205, 215, 231–3,
    252–6, 258–9, 265–73, 319, 342–6, 347–8
    see also theta
    definition 38–9
'exposure' see restated balance sheet assets
extraordinary general meetings (EGMs) 87–8, 90, 97,
    122–3, 131, 236, 238–9, 255, 308
extraordinary (special) dividends 55

fair values 219, 226–7, 261–2, 266–80, 284–6, 367–9,
    381–3, 402–3
Fazio, Antonio 252–5

Federal Reserve System 366
fees
    IPOs 69, 71–2, 83–4
    revolving margin loan facilities 323–4
    rights issues 88
    stock lending/borrowing transactions 26–9,
        41–2, 199–200, 228–9, 241–3, 317–18
Fiat 248–52
fiduciary banks 132–6
final exchange parts, equity swaps 305,
    313–16
final offering structures, IPOs 76
financial advisors, IPOs 69–87
financial covenants, equity financings 293–4
financial crisis from 2007 393–4
Financial Services Authority (FSA) 366
financing considerations 26, 65–6, 67, 103–40,
    287–325
    see also debt capital . . . ; equity capital . . . ; equity
        financings
financing repayment amounts, forward price calculations
    4–6
Fiorina, Carly 329–30
Fitch 293
fixed amount payers, dividend swaps 53–8
fixed amount per period, dividend swaps 53–8
fixed amounts 53–8, 59–64, 298–300
fixed parity mandatory convertibles 116–18
fixed strike, dividend swaps 53–8
floating amounts 6–26, 50–8, 59–64, 128–40, 224–9,
    249–52, 298–308, 311–16
fly put spreads 189–91, 193
follow-on capital raising 66–7, 87–102
    see also accelerated book-buildings; convertible
        bonds; equity capital market products; rights issues
foreign currencies see currencies
forfeiture terms, equity-based compensation plans
    259–86
Fortis Bank 103, 128–31
Fortis FRESH instrument case study 128–31
forward prices 1–6, 308–16, 330–2
forwards 1–6, 63, 121–4, 156, 207–8, 308–16,
    329–32
    see also equity . . . ; variance swaps
Fraport 229–33
FRESHs 103, 127–31
FSA see Financial Services Authority
FTSE 100 index 325
fund managers 105–6
    see also hedge . . .
futures exchanges 19–21, 22–6
FX risk 21–2, 23–4, 285–6, 369

gain-on-sale related to securitization transactions, Tier 1
    capital deductions 380, 383
gamma 42, 44, 59, 214–15
    see also delta
gamma-hedging 59
geometric Brownian motion 47–8
German disposal of Fraport with JP Morgan
    collaboration case study 229–33
Gileads' share repurchase program financed with
    convertible bonds case study 361–3

global coordinators 68–84, 92–5
  see also banks
Global Master Securities Lending Agreements (GMSLA)
    26–7
GMSLA see Global Master Securities Lending
    Agreements
going concerns, definition 367
'going public' process
  see also initial public offerings
  definition 66
Gold International case study 237–9
Goldman Sachs 83, 86, 141, 161–9, 243–8, 362–3
gone concerns
  see also Tier 2 capital
  definition 367, 376
goodwill 365, 380
  see also intangible assets
Google's Dutch auction IPO case study 85–7
grace/cure periods, early termination events 295
gradual sales, deterministic disposal of strategic stakes
    208–9
grant dates, equity-based compensation plans 258–86
the 'Greeks' (sensitivities) 42–5, 114–15
  see also delta; gamma; rho; theta; vega
'greenshoe' (overallotment) option, IPOs 79–80,
    83–7
gross dividends 11–14, 45–6, 202–3, 276–80
gross spread 71–2, 84–6
  see also fees; initial public offerings
group presentations, IPO roadshows 76, 77
guaranteed borrow maturities 27
guaranteed execution basis 333
guarantees 27, 288–300, 333

haircut uses
  see also credit risk
  stock lending/borrowing transactions 28–9
Hang Seng index 325
hard call term, convertible bonds 107–40
hard no call term, convertible bonds 107–40
hedge funds 105–6, 114–15, 156, 175–7, 200, 243–8
hedging 1, 13–17, 23–6, 44–5, 59, 63–4, 114–15,
    156, 175–7, 181–200, 216–29, 239–40, 243–8,
    250–2, 254–6, 257, 273–83, 285–6, 319–22, 341–2,
    363, 382–3, 388
  see also delta-hedging
  automatic exercise term (auto options) 282
  call options 186–9, 278–83
  collars 186–9
  dividend swaps 50–1
  equity swaps 13–17, 23, 24–6, 239–40, 273–80
  equity-based compensation plans 257, 273–83, 285–6
  fly put spreads 189–91, 193
  HSBC share performance awards 285–6
  knock-out puts 191–3, 219–24
  ladder puts 193–5
  pay-later puts 197–9
  put options 181–99, 319–22
  put spread collars 188–9
  put spreads 184–6, 188–93
  stock options plans 257, 273–83, 285–6
  strategic stakes 181–99
  summary of strategies 193
  timer call options 282–3

timer puts 195–7, 283
variance/volatility swaps 63
Hewlett Packard 329–32, 339–40
high coupon convertibles 104
high yield funds, convertible bonds 106
highly liquid assets, liquidity coverage ratios 394–6
historical volatility 40–1, 44–5, 59–64, 195–7, 282–3,
    366–7
hostile takeovers 67, 199–200, 236–56
  see also mergers and acquisitions
  defenses 236
HSBC 83, 257, 258, 283–6
hybrid instruments, bank regulatory capital 379–80,
    404–5

IAS 12 Income Taxes 381–2
IAS 19 Employee Benefits 384
IAS 39 Financial Instruments: Recognition and
    Measurement 382–3
IBM 30–52
IFIL 248–52
IFRS accounting 257, 259–65, 276, 369, 380, 382–3
implied dividends 52–3, 58
implied volatility 38, 39–41, 44–5, 47–9, 63, 64, 106–7,
    173–5, 185–6, 193, 267, 282–3, 320, 340
  see also options; skew; timer puts; vega; volatility
    smiles
  definition 39, 40
in-the-money options 31–2, 36–7, 42–4, 48, 113–14,
    200–1, 214–15, 227–9, 281, 339–43, 403
  see also intrinsic value...
incentive fees, IPOs 72
inception steps, dividend elections 203–4
income and expenditure accounts 261–5, 266–73,
    276–80, 286, 361, 381–2
indentures, bonds collateralized by equity stakes
    288–300
indexes see stock indexes
indirect issues of exchangeable bonds, deterministic
    disposal of strategic stakes 208, 211–12
Infineon convertible bond case study 103, 107–15, 127–8
ING rights issues case study 91–5
initial LTV, equity financings 288–300, 304, 308–16
initial prices, equity swaps 9–12, 15–26, 225–9, 249–52,
    276–80, 301–8, 309–16
initial public offerings (IPOs) 65–87, 141, 177–9, 345–6
  advisors 68–87
  'aftermarket' trading 79–81
  allocation of shares 66–70, 78–87
  analyst presentations 75–7
  benefits 67
  book-building IPO process 66–7, 76, 77, 82–5, 87
  concepts 65–87, 141, 177–9
  definition 65, 66–7
  drawbacks 67
  due diligence 69–87
  Dutch auctions 67, 85–7
  equity-story part of the analyst presentation 75–7
  fees 69, 71–2, 83–4
  financial advisors 69–87
  global coordinators 68–84
  Google's Dutch auction IPO case study 85–7
  'greenshoe' (overallotment) option 79–80, 83–7
  investor relations teams 80

lock-up periods 80, 84–7, 96
marketing-the-offering phase 68, 70, 72–3, 75–7,
    81–2
methods 66–7, 76, 87
offer prices 66, 70–6, 77–87
offering structure 70–1
phases 66–7, 68–81, 177–8
placement-of-the-offering phase 66–7, 68, 77–80,
    82
pre-IPO convertible bonds 141, 178–9
preparation-of-the-company phase 68–9
preparation-of-the-offering phase 68, 69–75, 81–2
product description 66–7
project structure 69–75
prospectuses 70, 72, 76, 77–84
'red herrings' 76, 77–8
risk factors 81–2
roadshows 68–9, 76–84
size of tranches 70–1
success factors 80–1
syndicates 70, 72–87
timescales 68, 72, 84–6
underwriters 69–87
valuations 72–5, 177–9
Visa Inc. case study 82–4, 87
insider information 328
    see also blackout periods
institutional investors 65–87, 106, 209–11, 247
intangible assets
    see also goodwill
    Tier 1 capital deductions 380
interest carry 5–6
interest flows
    equity swaps 6–26
    stock lending/borrowing transactions 27–9
interest payments
    see also coupons
    default events 293–4
    revolving margin loan facilities 323–5
interest rates 4–26, 38, 39–40, 44, 113–40, 177–9, 261–5,
    301–6, 323–5, 369
    see also rho
    equity swaps 6–26
    forward price calculations 4–6
    options pricing models 38, 39–40, 261–5
    risk 369
interim exchange parts, equity swaps 304, 312–13
Internal Capital Adequacy Assessment Process (ICAAP)
    366
internal ratings-based approach (IRB) 378, 383
International Swaps and Derivatives Association (ISDA)
    1–2, 6, 26–7, 307–8, 316
intrinsic value of an option
    see also at-the-money . . . ; in-the-money . . . ;
    out-of-the-money . . .
    definition 36–7
investment banks, indirect issues of exchangeable bonds
    207–8, 211–12
investor relations teams, IPOs 80
investors
    ABBs 65–6, 98–100, 115
    convertible bonds 103–4, 105–40
    IPOs 65–87
    profiles 78–9

IPE 157–61
IPIC disposal of Barclays stock ABB case study
    100
IPOs see initial public offerings
IRB see internal ratings-based approach
ISDA see International Swaps and Derivatives
    Association
issue dates 107–40, 142–79, 287–300
issue prices
    convertible bonds 107–40, 211–14
    exchangeable bonds 142–79, 211–14
ISVAP 254–5

joint/co-lead-managers 73–87, 96–8
JP Morgan 82–3, 86, 129, 229–33, 362–3

knock-out barriers 191–3, 219–24, 352–4
knock-out calls 352–4
knock-out puts 191–3, 219–24
KPMG 83

ladder puts, hedging 193–5
Laxey stock lending case study 241–3
LBOs see leveraged buy-outs
LCRs see liquidity coverage ratios
legal advisors, IPOs 68–9, 83–7
Lehman Brothers 86
lending fees, stock lending/borrowing transactions 26–9,
    41–2, 199–200, 228–9, 241–3, 317–18
LEPOs 141, 147–53
letters of credit 394
leverage 66–7, 258, 365–406
leverage ratios 393–4
leverage share savings plans 258
leveraged buy-outs (LBOs) 66–7
    see also private equity
Libor 6, 137, 301–6, 311–25
likelihoods of conversion, convertible bonds 141,
    161–72
liquidation procedures 296–7
liquidity 105–6, 107, 293–4, 324–5, 327–8,
    365–406
    bank regulatory capital 365–406
    convertible bonds 105–6, 107
    financial covenants 293–4
    share buybacks 327–8
liquidity coverage ratios (LCRs) 394–6
listed companies, M&As 236–56
Lloyds 103, 136–8
Lloyds ECN case study 136–8
loan to value (LTV), equity financings 288–300, 304,
    308–16, 318–22
lock-out periods, convertible bonds 107–40
lock-up periods 80, 84–7, 96, 111–12,
    253–4
lognormal returns, volatility calculations 40–1
Lombard loans see margin loans
long positions 6–26, 38–40, 105–6, 114, 278–9,
    386–7
low coupon convertibles 104
LTV see loan to value

maintenance covenants see financial covenants
make-whole clauses 126–7, 295, 297

management fees, IPOs 71–2
Mandalay Resort 126–7
mandatory convertibles 65, 66, 97–8, 100, 104, 115–40,
    207–8, 211–12, 248–52
    see also contingent convertibles; convertible bonds;
        equity-linked products; fixed parity . . . ; variable
        parity . . .
    advantages 115–16, 117–18
    Banco Santander fixed parity case study 116–18
    bankruptcy petitions 116, 130
    Basel III 372
    buyer perspectives 116, 118, 138
    conversion premiums 116, 121–2
    definitions 66, 97, 115, 116–17
    disadvantages 116, 118
    issuer perspectives 115–16, 117–18, 121–2, 138
    subordinated debt 116, 128–40
    UBS DECS case study 122–4
mandatory public offer requirements, M&As 235, 237,
    248–52, 254
manufactured dividends 28–9, 300–8, 320, 322
margin calls 294, 307, 316, 318–22
margin loans, equity financings 322–5
margining, equity financings 288–308, 309–16, 318,
    325
margins, futures exchanges 19–21, 22–6
mark-to-market values 193, 401
market abuses, share buybacks 328
market dribble-outs, deterministic disposal of strategic
    stakes 208–9
market risk 51, 247–8, 273–83, 320, 322, 367–406
    see also Value-at-Risk
    definition 367
market value of secured collateral, LTV 291–300,
    312–16
market vesting conditions, equity-based compensation
    plans 259–83
marketing-the-offering IPO phase 68, 70, 72–3, 75–7,
    81–2
Martin, John 361
Master Agreements 1–2, 26–7
maturities 4–6, 107–40, 142–79, 211–14, 232–3, 258–86,
    287–300
maturity dates, forward price calculations 4–6
Mediobanca 131–6
mergers and acquisitions (M&As) 67, 153, 199–200,
    224, 235–56
    AGMs 235–6, 240–3
    Agnelli family equity swap with Merrill Lynch case
        study 248–52
    antitrust authorities 237, 255–6
    arbitrage position enhancements 243–8
    bridge loans 235
    call options 252–6
    concepts 235–56
    defenses 236
    disclosure requirements 235, 236–7, 247, 251–2, 256
    equity derivatives 235–56
    equity swaps 238–40, 243–52
    hedge fund merger arbitrage position enhancements
        243–8
    Laxey stock lending case study 241–3
    listed companies 236–56
    locked-in acquisition prices 235

mandatory public offer requirements 235, 237,
    248–52, 254
    Mylan–King merger 243–7
    Perry's equity swaps with Bear Stearns and Goldman
        Sachs case study 243–8
    pre-offer blocks 235
    proxy contests 235–6, 237–40, 243–8
    put options 252–6
    qualified holdings 236–7
    regulators 235–56
    short-form disclosure statements 247
    stock lending/borrowing transactions 241–8
    success likelihoods 252–6
    Telefonica offer to Portugal Telecom case study 226,
        237–40
    transparent disclosure policies 240, 256
    Unipol takeover of BNL and call/put combination with
        Deutsche Bank 252–6
    voting rights 235–6
Merrill Lynch 83, 248–52, 329–32
MGM 126–7
Microsoft 49–50, 141, 169–70
Microsoft convertible plus call spread case study 141,
    169–70
minority interests 370–3, 374–5, 377–8, 397–400
Montalban Partners case study 237–9
monetization of dividend optionality 202–4
    see also scrip dividends
moneyness of options
    see also at-the-money . . . ; in-the-money . . . ; intrinsic
        value . . . ; out-of-the-money . . .
    definitions 37–8
Monte Carlo simulations 284
Moody's 293
Morgan Stanley 86, 101–2
mortgage servicing rights (MSRs) 380, 388–9, 393
MSRs *see* mortgage servicing rights
Mylan–King merger 243–7

negative covenants, equity financings 294
net dividends, equity swaps 11–14
net operating losses (NOLs), deferred tax assets
    381–2
net share settlement clauses 127–8, 167–9, 330–2
net stable funding ratios (NSFRs), bank regulatory
    capital 396–7
netting arrangements, restated balance sheet assets 394
Nikkei 225 index 325
non-core Tier 1 capital *see* additional Tier 1 capital
non-counterparty risk, definition 367–8
non-market vesting conditions, equity-based
    compensation plans 259–86
non-pre-emptive capital increases, definition 66
non-recourse equity financings, definition 299–300,
    320
non-vesting conditions, equity-based compensation plans
    260–86
notional amounts 9–14, 18–26, 30–50, 107–40, 142–79,
    182–205, 211–14, 227–9, 231–3, 250–2, 276–80,
    287–300, 302–8, 311–16, 320–2, 342–8
Novartis 141, 147–53
NSFRs *see* net stable funding ratios
number of shares 9–26, 118–24, 202–3, 211–12, 216–24,
    249–52, 283–4, 309–16, 330–2, 336

observation days/periods 40–1, 60–4, 196–7
off-balance sheet transactions 367–9, 394, 396–7
offer prices, IPOs 66, 70–6, 77–87
offering circulars, IPOs 76
offering structure, IPOs 70–1
official index divisor 57–8
offsetting dividend risks 45–7
Oliveira, Joaquim 141
OMRs *see* open market repurchase programs
one-speed range accruals 216–19, 220–1, 348–52, 353–4
one-to-one meetings, IPO roadshows 76, 77
open market repurchase programs (OMRs), share buybacks 327–9, 332–4
open/guaranteed borrow maturities 27
operational risk 365–406
option sensitivities 1
options 1, 30–51, 112–14, 121–4, 126–7, 147–79, 181–205, 207–8, 211–12, 214–15, 216–33, 252–6, 266–86, 318–22, 339–63, 373–4, 376–7, 401–3
  see also call . . . ; collars; 'Greeks' (sensitivities); put . . . ; stock options . . . ; warrants
  automatic exercise term 31–2, 282
  composite options 49–50, 162–9
  concepts 30–50, 252–6, 318–19
  corporate action adjustments 46–7
  definitions 30–6
  dividends 38–41, 45–7, 318–22
  embedded options 50–1, 112–14, 121–4, 156, 162–9, 173–7, 202–4, 261–86, 362–3, 385
  examples 30–44, 318–22
  LEPOs 147–53
  M&As 252–6
  Novartis LEPOs and put options with Deutsche Bank case study 141, 147–53
  offsetting dividend risks 45–7
  payoffs 32–6, 49–50, 162–3, 183–7, 191–2, 194, 200–1, 278–9, 341–2
  premiums 30–50, 181–205, 215–24, 231–3, 274–5, 280–3, 318–22, 339–40, 341–8, 362–3
  pricing models 36–7, 38–40, 45–6, 47–8, 261–5, 284
  quanto options 49–50
  rights issues 46–7
  straddles 58–9
  strike prices 30–50, 112–14, 162–9, 181–205, 252–6, 318–22, 341–61
  styles 30–6
  terms 30–5, 46–7, 161–2, 173, 182–3, 185, 200, 202, 214–15, 231, 252–6, 279–81, 283, 342–7, 402–3
  time value and intrinsic value 36–7, 110–11, 283
ordinary shares *see* common stock
OTC derivatives 50–64
  see also dividend swaps; variance swaps; volatility swaps
out-of-the-money options 36–7, 42–4, 47–8, 113–14, 186–9, 214–15, 280
  see also intrinsic value . . .
own credit risk gains and losses on liabilities, Tier 1 capital deductions 380, 383
own shares 327–8, 345–6, 385
  see also share buybacks

P/E ratios of comparables, IPO valuations 73
pay-later puts 197–9
payment dates, dividends 52–8
payoffs 3, 32–6, 49–50, 63, 162–3, 183–7, 191–2, 194, 200–1, 265–6, 278–9, 341–2
PCRPs *see* prepaid collared repurchase programs
pension funds, Tier 1 capital deductions 380, 383–5
performance vesting conditions, equity-based compensation plans 260–1, 280–3
Perry's equity swaps with Bear Stearns and Goldman Sachs case study 243–8
physically-settled CDSs 298–9
  see also credit default swaps
physically-settled equity forwards 1–6
  see also equity forwards
physically-settled equity swaps 6–26, 176–7, 227–9, 250–2, 276–80, 301–8
  see also equity swaps
physically-settled options 30–3, 159–61, 165–9, 182–4, 200–1, 214–24, 280–3, 320–2, 347–52
  see also options
Pillar 1 (Minimum Capital Requirements)
  see also Basel . . .
  definition 366
Pillar 2 (Supervisory Review and Evaluation Process), definition 366
Pillar 3 (Market Discipline), definition 366
'pilot fishing' category, pre-marketing of the IPO offering 76
placement-of-the-offering IPO phase 66–7, 68, 77–80, 82
pledge agreements 288–300, 308–16
portfolios 25–6, 51, 64, 105–6
  see also diversification
Portugal Telecom 141–7, 226
pre-deal research, IPOs 75–7
pre-emptive capital increases
  see also rights issues
  definition 66
pre-IPO convertible bonds 141, 178–9
pre-marketing of the IPO offering 75–8
pre-offer blocks, M&As 235
preference shares 141, 153–6, 294
premium payment dates, options 30–50, 214–15, 231–3, 342–6
premiums 30–50, 103–4, 107–40, 142–79, 181–205, 215–24, 231–3, 274–5, 280–3, 318–22, 339–40, 341–8, 361–3, 370–7
prepaid collared repurchase programs (PCRPs), share buybacks 338–40
prepaid forwards plus equity swaps, equity financings 308–16
preparation-of-the-company IPO phase 68–9
preparation-of-the-offering IPO phase 68, 69–75, 81–2
present values 41–2, 58, 122–3
price return equity swaps 7–26, 308–16
  see also equity swaps
pricing, convertible bonds 105–6
principal payments, default events 293–4
printers, IPOs 68–84
private equity 66–7
  see also leveraged buy-outs
private sales of put options, share buybacks 347–8

probability distributions 193
profits, Tier 1 capital 370–3
project structure, IPOs 69–75
prospectuses, IPOs 70, 72, 76, 77–87
proxy contests 235–6, 237–40, 243–8
public offer requirements, M&As 235, 237, 248–52, 254
publicly offered put options 346–7
publicly offered repurchase programs, share buybacks 345–6
put financing, equity financings 318–22
put options 33–50, 147–53, 181–99, 211–12, 216–24, 228–9, 252–6, 278–80, 318–22, 339–40, 346–7, 402–3
    see also collars; 'Greeks' (sensitivities); options . . .
    call/put deltas 43, 48
    definition 33–4
    Deutsche Bank exchangeable into Brisa case study 141, 156–61
    equity financings 318–22
    examples 33–4, 36–7, 42–4, 147–53, 318–22
    exchangeable bonds 156–61
    hedging 181–99, 319–22
    knock-out puts 191–3, 219–24
    M&As 252–6
    Novartis LEPOs and put options with Deutsche Bank case study 141, 147–53
    payoffs 34–5, 183–7, 191–2, 194, 278–9
    private sales of put options 347–8
    publicly offered put options 346–7
    share buybacks 346–8, 354–61
    strategic stakes 181–99, 211–12, 216–24, 228–9
    Swisscom's public offer of put options case study 346–7
    terms 33–4, 46–7, 182–3, 185, 252–6, 346–8
    Unipol takeover of BNL and call/put combination with Deutsche Bank 252–6
put rights, convertible bonds 110–11, 175, 178–9
put spread collars, definition 188
put spreads 184–6, 188–93, 318–19
put–call parity, definition 41–2

qualified holdings, definition 236–7
qualifying dividends, dividend swaps 54–8
qualifying shareholders, rights issues 88–98
quanto equity swaps 23–5
quanto options 49–50
quick ratios 293–4

R&R Holdings S.A. 153–6
Rabobank SCN case study 139–40
range accruals 207–8, 216–24, 348–55
    definition 216, 219, 220
    terms 216, 348–9
rating trigger events, equity financings 293
RDF see required stable funding
realized variance 59–64
realized volatility see historical volatility
rebates, timer puts 195–7
reciprocal stakes in unconsolidated financial companies, Tier 1 capital deductions 380, 385–9
record dates 52–8, 88–98, 205
record share prices, definition 45
recourse equity financings, definition 299–300

'red herrings', IPOs 76, 77–8
redemption amounts 107–40, 142–79, 232, 287–300, 319
redemption prices 96–8, 142–79
redemption rights, ECNs 137–8
reference entities, CDSs 298–300
reference obligations, CDSs 298–300
reference prices 6–26, 120–1, 202–4, 279–80
regulators 82, 97–8, 111–12, 128–33, 137–40, 230, 235–56, 308, 328–9, 332, 340, 365–406
    see also bank regulatory capital; Basel . . .
reinvestment of dividends, equity swaps 11–14, 302–8
relative value views 51, 64
relevant dividends 20–1, 54–8
repos 38, 39–42, 58, 144–7, 316–17, 394, 395–6
    see also stock lending/borrowing transactions
    definition 316
    rates 38, 39–42, 58, 316–17
    voting rights 317
required stable funding (RSF) 396–7
rescue capital raising
    see also accelerated book-buildings; convertible bonds; equity capital market products; rights issues
    overview 66
reserves 261–73, 370–3
reshuffled collateral, revolving margin loan facilities 324–5
resolutions of AGMs/EGMs 236, 238–9, 240–3
restated balance sheet assets, leverage ratios 393–4
retail investors, IPOs 65–87
retained earnings 269–73, 370–3
returns, volatility calculations 40–1
reverse convertibles 51
reverse triangular mergers 247
revolving margin loan facilities, equity financings 322–5
rho 42, 44
    see also dividend yields; interest rates
Richemont 141, 153–6
rights issues 46–7, 65, 66, 87–98, 115, 131–6, 248–9
    see also corporate actions
    advantages 89–90
    Banco Popolare convertible bond case study 95–8
    convertible bonds 95–8, 131–6, 248–9
    definition 65, 87–9
    disadvantages 89–90, 115
    dividends 91, 94–5
    fees 88
    historical price adjustments 93–5
    ING case study 91–5
    methods 87–8
    option terms 46–7
    product description 87–8
    risk factors 89–90
    roadshows 87–8
    shareholder alternatives 88
    success factors 90
    terms 89, 92–6
    TERP 89, 90–8
    timescales 89–90, 96–7
    underwriters 88, 89, 131–6
rights prices see subscription prices
risk management, bank regulatory capital 365–406

risk reversals
  see also delta; implied volatility; skew
  definition 48
risk–arbitrage spread trades 243–8
risk-averse investors 175–6, 181–4
risk-free interest rates 261–5
risk–return profiles, portfolios 51, 64, 105–6
risk-weighted assets (RWAs) 365–6, 367–9, 373, 376,
    377, 379, 387, 388, 390–2, 398–401
  see also credit . . . ; market . . . ; non-counterparty . . . ;
    operational . . .
  accounting considerations 369
  banking/trading-book operations 369
  call options 401
  computations 368, 373, 376, 379, 390–2, 398–401
  definition 365–6, 367–8
  reduction methods 401
risks
  see also counterparty . . . ; credit . . . ; FX . . . ; interest
    rate . . . ; market . . . ; operational . . .
  bank regulatory capital 365–406
  dividend swaps 52
  equity-based compensation plans 273–83
  IPOs 81–2
  offsetting dividend risks 45–7
  rights issues 89–90
  types 367–9
  underwriting risks 71, 74
roadshows 68–9, 76–84, 87–8, 107
RWAs *see* risk-weighted assets

S&P 500 index 21–2, 24–6, 325
  see also Standard and Poor's
safe harbour rules, share buybacks 328–9, 332, 334, 340
sale plus equity swaps, equity financings 300–8, 310, 313
SARs *see* stock appreciation rights
SCNs 128, 139–40
scrip dividends 11, 95, 202–4, 401–3
SEC 247, 332, 340
secondary placement products
  see also accelerated book-buildings; initial public
    offerings
  definition 66, 67
securities lending/borrowing transactions *see* stock
    lending/borrowing transactions
securitization transactions, Tier 1 capital deductions 380,
    383, 389
security mechanisms, exchangeable bonds 146–7
selling commissions (concessions), IPOs 71–2
sensitivities *see* 'Greeks' (sensitivities)
sensitivity analysis, TERP discounts 91–5
service vesting conditions, equity-based compensation
    plans 260–1, 270–3, 277–80, 286
settlement amount payment dates, dividend swaps 53–8
settlement amounts 32–50, 53–8, 59–64, 200–2, 225–9,
    276–83, 310–16, 319, 321–2, 330–2, 336, 344–6
  see also equity amounts
settlement dates 1–6, 9–14, 18–26, 30–50, 60–4, 100,
    110–11, 175, 178–9, 214–24, 225–9, 231–3, 247,
    250–2, 342–6, 349–52
settlement methods 1–2, 6–26, 30–58, 176–7, 182–4,
    214–24, 276–83, 298–300, 301–16, 320–2, 342–8
  see also cash . . . ; physically . . .

settlement prices 12–14, 16–26, 30–50, 183–205, 225–9,
    250–2
settlement terms, CDSs 299–300
share buybacks 75–7, 241–3, 327–63, 385
  accelerated stock repurchase programs 329–32,
    339
  Asian call purchases 343–5
  at-the-money calls 341–3
  blackout periods 75–7, 328–9
  call options 340–63
  concepts 327–63
  convertible bonds 361–3
  Corporacion Dermoestetica's public offer to acquire
    own shares case study 345–6
  deep-in-the-money call purchases 340–3
  definition 327
  double-speed range accruals 352–4
  double-speed range accruals with final put 354–5
  EPS adjustments 331–2
  equity forwards 329–32, 340
  Gileads' share repurchase program financed with
    convertible bonds case study 361–3
  Hewlett Packard's ASR with Merrill Lynch case study
    329–32
  Hewlett Packard's PCRP with BNP Paribas case study
    339–40
  in-the-money options 339–43
  liquidity improvements 327–8
  market abuse and safe harbour rules 328–9, 332, 334,
    340
  one-speed range accruals 348–52, 353–4
  open market repurchase programs 327–9,
    332–4
  own shares 327
  prepaid collared repurchase programs 338–40
  private sales of put options 347–8
  publicly offered put options 346–7
  publicly offered repurchase programs 345–6
  put options 346–8, 354–61
  range accruals 348–55
  regulators 328–9, 332
  stockbrokers 327–9, 332–4
  Swisscom's public offer of put options case study
    346–7
  transparency issues 332–3
  VWAP-linked repurchase programs 332–8
share plans
  see also equity-based compensation plans
  HSBC share performance awards 257, 258, 283–6
share-based payments
  see also equity-based compensation plans
  IFRS accounting definition 259–60, 276
shareholders 46–7, 65–98, 235–56, 257–86, 308, 324–5,
    327–63
  see also dividend . . . ; voting rights
short positions 26, 38–40, 50–1, 105–6, 114, 183–4, 186,
    188, 191, 193, 195, 199, 202, 215, 219, 227–9,
    242–8, 278–9, 308–16, 385–9
shortfall of the stock of provisions to expected losses,
    Tier 1 capital deductions 380, 383
skew 48, 185–6, 193
  see also delta; implied volatility; risk reversals
Societe Generale 173–4, 238–40

soft call term, convertible bonds 107–40, 162, 168–9
special clauses, convertible bonds 124–7, 174–5
special purpose entities (SPEs) 287–308, 309–16, 318–22, 374, 377, 399–403
specialized equity derivative products 1, 50–64
  see also dividend swaps; variance swaps; volatility swaps
speculators 243, 280
spot prices 4–6, 30–50, 183–4, 200–2, 216–24, 347–8
stakes in unconsolidated financial companies, Tier 1 capital deductions 380, 385–9, 403–4
standard deviations 40–1
  see also volatility
Standard and Poor's (S&P) 151, 229, 293
  see also S&P 500 index
standstill periods, M&As 235
steering committees, IPOs 69–75
stock appreciation rights (SARs) 257–86
  see also equity-based compensation plans
  accounting entries 263–5, 270–3
  call options 273, 278–83
  case studies 265–83
  definition 257, 263
  equity swaps 273, 275, 277–80
  hedging strategies 273–83
  payoffs 265–6
  risks 273–83
  terminology 258–9
  terms 258–9, 265–6
  treasury shares 273–5, 278, 279, 281
stock indexes 1–6, 17–26, 30–5, 56–8, 59–64, 265–83, 325, 387
  see also Eurostoxx . . . ; FTSE . . . ; Hang Seng . . . ; Nikkei . . . ; S&P . . .
stock lending/borrowing transactions 1, 4–6, 26–9, 41–2, 51, 114–15, 199–200, 204–5, 211–24, 228–9, 241–8, 317–18, 320–2, 329–32, 394, 404–6
  see also repo rates
  advantages 29, 317–18
  collateral 26–9, 114–15, 205, 241–8, 317–18, 405–6
  concepts 26–9, 114–15, 199–200, 204–5, 241–3, 317–18
  confirmation agreements 26–7
  counterparty credit risk 28–9
  definition 26–7, 317
  dividends 26–9, 51, 204–5, 241–3, 300–8, 317–18, 320, 322
  drawbacks 29, 317–18
  equity financings 317–18, 320–2
  haircut uses 28–9
  interest flows 27–9
  Laxey stock lending case study 241–3
  lending fees 26–9, 41–2, 199–200, 228–9, 241–3, 317–18
  M&As 241–8
  manufactured dividends 28–9, 300–8, 320, 322
  open/guaranteed borrow maturities 27
  strategic stakes 199–200, 204–5, 211–24, 228–9
  tax arbitrage schemes 29, 204–5
  transaction flows 27–8, 114–15, 241–3, 317–18
  voting rights 26–7, 241–8, 317–18, 320

withholding taxes 204–5
yield enhancement of strategic stakes 199–200, 204–5
stock markets 66–87, 158–61, 225–9, 236–56, 309–16, 327–63
  see also initial public offerings
stock options plans 257–86, 329–30
  see also equity-based compensation plans
  accounting entries 261–3, 266–73, 284
  call options 273, 278–83
  case studies 265–83
  concepts 257–86
  definition 257, 258–9
  equity swaps 273–80
  exercise prices 257–9
  fair values 261–2, 266–80, 284–6
  hedging 257, 273–83, 285–6
  HSBC share performance awards 257, 258, 283–6
  IFRS accounting 257, 259–65, 276
  risks 273–83
  terminology 258–9
  terms 265–6
  uses 257–9
stock splits 46–7
stock surplus component of Tier 1/2 capital 370–8
stock trigger events, equity financings 293
stockbrokers, share buybacks 327–9, 332–4
straddles 58–9
strategic equity transactions 141–79, 365
  see also bank regulatory capital; tax-driven . . .
strategic stakes 141, 161–70, 181–205, 207–33
  see also disposal . . .
  call options 141, 161–70, 186–9, 200–5, 207–8, 214–33
  call spreads 141, 161–70
  collars 186–9
  concepts 181–205
  covered call writing 200–2
  definition 181
  fly put spreads 189–91, 193
  German disposal of Fraport with JP Morgan collaboration case study 229–33
  hedging 181–99
  knock-out puts 191–3, 219–24
  ladder puts 193–5
  monetization of dividend optionality 202–4
  pay-later puts 197–9
  put options 181–99, 211–12, 216–24, 228–9
  put spread collars 188–9
  put spreads 184–6, 188–93
  stock lending/borrowing transactions 199–200, 204–5, 211–24, 228–9
  summary of hedging strategies 193
  timer puts 195–7
  withholding taxes 204–5
  yield enhancement methods 181, 199–205
strategies, share buybacks 327–63
strike prices 30–50, 59–64, 112–14, 162–9, 181–205, 214–24, 252–6, 261–86, 318–22, 341–61
  see also volatility smiles
  definition 38
structuring fees, revolving margin loan facilities 323–4
styles of options 30–6
  see also American . . . ; European . . .
sub-underwriters, IPOs 74–84

subordinated debt 116, 128–40, 294, 385–9
subscription agreements, bonds collateralized by equity
    stakes 289–300
subscription periods, rights issues 88–98
subscription prices 88–98
subscription rights, rights issues 88–98
subsidiaries 370–3, 374–5, 377–8, 397–400
sum-of-parts inputs, IPO valuations 73
swaps 1, 6–26, 50–64, 130, 142–7, 156, 176–8, 207–8,
    224–9, 238–40, 243–52, 273–80, 300–16
    see also cash-settled . . . ; dividend . . . ; equity . . . ;
        physically-settled . . . ; variance . . . ; volatility . . .
    CDSs 288–300
SWIFT confirmations 296
Swisscom's public offer of put options case study
    346–7
syndicates 70, 72–87, 89–98, 235–6, 255–6, 297–300,
    404–6
    see also underwriters
systemic risks 365–406

takeover make-whole clauses, convertible bonds 126–7
takeovers 67, 199–200, 236–56
    see also mergers and acquisitions
TARP see Troubled Asset Relief Program
tax-driven strategic equity transactions 29, 204–5
    arbitrage schemes 29, 204–5
    stock lending/borrowing transactions 29, 204–5
taxes 29, 147–53, 202–3, 204–5, 227, 257, 302–8, 316,
    346, 363, 380–2
    arbitrage schemes 29, 204–5
    convertible bonds 111–12, 363
    credits 381–2
    deferred tax assets 380–2, 388–9, 393
    ECN events 137–8
    equity swaps 227, 308, 316
    equity-based compensation plans 257
    havens 204
    withholding taxes 147–53, 202–3, 204–5, 302–8,
        346–7
Telefonica 226, 283
term financings, definition 322
term structure of implied volatility 48–9
termination dates 9–14, 18–26, 53–8, 60–4, 249–52,
    276–80, 298–300, 301–8, 309–16
termination events, equity financings 292–5, 309–16
TERP (theoretical ex-rights price) 89, 90–8
    see also rights issues
theta 42, 44
    see also expiration dates
third-party guarantees, exchangeable bonds 141–7
third-party issues, convertible bonds 141, 147–53
Thomas Weisel 86
Tier 1 capital 365–406
    see also Additional . . . ; bank regulatory capital;
        Basel . . . ; capital ratios
    Basel II 50/50 deductions 389
    calculations 372–3, 376, 393–4, 405–6
    capital instruments failing capital eligibility criteria
        393
    Commerzbank capital structure enhancement with
        Credit Suisse case study 404–6
    components 369–76, 377, 401–3, 405
    deductions 380–93, 394

definition 365–8, 369–70
    inclusion criteria 370–1, 374–5, 405–6
    leverage ratios 393–4
    minimum requirements 373, 376, 390–3, 398–400
    minority interests 370–3, 377, 397–400
Tier 2 capital 365–6, 367–8, 375–80, 386–9, 390–3,
    396–400
    additional inclusions 378
    additional Tier 1 capital 375–6
    Basel II 50/50 deductions 389
    calculations 378–9
    capital instruments failing capital eligibility criteria
        393
    components 376–8
    deductions 378, 386, 389, 392
    definition 365–6, 367–8, 376–8
    inclusion criteria 376–8
    minimum requirements 379
    trigger conditions for hybrid instruments 379–80
time value of an option 36–7, 110–11, 283
timer call options, hedging 282–3
timer puts 195–7, 283
    see also implied volatility
timing differences, deferred tax assets 381–2, 388–9,
    393
total return equity swaps 6–26, 130, 176–7, 224–9,
    238–40, 248–52, 275–80, 300–8
    see also equity swaps
    definition 6–7
    equity financings 300–8
    examples 7–14, 17–21, 275–80, 300–8
total shareholder returns (TSRs), HSBC share
    performance awards 283–6
TPG-Axon Partners 238–9
TPSs see trust preferred securities
trade dates 9–14, 18–26, 30–50, 53–8, 60–4, 183–4,
    200–2, 214–15, 216–24, 231–3, 247, 249–52,
    276–80, 298–300, 301–8, 309–16, 342–8
trade periods, rights issues 89, 96–8
trading book operations 365, 369, 386–7, 399–400
trading desks, delta-hedging roles 44–5
transaction costs 308
transitional arrangements, Basel III 392–3
transparency issues 45–6, 240, 256, 332–3
treasury shares 273–5, 278, 279, 281, 286, 327–63, 380,
    385, 401–3
    see also share buybacks
trigger events, equity financings 292–5
Troubled Asset Relief Program (TARP) 101–2
trust ESOPs (employee stock ownership plans),
    definition 258
trust preferred securities (TPSs) 405–6
trustees, bonds collateralized by equity stakes 288–300
TSRs see total shareholder returns
TUI buyback convertible case study 141, 175–7

UBS 83, 86, 103, 122–4, 238–40, 283
unconsolidated financial companies, Tier 1 capital
    deductions 380, 385–9, 403–4
underlying assets 1, 30–50, 53–8, 96, 107–40, 142–79,
    181–205, 211–15, 231–3, 249–52, 309–16
underwriters 69–87, 88, 89, 131–6, 248–9, 386
    see also syndicates
Unicredit 103, 131–6

Unipol takeover of BNL and call/put combination with
    Deutsche Bank 252–6
United Kingdom 366
United States (US) 83, 101–2, 332, 340, 366, 369, 380
    Bancorp 83
    GAAP rules 332, 340, 369, 380
    Treasury placement of Citigroup shares ATM case
        study 101–2
upfront fees, revolving margin loan facilities 323–4
use of proceeds 149

valuation dates, equity swaps 12–26, 311–16
valuation times, equity swaps 12–26, 311–16
valuations 12–26, 38–40, 47–8, 72–5, 110–11, 112–14,
    122, 177–9, 261–5, 311–16
    see also options pricing models
Value-at-Risk (VaR) 369
    see also market risk
vanilla options
    see also options
    definition 30
variable expiry timer puts 195, 196–7
variable parity mandatory convertibles 118–24
    see also dividend enhanced . . .
variable premium timer puts 195–7
variance strike 59–64
variance swaps 1, 58–64
    see also forwards; swaps; volatility . . .
vega 42, 44
    see also implied volatility
vesting conditions 258–86
Visa Europe 82–3
Visa Inc. IPO case study 82–4, 87
volatility 38–41, 42–5, 47–8, 51, 58–64, 106–7, 173–5,
    185–6, 193, 261–5, 267, 273, 276–7, 282–3, 285–6,
    318–19, 320, 340, 383
    see also historical . . . ; implied . . . ; variance . . . ; vega
    definitions 39, 40–1
volatility smiles 47–8
    see also implied volatility; strike prices

volatility swaps 1, 58–64
    see also swaps
volume-weighted average price per share (VWAP)
    15–17, 137, 144–5, 207–8, 216–24, 249–52, 307,
    331–40
voting rights 26–7, 103–7, 153–6, 183–4, 186, 187,
    190–2, 194, 199, 201, 211, 212, 214–15, 219, 226,
    229, 233–48, 308, 316, 317–18, 320, 347, 369–70,
    403–4
    convertible bonds 103–4, 106–7, 153–6, 211
    disposal of strategic stakes 211, 212, 214–15, 219,
        226, 229, 233
    M&As 235–6
    proxy contests 235–6, 237–40, 243–8
    repos 317
    stock lending/borrowing transactions 26–7, 241–8,
        317–18, 320
    strategic stakes 183–4, 186, 187, 190–2, 194, 199, 201,
        211, 212, 214–15, 219, 226, 229, 233
VWAP *see* volume-weighted average price per share
VWAP-linked repurchase programs 332–40

Wachovia 83
warrants 141, 153–6, 362–3
    see also options
    definition 154
Wells Fargo 83
withholding taxes 147–53, 202–3, 204–5, 302–8,
    346–7
    reduction methods 202–3, 204–5
    stock lending/borrowing transactions 204–5
WR Hambrecht 86

yield enhancement of strategic stakes 181,
    199–205
yield to maturity 148–79

zero-cost collars 186
zero-coupon convertibles/exchangeables 104, 147,
    151–3, 169, 231–3

Index compiled by Terry Halliday

Printed and bound by CPI Group (UK) Ltd, Croydon, CR0 4YY

23/04/2025

14660949-0003